# Communism in Latin America

# Communism
## in
## Latin America

ROBERT J. ALEXANDER

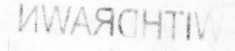

RUTGERS UNIVERSITY PRESS

*New Brunswick, New Jersey . 1957*

FOR MY PARENTS

# Foreword

IN RECENT YEARS much attention has been focused on the Communist movement in the United States and in certain countries of Europe and Asia. However, as in the case of most things Latin American, little heed has been paid to the Communist movements to the south of us. With the exception of Daniel James's excellent study of the Communist movement in Guatemala, no volume has appeared which attempts to analyse this important subject.

As a result, the public in the United States is almost completely ignorant of the extent of Communist influence in our sister republics. The average American citizen is startled when a "crisis" suddenly arises, such as that in Guatemala in 1954. He then tends to become panicky and to conjure up gigantic Stalinist forces in the Other America which do not, in fact, exist.

It is hoped that the present volume will do something to fill this gap in the information available to the reading public in the United States concerning the real nature of the Communist movement of Latin America. The author hopes that the result will be both to alert and to reassure. He hopes that this study will serve to allay any irrational fears concerning the strength of the Communists to the south; that it will help the public mind to distinguish between the activities of the Communists and the normal penchant of the Latin Americans for *coups d'état* and *pronunciamientos;* and, finally, that the book will arouse some awareness of the dangers which, in the long run, the Communist movement in Latin America will represent to the future of democracy and peace in this hemisphere and to the national security of the United States.

Thanks are due to those hundreds of individuals, Communist and non-Communist alike, both in Latin America and the United States, who have submitted to the author's interminable questioning, and who have provided much valuable written material. Special mention should be made of Dr. Ricardo Paredes, founder of the Communist Party of Ecuador, who not only allowed himself to be interviewed, but made available his personal files of early Communist literature; Ricardo Martínez de la Torre, historian of the labor and radical movements of Peru; and Earl Browder, formerly Secretary General of the Communist Party of the United States, who cleared up a great many questions concerning the relationships among the various Communist Parties of the hemisphere.

Very special appreciation is owed to the late Stephen Naft, one of the first experts on labor and radical activities in Latin America, who gave the author exceedingly valuable documents dating from the early days of the Communist movement in this hemisphere, including manuscript material which he collected when he was the Latin American representative for the Tass News Agency, a quarter of a century ago.

Most of the trips to Latin America for the material on which this book is based could not have been taken, had it not been for the aid of the Free Trade Union Committee of the American Federation of Labor. Special thanks are due to Jay Lovestone, the Executive Secretary of that Committee for his kind cooperation. The author also extends thanks to Serafino Romualdi, Assistant Secretary General of the O.R.I.T., with whom the author has worked for many years, and who has done his utmost to make these researches possible.

Finally, gratitude must be expressed to the author's wife, Joan Alexander, for her patience in living with "Communism in Latin America" for so long, and for her forbearance with the eternal ticktack of the typewriter necessary in getting the volume written.

Robert J. Alexander

Rutgers University
New Brunswick, N.J.
*December, 1956*

# Preface to the 1960 Printing

IN THE THREE YEARS that have elapsed since the publication of *Communism in Latin America*, the situation of the Latin American Communists has improved considerably. Political changes have given them new opportunities in several nations of the hemisphere, and in a number of others the Communists have energetically sought to exploit the recent expressions of pent-up anti-United States feeling that have come with greater political freedom. The position of the anti-Communist elements in the trade union movement has been undermined by the changing political situation. The Communists, on the other hand, occupy the most favorable position in organized labor that they have had since the decline of the Confederación de Trabajadores de América Latina in the immediate post-World War II period.

The anti-dictatorship trend in Latin America, already under way three years ago, has continued. Democratic regimes have been consolidated in most of the countries in which dictatorships had fallen by mid-1957. Other tyrannies have been overthrown since. In the spring of 1960 only four definitely dictatorial regimes were still in power.

The democratic, though conservative, regime of President Manuel Prado of Peru has been able to thwart all plots to overthrow it, and, currently, preparations for a democratic election to choose a successor to Prado are being discussed. In Honduras, the military junta which seized power from dictator Juan Lozano late in 1956 presided over democratic elections a year later. These gave the Liberal Party an appreciable majority in the new constitutional assembly. After writing a new constitution, the assembly, as its last act, named Liberal leader Ramón Villeda Morales as President of the Republic. He has so far been successful in beating off several attempted insurrections by dictatorial elements and in maintaining a relatively democratic regime in the small Central American republic.

Almost simultaneously with the first publication of this book, in May, 1957, the dictatorship of General Gustavo Rojas Pinilla of Colombia was overthrown after nation-wide rioting. After long negotiations between the two major parties, Dr. Alberto Lleras Camargo, a Liberal, was elected constitutional President, a year after the overthrow of Rojas Pinilla.

The process of re-establishing a constitutional regime in Argentina was completed on May 1, 1958, with the inauguration of President Arturo Frondizi. Although his regime has been constantly under threat of violent overthrow at the hands of conflicting elements in the armed forces, and has become widely unpopular among the civilian population because of its economic policies, Frondizi is still in the Casa Rosada. However, Argentine democracy remains incomplete because of the prohibition of the followers of ex-dictator Perón from participating as a recognized party in the country's politics. And it remains fundamentally insecure because of the violent and uncompromising antipathy of extremists in both Peronista and anti-Peronista camps.

The dictatorial regime of General Marcos Pérez Jiménez of Venezuela was overthrown on January 23, 1958, when the dictator fled abroad after a nation-wide civilian protest movement against his attempt to stay in power after his "constitutional" term of office had expired. The military-civilian junta which succeeded him carried out its promise to re-establish democratic constitutional government. It presided over elections in December, 1958, which were won by ex-President Rómulo Betancourt of the Acción Democrática Party. He was inaugurated as constitutional President on February 13, 1959. His coalition government began a process of fundamentally altering the economic and social institutions of Venezuela.

Almost a year after the fall of Pérez Jiménez, the dictatorship of General Fulgencio Batista was ousted in Cuba. The government of Fidel Castro, which came to power on January 1, 1959, set about a revolutionary program of agrarian reform, expropriation of foreign-owned property, and economic development under strict government control. The political direction of the Castro regime is still obscure.

In only one of the countries in which a strong-arm regime was overthrown in recent years was there a frank return to dictatorship. This was in Haiti, where after the overthrow of President Paul Magloire late in 1956, there was a succession of short-lived regimes. They culminated in the re-establishment of a dictatorship under President François Duvalier, victor in a one-candidate "election" in September, 1957.

As of spring, 1960, Duvalier's is one of the four obviously dictatorial regimes remaining in Latin America. The others are the governments of President Luis Somoza of Nicaragua, General Alfredo Stroessner of Paraguay, and Generalissimo Rafael Leónidas Trujillo of the Dominican Republic. All of these regimes are facing mounting opposition, and their tenure of power is problematical.

The overthrow of dictatorial regimes has resulted in much greater freedom of expression in the countries concerned. In newspapers, radio and television programs, and political meetings the people have been able to give vent to feelings and ideas which had been suppressed by the dictatorships, or had been allowed to be heard only when this suited the convenience of the dictator.

One of the most notable results of this greater freedom is a widespread outburst of indignation against the United States, and particularly against the policies which this country has followed in its relations with Latin America in recent years. This indignation commanded world-wide attention during the South American tour of Vice President Richard Nixon in May, 1958. It has continued to gain momentum in the two years following the Nixon incidents.

The United States has failed to react effectively to the widespread anti-Yankeeism which has become so obvious in recent years. The only adequate reaction would have been a frank reorientation of United States policy toward Latin America, a reorientation calculated to arouse the imagination of the molders of Latin American public opinion, and to convince the citizens of the other American republics that we were firmly determined to abjure past errors and to do our part in launching a new era in Inter American relations. Although the President and the Secretary of State of the United States have indicated more concern over Latin American affairs than they have done in the past, there has been no clear pronouncement that this country is firmly on the side of democracy in Latin America. Indeed, United States government policy on this subject has showed a schizophrenic quality, notably with regard to the worst of all Latin American dictatorships, that of Trujillo in the Dominican Republic. Whereas the State Department has become notably cool toward Trujillo, our military have been unnecessarily and even ostentatiously friendly. The announcement that the embargo on arms shipments to the Caribbean extended to the Dominican Republic was made many months after the announcement that it applied to Castro's Cuba. The United States Navy sent three admirals to visit Trujillo in the summer of 1959 at exactly the time he was being militarily attacked by exiles; and six months later it chose Ciudad Trujillo as the place for shore-leave for 4,000 United States Marines who had just finished a winter cruise.

Somewhat the same kind of an attitude has surrounded United States handling of economic relations with Latin America. Although the United States finally agreed in the summer of 1958 to go along with Latin American demands for an Inter American Bank, and for talks about stabilizing prices of the region's main export products, this was done in an almost off-hand manner. Little attempt was made to pick up the "Operación Panamérica" suggestion for hemispheric cooperation in economic development made by Brazilian President Jucelino Kubitschek in the middle of 1957. More or less routine handling of the suggestion resulted in its being all but forgotten—except by the Brazilians.

Such policies on the part of the United States do not add up to the kind of program which can arouse widespread sympathy and support among the Latin American public. They have done little to stem the tide of anti-Yankeeism among our southern neighbors. Anti-Yankeeism has favored the spread of the influence of the Communists. With considerable success they have sought to channel it in a pro-Soviet direction. They have been in a much better position to do so since the fall of various Latin American dictatorships than they were before those dictatorships were established. In this connection, the conclusions of *Communism in Latin America* have been completely borne out. The prediction that the Communists would emerge stronger from dictatorships than they were before the establishment of the tyrannies has been verified in the case of Peru, Colombia, Venezuela, and Cuba.

After the retirement of President-Dictator Manuel Odría in 1956 and the election of President Manuel Prado, Peru began a new democratic experiment, with the support of the democratic left-wing

Aprista Party. Although the Prado ad⸱
even conservative, regime, the Apri⸱
cause they felt that the all-importa⸱
of a military dictatorship. The ⸱
position. Under Odría, there h⸱
the official party nominally ⸱
pro-Odría group led by Sen⸱
there was no formal uniting o⸱
worked together as one in the trade ⸱

xiv

In Colombia
Rojas Pinilla
of the two
for almos⸱
parties ⸱
such ⸱
the ⸱
Th⸱
w⸱

The Peruvian Communists had gained
ganized labor during the dictatorship, since
not only the tolerance but also the backing of ⸱
had won control over the majority of the unions in ⸱
Puno, and Cuzco regions of southern Peru. They also con⸱
nation-wide Chauffeurs' Federation, and had a leading positi⸱
the miners' organizations in the central part of the country. All these
groups had been dominated by anti-Communist groups before the
establishment of the Odría dictatorship.

The Peruvian Communists used their influence in the labor movement to postpone for three years the affiliation of the re-constituted
Confederación de Trabajadores del Perú (C.T.P.) with the International Confederation of Free Trade Unions (I.C.F.T.U.) and its
American regional affiliate, the Inter American Regional Organization of Workers (O.R.I.T.). It was only after the Communists had
been routed in the miners' unions, and had lost control of the
Chauffeurs' Federation that the C.T.P. finally joined the I.C.F.T.U.
and the O.R.I.T. in 1959.

The Communist influence in the labor movement and in Peruvian
politics was strengthened by the fact that many individuals friendly
to the Luna Communists continued to hold positions in the Ministry
of Labor. In spite of Aprista pressure, President Prado did not oust
these people, apparently because of fear of agitation by the Communists. However, in spite of Prado's caution, the Communists took
a position against his administration. They worked with Fernando
Belaunde Terry, and others, who were violently criticizing the Prado
government. Upon several occasions President Prado felt it necessary
to declare martial law in some part of Peru for a limited time because
of crises brought about by these opposition groups. The Prado regime
has lived under constant fear that such a crisis might provide provoca-
tion for anti-democratic military elements desirous of establishing a
new military dictatorship.

, the overthrow of the dictatorship of General Gustavo
in May, 1957, was brought about largely by an alliance
traditional parties, the Liberals and Conservatives, which
a decade had been engaged in a virtual civil war. Both
were anxious to prevent a repetition of an army dictatorship
that of Rojas Pinilla. They agreed on a system of rotating
residency between the two parties during five presidential terms.
s system was crystallized in a series of constitutional amendments
hich were ratified in a plebiscite on December 1, 1957. Former
President Alberto Lleras Camargo, a Liberal, took office in August,
1958, as the result of agreement by the two parties.

The re-establishment of a constitutional regime in Colombia has
not resolved the social crisis which originally paved the way for the
civil war and the Rojas Pinilla dictatorship. Uneven land distribution, extreme rural poverty, and class hatred are widespread. General
Rojas Pinilla had stimulated the desire of large parts of the population for fundamental social reform, by making demagogic speeches
throughout the country—which he hoped would be a smokescreen to
hide the high-handedness and corruption of his regime.

President Lleras Camargo and other leaders of the constitutional
regime were well aware of the need for social reform, and by 1960 had
begun distributing government land to landless peasants as a first step
in a more general reform program. Meanwhile, however, the Communists have gained considerable ground, particularly in the labor
movement. In 1958 they recaptured control of the majority of the
unions in the petroleum industry. They also made considerable gains
among the workers in the industrial city of Cali and in other important centers. For the first time in a decade the Communists have
again become an element of importance in the Colombian labor movement, particularly in the ranks of the Confederación de Trabajadores
de Colombia (C.T.C.)—though by the middle of 1960 they had not
as yet been able to regain the control over the C.T.C. which they had
had during the 1940's.

Perhaps renewed Communist activity in the rural parts of Colombia
is even more important than growing Communist influence in the
ranks of organized labor; however, the rural activity is much more
difficult to document. Informed Colombians, including top officials
of the government, were admitting by early 1960 that the Communists were exceedingly active in the countryside, and that the government was fearful of their possible progress.

The same phenomenon of an improved Communist position resulting from a dictatorship has occurred in Venezuela, Colombia's eastern neighbor. The Communists emerged from the Pérez Jiménez dictatorship with a respectability, influence, and prestige they did not possess before the military tyranny was established in 1948.

The Venezuelan Communists, like their Peruvian counterparts, followed a policy of "dual Communism" throughout the ten years of dictatorship. The so-called "Red" Communists were the "official" party, and were in opposition to the tyranny; the "Black" Communists, on the other hand, were "unofficial," and supported the dictatorial regimes in power between 1948 and 1958. This fiction of two rival Communist parties was abandoned after the overthrow of Pérez Jiménez. Rodolfo Quintero and other leaders of the "Blacks" were quietly admitted to the "Red" party, and became its principal spokesmen in the high command of the reconstituted labor movement. Meanwhile, the Venezuelan Communists had gained much ground, in and out of the labor movement. The Red Communist party was treated quite mildly by the dictatorship, and hence was able to keep its underground organization intact to a degree that the democratic parties could not. Nevertheless, Communists of both colors played an active role in the agitation of late 1957 which resulted in the ousting of Pérez Jiménez on January 23, 1958. They participated as one of the four parties in the anti-dictatorial Patriotic Junta, to which Acción Democrática, the Catholic Partido Social Cristiano Copei, and the Unión Republicana Democrática also belonged.

The Venezuelan Communists thus received a fair share of the credit for the final triumph against the Pérez Jiménez regime. People tended to forget the support many of the Communists had given this government until only a few months before its overthrow. The Communists were able to penetrate numerous important groups, notably the members of the Caracas press, the teaching profession, the university students, and the labor movement.

Furthermore, after the overthrow of the Pérez Jiménez regime, the junta which succeeded it—and even the constitutional government of President Rómulo Betancourt—was under constant threat of a coup by military elements hostile to a democratic civilian regime. Great emphasis was put by all parties on the need for civilian unity in the face of this military threat. This mood helped to create a psychological atmosphere which for many months made it impossible for any group to disagree openly with or attack the Communists. By early 1960, however, this atmosphere was beginning to fade.

The most striking advances of the Venezuelan Communists were in the student and trade union fields. In both of these areas, the Communists had been isolated by 1948, before the fall of the democratic government of President Rómulo Gallegos. A decade later it was obvious that the dictatorship had served to bring the Communists out of their isolation and to give them unequaled strength among both the students and the organized workers.

The situation in the student movement was shown in the elections in the National University in Caracas, in March, 1960. The Communists by themselves captured the student representation in two of the university's ten faculties; they shared in victorious slates in half a dozen others. Only two faculties had clearly anti-Communist majorities in their student bodies.

In the labor movement the situation was particularly serious. After the fall of Pérez Jiménez, a labor coalition was formed by all four parties—Acción Democrática, Christian Social Copei, Unión Republicana Democrática, and the Communists. Unified unions were organized throughout Venezuela on an industrial and regional basis. The Communists shared in the leadership of most unions. The reconstruction of the Venezuelan labor movement was completed by a congress of December, 1959, which re-established the Confederación de Trabajadores de Venezuela. In this meeting, although the Communists had only about 25 per cent of the delegates, they were able to get most of the things they wanted. They forced the Acción Democrática, which had over 50 per cent of all delegates, to agree not to insist on having a majority of the members of the new fourteen-member executive committee of the Confederación. They also forced that party to agree to a policy of refusing to allow the Confederación to join the I.C.F.T.U. and the O.R.I.T., although these international groups had given valuable and continuing support both to the struggle against the Pérez Jiménez dictatorship and to the fight of both Acción Democrática and Copei trade unions in the underground.

The Acción Democrática and Copei trade unionists found it impossible to resist the Communists, because they felt that the general political situation of the country would not permit a break with the Communists in the labor movement—and the Communists threatened such a split unless they got their way on essential matters. The non-Communists were fearful of the results of the Communist Party going frankly into the opposition in the face of the continued threats to the constitutional regime from undemocratic military elements.

The stabilization of the Venezuelan democratic civilian regime to a degree that would permit a showdown with the Communists depends on the success of the regime's reform program. Basic is an agrarian reform, launched in February, 1960, after thorough study and discussion. Important, too, is a crash program for economic development. The Betancourt government also had extensive plans under way in the fields of education, improvement of health conditions, and social security. On one pretext or another, the Communists have opposed virtually all of the government's specific projects in all of these fields.

The Cuban Communists made some of the most extensive gains as a result of the events of the late 1950's. Although the Cuban Communists had been long-time allies of Fulgencio Batista, and did not join the military struggle against the Batista dictatorship until after April, 1958, they were able to capitalize on the revolution launched after January 1, 1959, and to call attention to the mistaken policies of the United States government in supporting the Cuban dictatorship between 1952 and 1959.

The Batista dictatorship was overthrown on January 1, 1959, after more than two years of civil war. This conflict began in November, 1956, when a small group of exiles, led by Fidel Castro, landed in the Sierra Maestra mountains in eastern Cuba. The military struggle was accompanied by the organization of an extensive underground in Havana and other cities. Twice, in August, 1957, and April, 1958, the Castro forces attempted to use this civilian underground to launch a revolutionary strike. Both efforts failed. The Communists did not support the general strike call on either occasion. In fact, there was little continuous contact between the Castro underground (and military) forces and the Communists until after the failure of the April, 1958, general walkout attempt. However, shortly thereafter, the Frente Obrero Nacional, which had been organized by the Castro forces in the labor movement, was amplified to include the Communists, and was rechristened the Frente Obrero Nacional Unido. At the same time, the Communists sent official liaison people to join the military forces of Castro in the mountains. A fairly large number of Communists participated in the military struggle during its last months.

Once the rebel forces were successful, the new Cuban leaders declared that they were not anti-Communist, and insisted that the raising of this issue would only serve to split the revolutionary forces. They permitted the Communists to function openly and, while emphasizing that they themselves were not Communists, refused to attack the Communists openly. However, a number of leaders in the Castro government disagreed with this position of Fidel, his brother Raúl Castro, and Ernesto Guevara—the Big Three of the government. These strong anti-Communists, including President Manuel Urrutia and Major Hubert Mattos, were eliminated from the government between August and October, 1959, and Mattos and a number of other military leaders of the Castro movement were given long jail sentences because of their attitude.

Coinciding with the purging of a number of outspoken anti-Communists from the leadership of the Castro government and its Rebel Army was a right-about-face of the Castro forces in the labor movement. The control of the trade unions had been seized on January 1st by partisans of Fidel Castro. During the succeeding six months, these provisional leaders called secret elections, and in most cases were confirmed in office. In many instances, the Castro 26th of July Movement lists of candidates in the unions were opposed by Communist slates—and in almost every such case, the 26th of July forces were smashingly successful. The same pattern was repeated in the national industrial union conventions, where the Communists proved to be a very small minority, and the overwhelming majority of delegates were 26th of July people.

By September, 1959, all the Cuban national industrial unions had held their conventions. By that time, too, the provisional leaders of the Confederación de Trabajadores de Cuba (C.T.C.), all of whom were 26th of July members, had decided by a sizable majority to keep the C.T.C. in the I.C.F.T.U. and O.R.I.T.

Suddenly, there was a change of policy and personnel within the labor movement. This occurred during and after the congress of the C.T.C. held early in November, 1959. This meeting was riotous, with violent oratory and even fist-fights. There was strong opposition among the delegates to the change Fidel Castro himself demanded in addresses to the congress. These changes were basically three in number. First, the congress reversed the decision taken earlier to keep the C.T.C. in the I.C.F.T.U. and the O.R.I.T., and instead voted to withdraw from those groups and to patronize the establishment of an autonomous Latin American labor confederation. Second, a slate of officers was elected which resulted in the removal of all but one of the principal anti-Communist spokesmen among the 26th of July leaders who had been in the Provisional Executive of the C.T.C. The one remaining strong anti-Communist was reduced from key secretary of organization to the least influential post on the Executive.

The third move of the C.T.C. congress was the establishment of a "purge committee," for the ostensible purpose of ousting from leadership of the national industrial unions all those who were "Batistianos," that is, who had had association with the fallen dictatorship. The fact was, of course, that all pro-Batista labor leaders had been removed on January 1, 1959, and the few days following that date. The new purge group set about ousting those leaders of national industrial unions who had been most outspoken in their opposition to the Communists. Thus, although the Castro regime continued to insist that it was not Communist, the most outstanding figures in its ranks who were publicly and continuously anti-Communist were removed during the last few months of 1959 and the early months of 1960. At the same time, the Castro government adopted a frankly "third front" position in international affairs, and showed increasingly violent hostility toward the United States.

The Communists, meanwhile, increasingly insisted that opposition to themselves was equivalent to opposition to the Cuban revolution and to the Castro regime. At the same time, they sought to picture as their own the program of social and economic reform being carried out by the Castro regime. However, the Communists' Partido Socialista Popular was not a part of the government, and, formally at least, had little to say in the formulation of government policy. Nor were avowed Communists given posts of importance in the labor movement. Those taking control of the C.T.C. after November, 1959, might best be described as "anti-anti-Communists." Although rumors were rife concerning the alleged Communist affiliation of some of the top officials of the Castro regime, little satisfactory evidence of such membership or association was actually presented.

The above developments in Peru, Colombia, Venezuela, and Cuba contributed considerably to Communist advances in the Latin American labor movement between 1957 and 1960; however, the Communists made progress in the trade unions of some other countries as well.

By 1960 the post-Perón labor movement of Argentina was divided roughly into four groups. These were the Peronista unions (known as the "62"), the Communist-influenced unions (the "19"), the strongly anti-Peronista groups (the "32"), and a considerable number of autonomous unions which did not belong to any of these factions. The Communist "19" group comprises several important unions, including the large Construction Workers' Union. They were perhaps the best-organized and most coherent of the four groups by the early months of 1960. Late in 1959 the "19" entered into a "unity of action" agreement with the Peronista "62" group, in spite of the fact that many Peronista union leaders were fearful of Communist infiltration in the ranks of their own organizations.

In Uruguay, too, the Communists gained considerable ground in the labor movement after 1957. The Confederación Sindical Uruguaya, which in May, 1957, was the largest of the country's central labor groups, declined in the following years, and a number of its affiliates withdrew. In November, 1959, a conference was held between a number of independent unions and those belonging to the Communist-controlled Unión General de Trabajadores. Out of this meeting came a provisional committee for a new Central Unica de Trabajadores, which undoubtedly included most of the militant unions of Uruguay, and probably a majority of all of the country's labor organizations.

The anti-Communist Confederación Costarricense del Trabajo "Rerum Novarum" suffered a decline after 1957 similar to that of the Uruguayan Confederación. A number of its affiliates broke away and became independent. Meanwhile, the Communists' Confederación General de Trabajadores Costarricenses became the largest central labor body of the country, although it represented a minority of all of the country's unions.

In Guatemala, too, the Communists have achieved a considerable resurgence in their trade union strength. They captured control of the Federación Autónoma Sindical de Guatemala, originally a Catholic union group. By 1960 this was the largest central labor body in the country with approximately a score of unions in its membership.

Finally, although the Communists could not boast a central labor body of any size in Mexico, they did show a considerable increase in trade union influence in 1958 and 1959. This influence was notable in the Railroad Workers' Union, the Teachers' Union, and some other important organizations.

On a hemispheric level, the Communists have sought to exploit this increase in their influence and to take advantage of the growth of anti-Yankee sentiments in the Latin American labor movements and in general public opinion. For this purpose, they adopted early in 1959 a new hemispheric trade union policy. Instead of building up their old hemispheric labor apparatus, the Confederación de Trabajadores de América Latina, they urged the establishment of a new "neutral" trade union federation for Latin America. This group would have no United States or Canadian affiliates.

The Communist-controlled Central Unica de Trabajadores de Chile took the lead in promoting this line early in 1959. Delegates were sent to various other Latin American countries for this purpose; and although their efforts were not immediately successful, in November and December of the same year, the congresses of the Cuban and Venezuelan labor movements gave friendly consideration to the establishment of a new "neutral" labor group, the former completely endorsing the idea and promising to take the leadership in it. These successes led the Communists early in January, 1960, to announce the liquidation of the Confederación de Trabajadores de América Latina, as a move towards "Latin American labor unity."

It is too early to predict what the net result of this new Communist hemispheric trade union policy will be. Its failure or success will without doubt depend largely on the general trend of Inter American relations. However, this policy does represent a comeback for the Communists in the labor movement of the Latin American countries, and it has arisen partly because of the attitudes of the United States. For the first time in more than a decade, the Communists have been gaining influence and prestige among the trade unionists of the hemisphere. At this juncture, it is necessary to view the situation of the Latin American Communists against the general picture of relations between the Latin American countries and the United States. The principal relevant factors in this picture, perhaps, are the widespread anti-Yankee feeling prevalent below the Río Grande and the efforts of certain elements in the Latin American countries to build up "neutralism" in the region. The Communists have given full support to this move.

The Castro Government in Cuba has taken the lead in attempting to develop this "third force." At least two of its major acts point in this direction: first, the summoning of a conference of underdeveloped nations to meet in Havana late in 1960; second, the signing in January, 1960, of a commercial agreement with the Soviet Union, whereby that country will purchase 1,000,000 tons of sugar a year for five years—approximately 20 per cent of Cuba's total annual output. Cuba has also made trade agreements with other Communist countries and with a number of uncommitted Asian and African states. The Cubans are anxious to influence other Latin American nations in the same direction. How successful they will be will depend a great deal upon the attitude which the United States takes both toward Cuba and toward Latin America in general.

Perhaps the developments among the Communists of Latin America since 1957, when this book was first published, may best be summarized by saying that the Communists have gained ground largely as a result of a growing anti-United States feeling in Latin America. That feeling is itself the result of the mistaken policies on the part of the United States. A recasting of United States policy toward Latin America on the basis of support for political democracy, and full-fledged cooperation in the economic development of Latin America, are still the best means that the United States can adopt to prevent further Communist gains below the Río Grande.

Robert J. Alexander

Rutgers University
New Brunswick, N.J.
*May, 1960*

# Preface to the 1963 Printing

THE YEARS THAT HAVE PASSED since the 1960 printing of this book have brought some successes to the Communists in Latin America. They have also brought some Communist failures and the seeds of what well may be a major crisis in the Communist movement in the Western Hemisphere.

The most notable success has come in Cuba. There, the Fidel Castro administration formally proclaimed itself an avowedly Communist government in May, 1961. This is the first such regime to appear in the Western Hemisphere.

The ousting of the democratic Leftist elements from the Castro government in the last months of 1959 marked a decisive turning point in the Cuban revolution. From then on, Fidel's regime was turned into a dictatorship, with the suppression of freedom of the press and freedom of assembly and organization for anyone critical of the regime, and the forceful seizure of the labor movement. With these developments, the opposition to the Castro regime grew. Hundreds of thousands of opponents, many of them former members of the Rebel Army and the 26th of July Movement, left the island. Others went to the hills, to organize once again a guerrilla movement against dictatorship. The old 26th of July underground was reorganized, and in the early months of 1961 engaged in an extensive campaign of terrorism against the regime. However, the underground and guerrilla opposition to the Castro regime was decimated as a result of the ill-fated and ill-advised invasion of Cuba in April, 1961, by exiled oppositionists under the patronage of the Consejo Revolucionario, and with the active backing of the United States government. Tens of thousands of people suspected of being disaffected were jailed; some leaders of the opposition, including Castro's first Minister of Agriculture, Captain Humberto Sori Marín, were executed.

In the meanwhile, the Castro regime had been moving steadily in the Communist direction. Increasingly large numbers of members of the Partido Socialista Popular were given posts in the administration. In the international arena, Castro began a series of harsh attacks on the United States, starting a chain of mutual recriminations between the Castro government and that of the United States. These recriminations reached a crisis stage in August, 1961, when the United States suspended purchases of sugar from Cuba. This was followed by a threat by Nikita Khrushchev "symbolically" to drop nuclear bombs on the United States if it intervened in the island, and by Castro's seizure of property owned by United States citizens and corporations in Cuba. The Soviet Union agreed to purchase the Cuban sugar that the United States did not take, as well as to extend considerable aid to Cuban economic development. Within a few months more than three quarters of Cuban trade was with the countries of the Russian bloc.

Even before the April, 1961, invasion, Castro and other strong men of the regime began to refer to the Cuban revolution as "socialist" rather than "humanist," the adjective they had previously used. On May 1, Fidel formally proclaimed the "socialist" nature of the revolution, within a context that made it perfectly clear that he was referring to the Communist brand of socialism.

This move was followed on July 26, 1961, with the announcement by Castro of the formation of the Organizaciones Revolucionarias Integradas (ORI). This was to be the preliminary form of a proposed Partido Único de la Revolución Socialista, and was to consist of a merger of the old Partido Socialista Popular with the remnants of the 26th of July Movement and the Directorio Revolucionario. The organization of the ORI was placed in the hands of an old-time Communist leader, Aníbal Escalante.

In the following months, old-line Communists moved into key positions within the Castro regime. In November, 1961, Lázaro Peña, who had led the Confederación de Trabajadores de Cuba between 1938 and 1947, as a result of the alliance of the Communists with dictator Fulgencio Batista, was reinstalled as formal head of the labor movement, which he had in fact been running for many months. At about the same time, Juan Marinello, former president of the Partido Socialista Popular and former member of Batista's cabinet, was named rector of the University of Havana.

Carlos Rafael Rodríguez, who had been the principal Communist liaison man with Castro, was given two important posts during this period. He succeeded Ernesto Guevara as the country's chief planning official, and a few months later succeeded Fidel Castro himself as president of the very powerful Instituto Nacional de Reforma Agraria.

The Communist nature of the Castro regime was confirmed beyond all possibility of doubt on December 2, 1961, in a speech by Fidel himself. This speech, to graduates of a training school for cadre members of the ORI, consisted largely of reminiscences of Castro's intellectual and philosophical development, but culminated in a proclamation that he was and always would remain a Marxist-Leninist. Throughout the speech he referred to the Partido Socialista Popular as "the party," and paid many tributes to it, admitting that it had been right throughout most of the revolution and he had been wrong.

Another country in which the Communists made considerable progress was Brazil. Although the Communist party led by Luiz Carlos Prestes remains illegal, at least in theory, it benefited from the fact that a more sympathetic government has come to power. President João Goulart, who took office in August, 1961, was much more willing than any of his predecessors to work with the Communists. As a result of the friendly attitude of the Goulart regime, the Communists reportedly were able to get many of their members and friends into posts in the lower and middle ranks of the administration. Cooperation was also evident in the ranks of organized labor, where at least until the middle of 1963 close associates of Goulart were supporting Communist elements to take over key organizations in the labor movement and organize a central labor federation.

The Communist party of Prestes strongly supported the Goulart regime. It did so in part because it approved of that administration's foreign policy, which was described by leading government spokesmen as "independent." This independence involved re-establishing diplomatic relations with the Soviet Union and other Communist-controlled countries, a considerable increase in trade with that part of the world, and disagreement with the position of the United States on the Cuban issue and others.

The Communists also experienced several failures in Latin America after early 1960. One of the most important of these was the sharp decline in the general popularity of the Castro regime. In spite of the almost universal support for the Castro government by elements of the Left and Center in Latin America during the first year or so, the increasingly dictatorial trend of that regime alienated the democratic Left. The formal declaration of Communist faith by Castro in 1961 removed whatever lingering doubts there may have been in this segment of public opinion before that time.

Another defeat for the Latin American Communists was their inability to muster support for a new Latin American labor confederation. The idea for such a confederation had been launched early in 1959 by the

Communist-controlled Central Única de Trabajadores de Chile (C.U.T.-Ch.). In November of the same year, the Confederación de Trabajadores de Cuba endorsed the idea, proclaiming its intention of taking the lead in organizing a "revolutionary Latin American Confederation of Labor."

The plans for this new confederation moved very slowly. Its sponsors were unable to obtain the support of important elements that they had hoped to bring into the group. Thus, at the end of 1960, the Confederación de Trabajadores de Venezuela, which had at first been in favor of the group, broke off all relations with the Cuban labor movement and declared its opposition to the proposed confederation. A year and a half later it joined the democratically oriented Organización Regional Interamericana de Trabajadores (O.R.I.T.). The Bolivian labor movement and the Peronista faction of the Argentine trade unions also refused to sanction plans for the new confederation.

As a result of these developments, when the Central Única de Trabajadores de América Latina (C.U.T.A.L.) was organized in a congress in Santiago, Chile, in September, 1962, it represented little more than a reconstitution of the defunct Communist-controlled Confederación de Trabajadores de América Latina (C.T.A.L.). The only new elements in the reconstituted confederation were the C.U.T.Ch., which had been under Communist control since its establishment a decade before, and the Brazilian Confederação Nacional dos Trabalhadores na Industria, which sent observers but not full-fledged delegates, and did not ultimately join the new C.U.T.A.L.

Of the national Communist parties, that of Venezuela suffered the most serious reverses between 1960 and 1963. At the end of 1960 it launched a policy of violent opposition to the government of President Rómulo Betancourt. Communists staged terroristic attacks in Caracas and other major cities, as well as in the oil fields, and attempted to establish a guerrilla war front. In spite of the fact that the campaign of violence caused considerable embarrassment to the Betancourt regime, it was a failure. As a result, the prestige and popular following of the Communist party of Venezuela suffered a disastrous decline. Whereas in 1958 and 1959 the influence of the Communists among the country's journalists was dominant, almost all such influence had disappeared by 1963. Whereas it was almost impossible for any political leader openly to attack the Communists in 1958 and 1959, even the most boisterous opposition politician in 1963 was careful to preface any reference to the Communists with "of course, I have no connection with the Communists, but. . . ."

Perhaps the most obvious indication of the decline of the influence of the Venezuelan Communist party was in the labor movement. In 1959 the Communists controlled perhaps 20 per cent of the country's unions. By April, 1963, when all of the opposition parties joined to form the rival labor confederation to the Confederación de Trabajadores de Venezuela, the Central Única de Trabajadores de Venezuela (C.U.T.V.), this new group claimed only four hundred of the country's thirty-four hundred registered unions. Even if the Communists controlled half of these organizations, this indicates a very sharp decline in Communist influence in organized labor.

More important than these setbacks, which might well prove temporary, was the crisis that began to develop in the Latin American Communist movement during the 1960 to 1963 period. This crisis had its roots in the Latin American area, but it also had its connections with the worldwide troubles in the Communist movement, arising from the growing split between the Russian and Chinese parties. The fundamental issue involved in this crisis was that of the road to power. Opinion was increasingly divided between those who felt that violence in the form of urban terrorism and guerrilla warfare was the only effective way by which the Communists could achieve power in the Latin American nations, and those who favored a more versatile approach to the problem. Not only did factions develop within the Communist parties, but the Communists and their allies began to differ, with potentialities of open animosity.

There was evidence of a difference of opinion in several of the Latin American Communist parties. In the Brazilian party, an actual split took place early in 1961. Although the contention centered on issues within the party, particularly the role that Luiz Carlos Prestes was to play in its leadership, the two groups took different sides on the question of the road to power and the Russo-Chinese split. The majority group, still led by Luiz Carlos Prestes, favored peaceful penetration of the Goulart regime as the road to power and the Russian side in the world-wide dispute. The smaller group, led by Mauricio Grabois and other former top leaders of the united party, violently opposed the Goulart regime and favored the violent road to power, while in international affairs siding with the Chinese.

By the beginning of 1963 an even more serious crisis had developed within the Venezuelan Communist party. The older leaders of the party were by that time in favor of abandoning the use of violence; however, their efforts to convince a party conference to accept this idea in January, 1963, failed. In June of the same year, Gustavo Machado was successful in convincing his party comrades to agree to a two-week suspension of the violence campaign, in the hope that the government would then come to terms with them. When it failed to do so, however, the violence was renewed.

In at least two of the Latin American Communist parties, pro-Chinese factions were expelled during 1962. This took place in the Chilean and Mexican parties. In several other parties younger members were growing restless at the "moderateness" of their leaders.

Perhaps of greater future importance was the growing problem between the Communists and their allies. These allies may be labeled the Jacobin Left, since they have characteristics similar to those of the Jacobins of the French Revolution. They are in favor of violent social change at whatever cost, they are xenophobic nationalists, and they are opposed to "formal" political democracy, as they are wont to call it.

The Jacobin Leftists in the various Latin American countries had developed in the years just preceding the Cuban revolution. With the victory of Castro, these elements saw in him the natural leader of their cause. He had demonstrated that it was possible to come to power in a Latin American country through guerrilla warfare, he had effectively defied the United States—the ambition of most Latin American nationalists—and there was little doubt about the fundamental nature of the reforms that he was bringing to the Cuban economy and society.

By 1963 the Jacobin Left still consisted of small and discordant groups in most of the Latin American countries in which it was active. In Venezuela it consisted of the small Movimiento de Izquierda Revolucionaria and a part of the Unión Republicana Democrática. In Peru it consisted of the Movimiento de Izquierda Revolucionaria (originally founded as the Apra Rebelde), the Partido Social Progresista, and perhaps the Trotskyite Partido Obrero Revolucionario. In Argentina it consisted of at least one faction of the much-splintered Socialist party as well as of various dissident elements of the Unión Cívica Radical Intransigente of ex-President Arturo Frondizi. In Uruguay, Chile, and Ecuador, all or part of the Socialist parties had joined the Jacobin Left. There were Jacobin Left groups in several other countries.

During the first years of the Cuban revolution, the Jacobin Leftist groups were a great asset to the Communists. Unlike nearly all other groups in Latin American politics, they were willing to work with the Communists, particularly in defense of the Cuban revolution; however, by the end of 1962 there had begun to develop important differences of opinion between the Communists and the Jacobin Left. It seems probable that the rift will become greater.

The Cuban missile crisis of October, 1962, served to bring out such divergences between the two groups. This arose over the presence of Soviet missiles in Cuba, and after President Kennedy ordered a blockade of the island, Premier Khrushchev agreed to withdraw the missiles. The Communist parties of Latin America were unanimous in their support of the action of Khrushchev in withdrawing the missiles. The Jacobin Leftists were generally highly critical of this action. Furthermore, during the week of the crisis itself, the the Communists were generally in favor of caution, whereas the Jacobin Leftists wanted to organize violent demonstrations against the United States. In Chile, for instance, the Communists succeeded only with great difficulty in dissuading the Socialists from calling a general strike of protest against the position of the United States.

Instances of discord between the Cuban Communists and their Jacobin Left allies were numerous in 1962 and 1963. There, in spite of the formal merger of the Communists and the Castroites, rivalry and controversy persisted between them. So many leading Communists had moved into key positions in the regime by March, 1962, that it seemed as if the Partido Socialista Popular was taking over control of the Castro government. Castro took prompt action. When in the early days of March the membership of the national executive committee of the ORI was announced, it contained only ten members from the old Communist party, while fourteen were from the 26th of July Movement and one was from the old Directorio Revolucionario.

Then on March 18 Castro began a series of violent attacks on the leaders of the old Communist party, accusing them of doing exactly what they were trying to do—take complete control of the regime. He attacked Aníbal Escalante personally, as a result of which Escalante fled to Czechoslovakia. Subsequently, most of the old Communists whom Escalante had put in charge of regional and local organizations of ORI were replaced with 26th of July people. A unique method was used for recruiting rank and file members of the new party. Groups of workers in factories, collective and state farms, and commercial enterprises were brought together to nominate members. From them, the local authorities of ORI chose those that they wanted. Thus, the old Communists were flooded by a group of newcomers, loyal to Fidel and not to them.

In the broader Latin American Communist field, Castro found himself in an equivocal position. His regime had come to depend economically almost completely on the Soviet Union, with 80 per cent or more of the country's trade being with the U.S.S.R. and other Eastern European countries. However, whether he liked it or not, he was the model and logical leader for those in and around the Latin American Communist movement who sympathized with the Chinese position. His revolution was the kind that the Chinese were advocating for all of the under-developed countries, and they made no secret of their recognition of this fact.

Castro reacted very strongly against the Soviet Union move to withdraw its missiles from Cuba in October, 1962, though subsequently he patched up his relations with the U.S.S.R. On a visit to Moscow at the end of April, 1963, he was the star of the Soviet celebration of May Day. Upon his return, he announced that the Russians were going to improve the conditions under which they had been purchasing Cuban sugar, but went out of his way to say that he had offered no political concessions in return for this generosity.

There is no doubt that Castro was aware of being caught in the growing split in the international Communist movement. Before and after his trip to Moscow, he made constant appeals to the divergent Communist groups to get together and not to let their differences of opinion result in an actual breakup of international Communism.

Thus, by the middle of 1963 the Latin American Communists found themselves deeply involved in the crisis of world Communism. Although their chances for coming to power in one or more Latin American countries had improved because of the pressure for rapid economic development and social reform, a possible split in their own ranks and the rise of a dynamic revolutionary group on their Left threatened to impede their movement from taking advantage of new opportunities.

ROBERT J. ALEXANDER

Rutgers University
New Brunswick, N.J.
*September, 1963*

# Contents

Communism in Latin America

# Part One

*The Communist Movement in Latin America—
Its Background, History, and Prospects*

## Chapter I

# Conditions Favoring the Rise of Communism in Latin America

COMMUNISM BREEDS ON DISCONTENT. Discontent is the historical background for the Communist movement in Latin America. Conditions of life in most countries south of the Rio Grande are still backward, poor, and in many cases oppressive. Wages are low; chances for advancement are limited; class and racial barriers are high. Yet this pattern is changing, and changing rapidly. For more than a generation there has been a widespread revolt against traditional conditions. The Industrial Revolution and social revolutions come hand-in-hand. It is this movement of revolt that the Communists have tried to exploit.

Latin America is still a predominantly agricultural region, in spite of the tremendous strides towards industrialization which have been taken since World War I. In many regions, agriculture has been truly feudal in its landholding patterns, and class differences have been intensified by a racial distinction between the landlord class and the tenants or peons.

Medieval methods of exploitation of land and labor have been particularly prevalent in the Indian countries: Peru, Ecuador, Bolivia, Guatemala, and Mexico. In the first two countries, these conditions still exist, though in the other three, more or less thorough moves have been made in recent years to abolish them.

In these countries, where Indians make up the great mass of the agricultural tenants and peons, there has been a struggle, ever since the Conquest, between white or mestizo (half Indian-half white) landlords and Indian agricultural communities, a battle in which the Indians have been generally the losers. The Indian has had little standing in the courts of law, and although in colonial times the King and, to a lesser degree, the Church sought to afford him some protection, the instruments of government have been largely in the hands of the Indian's oppressors. As a result, it was for centuries a comparatively simple procedure for the landlords to steal, bit by bit, the holdings of the Indian communities.

Those Indians who came under the control of the white and mestizo landlords were as good as bound to the soil. They were granted a bit of

3

land upon which to grow their corn and beans, but in return for this were obliged to till the soil of the landlord gratis. Until recent years, the Indians of Bolivia were obliged to spend six days a week thus laboring on the lands of their "patrons."

In these Indian countries and in most others, the personal relations between the landlord and his tenants and laborers were those of master and servant. It is still true in much of rural Chile that tenants and laborers must take off their hats in the presence of their employer. Any attempt to argue about the conditions under which they labor is regarded as "subversive." Much the same conditions obtain in rural Brazil, and until recent years were widespread in Argentina.

The income of most of the agricultural workers and tenants in Latin America has been hopelessly low. Most of the population of Latin America is still "out of the market"; that is to say, they receive little, if any, money income with which to purchase the output of manufacturing industries, native or foreign.

They live in more or less self-sufficient communities, where they grow most of their own food supply—a food supply which leaves most of them victims of malnutrition and the diseases which it breeds. They build their own huts of mud and wattle, or clapboard or sometimes stone; often they produce all or part of their own clothing. Such food and clothing as they cannot produce for themselves, they get in the local village, where purchase is often by barter rather than cash.

Most Latin Americans have little acquaintance with those material things which have become necessities in more advanced countries. Many, if not most, of them have never seen a moving picture. Scarcely any agricultural workers own radios, though in some cases they have become familiar with them through public loud-speakers in the village.

Until recent years, few rural workers of Latin America had travelled more than a few miles from their native village. Medical attention is still minimal, and incantations and local herbs have been the only protection against or cure for disease. Although scourges such as plague, yellow fever, smallpox, and more recently malaria have given way before growing public health services, many, if not most, of the rural workers and tenants of Latin America still suffer more or less constantly from diseases caused by intestinal parasites and undernourishment.

Of course, there have been exceptions to this state of affairs. The workers in the more modern forms of agricultural activity, particularly those producing commodities for sale in the world market, have lived under better circumstances. In the sugar fields of Cuba, Puerto Rico, and the northern part of the Pacific coast of South America, employers have been forced to pay their labor money wages, and have found it to their own advantage to provide the health services which will assure healthy workers, who can do a full day's labor. In Cuba and Puerto Rico, too, strong labor movements have grown up, which have greatly modified the ancient subservience of the agricultural worker to his employer.

The great plantations of the United and Standard Fruit Companies of Central America and the West Indies have also brought a different way of living for agricultural workers. They have not only provided excellent health services, they have built houses which are a considerable improvement over the huts from which these workers originally came, and are good even when compared with the habitations of the average Latin American city worker. These agricultural workers, also, have come into closer contact with the amenities of modern civilization: plumbing, schools, motion pictures. These companies have, however, found it hard to learn to treat their people as anything more than children who must be housed, fed, doctored, and entertained.

In recent years many agricultural workers have sought liberation by fleeing to the cities. The cities of Latin America have grown phenomenally in the last three decades. Mexico City, for instance, has more than quadrupled in size since the beginning of the Mexican Revolution in 1910, and has doubled since the middle 1930's. São Paulo has grown almost as fast and has become the biggest city in Brazil and the second largest in South America.

This tremendous increase in the population of Latin American cities has occurred in exactly the period during which the countries concerned have cut off immigration from abroad, so all the increase in urban population has come by reason of migration from the countryside. The East Coast countries of South America have, as a result, been faced with a serious shortage of agricultural workers.

Although the move of the Latin American worker from the countryside to urban industry has not as yet brought him a standard of living comparable to those of the workers of the more advanced industrial nations, it has brought him new social and economic freedom. The Latin American urban worker does not have the servile attitude of the agricultural tenant or wage worker. He is a man, a citizen, and often a trade union member, not a serf. With this improved status and greater freedom has come a desire to improve his position still more.

Insofar as the story of the Communists in Latin America is concerned, this increased independence and feeling of unrest of the urban workingman is more important than his actual low standards of living, and much more important than the lower standards of his rural brothers. For the movement of social unrest and revolt which has swept Latin America since World War I, has been with some few exceptions, an urban development.

The city has been in revolt against the chains which custom, history, and the law have imposed upon it. Conscious of its increased economic power, it has been unwilling to be content any longer with a secondary role in the life of the nations of the continent.

The social classes which have been particularly active in the Latin American social revolution have been the working class, both the white-collar and the manual workers, and the growing industrial (and to some degree commercial) middle class. It was their voices, their votes, their money, and their strong right arms which, upon occasion, broke the crust of the landholder-dominated, semifeudal Latin American society of the days before World War I.

The Latin American social revolution has had four basic components: nationalism, economic development, change in class relationships, and political democracy. The Communists have tried with greater or less success to use each and all of these factors in their propaganda and organization.

As nationalism has spread in the modern world, Latin America has caught the infection. Generally, the growing nationalism of Latin America has taken the form of a desire to be "free" from real or alleged subservience to certain of the Great Powers. This has often led to a feeling of unity among the Latin Americans themselves, and perhaps helps to explain why growing nationalism has not more often been turned against Latin American neighbors.

Latin American nationalism has been largely "anti-imperialism." During World War I and the post-World War I period, it centered on the struggle against United States interference in the internal affairs of the Latin American countries, against United States invasions of Nicaragua, Mexico, the Dominican Republic, Haiti, and other countries, and against evidences of Latin American subservience to the United States, such as the infamous Platt Amendment to the Cuban constitution.

With the Good Neighbor Policy, and the agreement by the United States to recognize the juridical equality of all of the American nations, the emphasis shifted from opposing overt intervention by the United States Government to resisting what many Latin Americans conceived to be the intervention by United States private business interests in the internal affairs of their nations.

There developed a widespread resentment toward foreign ownership of key elements in the Latin American economy. Expropriation of United States agricultural and petroleum interests in Mexico and of American petroleum interests in Bolivia before World War II, as well as repatriation of British and French investments in the public utilities and railroads of Argentina, Uruguay, and Brazil after World War II, were evidences of this feeling.

The two World Wars and the Great Depression undoubtedly fed the fires of nationalism in Latin America. During World War II, in particular, the Latin Americans were actively courted by both sides. They also were impressed with the importance to the Allied war effort of their provision of key raw materials and supplies. The importance of their role was even more evident to the citizens of Brazil and Mexico, because of the participation of their forces in the victorious armies.

The wars and the depression particularly aroused economic nationalism. The Latin American countries, whose role in the world economy had been largely that of producers of agricultural and mineral raw materials, became painfully aware of the dangers of an economy based on one or two such products.

In both wars and the depression, the Latin American countries had difficulty both in selling their mineral and agricultural products and in obtaining the manufactured goods which they needed from the industrial nations of Europe and North America. Those experiences convinced most thinking Latin Americans that their nations must become more self-sufficient. They became eager to diversify their countries' economies, and in particular to develop manufacturing industries.

This drive for economic development has become an integral part of the Latin American social revolution. Since the early 1930's, it has become almost an article of faith. Few politicians in the region would dare openly to proclaim opposition to industrialization and economic diversification. Virtually all of the countries have provided protection for infant industries, either through old-fashioned tariffs or through more newfangled exchange control devices. Many of the countries have established development banks or corporations, which have brought the government into active participation in the process of economic development.

The net result of this growing economic diversification has been to strengthen the urban against the rural elements in the economic and political life of the Latin American nations. It has also hastened the demands for fundamental redistribution of power in the economies and politics of the Latin American nations.

This class realignment is the third fundamental feature of the Latin American social revolution. It has taken two principal forms: a demand for agrarian reform, and moves to strengthen the position of the urban worker by organizing him for his self-defense and writing legislation on his behalf.

With the exception of Mexico, agrarian reform has at first been urged and promulgated by city folk. However, it has been the means of involving the agricultural worker and tenant in the civic and economic life of his community and nation. It is likely that pressure will come, increasingly, from the agricultural worker himself for an extension of agrarian reform in such parts of the region as it has not yet encompassed.

The growth of the trade union movement and of protective legislation has also been an integral part of the realignment of classes. It has been closely associated with the nationalist drive, since the first large conglom-

erations of wageworkers were usually those employed by foreign enterprises—railroads, public utilities, mines, factory farms, and manufacturing
enterprises—and labor organization thus took on a patriotic coloration.
Union organizations, strikes, and other movements aimed against foreign-
owned enterprises were often able to enlist a general sympathy in the community which they probably never would have aroused had the firms involved been owned and operated by nationals.

Labor legislation and trade unionism have been surprisingly advanced
for the type of economy which Latin America has possessed. By the end
of World War II there was virtually no nation in Latin America which
did not have its Labor Code—detailing the treatment of labor in factory
legislation, social security, regulation of collective bargaining, and support and control of trade unions.

In virtually every nation the great majority of "organizable" workers
—those on railroads, docks, and ships, in factories, in public utilities, even
in many factory farms—are now in trade unions. These workers' organizations are still weak, being too dependent upon the good will of a political party or the State, but they have succeeded in arousing the working
class to its possibilities and, in a more limited way, to its responsibilities.

The growth of strong middle and working classes has had profound
effects on the social, economic, and political structure of Latin America.
In Mexico and Chile power over the State passed from the landholding
aristocracy to the urban middle and working masses—though in the latter
case, the city folk had not dared even by the 1950's to attack the aristocracy in its rural strongholds and carry out an effective agrarian reform.

In other countries, too, political power changed hands. The Vargas
Revolution of 1930, despite all the subsequent vagaries, effectively took
control of the national government out of the hands of the rural landholders, though there, as in Chile, the new political forces did not dare
attack the aristocracy on its own home ground. The Perón Revolution,
whatever else it brought, ended once and for all the control of the rural
landlords and cattle barons over the destinies of Argentina.

The 1952 Revolution in Bolivia signalized the end of the feudal era in
that country. Events since the death of Juan Vicente Gómez in 1936 have
greatly undermined the position of the rural landholding element in Venezuela, though that unfortunate country had not by 1957 been able to
throw off the century-old curse of military domination of political affairs.

In all the countries in which the shift in class power has begun, it is a
continuing process, in most cases still far from completion. Even in Mexico, the Revolution which began in 1910 was still 45 years later a living
and evolving phenomenon.

In some countries the shift in class relations had not occurred by the
early 1950's. In Peru it lagged behind, the alliance of the military with
the traditional landowning and mercantile classes keeping a firm if un-

easy grip on the nation. Central America was still largely controlled by large landowners and military men. The dictatorship of Generalissimo Rafael Leónidas Trujillo had converted the traditional system of the Dominican Republic into a personal monopoly of power and wealth.

The shift in class relationships was accompanied by a struggle for political democracy. This is the fourth element in the Latin American social revolution.

The desire on the part of the masses of the people of Latin America for greater participation in the affairs of their government, and for the fundamental freedoms associated with political democracy, was profound indeed. However, the great danger in the Latin American social revolution has been that it might be diverted from democratic channels, that democracy might be sacrificed to achieve the other objectives of the revolution. This certainly occurred in Argentina under Perón. The Communists, too, have constantly sought—though frequently using democratic slogans —to direct the revolution into courses which would result in the establishment of their own particular brand of totalitarianism.

The Communists have consistently attempted to use all the slogans of the Latin American social revolution for their own propaganda. They have striven especially hard to portray themselves as ardent nationalists of the particular countries in which they were operating.

The Communists have embraced "anti-imperialism" with a vengeance. During most of their history they have been violently opposed to the United States' economic, political, and social influence in Latin America. Only during the late 1930's and the second part of World War II, when their "anti-imperialist" propaganda was directed against Axis influence in Latin America, have they modified their "anti-Yanquism."

During the 1920's and early 1930's the Communists had some success in enlisting Latin Americans in their world-wide campaign against "imperialism." Many Latin American intellectuals, including Haya de la Torre, people who were later active in the Venezuelan Democratic Action Party, and other non-Communists, were among the delegates to the World Congress Against War and Imperialism of 1928. Many of them continued to be active in the League Against Imperialism founded at the 1928 meeting and in the several Anti-War and Anti-Imperialist Congresses held in America.

Since World War II the Communist campaign against the United States in Latin America has been renewed with increased intensity. Campaigns "for peace" and "against Yanqui imperialism" became the principal preoccupation of the Latin American Communists.

In spite of the Latin American Communists' attempt to portray themselves as true-blue nationalists, it has been too obvious, in many instances, that their basic orientation was Russian, not Chilean or Brazilian or Argentine. This was particularly true during World War II. In the beginning they adopted a violent "anti-imperialist" position, aimed against the Allies and against the United States, and in some instances even bordered on anti-Semitism, so violent were their sympathies for the Axis.

Then, with the entry of the Soviet Union into the war, the Communists of Latin America, as everywhere else, adopted an equally violent pro-war attitude. So extreme was their position of "support for the United Nations," that they used their influence in the labor movement throughout the continent to put a damper on virtually all attempts at strikes and other movements upon the part of the organized workers. Frequently, such movements were denounced by the Communists as being of Nazi inspiration or worse.

During the war, too, they were less cautious about hiding their association with the Soviet Union. They tried to use the widespread sympathy for the Soviet Union's bitter struggle against the Nazis to aid their own positions in their respective countries. This tended to rebound upon them in later years, when popular sympathy for the Soviet Union had to a very considerable degree turned into hostility.

The Communists also have attempted to make use of the strong drive for economic development in the Latin American countries. This often fitted in very well with their opposition to the United States. They spread widely the idea that the United States was purposely trying to hold back the development of the Latin American countries. They were ardent advocates of the industrialization of Latin America and at the end of World War II went so far as virtually to advocate "calling off" the class struggle for a longer or shorter period of time, so as to form an alliance between the labor movements they controlled or influenced and the national employers' groups. At various times they toyed with the idea that the national employers were a "progressive" element in the economies of the various countries of Latin America, and sought to enlist their support in the campaign against United States influence in Latin America.

Of course, the Communists have attempted to take the leadership, when the opportunity presented itself, in upsetting traditional class relationships in Latin American countries. Their own doctrine has naturally made them seek a leading position in the trade union movements, and in some countries, such as Peru and Guatemala, Brazil and Cuba, they have attempted to develop support on the basis of appeals to suppressed racial groups—Indians in the first two instances, Negroes in the latter two.

From the early days the Communists have included in their programs demands for agrarian reform and other fundamental shifts in class and social relations in the Latin American countries. Only in Mexico and Guatemala have they had any real opportunity to take part in carrying out such changes, and in the former case they played only a very minor role.

At various times the Communists have attempted to theorize concerning the class changes which have been going on in Latin America. Their theories have varied with changes in the party line. Usually, however, they have urged that a bourgeois revolution of "national liberation" was the next step in the development of these countries; this was their line in Guatemala after World War II. However, they have also talked about a revolution which would result in the establishment of a "popular democracy" on the pattern of the early post-World War II regimes of Eastern Europe. This has been the line in Brazil and was adopted in Guatemala in the last months of the Arbenz regime. During the "Third Period" of the late 1920's and early 1930's the Communists tended to skip over the interim stages and seek the immediate establishment of an avowedly Communist regime. This was their line in Cuba, for instance, right after the fall of the Machado dictatorship in 1933, when they had the slogan of "Build the Soviets!" and actually attempted in some areas to establish their own governments on a local scale.

Finally, the Communists have attempted to capitalize on the fourth factor in the Latin American social revolution and depict themselves as supporters of democracy. There is no doubt that they have been severely persecuted by various Latin American governments from time to time, and they have pictured campaigns in defense of their own group as crusades for the general principles of political democracy and civil liberties. They laid particular stress on this role as defenders of the cause of democracy during World War II.

The Communists have thus attempted to use the rising tide of the Latin American social revolution as a means of bringing themselves to power. They have tried to seize the control of the revolutionary currents, and to divert them in the Communist direction. The surprising thing is not that they have occasionally succeeded in doing so, but rather that, in spite of the very profound feeling of revolt and change which has swept Latin America since World War I, the Communists have made comparatively little progress.

One of the key reasons why the Communists have not been more successful is that there have been other movements, of native Latin American origin, which have been able to seize and keep the leadership of the revolution in various countries. It is a very obvious fact that in any country in which there is another strong mass movement, the Communists have fared badly. Thus, in Peru, the Communists have never succeeded in getting any really wide base of support, and what importance they have had has come from the backing they have received from successive dictatorships. This has been due to the fact that the Aprista movement gained and held the support of the great masses of the people, who might otherwise have been influenced by Communist ideas and organization.

In Venezuela, too, the rise of the Democratic Action Party completely checked the progress of the Communists, and again the Communists' influence was largely something engendered by the dictators to act as a check on the influence of Democratic Action. In Cuba, the Auténtico movement had the same effect; in Costa Rica, the rise of the Liberación Nacional movement of José Figueres cut the very base out from under the Communists. In Puerto Rico the rise of the Popular Democratic Party of Muñoz Marín has undoubtedly prevented the Communists from getting a significant following.

Even in Argentina this same phenomenon has been repeated. The appearance of the Peronista movement in the middle 1940's undoubtedly had the result of checking the growing influence which the Communists had been enjoying inside and outside of the labor movement for about half a decade before the Peronista Revolution of 1943.

Chile and Guatemala further illustrate the fact that the best check for the Communists in Latin America has always been a native social revolutionary movement. The Communists in those two countries have been able to get real rank and file support and to wield tremendous influence on all aspects of the countries' life because of the lack of any such rival movement. In Chile such a movement existed in the decade of the 1930's, in the Socialist Party. However, as a result of a variety of circumstances the Socialist Party crumbled away, and the Communist Party gained an opportunity of which it made full use. Consequently, Chile was by the late 1940's one of the few countries in which the Communists had been able to build up a really substantial group of followers, who looked upon them as the only true defenders of the working class and the social revolution.

In Guatemala, the case was somewhat different, but equally informative. There, no rival social movement existed. As the result of peculiar circumstances, no leader and no party appeared able firmly to support and push forward the social revolution, but equally firmly reject Stalinism and all its works. As a consequence, in Guatemala the Communists achieved a degree of power which they probably have not obtained in any other Latin American nation and were able to build up a sizable body of popular support in the cities and in the countryside.

Those Latin American governments opposed to the social revolution have not infrequently worked with the Communists, in order to undermine the indigenous social revolutionary movements. This has been notoriously true of Peru and Venezuela. In the former country the Communists worked successively with the Sánchez Cerro, Benavides, Prado, and Odría dictatorships. In the elections of 1939 and 1950 Communists were elected to the dictator-controlled congress on the official ticket of the dictator. The Dictator-President Prado backed the Communists' bid for control of the labor movement, and General Odría in the late 1940's and early 1950's gave considerable help to the Communists in the labor movement.

In Venezuela, too, the dictatorial regimes opposed to the revolution worked with the Communists. While the democratically controlled trade unions were virtually destroyed after 1948, Communist-dominated unions continued to function with but little interference. Large public meetings were held by Communist trade unions, and they were allowed to hold regularly scheduled conventions. The work of the dictatorship was to turn control of a large part of the Venezuelan trade union movement over to the Communists.

Dictator Anastasio Somoza, of Nicaragua, and Dictator Generalissimo Rafael Leónidas Trujillo, of the Dominican Republic, both worked with the Communists during a short period in the middle 1940's, using them to bolster up their tottering dictatorships. In both of those countries the Communists got their first real chance as a result of this coquetting with the dictators.

The prevalence of dictatorial regimes in Latin America led to the development of a policy which may or may not have been consciously planned by the international Communist leaders responsible for the operations of the Communist Parties in Latin America. The widespread use of this new tactic, which was adopted in the late 1940's and early 1950's, makes it appear to be a well-designed, centrally directed move.

The tactic consisted of having more than one Communist Party in dictator-controlled countries. One party, usually the "official" one, engaged in more or less bitter opposition to the dictatorship; the other, "unofficial" but nonetheless, in actuality, just as official, supported the regime. This tactic was adopted in Argentina, Peru, Venezuela, and Cuba. In Mexico, more than one Communist Party was used, but for reasons which seem to be quite distinct from those in the other countries mentioned.

In Argentina the Communist Party had some difficulty making up its mind concerning what position to take in regard to Perón. At first, so long as World War II was on, they bitterly opposed Perón, coining the term "Peronazi" to describe his followers. However, after the war was over, and after Perón had been elected President of the Republic, they faltered. The official Party adopted a position of "critical support"; while a dissident faction broke away to form the Movimiento Obrero Comunista, under the leadership of former Politburo member Rodolfo Puiggros, which placed itself frankly in the Peronista ranks. In subsequent years, in spite of certain twistings and turnings, the official Communist Party tended to continue to regard itself as part of the Opposition, while the Movimiento Comunista was accepted as a fullfledged member of the Perón camp and came to have considerable influence in the inner circles of the Perón regime. It tried both to influence Perón and his followers in the Communist direction and to build up organizational strength in the Peronista trade unions.

In Peru the coming to power of the Odría dictatorship in 1948 resulted in the splitting of that country's Communist Party. The "official" group, led by Secretary General Jorge del Prado, was outlawed and went into opposition to the Odría regime. Another element, led by the Party's principal trade union figure, Juan P. Luna, allied itself with the Odría regime, formed a Workers Independent Electoral Committee, and won a senator and various deputies in the Odría congress.

In Venezuela the split in the Communist movement was older, dating from the middle 1940's, when the Communist Party split over the question of relations with the Medina Angarita dictatorship. Two separate parties were formed, one usually called the Red Communists, the other, the Black Communists. With the Army *coup d'état* in November, 1948, which ousted the Democratic Action government, the Black Communists adopted a policy of friendship towards the resultant military dictatorship and, as a result, were allowed to function quite openly, maintaining a significant hold on the country's trade union movement. The Red Communists, on the other hand, adopted a position of strong opposition to the military dictatorship and sought to work with the Democratic Action Party.

In Cuba the same tactic was used, but with a somewhat different twist as a result of General Batista's *coup d'état* in March, 1952. After a short period of hesitation, the Communist Party officially took a position of opposition to the dictatorship. However, a significant number of Communist trade union leaders withdrew from the party and joined the "Labor Bloc" of Batista's own Partido Acción Progresista. The P.A.P. was weak in labor support and welcomed them with open arms. The "unofficial" Communists were able to make some progress in rebuilding the Communists' trade union strength, which had been completely destroyed during the democratic administrations of Presidents Grau San Martín and Carlos Prío Socarras.

The split in Mexico has been of a somewhat different nature. It originated in considerable part from the prima donna attitude of Vicente Lombardo Toledano. During the 1940's Lombardo Toledano became the kingpin in the Communists' trade union activities in Latin America, but he refused to join the official Communist Party of Mexico, with whom he had fought many bitter battles in past years. Instead, he organized his own Partido Popular in 1947, which did not apparently lessen his position vis-à-vis the top leaders of the international Communist movement.

There is no doubt that, in some cases, democratic governments have also given aid and comfort to the Communists and have helped them to gain positions of importance. During World War II this tendency was widely prevalent. The Communists at that time were more pro-United Nations than the United Nations themselves, and their weight was welcomed in the fight against Naziism and Fascism both inside and outside of

Latin America. The Communists won more freedom of operation, and not infrequently actual aid, from the governments of Latin America during that period than during any other part of their history.

In particular cases, democratic leaders have worked with or used the Communists. This was true of President Lázaro Cárdenas of Mexico during the 1930's. He was in the midst of a severe struggle to carry forward agrarian reform and other aspects of his revolutionary program, and he welcomed any support he could get. The Communists were allowed to occupy important posts in the government-sponsored and oriented labor movement, the Confederación de Trabajadores de Mexico. During subsequent administrations the Communists lost most, if not all, of the ground they had gained during the Cárdenas period.

In Guatemala, too, the history of the late 1940's and early 1950's is one of the democratic government leaders working with and giving strong support to the Communists. Such instances have occurred, as well, in Chile under González Videla in 1946-47; in Ecuador on various occasions; in Colombia during the late 1930's and early 1940's, in Costa Rica during the administrations of Presidents Calderón Guardia and Teodoro Picado, to mention but a few examples.

One other factor has played a certain part in whatever success the Communists have had in Latin America—sympathy for the Soviet Union. It was to a very considerable extent admiration of the Russian Revolution which led to the founding of the Latin American Communist Parties. The Anarchists of Brazil were very sympathetic, and out of their ranks came the Brazilian Communist Party; the Socialist parties of Uruguay and Chile went over as such to the Communist International, largely because they wanted to be ranged alongside the "first workers' republic."

In the early years picturing the successes of "building socialism" in the Soviet Union was a very important part of the propaganda of the Latin American Communist Parties, and aroused a good deal of sympathy, perhaps more among the intellectuals than among the manual workers.

The great era of the Soviet appeal, however, was during the second World War. At that time the sympathy of the workers and the middle-class people of Latin America was overwhelmingly with the Allies, and there was very widespread admiration for the way in which the Red Army first stood off and then rolled back the armies of Hitler.

The Communists capitalized to the utmost upon this wartime sympathy for the Soviet Union. They became almost the principal spokesmen for the Russians—or at least seemed to be regarded as such by many in the Latin American countries. They urged closer relations with "our great ally," the Soviet Union, and various Latin American countries during this period recognized or re-recognized the Soviet Union. Relations were close between the new Russian embassies or legations and the Communist Parties of the various countries. There was little or no attempt to hide the close relationship between the Communists of Latin America and those of the Soviet Union. On the contrary, every attempt was made to capitalize upon this relationship.

The tide of sympathy for the Soviet Union ebbed after the War, a feeling of hostility developed in many parts as a result of the intensification of the Cold War, and the close relation of the Communists with the Russians lost its appeal. They became less ostentatious about it, and it seems likely that distrust arising from this relationship was a considerable factor in alienating a large part of the Latin American working class in the postwar years. Local Latin American nationalisms were ruffled by the professed adherence of the Communists to the Soviet Union.

In the early 1950's the Communists used their Soviet connections in still another way. Although they never ceased to picture the beauties of life in the Soviet Union, they began to lay emphasis on a somewhat more practical aspect of the subject. Resentment was widespread in many Latin American countries against the great dependence of their economies on that of the United States. The Communists, of course, helped in any way they could to stir up this resentment. One of their most potent arguments was to picture trade with the Soviet Union, Eastern Europe, and China as an answer to this excessive dependence on the United States.

The Chilean Communists were using this argument as early as 1946-47, when the González Videla government recognized the Soviet Union, a Soviet Embassy was established, and rumors flew that González was willing to negotiate with the Russians concerning the export of the country's copper output—which at that time was still selling at a low price fixed by United States authorities.

Later this became a theme exploited throughout the hemisphere. The success of some of the countries of Western Europe in negotiating limited trade treaties with the Soviet Union contributed to a widespread belief that such trade accords could be reached by Latin America. The negotiation of a treaty between Argentina and the Soviet Union in September, 1953, for the exchange of about $150,000,000 worth of goods each way further contributed to the popularity of this idea.

The Communists, naturally, did their utmost to publicize the virtues of the Communist countries as trading partners. In Bolivia they suggested such trade as a possible solution to the pressing tin problem. In Guatemala they encouraged the government actually to undertake negotiations with the Communist countries. Various Latin American groups attended the Moscow Economic Conference in 1952, though no concrete results seem to have been achieved by them there, and some of the delegates, at least, returned without any great enthusiasm.

Such success as the Communists have had in Latin America has been due, then, to three principal factors: their ability to exploit the Latin American social revolution; help which they have received from various governments, dictatorial and democratic; and their more or less close connection with the Soviet Union.

On the other hand, their chief stumbling blocks in the area have undoubtedly been indigenous social revolutionary movements which have been able to capture the imagination of the people of the various countries and to lead these people down the road to social, economic, and political change without making them instruments of international Stalinism and the Soviet State; and the ability of the United States and other non-Communist countries to demonstrate to the Latin American peoples that they can offer Latin America more effective aid in achieving its goals of higher living standards, more equitable distribution of income, and political democracy than can the Communists.

## Chapter II

# The General History of Communism in Latin America

THE INTERNATIONAL COMMUNIST MOVEMENT has passed through several fairly well-defined phases in its nearly four decades of history. Communism in Latin America has experienced each of these phases. In several instances, however, changes in the international "line" were applied somewhat late in the Latin American countries. This was particularly the case in the early 1930's.

The history of the Communist movement can be divided into at least seven periods.* The first of these extended roughly from the founding of the Communist International to the death of Lenin in January, 1924, and may be identified as the period during which Bolshevism triumphed both in Russia and in the Communist International. It was some time before it became clear just what sort of organization the founders of the Comintern were really intending to establish. Lenin and his associates had a very definite type of organization in mind. They were seeking to build a worldwide revolutionary political party, with a high degree of discipline and a unity of doctrine and tactics. Such an International left no room for reformist political parties which sought to attain their ends through parliamentary and democratic means, on the one hand, or for revolutionary trade union groups, such as the acutely undisciplined Anarchosyndicalists, on the other.

The second period extended from the death of Lenin to the beginning

* By the middle of 1955 it began to appear as if still another, eighth, period was emerging in the wake of Stalin's death. The speech of Nikita Kruschev to the Twentieth Congress of the Communist Party of the Soviet Union confirmed the trend away from at least some of the most obvious characteristics of Stalinism. However, by the end of 1956, this "second death" of Stalin seemed to have had relatively few repercussions among the Latin American "comrades." Their press began cautiously to criticize certain aspects of the Stalin epoch, and there were rumors of impending purges in some of the Parties, but there were no such examples of soulsearching and crisis in the Latin American Parties as appeared, for instance, in the Communist Parties of the United States and Great Britain. In spite of the apparent eclipse of Stalin we have frequently used the word "Stalinist" in this volume, as the most handy way of describing those who followed loyally his every word and deed throughout a quarter of a century.

of the collectivization and industrialization program in Russia, roughly in 1929, and marked the period during which Stalinism triumphed within the Communist movement.

The Third Period, so designated by Communist historians themselves, was the era of the first great efforts to industrialize Russia and destroy the independent peasantry there, and was marked outside of Russia by an extreme isolationism on the part of the Communist Parties. It extended approximately to the Seventh and last Congress of the Comintern in 1935, though the change in policy had actually begun before that date.

The Third Period was succeeded by the era of Popular Front tactics, marked by Russian cooperation with the West, by Communist collaboration with other leftist parties, and by intensified persecution, both in Russia and outside, of Communist dissidents. This period came to an abrupt end with the signing of the Nazi-Soviet Pact and the beginning of World War II. It was succeeded by another period of extreme isolation on the part of the various Communist Parties, a period of bitter controversy between them and other elements in the traditional Left.

A short period, this Stalin-Nazi Pact era was succeeded by the super-Popular Front of the latter part of World War II. During this era the Communists were not only willing to cooperate with other leftist and working-class groups, but they were willing to collaborate with anyone who would give even lip service to the Fatherland War of Liberation—Russia's military struggle against Nazi Germany. This era continued for a short while after the end of World War II.

The seventh period of the history of the international Communist movement is that which has come since the end of World War II. During this period the Communists have shown a much greater elasticity in tactics than in any previous epoch, but the lodestone of their tactics and strategy alike has been devotion to the Soviet Union and enmity towards the United States and (to a lesser degree) towards Great Britain.

The Latin American Communists have passed through all of these phases. In the beginning the Communist International attracted the attention and enthusiasm of very diverse groups in Latin America. The Brazilian Anarchists, the Uruguayan and Chilean Socialists, the Syndicalists of Cuba, the middle-class revolutionaries of Peru, the revolutionary generals of Mexico, were all attracted to the Comintern.

These groups regarded the new International as the home of all the more restless souls and idealistic radicals the world over. It was some time before the more rigid outlines of Bolshevik theory and organization became plain to the Latin American radicals and trade unionists. For different groups there were different events which tended to distinguish the "reformist" sheep from the Bolshevik goats.

One of these events was the issuing by the Comintern of the famous "Twenty-One Points" to which a party wishing to adhere to the International must agree. These points included the demand that the affiliating parties purge their more moderate leaders and the provision that each change its name to "Communist Party," regardless of what it had previously been. Particularly in the Latin American Socialist parties which were looking sympathetically toward the Comintern—those of Chile, Uruguay, and Argentina—this made many hesitate about joining the Third International. In Chile and Uruguay the majority of the party decided to accept the Twenty-One Points, but in Argentina they refused to do so, and the tiny Partido Socialista Internacionalista finally became the Comintern affiliate, instead of the much larger Partido Socialista.

With the Anarchosyndicalists an important turning point was the decision of one of the early Comintern congresses to permit affiliation of political parties only. Many Latin American Anarchists had followed the lead of the Spanish Anarchist National Confederation of Labor in hoping that the Comintern would consist of both political parties and trade union groups. However, the Comintern decided that it should consist only of parties and that a subsidiary group of Communist-controlled trade unions should be established, the Red International of Labor Unions (R.I.L.U.). This decision made many Anarchosyndicalists in Brazil, Argentina, and other countries turn their backs on the Comintern and affiliate instead with a new Anarchosyndicalist trade union center, the International Working Men's Association.

Because of their great distance from the center of world affairs and of Communist power, the Latin Americans were often slow to become aware of the fact that the Comintern had developed a very well-defined ideology and form of organization. For instance, it was not until he went to Europe and came into personal contact with the Communist Parties in Western Europe and Russia that the young Peruvian student leader, Víctor Raúl Haya de la Torre, was convinced that the new American Popular Revolutionary Alliance (A.P.R.A.) which he had founded should not become part of the Comintern. His fellow countryman, José Mariátegui, almost equally ill-suited to the Comintern's type of organization and ideology, died in 1929 without having fully realized that the Communists had a definite "line" and approved method of organization. His attempts to establish what he conceived to be a proper form of Communist organization for Peru were rebuffed at the 1929 congress of Latin American Communist Parties, and it was not until some months later that a clear division occurred among Mariátegui's followers between those who were willing to adopt the rigidity required for membership in the Comintern and those who did not think it appropriate for their country and their continent.

The second phase in Comintern history was a period of intense struggle between different factions, not only in the Russian party, but in other important affiliates of the International, including the French, German, and United States Parties. This was also true in Latin America. The Argentine and Chilean Communists were plagued with factionalism during the 1920's and early 1930's. The same was true of the Uruguayans and of the Cubans.

In most cases these splits were the result of personal rivalries for power and prestige among the leaders of the local Parties. However, as in the case of the European, Asiatic, and United States Communist Parties, these local quarrels often merged with the titanic struggle in the Russian Communist ranks, and the Latin American protagonists took the side of one or the other of the Russian groups. Thus Manuel Hidalgo's faction in Chile, and Sandalio Junco's in Cuba, took the side of Trotsky, while the Laferte and Vilar groups in those countries sided with Stalin.

However, it is interesting to note that in no case did a strong dissident Communist Party with international connections develop. In the case of Hidalgo's Left Communist Party in Chile, which in 1933 declared its adhesion to Trotsky's International Left Communist Opposition, the Party was of short duration and late in 1936 joined the newly formed Socialist Party of Chile. All that remained of Trotskyism in Chile was the inconsequential and insignificant Partido Obrero Revolucionario. A similar development occurred in Cuba, where Sandalio Junco's Trotskyites soon joined the newly formed Auténtico Party and became the core of that party's labor support, losing all connection with the international Trotskyite movement.

The only significant Trotskyite party which has appeared in Latin America, the Partido Obrero Revolucionario of Bolivia, did not come about as the result of the division of an existing Communist Party. Rather, it originated in a group of Bolivian intellectuals who were attracted by Trotsky's personality and writings and in the late 1930's oriented their newly organized party in the direction of the Fourth International. This party grew during the late 1940's and early 1950's, to become for a short time one of the world's two really significant Trotskyite parties—the other being that of Ceylon. By 1956 divisions within the P.O.R. had reduced it to a position of relative insignificance.

The Right Opposition, led in Russia by Bukharin, Rykov, and Tomsky, and abroad by Jay Lovestone in the United States and August Thalheimer in Germany, never had any following of importance in Latin America. Those Communists who split off to the Right of the Stalinist Party usually gravitated in the direction of the Socialists or some similar national radical reformist group.*

The Third Period, the era of extreme Communist isolation from other left-wing and working-class groups, was fully experienced in Latin American Communism. This period was perhaps more appealing than some

* The Titoist heresy of the 1940's did not make any inroads in the Latin American Communist movement, either. No important Latin American Communist leader sided with Tito, and no Titoist party developed in the area.

others to the Latin American temperament and state of political organization. The Latin American tradition of violent revolution made the extremism of the Communist Third Period more acceptable than it was in countries with stabler political systems, such as the United States and Great Britain.

The Third Period was, throughout the world, an era of Communist dual unionism. Each Communist Party set up a trade union movement in its own image and under its direct supervision and control, which affiliated with the Red International of Labor Unions. This was no less true of Latin America than of other parts of the world. Every Latin American Communist Party tried to set up its own trade union group, and these groups were brought together on a continental basis in the Confederación Sindical Latino Americana.

During this period the Communists were extremely isolated from all other radical and working-class parties. This led to some horrendous activities on their part. For instance, in Chile, the Communists were the only working-class group which opposed the short-lived "Socialist Republic" of June, 1932, and in so doing won opposition and hatred among other labor groups which it took them years to live down.

In Cuba, late in 1933, the Third Period attitude was epitomized by the violent attacks which the Communists made on the left-wing nationalist government of Dr. Ramón Grau San Martín, a government which was brought down as much by these Communist attacks as by the pressure of the United States Department of State. At this time the Communist Party of Cuba engaged in futile attempts to set up "Soviets" in various parts of the island where they had some influence among the workers. These adventurist activities were even criticized by the Comintern, as being too much of a good thing.

The extreme isolationism of the Third period was followed by the almost equally extreme collaborationism of the Popular Front period. The Latin American Communists were caught up in this movement, as were their brothers elsewhere in the world. In Chile they formed a part of the only avowed Popular Front established in the hemisphere. In Mexico they were ardent members of the coalition which supported the Cárdenas government, conceiving of this group as a Popular Front. In Brazil they took the lead in organizing a National Liberation Alliance, which they hailed as a Popular Front.

During this period, then, the Communists actively sought alliances with Socialist and left-wing nationalist parties which represented the reformist, moderate Left. In Chile, as we have indicated, they succeeded in joining the Socialists and Radicals in the Popular Front. In Argentina and Uruguay, on the other hand, the Socialists were unreceptive to Communist overtures.

In Peru the Apristas were politically unreceptive to Communist co-quetry, though the two groups did work together in the trade union field. In Cuba the Communists for a time actively strove for an alliance with Dr. Grau San Martín's Auténtico Party, but were rebuffed by the Auténticos and ultimately turned toward Colonel Fulgencio Batista. In Venezuela the Communists sought to work with the non-Communist Left, which ultimately crystallized into the Acción Democrática Party. In Colombia they worked closely with the left wing of the Liberal Party.

As in some European countries, where the Communists were often willing to bring into the Popular Front right-wing elements with which the moderate Left wanted nothing to do, in Latin America they were willing to make very peculiar alliances during the Popular Front period. Often these alliances were highly profitable to them.

Thus in Cuba the Communists, after having been rejected over and over again in their overtures to the left-wing Auténtico Party, finally sought an alliance with the military dictator of the time, Colonel Fulgencio Batista. Batista was anxious at that moment to become President through more or less honest elections, but he lacked any wide basis of popular support. Hence, he was willing to make an alliance with the Communists, who he thought might gain him such support. As a result, the Communist Party became legal, the Confederation of Workers of Cuba was established, and the Communists were put in control of it. This alliance long survived the Popular Front period.

In a similar move, the Brazilian Communists offered the olive branch to dictator Getulio Vargas in the late 1930's, in spite of the fact that he was holding their most prominent leaders in jail and had outlawed their Party. Vargas paid them little heed. In Peru they made a deal with Manuel Prado, the candidate of the then dictator, Marshal Benavides, whereby they supported Prado's candidacy in return for a place on his congressional ticket and a relatively free hand in the labor movement.

In these alliances with the dictators, the Communists were motivated by various factors. First of all, there was the international Communist "line" of the time, which was, to form the widest possible alliance for the purpose of thwarting those groups which were *avowedly* pro-Nazi and pro-fascist. Batista and Prado were not avowedly pro-fascist, and though Vargas was, he was faced on his Right with a more militant, more dogmatic fascist group, the Integralistas, to fight whom the Communists offered Vargas an alliance.

In the second place, these accords with the dictators were very fruitful for the Communists. Several of the dictators were anxious to build up popular support against democratic movements which were challenging their rule. For this purpose, they were perfectly willing to use the Communists. And for their part, the Communists were willing to use the dictators' support so as to have at least limited freedom for agitational and organizational activities and to build up a trade union movement under their own control.

The Popular Front period was perhaps most successful for the Communists in the trade union field. They merged their partisan trade union groups into the more moderate labor confederations. Communists played a leading part in organizing the Confederations of Workers of Chile, Mexico, Colombia, Ecuador, and Cuba, and the General Union of Workers of Uruguay. The Argentine Communists liquidated their independent trade unions in the Socialist-controlled General Confederation of Labor.

In the international trade union field, the Communists played an important role in the establishment of the Confederation of Workers of Latin America (C.T.A.L.). Following the policy of the international Communist leadership, which had dissolved the Red International of Labor Unions and instructed its affiliated groups to merge into those national trade union centers affiliated with the Socialist-controlled International Federation of Trade Unions (I.F.T.U.), the Latin American Communists urged the affiliation of national trade union confederations with the I.F.T.U.

The Popular Front epoch marked the first period during which the Communist parties of Latin America really assumed political importance in the life of the hemisphere. Although their activities had previously had some nuisance value in Colombia, Costa Rica, and elsewhere, this was the first time that responsible politicians in more than one country were willing to enter into alliances and agreements with Communists, and that they began to acquire really serious followings among the workers and intellectuals of the Latin American countries. They sowed the seeds during this period which were to flourish and grow into sturdy plants during the latter part of the second World War.

The Latin American Communists were again plunged into sudden isolation as a result of the coming of World War II. With few exceptions, the Latin American Communist leaders followed the International in its support of the Stalin-Nazi pact and in its general endorsement of the Soviet's benevolent neutrality toward Germany during the first phase of World War II.

The result was the isolation of the Communists from the other left-wing and working-class groups in Latin America. The Chilean Popular Front was broken up. The Communists in the labor movement of Mexico were isolated, and pro-Communist Vicente Lombardo Toledano was forced out of his position as Secretary General of the Confederation of Workers of Mexico, although he continued as President of the Confederation of Workers of Latin America. The C.T.A.L. itself was deprived of the financial support which one or more Latin American governments had been giving it during the Popular Front period.

Groups which had been allied to the Communists turned against them.

The Apristas of Peru, the Liberals of Colombia, the Socialists of Chile were violently in opposition to the Communists' pro-German line in World War II and attacked the Communists as tools of the Soviet State. In Argentina the pro-Communist Socialist Workers Party, which had broken away from the Socialist Party of Argentina in 1937 because of that party's unwillingness to work with the Communists, was decimated, with the great majority of its members returning to the Socialist Party.

Fortunately for the Latin American Communists, the period of Soviet-German friendship was relatively short. The entry of the Soviet Union into the War in the middle of 1941 ushered in another period of Popular Frontism, on an even more exaggerated scale than that of the late 1930's. This was the period during which the Communists of Latin America made their greatest gains.

There were various reasons for the Communists' success during this period. First of all, there was general sympathy among the workers and middle-class elements of Latin America for the Allied cause in the second World War, and after June 21, 1941, the Communists became the most vociferous supporters of the Allies. There was widespread admiration among the politically conscious Latin Americans for the mighty struggle which the Russians put up against the Nazi invaders, and there was a general tendency, in Latin America as elsewhere, to regard this military prowess of the Soviet armies as an indication that the charges which had been made concerning dictatorship and tyranny in Russia were not true.

The Latin American Communists basked in the reflection of this sympathy for the Soviet Union. They made no secret of the fact that they represented in Latin America what the Soviet Communists stood for in the U.S.S.R. At the same time, since they seemed to be such good supporters of the Allied war effort, the Communists found that other pro-Allied groups were willing and anxious to cooperate with them.

The Communists took the lead in organizing committees for the support of the Allies, such as the Junta de la Victoria in Argentina. They actively campaigned for Latin American countries breaking relations with the Axis and even for declarations of war by the Latin American countries. They worked as equals with, and were accepted as friends and allies by, Socialists, Liberals, Radicals, and others throughout the hemisphere.

During this period, of course, the Communists dispensed with talk of revolution and of dictatorship. They were democrats among democrats, and if they supported advanced programs of social welfare, they were only doing so because this was the best way to win popular support for the war effort—or at least, so they claimed.

As their European comrades were working in the Underground and in exile with liberal, anti-fascist Catholic groups, so the Communists were willing and anxious to work with such Catholic elements in the New

World. The most notable example of their success in this direction was the agreement made in Costa Rica between the Archbishop of San José, Monseñor Sanabria, and the Communist Party.

The Communists played down their past. In several instances they changed their name for the purpose of forwarding the broad alliance which they sought to make with all other elements supporting the War. In Colombia the Communist Party became the Social Democratic Party; in Cuba the Unión Revolucionaria Comunista was rechristened the Partido Socialista Popular. The Communist Party of the Dominican Republic also became the Popular Socialist Party. In Costa Rica the Communist Party became the Vanguardia Popular.

The Communists resumed the policy which they had followed in the earlier Popular Front period of allying themselves with the Latin American dictators, if those dictators would declare themselves in favor of the Allied war effort. Thus the Communists of Ecuador for a considerable time were allied with dictator Carlos Arroyo del Río, those of Nicaragua, with Somoza.

Old alliances, such as those of the Cuban Communists with Batista, of the Peruvians with Prado, were resumed. Juan Marinello, prominent Cuban Communist leader, actually served for a time as Minister Without Portfolio in Batista's Cabinet, thus becoming the first Latin American Communist to serve in a Latin American government. In Brazil the Communists succeeded early in 1945 in making a very fruitful working agreement with dictator Getulio Vargas, who was now eager to have their support in his attempt to have himself renamed President in the elections which he could not avoid calling.

Perhaps most striking of all was the short-lived alliance between the Communists of the Dominican Republic and the hemisphere's most monolithic dictator, Generalissimo Rafael Leónidas Trujillo. Trujillo, like Vargas, was anxious to go through the motions of a new "election," so as to establish himself as a "democrat." The Communists were willing to lend themselves to this maneuver, and for a considerable period they were given freedom of action, so that they could run an ostensible candidate against Trujillo, a candidate who they and he knew had no chance of winning, or even of having a respectable number of votes counted in his favor. Once he had used them, Trujillo sent the local Communists packing into exile.

Communist "anti-imperialism" was forgotten during this period. When Communists spoke of "imperialism" it was only the Axis brand to which they were referring. They attacked those who still insisted on speaking about British or American imperialism as saboteurs of the war effort. They discouraged all strikes and other activities against American and British-owned firms.

As a result of this attitude, the Communists were able to build up the most friendly relations not only with managers of local American and British-owned enterprises, but with local Allied diplomatic personnel. Their cooperation was sought in Allied propaganda efforts. Communist leaders, such as Senator Salvador Ocampo of Chile, were welcomed with splendid receptions when they visited the United States. Vicente Lombardo Toledano, by then widely regarded as pro-Communist, if not a Party member, was treated in a very friendly fashion by State Department officials and other U.S. leaders on his several visits to the United States, though President Roosevelt refused to receive him.

This apparent friendship between the Communists and the Yanquis strengthened the position of the Communists in Latin America. The Latin American governments, always anxious to keep in the good graces of Uncle Sam, took these friendly relations to mean that they, too, should court their local Communists. Or, if they felt inclined to treat the Communists in a friendly way in any case, the local government officials could point to the United States' attitude as an indication that this was what Uncle Sam wanted of them.

The Communists made particular headway during this period in the trade union movement. Although they tended to discourage strikes and even to soft-pedal peaceful presentation of demands on employers, and thus stirred up a certain discontent with their leadership among the rank and file trade unionists, the Communists' attitude of class collaboration and passivity won wide approval among the governments and employing classes of the hemisphere. In a region where the government plays such a dominant role in labor relations, this cordial relationship between Communist trade union leaders and government labor officials won the former more advantage than was lost them by the discontent these policies engendered among the rank and file workers.

As a result, the Communists made tremendous gains among the trade unions of a dozen different countries in Latin America. Their influence in the labor movements of Chile, Cuba, Argentina, Uruguay, Mexico, Colombia, Peru, Venezuela, and several other nations was greater than ever before. Furthermore, after the Cali Conference of the C.T.A.L. in December, 1944, the Communists formed a majority of the Executive Committee of the Confederation of Workers of Latin America.

The Latin American Communists were at the zenith of their power and influence during 1945 and 1946. Their Parties were legal or at least tolerated in virtually every country of the hemisphere. They had members of Congress in Cuba, Colombia, Peru, Ecuador, Brazil, Chile, Bolivia, Uruguay, Costa Rica, and members of lesser legislative bodies in several other countries. In the latter months of 1946 they had three members in the Chilean Cabinet, and seemed well on the way to achieving the first Communist government of the hemisphere in that country.

Since that period they have suffered severe defeats in virtually every country in the hemisphere. There are various reasons for these setbacks. First of all, they have followed the Communist international line in turning violently against the United States, and hence against every government in the continent which is friendly toward the United States.

On the other hand, many Latin American governments have tended to follow the lead of the United States in turning against the Communists. Frequently they have gone much further than the United States in this reaction, but in any case, the turn has limited the freedom of action of the Stalinists.

Perhaps more important was the fact that other political movements caught the imagination of the masses of several countries in which the Communists had been powerful. These nations included Argentina, where the rise of Perón stopped the Communists in their tracks; Brazil, where the *mística* of Vargas rose as that of the Communist leader, Luiz Carlos Prestes, fell in the late 1940's; Cuba, Colombia, Venezuela, and Peru, where left-wing democratic political parties stole much of the Communists' thunder.

At the same time, the Communists lost their position of dominance in the labor movement. Splits, government persecution, the rise of non-Communist trade union groups, help to the non-Communists from the United States labor movement, all tended to weaken the position of the Communists among the organized workers of the hemisphere.

Only in one country did the Communists make notable gains during the post-World War II period—in Guatemala. There they made great advances, due to vigorous propaganda and organizational activity by Communists from abroad, the inexperience of local left-wing politicians, and the advent of a major social revolution which the Communists more or less successfully identified with themselves. By 1953 the Communists controlled the labor movement in Guatemala, were an influential element in the government, although there were no avowedly Communist ministers in the Cabinet, and were edging their way towards the seat of power in that Central American republic. Even here, however, their progress was checked, at least temporarily, by the revolution which upset the Arbenz government in the summer of 1954.

After World War II the Communists tended to become increasingly isolated. Few of the Socialists, Radicals, Liberals, and other moderate leftists with whom they had cooperated during the war were inclined to follow them in their extremes of anti-United States propaganda and conviction. In most instances these groups had continued a more or less covert struggle with the Communists for control of trade union movements and other mass organizations, and although they had cooperated with the Communists for the temporary ends connected with the war, the rivalry had never really disappeared. It broke out again when the war was over.

This renewal of old interparty strife was made all the easier because the

Communists had shown on many occasions that they would be ruthless if they were once fully in control of the organized labor movement or any other organization. The most notable instance of this occurred in Chile during late 1946 and early 1947, when the Communists, having ministers in the government, began to act as if they controlled the whole administration—behavior which united almost the whole of the rest of the country against them.

There were other groups which had worked with the Communists during the war and which now began to turn against them. Liberal Catholic elements, which had been more or less sympathetic with them so long as they were fighting the Nazis, were not willing to accompany them on an equally energetic crusade against the United States and the countries of Western Europe. As their trade union following narrowed, the Communists tended to become more isolated from the mass of the workers in most of the Latin American countries.

The Communists' anti-United States line turned them into vociferous "nationalists," bitterly assailing what they claimed were United States attempts to dominate the economies and politics of the Latin American countries. However, many groups which in the past might have listened more willingly to the Communist attacks on the United States were now impressed with the Communist Parties' complete subservience to Russia and their willingness to justify anything which the Soviet Union did. To many staunch Latin American nationalists and opponents of United States penetration, it appeared that the Communists were not really Latin American nationalists, but, rather, special pleaders for the U.S.S.R. and its rulers.

Nevertheless, the Communists spent a large proportion of their time in the post-World War II period on the various "peace" drives of the international Communist movement. Hundreds of thousands of signatures were collected throughout the hemisphere for the Stockholm "peace" petition. Delegates from a number of countries participated in the numerous Peace Congresses. Vicente Lombardo Toledano played a leading role in the Peiping Congress of 1949, which organized the Far Eastern center of the Communists' World Federation of Trade Unions.

By the end of 1954, then, the Communists' political influence in Latin America was less than at any time since the late 1930's. In public opinion, politics, and the trade union movement, they certainly had lost most of the ground which they had gained as a result of World War II. Although they were still a potential power in the region, they remained a major force only in Chile, Brazil, and Guatemala.

Throughout their history the Latin American Communist Parties have followed the general pattern set by the international Communist movement. The Latin American Parties have faithfully reflected the changes in the "line," the internal dissensions, and the varying conceptions of strategy and tactics which have characterized the world-wide Communist movement. Any claim that the Latin American Communists are somehow "different," that they are "indigenous social reformers," that they are merely "agrarian reformers" or "anti-imperialists," is just so much nonsense. The Latin American Communist Parties are an integral part of the international Communist movement, and their role in Latin American affairs cannot conceivably be assessed with accuracy unless this basic fact is recognized.

Recognition of the true nature of the Latin American Communist Parties is all the more necessary, because the salvation of the region from the Communists lies precisely in the real indigenous social reformers, agrarian reformers, and radical nationalists or anti-imperialists. For it is characteristic of the Communists that they have grown to important proportions in exactly those countries where there have been no local, native radical movements which could catch the imagination and arouse the loyalty of the workers, students, and intellectuals of the nation.

The conservative elements and the continent's dictators aim at the impossible goal of damming up the social revolution which is sweeping the continent and gaining momentum with each passing year. The dictators frequently seek to justify their arbitrary power on the ground that they are "anti-Communist." This is, in most cases, the sheerest hypocrisy. In some instances they are anti-Communist because they are opposed to any kind of political activity in their countries except that which is devoted to their own aggrandizement; in others, they are not anti-Communist at all, but are perfectly willing to come to terms with the Communists, and to use them, if it seems expedient.

In any case, repression is but a stopgap measure if the Communists really have a hold on the imagination of the people of a country. Latin American dictatorships are volatile; they come and go; and a regime which has been based solely on force and has suppressed the Communists along with all other political groups, justifying its general tyranny by proclaiming its "anti-Communism," serves only to strengthen the Communists in the long run.

Only another political movement which can provide the workers and intellectuals of a Latin American country with a feeling of purpose, with hope, and with an outlet for their energies and emotions in the way that Communism is able to do, can permanently undermine the power of the Communists. It is exactly among these two social classes that the Communists have made their greatest inroads. Communist Parties in Latin America which have been able to become of some real significance in the life of their countries have had their mass base in the trade unions, with a periphery of intellectuals who were intrigued by the Party's certainty of purpose or were flattered by the Party's momentary adulation.

The Communists have been powerful, at one time or another, in Brazil, Chile, Cuba, Uruguay, Guatemala, Costa Rica, and Colombia. And in each of those countries the Communists were the dominant factor in the trade unions at the time of the zenith of Communist power. Likewise, the destruction of Communist power in the trade unions, wherever it has occurred, has fatally undermined the general political position of the Party.

In being so dependent for its mass backing on the trade union organizations which it has controlled, Communism in Latin America has followed the European pattern of Communist expansion rather than the Asiatic one. In Western Europe, generally, the influence of the Communists has depended in large part on their strength in the trade unions. In Asia, on the contrary, the principal source of Communist backing has been the countryside. In China, in Indochina, in Burma, in India, rural guerrilla armies have played an important part, and agrarian reforms have been the basis for the recruiting of membership in the Communist ranks.

In Latin America this Asiatic pattern has not been apparent. Although the Communists played a modest role in the Mexican agrarian reform program, and a fundamental one in the Guatemalan agrarian reform, the Communists in the first country never did achieve any very decisive influence, while in the second, it was their strength in the trade unions which enabled them to have some influence on events in the rural areas. By the middle of 1955 there was little evidence that the Communists of Latin America had shifted their emphasis to "Maoism"—a combination of agrarian reform and nationalism—as suggested by Daniel James in his *Red Design for the Americas: Guatemalan Prelude*. The basic strength of the Communists still lay among the urban workers and intellectuals. Though they were certainly using the slogans of agrarian reform and anti-Yanqui nationalism in the 1950's, the Communists had been using these same slogans and appeals in the 1920's.

The important problem is not what specific appeals the Communists use. In line with the post-World War II strategy of the international Communist movement, they will use whatever slogans seem useful at any given moment. The important question is whether the Communists will be able to exploit the Latin American social revolution for their own purposes. The only way to make sure that they will not be able to do so is for some other revolutionary group, of democratic tendencies, to carry out the reforms and fulfill the promises which the Communists say they will make good if only the workers, peasants, and intellectuals will place absolute power in their hands. This has been the most crucial question, throughout the history of Communism in Latin America.

*Chapter III*

# Latin American Communists, the Comintern, and the Soviet Union

THERE COULD BE no greater mistake than to believe that the Communists of Latin America are somehow "different," that because they are Latin American, they do not share the characteristics of Communists in other parts of the world. However, there are many politicians in the Latin American countries who have believed and still believe this. Many of them have had to learn the hard way that it is not true.

The Latin American Communists have never been without direction from the Communist International. This aspect of Communist affairs in the Americas is one of the hardest to trace. Although during the 1920's the Communists frequently disclosed the skeleton of their organizational structure in the hemisphere in various publications of the International and its subdivisions, they became increasingly reticent after Stalin achieved full control of the apparatus of the International—an event which occurred during the Sixth Congress of the Comintern in the late months of 1928, and in the months that followed this meeting.

However, in spite of this secretiveness of the Communists about their international apparatus in Latin America, there are bits and pieces of information which one can put together to get some kind of a composite picture of how the Comintern has worked there, who has pulled the strings, and how the Communist International has passed on orders and directives to its Latin American affiliates.

Obviously much of what follows has to consist of guesses and surmises on the part of the author. We hope that these are sufficiently correct to be in the category of "informed guesses."

In the very earliest days of the Comintern there were "delegates" of the International in the hemisphere, trying to bring Communist Parties into existence, and trying to lay down the "line" to those few which already existed. Two of the most interesting of these early emissaries of the international Communist movement were M. N. Roy and Sen Katayama.

Roy was an Indian, one of the founders of the Indian Communist Party, who later was expelled as a "right-wing deviationist," at the time of Nikolai Bukharin's fall in Russia, and became a bitter enemy of the Stalinists. Katayama was a Japanese, father of Socialism in his country, who had taken his small group of followers into the Comintern as soon as it was organized, and who was one of the most trusted figures in the early history of the Communist International.

Both Roy and Katayama made their headquarters in Mexico. Because of the Revolution then in progress in that country, this seemed in the early 1920's the logical place for a Latin American headquarters of the Comintern. Roy and Katayama each had a hand in the organization and alignment of the Mexican Communist Party, but their influence spread beyond this. Katayama, in particular, travelled widely in Latin America and is credited by Víctor Alba with having "discovered," among others, Victorio Codovilla, who was to become perhaps the Number One confidante of the Kremlin among the Latin American Communists.

Throughout the 1920's the Third International paid relatively little attention to the activities of the Latin American Parties. Their activities were supervised in a general way by two Swiss Communists, Stirner and Jules Humbert-Droz,* whose headquarters were in Moscow. However, although the Executive Committee of the Comintern sometimes sent open letters to one or the other of the Latin American Communist Parties, the latter were seldom considered important enough to justify such long-winded discussions at Comintern meetings, or sessions of the Enlarged Committee of the Executive Committee of the International, as were held "On the French Situation," "On the German Situation," and so on.

Latin American Communist leaders found their way to Moscow from time to time, even in the 1920's, sometimes to attend a Congress of the Comintern, sometimes on other business. As early as 1922, Luis Emilio Recabarren, founder and leader of the Chilean Communist Party, visited Moscow and came home to write a glowing pamphlet on what he had seen there.

During these early years certainly one of Moscow's principal sources of information concerning Latin American affairs was the Russian News Agency, Tass. None of the Latin American countries except Uruguay recognized the Soviet government during the 1920's, and so there was no such contact through diplomatic sources. However, the Tass Agency, with its American headquarters in New York City, had a network of correspondents among Communist leaders, pro-Communist intellectuals, and others in the various countries of Latin America.

The head of the Latin American Bureau of Tass was a German-American Anarchist, who was known at that time as Arnold Roller, but

* In the early 1930's Humbert-Droz withdrew from the Communist Party of Switzerland. Subsequently, he joined the Social Democratic Party, and eventually became its Secretary General.

who had been born Siegfried Nacht and, after leaving the Communists'
employ, became known as Stephen Naft. Although a sympathizer with
the Soviet Union in the 1920's, Naft had never joined the Communist
Party, and steadfastly refused to do so. Finally, he was given an ultimatum:
join or else. He still refused. Therewith, a cable arrived from Moscow:
"Liquidate Naft!" The manager of the New York office of Tass, unable
to replace Naft immediately, asked for a postponement of the dismissal of
the chief of his Latin American Bureau. Before long, another cable arrived: "Unliquidate Naft!"

Víctor Alba attributes the relative lack of interest in Latin American
affairs on the part of the Russian masters of the Communist International
during most of the 1920's to the Soviet Union's foreign policy during
those years. Always preoccupied with the danger of "encirclement," the
Soviet leaders saw the British and the French as the major threat, and so
concentrated their extra-European activities in the Asiatic and African
territories of those Great Powers. The United States was at that time a
minor foe, and so Latin America, the backyard of the U.S.A., was considered of small importance.

However, beginning in the middle 1920's, the leaders of the international
Communist movement began to take more interest in the affairs of Latin
America. A South American Secretariat of the Comintern was established,
with a membership which seems never to have been officially published,
though it is known to have included Victorio Codovilla, Rodolfo Ghioldi,
and José Penelón of the Argentine Communist Party. There was also at
least one European on this early Secretariat. On April 15, 1926, it com-
menced the publication of the fortnightly *La Correspondencia Sudamericana*, which carried informational articles on and instructions to the various Latin American Communist Parties.

A large number of Latin American trade unionists and Communist
leaders were invited to Moscow in connection with the celebration of the
Tenth Anniversary of the Bolshevik Revolution. It was during a meeting
of this group that the preliminary plans were laid for the establishment of
the first Communist hemispheric American labor organization, the Confederación Sindical Latino Americana.

At the same time, a meeting of leading Latin American Communists
was held to plan the strategy of the movement in these countries. Those
participating, according to the Peruvian, Eudosio Ravines, included
Ravines himself, along with Armando Bazán and Julio Portocarrero of
Peru; Ricardo Martínez of Venezuela; Victorio Codovilla of Argentina;
Astrogildo Pereyra, and Karracik of Brazil; List Arzubide, a Mexican poet,
described by Ravines as "a gay, demanding scoffer . . . an incisive critic
of this new society"; and Julio Antonio Mella of Cuba. One result of these
conferences, according to Ravines, was his decision to go back to his native country to establish formally a Communist Party of Peru.[1]

The Sixth Congress of the Communist International devoted little or no attention to the affairs of Latin America. There was no separate discussion of events in that part of the world or of the problems of the Communist Parties of Latin America. About the only concrete reference to the region in the resolutions of the Congress was a paragraph in a Thesis by Otto Kussinen concerning the problems of "colonial and semi-colonial" countries. It said, after listing a series of strikes which had occurred in recent years: "All of these events are full proof of the widespread nature and profundity of the revolutionary process, and most particularly of the increasing discontent of the countries of Latin America, against world imperialism."[2]

The Sixth Congress of the International was followed by the removal of the South American Secretariat of the Comintern from Moscow to Buenos Aires. The chief of this organization was a Lithuanian Communist, who went under the name of Guralsky, and who later disappeared in the Moscow purges of the late 1930's. He was an Old Bolshevik and had sided with Trotsky in the internal struggle in the Soviet Communist Party. Hence his dispatch to Buenos Aires was a sort of exile.

Guralsky's right-hand man was a Russian, known to the South American Parties as "Pierre." Víctor Alba concludes that he was probably there as a G.P.U. agent, to keep track of the activities of Guralsky and the leaders of the South American Communists. Other members of the South American Bureau were also from the Old World. They included a Tunisian, known as "Nemo," an Italian who was referred to as "Orestes," another Italian, Marcucci, and a Czech, Frederick Glaufbauf. Some or all of these gentlemen were using false names.

The activities of the Bureau were varied. Not only did it govern the operations and policies of the Communist Parties, but it also supervised the activities of all the peripheral organizations established by the various Communist Parties, such as branches of the International Red Aid, the Communist Youth International, the Anti-Imperialist League, and other groups.[3]

Alba reports that the only Latin American who worked closely with the South American Bureau was Victorio Codovilla, an Argentine of Italian birth, who was the Treasurer of the Bureau and chief of the Argentine Communist Party. His principal distinction then and subsequently was his blind obedience to the leadership of the Comintern, whoever its leaders might be.

In the middle of 1929 two important Latin American Communist congresses took place. The first was a meeting of delegates from all Communist and pro-Communist trade union groups of the hemisphere at Montevideo, Uruguay, in May, 1929. The other was The First Conference of Latin American Communist Parties, held in Buenos Aires, a few days later.

Thirty-eight delegates attended the Buenos Aires conference, representing the Parties of Argentina, Bolivia, Brazil, Colombia, Cuba, Ecuador, El Salvador, Guatemala, Mexico, Panama, Paraguay, Peru, Uruguay, and Venezuela. The Chilean Party was unrepresented, because the Chilean government would not give its delegates passports. Also present were representatives from the Comintern, the Young Communist International, the Communist Party of the United States, and the South American Secretariat of the Comintern.

At this conference, which lasted ten days, there were long discussions of various problems facing the Communists in the area. Much attention was paid to difficulties encountered in gaining adherents among members of the middle class. The problem of the colored races was debated at great length, and a resolution was finally accepted providing that the South American Bureau would be charged with directing the policy of each national Communist Party with regard to oppressed racial groups. The International had not yet adopted the policy of inciting racial nationalism among the Indians, Negroes, and other oppressed racial groups in America.

The South American Bureau of the Comintern was thereafter firmly established in Montevideo, Uruguay, which offered at that time the freest political climate in the hemisphere, hence making it possible for the Bureau to work with the least possible interference from the government authorities. Subsequently, other congresses under the auspices of the Bureau were held in Montevideo, notably in 1934, when the change in the line from the Third Period to the Popular Front Period was first announced by the Comintern to its Latin American affiliates.

It is not clear just how much territory the South American Bureau controlled, so far as the Latin American Communist Parties are concerned. Certainly for a number of years it controlled all the Parties in South America, and it may have supervised the Parties of the Caribbean as well.

However, there is considerable reason to believe that the Communist Parties of the Caribbean were directed from New York. Leaders of the United States Communist Party intervened in the affairs of the Mexican Communist Party at least twice during the 1920's. Later in 1937 Earl Browder, then head of the United States Communist Party, dissuaded the Mexican Communists from persisting in a split which they had engineered in the recently established Confederation of Workers of Mexico, and went to Mexico to seal the agreement. There he talked at great length with Vicente Lombardo Toledano, from whose Confederación de Trabajadores de México the Communists had originally split, and he believes that he had much to do with winning Lombardo to a sympathetic position towards the U.S.S.R. and the international Communist movement.

Apparently many of the Communist Parties around the Caribbean received all or part of their instructions through New York. American Communist leader Joseph Zack Kornfelder was active in the Communist

Parties of Colombia and Venezuela during the late 1920's and early 1930's. Instructions for the Salvadorean Party during 1931 and 1932, before the disastrous Communist uprising in January of the latter year, came from the New York headquarters of the Communist Party of the United States.

It seems likely that the International did not put all of its eggs in one basket. The author has been told by the man who was then Treasurer of the Chilean Communist Party that that group received financial contributions from the Comintern through New York City in the period following the overthrow of Dictator Carlos Ibáñez in September, 1931.

It is also true that Mexico was one of the bases of Communist operations in the hemisphere. There arrived in that country in 1927 one of the more mysterious figures of international Communism, a man known variously as Enea Sormenti, Arturo Sormenti, Carlos Contreras, and Vittorio Vidali, who has most recently been famous as the boss of the Communist Party of the late Free City of Trieste. There is little doubt that he was an agent of the Comintern, and perhaps of the G.P.U. Víctor Alba credits him with having directed the affairs of the Mexican Communist Party from behind the scenes, from the time of his arrival in 1927 until 1932, when he left Mexico for Spain.[4]

Mexico was at that time, as it is today, very hospitable to political refugees from all other Latin American countries. Not infrequently Communists, driven from their homelands, found refuge there. The case of Julio Antonio Mella of Cuba is well known. It also seems likely that the Communist officials in Mexico had a certain share in the direction of the Communist Parties of Central America. They are known to have helped organize the Guatemalan Communist Party in the 1920's, and perhaps some of the other Central American Parties as well.

An important gathering of Communist leaders took place in Moscow in connection with the Seventh Congress of the Communist International, which was originally scheduled for the late months of 1934. The Congress was postponed for almost a year, but the Latin American delegates who had arrived for the meeting were brought together to discuss their problems and to be more fully informed about the latest change in Comintern strategy.

Among the Latin Americans who participated in this session were Luiz Carlos Prestes, the Brazilian "Knight of Hope," who had recently joined the Communist Party while in the Soviet Union; Victorio Codovilla and Rodolfo Ghioldi of Argentina; Eudosio Ravines, who had lately escaped from prison in Peru; and delegations from Cuba, Mexico, Colombia, and Uruguay.

The increased importance which Latin America had assumed in Moscow's eyes was shown by the fact that most of the top figures of the Comintern participated in these discussions. These included the head of the Comintern, Manuilsky, and Dmitrov, who was to succeed him in this position. Also present were Klement Gottwald of Czechoslovakia, Kussinen of Finland, Wilhelm Pieck of Germany, Kolarov of Bulgaria, Togliatti of Italy, Ho Chi Minh of Indochina, Maurice Thorez and Raymond Guyot of France, and Van Minh of the Chinese Communist Party.

The chief subject of discussion was the application of the new Popular Front line in Latin America. The leadership of the Comintern was not itself unanimously agreed upon this line, upon which Stalin had not yet spoken. The President of the Comintern, Manuilsky, was much opposed to the new strategy, while Dmitrov was its chief proponent. The Latin Americans, too, were divided in sentiment. Luiz Carlos Prestes was against the plan, while Ravines, the Chilean Communists, and others favored it.

Eudosio Ravines, the chief source of information concerning what transpired at this conference, maintains that a compromise was reached in these discussions. It was agreed that an experiment with the Popular Front technique would be made in Chile, where the ground seemed ripe for such a movement, while in Brazil, Luiz Carlos Prestes would go forward with an attempt at insurrection—an attempt which resulted in the National Liberation Alliance uprising in November, 1935.* Eudosio Ravines himself was picked to carry out the Popular Front experiment in Chile.[5]

Earl Browder, Secretary General of the Communist Party of the United States, also participated in a meeting with the Latin American Communist Parties, during the stay of the various delegations in Moscow. He told the author that a number of the Parties had approached him, suggesting that an American continental Communist congress be held, but that this idea was turned down by the International. The Latin American Parties then suggested that Browder agree to become the principal advisor and consultant of their organizations. All the Parties of the Caribbean and the West Coast of South America entered into this agreement, except that of Mexico, which did not agree to accept Browder's services until after the 1937 split in the C.T.M.

From 1935 on, there were frequent conferences of leaders of individual Latin American Communist Parties with Browder and other United States Communist leaders in the New York Party headquarters. There were also several general meetings in which leaders of a number of Latin American Parties participated. Apparently Browder's viceroyalty included the Caribbean Parties and those of the West Coast of South America, including the Chilean Party, whose leaders conferred various times with Browder in the years that followed the Seventh Congress of the Communist International.

The influence of the American Communist Party on its Latin American comrade parties undoubtedly persisted for some time after World War II.

* It should be noted that Comintern publications talked of the Brazilian National Liberation Alliance itself as an application of the Popular Front line. The author is uncertain whether to regard the November, 1935, revolt of the N.L.A. as something which had been planned long in advance or as something precipitated by Varga's campaign against the N.L.A.

The certification of the "Red Communists" of Juan Bautista Fuenmayor as the approved Party in Venezuela, following the split in the ranks of the Venezuelan Communists, was carried out by the publication in Vicente Lombardo Toledano's paper, *El Popular*, and in the Cuban Communist Party's monthly *Fundamentos* of an Open Letter to the Venezuelan Communists from the United States Communist leader William Z. Foster, expressing his support of the Fuenmayor group. It is significant that this letter was not sent until six months after the split in the Venezuelan Party became official.

During World War II and the years immediately following the war, the Cuban Communist Party was undoubtedly also active in supervising the activities of some of its brother organizations in the Caribbean area. Cuban Communist representatives attended most of the Party congresses held in the Caribbean area during and after the second World War. The Cuban Party certainly played a major role in the organization of the Popular Socialist Parties of Haiti and the Dominican Republic.

Three other sources of influence and of orders for the Latin American Communists must be mentioned—the Argentine Communist Party, or more properly speaking, Victorio Codovilla; Vicente Lombardo Toledano; and the Guatemalan Communist Party. Codovilla spent most of the 1930's in Europe. He participated as a Comintern agent in the direction of the policies of the Spanish Communist Party during the Civil War, and did not return to the Americas until after that conflict had ended. He then returned to Argentina via Mexico and other Latin American countries. The purge of the Mexican Communist Party, which resulted in Hernán Laborde being succeeded as Secretary General by Dionisio Encinas, is said to have taken place as a result of his presence in Mexico.

In the postward period it is likely that Codovilla and in conjunction with him Rodolfo Ghioldi, who has always been his sidekick in the management of the Argentine Communist Party, have had an important role in directing the affairs of the neighboring Communist Parties. Codovilla and Ghioldi certainly have intervened at various times, from the late 1920's on, in the affairs of the Chilean Party, and it seems probable that they have had much influence in the Paraguayan and Uruguayan Parties as well. Rodolfo Ghioldi was in Brazil at the time of the 1935 N.L.A. revolt.

Vicente Lombardo Toledano has had a key position in the international apparatus of the Communists in this hemisphere, through his position at the head of the continental Communist trade union movement. It seems certain that the trade union policies of the Latin American Communist Parties have been largely set by Lombardo. He toured the whole continent during the second World War, driving home to the Parties and their labor movements the necessity of going all out to support the war effort of the Soviet Union and other United Nations. During this trip he cor.

ferred not only with the heads of the trade union groups affiliated with the C.T.A.L., but with the chiefs of the Communist Parties as well.

Subsequently, Lombardo has played an exceedingly important role in the Communist Parties of several of the Central American republics. This was notably true of Guatemala, where the Communists' strength was built largely upon their control of the organized labor movement, a control which was established with the help of Lombardo's C.T.A.L. He also had a good deal to do with the activities of the Communist leaders of Nicaragua and Costa Rica, who took refuge in Mexico when the going got hot in their own countries.

Lombardo Toledano attended personally the World Federation of Trade Unions' regional conference held in Peiping, China, in December of 1949. During that meeting it was decided that the publication of the W.F.T.U.'s Spanish-language publications should henceforward be in the hands of the C.T.A.L. headquarters in Mexico City. Apparently the C.T.A.L. was also promised a considerable increase in its budget. All of this suggests that Lombardo's position as the Communist gauleiter for Latin America, at least insofar as trade union affairs were concerned, was officially recognized.

Undoubtedly the Guatemalan Communist Party was also an important cog in international Communism's machinery in the Americas during the period when it had great influence with the government of President Jacobo Arbenz. It is certain that the Guatemalan Party's training school in Guatemala City was giving indoctrination and instruction to Communists from neighboring countries as well as to members of the Guatemalan Party. Exiled leaders of several neighboring Communist Parties sought refuge in Arbenz' Guatemala, where they received aid from the Guatemalan Party.

The case of the Brazilian Communist Party is a peculiar one. There seems to be general agreement among those who claim to know something about such matters that the Brazilian Communist Party has neither intervened in the affairs of other Communist Parties nor has it, in recent years, been subjected to intervention. Since the middle 1930's its master, always subject to orders from Comintern headquarters, has been Luiz Carlos Prestes. Although Rodolfo Ghioldi of Argentina was present in Brazil in 1935 at the time of the National Liberation Alliance revolt, and spent several years in jail as a result of its failure, he seems to have been there more as an aide to Prestes than as a director of the Brazilian Party's affairs.

It is certain that Prestes has followed policies which sometimes have differed from those of neighboring Parties, though never varying essentially from the stated Comintern policies. For instance, he severely criticized the Argentine Communists in 1945 for their opposition to Perón. Later, he was the first of the Latin American Communists to declare that members of his Party would support the Soviet Union in the case of a war between their country and the U.S.S.R.

After an extended trip through Latin America in 1946 and 1947, the author of this book came to the conclusion that at that time, the Latin American Communists received their instructions through four principal channels, as follows:

Argentina, Uruguay, Paraguay, Chile, Bolivia, and perhaps Peru were under the general supervision of Victorio Codovilla.

The Caribbean area, including the Caribbean republics of South America and Central America, and perhaps including Peru and Ecuador, were generally supervised by the Cuban Communist Party, which itself was watched over by the Communist Party of the United States.

Luiz Carlos Prestes was himself responsible for the activities of the Brazilian Communists.

Finally, the trade union activities of the whole Communist network in Latin America were guided by Vicente Lombardo Toledano, as chief of the C.T.A.L.

At this time the whole American Communist apparatus appears to have been managed from Moscow's branch office in Paris. Victorio Codovilla told the author that the Argentine Party's chief contact with the Communist Parties of Europe was through France. It is well known that the change in the line of the United States Communists which resulted in the ousting of Earl Browder was set off by an article in *Cahiers Comunistes,* a French Communist periodical, written by Jacques Duclos, who had recently returned from Moscow. These facts would indicate that in the immediate postwar years the American branches of the Communist International apparatus were managed through Paris.

Of course, this pattern has probably changed since the late 1940's. Undoubtedly for a time the Caribbean headquarters was moved from Cuba to Guatemala. It has probably become increasingly difficult for the United States Party—busy as it has been with its own troubles, and hampered by increasing restrictions on the travel of United States Communists to other countries and foreign Communists to the United States—to take as active a part in the affairs of the Latin American Stalinists as it once did. The decision of the Peiping W.F.T.U. congress seems to have raised considerably the status of Lombardo Toledano and the C.T.A.L. in the continental Communist setup.

The question remains as to what degree of direction the Communists of Latin American countries actually receive from outside the borders of their own nations. This, only one who has been on the the inside can know, and perhaps no single Communist leader in any Latin American country will be fully aware of the extent to which his Party has been influenced by outside orders, since the Communist International apparatus is notoriously inclined not to let the right hand know what the left hand is doing.

However, there are certain facts which are clear. At certain times the Comintern has given extensive amounts of money to the Latin American Communist Parties. This was certainly true in the early days of the Mexican Communist Party. It was certainly true in the 1930's of the Chilean Communist Party. It would seem to the author that it continued to be true in a number of countries—notably Argentina and Uruguay—as late as the 1940's and 1950's.* Many Latin American Communist Parties are notorious for the fact that in spite of a small membership and relatively limited influence, they have more money to spend on election campaigns and other propaganda than all the other parties in their countries put together.

The second thing which seems clear is that, in certain specific cases, outsiders have stirred up or settled quarrels within individual Latin American Communist Parties. This certainly occurred in 1930 in the Chilean Communist Party, where the South American Bureau of the Comintern intervened quite openly in the internal affairs of that Party. It also undoubtedly happened in the Mexican Communist Party on various occasions in the 1920's and 1930's, and as late as 1940. Daniel James, in *Red Design for the Americas: Guatemalan Prelude*, offers evidence that the decision taken at the end of 1951 to merge the two Communist Parties then existing in the country and to unite the three central labor organizations was taken as the result of orders which Victor Manuel Gutiérrez, chief of one of the Parties and one of the labor groups, brought back upon his return from an extended stay in the Soviet Union.

Another indication that the Communist Parties of Latin America are not their own masters is the alacrity with which they have followed the various twistings and turnings of the Communist Party line. They all obediently jumped from Third Period to Popular Front, from opposition to World War II to extreme support for the Allied cause, and back again to violent opposition to the United States.

Sometimes the Communist Parties of Latin America have received a kind of preview of a change in the international Communist line. Such was the case with the "dissolution" of the Communist International, carried out in 1943. Dissolution of the International had been discussed as early as 1938, at the Conference of Latin American Communist Parties held in Moscow. It had been suggested by Earl Browder, and Manuilsky and others present at this conference had said that it was a distinct possi-

* In May, 1955, the author was informed of certain peculiarities of trade treaties recently negotiated between Argentina and several countries behind the Iron Curtain. These treaties provided for Argentina's purchase of larger amounts from its trading partners than it sold to them. The balance was to be paid in Argentine currency to the respective Communist embassies in Buenos Aires. It seems distinctly possible that the funds thus obtained by these embassies went into Communist work in South America.

bility. Manuilsky had said, according to Ravines: "If the Communist International needs to be thrown overboard to save the ship, it will disappear as the First International, founded by Marx, disappeared once it had ceased to serve the purpose for which it was created."[6]

There is no doubt that sometimes the Communist Parties of Latin America, like those in other parts of the world, have been left high and dry by a sudden twist in the Soviet Union's policies. Ravines recounts the consternation and panic which seized the leaders of the Communist Party of Chile when the 1939 Pact between Stalin and the Nazis was announced —feelings which must have been much like those of the British Party, the Communists of the United States, and most of the other national Communist leaderships, who were not consulted in the least by Stalin about this latest veering in the Soviet Union's tactics, and were merely supposed to adapt their own policies to the change.

However, the Communists have soon been notified of changes and of the line which they are supposed to take in adapting their own policies to them. One ex-Communist leader of Chile told the author that the change in line from support of collective security to denunciation of it, which was made necessary by the Stalin-Nazi Pact, was transmitted to the Chilean Communists by Rodolfo Ghioldi of the Argentine Party.

So well do the Communists conform to the position of the international Communist movement at any given time, that one can travel from one country to the other in Latin America without noticing any important difference in what the Communists of the various countries are saying, insofar as international policies are concerned.

Every once in a while, the Comintern makes the Communist Parties of various countries jump through an ideological hoop to demonstrate their loyalty. This occurred soon after the second World War when the Communist Parties of various nations were made to come out and state that in case of war between their own nation and the Soviet Union, they would side with the Soviet Union.

The one lodestar of the Communist Parties of Latin America, as of those the world over, the one thing which has never changed, is loyalty to the Soviet Union. On this they never waver.

Dmitri Manuilsky, ex-head of the Comintern, summed up what has consistently been the policy of the Latin American Communists, in addressing a meeting of delegates of various Latin American Communist Parties in Moscow in 1928. He said:

Above all our force must be used in defense of the Soviet Union. This is the first duty of the parties, of the individual Communists, of our sympathizers, friends, and followers. The mark of a good Communist shall be precisely this: the fervor with which he defends the Soviet Union and its international policy, his eagerness to praise its works, the emphasis with which he teaches the people that the only just policy is that of the U.S.S.R. and that all other nations are un-just, provoking wars, and leading to world-wide conflagration. . . . The very soul of the Communist party's strategy is the vigorous defense of the Soviet Union; there can be but one policy, that of Russia, of Stalin. No Communist may have the right to defend any other. This must be clear to you all; remember it.[7]

This has been the credo of the Latin American Communists since the 1920's. At that time the Communists were stressing "defense of the Soviet Union" as the major objective of Latin American Communist policy. This motivated their sudden switch on the issue of the second World War. Subsequent to the war, they have pulled out all stops in their praise of the "Peace policy of the Soviet Union" and their denunciation of the "war camp" of the United States, Great Britain, and other opponents of the Soviet Union in the Cold War.

This supreme loyalty to the Soviet Union is the most pertinent thing about the Latin American Communists—or Communists anywhere else. It is the thing which distinguishes them not only from the Democratic Left in Latin America, but also from home-grown brands of totalitarianism in the region. The Latin American Communists are not only totalitarians, they are totalitarians whose first loyalty is to the Soviet Union, whose first duty is to serve the Soviet Union.

They are sometimes willing to sacrifice their individual national parties to this objective. This is certainly what occurred in Guatemala in the summer of 1954. The Communists recklessly pushed the Guatemalan Government into a position of violent opposition to the United States, rather than one of concentration on the essentially national revolution upon which the country was launched. The result was the overthrow of Arbenz and the suppression of the Communist Party, which was at the time the most promising Stalinist group in America.

Thus, the Latin American Communists are not "just another radical party." They are Stalinists, Communists, whose twin objectives are the achievement of absolute dictatorial power for themselves and support of whatever the Soviet Union chooses to do in the international field. They are part of the international Communist movement, receive aid and direction from it, and are blindly loyal to it.

## Chapter IV

# Communists in the Latin American Labor Movement

SINCE THE ORGANIZATION of the Comintern, the Communists have had some influence in the labor movements of the hemisphere. Even before the formal organization of Communist Parties in Latin America, important trade union groups had expressed their sympathy with the Russian Revolution and the Communist International.

The principal central body of trade unions of Chile, the Federación Obrera de Chile (F.O.Ch.), affiliated with the Red International of Labor Unions in December, 1921, even before the Partido Socialista Obrero, which controlled the F.O.Ch., joined the political International and became the Partido Comunista de Chile. It was the only central labor body in the hemisphere to go over *in toto* to the Communists, but the people who established the Communist Parties in several countries had more or less influence in the trade union movements of those countries.

In Argentina Communist influence appeared in both factions of the labor movement of the time: in the Anarchist Federación Obrera Regional Argentina of the Fifth Congress, otherwise known as the F.O.R.A. Comunista; and in the moderate Federación Obrera Regional Argentina of the Ninth Congress, which in 1921 became the Unión Sindical Argentina (U.S.A.). Thus, in its October, 1920, Congress the F.O.R.A. Comunista went on record as follows:

"The proletariat of the Argentine Region . . . expresses its solidarity towards the Russian Revolution and towards all the revolutionary forces which with energy and determination are bringing about the moral and material improvement of all the workers of the world; and particularly towards the Anarchists who in Russia, as everywhere, are fighting for the triumph of their ideals. . . .

Diego Abad de Santillán, the historian of the Anarchist labor movement of Argentina, comments that: "Reading between the lines, it is clear from the resolutions of this congress that two tendencies were struggling for control, one disposed to make concessions to the doctrine of the dictatorship of the proletariat, the other opposed to all such concessions. . . .[1]

For several years this struggle continued, but the pro-Communist element finally lost out when the F.O.R.A. Comunista joined the anarchosyndicalist International Working Men's Association, soon after the I.W.M.A. was established in 1922.

Meanwhile, in the other branch of the Argentine labor movement a similar struggle was under way, between Syndicalists and Socialists on the one hand, and Bolsheviks (or Communists) on the other. The Syndicalists triumphed in this struggle, and the Unión Sindical Argentina voted against affiliating to the Red International of Labor Unions. It maintained its independence of all international labor groups. Until the coming of the Third Period, therefore, the Argentine Communists were left as a minority movement in both of the major trade union bodies of Argentina.

In most other Latin American countries, too, the Communists were only minority groups within the trade union confederations during the 1920's. The majority element was either Socialist or Anarchosyndicalist, except in Mexico, where the dominant labor group of the time, the Confederación Regional Obrera Mexicana (C.R.O.M.), had a political orientation all its own.

The Red International of Labor Unions, which was the Communists' world-wide organization in the trade union field, had few Latin American affiliates in the early 1920's. The Anarchosyndicalist groups, which had been the principal trade union force in Latin America before World War I, for the most part joined the Anarchosyndicalist international body, the International Working Men's Association, established at a congress at Berlin, Germany, in 1922. A few groups joined the Socialists' International Federation of Trade Unions.

The R.I.L.U., or Profintern, as it is often called, was formally established two years after the organization of the Communist International. On July 15, 1920, an International Trade Union Council was established in Moscow as a "committee for the propagation of ideas of the revolutionary trade union movement." It had no definite program or tactics, but its objective was described as being "to unite the revolutionary trade unions under the slogan of the overthrow of capitalism and the dictatorship of the proletariat." In the beginning it included a great variety of groups, such as the Socialist-controlled General Confederation of Labor of Italy and the Spanish Anarchosyndicalist National Confederation of Labor.

However, in July, 1921, the First Congress of the organization was held for the purpose of clarifying its ideology. This Congress, which also met in Moscow, established "clearly defined ideals" of the organization. This "clarification" led to the withdrawal of various groups, including the Italian General Confederation and the Spanish C.N.T.[2]

Thus, the Anarchists and Socialists were clearly eliminated from the Communist international labor setup. For half a decade there was a violent polemic between Anarchist and Communist labor groups, in Latin America as well as in Europe. Concerning this, Alexander Lozovsky, the head of the Red International of Labor Unions, commented in 1929:

> Only in 1927 or 1928 did we begin to see in the majority of countries, an ideological crisis among the anarchists, which brought a certain number of anarchist or anarchosyndicalist comrades to understand that the revolution cannot be made by proclamations, that strikes cannot be made every twenty-four hours, and that to combat the bourgeoisie it was not sufficient to have a weekly paper and a few hundred members, but was necessary to have a sufficiently strong organization to continually combat and finally overthrow the capitalist State.[3]

As the 1920's progressed, the various Communist Parties of Latin America gained a certain following in the nascent labor movements of the area. In Chile they controlled the old F.O.Ch.; in some other countries they were successful in organizing trade union groups of their own; in still others they led "revolutionary opposition" groups in the majority trade union organizations.

The international Communist movement was anxious to organize the trade union forces of the various Latin American Communist Parties on a continental scale. However, this was a slow process. Before the formation of a continental Communist labor group, the Communists did what they could to discredit the only existing labor confederation of the hemisphere, the Pan American Federation of Labor, which was under the influence of the American Federation of Labor. One Communist, Ricardo Martínez of Venezuela, attended the 1927 Convention of the P.A.F.L., where he denounced the alleged subservience of the P.A.F.L. to "Yanqui imperialism," besides attacking several Latin American governments, against which he levelled the same charge.

A year later, Humbert-Droz, the Swiss who was currently charged with the control of Latin American Communist affairs, summed up the Communist attitude towards the Pan American Federation of Labor in a speech to the Sixth Congress of the Communist International:

> . . . Yankee imperialism endeavors to export not only its capital, but also the reformist method of corruption, of the American Federation of Labor, through the intermediary of the P.A.F.L., which is only the tool of Yankee imperialism in the ranks of the working class, the means by which the Wall St. financiers endeavor to insure their profits against the rebellion of the exploited.[4]

By 1927 only two Latin American trade union groups were affiliated with the Profintern, the Federación Obrera de Chile and the largely mythical Confederación Obrera Nacional de Colombia. However, the

Profintern was anxious to establish a Latin American affiliate. One of the first steps in this direction was a Continental Congress of Maritime Workers in 1926, in which Communist union groups cooperated with Anarcho-syndicalist seamen's organizations. It was attended by both the United States and Chilean I.W.W.'s and by maritime groups from Brazil and Uruguay, as well as delegates from the Profintern and the Russian Marine Workers Union. The Congress denounced the Pan American Federation of Labor, but did not adopt any overtly Communist resolutions.[5]

Another step towards establishing a Communist continental labor confederation was taken in December, 1927, during the ceremonies surrounding the celebration of the Tenth Anniversary of the Russian Revolution. Numerous delegations from Communist and sympathetic groups from all over the world were present in Moscow at that time.

The Latin Americans present held a meeting which adopted the following resolution:

> We delegates of working-class unions of Argentina, Brazil, Colombia, Cuba, Mexico, Uruguay, Chile, and Ecuador, who are in Moscow on the occasion of the tenth anniversary of the October Revolution, have met in the headquarters of the Red International of Labor Unions on December 11, 1927, and after having examined the problem of the working class and the unions in the countries of Latin America, have come to the following conclusion:
>
> Considering the growing aggressiveness of United States imperialism towards all the countries of Central and South America, and its aspiration to transform all of Latin America into a colony of American capital;
>
> Considering that the Pan-American Federation of Labor—organized by the reactionary leaders of American trade unions—is nothing more than an instrument of Wall Street and in fact an enemy of the working classes of South America as well as of those of Central and North America;
>
> Considering, that the weight of reaction in the countries of Latin America is directed against the working class, and considering that only the united efforts of the working masses of all of Latin America can restrain United States imperialism and bourgeois aggression of the Latin American countries;
>
> We unanimously decide:
>
> To proceed in all of the Latin American countries to the preparation of unity of all trade union organizations in the fight against United States imperialism, against the Pan-American Federation of Labor, against the offensive of the national bourgeoisie, and for the establishment of close fraternal relations among the working-class organizations, for the constitution of a single working-class international to include the unions of all countries, all races, and all continents, to fight in common against imperialist wars and for the integral emancipation of labor from the power of capital.

The undersigned promise to do all in our power to prepare for a conference of class-conscious unions of all of Latin America to meet in Montevideo towards the end of 1928 for the purpose of establishing a Latin American Trade Union Secretariat.

This resolution was signed by Attilio Biondi, A. Resnik, and Martin S. García from the Unión Sindical Argentina; Antonio Maruenda for the Autonomous Unions of Uruguay and the Unión Obrera Provincial de Córdoba, Argentina; Guillermo Hernández Rodríguez for the Sindicato Central Obrero de Colombia; Bernardo Lobo of the Confederación Nacional Obrera de Cuba; Rufino Rosas of the Federación Obrera de Chile; Pablo Méndez of the Liga Nacional Campesina de México; Prospero Malvestitti of the Unión Obrera Local (Autónoma) of Buenos Aires, Argentina; Ricardo Paredes of the Federación de los Ferroviarios del Ecuador and the Federación Obrera de Chimborazo, Ecuador; and a representative of the Minority of the Revolutionary Trade Unions of Brazil.

David Alfaro Siqueiros of the Miners Union of the State of Jalisco, Mexico, Montemayor of the Oil Workers of the State of Tamaulipas, Mexico, and Contreras of the Workers Transport Federation of Mexico, were present at the Moscow Conference but left before the Call was issued.[6]

It is notable that except for the F.O.Ch. of Chile, the C.N.O.C. of Cuba, and the U.S.A. of Argentina, no national trade union group endorsed the Call. The F.O.Ch. at the time was completely Communist-controlled, though it was losing strength under the battering of the Ibáñez dictatorship. The C.N.O.C. and the U.S.A. were both of Syndicalist orientation, though each had a certain sympathy for the Communists and had Communist minorities within their ranks. However, the pro-Communism of the C.N.O.C. was more marked than that of the U.S.A., which later refused to participate further in moves for the establishment of a regional Profintern affiliate in the Americas.

The actual manifesto convoking the Montevideo Congress was addressed "To the Workers' Organizations of Latin America and to the Proletariat in General," and was issued by another meeting in Moscow of Latin American trade union representatives, held in April, 1928. It called the proposed Congress definitely for May, 1929, and announced that a Provisional Secretariat had been established to make arrangements for the Congress.

The Call to the Montevideo Congress proclaimed that "we are living in the sharpest and most decisive period of the world struggle between the proletariat and the bourgeoisie, both because of the existence of the Soviet Union and because of the expansion and intensification of imperialism." It proclaimed "Yankee imperialism" to be "our nearest and most formidable enemy," and recited the history of United States intervention in Latin American affairs, charging the United States, as well, with responsibility for keeping the dictatorships of Machado, Ibáñez, Siles, Leguía, and Gómez in power.

The Call set forth an agenda for the Montevideo meeting:

1. Report of the Provisional Secretariat on its work.
2. The fight against British and American imperialism and native reaction.
3. The attitude towards the Pan-American Federation of Labor.
4. Program of economic demands.
5. National and international trade union unity.
6. Problems of immigration and emigration.
7. Problems of the Indians and the organization of the agricultural proletariat.
8. Creation of the Confederación Sindical Latino Americana.
9. Election of officials of the Confederación.

This Call was signed by delegates from the Jalisco State Miners Union, the Food Workers Federation, and the Railroad Workers Confederation, all of Mexico; the Confederación Nacional Obrera de Cuba; the Unión Obrera Revolucionaria of Venezuela; the Confederación Obrera Nacional and the Confederación Obrera of the Cauca Valley, of Colombia; the Federación Obrera de Guayas, the Federación Obrera de Chimborazo, the Confederación Ferroviaria, and the unions affiliated to the Socialist Party, of Ecuador; the Federación Obrera Local of Lima and the Federación Textil, of Peru; the Federación Obrera of Rio de Janeiro and miscellaneous unions of São Paulo, from Brazil. It was also signed by representatives of the Federación Obrera de Chile; the Federación Obrera Marítima, the Workers Unity Block, and a group of miscellaneous unions of Montevideo, from Uruguay; and the Unión Obrera Provincial de Córdoba, Red Trade Union Groups of Buenos Aires and Rosario, and Autonomous Unions of Buenos Aires, from Argentina.

Again, there were few national organizations, and most of the groups represented were local trade union groups under Communist influence. Also represented were Communist minorities within trade union federations in several countries.

The April, 1928, Moscow Conference adopted, in addition to this Call, a series of three resolutions—"The Tasks of the Trade Union Movement in Latin America," "For the Unionization of Agricultural Workers," and "Manifesto Against Reaction."

The first of these proclaimed that "The labor movement of Latin America is now passing through a period of tempestuous development," largely due to the growing industrialization of the area. It said that the atmosphere was also favorable to the development of trade unions because of the existence of a "continuous revolutionary effervescence" in the area. However, it noted that "the political life of the countries of Latin America

. . . are [sic] complicated by the bitter struggle between the American and British imperialisms."

The resolution pointed out that "The peasant class has a great importance in Latin America" and that in several countries this class is largely Indian. However, it notes that the trade unions have paid little attention to the peasants.

This resolution deplores the multitudinous splits in the Latin American labor movements, which are generally controlled either by Anarchists or reformists, both of which groups "debilitate the labor movement of these countries, diverting the working masses from the true revolutionary road and the proper methods of struggle." However, it notes that there is a growing element which is influenced by the Russian Revolution.

Finally, the resolution urges that there is a minimum program upon which the Latin American unions can be united: organization of the unorganized; struggle for organizational unity in each country and in the hemisphere; struggle for trade union liberty; struggle against the military dictatorships of the area; incorporation of the peasants into the trade union movement; struggle against the Pan American Federation of Labor; struggle against imperialism; and struggle "for a single class-conscious Trade Union international, to unite the workers of all countries, races, and continents."[7]

The actual founding congress of the Confederación Sindical Latino Americana was held as scheduled in May, 1929, in Montevideo, Uruguay. Labor groups from fifteen countries were present. The organizations represented and the delegates reported as attending the meeting were as follows:

*Argentina:* Unión Obrera de Luz y Fuerza de Avellaneda; Unión Gráfica Rosarina; Unión Obrera Telefónica de Rosario; Unión Obrera Provincial de Córdoba; Unión Obrera Local de Chivilcoy; Sindicato de Sastres de Chacabuco, and various local unions, represented by P. Iglesias, Francisco Monaco, Angel Luna, Antonio Maruenda, Lorenzo Luna, Pablo Lellas, Gildo Mello, Rafael Gnosza, Juan Gallicchio, Rafael Grecco, Domingo Díaz, Pedro Fernández.

*Bolivia:* Confederación Nacional Boliviana del Trabjo, Federación Obrera de La Paz, and Sociedad de Mineros "Primero de Mayo" of Potosí, represented by Francisco Blanco, Hugo Sevillano, and Romeo Castro.

*Brazil:* Confederação Geral do Trabalho Brasileiro; União dos Marítimos e Portuarios do Brasil, and Centro Cosmopolita de Rio de Janeiro, represented by José Santos, Antonio Gubinelli, Arnaldo da Silva, José Agusto, Teodoro de Oliveira, Guillermo de Aguiar; and Januario Vidal.

*Colombia:* Central Nacional Obrera y Campesina; Unión Sindical de Magdalena; Federación de Zona Atlántica; Federación Obrera de Bolivar; represented by Matallena Neira, Moisés Prieto, N. Arce, R. E. Mahecha, and F. Cuéllar.

*Costa Rica:* Asociación de Resistencia y Cultura Obrera de San José, as observer; Agrupación de Reorganización Sindical de Puerto Limón, represented by the El Salvador delegation.

*Cuba:* Confederación Obrera Nacional de Cuba and the Organización Obrera y Campesina de Cuba, represented by Pedro Torres, Sandalio Junco, Ramiro Ramírez, and de la Núñez.

*Ecuador:* Confederación Obrera y Campesina de Guayaquil; Unión de Chauffeurs and Sociedad Tipográfica de Pichincha; Consejo Central de los Sindicatos Agrarios de la Provincia de Guayas; Sindicato de Campesinos Indígenas y de Oficios Varios del Cantón Cayemba, represented by Felix Carrasco, Jorge Ramos, and Alberto Araujo.

*El Salvador:* Federación Regional de Trabajadores, represented by Serafín Martínez and Luis Díaz.

*Guatemala:* Federación Regional de Trabajadores, represented by Luis Aguirre and Armando Rojas.

*Mexico:* Confederación Sindical Unitaria de México and the Liga de Comunidades Agrarias del Estado de Veracruz, represented by David Alfaro Siqueiros, Elías Barrios, and Samuel Rodríguez Cercilla.

*Panama:* Federación Sindical de Obreros y Campesinos, represented by Jacinto Chacón and Eugenio L. Cossani.

*Paraguay:* Unión Obrera del Paraguay, Liga de Obreros Marítimos del Paraguay, Sindicato de Joyeros, represented by Recalde Milesi, Daniel Villalba, and Juan Denis.

*Peru:* Comité Pro-Confederación General de Trabajadores del Perú; Federación de Chauffeurs; Federación de Trabajadores Ferroviarios; Federación de Motoristas, Conductores y Anexos; Federación de Yanaconas; Federación de Campesinos de Ica; Federación de Trabajadores de Tejidos; Unificación de Obreros Cerveceros; Federación Gráfica; Federación de Tripulantes y Cabotajes; Sociedad Maritima Confederada de Callao, represented by Luis Suriva, Alberto Campos, Samuel Casanova, and Gilberto Arenas.

*Uruguay:* Confederación General del Trabajo del Uruguay, representado by Julio Baccino, José Lazarraga, Leopoldo Sala, J. Bacaicoa, F. Rodríguez, and Juan B. Massoni.

*Venezuela:* Agrupaciones Sindicales Revolucionarias, represented by Ricardo Martínez.

It is worthy of note that the C.S.L.A. founding congress met after the commencement of the Third Period in Comintern history. As a result the

Communists had already organized national central labor organizations of their own in Bolivia, Brazil, Mexico, Panama, and Uruguay, and were well on the way to launching one in Peru. All of these groups, as well as national labor organizations in Cuba, Guatemala, and Honduras which had passed under their control, were represented at the Congress.

The C.S.L.A. founding congress lasted for fourteen days. The subjects discussed included agricultural problems, trade union organizational matters, immigration, youth, Indian, and Negro problems. Long discussions centered on the supposed dangers of war and on the fight against imperialism, and the congress was reported to have "declared war upon British, and especially American imperialism."

The Congress devoted a great deal of attention to the problems of the Communist labor movements in particular countries. The meeting was said to have "considered plans for building a class-conscious labor movement in relatively virgin fields." It laid plans for mass demonstrations, particularly a continent-wide series of meetings against unemployment, to be held on March 30, 1930. A pact of solidarity was signed between the new C.S.L.A. and the Trade Union Educational League, the trade union propaganda agency of the United States Communist Party, which a few months later was converted into a rival of the American Federation of Labor under the name of the Trade Union Unity League.[8]

The Confederación Sindical Latino Americana was established as the Latin American affiliate of the Red International of Labor Unions. At least one Latin American, Ignacio Torres Giraldo of Colombia, sat on the Executive Committee of the Profintern as a representative of the C.S.L.A. He lived in Moscow for several years.[9]

The C.S.L.A. led a turbulent existence for half a decade. Communist-controlled labor federations were established in every country in which a Party existed, and these all joined the continental Communist labor group. Most of these national federations were more or less paper organizations.

The change in the international Communist "line" in the middle 1930's paved the way for the elimination of the C.S.L.A. and the merging of the Communist unions in different countries with other trade union groups. This led up to the formation in 1938 of the hemisphere's first real united front labor body, the Confederación de Trabajadores de América Latina (CTAL).

A preliminary move toward the formation of this new continental labor confederation was taken at the First American Congress of States Affiliated to the International Labor Organization, held in Santiago, Chile, in January, 1936. A group of the workers participating in that conference met and drew up the following proclamation:

> To the Workers:
>
> Meeting in Santiago de Chile on January 14, 1936, the undersigned trade unionists, who have come as delegates or observers to the Amer-

ican Labor Conference, have considered the situation facing the proletariat of America, and in particular the fact that there is no solid
organization for the defense of the workers' interests because of the
lack of unity among existing labor organizations; we have resolved:

To call upon the workers of the American continent to work for
the establishment of trade union unity in each country so as to better
achieve their aims.

At the same time, we observe that the proletariat of America has
problems which are common to the hemisphere, and that in order to
deal with these problems it is necessary, as soon as possible, to form a
vigorous continental organization of workers. We also consider necessary the closest cooperation among existing labor organizations to
work towards this end in their own countries. To attenuate the misery
which afflicts the proletariat of the continent, we propose the following bases for immediate action:

1. Defense of democratic liberties (freedom of speech, association,
press, the right to strike, etc.)
2. Maximum work week of forty hours, without decrease in present wages.
3. Increase in wages.
4. Strict fulfillment, and extension, of national labor laws and international labor conventions. For social security to protect the
worker against the risks of accident, illness, old age, unemployment,
and death.
5. Liberty for all political and social prisoners.
6. Opposition to fascism and war.

This proclamation was signed not only by Communists, such as Pedro
Chiarante of Argentina, Elías Laferte of Chile, and José Lazarraga of
Uruguay, but also by Socialists, such as Francisco Pérez Leirós of Argentina and Juan Díaz Martínez of Chile, and by workers of other political
coloration as well.[10]

The trade unions of the continent were not in fact united for another
two years. The initiative in calling the founding congress of a new labor
body for the hemisphere was taken by the Confederación de Trabajadores
de México, probably at the suggestion of the Mexican Government.

At that time the foreign relations of Mexico were severely strained, as
a result of the revolutionary program of the government of President
Lázaro Cárdenas. One of the fundamental principles of the political program of the Cárdenas regime was "Mexico for the Mexicans," and the
government had expropriated many foreign landholders, had seized the
foreign-owned National Railways of Mexico, and in March, 1938, had
taken over the country's oil industry, which had been largely in the hands
of the Shell, Standard Oil, and Doherty interests. The upshot of this last
move was that the British Government broke off diplomatic relations with
Mexico, and the international oil cartel declared a boycott of the newly

nationalized Mexican oil industry, thus preventing it from selling its products abroad and from purchasing necessary repair and replacement parts. As a result of all of these events, the international position of the Mexican Government was precarious, and the Cárdenas regime felt the need for some striking move to restore its prestige. Such a move was the summoning of the Latin American Labor Congress, which met in Mexico City in September, 1938.

All of the important national labor confederations then in existence were represented at the Mexico City Congress and became charter members of the C.T.A.L. These included the Confederación de Trabajadores de México; the Confederación General del Trabajo of Argentina; the Confederación de Trabajadores de Colombia; the Confederación de Trabajadores de Chile; and the Confederación Sindical de Trabajadores de Bolivia and Obrerismo Organizado of Nicaragua. The largely paper Confederación Nacional de Trabajadores of Paraguay and Confederación Venezolana del Trabajo were also represented. Finally there were represented one or more individual unions from Cuba, Peru, Ecuador, Costa Rica, and Uruguay.[11]

Various political groups in the labor movement were represented. The Mexican delegation was headed by Vicente Lombardo Toledano, the self-styled "independent Marxist," whom the Communists had tried to oust as Secretary General of the Confederación de Trabajadores de México the year before, but who was now veering in their direction. However, the loyalty of Lombardo and the other members of the Mexican delegation was chiefly to President Cárdenas, rather than to any outside influence.

The Cuban delegation included Socialists and Auténticos as well as Communists. The Peruvian delegation included Apristas and Communists. The Chilean delegation was made up of Socialists and Communists, as was that from Uruguay. Liberals and Communists came from Colombia. The Costa Rican delegates were Communists or Communist sympathizers. The Founding Conference of the Confederación de Trabajadores de América Latina was thus a real united front of virtually all the elements in the Latin American labor movement except the Catholics and the Anarcho-syndicalists.

The first Executive Committee of the C.T.A.L., with Vicente Lombardo Toledano of Mexico as President, and Fidel Velásquez, also of the Mexican C.T.M., as General Secretary, was certainly not dominated by the Communists. Francisco Pérez Leirós of Argentina was First Vice President, and José M. Argaña, also of the Argentine C.G.T., was Southern Regional Secretary; both were Socialists. The Second Vice President was Clodomiro Clavijo of Colombia, while Cristiano Costillo of Colombia was Central Regional Secretary; their political complexion is not known.

In spite of the fact that the Communists had only minority representation at best in the C.T.A.L. in its earliest days, the Communist influence was greater than the number of its personnel would indicate. Partly this was due to gains by the Communists in the affiliated national organizations soon after the C.T.A.L. was founded. In Cuba the various union leaders who had been to Mexico took the lead—in accordance with a pact which they had signed while still in the Aztec capital—in organizing the Confederación de Trabajadores de Cuba, which was finally established in January, 1939. The General Secretary of the C.T.C. was Lázaro Peña, Communist leader of the Tobacco Workers Federation, and subsequently a Communist member of the Chamber of Deputies.

The Communists' dominance in the new Cuban confederation owed much to the alliance which had been struck between them and the Cuban dictator, Fulgencio Batista. A similar situation in Peru, where Communist labor leader Juan P. Luna was elected to the Chamber of Deputies on the ticket of the dictator, Manuel Prado, in 1939, gave the Peruvian Communists a dominant voice in the labor movement of that country. However, the Peruvian unions were not confederated for almost half a dozen years.

The most important factor conducive to the decidedly pro-Communist tone of the C.T.A.L.'s pronouncements, particularly during the first twenty-one months of World War II, was the influence of the Confederación's President, Vicente Lombardo Toledano. His difficulties with the Mexican Communists inside his own Confederación de Trabajadores de México had disappeared, and Lombardo became increasingly sympathetic to the Stalinist position. He was particularly active in denouncing the presence of Leon Trotsky in Mexico. With the outbreak of World War II, Lombardo Toledano followed the international Communist "line," denouncing the war as an "imperialist" struggle, in which the workers had no interest. He could see no difference between the Western Powers and the German Nazis sufficiently grave to justify his taking sides in the war.

The pro-Communist position of the C.T.A.L. was confirmed at the first meeting of its Executive Council, which took place in Mexico City in June, 1940. Those present included Lombardo Toledano and Fidel Velázquez of Mexico and Pérez Leirós and Argaña of Argentina, all members of the Executive Committee. Also present were Bernardo Ibáñez of Chile and Lázaro Peña of Cuba, as well as fraternal delegates from the C.I.O. and the Spanish Unión General de Trabajadores (in exile).

The only avowed Communist in this group was Lázaro Peña. However, Lombardo Toledano was already far gone in his pro-Communist attitude, and Fidel Velázquez was his closest collaborator in the Mexican labor movement at that time. Pérez Leirós and Argaña were Socialists, who were working closely with the Communist group in the Argentine Confederación General del Trabajo. Bernardo Ibáñez was a Socialist.

The most significant resolution of this meeting of the C.T.A.L. Executive was one on "The Proletariat of America and the European War." It started by declaring:

The workers of Latin America consider the present war, like that of 1914, to be in its essence a struggle between two great groups of capitalist countries, fighting for economic and political domination, and this struggle is no concern of the workers, who have not provoked the crisis and are the only ones to suffer from it.

The resolution went on to say that not only were the Fascist dictators responsible for the war, but so were the "governments of the bourgeois democracies" which had not stopped the Nazis earlier. At a moment when France was falling, the leaders of the C.T.A.L. commented that the victories of the Germans were due to the vacillating policies of the British and their allies; they called upon the workers to continue to fight Fascism "as a social theory," but added that

the fight against Fascism doesn't signify for the workers of Latin America, in consequence, the rehabilitation of British imperialism or of the various forms which the bourgeois democracy of the West has adopted against popular interest but the struggle against all kinds of tyranny, so that from this great crisis may arise everywhere a true democratic government which will be the expression of the vital interests of the people.

There was no word of concern over the victories of the Nazis and no word of support for the British, who were still holding out against them. However, neither was there any praise of the "peace policy of the Soviet Union"; this would have probably been too much even for the tolerant Lázaro Cárdenas, who was still President of the country in which the C.T.A.L. Executive was meeting.[12]

A sudden change occurred in the C.T.A.L.'s position as soon as Russia entered the second World War. This was indicated by Lombardo Toledano's speech to the opening session of the First Regular Congress of the C.T.A.L. on November 22, 1941, exactly five months after the German attack on Russia. In discussing the war, Lombardo said:

President Roosevelt is waging an unquestionably vital battle in his country. We must aid this man to defeat the enemies he has in his own nation, who are opposing the helpful, public, and decided intervention of the United States in favor of those who are at this moment fighting against fascism in Europe.

The quicker the United States intervenes in the struggle the better. The quicker President Roosevelt can show his people that the isolationists are misleading them, the better. The quicker President Roosevelt can become a real factor in aiding the Soviet Union and England the better.[13]

During the rest of World War II, Communist influence in the C.T.A.L. grew by leaps and bounds. Communist policy was violently pro-Ally and thus coincided with the policies of the majority of the governments of

Latin America. As a result, relations between Communists, both inside and outside of the trade union movement, and governmental leaders in most of the Latin American republics were very good.

The Communists in Nicaragua worked on friendly terms with dictator Anastasio Somoza; Peruvian Communists worked closely with Dictator-President Manuel Prado. Communist cooperation with Colonel-President Batista of Cuba, established in the late 1930's, continued during the war, and Communist leader Juan Marinello actually entered the Batista Cabinet as Minister Without Portfolio.

Early in 1945 the Communists of Brazil were able to make a deal with dictator Getulio Vargas, who had persecuted them for a decade, whereby they promised him political support in return for a free hand in the labor movement. Even in the Dominican Republic friendly relations were established between the Communists and Generalissimo Rafael Leónidas Trujillo.

Undoubtedly this friendliness between the Communists and the governments of Latin America was a strong influence favoring the growth of Communist power in the trade unions. The governments of the area—and the employers as well—were perfectly willing to deal with Communist trade union officials, who, impelled largely by political motives, were actively in favor of class collaboration, peaceful settlement of labor disputes, and every other possible measure to prevent interference with production of goods needed by the Allies. The Communists were more amenable than were the Socialists, Anarchists, or even Catholics, who might give more consideration to the rights and wishes of the specific groups of workers whom they represented than to the political issues centering on World War II.

Communists in the trade unions no doubt also benefited from the very widespread sympathy for the Allied cause and admiration for the fight which the Russians put up against the Nazi invaders. The Communists pictured themselves as unconditional champions of the Allies and threw over themselves the mantle of Russian heroism. They worked together with Socialists, with Apristas, and even with some Catholics, in furtherance of the cause of the Allies, and many of those in contact with the Stalinists, inside and outside of the trade union movement, began to overlook whatever doubts they may previously have had about the "democracy" of the Communists.

The Communists made the utmost possible use of their heightened prestige in the ranks of organized labor. Several new national central labor bodies were formed under Communist leadership. Thus, the Unión General de Trabajadores was established in Uruguay in 1942; the Federación Sindical de Panamá and the Confederación de Trabajadores de Costa Rica were set up in 1943, the Confederación de Trabajadores del Perú and the Confederación de Trabajadores del Ecuador in 1944, and the Confederación de Trabajadores de Guatemala and the Confederación de Trabajadores de Nicaragua in 1945.

The heads of all these new labor confederations except the last two were admitted members of the Communist Parties of their respective countries. In the case of the Nicaraguan group, the leadership was in the hands of the Partido Socialista de Nicaragua, which, though it did not proclaim itself "Communist," was in fact the Communist Party of Nicaragua. In Guatemala there did not as yet exist an official Communist Party, but Communist influence in the C.T.G. was marked from the beginning.

Communist influence was notable in other organizations affiliated with the C.T.A.L. The C.T.C. of Cuba was still headed by Communist deputy Lázaro Peña, and the Communists were the dominant group in the C.T.C. In Colombia the Communists shared leadership in the Confederación de Trabajadores de Colombia with the Liberals, and attempts of anti-Communist members of the Liberal Party in 1939 and 1945 to break the dominant Communist orientation of the C.T.C. resulted only in short-lived splits, succeeded by situations in which the Communists and their allies were more definitely in the saddle than before. In the Confederación Sindical de Trabajadores de Bolivia, the Stalinist-oriented Partido de Izquierda Revolucionaria gained the upper hand in the early 1940's. Meanwhile, in Chile the Communists steadily increased their influence in the C.T.Ch., as the Socialist Party, which had controlled that organization since its inception in 1936, was wracked by a series of splits and wobbled unsteadily between a pro-Communist and an anti-Communist policy.

A very important factor in the growing Communist influence in the C.T.A.L. was the trend of events in Argentina. The Confederación General del Trabajo, which had been the strongest non-Communist element in the C.T.A.L., split in December, 1942. One faction was headed by José Domenech, leader of the Railroad Workers Union, and was strongly anti-Communist. The other group was led by Francisco Pérez Leirós of the Municipal Workers and Angel Borlenghi and José Argaña of the Commercial Employees Federation; but the bulk of the membership of this group was composed of unions under Communist control, such as the Construction Workers, Metallurgical Workers, and Packinghouse Workers. The two groups were known as C.G.T.#1 and C.G.T.#2 respectively.

C.G.T.#1 withdrew from the C.T.A.L., which continued to recognize Pérez Leirós and José Argaña of C.G.T.#2 as representatives of the Argentine workers. Argaña attended the July, 1943, C.T.A.L. Executive Council meeting in Havana in that capacity.

The military revolution of June 4, 1943, resulted in the suppression of C.G.T.#2 by the military government. Subsequently, unions which had belonged to it rejoined the C.G.T.#1 or were superseded by unions enjoying government support, and C.G.T.#2 went out of existence. C.G.T.#1 continued outside the ranks of the C.T.A.L. and came increasingly under the influence of Colonel Juan D. Perón, Secretary of Labor of the military government.

Among those unions which returned to C.G.T.#1 was the Federation of White Collar Employees, and this resulted in the withdrawal of Señores Borlenghi and Argaña from all activity in the C.T.A.L. Their place was taken by Rubens Iscaro, an avowed member of the Communist Party of Argentina. For some time Iscaro and Pérez Leirós continued to be recognized by the C.T.A.L. as the "representatives of the Argentine workers," but in the late 1940's this pretense was finally dropped.

With the split in the C.G.T. and its retirement from the C.T.A.L., the largest non-Communist element was removed from the Confederación de Trabajadores de América Latina.

Increased Communist influence in the national trade union centers affiliated to the C.T.A.L. was reflected in the occasional international meetings of that organization. For instance, those labor leaders attending the July, 1943, Conference of the Executive Committee of the C.T.A.L. were the following:

> Vicente Lombardo Toledano
> Lázaro Peña, Secretary General of the C.T.C. of Cuba, a Communist
> Ramón León Renterría, Vice Secretary General of the C.T.C., usually an anti-Communist
> Bernardo Ibáñez, Secretary General of the C.T.Ch., a Socialist
> Salvador Ocampo, Assistant Secretary General of the C.T.Ch., a Communist member of the Chamber of Deputies
> Enrique Rodríguez, Secretary General of the Unión General de Trabajadores of Uruguay, a Communist member of the Chamber of Deputies
> Víctor Cordero, representing the unions of Costa Rica, a Communist
> Wenceslao Medrano and Alberto Barda, delegates from the Confederación Dominicana del Trabajo of the Dominican Republic, "Trujillistas"
> Alberto Sánchez, delegate of the Confederación General de Trabajadores de Puerto Rico, a Communist
> Guillermo Rodríguez, official of the C.T.C. of Colombia, Vice President of the C.T.A.L., Communist
> José Morera, Angel Cofiño, Carlos Fernández, José Miguel Espino, and Angel Echevarría, from the C.T.C. of Cuba, all but Cofiño Communists at that time
> José Argaña, representing C.G.T.#2 of Argentina, a Socialist
> Fidel Velázquez, Secretary General of C.T.M. of Mexico and Secretary General of C.T.A.L., non-Communist.

Attending as fraternal delegates from Mexico were Luis Gómez and Mario Montenegro, neither of whom belonged to the official Communist Party, though Gómez belonged to a dissident Communist group.

At this Conference there was some protest against the growing influence of the Communists, and particularly against the practice of sending Communists as delegates from the C.T.A.L. headquarters on missions to various national affiliates. Argentine, Cuban, and Mexican delegates to the Havana Conference were among those protesting.[14]

The Communist trend in the C.T.A.L. was even more marked in the next gathering of its Executive Committee, which took place at Montevideo in February and March, 1944. Two interesting notes were struck at this meeting: the theme of national unity, to be increasingly emphasized after World War II; and the theme of hostility to the incursion of the A.F. of L. into Latin American Labor affairs.

Lombardo Toledano in his opening remarks to the Montevideo Conference spent much time in attacking the American Federation of Labor, and particularly Matthew Woll, for opposition to the establishment of the World Federation of Trade Unions (the preliminary conference of which was scheduled for June 5, 1944) and opposition to the C.T.A.L. in Latin America. Lombardo went out of his way to note the attentions which the A.F. of L. leadership had paid to Bernardo Ibáñez, Secretary General of the Confederación de Trabajadores de Chile, a Socialist, and at that time Lombardo's chief rival within the C.T.A.L. However, Lombardo added that Ibáñez was not being "misled" by such attentions.

A resolution of the Conference protested against attacks which it alleged were being made against the President of the C.T.A.L. by the American Federation of Labor. This resolution forbade any leader of any C.T.A.L. affiliate to accept invitations from any organizations "whose program opposes or is contrary to the work being carried on under the direction of the C.T.A.L."

In his opening address, Lombardo stressed the "national unity" line, which was then the international position of the Communist Parties. This was exactly the period when "Browderism" was dominant in the United States, when the United States Communist Party changed its name to American Communist Political Association and proclaimed that capitalists and workers, big businessmen and Communists could all live happily together, so long as they were "anti-fascist."

Lombardo's position was stated this way:

> . . . in the name of the workers of Latin America affiliated to the C.T.A.L., I issue a call to the industrialists, the bankers, the technicians, the men of the middle class, to all those factors which participate in the production of wealth, to tell them that the future can be one of adventure for our countries if all: the industrialists, the technicians, the bankers, the landlords and the workers, the peasants and Government join together for the purpose of planning the rapid and complete economic development of our countries, so as to leave behind the archaic capitalist epoch in which we live, and together enter into the historical period of modern life.[15]

From December, 1944, on there is no doubt at all that the Communists were in full command of the Confederación de Trabajadores de América Latina. In that month the C.T.A.L.'s Second Regular Congress met in Cali, Colombia. A new Executive Committee was elected at that Congress, consisting of Vicente Lombardo Toledano as President, and as members, Francisco Pérez Leirós and Rubens Iscaro of Argentina, Napoleón Molina of Colombia, Rodolfo Guzmán of Costa Rica, Lázaro Peña of Cuba, Juan Vargas Puebla and Juan Briones of Chile, Pedro Saad of Ecuador, Fidel Velázquez of Mexico, Juan P. Luna of Peru, and Enrique Rodríguez of Uruguay.

Of the twelve men on this new Executive Committee, seven were avowed members of the Communist Parties of their respective countries: Rubens Iscaro, Rodolfo Guzmán, Lázaro Peña, Juan Vargas Puebla, Pedro Saad, Juan P. Luna, and Enrique Rodríguez. Of the others, Lombardo Toledano was by that time closely following the Communist line, Pérez Leirós had been working closely with the Communists in his own country, and Napoleón Molina was a Liberal who was generally considered by his fellow party members a "fellow traveller." Only Juan Briones and Fidel Velázquez were definitely anti-Communists, and at this time even Velázquez was still following Lombardo's lead in international affairs.

The control of the Cali Congress was largely in the hands of the Stalinists and their close associates. Lombardo served as President, while the Secretaries included Bernardo Medina of Colombia, Miguel Escobar Madrid of Uruguay, Rodolfo Guzmán of Costa Rica, and Alejandro Carrillo of Mexico. Of these, only Medina was an anti-Communist, while Guzmán was an avowed Communist, and Escobar Medina may have been one. Of the four Commissions set up to prepare resolutions for submission to the plenary sessions of the Congress, three were headed by avowed members of the Communist Party. Pedro Saad of Ecuador headed the Political Affairs Commission, Enrique Rodríguez of Uruguay, the Organization Commission, Juan Vargas Puebla of Chile, the Social Affairs Commission. Only Fidel Velázquez of Mexico, who headed the Economic Affairs Commission, was not a Stalinist.

The resolutions of the Cali Congress reflected this Communist control. The Stalinist influence was particularly notable in the Report of the Political Affairs Commission, which followed in important essentials the Communist line current at that time. On the issue of treatment of Germany, the C.T.A.L. Congress adopted the extreme punitive position which was at that time favored by the Soviet Union and the various national Communist Parties. The Congress in its resolution on "The Structure of the Peace" resolved to insist on:

> The obligation of the German people to repair the damage caused to the peoples injured by Nazism, since all Germans have been implicated by their actions or their passivity in the crimes and destruc-

tion of this war; an obligation imposed not for vengeance but in the spirit of justice;

The analogous obligation of reparation, in conformity with their degree of responsibility, by the people of Japan, for the damage caused by the war in the Orient.

Although this extreme view on German war guilt was not, in December, 1944, confined to Communists, it certainly was their official position. It is interesting to note that the entirely different tone of this C.T.A.L. resolution when it discussed Germany and the European war, in which the Soviet Union was deeply involved, and when it talked of Japan and the Oriental war, in which the U.S.S.R. was still a neutral.

The section of this same resolution dealing with Spain said in part: "The C.T.A.L. and its affiliates will fight for . . . the liberation of the people of Spain, oppressed by the Nazi-Falangista dictatorship, lending all aid to the Junta Suprema de Unión Nacional, combatting Franco terror. . . ." Only a meeting in which Communist influence was very important would have worded a Spanish resolution in this fashion at that time, since the Junta Suprema de Unión Nacional was an invention of the Communists which was repudiated by all anti-Franco groups except the Communists and their closest collaborators, and a couple of years later was finally given up even by the Stalinists, when it failed to serve its purpose as a "front organization."

Another resolution introduced by the Political Affairs Commission of the Cali Conference, the one dealing with "The Immediate Objectives of the Proletariat in Latin America," contained a peculiarly Stalinist passage. It said:

> The C.T.A.L. and its affiliates will fight . . . against the leftish demagoguery of the Trotskyist type which, behind the mask of radical slogans which are out of accord with the present situation in America and the world, is attempting to force the Latin American masses into struggles for demands greater than those which are just at the present time.

Certainly no other political group had any particular interest at that time in attacking the Trotskyites. Only the Stalinists were driven by an anti-Trotskyite preoccupation verging on mania. The Stalinist origin of this resolution was further demonstrated by its next paragraph which contained the phrase, "against anti-Communist and anti-Semitic campaigns, and religious disputes raised by reactionary forces in America to divide the people and impede democratic action." Only the Communists themselves would thus speak of anti-Communism and anti-Semitism in the same breath.

The resolutions of the other Commissions of the Congress did not present positions which might not have been taken by almost any labor group in Latin America at that time. They urged the industrialization of the region, urged the United States to continue its wartime purchases of raw materials in Latin America into the postwar period, urged coordination of the economies of Latin America.[16]

Communist control of the C.T.A.L. was undisputed after the Cali Congress in December, 1944. This marked the high point of Communist influence in the labor movements of Latin America. For about three years longer the Stalinists continued to be without doubt the most powerful political force in the ranks of organized labor in the hemisphere. Until the end of 1947 the C.T.A.L., under the leadership of Lombardo Toledano and the Communists, remained united.

One more meeting of the C.T.A.L. leadership was held during this period, a conference of the C.T.A.L. Executive Committee in San José, Costa Rica, in December, 1946. The meeting was attended by the members of the Central Committee and by representatives of the Mexican C.T.M., the Cuban C.T.C., the Colombian C.T.C., the Costa Rican C.T.C.R., the Guatemalan C.T.G., the Nicaraguan C.T.N., the Federación Sindical of Panama, the Petroleum Workers Federation and Federation of Workers of the Federal District of Venezuela, the Mine and Metal Workers Union of Mexico, and several unions from El Salvador.

This San José meeting reflected the Cold War, which had already begun, and the shift in Communist emphasis from cooperation between the United States and Latin America to opposition to United States influence in Latin America. Thus, according to the *International Labor Review* report of September, 1947, the Conference resolved to fight against "international monopolies trying to dominate the natural resources, markets, and manpower of Latin America." It passed a resolution saying that any regional pact with the object of preparation for war without previous approval of the Security Council would be a violation of the U.N. Charter, thus opposing current moves to bind more closely the bonds of inter-American military solidarity.

Meanwhile signs had begun to appear of the forthcoming decline in Communist influence in the Latin American trade union movement. In Peru, for instance, the Communists had lost control of the Confederación Trabajadores when the Aprista Party was legalized in June, 1945. Soon thereafter, Communist deputy Juan P. Luna was ousted as Secretary General of the C.T.P. and was succeeded by Arturo Sabroso, an Aprista stalwart.

In Venezuela, following the revolution of October, 1945, which put the Acción Democrática Party in power, the trade union movement grew tremendously, and the new unions were principally under Acción Democrática leadership. This development culminated in November, 1947, in the establishment of the Confederación de Trabajadores de Venezuela, which refused to affiliate to the C.T.A.L.

Other new trade union groups appeared outside the ranks of the C.T.A.L. In Costa Rica, for instance, a new labor confederation, the Confederación Costarricense del Trabajo "Rerum Novarum," was established under the leadership of a young Catholic priest, Padre Benjamín Núñez. It seriously challenged the dominant position of the C.T.A.L.'s affiliate, the C.T.C.R. in the Costa Rican labor movement. After the May, 1948, Revolution, which resulted in the outlawing of the Communist Party of Costa Rica, Vanguardia Popular, the "Rerum Novarum" Confederation became the dominant group among Costa Rica's organized workers.

In Colombia a new trade union movement was established in 1946 under the patronage of the Jesuits. Padre Vicente Andrade, S.J., had been the Archbishop of Bogotá's representative at the Cali Congress of the C.T.A.L., where he had unsuccessfully demanded the floor to argue with some of the delegates, and had had a polemic in the newspapers with the C.T.A.L. leaders over this incident.

This same Padre Andrade was commissioned by the Colombian Church hierarchy to put into execution the Church's social policy. The result of his efforts was the establishment of the Unión de Trabajadores de Colombia in 1946. The U.T.C. was born at a time when the star of the Confederación de Trabajadores de Colombia, the C.T.A.L. affiliate, had begun to fade. The election of a Conservative President of Colombia in 1946 aided the growth of the U.T.C., since the C.T.C. was controlled by a coalition of Liberals and Communists, both of whom were inimical to the Conservative regime.

In Mexico various labor groups appeared in the early 1940's which did not join the C.T.A.L. These included several more or less important groups, such as the Confederación Proletaria Nacional, the Confederación Nacional del Trabajo, and the Confederación de Obreros y Campesinos de México.

In Haiti, after the January, 1946, Revolution, the workers were given freedom to organize for the first time. Several labor confederations developed during the next several years, but none of them joined the C.T.A.L. The only group which was for a while under Communist or near-Communist influence was the Fédération des Travailleurs Haïtiens, established early in 1946, but even it did not join the C.T.A.L.

Only in Guatemala and Brazil were new organizations established which joined the C.T.A.L. After the Revolution of 1944 in Guatemala, the field was thrown open for the organization of the Guatemalan workers. The C.T.A.L. sent in organizers and helped to bring about the establishment of the Confederación de Trabajadores de Guatemala early in 1945. The C.T.G. immediately joined the C.T.A.L.

In Brazil, the relaxing of the dictatorship of Getulio Vargas in 1944 and 1945 left the field open for trade union organizing activity, and the Communists stepped into this vacuum. They were able to gain control of a large number of the government's official trade unions. Throughout 1945 the Communists were active in laying the foundations for the establishment of a national trade union confederation. As a preliminary organizing group, they established the Movimento de Unificação Trabalhador (M.U.T.).

Although the M.U.T. was outlawed by the Dutra government early in 1946, Dutra's Ministry of Labor officials dealt with it on more or less equal terms when preparing for the First National Labor Congress, held in Rio de Janeiro in September, 1946. Out of this Congress, which split as the result of disputes between progovernment and pro-Communist delegates, the Confederação Geral dos Trabalhadores do Brasil was established, which affiliated to the C.T.A.L. The C.G.T.B. was officially outlawed early in 1947 and thereafter led a haphazard existence.

Splits in various national affiliates of the C.T.A.L. weakened the position of the Communists in the Latin American trade union movement. The oldest of these was that in the Unión General de Trabajadores del Uruguay, which occurred in 1942. It arose as the result of the action of Communist leaders of the U.G.T. in denouncing and trying to break a strike of packing house workers which it claimed—without justification—was fomented and directed by pro-Nazi elements.

As a result of this strike, most of the packing house workers—the most important group of industrial workers in Uruguay—withdrew from the U.G.T., to form a new Autonomous Packinghouse Workers Federation. The Socialists in the U.G.T. supported the packing house workers' walkout, and several important unions under their control, such as the Federation of Commercial and Industrial White Collar Workers, the Railroad Workers Union, the Newsboys Union, and a large element in the Metal Workers Union, also withdrew from the U.G.T.

Late in 1945 another split occurred in the U.G.T., and most of the unions which were under the leadership of the Batllista and Independent Nationalist parties withdrew from the Unión General. In subsequent years splits in the Communist Party of Uruguay itself resulted in dissident Communist trade union leaders taking the important Textile Workers and Urban Transport Workers Unions out of the U.G.T., and by the early 1950's the U.G.T. was reduced to the position of being the third Uruguayan national trade union center in size and influence.

None of the unions seceding from the U.G.T. made any move to affiliate to the C.T.A.L. Thus, as the Communist influence in the Uruguayan national trade union movement declined, Uruguayan representation in the Communist-controlled continental labor body was reduced in an equally drastic fashion.

An even more important split occurred in the Confederación de Trabajadores de Cuba. After several years of bitter struggle between the Communists and members of the Auténtico Party within the Cuban labor movement, a scission occurred in the middle of 1947, on the occasion of the C.T.C.'s Fifth Congress. The Auténtico faction of the C.T.C. was recognized as the official one by the Ministry of Labor, after some hesitation, and within the next two years virtually all of the country's national labor federations joined the official C.T.C.

By 1951 the Cuban Communists had ordered their trade union stalwarts to transfer their activities from the now largely moribund Communist C.T.C. to the official one. For practical purposes the C.T.A.L. had ceased to have a Cuban affiliate by that time, since the official C.T.C. made no attempt to affiliate to the C.T.A.L., and in fact took a leading part in the rival C.I.T. and O.R.I.T. organizations.

The Confederación de Trabajadores de Chile also split in 1946. Two organizations were formed, both of which called themselves C.T.Ch., and many unions stayed out of both factions. During 1946 and early 1947 the Communists undoubtedly had the majority of the country's unions in the ranks of their C.T.Ch. However, when President Gabriel González Videla turned against the Communists and attempted to smash their power in and out of the labor movement, the Communists lost much of their influence. Also, virtually all unions which were not directly under the control of the Communist Party withdrew from its C.T.Ch.

Early in 1953 unity was again established among Chilean unions with the organization of the Central Unica de Trabajadores. Non-Communist influence in the new C.U.T.Ch. was strong enough to keep it out of the C.T.A.L., though not sufficient to bring about its affiliation with the O.R.I.T.

In May, 1950, the Confederación de Trabajadores of Colombia was finally torn asunder by the fighting between Liberals and Communists in the organization. Two confederations with the same name were established. The Liberal group was recognized by the government as the official C.T.C.; it promptly joined the International Confederation of Free Trade Unions and subsequently affiliated also to the I.C.F.T.U.'s American regional group, the O.R.I.T. Communist attempts to keep a rival group going were fruitless, and the C.T.A.L. virtually ceased to have an affiliate in Colombia.

In Mexico the C.T.A.L. received a particularly severe blow. Early in 1948 C.T.A.L. President Vicente Lombardo Toledano was thrown out of the Confederación de Trabajadores de México, as the result of a quarrel with the principal leaders of the C.T.M. over the establishment of a new political party, and the C.T.M. withdrew from the C.T.A.L. For a short while several independent national industrial unions, such as the Petroleum Workers, Railroad Workers, and Mine and Metal Workers Unions remained affiliated to the C.T.A.L. However, by the early 1950's the C.T.A.L.'s representation in Mexico was reduced to the Unión General de Obreros y Campesinos de México, a tiny group under Lombardo Toledano's personal influence.

This centrifugal development of the C.T.A.L. was given impetus by the activities of the American Federation of Labor in the Latin American field. The A.F. of L. had conducted no official activity in Latin America for over a decade, but in February, 1946, it appointed Serafino Romualdi of the International Ladies Garment Workers Union as its Latin American representative.

During the next two years Romualdi gave moral and material support to those elements within the C.T.A.L. and its affiliates who were opposed to Communist influence, as well as to those labor movements which were growing up outside of the C.T.A.L. The upshot of his activities was the establishment in January, 1948, of the Confederación Inter Americana de Trabajadores (C.I.T.). It brought within its ranks most important groups outside of the C.T.A.L., except the Peronistas. These included the Cuban C.T.C., the Venezuelan C.T.V., the Peruvian C.T.P., the Socialist C.T.Ch. of Chile, the "Rerum Novarum" Confederation of Costa Rica, the U.T.C. of Colombia, and several smaller groups.

The C.I.T. remained in existence for three years. Then in January, 1951, it was succeeded by the Inter American Regional Organization of Workers (O.R.I.T.), which was established as the American affiliate of the International Confederation of Free Trade Unions. The principal difference between the C.I.T. and the O.R.I.T. was that the latter had within its ranks the Liberal C.T.C. of Colombia, the C.I.O. of the United States, the Canadian Congress of Labor, and after some hesitation, the Mexican C.T.M.

Still a third hemispheric labor group was formed in 1951 as the result of the activities of the Peronistas. The only two important national trade union groups included within the ranks of the Latin American Trade Union Unity Committee and its successor, the A.T.L.A.S., which was established in November, 1952, were the Argentine C.G.T. and the Mexican C.R.O.M., though a number of small and more or less insignificant organizations in Chile, Uruguay, Colombia, and other countries also joined the A.T.L.A.S. (Agrupación de Trabajadores Latino Americanos Sindicalizados).

In spite of the decline of the C.T.A.L.'s influence in America, the international Communist movement assigned it an important role in the world-wide organization. A meeting of the World Federation of Trade Unions held in Peiping, China, in December, 1949, was attended by Lombardo Toledano and other leaders of the Latin American Communist trade union movement. The C.T.A.L. was officially recognized as the W.F.T.U.'s regional grouping, and it was empowered to carry on all of the world organization's publication activity in the Spanish language.

For some time after this official recognition, the C.T.A.L. remained comparatively passive. Then in 1952 it announced that the Fourth Congress of the organization would be held in Quito, Ecuador, on the invitation of the Confederación de Trabajadores del Ecuador. However, newly elected President José María Velasco Ibarra refused to allow the meeting to he held, and it was postponed.

After the election of General Carlos Ibáñez as President of Chile in November, 1952, the Communist-controlled branch of the Confederación de Trabajadores de Chile invited the C.T.A.L. to meet in Santiago. This invitation aroused no opposition from the new President, and the Fourth Congress of the C.T.A.L. finally opened in the Chilean capital on March 23, 1953. However, from both the organizational and propaganda angles, this Congress was a failure.

Communist activities in the labor movements of Latin America have had several purposes during the first 37 years of Communist history. First of all, the trade union movements under Communist control were fertile recruiting grounds for the Communist Parties themselves. Through trade union activities, the Communists were often able to win the confidence of the workers, first in economic matters, and eventually in political affairs as well.

It is certainly historically true that the times and places in which the Communists have achieved considerable political influence have been those in which they have either controlled important labor movements or have had great influence in non-Communist labor movements. In Chile the key to Communist influence has been the Party's trade union work. The period during which the Party's influence was least was in the early 1930's, when the Communist-controlled Federación Obrera de Chile was at a low ebb. With the merging of the Communist unions and the more influential Socialist-controlled organizations to form the Confederación de Trabajadores de Chile, the Communists made rapid gains in the trade unions, which brought with them a similarly rapid increase in political influence in the nation at large. Communist power in Chile has been based on the great Communist influence in the coal and nitrate unions and, to a lesser degree, in the copper workers' organizations.

In Guatemala, again, the Communists' rise to influence and power came through their control of the trade union movement. First the Confederación de Trabajadores de Guatemala and then the Confederación General de Trabajadores de Guatemala were under Communist influence. With the labor movement firmly in its control, the Communist Party was able to make promises and threats to the governments of Presidents Arévalo and Arbenz, both of whom took them seriously. Through this trade union power, the Communists were able to work their way into important government positions and to gain considerable influence among the general public.

In Cuba there is little doubt that the rise of the Communists to influence in the late 1930's and the early 1940's was due to their deal with Batista, whereby they were given complete freedom of action and positive government aid in the trade union field in return for political support for

Batista's presidential ambitions. With the destruction of their control of the trade unions in the late 1940's, the Cuban Communists lost very heavily in popular support and ceased to have any significant influence in governmental circles.

In Brazil, too, the sudden rise of the Communists in 1945 and 1946 was the result of their great activity in the labor movement. The fact that they were able to keep a solid core of support in the late 1940's and early 1950's, even in the face of great hostile pressure by the government, was due to their strong influence in the ranks of organized labor.

The second purpose of Communist trade union activity in Latin America is closely connected with the Parties' role as sections of the international Communist movement and, in the last analysis, as agents of the Soviet Union. The possible use of key positions in the trade union movement for furthering the purposes of the international Communist movement has always been a primary consideration with the Latin American Communists.

As early as 1933 the agenda for the Second Congress of the Confederación Sindical Latino Americana included discussion of "concentration of forces in the fundamental branches of the economy of each country." During the second World War, the Communists first used their trade union influence to sabotage the delivery of goods to the Allies, and then, during the second part of the war, used it to get the largest possible contribution in effort and production from the Latin American workers for the cause of the Soviet Union and the powers associated with her. Since the outbreak of the Cold War the Communists again have made no secret of their desire to use the unions as a basis for ideological attack on the United States, and in case of war as a weapon to sabotage the delivery of needed supplies to this country.

Thus their relations with the trade unions have been a fundamental factor in the history of the Latin American Communists. Where they were strong in the unions, they were strong in the country. Where they had little influence in organized labor, they had little influence in the nation as a whole.

The same thing is likely to remain true for a long time to come. Although there is a tendency abroad to deprecate the Latin American trade unions, the fact is that they remain the most powerful mass organizations in Latin America today. They are a vital part of the Latin American social revolution and are perhaps the only institution in the region which can challenge the role of the military as the principal determinant of public policy and government. The Communists do not underrate their importance. It is essential that anyone trying to understand the role of the international Communist movement in Latin America be equally aware of their significance.

*Chapter V*

# Leaders of Latin American Communism

THE PRINCIPAL LEADERSHIP of the Communist Parties of Latin America has come from the intellectuals and the trade unions. There has been a sprinkling of leaders from other groups, such as the Army, the peasantry, and the idle rich, but the great bulk of the top figures and most of the secondary leadership have come from the intellectuals and trade union officials. The former group was much more important in the early days, while the latter has been rising in significance during recent years.

That the Communists should draw many of their principal figures from the ranks of the intelligentsia is not surprising. This group plays a more than ordinary role in Latin American politics. The number of people with advanced educations is very small, and the gulf between them and the masses of the people is extremely wide, so that the intellectuals play a role which is vastly out of proportion to their numbers in the area.

Intellectuals have played a leading part in the life of all of the political parties of Latin America. Not only do lawyers make up the great majority of the membership of the parliaments and cabinets of the Latin American countries—as they do in most nations—but the medical doctors, dentists, teachers, university professors, and poets are represented in both legislative and executive branches of the governments to a much greater degree than is general in most lands.

This has been no less true in the Communist Parties than in other political groups. Most of the early Communist leaders were intellectuals. People such as Ricardo Paredes of Ecuador, a doctor, Rodolfo Ghioldi of Argentina, a teacher, Luis Emilio Recabarren of Chile, a publicist, Manuel Mora of Costa Rica, a lawyer, Octavio Brandão of Brazil, a journalist, Diego Rivera, José Clemente Orozco, and David Alfaro Siqueiros of Mexico, artists, are among the outstanding Communist figures of the 1920's and early 1930's.

Subsequently, too, an important part of the Communist leadership has been drawn from the ranks of the intellectuals: Vicente Lombardo Tole-

71

dano (the Mexican "non-Communist" leader of the Communist trade union apparatus of the hemisphere), a teacher by profession; Pablo Neruda, one of Chile's two most famous poets; Juan Marinello, rated one of the leading literary figures of Cuba; Carlos Manuel Pellecer, Victor Manuel Gutiérrez, and José Fortuny, leaders of the Guatemalan Communists, Gilberto Vieira of Colombia, Jorge del Prado of Peru, and Sergio Almarás of Bolivia, all university students or members of the professions.

The Communists have been even more successful in bringing Latin American intellectuals into "front" groups than they have in actually integrating them into the Party membership and leadership. Thus in Mexico, Chile, Guatemala, and various other countries, Communist influence among the intelligentsia has been out of all proportion to the Communists' general influence in the community.

These intellectuals are very useful to the Communist Party in a variety of ways. They lend themselves freely to various international campaigns —"peace" congresses, "cultural" congresses, petition campaigns for one thing or another. They also are useful to the Party in establishing Communist influence in professional and other organizations which have great prestige in the national life of the various countries.

Finally, Communist sympathizers among the intellectuals lend themselves from time to time to "Trojan horse" maneuvers of the Communists inside other parties. This tactic has been particularly successful in Guatemala and Chile.

In spite of the large role which the intellectuals have played in the leadership of the Latin American Communist Parties, it is notable that no Latin American Communist Party has developed a first-rate theoretician, capable of making original contributions to Marxist and Communist thought. This is perhaps the more remarkable because of the penchant of the Latin American intelligentsia for philosophical ideas and abstractions.

There are probably various reasons for this. Most of the Communist Parties did not develop real strength until after Stalin had achieved control of the international Communist apparatus. Universally, Stalin's influence was exerted against such independent and original thinking. Most of the European Communist theoreticians were either driven out of the Communist ranks or were converted into mere automatons, whose function it was to express and justify Stalin's tactical maneuvers in turgid Marxist rhetoric.

Víctor Alba points out that the few Latin American Communist intellectuals who attempted to do some original theoretical thinking, such as Aníbal Ponce of Argentina and José Carlos Mariátegui of Peru, were virtually repudiated by the Communist apparatus. Those intellectuals who were capable of surviving were of the ilk of Lombardo Toledano, whose fame for saying nothing in long hours of discourse is international.

The trade unions have also been important sources of Communist leadership from the beginning. For instance, Elías Laferte, Juan Vargas Puebla, Salvador Ocampo, and many others in Chile have come from the ranks of the trade unions since the early 1920's. Eugenio Gómez of Uruguay was first a trade union leader, then a Communist. Many of the top figures of the Brazilian Communist movement have been drawn from the trade union ranks. Carlos Fernández R. and Lázaro Peña of Cuba, and Luis Gómez Z., Valentín Campa, Dionisio Encina, and Hernán Laborde of Mexico have been trade unionists. Most of the leadership of the Nicaraguan Partido Socialista was drawn from the trade unions. Many of the Venezuelan Communist leaders, such as Rafael Quintero, Jesús Farías, and others also came from this group.

There have been individual Communist leaders who have come from other social classes and groups. The ranks of the military have supplied a few Communist officials, notably Luiz Carlos Prestes and one or two of his associates in Brazil. In Mexico in the early days of the Party, several of the country's leading military men, including General Francisco Mújica, one of the outstanding figures of the Mexican Revolution, spent a longer or shorter time in the Communist Party.

Some leaders have come from the commercial middle class, such as Pedro Saad, the son of a reasonably prosperous Syrian immigrant merchant in Guayaquil, who succeeded Dr. Ricardo Paredes as chief of the Ecuadorian Party.

Of course, the sources of Party leadership differ from country to country. Almost everywhere, the Communist Party originated among the intellectuals, who then reached out to make contact with the trade unions. Naturally, in countries where the Party has been most effective in building up a following among the organized workers, it draws an increasingly large part of its leadership from the ranks of the trade unionists.

For instance, in Chile, where they have perhaps been most successful in building up an enduring following among the working class, a large part of the top leadership has come from this class. On the other hand, in Uruguay, where Communist trade union influence is less pronounced, this is much less true, and in fact the Party has lost many of its important trade union figures in recent years.

However, from whatever group the Communist leadership was drawn in any individual country, the important thing is that the principal Communists have become professional revolutionaries. Some of the Party officials have been little else. This can be said of Victorio Codovilla, for instance. He was the real founder and has been for many years the undisputed head of the Communist Party of Argentina, and for 35 years has had no occupation other than that of Party bureaucrat.

Following Lenin's dictum that the "leaders of the revolution" must be professional revolutionaries, the Communists have maintained in virtually every country a staff of people who have done little else but carry on

Communist activities—in the trade unions, in general politics, or in cognate activities. The legion of Communist Party functionaries is legendary in nearly every country in Latin America. In Chile, for instance, the Party is reported to have hundreds of individuals who are able to spend full time on union jobs, Communist Party organization and journalism, organizing demonstrations, and, in general, carrying on the work of the Party.

This is particularly notable in the trade union movement. Generally in Latin America trade union officials are part-time functionaries. They must earn their living working in a factory or in an office, and can only carry on their trade union activities after hours. But such is not the case with the Communist trade union officials. They are able to be on the job, in the trade union office, on the picket line, any time that they are needed. How they support themselves is a mystery to their fellow trade unionists, but the certain thing is that they are paid out of the ample financial resources of their Party.

Thus the Communists have built up throughout the hemisphere a skilled full-time organization of thousands of people, who are able to be on the job when their political rivals are busy earning a living, and who are able to step into key situations when their opponents are preoccupied with earning their bread and butter.

These people are not only full-time Communist functionaries—whether working within the Party apparatus proper, in the trade unions, or in some other occupation—but they are highly disciplined and highly trained. Communist discipline in Latin America is as it is in other parts of the world. One must accept the Party line, or get out. Few exceptions are made to this.

How doubters are handled is shown by the example of a leading Communist trade unionist of Chile. At the time of the Stalin-Nazi Pact in 1939, he had certain doubts about the Party line. He brought these out in discussions within the Party, and because of his key position in one of the major union groups in the country, he was not immediately expelled. However, he was forced to take a "leave of absence" both from the Party and from his union job. When, a few months later, he had resolved the problem and had decided to stay in the Party and accept its discipline, he was restored to his former position. Unfortunately for the Party, a few years later he began to doubt once more. By this time, however, the Party had built up other cadres in the union, his position was not so important to the Communists, and he was summarily expelled.

The Communists of Latin America, like their comrades in other parts of the world, are subjected to a continuous process of education and re-education. Each national Communist Party maintains an elaborate organization for the indoctrination of its leadership. Although this is intended mainly for the maintenance of the faith and discipline of the secondary figures in the movement, the major leaders are also forced to attend these "leadership training courses" from time to time. Probably only a few figures at the very top are exempt.

Perhaps typical of these Party training sessions is one reported in *For a Lasting Peace, For a People's Democracy*, the organ of the Cominform, on May 14, 1954. This item reads in part:

> The leadership of the Communist Party of Chile constantly stresses the necessity of raising to the maximum the political level of all its members. Five seminars for leading Party functionaries are now in progress in Santiago. The curriculum includes study of the decisions of the IXth National Conference of the Party, the Party plenums, the materials of the XIXth Congress of the CPSU, dialectical and historical materialism, political economy, and J. V. Stalin's "Economic Problems of Socialism in the USSR."
>
> The Party schools in Santiago include one for the leadership of the Santiago regional committee and several schools for the members of the commune commissions and committees. In addition study has been organized in short-term courses and in Party branches.
>
> This year, after a long interval, the Central Party school has been resumed in Santiago. Summer schools were held last year in Antofagasta and Valdivia with curriculums similar to that of the Central Party school. . . .

Where political conditions within a given country have not allowed the establishment of leadership training facilities, local leaders have been sent to regional training centers. Thus the C.T.A.L. headquarters in Mexico undoubtedly served as a leadership school for Communists from neighboring countries of Central America in the 1940's. Some time later, the Guatemalan Party certainly carried on an extensive program of training leaders from Honduras and other nearby nations. In South America the Chilean Party has doubtless frequently trained leaders from neighboring nations where conditions of dictatorship would not allow such activities.

On an international level, even the top-ranking leadership is subjected to training and indoctrination. From the middle 1920's the Lenin School in Moscow received a steady stream of trainees from the Latin American countries. In recent years the number of trips made behind the Iron Curtain by leading figures in the Latin American Communist movements has been enormous. Outstanding figures in the various national Parties and Party-controlled trade union movements have been taken to Moscow, Bucharest, or elsewhere for intensive indoctrination and training sessions lasting several months.*

From time to time Latin Americans have taken part in the administration of the international Communist movement's home office. Thus

---

* Daniel James and others have claimed that since World War II the principal training school for Latin American and other foreign Communists has been located in Prague, Czechoslovakia.

Ignacio Torres Giraldo, of the Colombian Party, was a long-time resident of Moscow as a member of the Executive Committee of the Red International of Labor Unions in the early 1930's. At about the same time Luiz Carlos Prestes, who had gone to the U.S.S.R. ostensibly to work as an engineer, played a leading role in determining Comintern policy in Latin America. Victorio Codovilla of Argentina spent the better part of the 1930's as an agent of the Comintern outside of Latin America.

More recently, Carlos Fernández R., one of the principal Cuban Communist trade unionists, spent the early 1950's as an official of the World Federation of Trade Unions in Vienna, as did Ferdinand Smith of Jamaica. The Guatemalan leaders were frequently called to Moscow for consultation in the late 1940's and early 1950's, and at least one of them, Carlos Manuel Pellecer (probably the most capable of the top Guatemalan Communists), headed for Moscow soon after escaping from Guatemala, following the debacle of the Arbenz regime in 1954.

The Latin American Communists are subjected, as are their brothers in other countries, to recurring purges and purifying processes. This has been going on since the 1920's. For instance, in 1929-30 the majority of the top leadership of the Chilean Communist Party was purged by the Regional Office of the Comintern in Montevideo, and others were put in charge.

In 1939-40 Victorio Codovilla, undoubtedly one of the key figures in the Communist movement throughout Latin America and one of the Latin American Communist leaders who was closest to Stalin, made a tour of the area, starting in the Caribbean and Mexico and proceeding southward, during which he carried out extensive purges of the various national Parties, for reasons best known to himself and the Comintern leadership. Most notable was the transformation in the Mexican Communist Party, where the old leadership, headed by Hernán Laborde and Valentín Campa, was displaced, and Dionisio Encina was put in charge of the Party machinery.

Of course, the process of purging is part and parcel of the Communists' method of operation. It is particularly necessary to them in cases where they have had to build up the Party membership rapidly in order to take advantage of a peculiar situation in a particular country.

For instance in Brazil, where in 1945-47 the Party was legal and grew in a few months from a handful of underground or imprisoned leaders to a mass movement having the support of 15 per cent of the electorate, it was inevitable that the Party should undergo a purge. Many of those who entered its ranks did so in the enthusiasm of the moment, or perhaps for opportunistic reasons. Those who would not adapt themselves to the Party's rigid discipline and swallow the Party's doctrine without question, or who became timorous in the face of subsequent government persecution, had to be dropped.

The result was that the Party membership shrank from 150,000 in 1946 to 50-60,000 in 1953. Undoubtedly, however, the smaller membership at the later date was better qualitatively, from the Party's point of view, than the larger group had been. Doubters dropped out, were expelled, or split openly as was the case with José Maria Crispim, who attempted to lead a scission movement in the early 1950's.

In Guatemala, too, during the administration of President Jacobo Arbenz, the Communists had to recruit many members into their ranks and into their leadership who in the end would not prove to be tractable and usable Party material. They had to accept people who would give them control of key positions in mass organizations and public administration, many of whom they would have to dump later.

Events moved too rapidly during the Arbenz administration for the purge technique to be applied. However, with the downfall of Arbenz and the scattering of the leadership of the Guatemalan Communist Party in exile, the situation changed. Carlos Manuel Pellecer and other important figures were summoned behind the Iron Curtain, apparently for further indoctrination and training, as well as for careful analysis of what had been the cause of the debacle. By the middle of 1955 it appeared that a purge of the Guatemalan Party's leadership in exile in Mexico had begun.

"Leadership" is at best a relative term in the Communist movement, in Latin America and elsewhere. Under "democratic centralism"—which despite its name means in fact blind acceptance of the decisions of the top figures in a national Party, who, in turn, must as blindly obey the leaders of the International—the top officials of a Communist Party in a specific country have virtually absolute power within their own organization's ranks, so long as they keep in the good graces of the international bosses.

The Party's organizational structure in each of the Latin American countries is adapted to this "democratic centralism," and in general is copied after the universal Communist pattern, first established by Stalin in the U.S.S.R. The chief functionary of each Party is the General Secretary. Associated with him in the top leadership is the body which is usually referred to as the Political Bureau (Politburo) or Political Committee.

Other important organs of the top echelon of each Party are the Control Commission and the Organization Commission. The first of these keeps track of the orthodoxy of the membership, from the Secretary General on down. The second is charged principally with strengthening the organizational structure of the group. Each is headed by a Secretary, who is generally a member of the Politburo.

One of the most important functions of the Politburo is to control the Party press. Every Latin American Communist Party which is able to function more or less legally has a great variety of publicity organs. Usually there is a daily newspaper, where this is at all possible, which is designed for the non-Party masses. There is frequently a monthly or bi-monthly "theoretical organ," which is principally intended to be read by Party members, consisting of articles of direct concern to the Party. In addition, there are frequently special periodicals, designed for young people, for women, for trade unionists, in addition to the countless publications by Communist front organizations such as "peace committees" and the like. There is nothing accidental about what appears in any of these Party-controlled publications.*

A structure similar to that in the top echelons of the Party is set up on a regional and local level in each country. Provincial Secretaries General are top men in their respective regions, and are assisted and watched by provincial committees and control and organization officials.

Ostensibly, the ultimate power in any Communist Party in Latin America, as elsewhere, rests in the Party Congress. Though supposed to meet at regular intervals, the Latin American Party Congresses are missed about as often as those of the Communist Party of the Soviet Union (which had no Congress, for instance, between 1939 and 1952).

More frequent than Congresses are the so-called "enlarged plenums" of the respective Parties' Executive Committees. These consist of members of the Central or Executive Committee of the Party, as well as the provincial General Secretaries and anyone else the Political Bureau or General Secretary sees fit to invite.

Both Plenums and Congresses of the Latin American Communist Parties are conducted along lines common to similar bodies throughout the world. The main business of such meetings is to hear reports from the General Secretary and from subordinate secretaries charged with organization, control, and other such matters, or from members of the Political Bureau specially deputed to discuss particular topics—such as the Party's policy in a coming electoral campaign, the Party's policy in the trade unions, etc.

Little or no discussion is allowed in such meetings. The proposals of the Party leadership are generally adopted "unanimously." The only time that this is not the case is when there is a split in the top leadership—but even then, such a problem has usually been resolved before the Plenum or Congress is called, and the larger meeting is summoned merely to ratify the results of the struggle for power in the top echelon.

That the Latin American Party officials are subordinate to the International (under whatever name it goes) has been frequently demonstrated.

---

* Leon Trotsky, writing in the late 1930's, charged that an important official in every Politburo, whether in Latin America or elsewhere, was the representative of the Soviet Secret Police. He alleged that frequently the other members of the Buro were not even aware of the identity of this agent, whose duty was to recruit local "talent" for the GPU's operations. There seems to be some evidence that the Mexican Communist Party in the 1930's had such a representative, but the author has little information as to whether such an official generally belongs to the Politburos of the Latin American Parties.

As early as the 1920's, the purging of the left wing of the Argentine Party by Ghioldi and Codovilla on instructions from the International, and the expulsion of Manuel Hidalgo and his associates from the top posts of the Chilean Party without benefit of a national convention of the organization, were cases in point.

More recently, the intervention by Browder in the Mexican Communist Party at the time of the Communist split in the C.T.M. in 1937, and the subsequent purging of the Laborde-Campa leadership of the Party by Codovilla and other International officials in 1940 are further indications of this remote control of the internal affairs of the Latin American Communist Parties.

Within the Latin American Parties the rigidity of control is indicated by the fact that with few exceptions there have been no organized factions within the Parties since the 1920's, when factionalism within the International itself was buried by Stalin. There have been dissident leaders aplenty, and there have even been splits in the Latin American Communist Parties, but in most of these cases the circumstances surrounding the splits and the relatively good terms upon which both groups remained with the International cast suspicion on the nature of the divisions. One is led to believe that they were scissions of convenience—as in Venezuela, Argentina, Peru—so as to have one Communist group with a dictator, and another against him, thus insuring the Communists' position no matter what happened.

Certainly no Communist Party in Latin America has dared to question the various turnings and twistings of the International "line." Individuals may have split away from time to time over the Popular Front issue, the Stalin-Nazi Pact, or something else, but the Parties as such have maintained a firm front.

Thus the leadership of the Communist Parties of Latin America, whatever its social origin, has come to form a compact, highly disciplined, highly indoctrinated group, subject to the discipline of the International, and allowing no dissension within its own ranks. It is a core of professional revolutionaries, who spend virtually all of their waking hours on Party business, be it within the Party apparatus itself or within some allied or outside organization. This leadership is well financed and extremely active, and has developed a tactical subtlety which a less Machiavellian type of political movement would find it impossible to achieve.

## Chapter VI

# The Latin American Communists as a Potential Military Danger to the United States

COMMUNISM WAS NOT PRIMARILY a military problem in Latin America by the end of 1956. Rather, it was an economic, political, and psychological one. It was a problem of winning the souls and minds of the people of Latin America.

However, more than in most parts of the world, ultimate power in Latin America rests in the hands of the military. Therefore, the problem of the Communists' influence and ultimate seizure of power there is intimately tied up with the question of their influence in military circles in the region.

The military in many parts of Latin America are an independent institution. They have a long tradition of domination over the civilian government; they frequently intervene, to oust one regime or install another, in the defense of "national honor," "national integrity," or "national unity."

In some parts of the hemisphere the open control of the government by the military is endemic. Thus in Venezuela there have been few times in the country's history when the chief executive has not been a military man. In Bolivia, at least until the Revolution of 1952, governments were made and unmade almost exclusively by the Army. Much the same could be said of Peru. In most of the Central American countries government by bayonet and bullet has been an integral part of the national history.

Even in countries such as Brazil and Chile, where the administration has usually been in the hands of civilians, the Army has always been the last court of appeal and has not infrequently intervened to oust a government, or at least to bring open pressure to bear upon a regime. In Argentina, which had a long tradition of civilian government, the last 25 years have seen the revival of militarism and a series of administrations which have depended in whole or in part on the will of the armed forces.

Perhaps only Uruguay and Costa Rica can be said to have thoroughly civilian governments. Only in those countries do the civilian politicians have the government firmly in their hands; only there can they operate without having to keep one eye cocked to see what the Army is going to feel and do about their decisions. And even there, the situation might change.

The chief challenge to the long-established power of the military in Latin American political affairs comes from the growing number of civilian organizations and movements which have appeared in the last three or four decades. The growth of these organizations reflects the fundamental economic and social changes taking place in the area since the turn of the century. The growth of the cities, the beginnings of in-dustrialization, the breaking down of the power and prestige of the landed aristocracy, have brought about a number of truly revolutionary developments in the social institutions of the Latin American countries.

Three types of organization have been particularly important: political parties, trade unions, and peasant organizations. With the transformation of civilian politics from a private preserve of the landed aristocracy to more broadly based participation, there have grown up in the Latin American countries a series of political parties of various types, which have tended to involve increasingly large numbers of people in their activities and which have created new loyalties and new threats to military domination of political life.

These parties have worn different political colors in different countries. In Uruguay, for instance, the traditional Colorado and National parties have taken on more decidedly ideological orientation with the extensive social reforms of Colorado President José Bâtlle y Ordóñez and his successors since 1910, and the reaction to these reforms which has been led by the Nacionales under the leadership of Luis Alberto Herrera. In Chile a whole series of parties, some of a Socialist nature, some patterned more or less after the French Radical Party, some of Christian Social orientation, have appeared and have come to dominate the country's politics.

In many countries a type of party has appeared which is perhaps best described as "Aprista" (taking the generic name from the Peruvian Aprista Party, the first institution of this kind). The Democratic Action Party of Venezuela, Muñoz Marín's Popular Democratic Party in Puerto Rico, the Febreristas in Paraguay, Pepe Figueres' National Liberation Party in Costa Rica, the Auténticos and Ortodoxos of Cuba, and the Movimiento Nacionalista Revolucionaria of Bolivia belong to this category of political organization.

These parties are nationalistic in their outlook; each has taken on the peculiar political coloration of the country in which it has appeared. But they have certain ideological tendencies in common. They favor widespread social reform, supporting the right to participation in the country's political, social, and economic life of depressed racial groups, be they

Negro or Indian, and of depressed social classes, particularly the urban workers, urban middle classes, and, to a lesser degree, the rural peasantry.

Being made up of economic nationalists, these parties favor the economic development of their nations and seek to restrict the freedom of activity of great foreign enterprises which operate within their frontiers. They have sought to push industrialization, diversification of agriculture, opening up of interior parts of their countries, while at the same time seeking national control over the fundamental industries such as railroads, public utilities, and heavy industry.

At the same time, these parties have been fundamentally democratic. Not only, as we have seen, have they sought to bring into active participation in their nations' political life social and economic groups which have hitherto been banned from such participation, but they have also sought to establish regimes providing more or less protection for the fundamental human freedoms: right to free speech, free association, free press, freedom of religion, and the like.

The Communists, too, have constituted one of the groups which have arisen as a result of this more general movement. Their appeal has been principally to the urban working class and intellectuals, and to a lesser extent to the peasantry and the urban middle class. To a degree depending upon the situation of each individual country, their importance has grown as these social and economic groups have participated more and more in their countries' political life.

Of importance equal to that of the new parties as a challenge to the continued domination of political life by the traditional groups, has been the development of what the Latin Americans usually call "social" institutions: the trade unions and the peasant organizations. Of these, the trade unions are by all odds the more important. Except where the landlords had been definitely defeated not only in the general politics of the nation, but in their own rural bailiwicks—in Mexico and Bolivia, and to a lesser degree, Guatemala—the influence of the peasant organizations was still very small in the middle of the 1950's. Only in the cities did mass organizations prosper.

Trade unionism has come hand in hand with industrialism in Latin America. By the late 1940's virtually all "organizable" workers in Latin America were in trade unions. Although the unions were still essentially weak and were closely tied either to political parties or governments, their potential force was tremendous. That the rulers of the Latin American countries were aware of this potential power was demonstrated by the extensive social legislation in the area and the plethora of laws designed both to favor and control the trade unions.

With the increasing complexity of the economies of the Latin American nations, organized labor, to a growing degree, held the power to bring all economic activities to a halt. The ability of the unions either to protect a government against a coup by the armed forces, or to bring down a regime by a concerted and successful general strike movement was something which every realistic politician in the area had to take into account. The possibility that well-organized trade unionists might actually confront the Army face to face was amply demonstrated by the events of October 17, 1945, in Argentina and the 1952 Revolution in Bolivia; on both occasions the organized workers defeated the military (though in a somewhat different manner in each case).

Insofar as the Communists were concerned, the importance of these rising trade union movements was likewise tremendous. Not only could Communist-controlled trade unions be a powerful weapon in the general political life of the various countries, but Communist-controlled labor might also be in a position of international importance, as a potential means of preventing the economic cooperation of these nations with the United States, and of cutting off supplies of minerals and agricultural raw materials from any enemies of the Soviet Union.

This possible interference with the shipment of strategic materials from Latin America to the United States and its allies is particularly important in the light of increased United States dependence on Latin America for essential raw materials and foodstuffs. The United States has traditionally received the bulk of its sugar, its coffee, and its bananas, much of its tin, a little of its copper, some of the scarcer metals, from Latin America. In recent years, with the approaching exhaustion of sources in the United States of first-grade iron, copper, and other minerals, our dependence on Latin America as a source for these has become even greater.

That the Communists could use their influence in the trade unions to prevent the shipment of these materials to the United States, their past history bears ample witness. As early as the 1920's they were engaging in campaigns to "prevent the shipment of any goods to the enemies of the Soviet Union." During the early months of the second World War, when the Germans and Russians were virtual allies, they were accused in Chile and elsewhere of trying to interfere with the shipment of goods to the Western Allies.

On the other hand, when the Soviet Union was attacked by the Nazis, and the "imperialist war" was suddenly converted into a holy war, the Communists subordinated everything else to the increase of production of those goods needed by Russia and its allies. They discouraged just demands by the workers, did all they could to prevent strikes, worked with anti-labor dictators who were "supporting the war effort," and denounced all those who sought to get wage increases and other gains for the workers as "traitors" and "saboteurs."

That the Communists would again use what influence they have in Latin American organized labor to "prevent the shipment of any goods to the enemies of the Soviet Union" is obvious. In the late 1940's when the Communist Parties of the world were called upon to proclaim that they would side with the Soviet Union in case of a war between their respective nations and that country, the Latin American Communists were most enthusiastic in their pledges of allegiance to the U.S.S.R. Luiz Carlos Prestes led off in 1946 with such a statement, even before the general wave of proclamations, but was followed later by every important Communist Party in the area.

In the middle 1950's the Communists had lost many of the key positions which they had held a decade earlier among the strategic workers of Latin America. However, they still had considerable influence among the maritime and port workers of Brazil, the railroad workers of Argentina, the United Fruit Company workers in Central America. Due to the suppression of the free trade union movement by the Venezuelan dictatorship, the Communists had one of the two union groups which were able to work among that country's key petroleum and iron-mining workers. In Mexico they still had a little influence among the country's mining and petroleum workers, and perhaps among the railroaders.

Of course, the political pendulum tends to swing violently in Latin America, and the fact that the Communists' influence among the workers was at a relatively low ebb in the middle 1950's does not mean that it will necessarily remain low. The only way in which their influence would be permanently minimized would be by the building of a succcessful democratic trade union movement, which could continuously push up the levels of living of the workers.

The extent to which such a democratic labor movement can be assured depends to a considerable degree on how much help the Latin American countries can get from the United States in their economic development plans. If industrialization has to be paid for completely out of these nations' own resources, capital accumulation will have to come to a considerable degree at the cost of a rising standard of living for the workers. They will be able to participate but meagerly in the fruits of the increased productivity of their nations' economies.

It is thus against the background of these two factors—the continuing key role played by the military in the political life of most of the Latin American countries, and the rising influence of civilian institutions challenging this traditional power of the Army—that the problem of the military influence of the Communists in Latin America must be discussed.

By the middle of the 1950's there were several areas in which the military potentiality of Communism was to be taken seriously. In at least two countries the Communists had some influence in the Army; in other nations their control of trade unions might become a military threat.

The two countries in which the possibility of actual Communist influence on the military was greatest were Brazil and Guatemala. In Brazil, due to the vastness of the country, the sparse population in its interior, and the peculiar circumstances of the history of the Communist Party, the Party had more or less close contacts with at least certain elements in the armed forces.

Guatemalan Communists demonstrated another way in which they might become a military menace to the United States. Because of the Communists' great influence in government circles during the administration of President Arbenz, the possibility that the Communists might sacrifice a Latin American country for the international objectives of the Soviet Union by provoking foreign intervention was made clear.

Brazil's Communist Party for 25 years has had a special connection with the country's armed forces. The principal leader of the Communists, Luiz Carlos Prestes, was a professional military man and won an almost fabulous reputation during the revolution and guerrilla war which he led in the interior of Brazil for three years or more in the middle 1920's.

Although few of Prestes' old comrades-in-arms followed him into the Communist Party, Prestes himself became almost a myth, and the Brazilian Army came to regard the campaign of the famous Prestes Column as an epic in its own history.

Several times in later years important elements of the Brazilian Army joined forces with Prestes and his civilian friends in attempts against the country's constituted authorities. A revolutionary uprising in 1935 saw parts of the garrisons of Recife, Pernambuco, and Rio de Janeiro revolting and proclaiming Luiz Carlos Prestes President of Brazil. This movement was suppressed in short order. However, many officers of the Brazilian Army were dismissed and numbers of them were jailed as a result of the 1935 uprising.

A decade later, when the Communist Party had been granted legality, Prestes applied for readmission to the Brazilian Army. Although his application was rejected, much consideration was given to the matter before a final decision was made.

In the early 1950's an alliance was formed between extreme nationalist elements in the armed forces and the Communist Party, which was again illegal. They joined in election campaigns in the Rio de Janeiro Officers Club, and in successful demonstrations against permitting foreign oil companies to develop the nation's petroleum resources.

The possibility that the Communists and the extreme nationalists in the military might join forces in something more than a political campaign was a real one by the middle 1950's. The country certainly would lend itself to such a campaign. The population is concentrated along the coast and particularly in the southeastern part of the nation. The interior of Brazil has a very sparse population. It contains no major cities, and is a region of great plains, forests, and jungles, with small centers of population in towns, villages, and plantations.

Although the Communists had not by 1956 made much progress in winning adherents in the interior of Brazil, the Party could probably raise the core of a guerrilla force among its disciplined adherents in the cities. Leadership for such a "people's army" could probably be provided by the military elements who were more or less closely connected with the Communists in their political activities.

It is unlikely that the Communists and their military allies could raise an army which could menace the country's principal cities or really endanger the heart of the nation. However, they could undoubtedly create a sufficient nuisance to increase vastly the country's military expenditures and intensify Brazil's already staggering economic difficulties.

This could be very serious for Brazil. The country has been in a state of exaggerated inflation for more than a decade, and such increased military expenditures, which would involve greatly expanded importation of military equipment and other supplies, would put a very great additional burden on the country's already shaky balance of payments and result in still further inflation.

It is almost certain that United States aid would be requested in the face of such a guerrilla campaign. If the situation got sufficiently critical, the aid of United States troops might even be requested. In any case, a Communist guerrilla war in Brazil would greatly strain the already thinly extended military power of the United States.

In addition, a Communist guerrilla campaign would give the Communists a new rallying point in their world-wide propaganda warfare against the United States. They would no doubt picture their military activities as a "people's war of liberation" against a government dominated by the "Yankee imperialists." This would be bound to distract the non-Communist forces in Latin America and even outside the area.

In Guatemala the Communists in the early 1950's revealed another kind of military threat to the United States. The Communists' influence in Guatemala under Arbenz was predominantly in the higher circles of the government. Although they had some following among the workers and the peasants, and perhaps could have formed a small guerrilla force from these elements, this was not their principal weapon.

The Guatemalan Communists used their influence to force the Arbenz government into an increasingly belligerent attitude towards the United States and all things "Yanqui." They and their superiors in the Kremlin showed that they had little concern for the fate of Guatemala or the Guatemalan Revolution, and would readily sacrifice them to the interests of the Soviet Union and world Communism. In the years to come, those interests might be served, in some similar case, by pushing a Latin American government into such an extreme position as to provoke open United States hostility.

The Guatemalan situation indicated the kind of danger which might arise, were the Communists successful in pushing a Latin American government into such a position as to provoke armed intervention by the United States. Although there was no such intervention involved in the overthrow of President Arbenz, the Communists succeeded in arousing a world-wide campaign of attack and abuse against the United States, representing the latter as following a policy of "dollar diplomacy" in the Caribbean republic.

A "diversion" in Guatemala, if it had come about, would also have played into the hands of the Soviet Union by spreading still further the limited military resources of the United States. Moreover, it would have increased United States difficulty in getting necessary mineral and agricultural resources from the other Latin American countries.

The Guatemalan experience demonstrated still another kind of potential military danger from the Latin American Communists. The Communists had great influence with President Arbenz. Because of this, they were able to penetrate virtually all branches of the Guatemalan civil administration, placing people in whom they had confidence in key positions.

There is little doubt that they were attempting the same kind of penetration in the country's armed forces. They sent several important officers of the Guatemalan Army on all-expense tours to various Iron Curtain countries. They played up key military men in their press. They encouraged the Arbenz government to bribe important military men with well-paying civilian jobs which they could use to enrich themselves surreptitiously. Finally, Arbenz, with Communist support, followed a policy of giving extensive privileges to the officer corps of the Army, such as high salaries, extra perquisites of office, official cars, and the like, which they would not want to endanger by opposing the regime.

The final objective of this policy of the Guatemalan Communists undoubtedly was not only to "soften up" the armed forces and make them incapable of resisting anything which the Party, through Arbenz, might propose, but to undermine the armed forces as an institution. There is little doubt that the Communists in Guatemala had set up the skeleton for a military force of their own, based on their trade union and peasant followers. Their hope was that ultimately this group could be armed and in case of a showdown with the regular Army, could overcome it.

The Communists were unsuccessful in Guatemala. Although many officers who had opposed Communist penetration of the government were ousted from the Army, many of those who remained were still unfriendly towards the Communists. When a crisis arose in the shape of the Castillo Armas "invasion" of Guatemala in June, 1954, they reacted against the Communists. They refused to allow the arming of the latter's civilian followers, and finally they demanded the resignation of Arbenz himself and an armistice with the strongly anti-Communist Castillo Armas.

The Guatemalan incident illustrates more than anything else the dangers which may arise from a situation in which there is no real ideological force to challenge the Communists as leaders of the Latin American social revolution. Although there were other "revolutionary" parties in the Arévalo and Arbenz administrations, they had no ideology and discipline of their own which set them apart from the Communists. The latter were able, therefore, to obtain great influence in these parties and in the government supported by them. The Communists were able to penetrate to the highest echelons of the administration itself, with the results that we shall describe in more detail in Chapter Sixteen.

It follows that one of the most important ways to prevent the Communists achieving a position from which they can become a military menace to the United States, is to make sure that they are never in a position to obscure the real differences which exist between themselves and those other groups which are anxious to carry out the Latin American social revolution.

This means that the United States Government must always bear in mind that the struggle against Communism in Latin America is not now principally a military one; that to be successful, it must be prevented from degenerating into a military conflict. For this, a clear understanding of the nature and role of the Latin American armies is essential.

The Latin American military are largely overgrown police forces. Although the author knows little or nothing about military tactics and strategy, he believes that it is fair to say that at most there are only two or three armies in Latin America which would be capable of putting up a serious defense of their nations against a major invader even for a few days.

If this is true, it is worse than folly to pour armaments into the Latin American countries. It is worse than useless to give them antiquated World War II airplanes and tanks, rapid-fire small arms, and machine guns. These weapons would be of little or no use in repelling a serious invader. But they are of tremendous value in maintaining the armed forces' superiority over the civilian populations of their respective countries, and thus of maintaining military dictatorships.

One of the factors which has considerably ameliorated the Latin American penchant for military dictators has long been the fact that they were comparatively easy to overthrow if the civil population really wanted to do so. A rifle in the hands of a civilian could kill or wound as surely as one in the hands of a "soldier." If the armaments of the military and the civilians were somewhere near on a par, military dictators were never quite so secure from a civilian uprising as they would like to be.

However, in recent years, largely due to the United States' arming of the Latin American military forces, this balance of power in Latin American politics has shifted. One civilian armed with a rifle is not equal to one soldier armed with a heavy machine gun. Armed civilians can do little against tanks, and nothing against airplanes.

Therefore, Latin American military dictatorships are now infinitely less subject to civilian pressure. Now only a division within the armed forces can upset a military regime which is careful not to allow the development of a strong labor movement. Civilians are hopelessly at the mercy of a military tyranny unless such an eventuality occurs.

Thus if the United States continues to follow a policy of giving more and more armament to Latin American military forces, it is aiding the armed forces of these countries to install and maintain dictatorships. To do so is to play directly into the hands of the Communists.

A military dictatorship helps the Communists on two counts. Using their policy of "dual Communism," the Communists will very likely first allow one branch of their organization to make its peace with the dictator, who, looking for civilian support, will welcome the Communists' co-operation. This has happened in various Latin American countries.

In the second place, the wing of the Communists' apparatus which takes a posture of opposition to the dictatorship will inevitably be thrown into the company of the democratic parties which are also fighting the tyranny. In the face of the persecutions of a common military tyrant, the differences between the various civilian political groups will become obscured. The experience of Europe during the Nazi occupation, where Communists and anti-Communists worked together in the Resistance, gave ample evidence of this. Similar evidence could be cited in half a dozen Latin American countries.

Apparent United States support of the military dictatorships gives the Communists ample "evidence" to prove to their fellows in the Opposition that the United States is really responsible for the tyranny under which they are all suffering. It allows them to put forward the logical argument that "the friends of our enemies are our enemies" to the disadvantage of the United States, and the companion bit of logic that "the enemies of our enemies are our friends" to the advantage of the Soviet Union. In a word, the United States support of military dictatorships in Latin America is one of the surest ways possible to break down the barriers between those genuine advocates of the Latin American social revolution and the Communists.

The situation is made a good deal worse when the United States not only supplies arms to the dictators with which they can suppress their peoples, but heaps honors upon them as well. This occurred several times in the early 1950's. In 1953 the President of the United States conferred the Order of Merit upon Peruvian dictator, General-President Manuel Odría. In the following year he conferred a similar medal on the even worse tyrant, Colonel Marcos Pérez Jiménez, Dictator-President of Venezuela.

If the United States were purposely to seek a way to enrage the democratic elements in the dictator-ridden countries, and to encourage them to join forces and forget their differences with the Communists, this country could not find a more efficient means than to bestow decorations on a Latin American military, strong-arm ruler. Such a move confirms all of the natural anti-Yanqui prejudices of the Latin Americans and throws them directly into the hands of the Soviet Union and its Latin American servants.

There is more than a little reason to believe that the United States attitude toward the military of Latin America is determined by the Defense Department. It would be well for the United States Government to remember that the Defense Department's job is to prepare for and to fight military combats; the State Department's job is to conduct diplomatic relations. The State Department officials are much more acutely aware than the Defense Department of the psychological and political damage done by the apparent United States courting of Latin American dictators. It would be well for the President to allow his diplomats to guide him in his relations with the countries to the South, rather than turn this job over to the military.

In yet another way, the Communists' ability both to launch guerrilla efforts and to use the trade unions against the United States will depend on the U.S.A. itself. This will involve the ability of the United States to cope with the rising nationalism of the Latin American countries. Because of the great economic, cultural, and political influence of the United States in Latin America, that nationalism tends naturally to be turned against this country. It will take skillful diplomacy, a consistent policy of trying to aid the fulfillment of the Latin Americans' desire for economic development, and ample and continuous demonstration of this country's real concern for political democracy in the other nations of the hemisphere, to convince the Latin American workers and middle classes that the Colossus of the North has changed its ways. Unless they can be so convinced, the long-run chances of keeping the Communists from becoming not only a political menace, but a first-class military danger in Latin America, will be small indeed.

# Part Two

*The Communist Movement in Individual*
*Latin American Countries*

## Chapter VII

# Luiz Carlos Prestes and the Partido Comunista do Brasil

SEVERAL CHARACTERISTICS DISTINGUISH the Communist movement of Brazil from those of other Latin American countries. First, it sprang from the Anarchist, not the Socialist, movement. Second, the Party has had peculiar and intimate connections with military men ever since the early 1930's. Finally, it has been much more "personalist" than is usual in the Latin American Communist Parties.

The Russian Bolshevik Revolution aroused a great deal of early enthusiasm among the Brazilian Anarchists, who until the end of World War I were the principal leaders of the labor movement. The Anarchist newspaper, *A Plebe,* carried a fervent pro-Soviet appeal by Maxim Gorki in its February 22, 1919, number. The same issue had a long letter from one "Kessler," who described himself as "Delegate of the Socialist Republic of the Russian Soviets to the workers of the Bourgeois Republic of the United States of Brazil." Subsequent issues of the paper carried articles by Lenin on the Brest-Litovsk peace treaty with Germany, by the Argentine Socialist, José Ingenieros, on "The Historical Significance of Maximilism" (another name for Bolshevism), an article on "The Figure of Carl Liebknecht," and another letter from "Kessler."

Some Brazilian Anarchists soon became disillusioned with the Bolshevik Revolution, and the Anarchist press became a forum for the conflicting opinions of the pro-Bolsheviks and the anti-Bolsheviks. Octávio Brandão, one of the principal leaders of the pro-Bolshevik group, wrote in *A Plebe* on March 5, 1921, "I believe that the only program of this journal should be this: The intense propaganda of Bolshevism, for the glorification of the Russia of the Soviets."

A few months later Brandão, in a speech to the Civil Construction Workers Union of Rio de Janeiro, declared that the ideal of the Brazilian Anarchists "should be the conciliation of Marx and Bakunin, of Lenin and Kropotkin, between centralism and federalism."[1]

Among the other Anarchist leaders who sided with the Bolsheviks were

Astrogildo Pereira, later to become the Brazilian Communist Party's delegate to the Fifth Congress of the Comintern in 1924, and one of the principal figures in the Communist leadership for thirty years; Antonio Canella, leader of a great textile strike in Rio in 1919, who joined the Communist Party soon after it was formed, became a member of the Central Committee of the Party, went to Russia in a Communist delegation, and resigned from the Party on his return home early in 1924;[2] and Roberto Morena, one of the younger Anarchist leaders, who later became the principal Communist spokesman in the trade unions.[3]

However, there was a powerful group of Anarchist leaders who became strongly opposed to the Bolsheviks. One of the first articles in the Anarchist press in pronounced opposition to the Leninists appeared in *A Plebe* on March 5, 1921, and was written by Angelo Vizzotto. It said that the dictatorship in Russia was not controlled by the proletariat, but by the Bolshevik Party, and was "the most brutal expression of authority." The article ended with the statement that one can be for dictatorship or for Anarchism, but not for both at the same time.

A less passionate anti-Bolshevist statement appeared in the March 18, 1922, issue of *A Plebe*, signed by Edgard Leuenroth, Secretary General of the Anarchists' Confederação Operária Brasileira, and other leading Anarchists, including Rodolpho Felippe, Antonio Domingues, and Ricardo Cipolla. It started out by expressing general sympathy with the Russian revolutionary movement, and then went on to say:

> Supported in the so-called proletarian dictatorship, Bolshevism maintains the State as its administrative machine and continues its centralist policy, imposing in an authoritative manner its orders upon the masses . . . destroying those proletarian individuals, groups, and organizations which are trying to take advantage of the social gains and the consciousness aroused in the people to direct the renovating action of the revolution along Anarchist lines. . . .

One of the crucial issues leading to a split between the pro-Communist and anti-Communist factions of the Anarchist labor movement was the problem of international affiliation. In 1922 the international Anarchosyndicalist labor movement decided not to become part of the Communists' Red International of Labor Unions, and resolved instead to establish its own International Workingmen's Association with headquarters in Berlin. The question immediately arose in Brazil whether the Anarchist unions there should join the Berlin International or that of Moscow. The majority of the Brazilian group finally decided that the Confederação Operária Brasileira should join the Berlin International Workingmen's Association.[4]

In the process of the struggle over this and other issues, the pro-Bolsheviks established the Brazilian Communist Party. It was first organized in Rio de Janeiro in 1921, with twelve charter members.[5] Growth of the new Party was not very rapid. In December, 1922, its single delegate to the Comintern's Fourth Congress in Moscow reported that it had five hundred members.[6] Two years later its report to the Fifth Comintern Congress indicated that there were only 350 members.[7]

Some idea of the scope of the Communists' activities in the early years of the movement can be gained from the fact that some 1440 people attended a series of 240 lectures which the Communists gave over a period of thirty weeks, late in 1925 and early in 1926. These lectures included discussions of imperialism, revolutionary theory, religion, and other subjects; and Lenin's *Radicalism, the Infantile Disease of Communism* was used as a textbook. During the first seven months of 1926, about 254,000 pieces of propaganda literature were distributed by the Party.[8]

The fledgling Party had difficulties with the police almost immediately. Octávio Brandão commented that because of their more or less underground existence, the Brazilian Communists "had much in common with the ants." Three different times they were forced to suspend lecture courses.

The Communists' theoretical magazine, *Movimento Communista*, only survived for 24 issues, being forced to suspend in June, 1923, when the printing press, archives, and bookstore of the Party were seized by the police.[9] This magazine was followed by a weekly propaganda journal, *A Clase Operária*, the first issue of which appeared in Rio on May Day, 1925; it achieved a circulation of 9500 copies before it was suppressed, after its twelfth number. Although it reappeared some time later, the paper was frequently suspended for longer or shorter periods by the authorities throughout the 1920's.

Three other papers, issued by trade unions but edited by Communists, had somewhat less difficulty. These were: *Voz Cosmopolita*, organ of the Hotel and Restaurant Employees Union of Rio; *O Solidario*, organ of the Foodworkers Union of São Paulo; and *Alfaiate*, organ of the São Paulo Tailors Union.[10]

Many of the Communists' worst difficulties arose from the conflict, both inside and outside the labor movement, between the Communists and their ex-comrades who stayed loyal to Anarchosyndicalist ideas. The Anarchist attack on the Communists grew in intensity. The July 8, 1922, issue of *A Plebe*, for instance, reported a greeting from R. Vaterland of the South American Bureau of the Comintern to the Brazilian Communist Party and remarked that it "indicates the dictatorial mentality of the Bolshevik Communists," particularly in its statement that "The Communist Party of Brazil is destined to give orders of the day to the exploited class. . . ." The *A Plebe* writer added indignantly, "The Brazilian working class is not destined to take orders from anyone." An article by Emma Goldman on "How Bolshevism Killed the Russian Revolution" appeared in the September 23, 1922, issue of the same newspaper.

The Anarchists and Communists fought it out during the 1920's for control of the Brazilian labor movement. The Communists were unable to capture the old Anarchist Confederação Operária Brasileira. However, they did have influence in a number of unions and sought to form a rival to the C.O.B., which functioned only sporadically in any case.

The first central organization under Communist control seems to have been the Confederação Sindicalista Cooperativista, of which Sarandy Reposo was the principal figure; this existed during 1924,[11] but does not appear to have lasted for very long.

In 1927 a congress of unions of Rio de Janeiro was held in the Teamsters Union Hall, and the Federação dos Trabalhadores do Rio de Janeiro was formed, which included workers from the capital city, as well as from the neighboring cities of Niterói, Petrópolis, etc. Both the Communists and Anarchists had influence in this federation, though the Communist element seems to have been dominant. A second congress of the Federação was held in 1929 and launched a Committee for the Confederação Geral do Trabalho do Brasil.[12]

By 1928 Rodolfo Ghioldi, an Argentine Communist who was in close contact with Brazilian affairs, reported that "the Communist movement has ousted the Anarchists from their leading position" in the labor movement.[13]

In addition to their strength among the Rio de Janeiro unions, the Communists controlled the graphic arts workers, shoeworkers, and hotel and restaurant workers of São Paulo City, and various provincial union groups in the State of São Paulo. In Recife, on the Northeast Coast, almost all of the unions, federated in the União Geral de Trabalhadores, were described by official Communist sources as "revolutionary," meaning pro-Communist. It was also reported that in other states various groups sympathetic to the Communists were "on the way to crystallization."[14]

The work of the Committee for the C.G.T.B. was successful, and in April, 1929, the founding congress of this national Confederation was held in Rio. Representatives were present from the principal states, and it was said that about 60,000 workers were represented. It was agreed to send delegates to the founding conference of the Communists' Confederación Sindical Latino Americana in Montevideo the following month.[15]

In 1929-30 strikes of the Graphic Workers of São Paulo and the Food Workers of Rio, which were suppressed by the police, gave the government the excuse to crack down on both the C.G.T.B. and the Communist Party. The 1930 convention of the C.G.T.B. was prevented from meeting by the police, the two Communist members of the Municipal Council of Rio were arrested, and the labor movement was generally terrorized.[16]

In the meanwhile the Communists had also been active in the general political arena. The Party first ran candidates for public office in the municipal election of 1925 in the port town of Santos, which had already become a Communist stronghold.[17] In 1927 the Communists organized the Bloque Operária e Camponêsa, as an electoral front for the Communist

Party. This "front organization" became particularly useful after 1928, when the Communist Party was declared illegal by the government of President Washington Luiz.[18] The Bloque ran two candidates for parliament in that year, João da Costa Pimenta and Azevedo Lima. The latter was elected, and Pimenta received three thousand votes, four thousand being necessary for election. In 1928 the Bloque Operária e Camponêsa ran candidates for the municipal council of Rio de Janeiro. Octávio Brandão and Minervino de Oliveira, a marble worker, were elected to the municipal assembly.[19]

The Bloque Operária e Camponêsa was discussed in international gatherings of the Communist movement. Humbert-Droz, the Swiss Communist who was more or less in charge of Latin American affairs of the Comintern, reported to the Sixth Congress of the International that the Brazilian Communists had at first considered forming "a Kuomintang, which was to coordinate the organizations of the revolutionary petty bourgeoisie, those of the working and peasant classes, trade union organizations, and the C.P." They gave this up, said Humbert-Droz, when Chiang Kai-shek's Kuomintang turned on the Communists in China. Instead, they formed a "workers and peasants bloc which coordinates labor and peasant organizations" under Communist leadership and control. However, Humbert-Droz expressed fear that it might be captured by "certain petty bourgeois elements."[20]

The Brazilian Communists in these early years played an active part in the affairs of the Communist International. They seem to have been represented at every Comintern Congress from 1922 on. In 1928 Lacerda, one of the Brazilian delegates to the Sixth Congress of the Communist International,[21] was elected to the Executive Committee to represent the South American Parties, besides being on the Program Commission of the Congress.[22] The Brazilians had two votes at this Congress.[23]

The first important split in the Communist Party of Brazil occurred in 1929, largely as a result of the adoption of the international Communist "line" of the Third Period. This line called for an extremely sectarian position on the part of the Communists in the trade unions, and brought them into conflict with trade unionists with whom they had formerly worked more or less closely.

The upshot was that many of the trade unionists in the Party objected to its new policy and formed what came to be known as the Oposição Sindical. It was led by Barbossa, the Trade Union Secretary of the Party, and by João da Costa Pimenta, printing trades leader and outstanding figure in the Rio trade union movement. The Oposição Sindical was expelled by the Party's Third Congress in 1929. Barbossa returned to the Communist ranks in 1943; da Costa Pimenta became a Trotskyite, and then in the late 1940's joined the newly established Socialist Party of Brazil.[24]

In the same year another split occurred in the Party, when the followers of Leon Trotsky withdrew. Those who were to become members of the

Trotskyite group were for the most part members of the Communist Youth. They included Mário Pedrosa, Livio Xavier, Rodolfo Coutinho, Arístedes Lobo, and Hilcar Leite.

The Trotskyite split came about as a result of two separate developments. On the one hand, Mário Pedrosa went to Germany, where he joined the Communist Party of Germany and studied in the Economics Faculty of Berlin University. There he learned of the split in the Communist International between the Stalinists and Trotskyites, and sided with the latter. As a result, he did not go on to Moscow to study in the Marx-Engels-Lenin Institute of the Comintern, as had been planned.

Instead, Pedrosa went to Paris and became associated with the French magazine *Clarité*, which was being published by the Trotskyites under the editorship of Pierre Nevile. Pedrosa sent various copies of this to Brazil and began to write his friends in the Brazilian Communist Youth about what was going on in the International. Upon his return to Brazil, there was quite a group ready to associate with him.

In the meanwhile Rodolfo Coutinho had gone to the Sixth Congress of the Communist International as one of the Brazilian delegates. This was the Congress which ousted Trotsky, and Coutinho sympathized with the expelled Russian leader. When he returned home, he was ready to join the Trotskyite ranks.

The first Trotskyite group was called the Grupo Comunista Lenino. In 1931 they reorganized as the Legião dos Comunistas. The Trotskyites were strong in the beginning, controlling the key Graphic Workers and Metallurgical Workers unions in Rio and São Paulo. During the years just following the 1930 Revolution, the Trotskyites had more popular support and trade union influence than their Stalinist rivals.[25]

The Communists were confused about what position to take toward the Revolution of 1930. This Revolution came in October, after the government had "counted out" Getulio Vargas, the opposition candidate for President in the election earlier that year. Vargas was Governor of Rio Grande do Sul, the most southerly of the United States of Brazil, and for some months before the outbreak of the Revolution it was an open secret that he and his Minister of Finance, Oswaldo Aranha, were busy lining up support for the uprising.

Although Vargas had the backing of the "Tenentes," the famous Army revolutionary group of the 1920's,* as well as most left-wing civilian ele-

---

* The Tenentes were an element among the young officers dissatisfied with the status quo of the 1920's. They were nationalist and vaguely socialist in their attitude, though neither then nor later did they succeed in organizing a political party with a precise doctrine. They led several revolts in the armed forces in the 1920's, including that which gave rise to the famous Prestes Column in 1924. They were the principal force in the successful revolt of 1930, which put Getulio Vargas in power, and from that day to this ex-Tenentes have controlled the Army and have played a leading role in the nation's political life. The word "tenente" means "lieutenant."

ments, the Communists did not back the movement. In fact, in the months preceding the Revolution the Communist-controlled Confederação Sindical Regional of Rio Grande do Sul took the lead in a series of violent strikes in the state, creating an embarrassing problem for the Vargas regime, which was picturing itself as a "friend of labor." Leaders of the Communist Party in the state, including Plinio Mello, were exiled across the border to Uruguay and took refuge in that republic's capital, Montevideo.

Some time before the October, 1930, Revolution a meeting of the leadership of the Brazilian Communist Party, in conjunction with the South American Bureau of the Comintern, was held in Montevideo. Octávio Brandão, Astrogildo Pereira, and the other principal figures in the Brazilian Party participated in this meeting, during which the policies of the Party were submitted to wide "self-criticism."[26]

The meeting did not change the Communist attitude toward the coming Revolution. The Party did not support the Revolution once it took place. It denounced the politicians on both sides as being "tools of the imperialists" and against the interests of the workers, peasants, small businessmen, etc., and it urged formation of a "democratic government of workers and peasants," in which the proletariat would have the hegemony and lead the mass of the exploited and oppressed of the fields and the cities. The Party proclaimed that this revolution "would not be accomplished by means of isolated barracks uprisings, directed by lieutenants, generals, or other caudillos, but by a true insurrection of the masses of all Brazil, in the front of which would be found the organized proletariat and its party, the Partido Comunista do Brasil."

The Party issued a program calling for "destruction of the latifundia, division of the land among those who work it, expulsion of the imperialists, repudiation of foreign debts, nationalization of imperialist enterprises and socialization of the means of production and distribution."[27]

Seventy-three leaders of the Communist Party were arrested in August, 1932, and were jailed in the Dois Rios correctional colony on Ilha Grande. They were freed at the end of the year.[28]

In spite of the generally negative attitude of the Communists toward the Revolution of 1930, there was some confusion. Plinio Mello, fresh from the Brazilian Communist Party's executive meeting in Montevideo, returned to Brazil, going to the port town of Santos, where the Communists had a small nucleus. Mello, Josias Leão, Luiz de Barros, and other Communist leaders organized a regional committee of the Party.[29]

These Communist leaders received from João Alberto (brother of Luiz de Barros), the revolutionary Governor of the state of São Paulo an authorization which read as follows:

> This document grants Srs. Plinio Mello, Josias Carneiro Leão, and Luiz de Barros authorization, in the name of the Partido Comunista do

Brasil, to establish its headquarters, carrying on work of party organization, holding elections and propaganda or doctrinal meetings, and editing publications of a political character. The aforesaid gentlemen have, furthermore, entire responsibility for whatever material of a subversive character is promoted by that Party.[30]

At that time the labor movement was in a very effervescent state, and this Communist State Committee wanted to try to set up a sort of dual power, a kind of Soviet. For this purpose, they got together all the working-class groups in São Paulo, including the Trotskyites and the Anarchists. However, the Anarchists would have nothing at all to do with the "bourgeois" revolution, and since they still had considerable influence in the labor movement, this "soviet" scheme fell through.

In spite of the influence possessed by the legal State Committee of the Communist Party of São Paulo, it was repudiated by the national leaders of the Party. Mello and others were expelled from the Party. A general position of opposition to the 1930 Revolution was ordered by the Party leadership.[31]

In the meanwhile the Communist Party had gained a new adherent in the person of Luiz Carlos Prestes. A professional military man, Prestes first gained fame during a revolution and subsequent guerrilla war which took place between 1924 and 1927.* Then a young Army captain in his middle twenties, he was chief of staff of the guerrilla forces and their chief tactician. He won a fabulous reputation as the "Cavalier of Hope," which was still not entirely dimmed a generation later.

The 1924 Revolution broke out first in the city of São Paulo on July 5. The Paulista rebels were headed by Isidoro Dias Lopes, and included numerous leaders who then and later were to acquire nation-wide reputations and to play leading parts in the political life of their country.

For two weeks the rebels held the city of São Paulo and defeated government troops sent to oust them. The leaders of the revolt then decided to withdraw from the city and seek support in the interior, where the risks of open battle would be less and the ability of the rebels to maintain themselves off the country would be greater. The rebels retreated southwestward, towards the Paraná River.

It was not until three months later that Captain Luiz Carlos Prestes, second in command of the Santo Angelo fortress in Brazil's southernmost state, Rio Grande do Sul, seized control of the fortress and declared himself in revolt against the federal government of President Arturo Bernardes. At the head of fifteen hundred men, Prestes then set out to join forces with the São Paulo rebels. He was not able to do so until April 11, 1925, when,

* According to Raquel de Queiroz, Prestes was sick of typhoid fever at the time of the earlier 1922 Revolution which broke out in São Paulo. He later apologized frequently for not having been able to take part in this uprising. (*Vanguardia Socialista,* October 12, 1945.)

with scarcely eight hundred soldiers remaining under his command, and after a spectacular series of adventures during a march of more than two hundred leagues, the Prestes Column and the Paulista Column joined forces at the falls of the Iguaçu.

For the next two years the united forces, all of which came to be known as the Prestes Column, wandered back and forth across the interior of Brazil. In its wanderings the Column touched every state in the Brazilian federation. It marched 36,000 kilometers and fought hundreds of skirmishes and scores of pitched battles with government troops. It came within a few miles of the Atlantic Coast in some areas, menaced some of the chief cities of the republic.

During its meanderings the Prestes Column sought to arouse a spirit of rebellion among the people of the back country, among the serf-like agricultural workers on the coffee plantations and the cattle ranches. However, the time was not yet ripe for such uprisings. The rebels met almost unanimous opposition from the rural workers, who, under the leadership of their masters, fought against the marauding soldiers.

Prestes' fame became legendary. Few saw him, but all knew about him. In the popular mind he became a kind of Robin Hood. Even newspapers supporting the government against which he was rebelling credited him with being "a greater general than Hannibal." He became a symbol of the protest of the poor against the rich, of the middle class against the landlords who had controlled Brazil since colonial times, of the people against the "oligarchy."

This myth-like character of Prestes was to stay with him for a generation. He was seldom to be seen. For more than a quarter of a century he was either in exile, in jail, or in hiding. Only for two years, from May, 1945, until early 1947, was he in active and open contact with the Brazilian masses.

A *mística* grew up around Prestes. He developed a tremendous and lasting popular following. The "Prestistas" became a potent factor in Brazilian politics. In later years, after Luiz Carlos Prestes became the chief leader of the Brazilian Communist Party, the popularity of that Party was based in a large measure on the personal following of Prestes himself.

For another reason, too, the Prestes Column was to have a lasting influence on the history of Brazilian Communism. Prestes had serving under him or with him in this campaign many who were to become leading figures both in Brazilian politics and the Brazilian Army. Some of the young officers who took part in the Great March turned from military life to politics, as did João Alberto.

But others were to remain in the Army, though not for that reason being completely out of politics. A generation later they were the principal leaders of the Brazilian armed forces. Among them were Eduardo Gomes, who was to be the first chief of the Brazilian Air Force; Estilac

Leal, who became Commander-in-chief of the Army and Minister of Defense; Juárez Tavora, who became Chief of Staff, and in 1955 candidate for the presidency; and Cordeiro de Farias, one of the most important figures in the Army high command, and in the early 1950's Governor of the state of Pernambuco.

Although none of these men followed Prestes in joining the Communist Party, it is not likely that they completely lost their respect for Prestes the man and Prestes the fabulous military leader. Their juniors in the armed forces also maintained considerable respect for the "Cavalier of Hope," and from time to time showed an inclination to work with him and his Party at crucial moments.

Once his little band of six hundred surviving warriors had laid down their arms after crossing the frontier into Bolivia early in 1927, Luiz Carlos Prestes took refuge in Buenos Aires, Argentina. There he remained until leaving for Russia sometime in 1931. It was in Buenos Aires that Prestes became a Communist.

Upon his arrival in the Argentine capital, Prestes was the outstanding figure among the Tenentes, and as such the leader of an amorphous, mainly middle-class, movement without any very well-defined ideology. Although Prestes was generally looked upon as being more left-wing than most of his associates, he certainly was not a Communist.

Prestes was courted by both the Stalinists and Trotskyites. As soon as the Prestes Column crossed the Bolivian frontier, Prestes was interviewed by Communist leader Astrogildo Pereira, in the latter's capacity as reporter for the Rio de Janeiro paper, *Esquerda*.[32] Somewhat later João Caudeira Leal was sent to Buenos Aires by the Brazilian Communist Party to win over Prestes, and was aided by the South American Bureau of the Communist International.[33]

In the meanwhile Aristides Lobo of the Trotskyites also went to Buenos Aires in an attempt to win Prestes over to that group. Lobo claims credit for persuading Prestes to give up his own Liga Revolucionaria and throw in his lot openly with the Communist movement, of which, of course, the Trotskyites at that time still claimed to be a part—the "Left Opposition." Lobo came to be very close to Prestes for a while and drafted several of the statements which the ex-guerrilla chief issued over his own signature.[34]

However, the Trotskyites lost out in this competition for Prestes' loyalty. He became a Stalinist, and in his *Open Letter* of March 12, 1931, Prestes attacked the Trotskyites, and in particular Aristedes Lobo, whom he accused of having "informed the police that there are close relations between me and the South American Secretariat of the Communist International. . . ."[35]

Meanwhile many of his old friends were busy preparing a new revolutionary attempt in Brazil. They naturally looked for leadership and cooperation from Luiz Carlos Prestes. In fact, Prestes took an active part in early preparations for the 1930 Revolt. He visited Oswaldo Aranha in Rio Grande do Sul, and subsequently there was much commuting back and forth between Brazil and Prestes' Buenos Aires residence.

However, the former guerrilla leader is himself the authority for the statement that these negotiations came to naught because Prestes was fundamentally out of sympathy with the other conspirators. He objected to the "ridiculous material help" given the Tenentes by old-line politicians anxious to use them as a vehicle to return to power. He strongly disapproved of his old comrades' willingness to work with these people.

His own ideas were becoming more and more radical. He wrote a letter to a friend, Lieutenant Silo Meirelles, which sowed a good deal of consternation among the Tenente group for its "advanced Socialist" ideas, and sent two of the group, João Alberto and Siqueira Campos, hurrying off to Buenos Aires once again, in a final effort to enlist the support of Prestes for the proposed revolutionary venture and to sound out his general ideological position. They came away convinced of Prestes' increasingly pro-Communist attitude.

However, it was May, 1930, before Prestes himself gave any public indication of leaning in this direction. About a month before he had indicated a program of unity among anti-government forces which offered little hint of the type of profound social change he was to advocate soon afterward. His "Summary of a Political Program" listed the following points:

Political Liberties:

1. Full re-establishment of the individual rights guaranteed in the Constitution.
2. Abolition of the Press Law which is an instrument to coerce the liberty of thought and of free criticism of public affairs.
3. Re-establishment of the right of free circulation through the mails of publications which study or propagate whatever political, philosophical, social, or religious principles, abandoning all decrees, laws, circulars, etc. which interfere with free transit of posts guaranteed by the Constitution.
4. Assurance in an unequivocal manner of the right of free association in public or private meetings, today abolished under one pretext or another. Consequently all laws, decrees, or other measures which prevent such free association must be abolished.
5. As an absolutely necessary complement to the right of association, the right to form centers for professional activities, which will serve to orient the public concerning criminal acts of those who attempt to enrich themselves through adulterations or monopolies.
6. The abolition of laws which provide for the expulsion of for-

eigners who, coming to Brazil, give their physical energies for
the development of the national riches and in doing so in no way
give up their right of conscience and their right to propagate
the principles in which they believe.

Political Action:

1. Dissolution of the Municipal Councils, the State Legislatures,
   and the Federal Congress, which do not represent the will of the
   people or the interests of the Brazilian nation because they are
   made up of professional politicians.
2. Amplification and systematization of the powers of the Municipal Councils as a basis for the federal system of the Republic.
3. Absolute respect for the autonomy of the States, putting an end
   to federal intervention in their affairs.
4. Prohibition of re-election of members of legislative bodies.
5. Abolition of the discretionary use of the State of Siege which
   the Government now possesses.

Rural Problem:

1. Organization, on government-owned lands, of national colonies
   (identical with the foreign colonies in Rio Grande do Sul), in
   which the lands would be sold on reasonable terms, and the
   necessary means of transport would be provided by the government.
2. Distribution in present agricultural centers of tools and seeds
   which will aid the people to cultivate the land.

Then came the famous May Manifesto, which was addressed "to the
suffering proletariat of our cities, to the oppressed workers of the *fazen-
das* and ranges, to the miserable masses of our hinterland, and very specially to sincere revolutionaries, to those who are disposed to fight and
sacrifice for the profound transformation which we so badly need."

After a discussion of the manner in which the presidential campaign
then under way was being carried on, and particularly of the role of the
Liberal Alliance, which was being supported by most of his old Tenente
comrades-in-arms, Prestes commented:

> The Brazilian revolution cannot be made with the innocuous pro-
> gram of the Liberal Alliance. A simple change of men, a secret vote,
> promises of electoral freedom, of administrative honesty, of respect
> for the Constitution and for stable money, and other panaceas will
> resolve nothing in any way which could possibly interest the great
> majority of our population, without the support of which any revo-
> lution which may be made will be only a simple struggle among the
> dominant oligarchs.

He proclaimed "great landed property and Anglo-American imperialism" to be the "two fundamental causes of the political oppression in

which we live and of the successive economic crises in which we find our-selves." He ended his Manifesto with a call for a more fundamental revo-lution than that envisaged by the Liberal Alliance, one designed to deal with what he claimed were the root causes of Brazil's troubles:

> To carry out the program of the revolution which we propose—the only one which we think is in the national interest—the future government must be founded on the true masses of the workers of the cities and the hinterland. A government capable of guaranteeing all the most necessary and indispensable social legislation: limitation of hours of work, protection of women and children workers, insurance against accidents, unemployment, old age, invalidism, and sickness; the rights of strike, assembly, and organization. The victory of the revolution, in that moment, will depend more on the certainty with which we are guided than by the opposition offered by the present rulers, who are frankly disorganized and ineptly led.
>
> We proclaim the agrarian and anti-imperialist revolution carried out and sustained by the great masses of our population. We struggle for the freedom of the agricultural workers submitted to all forms of feudal and colonial exploitation, for the confiscation, nationalization, and division of the land; for the free granting of the land to those who work it. For the liberation of Brazil from the yoke of imperial-ism, for the confiscation and nationalization of nationalist enterprises, of latifundia, concessions, rights of way, public utilities, mines, banks, and the repudiation of all foreign debt. For the institution of a gov-ernment really coming from the workers of city and country, in complete accord with the revolutionary anti-imperialist movements of the Latin American countries, and capable of wiping out the privileges of the present exploiters and of carrying out the revolu-tionary demands. Thus will we triumph.[36]

As Abguar Bastos, one of Prestes' biographers, says, this was not a defi-nitely pro-Communist document, though it indicated certain tendencies in that direction. Prestes apparently was anxious to form an alliance be-tween his old Tenente comrades and the trade unions and other organiza-tions of the working class.

The Manifesto met strong opposition from Prestes' former associates in the 1924 revolt. His former chief, General Isidoro Dias Lopes, and associ-ate, Juarez Távora, both issued replies to the Manifesto. They dissociated themselves from his advocacy of the leading role of the proletariat and his implied support of a Soviet or similar form of government, on the grounds that this was not suited to the Brazilian milieu, which demanded leadership from such groups as the Tenentes, rather than from the weakly organized and divided labor movement.

The third Tenente uprising occurred in October, 1930. It resulted in placing in the presidential palace Getulio Vargas, former Governor of the state of Rio Grande do Sul, and unsuccessful candidate in the 1930 presidential election against Julio Prestes (no relation to Luiz Carlos Prestes), the nominee supported by President Washington Luis. The revolutionary movement represented an alliance between the Tenentes and certain old-line politicians, such as Vargas and Arturo Bernardes, President from 1922 to 1926, the man against whom the Prestes Column had carried on its three-year campaign.

For some months after the 1930 Revolution Luiz Carlos Prestes remained silent. Then on March 12, 1931, he issued his first *Open Letter* to the People of Brazil. In this he violently attacked his former associates of the Tenente movement, accusing them of having become agents either of the British or of the American imperialists, of having done nothing except oust the former oppressors of Brazil so as to convert themselves into oppressors.[37]

Prestes noted that he had had in May, 1930, "no clear comprehension of Marxism," that he had therefore attempted to form a "League of Revolutionary Action as an instrument to give technical aid to the proletariat and its party," and that for this purpose he had sought to rally a number of his former associates who still claimed to be revolutionaries. However, he noted that he had taken the wrong course with this League, and went on to say:

> In these conditions and with this experience, we, the revolutionaries of the petty bourgeoisie, the elements who honestly and sincerely wish to fight alongside the proletariat against imperialism, who wish with the Agrarian and Anti-Imperialist Revolution to initiate the Proletarian Revolution, must understand the justice and correctness with which the Communist Party of Brazil combats the elements which . . . do not comprehend that only with a class-conscious party, a genuine party of the proletariat, free of any influence of the petty bourgeoisie, be it "tenentista," "aliancista," or "Trotskyite," will it be possible really to lead the proletariat to the achievement of its aims, to give the land to him who cultivates it, to expel the imperialists and organize a Government of Workers', Peasants', Soldiers', and Sailors' Councils.

Prestes' reference to the Trotskyites, whom he attacks bitterly in the *Open Letter*, is indicative of how closely he had by this time come to be allied with the Stalinist Communists. This alliance he confirms when he says:

> To all, then, who ask me about "Prestismo," to all sincere and honest revolutionaries . . . I can only indicate one road to follow—the Agrarian and Anti-Imperialist Revolution, under the incontrovertible hegemony of the party of the proletariat, the Partido Comunista do Brasil, Brazilian section of the Communist International.

Prestes received several letters from his old followers and associates, protesting his position. Some of these expressed dissatisfaction with the progress of the 1930 Revolution, and particularly with the association of the Tenentes with old-time politicians such as Arturo Bernardes and Getulio Vargas. However, they did not approve of Prestes' support of Communism.

In reply to these people, Prestes issued another *Open Letter* on March 20, 1931. After again accusing his old associates of being office seekers and servants of British and American imperialism, Prestes says:

> . . . They fear the specter of Communism. And without wishing to do so, they are indicating to the masses the true road they should take. They all know from whence comes the danger, that there is only one—Communism. For this reason they combat it with all of the means at their command, no matter how vile or criminal. But they cannot prevent the masses in the cities and in the countryside from uniting behind their class party, which will lead them to victory— the Communist Party. The workers are preparing to resist new blows which are being prepared against their class and its vanguard. They are discussing their own problems, uniting and organizing solidly in revolutionary trade unions and in the ranks of the Party which, by means of a correct tactic, will destroy all of the apparatus of the bourgeois State and will establish the dictatorship of the proletariat. The soldiers and sailors will turn their arms against their own officers, lackeys of the bourgeoisie, and will organize their councils and will fraternize with the workers, aiding them in seizing the land, the factories, the banks, the railroads, and organizing their own government. Long live the unity of all the workers, peasants, soldiers, and sailors! The land for the peasants, the factories for the workers! Long live the government of the councils of workers and peasants, soldiers, and sailors! Long live the Communist Party! Long live the Proletarian Revolution![38]

In spite of Prestes' endorsement of the Communist Party and its position, "Prestismo" remained an important political current in Brazil independent of the Party. Both Prestes and the Communists were aware of this and tried to combat it. Thus Fernando Lacerda, one of the top leaders of the Party, attacked "Prestismo" as "an ideology which has its origins in the unsure and unfirm mentality of the petty bourgeoisie, that intermediary, vacillating group between the two principal classes of capitalist society, the proletariat and the bourgeoisie." He attacked its "lack of confidence in the proletarian and peasant masses . . . and its lack of faith in the capacity of the proletariat to direct its own revolution." Lacerda also attacked "Prestismo" for "its belief in 'elites,' 'heroes,' or 'cavaliers of hope,' " and declared that it was retarding the development of a real revolutionary mentality.[39]

Prestes himself attacked "Prestismo." At the time of the 1932 civil war in the state of São Paulo he accused certain elements in that state of using his name "to lead the masses in the war." He added that the real need was to strengthen the Communist Party and that "Prestismo" was a great obstacle, a "petty bourgeois ideology."[40] Although Prestes had now completely endorsed the Communist Party, it is interesting to note that in 1931 he wrote one of his friends in São Paulo recommending that "All propaganda should be made in the name of the Chief." (Aristides Lobo, in *Vanguarda Socialista*, April 5, 1946.)

There was apparently a conflict within the ranks of the Communist Party of Brazil over the issue of Prestes. Some of the older leaders, such as Astrogildo Pereira and Octávio Brandão, were jealous of Prestes and feared the effects on themselves of the entry of Prestes into the Communist ranks. They were exceedingly anxious to point out any of his "deviations" from Communist orthodoxy, and the newspaper *O Jornal* of Rio de Janeiro, which published Prestes' various pronouncements, also carried lengthy replies by Octávio Brandão in the name of the Communist Party of Brazil.[41]

Prestes went to Moscow in 1931.[42] There he was first set to work directing the construction of workers' housing projects. Soon, however, he began to take an active part in counselling the Communist International on South American affairs, working very closely with its South American Secretariat,[43] and assumed a post on the International's Executive Committee.[44] However, Prestes maintains that he did not actually join the Brazilian Communist Party until his return to his native country in 1934.[45]

Upon returning to Brazil, Prestes became a member of the Political Bureau of the Brazilian Communist Party and, in effect, its principal figure. A statement was issued by the Party to explain why he was being integrated into the top leadership so soon after becoming a Party member. This was done, the statement said, because of "the situation of Brazil, and the special role and work hitherto carried out" by Prestes. "The more we are able now to establish a complete, firm, and indivisible bond between the proletarian leadership of the Party and the national popular hero, the more easy it will be to overcome the difficulties of the various stages of the revolution in Brazil."

The Party therefore recognized Prestes' "equal rights in the administration" of its affairs, and said that his "particular position" did not represent a weakness in the Party, but rather "a great positive value and reinforcement for the Party." Prestes, the leadership proclaimed, had evolved "from a petty bourgeois revolutionary" into a Bolshevik.

The assumption by Prestes of the leadership of the Communist Party of Brazil thus represented the culmination of a long process of development. Abguar Bastos has traced this development as follows:

> . . . the revolutionary position of Prestes experienced definite trans-
> formations. . . . The first was when he broke with the revolutionary

liberals and founded the Liga de Acção Revolucionaria. The second began when Prestes dissolved the Liga. . . . The third period was when he launched the slogan of the agrarian and anti-imperialist revolution and accepted the leadership of the Communist Party. The fourth began when he definitely joined the party system of the Communist International, and after a prolonged period of politicalization and because of his "special position" as a popular national hero, he became a member of the Executive Committee of the Third International. The fifth is when he assumed a leading position in the Communist Party of Brazil.[46]

The return of Luiz Carlos Prestes to Brazil coincided with the adoption of the Popular Front policy by the Brazilian Communist Party. The application of this policy in Brazil involved both the unification of the labor movement under Communist leadership and the formation of a wider political group, the National Liberation Alliance.

The Communists were instrumental during 1934 and 1935 in calling local trade union unity conventions and preparing for a national trade union unity congress. The unions involved were those "which have the greatest character," according to official Communist reports.[47]

The Communists succeeded in bringing together not only old-line trade unions, but also some of those labor organizations which had been established under the Labor Law of the Vargas government early in 1931. This latter type of union had legal recognition from the government, and employers were legally bound to deal with them, but these unions were also subjected to more control by the federal government than were the "free" unions. Great emphasis was now laid by the Communists on detaching these "legal" unions "from the influence of the government . . . so as to realize labor unity."[48]

A labor unity convention was finally called by the Communist Party and the National Liberation Alliance in May, 1935. Three hundred delegates, claiming to represent 500,000 workers, attended the convention. Among the groups represented were the Federation of Seamen, claiming 200,000 port and river workers, and the National Federation of Railwaymen, with 10,000 members. The upshot was the establishment of the Confederação Sindical Unitária do Brasil.[49]

Even more important than trade union unity, insofar as the Communists were concerned, was the formation of the National Liberation Alliance. The N.L.A. was mentioned by Georgi Dmitrov, President of the Comintern, as "a correct foundation for the development of the united anti-imperialist front," and he gave the Communist Party of Brazil credit for having organized the Alliance.[50]

Lacerda, Brazilian delegate to the Comintern, writing in *International Press Correspondence*, August 17, 1935, commented thus on the role and activities of the National Liberation Alliance:

The next stage in the struggle in Brazil, which is at a turning point in history, is the establishment of the anti-imperialist People's Front under the banner of the National Liberation Alliance. The People's Front Government, to which the victory of the Popular Front will lead, will not yet be the democratic dictatorship of the workers and peasants, but only a stage towards it. The peasants have a key position in the establishment of the People's Front; we must win them in the first place, and we must secure hegemony of the proletariat through a persistent, genuine, day-to-day struggle for all the demands of the masses. We would, however, become a sect if we did not make the most of the contradictions within the camp of the ruling class. The People's Front movement can only lead to the goal if it is combined with the consolidation of the ranks of our party.

The National Liberation Alliance was a very broad coalition of groups and individuals opposed to the Vargas administration. It was described by an article in the *Communist International*, May 20, 1935, as being supported by "very wide masses of working-class organizations, of office employees, students, important sectors of the army and navy, various peasant organizations, the petty bourgeois 'travaillists' and 'tenientes' parties, some national reformist groups, numerous socialist 'parties,' big trade unions, and mass young people's organizations."

Luiz Carlos Prestes was elected honorary head of the National Liberation Alliance.[51] Other old Tenentes actively participated in the Alliance. Miguel Costa, Prestes' onetime chief in the so-called Prestes Column, headed the N.L.A. in the state of São Paulo.[52] Heroclino Cascardo, who had led a naval mutiny coordinated with the Army uprising of Prestes and others in 1924, was the National President of the Alliance.[53]

On July 5, 1935, the National Liberation Alliance issued a program calling for suspension of payment on the country's foreign debt, Brazilian control of public utilities, expropriation of large estates and their division among peasants, and separation of Church and State. Other demands of the Alliance included those for an eight-hour day, minimum wages, and a social insurance system.[54]

The activities of the National Liberation Alliance were varied. It sponsored the trade union unity conference of May, 1935; it carried on campaigns against the Brazilian fascists, the Integralistas; it cooperated with the trade unions in protesting a clash between strikers and Integralistas in Petrópolis. It issued an appeal to the "Catholic masses and to the poor clergy." It fought alongside the peasants in Minas Geraes against evictions by landlords. It carried on a general campaign for minimum wage legislation and backed a demonstration of 20,000 bank clerks for a minimum wage.[55]

The Vargas government was strongly opposed to the National Liberation Alliance. On July 12, 1935, President Vargas declared it legally dissolved, but it continued to function in spite of this.[56] It was not until November that there was a violent clash between the N.L.A. and the government.

After the outlawing of the Aliança Libertadora Nacional, tension between it and the Vargas government grew. In October, 1935, there was a walkout on the Great Western Railway, supported by the N.L.A., and although the workers were offered a 30 per cent wage increase, they did not return to their jobs. The strike spread and threatened to become general. In Recife troops refused to fire on strikers. There were evidences of unrest in the countryside.

Faced with this situation, the leaders of the National Liberation Alliance met and concluded that the time had come for a showdown with the government. They alerted their military supporters, and an armed uprising began. The principal rebel group consisted of a portion of the Rio de Janeiro garrison. The insurrectionists proclaimed Luiz Carlos Prestes to be President of Brazil, and there was severe street fighting in the capital for eight or nine hours before the government finally suppressed the rebels.[57] There was also some fighting in Rio Grande do Norte and Pernambuco in the North, but government troops were quickly victorious there.[58]

With the suppression of the revolt, the Vargas regime moved to crush the N.L.A. and the Communist Party. There were widespread arrests, and those jailed included deputies Domingos Velasco, Abguar Bastos, João Mangabeira, and Ottavio de Silverio, and Senator Abel Chermont.[59] Also arrested was Pedro Ernesto Baptista, Mayor of Rio de Janeiro at the time of the uprising.[60] Luiz Carlos Prestes evaded the police for some time and was not finally arrested until March, 1936.[61]

The secret trial of Prestes and other leading figures took place in May, 1937. Thirty-five defendants were in the dock. Prestes was given a sentence of sixteen years and eight months in prison. Arthur Ewert, a German Communist who played a leading part in the N.L.A., was given fourteen years; Pedro Ernesto Baptista received three years and four months, and the Argentine Communist leader, Rodolfo Ghioldi, was sentenced to four years. Hercolino Cascardo, President of the National Liberation Alliance, and João Mangabeira were acquitted, after spending ten months in prison.[62]

Of course, after the collapse of the National Liberation Alliance revolt, Communist activities were driven underground. For some time the Communist paper, *A Clase Operária*, continued to appear, as did the official organ of the N.L.A., *Libertador*. Clandestine meetings of the Party were held, and even occasional open street meetings, though these were generally broken up by the police.[63]

Non-Communist political leaders who had been associated with the N.L.A. continued to be active. In Rio a People's Front for Democracy was organized, under the leadership of deputy João Cafe Filho.* In São Paulo a similar group called the Radical Democratic Union was established by General Miguel Costa, one of the old Tenentes. In the state of Rio Grande do Sul a Democratic National Union was established under the sponsorship of Professor Bruno Lima. A National Democratic Students League was active for a while, though it did not gain any great degree of support.[64]

The Communist Party continued to follow the Popular Front policies which were the international Communist "line" at the time. Thus the Party's May Day manifesto of 1936 said "the time is not yet ripe in Brazil for a workers' and peasants' dictatorship, and even less for a proletarian dictatorship." It stressed the necessity for the Communists to struggle beside "honest democrats, anti-imperialists, and nationalists."[65]

The attitude towards Getulio Vargas underwent a considerable transformation. In January, 1937, Octávio Brandão was still talking about "the toadies of the Vargas government," and wrote: "Hitler's aim to set the world on fire, and to burn and destroy, is equally the aim of Vargas, Hitler's ally in the struggle against 'Communism,' that is, against world peace and world democracy."[66]

However, in November, 1937, President Vargas turned on his former associates, the Integralistas, Brazil's own green-shirted fascist movement. He outlawed the party, deporting its leader, Plinio Salgado, to Portugal. At the same time he abrogated the democratic Constitution of 1934 and proclaimed a new Constitution, patterned on that of Mussolini's Italian Fascist State, announcing the foundation of a Brazilian corporate regime under the name of the "Estado Novo" or "New State."

This turn of events apparently won the approval of the Communists, for in the June, 1938, issue of *International Press Correspondence*, Octávio Brandão wrote that "Fascism in Brazil has suffered a defeat, but it is not yet finally beaten. The fascist danger is still in existence, particularly in the states of Santa Caterina, Paraná, São Paulo, and Rio Grande do Sul."

However, the "fascist danger" was apparently no longer considered by the Communists to come from the Vargas regime. Brandão discussed, somewhat tentatively, the "democratization" of the Vargas regime, noting that the President had restored legal status for the Freemasons and had acquitted 21 army officers on trial for lack of energy in suppressing the N.L.A. revolt. He concluded:

> All this shows that the bloc of November 10, 1937 (the bloc of semi-feudalists and the reactionary bourgeoisie, with the militarists, with the Integralista leaders, and the Nazi groups), is breaking up, and that, on the other hand, a new development of the democratic

* Cafe Filho remained a strong opponent of Vargas throughout the rest of Vargas' dictatorship. However, the turn of the political wheel of fortune made him Vice President under Vargas after the election of 1950. Cafe Filho succeeded to the presidency after Vargas committed suicide in August, 1954.

movement has begun. There has been a partial defeat of fascism, which is of great importance not only for Brazil, but for the whole world.

Two months later the Comintern's *World News and Views* of August 6, 1938, reported that the Communist Party had issued a new program "for democracy and independence," consisting of the following points:

The State apparatus to be cleared of the fascists and other traitors to the country; release of the defenders of democracy and national independence; amnesty for all sentenced, imprisoned, and fugitive anti-fascists; democratic orientation of home and foreign policy; establishment of a national smelting and heavy industry; solution of the problem of high prices and economic crisis; suppression of profiteering and usury; practical application of the law on minimum wages, and other laws promoting the interests and wishes of the people.

The Comintern organ noted that the Brazilian Communist Party presented this program as a basis for "a national front which will unite people and government." It announced that "the democrats—above all, the Communists—are calling upon the people to support the government with weapons in hand, against any Integralist putsch, and for the integrity and independence of the country."

Meanwhile the Communist Party had suffered a split. This schism developed over the question of what the Party's attitude should be towards the 1937 election, an election which finally was never held, because of President Vargas' November, 1937, *coup d'état* and the proclamation of the Estado Novo. Prior to the coup President Vargas was officially supporting the candidacy of the writer and journalist, José Américo, and there was a faction of the Communist Party, headed by Laudo Reginaldo da Rocha (known generally as Bengu), which wanted to back the Américo candidacy. The other faction proposed that instead the Party launch the symbolic candidacy of Prestes.

Although the group in favor of an independent campaign had a majority in the Brazilian Communist Party, the International decreed that it should support Américo. A split resulted. The majority, now turned minority, continued in control of the São Paulo Regional Committee of the Party. It also had control of the Communist organization in the state of Paraná, as well as a part of the apparatus in the state of Minas Geraes and some fragments in Rio Grande do Sul and Recife.

As soon as the dissident group broke with the Communist Party they were subjected to a tremendous attack from the whole force of the still potent Communist propaganda apparatus. Within a year they were reduced to a handful of less than a hundred people. These joined the Trotskyite movement and formed the Partido Socialista Revolucionario. Until the advent of the Estado Novo they published a semi-legal paper called *Orientación Socialista* and thereafter, for a while, were able to get out an illegal journal, *Luta de Classes,* which was sometimes printed and sometimes mimeographed.[67]

Both the P.S.R. and the older Trotskyite group, led by Mário Pedrosa, Hilcar Leite, and others, joined the Fourth International when it was formally organized in 1938, and Pedrosa was present at the founding congress. However, the Partido Socialista Revolucionario finally became the orthodox Trotskyite group in Brazil and the official affiliate of the Trotskyite International.[68]

None of the Marxist groups was able to function effectively after Vargas' proclamation of the Estado Novo. Their leaders were dispersed, being jailed, put in concentration camps, exiled, or driven into inactivity. They were not able to publish any kind of legal periodicals, and the risks and penalties for putting out illegal ones were formidable.

The Communists were quiescent during most of Word War II. However, there is little doubt that they supported the Vargas government's participation in the war from 1942 to 1945. Blas Roca, Cuban Communist leader, who visited Luiz Carlos Prestes in jail in July, 1942, reported that Prestes urged an all-out effort against the Axis to win the war. The Blas Roca-Prestes interview, which was reported in the pro-Communist *Allied Labor News* of July 22, 1942, was arranged by Foreign Minister Oswaldo Aranha, to whom Blas Roca referred as "a brilliant exponent of Brazil's Pan American and anti-Axis policy."

The Communists were not able to be active in the trade union movement. The Vargas regime did not permit the election of Communists or other known oppositionists to posts in the trade union movement. When such people were elected, they were not allowed by the Ministry of Labor to take office.[69]

An important wartime event was the visit to Brazil in March, 1944, of Vicente Lombardo Toledano, the pro-Communist leader of the Confederación de Trabajadores de América Latina. Lombardo addressed a big meeting in Rio, run by the National Defense League and the Mexican-Brazilian Institute. On the speakers' platform were the Chilean and Venezuelan Ambassadors to Brazil.[70]

Lombardo Toledano interviewed Vargas' Labor Minister, Marcondes Filho. The government-controlled Brazilian radio reported on April 4, 1944, that "The words of the illustrious labor leader are of special importance at this time, because they confirm the good results of our internal and international policy."

Several months later a group of Brazilian maritime workers, then in the United States, sent a message to Lombardo Toledano, who was attending the International Labor Organization Conference in Philadelphia. They called him "not only the greatest leader of the workers of the other brother countries, but also the greatest leader of the workers of Brazil, an integral part of the Latin American proletariat." They expressed opposition to fascism and expressed hope that Brazilian workers would soon be associated with those of the rest of Latin America.[71] Of course, such expressions as these were, in the context of the time, no necessary indication of Communist affiliation on the part of the workers concerned.

Late in 1944 opposition to the Vargas regime began to increase sharply. The União Democrática Nacional was formed as a rallying point for the anti-Vargas forces. One pro-Communist news source reported that it included "industrialists, students, landowners, workers, part of the 'tenientista' army group which brought President Getulio Vargas to power, members of the National Liberation Alliance, and the Communists."

The first item in the first Manifesto of the U.D.N. was interesting, in view of the position which the Communists took a few months later toward President Vargas' continuation in the presidency. This item called for "Organization of a provisional government junta, including army representatives whose past guarantees execution of this program."

There is little doubt that the Communists supported the U.D.N. at its inception. The New York Communist paper, *Daily Worker*, noted on January 8, 1945, that "The National Democratic Union wants real elections and constitutional government." Two months later, on March 25, 1945, the *Daily Worker's* Latin American correspondent referred to General Eduardo Gomes, the leader of the U.D.N., as "Brazil's future presidential candidate" and noted that he "proceeds from the 'tenientista' movement, a movement that has written so many great pages of democratic history."

The formation of the U.D.N. was made possible by a relaxation of the Vargas dictatorship. *The New York Times* reported on March 3, 1945, that:

> Rumors that the Communist party was getting ready to reorganize gained credence after reports had come from Mexico, Washington, and London that Brazil would recognize the Soviet Union. . . . Recognition of Russia is now under study, the President said. "Russia has given the world a great sample of her courage and tenacity," he remarked.

On April 21, President Vargas released Luiz Carlos Prestes and 147 others in an amnesty for political prisoners. Of these, 130 were said to be Communists, though the New York *Daily Worker* commented on April 22 that "Obviously the term 'Communist' is rather loosely applied and may refer to many non-Communists who had participated in the anti-fascist movement."

The release of Prestes from jail marked the beginning of a two-year period of activity and progress for the Communist Party such as it had never seen before. With the exception of some minor molestations, the Party was allowed to function legally; it presented candidates in the 1945 and 1947 elections; and it assumed a leading position in the trade union movement. Intellectuals, trade union leaders, even opportunistic politicians flocked to the Communist Party and its periphery.

A hint as to why the Communists were suddenly allowed such freedom of action was given in Prestes' first public speech after getting out of jail. Delivered on May 25, 1945, to a vast crowd of 70,000 people in the Vasco da Gama Stadium in Rio, Prestes' discourse confounded and shocked many of his supporters, when he said that for Vargas to resign from the presidency would be "desertion" and would produce confusion and chaos.[72]

To people who had been fighting Vargas for more than a decade and who were looking forward with enthusiasm to the elections Vargas had promised for December, 1945, Prestes' new position in support of Vargas was a shock indeed. Many of them immediately jumped to the conclusion that there had been a "deal" between Vargas and Prestes, and that the latter had been released only after agreeing to support the President's continuation in power.[73]

The Communists, of course, refused to admit any such agreement. In an interview with the author on August 27, 1946, the then Senator Prestes denied categorically that there had been any deal between himself and Vargas, and particularly denied the rumor that Vargas had visited Prestes in his jail cell. Prestes' explanation for the Communists' support of Vargas in the months before the latter's overthrow was that the policies of Vargas and the Communists tended to coincide—since the militarists who were Vargas' chief enemies were even more against the Communists than they were against the President. Both Vargas and the Communists, said Prestes, worked to maintain Vargas in power and to have free elections for a Constituent Assembly.

This was more or less the line which the Communist Party took at the time. The official Communist newspaper in Rio de Janeiro, *Tribuna Popular*, remarked of Vargas on September 16, 1945, that "If he desires to march with the people, the Party will march with him!" Prestes himself was reported by the *Daily Worker* of August 30, 1945, as saying in a speech to the National Committee of the Communist Party: "We affirm that we have no commitments except with the people. If our policy coincides with the personal objectives of Vargas or of any other citizen that is not our fault but that of history."*

Whatever their motives, it is certain that the Communists sought to maintain the Vargas regime in power. In the middle of September the Communist Party and the trade union group which it quickly organized, the M.U.T., held mass meetings all over the country, urging postponement

---

* The change in Prestes' personal attitude towards Vargas is the more surprising in that Vargas had kept Prestes a prisoner for nine years and had turned his wife and daughter over to the Nazi Gestapo. Olga Prestes was killed by the Nazis; Prestes' daughter was returned to him after World War II.

of the presidential elections and the calling instead of a Constituent Assembly.[74]

Early in October, 1945, the Communists held a great demonstration for Vargas outside the presidential palace. The Socialist weekly, *Vanguarda Socialista*, in its issue of October 19, 1945, described the meeting thus:

> Getulio Vargas agreed to receive the leaders and the masses of the Communist Party, who went to the Guanabara Palace to cheer him and to ask the convocation of the Constituent Assembly. Thus was officially sealed the Getulio-Prestes alliance. The Prestistas and the Queremistas* form today a single bloc which attempts to impede the progress of the movement to re-democratize the country, and thus to restore the regime of force and oppression under which we have lived during the last seven years of the Estado Novo, though this time with a more pronounced totalitarian character.

Vargas, addressing this same meeting, was reported by the *Daily Worker* of October 25, 1945, to have said, "I favor the Constituent Assembly. I would not take responsibility for any move which would provoke bloodshed among Brazilians." He added that all parties would be consulted on what policy to follow, and that "They must tell whether they favor the people's aims or prefer to maintain themselves within reactionary ranks." He thus endorsed the Communist program of postponing the presidential election, keeping himself in office, and having elections only for a Constituent Assembly.

The Communists rushed to Vargas' defense when United States Ambassador Adolf Berle, in a speech before the journalists of Rio de Janeiro, welcomed the holding of the elections on December 2 for both the President and Constituent Assembly, and said that this confirmed Brazil's belief in the democracy for which both the U.S. and Brazil had fought in World War II. Prestes commented that "Berle takes the attitude of a counsellor on Brazilian political questions. We ourselves will resolve our own probems. In the struggle of the peoples for liberation, we participated on the battlefields and we, too, have won the right of self-determination." Roberto Morena, chief trade union strategist of the Party, declared that Berle's speech was "incompatible with the Good Neighbor Policy."[75]

The Communists' support of Vargas brought a violent break with their old allies in the União Democrática Nacional, who continued the fight against the Vargas regime which the Communists had now abandoned. Early in June Prestes withdrew the Party's support from General Gomes, leader of the U.D.N., saying that he did not favor either presidential candidate, since both were generals and were alike in their policies.[76]

Rodolfo Ghioldi, the Argentine Communist who was long a close

* "Queremistas" was the term used for those of Vargas' supporters who urged him to remain in office in spite of his promises of a presidential election. The name comes from their slogan "Queremos Vargas" (We want Vargas!).

associate of Prestes and was his jail mate in Vargas' political prison for some years, confirmed the changed attitude toward the U.D.N. when, in an interview with the *Allied Labor News* on June 21, 1945, he said:

> The Oppositionists are not against the Estado Novo. . . . They were the theoreticians of corporatism while Fascism was in the ascendancy throughout the world and were admirers of Vargas from 1936 to 1942. . . . They resent democratization, and their new techniques consist in appealing to the opposition candidate to assume a dictatorship. They are using the honorable name of Brig. Gen. Eduardo Gomes in this way as a smoke screen for their reactionary intrigues.

For his part, General Gomes some months later attacked the Communists "bitterly," and after the fall of Vargas, the Communists' official paper was calling Gomes "a menace to the progress of Brazil."[77]

In the meanwhile the Communist Party had been growing by leaps and bounds. Within a year and a half after Prestes' release from jail it grew from a mere handful of members to a Party claiming 130,000 card-carriers.[78] State committees were established throughout Brazil, one of the first of these being that of São Paulo, which was inaugurated with a speech by Prestes early in June.

On May 23, 1945, the Communists began publication of an official daily newspaper in Rio de Janeiro, *Tribuna Popular*. Pedro Motta Lima was listed as publisher, and Aydano do Couto Ferraz as editor-in-chief. It was followed soon afterwards by regional papers in various of the state capitals.

A National Convention of the Party, the first legal one ever held, met in August, 1945. Aside from electing Prestes Secretary General of the Party, this convention drew up a Party program and urged President Vargas to convoke a Constituent Assembly "in the shortest possible time."[79]

To a very considerable degree, the Communist Party of Brazil during the 1945-47 period was a Prestista party almost more than it was a Communist Party. The author travelled fairly widely in Brazil late in 1946, talked to numerous Communists, both inside and outside of the labor movement, and was very much impressed with this fact. Workers' loyalties were very generally divided between Vargas and Prestes, with those favoring Vargas generally being more or less closely associated with his Partido Trabalhista, and those who were more or less enthusiastic about Prestes being in the orbit of the Communist Party.

Prestes was certainly the chief selling point of the Party. He travelled up and down the country, in one tour speaking to an estimated 800,000 people. Prestes himself reported in the *Daily Worker* of October 27, 1945, on returning from this tour, that "Everywhere you feel the people pin their hopes on the Communists . . . besides those people who lean towards the Communists, the rest favor Vargas."

The Communists were particularly active in the labor movement. As early as April, 1945, they organized the Movimento Unificador do Trabalhadores. It was established outside the government labor setup, as a sort of Communist general staff. Moreover, the Communists quite deliberately made the decision that they would not form rival unions to those which had been established under the patronage of Vargas' Estado Novo, but instead would try to win over the official unions.

This policy of infiltration in the official labor movement had several advantages over the policy of dual unionism. First of all, it would not bring the Communists into direct conflict with the legal obstacles which would face unions organized outside the Estado Novo apparatus. Only recognized unions could appear before government Labor Courts or sign legal collective agreements with their employers, and thus be in a position to provide bread-and-butter gains for their members quickly.

In the second place, under the Vargas system, there was a compulsory contribution by every worker of one day's pay a year to the official unions. If the Communists were able to gain control of a sizable number of official unions, they would have ample funds for union activities—and for the Party.*

Under the sponsorship of the M.U.T., state labor congresses of official unions were held in various states, including Ceará, Bahía, the Federal District (Rio de Janeiro City), and São Paulo. The pronounced Communist orientation of the last of these meetings was shown in its final session. Only Communists or pro-Communists were allowed to speak. João Amazonas, recently elected Communist deputy, was the principal orator. He devoted a great deal of his speech to extolling the Communist Party, commenting in passing that there was only one party of the proletariat "and that all others were little more than fascists who were trying to infiltrate the laboring masses in order to lead them to fascism." He specifically attacked Socialists, Trabalhistas (Vargasites), and Trotskyites, and accused them of being "traitors and facists." When Socialist delegate Plinio Mello rose to protest this allegation, he was reduced to silence amid shouts of "Down with Trotskyism." Amazonas then ended his speech with a peroration attacking the record of the Trotskyites in Russia and Spain.[80]

Late in October, 1945, Getulio Vargas was overthrown by an Army *coup d'état*, when he attempted to appoint his brother Chief of Federal Police, a move which military authorities interpreted as presaging the cancellation of the elections scheduled for December 2. The ousting of

---

* Later, when the Communists had members of Congress, *Vanguarda Socialista* reported on July 30, 1946, that Communist deputy João Amazonas spoke strongly against a motion introduced by Socialist deputy João Mangabeira to abolish this compulsory deduction from the workers' pay.

Vargas was accompanied by a certain amount of confusion; the Communist paper, *Tribuna Popular,* was temporarily suppressed, and Prestes was variously reported as taking refuge in a foreign embassy and as being under arrest.[81]

The Communists condemned the overthrow of Vargas. In its first statement after his fall, the Party was reported by the New York *Daily Worker* of November 8, 1945, as saying that "the coup was on the surface directed against ousted President Getulio Vargas, but was really directed against the people, democracy, trade union organizations, and the Communist Party." It attacked Vargas for allowing organization of "reactionary groups, who, along with the military candidates, unleashed the coup," and said that the nation was on the brink of civil war.

However, civil war did not come, and when the new regime indicated that it would go on with the elections planned for December 2, the Communists resolved to take part in them. On November 24 they announced the nomination of a candidate of their own, Yeddo Fiuza, former Mayor of Petrópolis and at one time Vargas' Director General of Public Works.[82] They had already nominated congressional slates in most of the states.

The nomination of Fiuza did not raise any great enthusiasm among the Communist rank and file and their friends. Virginia Prewett reported in the Chicago *Sun* of November 30, 1945, that "Fiuza is a controversial figure over whom the Communists themselves are divided." The United Press reported on November 29 that he was not nominated as a Communist candidate, "but as a democratic candidate supported by the Communist Party."

The Communists issued an election program, to which it was announced that all Communist Party candidates were pledged as a "program of national union." The use of this phrase "national union" is interesting, because it indicates the adherence of the revived Brazilian Communist Party to the international Communist slogans of that time.

Among the policies which were emphasized in this program, as reported in *Tribuna Popular* of November 14, were agrarian reform and a democratic constitution, which among other things should follow the People's Democracy pattern of having "a president of the republic . . . elected by the assembly of people's representatives" who "should not have superior powers to them."

The Communist program also declared "for the solidarity of the United Nations, in support of the Charter of San Francisco and of the policy of peace and collaboration under the guidance of the World Security Council and of the three great democratic nations, the United States, England, and the Soviet Union."

The Communists threw great energy into the campaign, striving particularly for the election of members of their Party to the Constituent

Assembly. The windup meeting of their campaign was held in the Carioca Square in Rio, and it was variously reported that 130,000 to 200,000 people were present. Prestes, naturally, was the principal speaker.

The Communists did very well in the elections. They received some 700,000 votes, 15 per cent of the total. Prestes was elected Senator from the Federal District and deputy from São Paulo, Estado do Rio, Pernambuco, the Federal District, and Rio Grande do Sul. He had headed the ticket in every state. He finally chose to sit in the Constituent Assembly as Senator from the Federal District.

The Party elected fifteen deputies and one senator. Four members of the Party's Central Committee were elected: Prestes, M. Grabois, and Agostinho Dias de Oliveira from Pernambuco, and José Amazonas from the Federal District. Also elected were: Mário Scott, José Maria Crispim, Jorge Amado (the famous novelist), Milton Caires, and Caio Prado Junior (a well-known historian) from São Paulo; Batista Neto from the Federal District; Alfredo Richmond and Alcedo Coutinho from Pernambuco; Caludino José da Silva and Alcides Rodrigues Sabença from Estado do Rio; Abilio Fernandes for Rio Grande do Sul; and Carlos Marighella from Bahía.

The Communists received more votes than any other party in a number of state capitals and industrial cities, including São Paulo, Santos, Campinas, Sorocaba, Birigut, Recife, Olinda, Natal, and Aracajú.[83]

For more than a year after the December, 1945, election the Communist Party functioned legally, openly, and with only minor restrictions upon the part of the government. Occasionally the government of President Dutra, who was also elected in December, 1945,* used the Communists as scapegoats when there were street riots or other embarrassing events. The author still remembers with some consternation how he arrived one day in September, 1946, at Communist Party headquarters in Rio to keep an appointment with Luiz Carlos Prestes, only to find that the police had seized and temporarily closed the building in which the headquarters were located.

Prestes and other Communists took an active part in the deliberations of the Constituent Assembly and were particularly active in supporting the social clauses of the new constitution. However, the Party's principal field of activity during these months lay in the trade union movement.

The Communists had considerable influence in the labor movement, particularly among the rank and file and the lower-echelon leadership. There were some who felt that the Party was using this influence more for its

---

* Before the overthrow of Vargas, General Dutra had ostensibly been the government nominee. However, he was reportedly upset because Vargas was giving him little aid. At one point he contemplated withdrawing from the race, but was prevailed upon by his rival, General Gomes, not to do so. After Vargas' ouster, Dutra received Getulio's endorsement a few days before December 2. Vargas' backing was generally credited with having elected Dutra.

own benefit than for that of the workers. Ex-Communist Hilcar Leite wrote in the Socialist weekly, *Vanguarda Socialista*, on May 17, 1946:

> Prestes & Co. are every day giving more incentive to reaction, using in their adventures the trade union organizations whose executive committees the Communists have captured. Trying to use the labor movement as an instrument in their struggle against the government, the Communists are running the gravest risks for the labor organizations, which will be sacrificed in the Communist-government struggle.

The M.U.T., the Communist vehicle among the trade unions, had had in view since its inception the project of establishing a General Confederation of Labor of Brazil (C.G.T.B.). Some months after the election the M.U.T. issued a formal call for a Labor Congress to establish the C.G.T.B., to meet on September 25, 1946.

The government countered the move of the M.U.T. with several measures. First, it declared the M.U.T. illegal in May, 1946. Second, the Ministry of Labor suddenly called a national Labor Congress of its own, to meet on September 9, with an agenda which was virtually identical with that of the meeting summoned for two weeks later by the M.U.T.

After some confusion, the M.U.T. leaders decided to cooperate with the Ministry of Labor on the arrangements for the meeting which the government had called, and to call off its own convention. Compromises were reached between Labor Ministry and M.U.T. officials on detail concerning the Congress.[84]

The sessions of the Labor Congress were stormy. The author attended its opening meetings, and it was fairly obvious from the beginning that there were at least two well-organized groups represented—one favorable to the Ministry of Labor, another composed of Communists and their allies, who had a well-organized caucus, with floor leaders, and a definite program to present.

The Communists favored the immediate establishment of the C.G.T.B. Their opponents favored the establishment of various national federations and confederations along industrial lines, as provided for in the labor setup in the Estado Novo. In the third plenary session of the Congress these two points of view came into open conflict. Representatives of the Federação de Empregados do Comercio of São Paulo objected to the decision of the Congress commission which had recommended the establishment of the C.G.T.B., and when they were rebuffed they walked out of the session, followed by several hundred other delegates. The secessionists reconvened across the Bay in the city of Niterói, where they drew up a resolution urging that the Minister of Labor dissolve the Congress. This he soon did.

However, the pro-Communist unions continued to meet and formally organized the Confederação dos Trabalhadores do Brasil. They elected a provisional executive, with Manuel Lopes Coelho Filho of the Rio de Janeiro Metallurgical Workers Union as Secretary General. Three months after the Congress, the C.T.B. claimed to have two hundred unions affiliated with it. The C.T.B. formally joined the Confederación de Trabajadores de América Latina (C.T.A.L.). The Confederação de Trabalhadores do Brasil continued to have a legal existence for about six months after its organization.[85]

The Communists participated in the elections of January, 1947. They added four more deputies to their delegation in the national Chamber of Deputies and gained various seats in the Rio de Janeiro municipal council and state legislatures. However, they received considerably less votes than they had gotten in the December, 1945, poll.[86]

In spite of this decline in popular support of the Communists, the government moved to outlaw the Communist Party. A suit was filed with the Supreme Electoral Court, asking that body to rule that the Communist Party was not a legal political organization. However, for some time the Court hesitated to act, and President Dutra resisted pressure to outlaw the Party by executive decree. Nonetheless, the administration carried on a constant propaganda barrage against the Communists and against the Soviet Union on the government-controlled radio stations.

Finally in May, 1947, the Supreme Electoral Court ruled that the Communist Party was not a legal organization. A few days later the C.T.B. was also declared illegal.[87] However, it was October, 1947, before Congress passed a measure ousting the Communist Party's deputies and senators from its midst.[88]

Although after May, 1947, the Communist Party was once again illegal, it did not cease to function. However, it suffered considerably in terms of membership. Just before being outlawed it claimed some 200,000 members.[89] A few years later it was reported to have fallen to no more than 80,000 card carriers.[90]

The Communist Party was in effect semi-legal. Although it could not register and run candidates under its own name, it did succeed in placing various candidates, some of whom were elected, on the tickets of other political organizations. Although orders went out for the arrest of various members of the Communist Party leadership, including Luiz Carlos Prestes, few of them were actually picked up by the police.

The newspaper *Correio da Manhã* of Rio, virtually the *New York Times* of Brazil, commented editorially, October 18, 1953, on this situation, as follows:

It is now three years since the criminal courts ordered the apprehension of Luis Carlos Prestes and other Communists, indicted under the law. It was the Supreme Court which issued the decree ordering the judge in charge of their case to bring this about. . . . However, only two of the accused have been picked up, one working tranquilly at his job in this city, and the other because, having committed new and subsequent crimes, he is serving his penalty in the Seventh Military Region jail. The rest are at liberty, freely moving about, writing in periodicals under their own names, speaking at meetings, organizing and launching strikes, and even being seen in meetings of homage of "yellow" unionists to Minister João Goulart. The Communist Party has no legal existence. But it has strength enough to protect its members from the action of the law. It goes even further: it issues money for internal circulation, acting, according to the declaration of Orlando Ribeiro de Castro, as if it were "a State within a State."

The representative of the Law made a confession that the civil police is technically unable to make the arrests ordered by the Supreme Court. . . . In any case, the Communists should not continue to have the privilege of evading penal justice.

The Party organization continued to function. The National Committee held meetings periodically. Lower-echelon bodies no doubt also met with more or less regularity. The Communists succeeded in building up a number of front organizations, such as the Movement of Partisans of Peace, the National Federation of Women, and the Committee for the Defense of Petroleum.[91]

The Party continued to recruit members. For instance, during a printers' strike in São Paulo in 1952, which lasted 64 days, the Party claimed to have gained 270 new members from among the strikers.[92]

As was the case with other Communist Parties the world over, the Communist Party of Brazil spent much of its time and energy in the post-World War II period in its campaigns for "peace." The Brazilian Communists followed the international Communist "line" in its trend away from friendship for the wartime Allies and towards intransigent, violent, and vituperative opposition to the Western Powers, particularly the United States.

Luiz Carlos Prestes was one of the first to take this anti-United States line. Early in 1946 he made a widely noted statement concerning the position Brazil should take in the case of a Russo-American conflict. He explained this statement to the author some months later, on August 27, 1946. He said that he had been asked what would be the Communist attitude in case of an imperialist war of the United States against Russia. His reply had been that such a war was unthinkable, since neither the United States nor Russia wanted it, and that so long as the United States remained democratic, the people wouldn't allow such a war. But if such a war did come, any war against the workers' state, the Soviet Union, was an attack upon the workers all over the world, Brazil included, and the workers would therefore react against it. In case Brazil was drawn in on the side of the United States, the workers of Brazil should do all they could to aid the

Soviet Union. This, he said, was in line with the traditional policies of the Communists from the time of Lenin.

The Brazilian Communists carried on a very active campaign for the collection of signatures for the "Stockholm Peace Appeal." They set a target of four million signatures in Brazil, and the Communist magazine *Problemas* reported in its November-December, 1952, issue that they had actually gotten five million names.

Subsequently, when the campaign to hold "Peace Congresses" all over the world was in full swing, the Brazilian Communists undertook to organize such a meeting in Brazil. Late in 1952 the National Committee of the Party published in the November-December issue of *Problemas* a directive which read in part:

> The National Committee of the P.C.B. decided that the whole Party will mobilize to give the maximum aid to assure the success of the preparation in Brazil of a Congress of Peoples for Peace. It is the fundamental task of all the organs and militants of the Party to assure the effective participation of the Brazilian people in this great meeting of peoples. . . .

This meeting was finally prohibited by the Vargas government.

The Communists carried on a great deal of propaganda about the Korean War. Prestes wrote in the September-October, 1951, number of *Problemas* about "the criminal war against the people of Korea by the government of the United States." The Communists were particularly anxious that Brazil should not send any troops to participate in the war, and violently attacked all those who were even hinting at such a possibility. Thus the National Committee of the Party published in the March-April, 1951, issue of *Problemas* a manifesto which said:

> The native reactionary forces and the American aggressors are developing in Brazil, on an increasing scale, the work of psychologically preparing for war, attempting to mislead our people. Through the press and through criminal declarations such as those of Raul Fernandes, João Neves, Cordeiro de Farias, Eduardo Gomes, deputies and senators of all the reactionary parties, they openly defend the sacrifice of Brazilians in Korea or in any other aggression unleashed by the Americans.

Brazilian Communists took a very active part in the "germ warfare" campaign. A Brazilian, Dr. Samuel Pessôa, was on the mission of scientists which the Chinese and Koreans invited to come to "verify" the charges against the United States. The author talked with Pessôa on June 15, 1953. The São Paulo University professor, a particularly violent and passionate enemy of the United States,* said that he had spent eleven days in Korea

---

* Pessôa's antipathy to the United States is particularly interesting in the light of his ancestry. His maternal grandfather was a Confederate, who left his native country after the Civil War to escape the effects of Emancipation.

and had been particularly impressed by the brutality of the United States bombings of the cities of North Korea.

Pessôa claimed to have seen "proof" of United States bacteriological warfare. This "proof" consisted of interviews with United States majors and colonels who "confessed" to having dropped bacteriological bombs; a bibliography compiled by the Chinese Communists of articles and books which had been published in the United States in recent years concerning the problem of germ warfare; and germs which the Chinese told him had been dropped in Korea by American planes. These, he said, were undoubtedly real disease germs.

Early in 1952 the Communists organized demonstrations and issued manifestoes against a visit to Brazil by United States Secretary of State Dean Acheson. At about the same time they were engaged in a violent campaign against a proposed Mutual Defense Agreement between the United States and Brazil. The fantastic lengths to which their campaign on this issue went is shown by a Resolution of the National Committee of the Party published in the November-December, 1952, issue of *Problemas*, which read in part:

> We affirm that the "Military Accord" completely submits the Brazilian armed forces to the control of American imperialists, who are seeking to transform these forces into a mercenary corps under the command of Yankee generals and officers, to be used not only against the Koreans and other free peoples, but even against our own people, who are opposed to imperialist war and have already demonstrated that they are not disposed to die slowly of famine or be enslaved by the fascists and agents of American imperialism.
>
> We emphasize, too, that by the terms of the new "Accord," the Vargas government hands over gratuitously to American imperialism all the riches of the nation, opens completely the doors of the country to the invasion of all kinds of Yankee agents and spies under the cloak of diplomatic immunity, and cynically violates the laws of the country, assuring the agents of Yankee imperialism extraterritorial rights and freedom from control by our courts.

As part of their anti-United States campaign, the Brazilian Communists were particularly active in opposition to the Vargas government's proposal to permit American oil companies to participate in the exploration for and exploitation of Brazilian petroleum resources, through a monopoly, Petrobras, in which both the Brazilian government and United States oil companies would have an interest.

Their chief instrument in the petroleum campaign was the Centro de Estudos e Defesa do Petróleo e da Economia Nacional. The Communists reported that "around this organization are united many elements of the Brazilian people and representatives of the national bourgeoisie."

The Centro held various National Conferences for the Defense of Petroleum. The third of these, held from July 5 to 7, 1952, drew up resolutions against the Vargas government's Petrobras proposal and suggested that instead there be established a purely Brazilian government monopoly of the extraction, refining, and sale of petroleum. It also went on record "against the pillage of the natural resources of the country and against the colonial policy of the United States in Brazil."

The Communists sought wide support for the decisions and activities of the Centro de Estudos e Defesa do Petróleo. They boasted that the decisions of the Third Congress of the organization had been supported "by many state legislative assemblies and municipal councils, and by some deputies in the National Congress, and by representatives of the armed forces, among them twelve generals and one vice admiral."[93]

The Party was very active among the trade unions. However, it was not permitted by the government to get control of any of the federations and confederations which developed during the Dutra administration and the second Vargas period. Nor was it allowed to get complete control of any large number of local trade unions.

The Confederação dos Trabalhadores do Brasil, which the Communists had organized in September, 1946, ceased after May, 1947, to function as an effective central labor organization. Many of its leaders were arrested, and some of them dropped out of trade union and political activity as a result of government persecution.[94] However, the Communists maintained the fiction that the C.T.B. still existed, using it rather as a general staff for their activities in the trade union movement than as a real central labor organization. It was not possible for any trade unions or federations or confederations legally to affiliate with it after it was outlawed in May, 1947. Roberto Morena, who during the Communist Party's legal period had been in charge of the Party's trade union work, but had then gone to work for some time in the headquarters of the C.T.A.L. in Mexico, returned to become the Secretary General of the C.T.B.[95]

In spite of the difficulties involved in their Party's being illegal, the Communists continued to be active in the rank and file of the trade unions. They held office in many of them, though they were usually elected on a joint slate with other political groups, rather than as representing an independent force in their own right. They even held important positions in some of the higher-echelon organizations of the Brazilian labor movement. A Communist was Vice President of the Journalists Federation,[96] and Communists held important posts in the Maritime Workers Federation, where they carried on a running battle against the leadership of that organization.[97]

The Communists took an active role in various strike movements, though usually they shared the leadership with members of other political groups. For instance, in a widespread walkout in São Paulo in April, 1953, in which the metal, wood, textile, and glass workers participated, and which lasted 27 days, the Communists took part in the leadership of the walkout and tried to capitalize on it. However, they were only one of at least five political groups represented, and they did not have a decisive say in how the walkout was conducted.[98]

In the maritime strike of June, 1953, the Communists were also active. However, in this strike there was also a good deal of political influence from elements within President Vargas' own Partido Trabalhista.[99]

In spite of their illegal status, the Communists continued to engage in electoral activity. They particularly took advantage of the 1950 presidential election campaign to place candidates on the tickets of other parties. They succeeded in electing one deputy, Roberto Morena, the Party's principal trade union figure, to the Federal Congress. He was elected officially on the ticket of the Partido Republicano Trabalhista, which had been organized specially for the 1950 election. Also elected, on this same party ticket, were four members of the Rio de Janeiro City Council.

The Communists were able to elect members of various State Legislatures, including one who was successful on the ticket of Vargas' own Partido Trabalhista in the state of Pernambuco. Other parties were willing to make such deals because they needed votes, and the Communists had them.[100]

In the state of São Paulo the Communists worked inside the Partido Social Trabalhista and the Partido Nacional Trabalhista, both of which had split off from the Vargas party. They elected two City Councillors on each of these parties' tickets. However, the election of the Communists was declared null and void by the electoral courts, and other representatives of the two parties were named in their stead.[101]

By all rules of political logic, the Communists should have made appreciable gains after the re-election of Getulio Vargas to the presidency in 1950. There were three major elements in the country's political picture at that time. The conservative elements were generally grouped in the União Democrática Nacional and part of the Partido Social Democrático. Among the masses there were but two visible forces, the followers of Vargas and the Communists.

After his re-election Vargas lost popularity very rapidly. His second government was democratic, but did virtually nothing. In spite of extravagant promises made when he was out of office, Vargas was unable to do anything about stopping the inflation which was the workers' most pressing problem. He lost influence among the trade unions, the lower echelons of which tended to take an increasingly independent attitude. Vargas' star had waned disastrously by the beginning of 1954, and his moves during that year to double the minimum wage and expand social security only partially offset this decline. Even his suicide, which was accompanied by demagogic letters saying that he had killed himself because he had been thwarted in his desire to help the workers, only momentarily united some of his old working-class followers around the banner of their fallen leader.

In the face of this situation, the Communists should have made rapid gains. There was a vacuum in Brazilian politics. Virtually all the workers had followed either Vargas or the Communists, and with the decline of Getulio the Communists should have profited.

However, they did not do so to any marked degree. In fact, they suffered several notable defeats. The most crushing one was in the mayoralty elections in the city of São Paulo in the middle of 1953. An unknown politician, Janio Quadros, supported only by the small Socialist and Christian Democratic parties, swept the polls. The Communists, who had polled 300,000 votes and had been the largest party in the city in 1947, received only 20,000 for their nominee in 1953. Their voice was unheeded. Furthermore, they lost control of virtually all the most important unions in the city and state of São Paulo to independent elements not affiliated with either the Partido Comunista or Vargas' Partido Trabalhista.

The Communists sought to capitalize on Vargas' suicide. Even before this they had formed a tacit alliance with João Goulart, who in 1953 and 1954 had served as Vargas' Minister of Labor and was seeking to inherit Getulio's mantle as "father of the poor." Followers of Goulart worked with the Communists in the maritime strike of July, 1953, and negotiations were afoot for an electoral alliance between the two groups at the time of Vargas' death.

However, the Communists' attempts to wrap the Vargas banner around themselves after Getulio's death brought only slim results. They seemed unable to take advantage of the death of their chief rival to gain support among the workers.

Perhaps the explanation of this lies in the fact that by the time of Getulio's death, the Vargas era was a thing of the past in Brazil. Brazilian citizens of all classes were tired of the faces which had decorated the political rostrum ever since the 1930 Revolution. They were seeking for a new leadership which did not have any connection with the corruption, demagoguery, and mild totalitarianism of Vargas.

This factor probably explains the victory of Janio Quadros, a virtual unknown, in the mayoralty elections in 1953 and the São Paulo State gubernatorial elections in November, 1954. It also explains the failure of the Communists to capitalize more on the decline of Vargas. The Communists had had too spotty a record with regard to Vargas, particularly since May, 1945. They had supported him during the last months of his dictatorship, had worked with him in the opposition during the Dutra administration, and had backed him in the 1950 presidential election. Although they had severely criticized him during his second presidency, they had shown themselves willing enough to work with the most demagogic fringe of Vargas' followers right down to the old dictator's death, and had sought to be more Vargasista than Vargas after his suicide.

This opportunism did not appeal to the Brazilian workers. They seemed to be more sophisticated and aware of the facts of politics in their country than the Communists had given them credit for. The upshot was that the Communists made surprisingly little headway among the country's urban masses, in spite of what would seem to be exceptionally favorable circumstances.

This decline in the fortunes of the Communists would probably have continued if an effective alternative to Vargas and the Communist Party had appeared with the decrease in popularity of these two groups. However, this did not occur. Although the Socialist Party haltingly attempted to provide such an alterntaive, it was itself too torn between the attractions of Getulismo and Communism to be successful.

The result was that by the end of 1956 the Communists were again beginning to gain ground, to such a degree that they might within a foreseeable period become a major factor in the struggle for power in Brazil. This change was brought about by three developments:

First of all, after the death of Vargas, there ensued a struggle for power within his Partido Trabalhista Brasileiro. In the course of this contest, many leaders of the party were willing to call to their support Communists and fellow travellers. By the end of 1956 Communist infiltration in the P.T.B. had become a serious problem.

In the second place, the disintegration of the P.T.B. and the failure of any new force to assume effective leadership in the trade unions had the result of preparing the ground for further Communist penetration in these vital organizations. Hence, in São Paulo, the Communists were able to capture the State Textile Workers Federation as well as the powerful Metal Workers Union of the city of São Paulo.

Finally, a split in the anti-Vargas ranks as a result of the hotly contested 1955 presidential election gave the Communists another opportunity to make contact with elements in the armed forces. When General Lott, Chief of General Staff under President João Cafe Filho, carried out a coup to assure the inauguration of President-elect Jucelino Kubitschek, this caused a serious division in the armed forces. The Communists by supporting and lionizing General Lott, were able to establish friendly relations with at least some of those in his faction of the Army.

The leadership of the Communist Party after 1947 manifested a great deal of concern for the ideological purity of the organization. We have noted that during its short period of legality the Brazilian Communist Party had been largely a "Prestista" organization, gaining its rank-and-file membership in large part through the personal popularity of the almost mythical Luiz Carlos Prestes. After it became illegal many members deserted the Party. The leadership being much concerned with the ideological indoctrination of those who were left, there is little doubt that by the early 1950's the Communist Party was a smaller, but much better disciplined and indoctrinated organization.

During the intervening years there was much emphasis in the Party's publications on the need for "self-criticism." The National Committee in a proclamation published in the March-April, 1951, issue of *Problemas* stressed the ideological weakness of Brazilian Communism. It said:

> . . . the fundamental weakness of our Party is ideological, from it come other political and organic weaknesses. The majority of the members of the Party were educated in the period in which we were guided by a political orientation based on class collaboration, and as yet do not have a Marxist-Leninist-Stalinist formation, thus being easily swerved by influences foreign to the proletariat. Class illusions are still strong in our ranks, particularly reformist illusions. And it is because of insufficient ideological preparation that our Party is faced with serious difficulties in its activities.

A few months later João Amazonas, a member of the National Committee, wrote in the July-August, 1951, issue of *Problemas* about what had been done to try to raise the ideological level of the organization:

> There is no doubt that we have taken steps towards elevating the ideological level of the Party. There were carried out in various parts of the country courses of short duration, and now we have initiated another series averaging three weeks. This task has great importance in the struggle to overcome our weaknesses and must be carried out with more perseverance and firmness. Furthermore, little initiative is forthcoming for the organization of study circles and we lag in the improvement of our press and in the publication of Marxist books and pamphlets. The distribution of our press is small, as is that of our literature.

Much emphasis was laid on the importance of the study of Stalin's works as a means of indoctrination of the Party membership. Thus an editorial in *Problemas* of November-December, 1952, said:

> In the materials of the XIX Congress of the Communist Party of the U.S.S.R. and in the speech of Stalin, the Brazilian Communists have a powerful weapon and a sure guide in the struggle which they are carrying on for peace and the liberation of our country from the imperialist yoke.

One reason for the concern with the ideological training of the Party was the fact that there was a good deal of dissension within the ranks. This was referred to, if obliquely, in the party organs from time to time. Thus the National Committee stated in its thesis published in the March-April, 1951, issue of *Problemas:*

> . . . there have arisen sectarian tendencies in the activities of the Party, which tend to discount the struggles for immediate demands

and legal forms of struggle. These tendencies have been endangering the correct application of the present political line and tactics, and are contributing to the weakening of the Party.

The only open break in the Party's ranks was the secession of a small group in the state of São Paulo under the leadership of José María Crispim, one of the Party's deputies in the 1945-47 period. Crispim's break was widely reported as being a Titoist split in the Party. However, this interpretation is dubious at best. It is not likely that the Crispim split was a basic break with Stalinism. Crispim had a fight with the Brazilian Communist leaders and as a result was ousted from the Party. His group started publication of a journal, *Unidade,* which Crispim sent to the Cominform, seeking the international Communist movement's support for his position.[102]

Ideological discipline was perhaps more essential in the Brazilian than in any other Communist Party in Latin America. This was because of the special role which seems to be reserved for the Brazilian Communists, if the occasion should arise. Because of the vastness of the country and its bad communications, as well as because of the peculiar relations of the Brazilian Communists with some elements in the country's military, it seems likely that the Brazilian Communist Party was prepared in the late 1940's and early 1950's to engage in guerrilla warfare if the orders to do so were given.

This potential military role of the Brazilian Communists was emphasized by Diógenes Arruda in the name of the Executive Commission to the Plenum of the National Committee of the Party in February, 1951, as reported in *Problemas*, March-April, 1951. In discussing the Democratic Front of National Liberation which the Party had undertaken to organize, Arruda said that the local committees of this Front should be organized "in all places of labor and centers of population . . . to unify all the patriotic and democratic forces of our people, attempting to win for the program of the Frente Democrático de Libertação Nacional all the mass and popular organizations which now exist, as well as personalities of local prestige."

Arruda went on to say that the Party must use "all forms of mass struggle": "It is certain that at the present time the principal form of struggle is the struggle of the masses—protests, demonstrations, economic and political strikes—which, especially in the countryside, tend to become rapidly transformed into partial combats, in armed struggles for concrete objectives." The Party "must in no way fear" this development, according to Arruda.

He urged that:

> If in the interior of the country, where the forces of state reaction are generally weaker, it is essential to arouse the masses and lead them in struggles which rapidly attain the highest forms, including

armed struggle, in the great urban centers where are concentrated the principal armed forces of imperialist reaction, the essential task consists in discovering the most adequate forms of struggle which will unite the forces of the working class, which will politically and ideologically educate them and prepare them for the decisive combats.

Arruda quotes Prestes as saying:

We must learn to use all the forms of struggle which the tense international situation requires. Since we are at the front of the masses, we must not recoil from using the highest forms of struggle, including violent shocks with the forces of reaction, partial combats to which we will sometimes be forced, especially in the interior of the country, in the struggle of the masses against feudalism and police brutality. Situations may arise, too, in which local or regional power weakens. In such cases, we must never vacillate in taking power, to realize within that locality our agrarian and anti-imperialist program, which will then become known to the masses, even though our stay in power may be brief. In addition, as international contradictions arise as a result of violent conflicts between various factions of the ruling classes, we must intervene as an independent force in these conflicts, as best we may, supporting, as the circumstances dictate, one side or the other, always seeking to transfer these combats into mass struggles for national independence, against imperialism, for liberty and democracy, for land for the peasants, for better wages and working conditions for the proletariat, for a popular democratic and progressive government.*

Words could hardly be clearer concerning the orientation of the Brazilian Communist Party. The actions of the Party lend support to the statements of Arruda and Prestes about Communist intentions. There is no doubt that the Communists established close contact with an element among the military.

During the period when the Party was still legal, there was a strong move made to get Prestes' Army commission restored to him. Although it failed, he succeeded in arousing a good deal of support for this move. There is little doubt that Prestes' reputation as an old Tenente and as the leader of the famed Prestes' Column had preserved for him a certain sympathy among the ranks of the Army, many of whose leaders of the 1940's had been associated with Prestes in the events of the 1920's.

Two subsequent events highlighted the continuing Communist attempt to build or maintain good relations with elements in the armed forces. One of these was the association of various military men with the cam-

* In spite of these proclamations, the author has found no evidence to substantiate the story published in a widely circulated United States periodical in the summer of 1954 to the effect that Prestes was at that time actually leading a guerrilla army in the interior of Brazil. However, the Communists are taking the lead in localized insurrections. One such uprising occurred in April, 1956, in rural areas of the state of Goias, where a movement by small landholders against large landowning neighbors who were attempting to seize their land was exploited by the Communists.

paign against foreign participation in the development of the country's oil resources, a campaign in which the Communists took a leading part. The Centro de Estudos e Defesa do Petróleo succeeded in getting twelve generals, a vice admiral, and various lesser officers to sign its proclamation against foreign investment in Brazilian petroleum.

The other incident was a much-publicized election in the Officers' Club of Rio de Janeiro early in 1952. The election of officers of this club has long been the weathervane of opinion in Brazil's officer corps. The 1952 elections in the Club seemed to pose the issue as to whether or not the officers of Brazil's Army were sympathetic with the extreme nationalists who were friendly to the Communists. Candidate of the nationalists was General Estilac Leal, an old Tenente; his opponent was General Alcides de Etchegoyen.

The moderates won in the Officers' Club election, but the incident served to point up the problem of the alliance of the Communists and extreme nationalists in the armed forces. Even with the defeat of the Communist-favored candidate in this poll, the fact remained that the Brazilian Communists had closer contact with their nation's armed forces than any other Latin American Communist Party, and that Brazil was the most likely country in all of Latin America to be the scene of a Communist guerrilla-warfare campaign which would serve as a "diversion" against the Western Powers, and particularly the United States.

This danger was highlighted by the election of October, 1955, and the events which followed it. The Communists threw their support behind the "Vargasista" candidates, Jucelino Kubitschek and João Goulart, nominees for President and Vice President of the Republic, respectively.

With the victory of the Kubitschek-Goulart ticket, there was strong sentiment both in the Army and among some civilian politicians against permitting them to take office. In a move to forestall such resistance, the Chief of the General Staff, General Lott, led a *coup d'état* on November 11, which resulted in placing Senator Nereu Ramos temporarily in the Presidential Palace.

The Communists supported this *coup d'état*. They pictured the opponents of the Kubitschek-Goulart combination as "fascists" and "tools of the Yankee imperialists," and urged the new interim government to take strong measures against the "golpistas," while at the same time insisting that it should once again legalize the Communist Party.

At the end of 1956, then, the Communists remained an important factor in Brazil's political picture. Although they had declined in political influence from their peak in 1945-47, they continued to have considerable popular support, and had a tightly disciplined and seasoned organization such as they had not commanded when they were legal. They were one of the continent's most potent and potentially dangerous Communist organizations.

*Chapter VIII*

# Communism in the Río de la Plata Hinterland

## URUGUAY

DEMOCRACY AND COMMUNISM don't mix. Little Uruguay bears witness to this. Uruguay is a synonym for democracy and social progress in Latin America. Not only are civil liberties and representative government more firmly established there than in almost any other country in the hemisphere, but the country has a long, proud history of social legislation and free trade unionism.

Uruguay has had no really serious dictatorship during the twentieth century. Though President Gabriel Terra governed by strong-arm methods for a few years in the 1930's, he left most of the basic freedoms intact, and, furthermore, the Uruguayans are still deeply ashamed of this near approach to dictatorship.

Uruguay has had no successful revolution for two generations. The citizens of the little republic have become used to changing their government by ballots, not bullets. The Army has been kept small and unobtrusive, and government is firmly in the hands of the civilians.

The country has been not only democratic, but prosperous. A land of rolling hills sloping down to a coastal plain rich in agricultural soil and glittering sandy beaches, Uruguay has remained fundamentally a grazing country. However, in recent years there has developed an increasingly prosperous agriculture, and in the capital city of Montevideo there have grown up a wide variety of light manufacturing industries.

Following the lead of its most famous citizen, President José Batlle y Ordóñez (1903-07 and 1911-15), Uruguay early became well known for bold social experimentation. It took the lead among Latin American nations in enacting protective labor legislation, in establishing social security, in developing a public housing program, and in "yardstick" government operation of essential public services.

Progressive and democratic Uruguay has not provided very fertile soil for Communism, in spite of the fact that it is one of the few countries in the hemisphere where the Communist Party has never been illegal. Although for several years the little country was the center of Communist activities in Latin America, it was itself relatively little affected by these activities.

Uruguay is one of the two countries in Latin America in which the Socialist Party joined the Third International and changed its name to Partido Comunista. The Socialists had made considerable progress during World War I, winning two seats in parliament and gaining a good deal of influence in the labor movement, particularly in the Federación Obrera Marítima. It was particularly in the ranks of the Socialist maritime workers, led by Eugenio Gómez, that the Russian Revolution aroused widespread sympathy. When the Communist International came into existence in 1919, there was much sentiment among these workers for affiliation of their party with the new group.

The pro-Communist sentiment was opposed most strongly by the founder of the Socialist Party, Dr. Emilio Frugoni, one of its two members of the Chamber of Deputies. His opposition was intensified after the Comintern published its "Twenty-One Conditions," which all parties wishing to affiliate with the Third International had to fulfill.

A controversy raged for several months early in 1921 in the party's daily paper, *Justicia*, over the issue of international affiliation. For instance, on April 1, 1921, Frugoni published an article entitled "On the 21 Conditions," in which he expressed his sympathy with the left-wing sentiments of many in the Socialist Party, and said that if it were not for the Twenty-One Conditions, he would have favored affiliation with the Comintern as a gesture of solidarity with the Russian Revolution and as a repudiation of the rightist and nationalist trends in the world Socialist movement. However, he added, he did not think that the Uruguayan Socialist Party should accept these Conditions.

Eugenio Gómez, writing in *Justicia* the next day, answered Frugoni by saying that the Twenty-One Conditions were "indispensable to maintain the purity of the parties" joining the International. He added, "For this reason I believe that the party should approve the 21 Conditions. Thus all of the party will march on the true road to the emancipation of the proletariat."

This polemic was preparatory to the Party's regular convention, held in the middle of April, 1921. Two motions on the issue of international affiliation were presented to this Congress. The first simply stated that "the Congress ratifies its adhesion to the Communist International." The second ratified affiliation with the Comintern but refused to accept the Twenty-One Conditions. The final vote was 1007 in favor of unconditional affiliation to 110 for the opposing resolution. The Congress then went on to change the party's name to Partido Comunista.[1]

The dissidents withdrew to re-form the Partido Socialista, under Frugoni's leadership. There was a bitter fight for control of the old party's property, a struggle which was won by the Partido Comunista. Frugoni, meanwhile, resigned his seat in the Chamber of Deputies, since he could now no longer represent the party which had elected him.[2]

Since the Communists grew out of the trade union wing of the Socialist Party, it was natural that they should devote much of their time to the problems of the labor movement. They launched a trade union newspaper, *El Sindicato Rojo* (*The Red Trade Union*), and set about the task of building a Communist labor movement.

The principal trade union center at the time was the Federación Obrera Regional Uruguaya, under Anarchist control. However, many unions which were opposed to doctrinaire Anarchism had withdrawn from the F.O.R.U. and had established the Comité Pro Unidad Obrera (C.P.U.O.). The Communist-controlled Federación Obrera Marítima joined this C.P.U.O. in which, however, the Communists were a minority group. The control of the Comité was in the hands of trade unionists of Syndicalist persuasion.

The Communists violently attacked the majority group in the C.P.U.O. For instance, an article in *El Sindicato Rojo* in February, 1923, denounced "The Degeneration of Anarchosyndicalism." The Communists complained that their Syndicalist rivals were unworried by "the menace of a new war in Europe" and were leading the trade union movement down a blind alley.

The Communists were anxious that the new trade union central organization which the C.P.U.O. was seeking to establish should join the Red International of Labor Unions.*

The February, 1923, issue of *El Sindicato Rojo*, which published two proposed texts of the statutes of the new central labor organization to be set up by the C.P.U.O., indicated that the Communist-sponsored version provided for affiliation with the R.I.L.U. The Syndicalist proposal did not.

The R.I.L.U. itself sent a special message to the C.P.U.O. National Congress in September, 1923, over the signature of Heinrich Brandler. It denounced the other international trade union groups and said that it was sure that the Uruguayan workers, firmly united in this Congress, would decide to affiliate to the R.I.L.U.[3]

However, things did not turn out the way the Communists hoped. Of the 53 trade unions represented in the Congress, 32 opposed R.I.L.U. affiliation, while only 21 favored it. Since voting was on the basis of unions, not total membership, the proposition thus lost, though the Communists claimed that the pro-R.I.L.U. forces represented unions with

---

* A representative of the Anarchist F.O.R.U. who attended the 1922 Red International of Labor Unions World Congress was reported in the June 30, 1922, issue of the Socialist paper, *El Sol*, to have been denied admission because of his Anarchist proclivities.

2869 members and their opponents represented only 2354 union members.

Two and a half years later, the Communists claimed that there were 36 unions in the country which were "favorable to the R.I.L.U.," and that these had 3610 members. These included unions in the C.P.U.O.'s successor, the Unión Sindical Uruguaya, and several independent groups. The Communist-controlled unions included those of shoemakers and wood workers. They controlled the printing trades workers union until December, 1925, but lost it in that month.[4]

The Communists, though their unions were for the most part in the Unión Sindical Uruguaya, were hostile to the dominant element in the U.S.U. For its part, the U.S.U. leadership refused to cooperate with the Communists, who urged various joint demonstration campaigns, such as a "popular anti-militarist movement." Six months after the organization of the U.S.U. the April, 1924, issue of *El Sindicato Rojo* published an attack on the "new Anarchist" control of the organization and added that the U.S.U. executive had lost many opportunities to lead the workers militantly and to bring autonomous unions into the organization.

Communist efforts to capture the U.S.U. were blocked by that body's leadership, which expelled some Communist unions and refused to admit new Communist groups. In 1927 the Communists organized the Bloque de Unidad Obrera within the U.S.U. Its aims were stated to be "to combat the sectarianism and divisionism inside the U.S.U.; to transform the U.S.U. into a really class-conscious central labor organization; to propagate the principles and tactics of true revolutionary syndicalism. . . .

The U.S.U. leaders regarded the formation of the Bloque de Unidad Obrera as dual unionism and expelled all unions affiliated with it. Undaunted, the Communists claimed that more than half of the U.S.U. unions had followed them out of the Unión Sindical, and they set about to "reunite" the labor movement.[5]

In spite of their separation from the U.S.U., the Communists did not give up their attempts to woo the leaders of the Unión Sindical. When the R.I.L.U. launched its plans to organize a continental labor confederation, they invited the U.S.U. to participate, an invitation the U.S.U. leaders refused.[6]

In 1929 the Communists converted the Bloque into the Comité Pro Iniciativa Pro Congreso de Unidad Nacional, with the avowed purpose of establishing a new Communist-controlled central labor group. This move was in conformity with the general Third Period Communist "line" of establishing Communist-controlled labor confederations in every country.

The new Confederation was established in May of that year as the Confederación General del Trabajo del Uruguay. It claimed 14,500 dues-paying members, which the Communists maintained "is to say, almost all of the organized forces of the country." The C.G.T. unions included con-

struction workers, municipal employees, the old Federación Obrera Marítima, shoe workers, telephone workers, and various other groups.[7]

Within the C.G.T. there was a small group of Anarchosyndicalists who,
though sympathetic towards the Soviet Union, were still loyal to their
traditional "apoliticism." They opposed moves by the Communists to
use the C.G.T. as an electioneering vehicle for the Party and argued that
the Communist Party should not participate openly in deciding the policies
of the labor organization. When these problems were discussed in the
first "plenum" of the C.G.T., the Anarchosyndicalists were defeated by a
vote of 90-4.[8]

In the meanwhile the Communists had been active in other fields. The
Party carried on regular electioneering activity. When it joined the
Comintern it had two members of Congress, but one of these, Frugoni,
quit the Party and resigned his parliamentary seat, leaving the Communists with only one deputy. In the 1922 elections, the Communists received only 2900 votes, which was 1000 less than the Partido Socialista
had gotten in 1920. However, Communist deputy Celestino Mibelli was
re-elected, and four Communists were chosen members of the Montevideo
Departmental Assembly.[9]

The Communists participated in the 1926 presidential election. Their
candidate was Elias Sosa, a farmer whom they ran on a "workers' and
peasants'" ticket.[10] He received only 4000 votes, compared with the 4800
the Communists had received in congressional elections the year before,
but they consoled themselves with the thought, expressed in *La Correspondencia Sudamericana*, December 21, 1926, that "the 4000 votes we
received are 4000 secure and firm votes for our party."

The Communists were particularly active in organizing "anti-militarist"
activities. At the end of 1923 the Minister of Defense introduced in parliament a law for compulsory military service. The Communists reacted
violently against this. Mibelli opposed it in Congress, and outside the Communists organized a network of "anti-militarist committees." The Communists undoubtedly contributed to the success of the campaign against
this measure; finally the Minister withdrew the proposal.[11]

The Communists also established various "front" organizations. By
1928 they had: an Anti-Imperialist League; a branch of the Communists'
world-wide legal aid organization, the International Red Aid; and a Red
Sports Federation, which boasted 2000 members. There was also a Party
youth organization, the Liga de Juventudes Comunistas.

The Uruguayan Communists followed closely the various orders of
the Comintern with regard to Party organization. In the late 1920's they
undertook to reorganize the Party on a "nuclei basis," that is to say, on the
basis of factory and workshop organizations, rather than neighborhood
units. Late in 1928 it was reported that this reorganization was not pro-

ceeding satisfactorily, but that the Uruguayan Communists hoped to do better in the future.

The Uruguayan Communist leaders also tried to follow the Comintern's orders to increase the number of "workers" in the Party. *International Press Correspondence* reported on November 16, 1928, that 80 per cent of the members of the Party were manual workers, while 20 per cent were white-collar workers and peasants. In the following year the Uruguayan Party reported to the continental Communist congress that 90 per cent of the Party members were wage or salary workers.[12]

With the onslaught of the Great Depression, the Communists intensified their activities. In the Chamber of Deputies Communist representative Eugenio Gómez introduced a bill proposing the establishment of unemployment insurance which would give one peso a day to each unemployed worker. In Montevideo Communist city council member Leopoldo Sala proposed that the city also pay one peso a day to all unemployed, and that the prices of basic articles in the workers' budget be reduced and all taxes on the unemployed be removed.[13]

The Communists did not get along very well with President Gabriel Terra, who came into office in 1931. In February, 1932, the government closed down both the Party headquarters and the Communist newspaper, *Justicia*. The non-Communist papers maintained that this was done to head off a plot to overthrow the government, a charge which the Communists claimed was untrue.[14]

Early in 1933 President Terra carried out a bloodless *coup d'état*, suspending the Constitution and dissolving the Council of State which President Batlle had introduced fifteen years before to limit the powers of the presidency. At the same time Terra cracked down on the Communists. Many Communist leaders were arrested and jailed. Their homes were raided, and the Party's activities were seriously circumscribed.[15]

However, in spite of initial persecution by Terra, the Communist Party was never made illegal, and continued to hold public meetings. With the change in the Comintern's "line" from the Third Period to the Popular Front, the Communists attempted to join forces with other groups in opposition to the Terra regime. They participated in student demonstrations against Terra's proposal to abolish the autonomy of the University of Montevideo.

The May Day demonstration of 1936 brought together workers of various political shades. The Communists claimed that some 40,000 workers participated in this demonstration. Banners urging the formation of a Popular Front were prominent, as well as others demanding the freedom of Luiz Carlos Prestes and Rodolfo Ghioldi, who had been imprisoned in Brazil following the failure of the Communist-inspired November, 1935, revolt there.[16]

Support of the Spanish Republic in the Civil War of 1936-39 served as a rallying point for united efforts of all liberal and radical political elements in Uruguay. Francisco Pintos, the Communist historian, notes that this campaign

> sealed the unity of a powerful movement such as had never existed before. . . . Compact masses throughout the country, belonging to all of the democratic parties, workers, artisans, small merchants, and small industrialists joined this common effort. Montevideo was covered with a network of Committees for Aid to the Spanish Republic.[17]

Communist efforts to form a Popular Front were to no avail, however, and even the attempts to form a united trade union movement came to naught during this period. In later years this failure was attributed by the Communist leaders to weaknesses within their own Party. Thus Franscisco Pintos wrote:

> The internal situation in the Communist Party, its social composition in which the workers in basic industries did not predominate, the continuance in its ranks and even in its leadership of elements foreign to a true Communist Party, made difficult the application of a correct line suitable to national conditions at that moment.[18]

Certain it is that there was some dissension within the Party at this time. Pintos notes the existence in the Party of certain "Trotskyite" elements,[19] some of whom were expelled in 1937 when the Trotskyite Liga Obrera Revolucionaria was formed. Some Trotskyites had left the Party as early as 1929, and this new scission added to their ranks.*[20]

With the outbreak of World War II the Uruguayan Communists adopted the line of world-wide "opposition to imperialist war," vigorously denouncing the Allied cause. They organized a "Peace Congress" in Montevideo in 1940.[21] An example of the Communists' propaganda during this first part of the war is the following, taken from *Hambre en el Uruguay*, a pamphlet about labor conditions in the Uruguayan countryside, written by Eugenio Gómez and published by the Party in April, 1941:

> Each union and the whole working class, which is fighting for better wages, must combat the imperialist war. The imperialist war is throwing the workers on the battlefields to fight and die for the interests of their exploiters. . . . All of America is in danger. The North American Government is already virtually in the war. It is fighting to dominate the Latin American peoples by means of the Export-Import Bank and economic cartels. And it wishes to take us with it into the war. At the same time Nazi imperialism conspires with Herrera to prepare *coups d'état* in combination with the Nazis of Argentina and Uruguay, to turn our country over to German-Italian-Japanese imperialism. War menaces Uruguay. And those who are bringing this

---

* An even earlier split in the Party had been that of Celestino Mibelli, the Communists' first member of the Chamber of Deputies, who withdrew from the Party in the late 1920's. He seems to have withdrawn completely from politics thereafter.

war to us are the owners of the great firms which enslave our country: the railroads, the packing houses, the trolley car companies, the cement plant, the gas works, the construction company of the Río Negro. . . . Must we workers kill one another in the interest of these firms? . . .

The extent to which the Uruguayan Communists went in their opposition to the Allied war effort was pointed out in the New York Trotskyite weekly, *Labor Action*, of August 12, 1940, which disclosed that the principal Spanish-language Nazi periodical in that country was being printed on the presses belonging to *Unzer Freund*, the Communists' Yiddish-language newspaper. When this was brought to light, the Communists somewhat lamely explained that they had agreed "to print only that part" of the Nazi paper "which is not anti-Semitic."

The Communists' attitude towards the war made relations between them and other elements in the labor movement very difficult. The Socialists and other political groups operating in the trade unions were frankly pro-Ally. The Comité de Unidad y Organización Obrera, which was set up in 1941 to try to establish a united trade union movement, was violently torn between the pro-Ally group and the Communists, who wanted the Comité to go on record denouncing the war as an imperialist plot.[22]

The invasion of Russia brought an abrupt about-face in the Communists' attitude. They became the most passionate supporters of the Allied cause. Typical of their changed position was a pamphlet by Eugenio Gómez, *Unite the Uruguayan People to Defeat Nazi-Fascism*, issued a few weeks after the invasion of the Soviet Union. At one place in this pamphlet Gómez says:

> England and the Soviet Union have just signed a pact of great importance to all humanity, which everyone who struggles for progress and against barbarism applauds without reserve: England and the Soviet Union have promised not to sign a separate peace. Today, when these two great peoples, the Soviet and the English have promised to carry forward to victory the fight against the Nazi aggressor, today when Roosevelt has declared that he hopes for the triumph of the Soviet arms and is disposed to aid it, we must fight to unite Uruguay with this struggle. And since Uruguay itself is menaced, all of us who are enemies of Nazi-Fascism must unite and fight to the end.

This change in their position towards the war caused the Communists considerable embarrassment. Of course, they had suddenly to reverse their position in the Comité de Unidad y Organización Obrera. More serious was the fact that they had scheduled for July 1, 1941, a large mass meeting to denounce the war, which they had publicized weeks in advance. It was to be the culmination of a long "anti-war" campaign. They had quietly to cancel the meeting and hope the public would forget about it.

Still more embarrassing was the fact that they had scheduled for June 22 a one-day general strike by the unions under their control, as a protest against the war. With the invasion of the Soviet Union, the Communist Party executive was called together the evening of June 21; it was then announced that the work stoppage next day—which it was too late to cancel—would be a demonstration in favor of the Allies instead of against them.[23]

The lengths to which the Communists were willing to go in their prowar phase may be seen by their position on the issue of compulsory military service. Uruguay had never had conscription, since the people had a proper fear of the dangers to their democratic government inherent in a large military force. Nonetheless, during the war President Baldomir proposed that the country adopt a system of universal military service.

The Communists were among the few political groups to give unqualified support to this idea. Their attitude was shown in a pamphlet by Eugenio Gómez, *Servicio Militar Obligatorio*. In this Gómez declared:

> The problem is the defense of our independence, and for this it is necessary to create A LARGE NATIONAL ARMY, capable of repelling aggression, WITH COMPULSORY MILITARY SERVICE, which would bring into active service all men capable of bearing arms. Obligatory military service must therefore be the core of the national defense.

The Communists' shift made a united trade union movement possible for the first time. Trade unions controlled by the Communists and Socialists, as well as groups influenced by one or another of the larger parties, were brought together in the Unión General de Trabajadores, which was founded in 1942. The two principal political groups represented in the U.G.T. were the Communists and the Socialists. The Secretary General was a Communist, Enrique Rodríguez, who had formerly been head of the shoemakers' union. The principal Socialist leader in the Union was Juan A. Acuña, who occupied the post of Secretary of Social Affairs.

This new-found labor unity did not last for long. The first split in the U.G.T. occurred early in 1943, as a result of the Communists' insistence on subordinating all other considerations to the need for aiding the Allied cause. In December, 1942, a strike broke out in the packing houses, which represented the country's principal manufacturing industry, and were then supplying large quantities of meat to the Allied armies. The majority of the Executive Committee of the U.G.T., led by the Communists, denounced the walkout. Later Enrique Rodríguez explained in an interview with the author (October 10, 1946) the reasons for this action. He said that the war was at that time at its lowest ebb, for the Germans were at Stalingrad; the strike was part of an attempted *coup d'état* against the government; and there were Nazi agents mixed up in it.

The leaders of the strike denied these charges and claimed that the walkout was of a purely economic nature. In this they were supported by the Socialist members of the U.G.T. executive, who resigned in protest at the U.G.T. attitude towards the walkout. The Socialist-controlled unions soon withdrew from the U.G.T.[24]

A further small spit in the U.G.T. occurred in 1945, when the Communists apparently decided that they no longer needed window dressing in the form of trade unionists from other parties on the Executive Committee of the organization. At that time the Committee contained only three Communists, with three members of the Independent Nationalist Party, two of the Batllista Party, and one of the Baldomirista Party.

When the non-Communist members of the Executive Committee insisted on denouncing certain disruptive activities of Communist elements at a meeting which the U.G.T. had run to protest conditions in neighboring Paraguay, the Advisory Council of the U.G.T. was hurriedly called together. This body had the power to discipline members of the executive and was controlled by the Communists. It proceeded to expel Nicasio Zeballos Calzado, the leading Independent Nationalist member of the executive. The other non-Communist members then resigned in a body and were replaced by a Communist slate. From then on, the U.G.T. was a completely Communist body.[25]

In spite of these disaffections, the U.G.T. gained much force during the war. The labor movement expanded rapidly, and the U.G.T. profited most from this growth. By 1946 the organization claimed some 50,000 members and certainly controlled a considerable majority of the organized workers of Uruguay.

The year 1946 saw the high-water mark of Communist influence. Its rise during the five preceding years had been due principally to two factors. In the first place, the Communists had been, after June 21, 1941, the most vociferous supporters of the Allied cause, and public opinion in Uruguay, and particularly in Montevideo, where most of the Communist strength was centered, was strongly in favor of the Allies. The Communists were able to ride this wave of pro-Ally sentiment, which was inevitably pro-Russian sentiment in part. In Uruguay as in other countries the Communists did not hide, during this period, the fact that they were the local representatives of the "mighty Soviet Union."

The second thing which aided them was undoubtedly the development of the labor movement under conditions which found them largely in control of its most important organizations. Industries grew apace in Montevideo during the war years, a democratic government was in control, and it was possible for the new industrial workers to unionize. Furthermore, the country was prosperous, and the new labor organizations were more than usually successful in winning gains for their members—and generally without a violent struggle.

The upshot of this was not only a great growth in Communist strength in the labor movement, but a large increase in the Party's membership and voting power as well. For the first time the Communists made considerable headway in the countryside. Commenting on this to an Extraordinary Congress of the Party which met in August, 1941, Eugenio Gómez said: "Comrade Alvarez informed me that in one meeting, attended by 50 workers, 48 of them joined the Party. In another, attended by 28, all present signed application cards; in still a third, where there were 30 present, 28 joined, and so on."[26]

As the war progressed, the Uruguayan Communists adopted the universal Communist slogan of "National Union." In the 1942 elections they attempted to get all of the parties but the pro-Axis Herreristas to join in naming a presidential candidate. However, when they failed in this, they put up their own ticket, headed by Gómez for President and Julia Arévalo de Roche for Vice President.[27]

They gave unlimited backing to the pro-Allied administration of President Baldomir. Thus when the President temporarily assumed dictatorial powers on February 21, 1942, to amend the Constitution so as to eliminate a provision which gave the pro-Axis Herrerista Party half the members of the Senate, the Communists applauded his move. They issued a pamphlet, under Gómez's signature, entitled *What Happened on February 21?* to explain and defend the President's action.

The Communists made considerable headway among the Uruguayan electorate. In the 1942 congressional elections they tripled their previous poll, receiving 15,000 votes. This increase in Communist electoral strength continued for some time after the end of World War II. In the November, 1946, election, the Communists for the first time won a seat in the Senate, to which Julia Arévalo de Roche was elected. They also won five seats in the Chamber of Deputies in place of the three which they had had before. In all they polled about 33,000 votes, more than double what they had received in any other election.[28]

The tide turned against the Communists because of the Cold War and because the workers got tired of the Communists' practice of using their organizations for political purposes. As the global struggle between Communist Russia and the West developed, the great majority of the Uruguayan people were on the side of the West. The Communists, of course, made no secret of the fact that their loyalties lay with the Soviet Union.

The true position of the Communists was recognized by other working-class groups. For instance, the Socialist weekly, *El Sol*, editorialized in its edition of the first week of June, 1945:

In place of capital, Russia has made "political investments" in the world; the Communist Parties. If they are not as efficacious as the other for assuring political control over the American people, they are capable of being important factors for supporting the offensive and defensive measures taken by her against the other great power in the balance, the United States. And, as games of diversion, as tactical elements, the political position of the South American Communist Parties will automatically reflect the relations—the conflicts and the understandings—between the great powers.

The attitude of the Soviet Union towards small countries did not help the Uruguayan Communists in maintaining their popularity. Uruguay itself encountered this attitude when in April, 1945, the Soviet Minister protested to the Uruguayan Government against attacks on the Soviet Union in the Uruguayan press. The little country's Foreign Minister replied that Uruguay's free press could not be censored, and invited the Legation to sue any papers involved.[29]

The Communists' worst decline was in the labor movement. Numerous small unions left the U.G.T. Several important affiliates of the U.G.T. withdrew when their leaders quarreled with the Communist Party. The Textile Workers Union, headed by Héctor Rodríguez, onetime Communist Party member of the Chamber of Deputies, left the U.G.T. when Rodríguez was thrown out of the Party.

However, the Textile Workers Union did not join with the other non-Communist unions, and some non-Communist leaders were in fact doubtful about the sincerity of Rodríguez's quarrel with the Party. Rodríguez continued urging the "unity" of the labor movement, a unity which included the Communist-controlled unions.

More certain was the splitting away of the bus-drivers' unions from the U.G.T. Early in 1952 there was a violent struggle inside this group, a struggle won by the anti-Communists after one of their leaders had been slain. The unions then withdrew from the U.G.T. and resisted moves by the Communists to involve them in further political demonstrations. However, by the middle of 1954 the Communists seemed to be on their way back to control of the group.

Whatever caused the withdrawal of various unions from the U.G.T., that organization shrank from 50,000 members to perhaps 15,000 by the middle of 1954. An equally catastrophic decline occurred in the Communist vote. In the 1954 election the Communists lost their seat in the Senate and three of their five seats in the Chamber of Deputies.

One result of the severe defeat which the Communists suffered in the 1954 elections was the intensification of the factionalism which had been rampant inside the Party for several years. The principal victims of this were the founder of the Uruguayan Communist Party, Eugenio Gómez, and his son, Eugenio, Jr., both of whom were expelled from the Party late in 1955. Some months after their expulsion, the Gómezes proclaimed themselves Stalinists and attacked the attempt—concurred in by the Uruguayan Communists—to downgrade Stalin.

The Uruguayan Communists, even at the height of their influence, were never a major factor in Uruguay's politics. Even in 1946, they did not receive much more than 10 per cent of the total vote. The great majority of the voters of Uruguay have remained loyal to the traditional parties, the Partido Colorado and the Partido Nacional. The Communists have merely competed for the 10 to 15 per cent of the vote which has traditionally gone to the left-wing minority parties. When the Communists have gained, the Socialists have lost, and vice versa. The Communists have never had a close alliance with the government or with a major political party. No political group has felt the necessity for seeking the Communists' backing.

Because of the farsightedness of President José Batlle y Ordóñez, Uruguay has been spared both the tyrannies and the revolutionary movements which have plagued most Latin American countries. The conversion of Uruguay's society from one dominated by a landlord aristocracy to a modern democratic state, with a more or less balanced economy and a relatively high standard of living, was achieved by the succeeding Partido Colorado governments, which have been in power since the beginning of the twentieth century.*

Because others took the lead in bringing about social reforms and raising the standards of living of the masses, the Communists have not been very successful in capitalizing on the promise of such gains. If the future governments of Uruguay continue the progressive social policy of their predecessors, the Communists will never be able to make effective use of social issues in their drive to power. The principal area in which reform is still necessary is in the countryside where large landholding is still the rule and illiteracy and poverty are still distressingly acute problems.

Lacking social issues, the Communists have one other possible rallying cry—nationalism. Whether this is effective or not will depend very much on the actions of the United States. Uruguay, like all other Latin American countries, has become increasingly nationalistic in recent years. Because of the predominance of the United States in the hemisphere, Latin American nationalism tends to become anti-Yanquismo, opposition to the United States.

The Uruguayan Communists have dwelt most persistently on the nationalist theme, trying to paint the United States as responsible for everything which has gone wrong in the country since World War II. This

* Due to the peculiar electoral laws of Uruguay, it has been possible for the two major parties to split, while all of their factions have been able to make use of the banners of the Partido Colorado and the Partido Nacional. Since the days of President Batlle the dominant faction in the Partido Colorado and the nation as a whole has been the Partido Colorado Batllista.

strident anti-Yanquismo was not as successful in the postwar period as the Communists might have wished, because the Uruguayan people were basically sympathetic with the United States and democracy, rather than with the Soviet Union and totalitarianism. Furthermore, faced with another kind of totalitarianism across the Río de la Plata, they counted on the United States for support in case of any disagreeable incidents with Perón. Finally, other parties, particularly the Socialists, have rallied support behind the nationalist banner, without agreeing to work with the Communists or becoming tools of the U.S.S.R.

In the mid-1950's Uruguay's democracy and social progress remained the country's best defense against Communism.

## PARAGUAY

The Communists have so far made but little progress in Paraguay. The country has been governed in recent years by a series of dictators, who have allowed little room for opposition of any kind, least of all that of the Communists. But Paraguay's recent dictators have not been unaware of social problems. They have carried on a comparatively enlightened agrarian reform, have enacted considerable labor legislation, and have laid the foundations for a social security system.

One of these dictators, Colonel Rafael Franco (in power in the late 1930's for one year), was able to arouse the imagination and support of the nation's humble folk, and to establish a political party which, in the rare periods of political liberty the country has enjoyed since, has been able to offer the Communists serious competition for leadership of the movement for social revolution in Paraguay.

In Paraguay the urban working class, to whom the Communists usually make their principal appeal, is still very small. The country remains one of the poorest and most underdeveloped of the South American nations, in spite of her possession of extremely fertile soil and considerable mineral resources.

The reasons for this backwardness are to be found in Paraguay's turbulent history. During colonial times, the country was the scene of bitter struggles between the Jesuits, whose missionary colonies contained several hundred thousand Indians, and the descendants of Spanish settlers, eager to enslave the Jesuits protégés. During its first sixty years of independence, Paraguay was ruled by three of the most authoritarian and picturesque tyrants in the history of the continent. Dr. Francia, Carlos Antonio López, and the latter's son, Francisco Solano López.

The last of these dictators involved the country in a war with its three neighbors, Argentina, Brazil, and Uruguay, which lasted five years and was not concluded until virtually all of the adult male population of Paraguay had been destroyed. In the 1930's, after two generations of respite and reconstruction, the country was again engaged in a disastrous war, this time with Bolivia over the desolate Chaco region. From this conflict, Paraguay has not yet recovered.

Most Paraguayans, of all social classes, have in their veins the blood of both of Guaraní Indians and their Spanish conquerors. The great majority are peasants, living on subsistence farms. Recent governments have been carrying out a program of agrarian reform, which has sought to provide all those Paraguayans who desire it with enough land to grow their own food and a small money crop. It does not seem likely, even under a regime which gave the Communists complete freedom to carry on their propaganda and organizing activities, that the Stalinists would be able to make much headway among this class of small peasants.

It is probable that greater susceptibility to Communist propaganda would be found among workers for the foreign companies which exploit the country's forest resources. These laborers are hired at small wages to spend months in the forest areas gathering the valuable tanning extract, *quebracho*, or the famous Paraguayan tea, *yerba maté*. Until recently they were treated in the most oppressive fashion, and although conditions among them are reported to have improved considerably in late years, the kind of social-national appeal at which the Communists are experts would undoubtedly achieve a degree of success among them.

The urban working class is confined largely to Asunción and a handful of provincial cities and towns. There a few manufacturing industries have been established—textile manufacturers, industries processing the country's raw materials, the construction trades. The workers employed by these industries, in addition to the railroaders and those employed in the very important river transport industry, make up the sum total of "organizable" workers.

Trade unionism began among the maritime workers even before World War I. From then until the middle 1920's the leadership of the organized workers was in the hands of the Anarchists. The Paraguayan Anarchists, like those of other Latin American countries, were influenced by the Russian Revolution, and many were very sympathetic to it during its first years.

At the same time, a group of young intellectuals, led by Odilio Barthe, declared themselves to be Communists. Ibarola, who represented the Paraguayan Communist Party at the Sixth Congress of the Communist International in 1928, was reported by *International Press Correspondence*, October 25, 1928, as saying that "the Communist Party has successfully held a number of meetings." A few months later a member of the Paraguayan Communist Party described it as being "numerically weak" and added that it "has not so far been able to convert itself into a mass organization, but its influence is becoming constantly greater among the masses of workers and peasants of the country.[30]

The Communists were anxious to get the Paraguayan labor movement to affiliate with the Red International of Labor Unions and to participate in the continental trade union congress which they organized in Montevideo in May, 1929. There were two central labor organizations in the country at this time, the Unión Obrera del Paraguay and the Centro Obrero Regional. Both were more or less of Anarchist orientation, and the former was the more important of the two, having the Liga de Obreros Marítimos, the country's largest trade union, in its ranks.[31]

The Unión Obrera issued a proclamation late in 1928, published in the Communists' Latin American labor paper, *El Trabajador Latino Americano*, on December 31, 1928, which, in view of the threat of a war between Paraguay and Bolivia over the Chaco, urged the summoning of a continental labor congress to work against such a war. It ended: "We await, above all, the actions of the international organizations such as the International Federation of Trade Unions, the Red International of Labor Unions, and the Committee for the Latin American Trade Union Confederation." The last-named was the organizing committee for the Communists' continental labor congress.

Late in 1928 Daniel Villalba, Secretary of the Liga Marítima and Francisco Gaona, a Communist and Secretary of Organization of the Railroad Workers Federation, visited Montevideo, apparently to discuss the forthcoming Communist continental labor congress. However, in spite of these exploratory conversations, no major Paraguayan labor group joined the Confederación Sindical Latino Americana when it was established in Montevideo the following May.

The Communists were particularly bitter about the failure of the Liga de Obreros Marítimos to join the C.S.L.A. *El Trabajador Latino Americano* in its issue of February, 1932, attacked Daniel Villalba, head of the union, as a "traitor" and a "fascist unionist," and claimed that the refusal of Villalba and the union leadership to join the Communist organization ran counter to the wishes of the Liga's membership.

As a result of this, the Communists organized their own trade union group, in conformity with the general Third Period policy of the Comintern of establishing purely Communist central labor groups in each country. They named their organization the Comité Sindical de Unidad Clasista. It claimed influence among the railroad workers, as well as the bricklayers and some other craft unions.[32]

The Communists opposed the Chaco War with Bolivia and suffered severely for this. Party leaders, including Obdulio Barthe, were jailed in Asunción. Oscar Creydt and Marcos Kaner, a leading Communist trade unionist, were arrested in Argentina and then were turned over to the Paraguayan government.[33]

However, in spite of these measures, the Communist Party apparently continued underground activities. It was reported by the Comintern's

*International Press Correspondence*, March 9, 1934, to have held its first "national conference" late in 1933 or early in 1934. The same periodical reported on February 9, 1935, that

> the best elements in the anarcho-syndicalist and petty-bourgeois movements have gone over to the Communist Party. Communist groups are being formed not only on the Argentine frontier, but also in the interior of Paraguay. In the last few months a number of youth groups against war have been formed. The Communist Party also issues propaganda material in the language of the Guaraní Indians, and its literature reaches the front and is read by the soldiers.

Once the Chaco War was over, Paraguay was in a state of ferment. Paraguay's war losses had been heavy, although the country had "won" the conflict. The returning soldiers were not willing to go back to the status quo ante bellum. There was widespread feeling that Paraguay's social, economic, and political institutions should be brought up to date.

Colonel Rafael Franco, one of the heroes of the war against Bolivia, took the lead in the movement to crystallize this sentiment. Calling on the Army to support him, he rose in revolt, and was proclaimed Provisional President of Paraguay.

The Franco regime was exceedingly controversial at the time. It was greeted abroad as "totalitarian" and even "fascist." It took drastic measures against the old regime, and all political parties were "temporarily" outlawed. A law providing for government recognition and support of trade unionism was decreed. The government outlined a program for expropriation of large landholdings and their division among veterans of the Chaco War.

The Franco regime lasted little more than a year. It was finally ousted by elements of the Army who were alienated by Franco's jailing of General Estigarribia, Commander-in-chief of the Paraguayan Army during the war. However, in spite of its short duration, the Franco regime was able to arouse widespread support among the workers and younger intellectuals, as well as among the junior officers of the Army. On the basis of this support, Colonel Franco organized in exile a political party, named Febrerista after the month in which Franco had seized power.

The Febreristas immediately became the principal competitors of the Communists for the support of those elements in the Paraguayan population who wanted a social revolution. During the Franco administration the Confederación de Trabajadores del Paraguay had been organized under the control of the Communists, though the followers of Franco were their chief rivals in the Confederación.

During a large part of the regime of President Higinio Morínigo, which lasted for most of the 1940's, both the Communists and Febreristas were illegal. In 1943, the Communists, following the international Communist "line," proposed the formation of a National Union of all of the opposition parties. The Political Commission of the Party published the following statement in the May 14, 1943, issue of *Unidad Paraguaya*, a periodical for the anti-Morinigo exiles in Buenos Aires:

> The time is critical, but perspectives are opening for the development of a growing Unión Nacional. There is still time effectively to unify all Paraguayans—civilians and military men who are for constitutional normalcy—in defense of the Fatherland and of democracy. There are favorable conditions for joint action, and the gravity of events teaches us that there is no time to lose. All patriots should take their positions in this situation and join in declarations of concrete common action, unifying all the partisan forces of national independence and liberty. . . .
>
> We will organize immediately full discussions on the program of unity and we will form a Committee of National Union in defense of public liberties for a general amnesty, civil and military, for the strictest collaboration with the United Nations and against the corporative reform of the Constitution.

Those Communists who remained in Paraguay received rough treatment from the government of Morinigo. Among those reported by the New York *Daily Worker* of May 23, 1943, as being imprisoned, were Augusto Cañete, General Secretary of the Party, who was kept six months in a concentration camp in the Chaco, and Cirilo Aguayo, Communist maritime leader, who had been a Paraguayan delegate to the founding congress of the Confederación de Trabajadores de América Latina in Mexico in 1938.

On November 15, 1944, President Morinigo announced his intention of allowing all political parties, including the Communist Party, to organize legally. He also announced his intention of allowing free organization of the labor movement. This offer was accepted by the Consejo Obrero Nacional, which had been organized as the spokesman for the Confederación de Trabajadores del Paraguay after the latter had been declared illegal in 1941,[34] and the Consejo immediately began to operate openly.

However, this truce did not last very long, and by the end of 1945 the Communists and other opposition elements were again in difficulties with the Morinigo regime. Among others, Bernardo Leiva, who had been Paraguayan delegate to the C.T.A.L. conference in Cali, Colombia, in December, 1944, spent some time in a concentration camp in the Chaco.[35]

In 1946 another truce was arranged between Morinigo and the opposition. Members of the Liberal and Febrerista parties entered the Morinigo cabinet, and the Communist Party and the labor movement were again allowed to organize more or less freely.

During the few months during which this truce existed, the Communists gained considerable influence, adding several thousand to their membership. This increase in Communist power brought reaction, particularly from the Catholic Church. Communist leaders Oscar Creydt and Obdulio Barthe attempted to head off religious opposition by a visit to the Auxiliary Archbishop of Asunción to declare that they had no intention of harming the Church.[36]

As a result of the activities of all of the political parties in trade union affairs during these few months of freedom, the Consejo Obrero was split. The Communists continued to control the Consejo, which represented only part of the organized workers. Each of the other parties—Partido Colorado, Partido.Liberal, and Febreristas—had its own central labor organization.

The end of the political truce came early in 1947 with the outbreak of a civil war, backed by the Liberals, Febreristas, and Communists, and led by Colonel Franco. The rebels lost. The victor was the Colorado Party, which has controlled the government since that time.

The Communists have been illegal since this revolt. They have been severely persecuted by the succeeding Colorado Party governments, and although in mid-1955 they were generally credited with retaining some influence among the city workers, they were given little opportunity to show it legally. Although some Communists undoubtedly held posts in the unions belonging to the Confederación Paraguaya del Trabajo, established in 1951 under the patronage of the government of President Chaves, they had to be careful not to be too obvious about pressing the Party "line," or they were certain to lose their union positions and perhaps go to jail. Thus, the Paraguayan Communist Party has remained a factor of secondary importance in the political life of the republic.

## Chapter IX

# The Stalinists of the Pampas—Argentina

THE ARGENTINE COMMUNISTS pride themselves on the fact that their Party was a founding member of the Communist International. The Argentine Communist Party was established in January, 1918, as the Partido Socialista Internacionalista. Its creation was the outcome of a division of opinion which had existed for several years in the ranks of the Socialist Party of Argentina.

A left wing had begun to develop within the Socialist Party even before World War I. On a theoretical plane, the Argentine left-wing Socialists opposed the moderate "revisionist" ideas of the German Socialist Eduard Bernstein, which had much currency in the Argentine Socialist ranks.[1] On a more practical plane, the left wing attacked what it claimed was the party's excessive concentration on parliamentary activity and denounced the party's trade union policy of refusing to cooperate with more radical political groups in the labor movement.[2]

The left wing was particularly powerful in the ranks of the Socialist Youth, which was founded in 1912 and was generally more radical than the older group in the party. However, the Left also had the support of a sizable number within adult party organizations.[3]

The struggle between the two factions came to a head over two issues: the Socialist Party's attitude towards the first World War and its attitude towards the Russian Revolution. The war issue was bitterly disputed. The Socialist members of Congress were consistently in favor of aiding the Allies. A large section of the party—those who later formed the Partido Socialista Internacionalista claimed a majority at this time—supported a policy of strict neutrality. These issues were fought out in a series of party congresses and conferences during the war.[4]

The Partido Socialista Internacionalista, in a proclamation to the Socialist parties of the world issued soon after its establishment, summed up its attitude on the war question thus:

> The Socialist Party, by approving the capitalist war, completely estranged itself from the Socialists who, amidst the horrors of the

conflagration, are working indefatigably in Europe and the United States for permanent peace through Socialism in conformity with the resolutions of the Socialist Congresses of Stuttgart, Copenhagen, and Basle, confirmed by the recent Zimmerwald and Kienthal Congresses.[5]

The left wing differed violently with the Socialist Party leadership on the Bolshevik Revolution in Russia. Their stand was defended thus:

> ... to make more patent the absolute divorce of the Socialist Party from Socialism, the official organ of the party, in commenting on the Maximalists (Bolsheviks), called them "the worst enemies of the Russian revolution" as though the rise to power of the first genuine Socialist government in history was a thing to be deplored. When an aggregation which calls itself Socialist condemns a people which proposes to bring about world peace, to overthrow the capitalist system and supplant it with the longed-for Socialist Industrial Republic ... can it honorably keep on displaying the Socialist label?
> ... The Russian Maximalists, heroic vanguard of international Socialism, have laid the foundation of a new humanity, the redeemed humanity of the future, without castes or social privileges, without wars and without tyrants. ... Stimulated by the red dawn that sheds its first glorious radiance in Europe, let us be united in our work, let us all cooperate in it. ...[6]

In April, 1917, the Third Extraordinary Congress of the Socialist Party was held in Buenos Aires. There a resolution introduced by delegates Ferlini, Penelón, and Muzio was passed repudiating the pro-Ally actions of the party's members of Congress. However, the right wing remained in control of the party's machinery.

In the face of this resolution, the party's members of Congress presented their collective resignation and a referendum of the party membership was held to determine whether or not their resignations should be accepted. The result was a victory for the party's representatives in Congress and for the right wing.

In September, 1917, the Socialist parliamentarians voted in favor of breaking off diplomatic relations with Germany. This gave rise to the formation of the "Committee for the Defense of the Resolution of the Third Extraordinary Congress" by the left wing. The Committee was set up by Victorio Codovilla, Rodolfo Schmidt, José F. Grosso, Carlos Pascali, Juan Greco, César Ferlini, and Arturo Blanco. Among the signers of a manifesto issued by this Committee were Juan Ferlini, José F. Penelón, Rodolfo Ghioldi, Ricardo Cantoni, Concilio Tomeo, Pablo López, Miguel Contreras, González Mellén, Luis Miranda, and Carlos Caltaaris.[7]

When the Committee was ordered by the party's Executive Committee to dissolve, the left wing refused. As a result, its members were expelled from the Socialist Party; they were soon joined by a centrist group which had hitherto tried to maintain peace in the party.

The Socialist dissidents assembled on January 5-6, 1918, to form the Partido Socialista Internacionalista. The delegates present claimed to represent 766 party members, mainly from the city of Buenos Aires, the province of Buenos Aires, and the province of Córdoba. In the months that followed other groups left or were expelled from the older party and joined the new one.[8] By the beginning of 1919 the latter claimed 33 branches and 1400 members and was issuing a weekly newspaper, *La Internacional.*[9]

The founding congress of the Partido Socialista Internacionalista adopted a resolution expressing its solidarity with the Russian Bolshevik regime; approved a declaration of principles and the statutes of the party; and issued a manifesto to the people of Argentina, announcing the party's foundation. It also established the obligation of each party member to belong to the appropriate labor union in his trade or occupation.[10]

Although the Partido Socialista Internacionalista sent a message to all the parties which had been affiliated to the pre-war Socialist International, announcing its own existence and urging that it, and not the old Socialist Party, be recognized as the Argentine member of the International, the sympathies of the new group were not with the old-line Socialist parties. On the contrary, though the Partido Socialista Internacionalista was not itself able to send a delegate to the founding Congress of the Communist International which met in Moscow in March, 1919, it empowered the delegate of the Italian Socialist Party to be its spokesman. It is for this reason that the Argentine Communists regard their Party as a founding member of the Communist International.[11]

In December, 1920, the First Extraordinary Congress of the Partido Socialista Internacionalista adopted the name Partido Comunista, in conformity with the decisions of the Second Congress of the Comintern, which had issued the famous Twenty-One Conditions to which all parties wishing to belong to the Communist International had to conform. The two principal speakers endorsing the decisions of the Comintern and urging the change in name were Victorio Codovilla and Rodolfo Ghioldi. The decision was taken unanimously.[12]

The Communists were very active in the trade union movement. At the time of the "Tragic Week" in January, 1919, when troops fired on a group of strikers and precipitated a veritable labor uprising in Buenos Aires, the party issued a manifesto saying in part: "The Partido Socialista Internacionalista protests energetically against the massacre of the Vasena workers. It urges the solidarity of all labor with these workers to aid them to triumph. . . ."[13]

The Communists did not have any distinctive trade union groups of their own at this time. The labor movement was split into two central organizations, both called Federación Obrera Regional Argentina. The larger, which was generally known as the F.O.R.A. of the Ninth Congress, was of Syndicalist orientation, though the Socialists also had considerable influence in it. It was within this group that the Communists principally operated. The other F.O.R.A., "of the Fifth Congress," was doctrinaire Anarchist in its political ideology.

During the first several years the Communists urged the unification of the two labor organizations. Subsequently, with the formation of the Red International of Labor Unions in 1921, the Communists sought to have both F.O.R.A.'s affiliate with the new Communist international trade union center.

The issue of affiliation with the Red International of Labor Unions was hotly fought out in both the Argentine central labor bodies. The Anarchist F.O.R.A. of the Fifth Congress was initially very sympathetic to the new Communist International and applied for admission to the R.I.L.U. It was recognized by the R.I.L.U. for a time as an affiliate with "consultative" status. However, the Argentine Anarchists, like their brothers in Spain, soon became disillusioned with the Bolsheviks, and when the Anarchosyndicalist International Working Men's Association was formed in 1922, the F.O.R.A. of the Fifth Congress severed its connections with the R.I.L.U. and joined the I.W.M.A.[14]

In the meanwhile, in the F.O.R.A. of the Ninth Congress there appeared among the delegates to the organization's Convention of December, 1918, a faction which was decidedly sympathetic to the Bolshevik Revolution. The Congress as a whole sent greetings to the Russian and German revolutionaries.[15] However, during the next year the F.O.R.A. of the Ninth Congress applied for admission to and was accepted in the reorganized International Federation of Trade Unions (I.F.T.U.), which in Europe was in general dominated by the Socialists.[16]

In 1922 the F.O.R.A. IX was reorganized as the Unión Sindical Argentina, which, minus the railroad workers' organizations which refused to join the reconstituted group, was weaker than the F.O.R.A. IX. There was bitter discussion within the U.S.A. concerning whether it should affiliate with the Red International of Labor Unions. The Communists had considerable influence in the organization, but by no means enough to win support for affiliation.

In October, 1922, the U.S.A. had a referendum to decide whether to send delegates to the R.I.L.U. or to the new Anarchosyndicalist I.W.M.A., both of which were soon to hold congresses. Although 5167 members voted to send delegates only to the R.I.L.U. congress, and 3879 voted to send delegates to both congresses, 17,557 were against being represented at either meeting.[17]

The Communists, in spite of their failure to make any serious imprint on the major central labor groups during the 1920's, had some minor union strength. When the shop crafts, maintenance of way employees, and all train personnel except locomotive engineers, firemen, and wipers were united in Unión Ferroviaria in 1922, the Communists led a dissident group among these workers who established the Federación de Sindicatos Ferroviarios. Rodolfo Ghioldi reported in 1926 that this group had about 2000 members, compared with some 60,000 in the Unión Ferroviaria. In the F.S.F. Congress of that same year, Ghioldi reported that 70 per cent of the delegates were Communists, 25 per cent were Anarchists.[18]

The Communists also had some influence among the metallurgical and construction workers. They had controlled unions in these industries since the end of World War I.[19]

The Communist Party carried on electoral activity in the 1920's. As early as October, 1918, it elected its first City Councilman in Buenos Aires, Juan Ferlini.[20] Then in November, 1920, it elected another Councilman, José F. Penelón, in the capital city.[21] In the provinces, too, the Communists made some headway, electing a member of the provincial legislature in Córdoba,[22] and receiving 3114 votes in the province of Mendoza in the 1920 election, compared with the 2000 received by the Socialist Party.[23]

However, the Communists remained a very small group. They reported to the Fourth Congress of the Communist International in 1922 that they had 3500 members, according to *International Press Correspondence* of December 14, 1922. They sent two delegates to this Congress.

In 1921 the Communists received a new group of recruits from the Socialist Party. Many in the older party favored adherence of that group to the Third International. They were led by the party's Senator, Enrique del Valle Iberlucca. When the pro-Comintern faction was defeated in the party's 1920 Congress, del Valle Iberlucca submitted to the party decision, but most of the other members of the group did not.

The dissident Socialists were organized in a group which they called "Claridad." They called a congress of their group to determine what to do. Among the important delegates to this meeting were Silvano Santander, who in later years was to become a deputy for and outstanding leader of the Radical Party; and Orestes Ghioldi, brother of Rodolfo.* The majority favored unconditional affiliation with the Communist Party; a minority favored affiliation only after negotiations with the Communists.[24]

Orestes Ghioldi, a few months after joining the Communist Party, took the lead in forming the Communist youth group, the Juventud Comunista. It immediately began to publish a periodical entitled *Juventud* and a children's paper, *Compañerito*. Youth work was from then on an important part of the Party's activities.[25]

In these early years the Party was wracked with factionalism. During

* A third brother, Américo, remained in the Socialist Party, was a Socialist member of the Chamber of Deputies, and Secretary General of the Socialist Party and in the early 1950's served as the Socialists' official representative-in-exile in Montevideo.

the 1920's there were at least five important intra-party struggles, three of them involving a left-wing opposition group, the other two against right-wing elements.

The first dissident group was a left-wing element headed by a certain Karothy, who in the first months of the Party's existence took the position, widely held in various nascent Communist Parties at that time, that the new organization should not participate in "bourgeois elections." This faction was expelled without any serious repercussions.

The second rebel group was also of a leftist nature. It appeared during the Party's Third Congress in April, 1920, and was led by Tomás Velles of Rosario. These dissidents revived a controversial issue which had been a favorite of Socialist Party left wings in many countries before World War I. Velles proposed that the Party give up its "immediate demands" and issue a program which consisted only of four or five points "which will be sufficiently advanced to differentiate us clearly from the other political parties of the country."

This fight continued for several years. The left-wing group had a majority in the Party's third, fourth, fifth, and sixth Congresses, held in April, 1920, January, 1922, July, 1923, and July, 1924, and prevented the passage of any program of "immediate demands." However, in spite of supporting the ideological position of the Left, each of these meetings but the last elected a right-wing majority to the Executive Committee of the Party.

The leaders of the right-wing group included Victorio Codovilla, Rodolfo and Orestes Ghioldi, and José Penelón, while the left-wing included Cayetano Oriolo, a leading Communist trade unionist, Miguel Contreras, leader of the Party in Córdoba, and Tomás Velles.

Between the Sixth and Seventh Congresses of the Party, the right wing threw all of its energies into the factional battle. Although at the Sixth Congress the left wing had for the first time captured control of the Executive Committee, the right wing soon negated this by winning over one or two of those elected by the leftists. The next move was for Codovilla to take the matter up with the Communist International, to several of whose early Congresses he had been a delegate. He went to a meeting of the Enlarged Executive Committee of the Comintern at which "the Argentine Question" was taken up exhaustively. The result was an Open Letter from the Comintern to the Argentine Party, supporting the position of the right wing and expressing amazement that "a party of Marxist origin such as yours has been able to maintain during a long period a program of action—which should be based on concrete points which reflect the immediate necessities of the masses—which is a simple declaration. . . ."

Upon Codovilla's return from the Comintern meeting the Argentine Communist Party held an Enlarged Executive Committee meeting, presided over by Rodolfo Ghioldi. After Codovilla's report on the Comintern session, the Executive Committee decided to accept the Comintern's Open Letter, and to demand that all the leftists also accept this Letter. Codovilla, the two Ghioldis, Penelón, and others then went to the base units of the Party to urge the acceptance of the position of the Executive Committee.

When an element among the leftists tried to organize against this onslaught of the right-wing majority in the Executive Committee, and began issuing an organ called *La Chispa* under the editorship of Cayetano Oriolo, they were disciplined. Oriolo and other left-wing leaders were expelled from the Party. Other leftists then relapsed into silence.

Only after this extensive preparation did the right-wing majority summon the Seventh Congress of the Party in December, 1925. This Congress for the first time adopted an extensive program of immediate demands. However, in spite of the pre-Congress purge, the controversy in the Seventh Congress was a violent one, and one of the right-wing leaders, Enrique Muller, was assassinated while making a speech from the Congress platform.

The expelled leftists organized a rival party, the Partido Comunista Obrero. It published *La Chispa* as its official paper and continued in existence until 1930. Some of its members became Trotskyites, while others entered the Socialist Party. Some of the leftist leaders stayed in the Partido Comunista, including Miguel Contreras, who was in the early 1950's the Party's principal spokesman in the province of Córdoba.

The Communist International itself came to the support of the official Party after this split. Humbert-Droz, in the name of the Central Committee of the Comintern, sent the following wire, dated May 26, 1926 (according to *La Correspondencia Sudamericana* of June 15, 1926), to the Argentine Party: "Committee resolved meeting today to send your party letter solidarity for bolshevizing action your Central Committee confirmed in recent Congress, and to denounce so-called Partido Comunista Obrero as organization enemy of Communism."

Meanwhile the Party leadership was also faced with a right-wing opposition group. For a short while, particularly during the Communists' Fourth Congress, this group for tactical reasons allied itself with the extreme Left, but it was eliminated from the Party even before the conclusion of the struggle with the Left.

The leaders of this right-wing group included Silvano Santander, Luis Koiffmann, and various others. They established a factional organization within the Party and issued a periodical *Nueva Orden*, which urged the liquidation of the Communist Party and its members' re-entry into the ranks of the Socialist Party. They apparently got in contact with the Socialist leaders, and Dr. Juan B. Justo, leader of the Socialists, published an editorial in the Socialist paper, *La Vanguardia,* inviting the Communists to return and suggesting that problems of liquidation of Communist property could be settled "by common agreement."

The majority of the Communist Executive Committee then gave the right wing an ultimatum. They must either dissolve their faction and cease publishing their periodical, or be expelled from the Party. When the right wing refused to comply, they were thrown out. They apparently did not organize a rival party. Some of them returned to the Socialist Party; Silvano Santander joined the Radical Party.

The final scission in the Communist Party in the 1920's was led by José Penelón, who was the Party's second member of the Buenos Aires City Council. Penelón had worked closely with Codovilla, Ghioldi, and other dominant elements in the Party until after his second election to the City Council in 1927. He tended thereafter to concentrate most of his attention on municipal problems. He also opposed various policies of the Party leadership, including the factional activities of the Communists in the labor movement, and the Party policy which was summed up in the slogan, "No wheat, no meat, nothing for the enemies of the Soviet Union." Penelón argued that a conscientious enforcement of this latter policy would bring hunger and misery to the workers and peasants of Argentina without contributing anything very concrete to the Soviet Union.

For some time in 1928 an associate of Penelón, Romo, was Secretary of the Party, while Codovilla and Rodolfo Ghioldi were absent in Europe, attending the Anti-Imperialist Congress in Brussels and the Sixth Congress of the Comintern in Moscow. However, even before the return of Codovilla and Ghioldi, the Penelón group found themselves in the minority and withdrew to form a new Partido Comunista de la Región Argentina.

With the return of Codovilla and Ghioldi, a number of the followers of Penelón withdrew from the dissident party, including some of its principal figures, among them Pedro Chiarante and Luis Sommi. Nevertheless, the Partido Comunista de la Región Argentina has continued down to the present time, changing its name first to Partido Comunista de la República Argentina, and later to Partido Concentración Obrera.\*

The Penelón split was the last serious division within the ranks of the Argentine Communist Party. When Codovilla and Ghioldi returned from Europe, the Argentine Communists may be said to have entered the Stalinist period; open factionalism within the Party was ended, and the organization became "monolithic." Although individuals quit the Party from time to time, for almost twenty years they were not able to take any sizable portion of the Party with them, and the control of Codovilla and Ghioldi over the Party apparatus was complete.[26]

---

\* The Partido Concentración Obrera was still in existence in 1956, though it was of absolutely no importance in the country's political life.

With the beginning of the Third Period, the Argentine Communists entered into a campaign to establish their own central labor organization. They first made a final attempt to capture the Unión Sindical Argentina, or at least to get it to affiliate with the Red International of Labor Unions.

Representatives of the Unión Sindical Argentina attended the Moscow celebration of the Tenth Anniversary of the Bolshevik Revolution in November, 1927, and signed a document calling for the formation of a new revolutionary confederation of Latin American trade unions.[27] However, when it came to planning the details of the founding congress of this regional trade union confederation, the U.S.A. delegates differed with their Communist confreres. The U.S.A. officials insisted that the new group not be subordinated to any political ideology and that it deal exclusively with trade union and not political questions.[28]

Although the U.S.A. Executive Committee submitted the question of participation in the continental labor congress to a referendum of its membership, with the recommendation that attendance be approved, the U.S.A. finally decided against it.[29] The editor of the U.S.A.'s journal, *Bandera Proletaria* (as reported by *El Trabajador Latino Americano* of February 28-March 15, 1929), explained the final decision by pointing out that the agenda of the congress included many political items to the discussion of which the U.S.A. was opposed. The U.S.A. leaders also objected to the representation at the congress of small Communist trade union groups on an equal footing with the U.S.A. The basic issue, apparently, was the obvious Communist control which was to be exercised over the continental congress.[30]

By the time the founding congress of the Confederación Sindical Latino Americana (C.S.L.A.) was held in May, 1929, the Comintern had already entered into its Third Period and its policy of dual unionism. As a result, the Congress adopted a resolution on the Argentine situation, endorsing the formation of a Committee of Revolutionary Unions, as proposed by the Argentine Communist-controlled unions there represented—a local central labor body from Córdoba and small unions of electric power, textile, and metallurgical workers. An Argentine Communist, Miguel Contreras, was elected Secretary General of the C.S.L.A.[31]

After the failure to win over the Unión Sindical Argentina, the Communists established their own central labor organization, which they called the Comité de Unidad Clasista. This group undertook various organizing activities. It established the Sindicato Obrero de la Industria de la Carne and sought to organize the packing-house workers into this new union. Late in 1931 it called a general strike at the Frigorífico River Plate, which was reported in *El Trabajador Latino Americano* of January-February, 1932. This walkout won two months' dismissal pay for certain workers who had been discharged by the company.

The Communists also undertook to organize the oil workers in Comodoro Rivadavia, in the southern part of the province of Buenos Aires. It established the Unión General de Obreros Petroleros, with a charter membership of three hundred workers. Within a few months 800 of the 7780 oil workers had joined. The new union called several strikes, all of which were suppressed by the government.[32]

A congress of the Comité de Unidad Clasista held in Rosario in October, 1932, was reported in *El Trabajador Latino Americano* of November, 1932. There were 77 delegations reported as representing 54 unions and 20 "revolutionary oppositions"—Communist groups inside other unions. The Congress claimed to represent 20,000 workers. Some idea of what kind of workers belonged to the Communist trade union organizations can be obtained from a meeting called late in 1931 to protest a decision of the Uriburu dictatorship to deport "alien undesirables." The meeting was attended by representatives from the Packinghouse Workers Federation and unions of tailors, waiters, metal workers, textile workers, cooks and pastry cooks, painters, carpenters, and Communist minority groups among maritime and port workers, railroaders, and others.[33]

The Argentine Communists suffered severely at the hands of the Uribura dictatorship, which seized power in a military *coup d'état* in September, 1930. Of the four hundred political prisoners which the military regime put in Villa Devoto penitentiary, two hundred were reported to have been Communists. The Communists organized protest demonstrations against the regime in various parts of the country.

The Uriburu regime organized the infamous Special Section of the Federal Police, the principal purpose of which was to persecute the Communists. Hundreds of them were jailed, including many of the Party's principal leaders—Miguel Contreras, Héctor P. Agosti, Juan J. Real, Orestes Ghioldi, and Paulino González Alberdi. Many Communist leaders were sent to the notorious concentration camps which the regime established in the southern part of the country.

During this period the Communist Party was illegal, and as its official history says:

> The directing bodies of the Party, rather than being elected were named in secret meetings. Its press was frequently suppressed. In 1932 its daily, *Bandera Roja*, was suppressed by the Justo government [which came after Uriburu], so the Party began issuing another paper, *Mundo Obrero*, which was likewise suppressed. It was succeeded by *Frente Unico*, which in its turn was closed by the government.

The Party's weekly paper, *La Internacional*, continued to appear more or less regularly. However, in December, 1934, Héctor P. Agosti was indicted for "incitation to rebellion," and "disrespect for the president of the republic" in his capacity as editor of both *Bandera Roja* and *La Internacional*.[34]

In spite of the fact that the Uriburu regime concentrated much of its police efforts on the Communists, other groups, including the Anarchists, the Socialists, and even the members of the country's majority party, the Radicals, were also severely persecuted. This seemed to have no effect on the Argentine Communist Party of the Third Period, in the direction of making it more sympathetic toward other opposition groups.

Typical of the Communists' attitude are their assailing the followers of the mildly left-wing Radical, ex-President Hipólito Irigoyen, as "equal to German Nazis," their description of liberal Senator Lisandro de la Torre as "an agent of Anglo-Yanqui imperialism," and their picturing of Juan B. Justo, founder of the Socialist Party, as "an ally of reaction."[35]

The position of the Communists with regard to the Radicals was particularly sectarian during this period. Writing years later, with the wisdom of hindsight and a different Party "line," the Communist Party's official historian summed up the situation during the early 1930's as follows:

> The majority of the leaders of the Party did not understand that the role of the working class and of its vanguard party consisted not of fighting against Radicalism as such, but on the contrary of seeking an alliance with the Radicals.
>
> If they had taken this into account, it would have been possible to impede the consolidation of the Uriburu-Justo governments, to oust the oligarchy from power, and to form a democratic government which would continue the liberal and progressive tradition of Irigoyen.[36]

Actually, of course, the Argentine Communist Party, in concentrating most of its attacks on the Radicals rather than on the military dictatorship, was following the world-wide policy of isolation from the democratic Left which was the hallmark of the Comintern's Third Period. Whoever had been in executive positions in the Argentine Party at that time would have been expected by the Communist International to follow more or less the policy which the Party did in fact pursue.

With the change in the Comintern's strategy, the position of the Argentine Communist Party also changed. This alteration was epitomized by the dissolution of the sectarian Communist unions and the entry of their members into the unions of the Confederación General del Trabajo, which had been formed in 1930 as a result of a merger of the syndicalist U.S.A. and the Socialist-controlled Confederación Obrera Argentina. Reporting on this in the October-November, 1935, issue of *El Trabajador Latino Americano*, Miguel Contreras wrote that Communist-controlled union groups in Buenos Aires, Santa Fé, Córdoba, Tucumán, Chaco, Misiones, and Patagonia were "pushing with all their enthusiasm for unity in each industry, and they are calling on the workers of all tendencies to enter the C.G.T. to make it the single great central body of the Argentine proletariat."

The more conciliatory attitude of the Communists was accompanied by a leftward movement in the Socialist Party. A group of younger members of that party, led by Benito Marianetti, Ernesto Guidici, and others, urged a Popular Front including both the Socalist and Communist parties. When their point of view was defeated, the dissidents withdrew from or were thrown out of the party. The majority of the rebels formed the Partido Socialista Obrero, which continued in existence until the middle 1940's, when it was dissolved and most of the remaining members joined the Communist Party. Soon afterwards Marianetti became a member of the Communist Party Central Committee.[37]

A few of the Socialist dissidents entered the Communist Party as soon as they were thrown out of the Socialist Party. The most important figure in this group was Ernesto Guidici. The majority of the members of the Partido Socialista Obrero, however, probably returned to the Socialist Party in the late 1930's.[38] A few members of the P.S.O. became Trotsky- ites.[39]

The campaign for a Popular Front did not bear fruit in Argentina, in the sense of resulting in the formation of a broad political alliance of the Left. The Radical Party had a traditional policy of maintaining com- plete independence of all other political groups, and the Socialist Party, with the exception of its left wing, was not receptive to the Popular Front idea.

However, there were occasions when various parties of the Left took joint action. Perhaps the most important of these was the May Day dem- onstration in 1936 at which the speakers were José Domenech, Secretary General of the C.G.T., for that organization, Arturo Frondizi for the Radical Party, Paulino González Alberdi for the Communists, Senator Mario Bravo for the Socialists, and Senator Lisandro de la Torre for the Progressive Democratic Party.[40]

One of the issues in the late 1930's which made it easy for the Com- munist Party to have more or less friendly relations with other left-wing parties was the Spanish Civil War, around which it centered many of its activities. The Communists played a key role in the formation of the Federación de Organismos de Ayuda a la República Española, an Argen- tine equivalent of the North American Committee to Aid Spanish Democ- racy, and they seem to have exercised somewhat the same kind of control over the F.O.A.R.E. that their United States comrades had over the North American Committee.[41]

In pursuance of the Popular Front "line" the Communists threw their support in the 1937 presidential elections to the Radical Party candidate, ex-President Marcelo T. de Alvear. They launched the slogan "All Power to de Alvear."

However, when de Alvear was defeated by Dr. Roberto Ortiz, the Communists showed their versatility by attempting to make their peace with the new chief executive. After noting that Ortiz was supported largely by the pro-British big landowners and the politicians most closely associated with them, the Party argued that

> Ortiz is not yet a fascist, and does not propose to establish a fascist regime. All facts permit us to speculate that he will try to impede the development of fascism, and will attempt to establish a moderate democratic government which, in Argentine conditions, will be a positive act, as compared with the present administration.[42]

The Communists gained a good deal of ground in the trade unions after the dissolution of their Comité de Unidad Clasista and the entrance of Communist trade unionists into the C.G.T. and its constituent unions. The most powerful union under Communist control was the Federación Nacional de la Construcción, established in 1937, which by the time of the 1943 Revolution claimed 100,000 members, of whom 62,000 were reported as being dues-payers. This union claimed to be the second largest in the country. Another important Communist union was the Federación Nacional Metalúrgica, which claimed 40,000 members in 1943, with 20,-000 of them paying dues.[43] The Communists also controlled the small Packinghouse Workers Federation and the Federación Obrera Textil, which they had established in the late 1920's and which grew considerably during the 1930's.[44] Various unions of woodworkers were united during this period, and the unified organization also fell under Communist influence.[45]

The Communist Party enjoyed a semi-legal status at this time, and its publications were allowed to appear more or less freely. On October 28, 1936, the first issue of *Orientación,* the Party's official weekly, was published. In January, 1940, the Party began publishing a daily newspaper, *La Hora.*[46]

From time to time the Communists expelled more or less important figures among their leaders. "Deviationists" of Right and Left fell by the wayside. On the one hand, there were those who sought to go even farther than the Party "line" concerning Popular Front policies. They sought to abolish the Party cells inside the unions, so to remove this cause of dissension and distrust between Communists and trade unionists of other parties. This element was quashed and its principal figures were expelled from the Party at a meeting of the Central Committee in July, 1938.[47] Some time earlier there had been expelled a left-wing element, which objected to the Popular Front "line," led by Jacobo Cosín, member of the Party's Executive Committee and the Party's Secretary General in the city of Buenos Aires.[48]

Unlike the situation in the previous decade, these expulsions did not result in splitting the Party. The control of Codovilla and Rodolfo Ghioldi over the Party was firm, in spite of the fact that they were both out of the country during most of these years. Ghioldi had been sent as a Comintern agent to help organize the National Liberation Alliance in Brazil. When a revolution called by this Alliance failed in November, 1935, Ghioldi was arrested and sentenced to five years in jail.

Codovilla was one of the principal Comintern agents in Republican Spain during the Civil War. There he gave orders to the local Communist Party and helped to organize that Party's effort to substitute a Communist dictatorship for the democratic Republican government.[49] He returned to Argentina early in 1941, after visiting and carrying out purges in a number of the Latin American Communist Parties.

Codovilla exercised control over the Argentine Communists even when he was away in Europe. Rodolfo Puiggros, himself a leading Communist during this period, has described how Codovilla sent a special agent "with full powers" to Argentina in 1938 to carry out the purge of the right-wing elements which we have already noted.[50]

In Argentina, as everywhere else, the Popular Front period came to a sudden halt with the Stalin-Hitler Pact of August, 1939. During the period of the Pact, the Argentine Communists, like their brothers in other countries, were isolated from other elements in the political arena. Interestingly enough, this period is hardly mentioned in the Party's official history, written in 1947. The Party took a strong position against the Allies. This attitude was characterized by a headline in the Communist weekly, *Orientación*, on May 1, 1941, which read "For Peace, Against the Imperialist War!"[51]

Relations between the Communists and other parties of the Left were very bad at that time, notably in the trade union movement. The important Unión Obrera Textil, which had been largely controlled by the Communists but which contained a strong Socialist minority, was split early in 1941 over the issue of the Communists' "anti-war" attitude. The Socialists formed a rival organization with the same name, which claimed by the time of the 1943 Revolution to have a majority of the textile workers in its ranks.[52]

However, once the Soviet Union entered the war, the Communists took a violently pro-Ally position and made a fresh right-about-face in internal political affairs, seeking to align themselves with anyone who would proclaim himself in favor of the Allied cause in and against the pro-Axis "neutrality" of the government of President Ramón S. Castillo. The Communists summed up their attitude during this second part of World War II in a declaration "All those who are in favor of the triumph of the U.S.S.R. and its allies are our friends. All those who are against them, openly or covertly, are our enemies."[53]

The Communists were active in raising funds to send food and equipment to the U.S.S.R. They established for this purpose the Confederación Democrática de Ayuda, which consisted of 280 local groups throughout the country. They also took a leading part in setting up the Comisión Sanitaria to send medical supplies to the Allies, and the Junta de la Victoria, the principal pro-Ally women's organization.[54]

In the field of national politics, the Party sought an alliance with the pro-democratic parties. In preparation for the presidential election scheduled for late 1943, the Party proposed the organization of a Unión Democrática to unite the opposition against President Castillo's nominee. In February, 1943, a committee of the Communist Party met with a similar group from the Radical Party to lay plans for a united campaign at the end of the year. The police surrounded the Casa Radical, where the meeting was in progress, and arrested the Communist leaders, Victorio Codovilla, Rodolfo Ghioldi, Juan José Real, Arnedo Alvarez, and Florindo Moretti. Several of these were sent to jail.[55]

In spite of their appeals for unity in the political field, the Communists contributed directly to splitting the C.G.T., the country's principal central labor organization, in December, 1942. This incident, again, is not mentioned in the Party's history, published in 1947. The Communists had for some years been gaining strength in the C.G.T., and in the early 1940's they allied themselves with a group of Socialist trade union leaders dissatisfied with the domination of the C.G.T. by the Railroad Workers unions. The principal figures among these dissident Socialists were Francisco Pérez Leirós, of the Municipal Workers Union, and Angel Borlenghi, head of the Commercial Employees Federation.

The struggle between the two groups—the Unión Ferroviaria leaders and their allies, and the dissident Socialists and Communists—came to a head in the C.G.T.'s Congress in December, 1942. The first group renamed C.G.T. Secretary General José Domenech, a railroad worker, as candidate for the top post in the Confederation. The dissident Socialist-Communist coalition named Francisco Pérez Leirós as Secretary General.

There was a serious dispute concerning who was really elected, and the C.G.T. was split. Because Domenech had been nominated on list #1, at the Congress, the C.G.T. of which he was Secretary General became known as C.G.T.#1, that of Pérez Leirós, C.G.T.#2. The two rival organizations continued to exist until some time after the Revolution of June 4, 1943.[56]

An epoch in the history of Argentina and in the history of the Argentine Communist Party ceased with the Army *coup d'état* of June 4, 1943. This successful uprising brought to an end the negotiations for the nomination of an anti-Castillo candidate in the 1943 elections, because the elections were cancelled. It had a profound effect on the trade unions, finally resulting in their rank and file and most of their leaders going over to the banner of Colonel Juan Domingo Perón, and thus cutting away the mass base not only of the Communist Party, but the Socialist Party as well. It brought to a sudden halt the rise of Communist influence inside and outside the trade union movement.

One of the first acts of the military dictatorship was to attack the trade unions. C.G.T.#2 was outlawed on the grounds that it was "Communist-controlled." Several of the country's principal unions, including the two railroad-workers organizations, Unión Ferroviaria and La Fraternidad, and Pérez Leirós' Municipal Workers Union, were "intervened" by the government—that is, their elected officials were ousted, and military men were put in charge of them.

Soon afterwards Colonel Perón was named Secretary of Labor and Social Welfare. In this post he made a determined attempt to rally the workers to his personal standard. He decreed a social security system. He helped workers such as those in the packinghouses, and the sugar cane fields of Tucumán Province, who had never been able to organize strong unions because of employer and government opposition, to establish their own trade unions. He forced employers to accept collective contracts which granted their workers sizable wage increases, resulting for a few years in a very definite advance in the real wage of the average Argentine urban worker.

At the same time, Perón and the regime saw to it that those unions and union leaders who would not cooperate with him were deprived of their positions of leadership. When the union leaders were obstinate, rival unions were established and were given government recognition, under a new decree-law* issued by Perón according to which a union had to have legal recognition in order to be able to engage in collective bargaining. Thus the old organizations were effectively driven out of business.

The Communists suffered severely under these measures. The government organized rivals to the Communist-controlled construction and metallurgical workers unions, and before long most of the workers in these industries had deserted the Communist organizations. The Packinghouse Workers Federation was virtually taken away from the Communists by the Peronistas, and the Communists were left with little or nothing in that field.

At the same time, the Communist union leaders who would not bow to Perón were summarily dealt with by the government. Hundreds of Communist leaders, both inside and outside the trade unions, were jailed or sent to concentration camps, and a considerable number met death at the hands of the Peronistas.

The Communist Party, which had enjoyed a semi-legal status during the late 1930's and early 1940's, was driven far underground. Its publications were suppressed; its leaders were jailed or exiled. Codovilla took

---

* A decree-law is an administrative decree with force of law, the favorite legal instrument of legislature-less dictatorships in Latin America.

refuge in Chile; Rodolfo Ghioldi went to Montevideo, Uruguay, where he played a leading part in the activities of the exiled oppositionists.[57] Codovilla was not allowed to go into exile until a great deal of pressure had been put on the Argentine government from outside. President Roosevelt personally intervened in his behalf, after Earl Browder, then head of the United States Communist Party, had sought his aid in the matter.[58]

The Communist Party during this period followed an unyielding policy of opposition to the military government and to Perón. It could not have done otherwise. Very soon after the military regime seized power, it became clear that its leaders favored the Axis in World War II. This made any compromise between the Communists and the government inconceivable.

The Communist position was made clear upon the occasion of the first Packinghouse Workers' strike in September, 1943. One of the strikers' demands was for the return of José Peter, leader of the Communist-controlled Federation of Packinghouse Workers, who had been sent to a concentration camp in the southern part of the country. Bowing to this request, Colonel Perón personally sent an airplane to bring Peter back to Buenos Aires.

Instead of showing any softening toward the government for having released him, Peter used the opportunity of an address to the strikers not only to urge them to return to work, on the grounds that the strike was hurting the Allied war effort, but to denounce the government as of "Nazi" inspiration.

Peter's exhortations resulted in the workers returning to their jobs, but a few days later they were in the streets again. This time, the strike was under entirely different leadership, and the influence of the Communists among the packinghouse workers was at an end, at least for the time being. The Peter incident was repeated many times over throughout the country.[59]

The Communists' relations with the other opposition parties during this period were very close. Abroad the Communists played a leading part in the group known as "Patria Libre," formed by exiles in Montevideo. Both at home and abroad they urged a united front of all opposition groups to fight the dictatorship. Thus Codovilla, in an *Open Letter to Anti-Fascist Patriots* said: "For the people to triumph, it is necessary to forge trade union unity and bring together all democratic forces opposed to the dictatorship under a Single Command."

Early in 1945 the military regime began to take steps to make itself constitutional. Elections were promised, the government agreed to allow the political parties to reorganize, certain restrictions on freedom of the press were lifted, exiles were invited to return, and political prisoners were freed.

At that point, Perón, who was obviously the regime's candidate for the presidency, was anxious to rally the support of one or more of the already existing political parties. Overtures were made to the Communist Party, among others. Several members of the Party's high command had an interview with Admiral Tessaire, one of Perón's right-hand men. Tessaire said frankly that Perón was a candidate for the presidency and that the regime lacked popular support. He offered the Communists a "deal," saying that the government would be willing to restore the legality of the Communist Party for the first time in twenty years, would allow it to re-establish a legal press, and in other ways would extend its backing to the Party, if, in return, the Communists would support the regime.[60]

This offer was made in March, 1945. The second World War was drawing to a close, but was not yet ended. The Communists were at the height of their "anti-fascist" period, and in view of the still pronouncedly pro-German orientation of the military dictatorship, they could not yet make any compromise with the regime.

The Communists therefore rejected the offer made to them by Tessaire. In spite of this fact, the government went through with much of what it had promised. When the other parties were restored to legality, the Communists, too, were allowed to register their organization as a legal political party. On April 7, 1945, they began publishing a legal weekly, *El Patriota*, which continued to appear until the re-establishment in November of the same year of the Communist daily, *La Hora*. Meanwhile, in August, the regular weekly periodical of the party, *Orientación*, resumed publication.[61]

During the presidential election, in which Perón was named chief executive, the Communists supported the candidate of the Unión Democrática, Tamborini. The parties which joined in the Unión Democrática did not put up joint tickets for members of Congress. The Communists put up their own candidates, running in some areas on a joint ticket with the small Progressive Democratic Party.

The Communist candidates for Deputy did better than they had ever done before. In the Federal Capital, the city of Buenos Aires, Rodolfo Ghioldi, running for Senator, received 67,577 votes, and Arnedo Alvarez, the Party's candidate for Deputy, received 67,955 votes. In the province of Santa Fé, the joint lists of Communists and Progressive Democrats gave the Communist candidate for Deputy 71,239 votes. In the province of Buenos Aires, the Communist candidates for Deputy received about 25,000 votes. In the province of Mendoza the Communists elected three provincial Deputies. Throughout the country the Communists received enough votes to have given them 12 Deputies in the national Chamber, had the seats been apportioned according to the total number of votes throughout the nation.[62] They thus showed themselves to be a national party of consequence, a force to be reckoned with in the national picture.

After the election of Perón as President, the Communists altered their position toward the government and toward the Peronista movement.

For one thing, they disbanded the anti-Peronista trade union movement which they had maintained during the first three years of the dictatorship. Victorio Codovilla explained this to the author, on November 19, 1946, by saying that the Communists had maintained separate unions before the election because they were sure that Perón would be defeated. However, the elections had indicated that the majority of the workers were with Perón, and if the Communists were going to influence the workers, they would have to go where the workers were, in the Peronista unions. Furthermore, Codovilla added, if the Communists had not gone into the Peronista unions, the real Nazis on the fringe of the Peronista movement —the Alianza Libertadora Nacionalista—would no doubt have become important in the unions on which they were concentrating much of their energies.

Within the Peronista unions the Communists were very active. The official Party published a monthly newspaper addressed particularly to the members of the trade union movement, which received wide circulation among the workers. They were able to build up important cadres in many of the dictator's unions. Of course, under conditions of a dictatorship it is hard to verify such things, but the author had the impression in the course of visits to Argentina in 1952, 1953, and 1954, that the Communists were the principal non-Peronista group within the Peronista trade unions.

There were various reasons for this Communist strength in the unions. First of all, the Communists did not suffer persecution from the government after 1946 to the degree that, for instance, the Socialists did. In any case, the Communists were better equipped than were the Socialists for the kind of underground political guerrilla warfare which was necessary in the Peronista trade unions. Moreover, their financial resources for work among the union members were infinitely greater.

Another reason for the strength of the Communists in the Peronista unions was the absence until 1954 of any organized trade union activity on the part of the Radical Party. It was not until Arturo Frondizi captured control of the Radicals, the principal opposition party, that an organized attempt was made by this party to build up disciplined Radical groups in the unions. The beginning of this campaign by the followers of Frondizi brought an immediate violent attack from the Communists.[63]

Soon after the election of Perón the Communists split, in the first serious scission in twenty years. The leader of the dissidents was Politburo member Rodolfo Puiggros, who had conducted the Party's negotiations with Admiral Tessaire the year before. He and his group felt that the Communist Party should come out frankly in favor of the Peronista Revolution and try to influence it from within.

The Puiggros group compared its position vis-à-vis Perón to that of the Chinese Communists in the early days of the Kuomintang. In the time of Sun Yat Sen the Communists accepted the objectives and doctrines of Sun Yat Sen, but they wanted to go far beyond these. So they cooperated with Sun Yat Sen for the fulfillment of the immediate program he had set forth, which would lay the groundwork for their own work thereafter. They also fought the reactionaries in the Kuomintang camp. In a similar manner, said the Puiggros group, they were for cooperating with Perón, with whose program of Economic Independence, Political Sovereignty, and Social Justice, they were in agreement, though they wanted to go further. So, too, they would oppose the "reactionaries" within the Peronista camp.

Furthermore, the Puiggros people argued that Perón was an empiricist, with no particular theory of his own. They believed that if they worked closely with Perón, they could provide the philosophical and ideological basis for his regime.[64]

The Movimiento Obrero Comunista formed by the Puiggros group operated openly. It published a periodical, *Clase Obrera*, which bore the subtitle *Por el Frente Nacional Anti-imperialista. Clase Obrera* was full of references to Perón as "El Conductor de la revolución nacional emancipadora." It carried on tireless polemics with the official Communist Party.

That the Puiggros group still had some standing with the international Communist movement is indicated by the fact that Puiggros made a special trip to La Paz, Bolivia, in November, 1952, to meet Vicente Lombardo Toledano, principal leader of the Communist trade union apparatus in Latin America.[65] A further indication is the attitude which the periodicals of this group took with regard to the Soviet Union. The attitude was consistently friendly, and citations of Stalin—as the fount of all given doctrine—were frequent.

The Puiggros group made some headway among those Communists who had been active in the labor movement. In 1952 Puiggros himself claimed that a majority of the trade union activists of the pre-1946 Communist Party were in his group.[66] Non-Communists gave members of the group credit for leadership of the January, 1951, strikes of the railroad workers, which were general throughout the country.[67]

The official Communist Party remained more or less a member of the Opposition, though other opposition groups lost all faith in the Communists, having no assurance as to the direction in which their "line" would take them. The Communist Party, despite its being in the Opposition, no longer was so violent in its attitude towards the Perón regime.

The change in attitude of the official Communists after the 1946 election was shown in a speech of Victorio Codovilla on June 1, 1946, when he said, among other things:

> All Argentines—natives and other inhabitants of the country—who are in accord with a program of social justice and national prosperity,

whether they are members of the parties which made up Unión Democrática or adherents of the parties which supported the candidacy of the president-elect, must unite in a strong National and Social Liberation Front of the Argentine people.[68]

This was a far cry from the abuse of "Peronazis" which the Communists had levelled against all Peronistas before and during the 1946 election campaign.

The position of "constructive opposition" taken by the Communists during the early part of the Perón administration brought the Party certain dividends, insofar as their press and public activities were not submitted to the same kind of persecution as those of other opposition groups. *La Hora*, the Communist daily paper, continued to publish while the periodicals of the Socialist, Radical, and Laborista parties were shut down. It was not until early in 1950 that *La Hora* was finally closed by the government.

The Party criticized various aspects of the Peronista regime. For instance, the Amplified Central Committee meeting of July, 1951, assailed the Peronista agrarian reform campaign as serving to extend the holdings of the large landholders rather than destroy them, attacked the "anticapitalist demagogy, and pseudo social justice" of the government, and characterized elections under the Peronista regime as "plebiscites of the fascist type."[69]

Only once, in 1952, did the Communist Party seem to shift its line to one of open and more or less complete support of the Peronista regime. At that time Victorio Codovilla was abroad, and Juan José Real was left in charge as interim Secretary General. Under his leadership, the Communist Party veered sharply towards support of Perón.

The most outspoken activities of the Communist Party in favor of Perón during this period revolved around the call by Perón for a "United Popular Front" of all Argentines behind his government. The Communists responded favorably. An unsigned editorial in the Party's magazine, *Nueva Era*, for March-June, 1952, said:

> . . . the Communist Party considers necessary and opportune the proposal of Perón to form a "United Popular Front" to impede a possible *coup d'état* of the oligarchs and Imperialists, and to defeat such a move if it be made.
>
> However, it is necessary to remember the fact that the large landowners and capitalists leagued with the Yankee imperialists are those who organize and finance *coups d'état* so as to defend their antinational interests based on the old economic and social structure of the country. Taking this into account, it is clear that it is necessary to take measures not only to impede and defeat a pro-Yanqui reactionary *coup d'état*, but to prevent its repetition. For this, there is no other way than to extirpate *the causes* which generate reactionary, oligar-

chical-imperialist *coups d'état* by carrying out an economic and social program which would liquidate the material basis for such movements and permit steps towards solving the problems of the agrarian revolution and anti-imperialism.

The Party, continued the policy indicated in this and other statements favoring rapprochement with Perón until the return of Codovilla from Europe. Those who opposed this trend, including Rodolfo Ghioldi, were disciplined, and rumors spread that Ghioldi was actually in danger of being expelled from the Party by Real.

However, with Codovilla's return from the Nineteenth Congress of the Communist Party of the Soviet Union, the Party went back to its old policy of opposition to the regime. In a long speech to the Central Committee of the Party, Codovilla violently took Real to task, denouncing his "deviationism." As a result, Real was removed from all positions of influence and sent back to the rank and file; while Ghioldi was relieved of all disciplinary measures which had been applied to him up to that time.[70]

Codovilla summed up the position of the Communist Party towards Peron, in his speech to the Central Committee:

> We say that, in spite of its anti-oligarchical and anti-imperialist declarations, the Peronista government has not resolved any of the fundamental problems of the agrarian and anti-imperialist revolution. What has been called the agrarian reform of the government . . . has done little . . . and the large landholdings have remained *fundamentally* untouched; the great foreign monopolies (packinghouses, electricity, etc.) continue in existence; the foreign firms have increased in quantity and size; the privileges of the large capitalists have not been touched, and the policy of the government was and is to conciliate the interests of capital and labor, though inclining in the direction of capital; the cost of living has risen; the "organized democracy" has turned out to be a corporate state of fascist type, even if it is labelled "social justice"; the "third position" has not kept the Peronista government from adapting the economy of the country and its foreign policy to the exigencies of Yanqui imperialism. . . .[71]

Thus the official Communist Party continued to maintain a policy of opposition to the Peronista regime, while another branch of Argentine Communism, the Movimiento Obrero Comunista, had a position of considerable influence in the Peronista movement.

The Communists played little or no role in the overthrow of Perón and the events surrounding it. They were not granted seats in the National Consultative Assembly which was established by the Lonardi government and continued by its successor under General Aramburu.

Both groups of Communists were hostile to the Aramburu government. They did not publicize their activities very widely, perhaps so as not to arouse retaliation on the part of the Provisional Government. However, they were exceedingly active among the trade unions, where they sought to gain leadership among the Peronistas, most of whose former leaders were in exile, under arrest, or were in hiding.

The Communists themselves suffered a certain amount of persecution at the hands of the Aramburu Government. Upon the occasion of a transit strike in Buenos Aires in the middle of May, many of the Communists were rounded up by the government. Some of the Communist leaders, including the head of their trade union general staff, Ruben Iscaro, were reported as being deported to concentration camps the Provisional Government established in Patagonia.

The Communists seemed destined to gain some support from among the Peronistas. Their chances were particularly good of recruiting the most fanatical followers of the former dictator, whose hatred for the Provisional Government was most intense.

## Chapter X

# Communism in the Shoestring Republic—Chile

THE COMMUNISTS OF CHILE have been a factor of importance in their country's politics longer and more consistently than have their comrades in any other country of Latin America. For over thirty years they have been an important element in the labor movement, and during much of this time they have been the principal political force among the country's workers.

The only period in their history during which the Communists have not enjoyed widespread support among the workers was when they were aced with another party which caught the imagination of the Chilean workingman. This was during the 1930's, when the Socialist Party was the chief spokesman for Chilean labor, controlled a majority of the trade unions, and was one of the country's foremost parties. Only with its splitting and the destruction of its influence were the Communists able to reassume the role of the principal workingmen's party.

The history of the Chilean Communist Party, particularly since 1939, presents the best example in Latin America of how a Communist Party, with a relatively small membership and only limited popular following, is able to wield wide influence for a long period of time. Its importance has been due largely to the Communists' rigid discipline, their ability to play upon popular prejudices and issues, and their versatility in creating and exploiting the inferiority complex from which all their rivals in the Chilean Left have suffered for more than a decade.

The Chilean Communist Party is one of the two Latin American Communist groups which had its origin in the affiliation of the nation's Socialist Party to the Communist International. The Partido Socialista Obrero, founded in 1912 by the labor journalist, Luis Emilio Recabarren, had already gained an important position on the country's political scene and had become the dominant factor in the trade union movement when in 1921 its Convention decided to join the Third International and change the party name to Partido Comunista.

The proposal to join the Comintern had been made originally at the

party's 1920 Convention by Recabarren. However, final action was postponed until the following year, at which time the party decided to accept
the Twenty-One Conditions laid down by the Comintern for admission.[1]

In contrast to the situation in Uruguay, where the Socialist Party's
decision to affiliate to the Comintern led to an important split in the party,
only one significant leader (Carlos Alberto Martínez) and no important
groups of members withdrew from the Partido Socialista Obrero Chileno
when it became the Partido Comunista. The delegates were unanimous in
ratifying affiliation to the Comintern. There were several important
leaders who would have preferred to keep the name Partido Socialista
Obrero, but Rodolfo Ghioldi, the Argentine Communist leader who was
the Comintern's representative at the Party Congress, made it clear that
the change in name was mandatory.[2]

In the election of 1920 the P.S.O. had placed two members in the
Chamber of Deputies, Recabarren and Luis Víctor Cruz. Recabarren was
not re-elected in 1923, at which time he was in the Soviet Union, though
another Communist was elected to take his place.

The Communists were particularly active in the trade union movement.
They controlled the Federación Obrera Chilena, which in the early 1920's
claimed 200,000 members. The F.O.Ch. was strong among the nitrate
miners in the country's northern deserts. It had resolved to join the Red
International of Labor Unions a week before the P.S.O. took the decision
to affiliate with the Comintern.

Recabarren went to the Soviet Union in 1922, to attend congresses of
the Comintern and the R.I.L.U. Returning in 1924, he gave a series of
lectures in which he praised the Soviet Union as "the country of the
future."

A few months after Recabarren's return from Europe, a military *coup
d'état* ousted President Arturo Alessandri, who had been elected as Chile's
first "middle-class" President in 1920, and opened a new chapter in Chilean
political life. During the first three years of his administration he had been
faced with a hostile Congress, which did its utmost to defeat his attempts
to bring about fundamental reforms in Chilean political life. Alessandri
had sponsored a Labor Code to enact needed social legislation and provide
legal recognition of the trade unions. He had sought to achieve the
separation of Church and State, and had urged the rewriting of the nation's constitution to strengthen the power of the chief executive, who had
been rendered virtually helpless in the hands of a fickle Congress under
an extreme version of the parliamentary system.

None of these measures had been enacted by Congress, and Alessandri
had been blocked at every step, in spite of the fact that he had widespread
popular support. Even after a pro-Alessandri Congress was elected, late in
1923, its members devoted their time to discussing a bill to raise their own
salaries, instead of passing the legislation urged by Alessandri.

This situation reached a crisis in September, 1924, when a group of young military officers demonstrated in the balconies of Congress, while its members were discussing the congressional salaries bill. When the officers were backed up by the leaders of the armed forces, President Alessandri called in the commanders of the Army and Navy and asked them what it was they wanted.

The officers presented Alessandri with a list of demands, most of which were included in the President's own program. According to General Juan Bennett, a member of the three-man military junta which ousted Alessandri a few days later, the officers included the President's demands so as to make their principal desire, an increase in their own pay, seem a little less unpatriotic.[3]

Alessandri accepted the military men's demands, on the condition that once they had been passed through Congress, the Army would retire to its barracks. However, when the military men did not relinquish political activity as promised, Alessandri resigned and was succeeded by a three-man military junta, which ruled the country until January, 1925.[4]

During this period of crisis the Communist Party took a wait-and-see attitude. It neither supported nor opposed the military regime. The Party continued its normal activities, since the revolutionaries did not interfere with freedom of speech and political life.

The most important event for the Communist Party during the few months the military junta ruled Chile was the suicide of Luis Emilio Recabarren. Why he killed himself is still a matter of controversy. At the time, the belief was widespread that Recabarren had been killed by the Junta, because they were afraid of his influence with the workers.[5] Some argued that Recabarren committed suicide because of his disillusionment with what he saw in the Soviet Union. However, Manuel Hidalgo, who succeeded Recabarren as chief of the Communist Party, has told the author (December 17, 1946) that the cause of Recabarren's death was his mental instability. A very moody man, he took his own life in a fit of despondency.*

Meanwhile the young Army officers who had made the September, 1924, Revolution were dissatisfied with the three senior military men whom they had installed in place of President Alessandri. As a result,

* The question of the Communists' relationship with Recabarren is one of the most intriguing in the history of the Chilean Communist Party. Although in recent years the Communists have taken Recabarren's name as a banner, and have attempted to monopolize his memory, they did not always do so.

During the Third Period, the Communists severely criticized Recabarren and the role he had played in the Party. The Report of the Party's 1933 Congress claimed that "it is evident that his ideology was that of a Liberal." It went on:

"He spoke of social revolution and never of workers' and peasants' revolution, he did not understand the role of imperialism, nor of the workers' and peasants' alliance. The C.P. was, according to him, the party of all the poor and not the party of a single class, the proletariat. He had great democratic illusions."

early in January, 1925, a military junta of young officers, led by Lieutenant Colonels Carlos Ibáñez and Marmaduque Grove, deposed the three-man government. They summoned President Alessandri back from Europe, and he arrived in Chile a few weeks later.

With his return from exile, Alessandri launched a nine-months period of drastic reforms. The principal achievement was the writing of a new Constitution. To draw up this document, President Alessandri named a commission of one hundred members, of whom six were members of the Communist Party. The Communist delegation was headed by Manuel Hidalgo, the new leader of the Party.

Hidalgo was an active member of the Constitutional Commission. He proposed a clause which would have suppressed private property in Chile. After long discussion a compromise was reached, which declared the sanctity of private property but said its continued existence would be conditional upon its contribution to the well-being of the country.[6]

Meanwhile the Communists were conducting a campaign throughout the country against governmental registration of trade unions. Legalization and registration of the unions were among the measures provided for in the legislation passed in September, 1924, but it was not until the reinstallation of Alessandri in January, 1925, that the government took active steps to have the unions register under the law.

The Communists feared that the registration of unions would result in their falling under the government's political control, thus undermining the position of the Communists, who until that time had dominated the labor movement. It was not until the middle 1930's that the Communists allowed unions under their control to seek government registration. In 1925 the Communists fought bitterly the activities of the government commissions sent out by Alessandri to encourage union registration throughout the country.

The Party not only opposed the union registration law, but most of the other measures which had been passed in September, 1924, and which Alessandri attempted to put into execution in 1925. It was particularly active in agitating against the two laws which established Social Security Funds for manual workers and white-collar workers.[7]

During this period the Party had a considerable press. It issued five daily newspapers, *Justicia, El Despertar de los Trabajadores, El Comunista, La Jornada Comunista,* and *La Defensa Obrera,* in various parts of the country. It also published several weekly newspapers and magazines.[8]

Soon Alessandri again fell victim to the military. Upon his return from Europe, he appointed Colonel Carlos Ibáñez as his Minister of War. It soon became obvious that Ibáñez had presidential ambitions, and in September, 1925, he forced the resignation of President Alessandri for a second time.

A presidential election succeeded the resignation of Alessandri. The candidate of all the parties except the Communists was Emiliano Figueroa Larraín. The Communists threw their support to José Santos Salas, who had been Minister of Health in Alessandri's 1925 Cabinet and had made a considerable name for himself, particularly among the workers. Although without any other party support, Santos Salas made a surprisingly strong run against the victorious Figueroa Larraín.

For the year and a half after the election of Figueroa Larraín in November, 1925, constitutional government passed through a serious crisis, with Colonel Ibáñez' power increasing as that of the President declined. The position of the Communists *vis-à-vis* the government became increasingly difficult during this period, though the Party made considerable electoral gains.

In the elections for Congress in 1926 the Communists succeeded in adding considerably to their parliamentary delegation. Manuel Hidalgo and Juan Carmona were elected to the Senate, while seven Communists were placed in the lower house.

Senator Manuel Hidalgo, the Party's principal leader, was a particularly vigorous opponent of Minister of War Carlos Ibáñez. When rumors spread that Ibáñez was plotting against President Figueroa Larraín, Hidalgo called a group of seven senators together and suggested the formation of the court martial to try Colonel Ibáñez and, if he was guilty, to have him executed. This move came to nothing, but it made Hidalgo and Ibáñez bitter enemies.

Soon afterward Ibáñez had a fracas in the Chamber of Deputies, where he was defending his own policies, and as a result of this incident, President Figueroa resigned. That same day ten senators and deputies were jailed, among them Hidalgo. He thought that he was going to be shot, in revenge for his recommendation of the same treatment for Ibáñez. However, he was deported, first to Ecuador and then to Peru. There he made contact with Chilean sailors, who belonged to the Anarchosyndicalist I.W.W., and they smuggled him back into Chile three months after he was deported.[9]

As a result of President Figueroa's resignation, another presidential election was necessary. Carlos Ibáñez was the principal candidate. His only opponent was Elias Laferte, Communist Secretary General of the Federación Obrera Chilena.

Laferte had been arrested on February 22, 1927, when Carlos Ibáñez became Minister of Interior, and had been deported to the Pacific island of Más Afuera, a bleak prison colony a thousand miles off the Chilean coast. On June 10 a Chilean man-of-war arrived with a new boatload of prisoners, and Laferte found out for the first time that he had been a candidate for the presidency when officers of the ship came ashore to see the man who had dared to run against Ibáñez.[10]

For the next four years Carlos Ibáñez was the dictatorial President of

Chile. Not only the Communists, but all the other political parties, had a difficult time. Leaders of all parties were deported or jailed, including ex-President Alessandri, Colonel Marmaduque Grove, who had been Ibáñez' associate in the 1924 and 1925 revolutionary movements, ex-President Emilio Figueroa, and others.

The Communists suffered particularly heavily. The 1927-31 period marked the growth of the legally recognized trade unions at the expense of the non-recognized unions under Communist and Anarchist control. By the end of the Ibáñez regime, most of the country's unions belonged to the Confederación Nacional de Sindicatos Legales, and a new type of Socialist-oriented leadership had appeared in these organizations.

The Eighth Congress of the Communist Party had been held in December, 1926. This Congress elected a new Central Committee, replacing one which was accused by the Comintern of "certain opportunist deviations." At least part of the ousted leadership left the Party, to form what its members called the Vanguardia Nacionalista. The new Central Committee undertook to "revolutionize" the Party.[11]

In February, 1927, persecution of the Communists began, and in May, 1927, almost all the members of the Central Committee of the Party were arrested. The only ones who escaped were Bascuñan, López P., Iriarte, and Donoso. Iriarte, Donoso, and Bascuñan formed a new Central Committee, which lasted until August, 1928. After that new elements entered the Committee, including Galdames, Zavala, and Rosas, who had just returned from the Soviet Union. These men tried to reorganize the Party on the basis of three-man cells.

The Party's Local Committee of Santiago opposed this method of organization. The group, which was composed of M. Contreras, E. Torres, Humberto Mendoza, H. Godoy, M. Araya, A. González, and O. Moreno, was very active and had divided the city into sectors, which were then broken down into neighborhood cells. It edited a regular mimeographed bulletin. When it tried to extend this method of organization outside the city to the province of Santiago, it was blocked by the Central Committee of the Party.

Early in 1929 virtually all the members of the existing Central Committee were jailed, and on April 20, 1929, a new Committee was organized, composed of H. Godoy, H. Figueroa, Manuel Hidalgo, G. Valdés, and Humberto Mendoza, most of whom were from the Santiago Local Committee. It was officially recognized by the South American Secretariat of the Communist International.

However, differences developed between the new Central Committee and the South American Secretariat. Finally, the Montevideo Comintern regional headquarters sent to Chile one Sotelo, who had never played a major role in the Party's leadership, to reorganize the Party there. The Central Committee countered by calling a meeting of delegates from various parts of the country and expelling Sotelo from the Party. With the backing of the South American Secretariat, however, Sotelo continued to maintain contact with those who were not in conformity with the position of the majority of the Central Committee.

The delegate conference which expelled Sotelo (which met in January, 1930), elected a new Central Committee, consisting of Godoy, Mendoza, Figueroa, Carlos Contreras Labarca, Elías Laferte, Galdames, and R. Rosas, with Manuel Hidalgo, Cruz, M. Araya, Braulio León Peña, and Luis Peña as alternate members. Rosas, Laferte, and Galdames were exiled or deported, and Contreras Labarca was out of contact with the leadership; it was virtually impossible for the newly elected Committee to function.

Soon afterwards, therefore, a new meeting was held in one of the offices in the Congress building, and Hidalgo, Cruz, and Araya were named as a Provisional Central Committee, with full powers to act for the Party. However, soon after that the Ibáñez government arrested most of the Communist leaders. When a new delegate conference of the Party was held in August, 1930, all those participating in it were arrested.

Because of these arrests, still another Central Committee was organized in a meeting in Valparaíso. It consisted of Braulio León Peña, Galo González, José Vega, and Contreras Labarca. This Committee entered into friendly relations once again with the Secretariat of the International in Montevideo.

As a result of the constant disputes between the Hidalgo-Humberto Mendoza faction, which controlled the Chilean Communist Party for most of the Ibáñez period, and the South American Secretariat of the International, the Communists emerged from the Ibáñez period as two distinct parties. The causes for this division in the Party's ranks were stated by the Hidalgo-Mendoza faction to be eight in number:

1) The South American Secretariat kept up constant correspondence with a group in Antofagasta without going through the Central Committee in Santiago, in spite of constant protests by the Central Committee.

2) The Central Committee wanted to form a legal Party, keeping power in the hands of the illegal one. The South American Secretariat sent a flat refusal to agree to this proposal, without offering any reasons for the refusal.

3) The Central Committee asked the Secretariat to send two of its members to sit as members of the Committee and give it technical advice; the Secretariat refused.

4) The Secretariat sent Sotelo "with full powers to replace the Central Committee, because it would not follow the bureaucratic mandates of the Secretariat."

5) There was a lack of adequate contact between the Secretariat and the Central Committee—for instance, the Secretariat notified the Central Committee of a meeting of the Comintern only ten days before that meeting was due to take place. At the same time, the Secretariat refused to send funds so that the Chilean Central Committee could send students to training schools in Moscow, or even to receive training in Buenos Aires or Montevideo.

6) Actions were performed by the Secretariat which were against the program of the Comintern. (No details were offered concerning these actions.)

7) Relations were maintained by the Secretariat exclusively with the Secretary General of the Chilean Party, instead of with the full Central Committee, and the Secretariat refused to put on its letters proof as to their authenticity.

8) The Secretariat refused to call a Congress of the Chilean Party.[12]

The pro-Secretariat faction of the Party accused the Hidalgo-Mendoza group of having been too submissive to the Ibáñez regime. They claimed that Hidalgo had upon occasion complimented Ibáñez and said that his policy of asserting "the regulatory action of the State over all social forces reflects perfectly our Communist doctrines." They also accused Hidalgo of having called Ibáñez "the first Republican" and of having voted for a Law on the Interior Security of the State.[13]

The Hidalgo-Mendoza group was undoubtedly influenced by the Stalinist-Trotskyite feud in the Comintern. Seeking allies against the Stalinist-controlled South American Secretariat, they naturally gravitated towards the Trotskyite Opposition. This tendency was reinforced by Trotskyite literature printed in Spain which circulated in Chile during the Ibáñez period. This literature particularly criticized the bureaucratic attitude of the Comintern, and this was a criticism with which the Chilean Party leadership had come fully to agree.[14]

With the overthrow of Carlos Ibáñez in July, 1931, the split in the Communist Party became public. The two factions organized as separate parties. The pro-Comintern policy continued under the leadership of the last Central Committee which had been organized while the Party was illegal. The Hidalgo-Mendoza group established a new Central Committee of seven members, later expanded to 15, with Humberto Mendoza (who used the pseudonym of Jorge Levin) as Secretary General. It organized local groups in Santiago and several nearby towns, in Antofagasta, Tocopilla, and Coquimbo in the North, and in various southern towns. It also established a youth organization. This faction continued to call itself "Communist Party, Chilean Section of the Communist International."[15]

The two groups were in disagreement on a number of issues. For one thing, the Laferte-Contreras Labarca faction, which was aligned with the

Comintern's South American Secretariat, sought to reorganize immediately the Federación Obrera de Chile, of which Elías Laferte was still nominally Secretary General. This attitude conformed perfectly to the Comintern's Third Period "line" of Communist dual unionism, which was then in vogue.

The F.O.Ch. was credited with having about 25,000 members right after the overthrow of Ibáñez, though this was only a small fraction of the trade union membership at that time.[16] A convention of the F.O.Ch. was held on September 20, 1931, and was attended by delegates from the coal and nitrate mining areas, and by representatives of various unions in the principal cities. There was also a scattering of representatives of agricultural workers' organizations.[17]

This congress of the F.O.Ch. "expelled" Manuel Hidalgo and other leaders of the dissident Communist group, which was strongly opposed to the revival of the F.O.Ch.[18] The Hidalgo group argued that the great majority of the workers were by that time in the legally recognized unions, which the F.O.Ch. congress attacked as "fascist" organizations,[19] and that the Communists should therefore work within these unions.[20]

There were various other bones of contention. The Hildago faction opposed the Comintern's policy of attacking all other left-wing groups as "social fascists," and opposed the Comintern slogan of a "united front from below." They felt that if there was to be an alliance of the Communists with other left-wing groups, it should be brought about by negotiation among the responsible leaders of the various parties.[21]

A general election was called soon after the overthrow of Ibáñez. Both factions of the Communist Party put up candidates, Laferte running for the "official" group and Hidalgo for the dissident party. Arturo Alessandri was also a candidate, and there was a nominee for the right-wing parties. However, the victorious candidate was Juan Esteban Montero, a member of the Radical Party, who was very popular because of the active part he had taken in bringing about the downfall of Ibáñez.[22] Hidalgo ran considerably ahead of Laferte in the voting, but behind the other three candidates.

While the election campaign was in full swing, a mutiny occurred in the Chilean fleet, stationed at Valparaíso. Although the Communists had nothing to do with bringing about this uprising, both factions attempted to take advantage of it. The official Communists attempted to arouse support on land for the rebellious sailors, and they talked airily of establishing "soviets," but nothing concrete came of this talk.[23] The Opposition Communists organized a Revolutionary Committee among their sympathizers, to win support for the mutineers.[24] The leader of the rebellious mariners, Pacheco, later joined the official Communist Party.[25]

The few months during which Montero remained President of Chile were turbulent ones, marked by strikes, plots, and widespread unrest. The most important activity of the Communists during this period was an attempt by members of the official Party to seize the barracks of the Esmeralda regiment in Copiapó on Christmas Eve, 1931, when most of the soldiers were on Christmas leave. The Communists held the barracks for three hours and then were driven off by soldiers and members of the national police.[26]

The Montero regime came to a sudden end on June 4, 1932, with a *coup d'état* of military men and civilians, which proclaimed a "Socialist State." The leader of the movement was Colonel Marmaduque Grove, leader of the 1924 and 1925 revolutions and founder of the Chilean Air Force, who had returned from exile after Ibáñez' overthrow to become chief of the air arm. Closely associated with him were Eugenio Matte, leader of one of the many Socialist parties which had arisen following Ibáñez' ouster, and Carlos Dávila, Ibáñez' former Ambassador to Washington.

Since the Grove regime stayed in power only a few days, it was not able to accomplish very much. However, it did decree the establishment of a National Bank; it ordered the return to working class women of the sewing machines which they had pledged with the National Pawn Shop; it proposed to nationalize the coal, copper, and nitrate mining industries. It pledged—and gave—full encouragement to the trade union movement, one trade union leader actually serving in the Cabinet during this short-lived regime.[27]

Grove's Socialist Republic also declared an amnesty for all political prisoners, particularly those sailors who had participated in the November, 1931, mutiny. It suspended the eviction of all delinquent renters paying 200 pesos or less until the government should have time to work out a long-range program in this field. Finally, it reinstated all teachers ousted during previous regimes for political reasons.[28]

The official Communists had participated in the early stages of the negotiations which resulted in the June 4 uprising. However, Laferte, returning from Moscow a few weeks before the coup, ordered the Party to withdraw from these negotiations. When the coup actually occurred, the Laferte party was in opposition.

The attitude of the Laferte Communists is shown by a manifesto which they issued right after the Socialist Republic was proclaimed. It started: "Against Monteroism, the assassin and starver of the workers! Against the socialistic demagoguery of Grove, Dávila, and Company!" and ended: "*Viva* the Workers and Peasants Revolution! Recognition of the Soviet Union! *Viva* the Soviet Union! *Viva* the Communist Party!"

The F.O.Ch., of which Laferte was still Secretary General, also issued a pronunciamento, which said of the leaders of the Socialist Republic:

> They all represent the class interests of a sector of the bourgeoisie, allied to imperialism, which, in the midst of the insoluble situation in

which they find themselves, wish to save once again their class privileges and distract the independent struggle of the great masses from the conquest of their demands. . . .

The F.O.Ch. proclamation claimed that "The road to socialism and the social revolution is nothing less than the Workers and Peasants Revolution, which must be made by the great masses through the establishment of a government of Councils of Workers, Soldiers, Peasants, and Sailors."[29]

As soon as the June 4 uprising occurred, various left-wing groups seized the buildings of the University of Chile, in the center of Santiago and only a few blocks from the presidential palace. There they established the Consejo Revolucionario de Obreros, Campesinos, Soldados y Marineros, composed of representatives of the Students' Federation, the two Communist Parties, various smaller political groups, and some workers' organizations.

Within this Revolutionary Council a struggle took place between the two Communist elements. The Laferte party wanted to use the Council to carry on an all-out attack upon the Grove regime. The dissident Communists wanted to give Grove qualified support, though saying that the revolution, good so far as it went, should go further. The dissidents suggested to Grove a seven-point program which they urged him to follow.

The official Communists were particularly anxious to win over the students, most of whose leaders were with the Hidalgo party. A Comintern representative (a Rumanian), who arrived in Chile the day after the Grove coup, offered to readmit the dissident Communist student leaders to the Comintern-backed Communist Party if they would publicly state their "errors." This the dissidents refused to do, and the struggle continued.[30]

The official Communists were well financed during this period. The man who was the Party's treasurer at this time told the author many years later that the Party had received $10,000 from the Comintern during the month of June, 1932, in comparison with the $1800 per month which it had been receiving previously.[31]

The official Communists remained in control of the Comité Revolucionario, and the dissident Communists withdrew to form the Alianza Socialista Revolucionaria de Trabajadores, in conjunction with Eliodoro Domínguez' Partido Socialista Marxista and other small groups. Branches of this Alliance were quickly established throughout the country.

When Grove fell, after only twelve days in power, a general strike in his support was organized by the Alianza. It lasted three days and was supported with particular firmness by the railroad workers, by most construction workers (among whom the influence of the dissident Communists was particularly strong), and by most factory workers. The trolley-car workers of Santiago and Valparaíso also backed the walkout. However, it was finally defeated.[32]

Carlos Dávila, who had split with Grove and withdrawn from the government of the Socialist Republic four days after the June 4 revolution, was responsible for ousting Grove. He took over as President of what he continued to call the Socialist Republic, remaining in power just about one hundred days. Grove, meanwhile, was sent off into exile on Más Afuera Island in the Pacific.

With the ousting of Dávila, in September, 1932, new elections were called. The two principal candidates for the presidency in this poll were Arturo Alessandri, who now represented a coalition of most of the country's traditional parties, from the Conservatives to the Radicals, and Marmaduque Grove, put forward by a heterogeneous group of small parties, which had backed his short-lived regime and for which he had become a symbol after his overthrow. This latter group of parties included the dissident Communists, led by Manuel Hidalgo and Humberto Mendoza.

The official Communists again nominated Laferte, and were violently opposed to Grove's candidacy. Theirs was a full-blown Third Period position, in the face of the problems facing the country. They attacked Grove and those supporting him, saying "Grovism objectively defends imperialism and feudalism by not proposing expropriation without indemnification of all foreign-owned enterprises," and "Grovism is a bourgeois party, intimately allied to the landowners and imperialists." They talked of the "reactionary nature of Grovism, its position in defense of imperialism and *latifundia*, its alliance with Ibáñez, its increasing fascization, its methods of misleading the masses."

The official Communists were particularly violent against Hidalgo and his party, calling the latter "a bourgeois-Grovist agent in the heart of the working class." They called Hidalgo himself "a professional collaborator with the bourgeoisie, a professional traitor."[33]

Although Arturo Alessandri was once again elected constitutional President of Chile, the Grove forces made a very strong campaign, particularly in view of the fact that Grove himself only returned from exile a few days before the end of the campaign. Although he was not elected, the forces which gathered around him at that time under the banner of Socialist Revolutionary Action laid the foundations for the formation of what was to become one of the country's major political groups for more than a decade. It took definite form with the establishment of the Socialist Party of Chile in the early months of 1933.

Both the Communist Parties elected members of Congress in this campaign. The official Party elected Contreras Labarca to the Chamber of Deputies on a ticket which it shared with the Liberal Democratic Party.[34] The dissident Communists elected Manuel Hidalgo to the Senate on a joint list with the Radical Socialist Party, and Emilio Zapata to the Chamber of Deputies from Santiago on a joint ticket with the Partido Socialista Unificado.[35] However, this small representation of the two groups was some indication of the great decline in Communist influence among the workers and the voting public in general since the middle 1920's, a decline brought about largely by the rise of rival socialist elements enlisting support from the same groups to which the Communists directed their appeal.

During 1933 both parties held national Congresses. The official Party devoted much of the time of its conference in July, 1933, to problems of organization. It decided to launch a campaign to form groups of "activists," composed of fifty members each in Antofagasta, Valparaíso, and Santiago, and of thirty members each in Iquique, Talca, Temuco, and Valdivia. It also drew up a program which was in key with the Third Period Communist "line." It demanded confiscation without compensation of all foreign firms and all large landholdings. It listed a number of immediate demands for reforms in favor of the workers, such as 15 days paid vacation, a minimum wage, and a 12 week rest period for working mothers.

True to the Third Period "line" throughout the world, the official Communists demanded "self-determination" for the country's racial minority. Although there are only a few thousand full-blooded Araucanian Indians in the southern part of the country, most of them living on reservations, the Communists demanded the formation of an Araucanian Republic.[36]

The dissident Communists held their Congress in March, 1933. Its principal decision was to affiliate officially with the International Left Communist Opposition, thus becoming a Trotskyite group.[37] The party, which soon took the name Left Communist Party, maintained its independent existence until 1937, when it merged with the Socialist Party of Chile, taking this action because its leaders had reached the conclusion that the "Fourth International" being sponsored by Trotsky was destined to be more a paper organization than a real one.[38]

Through the rest of the 1930's the Stalinist Communists devoted much of their energies to the labor movement. Until 1936 they acted principally through the Federación Obrera de Chile, of which Laferte remained Secretary General until 1935, when he was succeeded by another Communist leader, Salvador Ocampo.

With the change in the Communist International line in 1934-35, the Chilean Communists began to put that line into effect in their own country. They no longer opposed attempts to unite the labor movement. The first move in this direction was a meeting called on the initiative of the Socialist-controlled Confederación Nacional de Sindicatos Legales in June, 1935. However, this meeting merely explored the problem without reaching any concrete conclusions about uniting the various trade union groups then in existence.

The next move came after a widespread railroad strike in 1936 when the Frente Nacional de Unidad Sindical was established, with representatives of both the F.O.Ch. and the Confederación Nacional de Sindicatos Legales, as well as several independent unions, such as the Millers Federation and the Railroad Workers Federation. Luis Solís of the C.N.S.L. was Secretary General of this new group, and Salvador Ocampo of the F.O.Ch. was Sub-Secretary General.[39]

The Frente Nacional paved the way for a unity congress which met in December, 1936, and established the Confederación de Trabajadores de Chile (C.T.Ch.). The facade of unity was somewhat cracked by the struggle in the Congress between the Communists and Socialists for the Secretary Generalship of the Confederación. A Socialist, Juan Díaz Martínez, was the victor.

The Communists and Socialists continued the struggle for power in the unions within the C.T.Ch. The second Congress of the C.T.Ch. was held in 1939, and again a Socialist, Bernardo Ibáñez, was elected Secretary General. However, the Communists refused to accept this and withdrew from the C.T.Ch., establishing their own organization, with the same name, headed by Salvador Ocampo. Negotiations between the two groups were soon undertaken, however, and resulted in a reunification, with Ibáñez remaining as Secretary General and Ocampo as Assistant Secretary General.[40]

In the meanwhile, political changes were taking place which were advantageous to the Communists' new Popular Front line. The Alessandri administration, which had been put in office as a moderate leftist regime, with the support of the Radical Party, moved increasingly to the Right. After the 1936 railroad strike, the Radical Party quit Alessandri's cabinet, which from then on was made up largely of the right-wing Liberal and Conservative parties.

The Left, on the other hand, tended increasingly to unite. The left-wing elements consisted principally of the Radical Party, which was particularly strong among urban middle-class elements, especially government employees, and the Socialist Party, which in the 1930's represented the majority of the urban working class.

The first move towards unification of the Left was the formation of the Bloque de Izquierda in 1935 with the inclusion of the Socialist Party, the Democratic Party, the Left Communists, and the Radical Socialists. A year later this alliance was expanded, and the continent's only Popular Front was established, with the Communist Party, the Radical Party, and the Confederación de Trabajadores de Chile joining the left-wing alliance.[41]

The Communists were a minor element in the left wing in the 1930's. However, the Comintern apparently picked Chile for a South American experiment in the Popular Front technique. Eudosio Ravines, founder of the Communist Party of Peru and for a while a Comintern agent in Spain, was sent to Chile to take charge of the effort of the Communists to penetrate and if possible capture the growing movement toward left-wing unity.

Ravines, in his book, *The Yenan Way*, describes the manner in which the Chilean Communists began their campaign to divide the parties allied with them in the Popular Front, while ostensibly being all in favor of "unity." Adroitly, they played upon the petty jealousies and personal ambitions of leaders of the other left-wing groups. They enveloped in a wave of flattery and adulation those who would do their bidding, while implying or openly stating "doubts" about the loyalty and good faith of those leaders of the other parties who refused to become subservient. To those who helped them, the Communists could offer financial support and wide publicity. Those who opposed them were threatened with the full fury of the whole disciplined Communist propaganda machine—press, platform, and parliamentary tribune—a threat which engendered increasing fear as the strength of the Communists grew. This procedure, begun under Ravines' direction in the late 1930's, was continued through the next two decades, long after he had abandoned the Comintern ranks.

While thus trying to split their allies in the Popular Front, the Communists sought to bring strange elements into the left-wing combination. They tried to recruit the ex-dictator, Carlos Ibáñez, who was then associated with the Chilean Nazi Party, into the Popular Front. Carlos Contreras Labarca, in his November, 1938, article in *The Communist*, explained this move thus:

> In its famous "Message to the People of Chile," in November, 1937, the Communist Party called for the unification of all the democratic forces. Regarding Ibáñez, it stated, after criticizing his past, that if he severed all connections with the Nazis and adhered to the anti-Fascist movement, the entrance of the democratic forces supporting him, and of himself, into the People's Front, must be facilitated, if his acts were in accordance with his words.

The first test of the Popular Front came in the congressional elections of April, 1937. The Front as a whole won ten out of the 25 seats in the Senate and 66 out of the 146 positions in the Chamber of Deputies. The Communists elected Elías Laferte to the Senate and seven members, including Carlos Contreras Labarca, the Party's Secretary General, to the Chamber of Deputies. The Socialists won 15 seats in the Chamber.[42]

As the 1938 presidential campaign approached, the question of left-wing unity became increasingly important. One of the principal problems was the selection of an appropriate candidate. The Socialists put forward the name of their leader, Marmaduque Grove, and for some time were very insistent that he be the candidate of the united Left. However, the Radicals, who formed the other major element in the new left-wing coalition, insisted that the nominee be a member of their party.

The problem of the presidential candidate was the principal item for discussion at the Convention of the Left held early in 1938, and this played directly into the hands of the Communists, enhancing their importance, which otherwise would not have been very great at the gathering. The Radicals and Socialists were virtually deadlocked in support of their respective candidates, Pedro Aguirre Cerda and Marmaduque Grove. The Socialists had already lost the first round before the Convention met, since their proposal for a referendum instead of a convention to choose the left-wing nominee had been defeated.

The Communists were not committed to either candidate, and as Contreras Labarca said, "Both solicited the support of the Communist Party." The Communists sought to break the deadlock between the Radicals and Socialists, "urging them, in the name of the people, to lay aside their partisan and selfish interests and seek jointly the one candidate who would unite all the democratic forces of the country." The final result was that Aguirre Cerda won the nomination, which for political purposes was made unanimous.

The election of December, 1938, was the most closely fought contest since 1920, when Arturo Alessandri ran for the presidency for the first time. The results were so close that there was some question as to whether the right-wing forces, who lost the poll, would accept the results. It was not until Arturo Alessandri, the retiring chief executive, announced that he would not allow the results of the election to be violated, although his nominee, Gustavo Ross Santamaria had lost, that it became clear that the Popular Front's candidate would become President of the republic.

With the inauguration of Pedro Aguirre Cerda, the question arose of Communist participation in the new government. Even before the election, the Party's Secretary General, Carlos Contreras Labarca, wrote:

> The Communist Party declares that its inviolable and exemplary fidelity to the People's Front . . . has never been inspired by the wish to obtain any participation in the government, and that it has never had any interest but that of satisfying our people's noble desires crystallized in the People's Front program. The Communist Party considers that its responsibility in carrying out this program can be fulfilled outside the government. . . . Consequently it leaves the People's Front entirely free to decide, in the best interests of the people, what executive tasks may devolve upon the Communist Party.

This is one interpretation of why the Communists stayed out of the Aguirre Cerda cabinet. Another might be that they were adopting the tactics employed by their French and Spanish comrades two years before, when they stayed out of their countries' Popular Front governments so as to be in a position to snipe at fellow members of the Popular Front, when that seemed advantageous, at the same time taking credit for the good things which the Popular Front regime did.

The Aguirre Cerda government took office in December, 1938. A few

months later came the second World War, which caused dissension between the Communists and their associates in the Popular Front. The
Chilean Communists followed the international Communist "line" during
the first months of the war, shifting from violent support of "collective
security" to even more violent opposition to it and denunciation of the
Allies. The Socialists and Radicals, on the other hand, were sympathetic to
the Allies, and this fact led to violent clashes between the Communists and
the other parties, particularly the Socialists.

The Chilean Communists' attitude toward the war during its first 22
months is shown by an official resolution of a Plenary Session of the
Party's Central Committee: "By means of this criminal war the imperialists
fight to divide among themselves the colonial and semi-colonial and dependent peoples and nations, at the same time that they involve them in
the conflict and force them to work, suffer, and die for the winning of
*THEIR* war."[43]

Humberto Abarca, one of the Communists' members of the Chamber of
Deputies, commented:

> Chile must stay neutral. Our country has nothing to gain in this war;
> on the contrary, its participation in it, in favor of whichever side it
> might be, would put in immediate danger the existence of our national
> independence and our democratic regime. The participation in the
> war interests only the oligarchy and imperialism.[44]

The Chilean Communists applauded every move of the "Soviet Fatherland." For instance, Elías Laferte claimed, "This Socialist Fatherland has
liberated 23 million workers of the Ukraine and Byelorussia, the working
peasants of the Baltic States, of Bessarabia, and of Bukovina. . . ."[45] When
the Russo-Finnish war occurred, Salvador Ocampo, then in the United
States, wrote in the December 19, 1939, *Daily Worker*, "The government
of Finland allowed itself to be used by England, France, and Germany
against the Soviet Union." He added, "The Chilean people have no part
and want no part in the European war. And we hope other countries will
follow our example."

The Socialist Party took particular umbrage at the Communist position.
Socialist Minister of Development Oscar Schnake, in addressing the Socialist Party's Seventh Ordinary Congress on June 4, 1941, said that though
he did not condemn the Russian government in fighting for peace, he
did condemn "it and its representatives in Chile, when they attempt to
place the welfare of the Chilean workers and the future of Chile at the
service of the peace and welfare of the Russians."

Bernardo Ibáñez, Secretary General of the Confederación de Trabajadores de Chile and a Socialist deputy, speaking to the same meeting, made
the accusation that "The international Communist leaders join with Naziism and Fascism to destroy democracy and the most sacred things which

mankind has constructed during long centuries in the fight for liberation."[46]

So acrid did the controversy between the Communists and Socialists become that the Central Committee of the Socialist Party recommended that the Communists be expelled from the Popular Front. This demand was refused by the Popular Front, however,[47] and as a result, the Socialists themselves withdrew from the formal organization of the Popular Front.

Before the 1941 elections, Congress passed a bill, sponsored by the opposition Liberal Party, which outlawed the Communist Party.[48] In spite of this law, the Communists participated in the 1941 election, under the name of the Proletarian Party.[49]

The Communists made greater gains in the March, 1941, election than they had ever achieved before. Their vote increased from 17,162, which they received in 1937, to 55,000 in 1941. They elected three senators and seventeen deputies. For the first time they surpassed the Socialist representation in parliament, though their vote was considerably behind the Socialists'; the Communists profited from an alliance with the Radicals, while the Socialists went it alone.[50]

Thus, although their attitude during the first months of the second World War temporarily alienated the Communists from the Socialists, it had the effect of isolating the latter rather than the former, and did not prevent the Communists from making considerable gains among the workers. One of the reasons for this success of the Communists was the fact that the disintegration of the Socialist Party had begun.

The Socialist Party, as established in 1933, was a unification of a large number of small political organizations, each with its own leader. In the first years, the two principal figures in the party were Marmaduque Grove and Eugenio Matte, both of whom had been members of the 12-day government of the Socialist Republic. With the death of Matte in 1935, Grove became the undisputed chief of the party.

Although there were rivalries within the party among the various leaders, who had more than the usual tendency toward striking prima donna attitudes, these conflicts of ambition did not become serious until after the Socialists entered the Popular Front government, and the desire for office reinforced the centrifugal forces already at work. In December, 1938, Socialist ministers joined those of the Radical Party in the government of Pedro Aguirre Cerda.

Although the Socialist ministers, and particularly Minister of Development Oscar Schnake, did a good job, the government itself ran into numerous difficulties. Only a month after it took office, the country was shaken by one of the worst earthquakes in its history, and whole cities were razed. The government was thus faced with the necessity of spending large amounts of money on rebuilding these devastated areas, which interfered seriously with its carrying out the program of economic development and social legislation upon which it had been elected. A further difficulty was added when, less than a year after Aguirre Cerda took office, the second World War began.

Before the first year of the Aguirre Cerda regime was out, a strong body of opinion appeared within the Socialist Party which felt that the Socialists should withdraw from the government. This faction argued that the party was losing prestige through its participation in a government which could not fully carry out those things which it had promised to do. Many realized also that the chief gainers at the Socialists' expense were the Communists, who remained outside the government and were openly and quietly implying and alleging that "certain elements" in the Popular Front government were "betraying" its program.

The controversy within the Socialist ranks became so acute that there were fist fights between members of the different factions at regional meetings of the party. Finally, early in 1940, the dissident elements withdrew to form a new party, the Partido Socialista de Trabajadores. The leader of the dissidents was deputy César Godoy Urrutia.

The Communists claimed to sympathize with the majority group of Socialists under Marmaduque Grove's leadership, and denounced Godoy Urrutia and others of the P.S.T. as "Trotskyites." Within the C.T.Ch. the Communists helped the Socialists oust Carlos Acuña and Carlos Videla, P.S.T. members on the Executive Committee of the Confederación, and replace them with men loyal to the Grove Party.[51]

The Communists certainly were not dismayed by this weakening of their chief rival for support among the Chilean workers. Some years after, in 1944, the leadership of the P.S.T., including deputies Godoy Urrutia and Natalio Bermán, joined the Communists.[52]

In the meantime the Party had changed its international position after the invasion of the Soviet Union by the Nazis. Daniel Palma, one of the leaders of the Young Communist League, explained the change in the Communist attitude:

> The war then was a war . . . in spite of the wishes of the people and against their interests. It was a war which the imperialists of all the world had been preparing for many years. . . . Today there is a fundamentally different situation. Hitler Fascism has launched the most criminal attack that could be conceived against the country which is the hope and pride of youth, where young people live the happiest lives, where work is assured, against the country with most students in the world, a children's garden, the paradise of sportsmen, the country where girls are equal in rights with the young men, the most free and most democratic country in the world: the Soviet Union. . . . Hitler attacked the U.S.S.R. . . . because its policy of peace was the major obstacle to the realization of his rapine plans. . . .[53]

With this shift in the Communists' attitude, their relations with other left-wing parties, particularly the Socialist Party, improved. It became possible once again to establish the Popular Front, with Socialist participation, under the name of Alianza Democrática. The Communist-Socialist truce was particularly evident in the labor movement. Although the rivalry between the Socialists and the Communists for control of the Confederación de Trabajadores de Chile did not by any means disappear, there was an end to the open warfare which had existed during the first months of the world conflict.

At the Third Congress of the C.T.Ch., which was held in December, 1943, there was no conflict between the two parties for control of the Confederation. Rather, a joint ticket was presented, which continued Socialist deputy Bernardo Ibáñez, as Secretary General, and Communist deputy Salvador Ocampo as Sub-Secretary General.[54]

Throughout the remainder of the war, the Communists continued to gain ground, both in the labor movement and among the general public, while the Socialists increasingly lost support, both among the workers and the voters. Further Socialist splits were to a considerable degree responsible for this. There is little doubt that these constant scissions in the Socialist Party strengthened the Communists, and there is reason to believe that the Communists were more than passive spectators of some of them.

The most serious Socialist division after the formation of the P.S.T. was the struggle which broke out in 1943 between the party's Secretary General, Salvador Allende, and its lifetime President, Marmaduque Grove. The Socialists had tended to lionize Grove, trying to make the most of the aura which still surrounded him as the "hero of the Socialist Republic." However, Grove, a career military man, was not an adroit politician. He tended too much to take at face value the encomiums which his Socialist comrades heaped upon him, and to feel that he was "bigger than the party." Aside from personality clashes between Grove and other leaders of the party, two issues caused the split. One was the old question of participation of the Socialist Party in the government—now the administration of President Juan Antonio Ríos, a member of Aguirre Cerda's Radical Party, who had been elected chief executive after Aguirre's death in 1942. The other was the problem of organic unity among the Socialists, Communists, Partido Socialista de Trabajadores, and Partido Democrático. Grove favored continued participation in the government and the formation of a *partido único* (united party), his antagonists opposing both these measures.

The first open break between the two groups took place at the Ninth Congress of the Socialist Party in January, 1943. Defeated in this Congress, Grove and the delegates supporting him withdrew and elected a rival Central Committee in opposition to that named by the majority of the delegates.[55] However, party unity was restored a few weeks later, when a six-man steering committee, equally divided between the two factions, was established, with Grove as President and Allende as Vice President of the party.[56]

A final split between Grovistas and Allendistas took place in the middle of 1944. The Grovistas organized a new party, the Partido Socialista Auténtico, while the Allendistas remained in control of the majority of the party, with Bernardo Ibáñez, Secretary General of the Confederación de Trabajadores de Chile, also assuming the party's Secretary Generalship.[57]

There is no doubt that the Communists were very active in bringing about this division in the ranks of their chief rival. One of the issues involved was whether or not the Socialists should accept the Communist suggestion for the merger of the two parties. Also, it seems likely that some of those around Grove were either secret members of the Communist Party or at least close sympathizers with the Communists. Asdrubal Pessoa, who became Secretary of Organization of the Partido Socialista Auténtico, split away from the P.S.A. a few months after it was founded, and soon afterwards formed a trade union and political alliance with the Communist Party.[58]

The Communists quite openly sympathized with Grove and his faction in this split. They "built up" Grove in their press and played upon his vanity and lack of political astuteness, with disastrous results for the Socialist Party.[59]

The anti-Grove faction kept the loyalty of most of the Socialist trade unionists, both officials and rank and file. The selection of Bernardo Ibáñez as party Secretary General had been designed to assure this. As a result, the rivalry between the Socialists and the Communists in the labor movement became increasingly acute after the split.

The Socialists had maintained control of the C.T.Ch. throughout the period of the second World War. How they had done this was outlined by Socialist Secretary General Salvador Allende in a report to a Plenum of the Socialist Party in 1944, when he said:

> The Secretary General of the C.T.Ch. is our comrade Bernardo Ibáñez, and we can say that until now the positions taken by the Socialist councillors have had the support of the Radical, Falangista, and Democratic members, which has practically given the Party an absolute majority in the National Executive Council of the C.T.Ch.

The Sub-Secretary General of the Socialist Party reported to the same party meeting concerning the political situation within various important unions in the C.T.Ch. He noted that in the White Collar Workers Federation the Socialists and Communists were allied against the Radicals, who controlled the Federation. In the Bakers Federation all political factions agreed to present a single list of officers. In the Maritime Workers Federation there was also such a united caucus, but the Socialists had a majority. In the Railroad Engineers and Firemen's Union the Socialists had a majority. In the Railroad Workers Federation, a Communist President had been replaced by a Socialist through an alliance of the Socialists and Radicals.[60]

The Communists did not attain a majority in the leadership until January, 1946. The occasion for the shift of the Radical Party, Democratic, and Falangista (Social Catholic party) members of the C.T.Ch. to the side of the Communists, which gave them control of a majority, arose with a pair of general strikes against the government of President Juan Antonio Ríos.

The occasion for the first general walkout was the withdrawal of legal recognition from two small unions in the nitrate fields as a result of a wave of illegal strikes in the months after the end of World War II. The government had been powerless to prevent these walkouts, and one of the last cabinet meetings attended by the ailing President Juan Antonio Ríos early in January, 1946, decided to take drastic measures by withdrawing legal recognition from two unions which were then on strike. The C.T.Ch. had already planned a series of meetings to protest the high cost of living; now, these meetings were converted into gigantic demonstrations against the government's action. The principal meeting was held in the Plaza Bulnes in Santiago, right in front of the presidential palace. As a result of circumstances which it is difficult to determine accurately, armed police fired into the crowd, and six of the Plaza Bulnes demonstrators were killed while several others were wounded.

The Executive Committee of the C.T.Ch. held an emergency meeting right after the Plaza Bulnes "massacre" and determined upon a one-day protest strike, at the same time demanding that the cabinet be changed and those responsible for the "massacre" be punished. The government countered by ordering the arrest of the principal leaders of the C.T.Ch., a move which the labor leaders met by decreeing a second general strike to continue until the demands of the C.T.Ch. were met.

Meanwhile negotiations were going on for the formation of a new cabinet. Acting President Alfredo Duhalde (who had taken over the chief executive's office when President Juan Antonio Ríos became sick) and Socialist trade union leader Bernardo Ibáñez told the author that the Communists had demanded the entry of their Party into the cabinet before the proposed second general strike would be called off. This charge was denied to the author by Salvador Ocampo, the principal Communist trade union leader.

On the afternoon before the second general strike was supposed to begin, Acting President Duhalde invited members of the Socialist Party to join his cabinet. The Socialists agreed, on the conditions that the withdrawal of recognition from the two nitrate unions be cancelled, that the orders for the arrest of C.T.Ch. leaders be withdrawn, that those responsible for the Plaza Bulnes massacre be punished, and that steps be taken to curb the rising cost of living.

After the Socialists had decided to enter the cabinet, they attempted to get the general strike called off before it began. To achieve this, Bernardo Ibáñez got on the radio, speaking from the presidential palace, and told the workers that the objectives for which the strike had been called had now been achieved and that therefore there was no need for the strike.

As a result of Ibáñez' speech, the C.T.Ch. split. The Communists in the C.T.Ch. executive claimed Ibáñez had no right to call off the walkout singlehanded, and decided to continue with plans for the strike. In this decision the Radical Party, the Falange Party, and some of the Democratic Party members of the executive sided with the Communists. This group "deposed" Bernardo Ibáñez as Secretary General and elected a Communist, deputy Bernardo Araya, in his place.

The Socialists reorganized their faction of the C.T.Ch., retaining Ibáñez as Secretary General and filling the posts on the Executive Committee formerly held by members of those parties which had gone along with Bernardo Araya's C.T.Ch. The replacements were Socialists and members of the faction of the Democratic Party which sided with the Socialists.

For the following year and a half the Communists and Socialists fought for control of the organized labor movement. The majority of unions undoubtedly went with the Communist-controlled C.T.Ch. within the first six months of the split. The Communists themselves controlled the important Miners Federation, the Metal Workers Federation, the Construction Workers Federation, and the smaller Agricultural Workers Federation. The Radicals, who sided with the Communists, controlled the C.T.Ch.'s White Collar Workers Federation. The small Millers Federation, controlled by the Falange Party, also sided with the Araya C.T.Ch. The Railroad Workers Federation, because the Communists and Radicals together had a majority, also joined the Araya C.T.Ch.

The principal unions to stay with the Socialist-controlled C.T.Ch. were the Chemical and Pharmaceutical Workers Federation, the Hospital Workers Federation, the Woodworkers Federation, and a small railroad workers' organization. Other important organizations split, with separate groups being established in both C.T.Ch's. The Maritime Workers Federation and the Textile Workers Federation were the most important bodies thus affected. Many unions dropped out of the C.T.Ch. entirely.

Between January and September, 1946, the influence of the government was thrown on the side of the Socialist C.T.Ch. Subsequently, however, with the victory of Gabriel González Videla in the elections held in that month, the government's backing went to the Communist-controlled labor group.

President Juan Antonio Ríos died in the middle of 1946, which necessitated an election to determine his successor. There were four candidates the day the poll took place. One of these was Gabriel González Videla, who was backed by the Radical Party, the Communists, and several smaller groups. Eduardo Cruz Coke, a leader of the Social Christian Wing of the Conservative Party, was supported by that party, by the Falange Party, and by Marmaduque Grove's Partido Socialista Auténtico. The right-wing elements in Chilean politics generally supported Senator Fernando Alessandri, son of ex-President Arturo Alessandri. The fourth candidate was Bernardo Ibáñez, nominated by the Socialist Party after the with-drawal of Vice President Alfredo Duhalde, whom they had first sup-ported.

Although Gabriel González Videla received the largest number of popular votes, he did not receive a 51 per cent majority; hence it was necessary under the Chilean Constitution for Congress to choose between the two candidates having the highest number of votes. A great deal of horse-trading preceded the final decision. The Radicals and Communists in Congress naturally pledged their votes to González Videla. The Socialists of both factions did likewise. The members of the Conservative and Falangista parties, on the other hand, pledged themselves to vote for Señor Cruz Coke, whom they had backed in the popular election. The final choice, therefore, rested with the Congressmen of the Liberal Party. Their leader, ex-President Arturo Alessandri, was in 1946 President of the Senate, and the Liberals had voted in the popular election for Alessandri's son, Fernando. So Arturo Alessandri once again became the key to the presidential succession.

Alessandri and his friends negotiated at great length with González Videla. The two groups finally reached an accord, whereby the Liberal Congressmen would vote for González Videla, in return for which González Videla would admit three Liberal Party members to his cabinet, to serve alongside three members of his own Radical Party and three Communists.

Thus members of the Communist Party entered the Chilean government for the first time. Although they were not the first Latin American Communists to enter a ministry, as is often maintained (Communists had before this served in the Cuban and Ecuadorian governments), they were the first Communist ministers to have designated portfolios. Carlos Contreras Labarca became Minister of Communications and Public Works, Miguel Concha became Minister of Agriculture, and Victor Contreras was named Minister of Lands and Colonization by the President.[61]

During the five months in which Communist ministers served in the government of President Gabriel González Videla, the Chilean Communist Party made great strides. It made particular headway in the labor movement. Both factions of the C.T.Ch. held congresses in Santiago about the middle of December, 1946. The contrast between the two meetings was a measure of the relative strength of the two labor groups. The Socialist C.T.Ch. held its opening meeting in a comparatively small auditorium in town, with perhaps a couple of thousand people in attendance. The Communist C.T.Ch. held its inaugural session in the National Stadium, with perhaps 15,000 to 20,000 people present. The Communist meeting was addressed by President Gabriel González Videla and several of his ministers, in addition to representatives of virtually all the country's left-of-center parties. Many of the delegates to the Communist C.T.Ch. Congress were reported to have had their way to the meeting paid by the government, and special cars were put at the disposal of these delegates by the National Railways.

The Communists used their presence in the government to attempt to penetrate the countryside, which had been virtually closed to them heretofore. González Videla had promised during his campaign to permit the legal organization of trade unions among agricultural workers, something which had not been allowed by any previous government. The Communists set about to capitalize on this promise, with some degree of success.

There was unremitting pressure on González Videla from the Communists for more and more concessions. Unions under their control carried on a constant campaign of "quickie" strikes, and González Videla spent much of his time negotiating settlements of these walkouts.

To the author, who was in Chile during most of this period of Communist participation in the government, it seemed that the Communists made the great error of acting as if they were already in full charge of the government. They set out to terrorize the opposition, particularly the elements opposed to them in the labor movement. To a certain degree, they were supported in this by President González Videla.

Leaders of non-Communist unions were afraid to call their members out on strike, lest the government "intervene" in their organizations, remove the non-Communist leaders, and turn the unions over to the Communists. Even where the great majority of the workers were anti-Communist, as in the case of the Hospital Workers Federation, President González Videla insisted on dealing only with the small rump group established by the Communists.

Most striking was the Communist use of terrorism against the Socialists and the Anarchists. This began with a series of street clashes, where gangs of Communists attacked representatives of the other two groups and in several instances assassinated them. A leading member of the Young Socialists Federation was the principal victim of such an assault.

However, the opposition elements in the trade unions did not take these attacks lying down. They soon organized strong-arm squads of their own, and several Young Communists were also slain in the streets of Santiago. In general, after the first demoralization of their defeat, the Socialists and

Anarchists in the trade unions rallied and three months after the inauguration of González Videla were on the offensive once again.

Indeed, the principal result of the onslaught of Communist strong-arm men was the unification of all of those elements which were outside of and opposed to the González Radical-Communist-Liberal coalition. Upon the occasion of the burial of the assassinated Young Socialist leader, a huge funeral cortege was organized, in which the principal leaders of the Socialist, Democratic, and Conservative parties marched, along with thousands of workers, to the gates of the cemetery. The Communists made no attempt to challenge this demonstration.

There was considerable uneasiness among the Communists' allies, the Radicals and Liberals. It appeared as if the Communists were the chief gainers from this coalition, while the other two parties were quickly losing ground. These doubts were intensified as a result of municipal elections in April, 1947. The elections showed a considerable gain by the Communists, the Socialists, and the Conservatives. The general conclusions to be drawn from this poll were that the Communists were gaining rapidly among those who had formerly voted Radical, but were losing considerably among the workers, who had previously voted for González Videla but were now tending to return to their old Socialist allegiance. Finally, it seemed obvious that many of those right-wing voters who normally voted Liberal were perturbed by the unnatural alliance of their party with the Communists, and had chosen to support the other right-wing party, the Conservative, as a result.

The elections were followed by a week of political maneuvering. The leader of the Liberals in Congress announced that he felt his party should resign from the Radical-Communist-Liberal coalition. His words were echoed by various other Liberal spokesmen. Voices of alarm were also raised within the Radical Party, and the suggestion was heard that the Radicals were gaining little and losing much from their too close association with the Communists.

Arturo Alessandri, meanwhile, remained silent. His apartment off the Plaza Mayor was the scene of constant goings and comings of politicians of all parties, including the Communists. Finally, he gave an interview to the Liberal paper, *El Mercurio,* a week after the election; in this, after a long disquisition on the meaning of the Constitution and its role in the current crisis, he said in an apparently offhand way that he thought the Liberals should retire from González Videla's government.

The next day the Liberals did resign. They were followed by the Radicals. Only the Communist ministers refused to leave the cabinet, and it became necessary for President González Videla to request their resignations.

That night was a notable one in Santiago. A "spontaneous" torchlight parade and demonstration was organized by the Communists. The marchers chanted "No se puede gobernar sin apoyo popular" (You can't govern without popular support), meaning, of course, that González Videla would soon find that he could not govern without the Communists.

The Communists did not immediately declare war on González Videla. Although there were some strikes, particularly in the coal fields, by Communist-controlled unions protesting the dismissal of the Communist ministers, the Communists adopted a wait-and-see attitude for about a month. President González had meanwhile organized an all-Radical government with the tolerance of the Liberals in Congress, and apparently the Communists were not sure whether or not their exit from the cabinet was final.

After about a month of waiting, however, the Communists undertook a species of guerrilla warfare, using the trade unions as their principal weapon. "Quickie" strikes, designed to embarrass the González government, again became the order of the day. Finally, González Videla broke definitively with the Communist Party, and moved swiftly against them.*

Now, in October, 1947, González broke off diplomatic relations with Czechoslovakia and the Soviet Union (and a few days later Yugoslavia). At the same time the government rounded up two hundred of the country's top Communist leaders and issued warrants for the arrest of three hundred more.[62]

The occasion for this showdown was a strike which the Communists had called in the coal fields near Concepción. In breaking the strike, González asked the cooperation of the Socialist C.T.Ch., which recruited workers from other parts of the country to man the coal mines abandoned by the Communist-controlled union.[63] The strike was quickly broken.

González Videla made clear his reason for breaking with the Communists. He issued a statement which appeared in *The New York Times* of October 23, 1947, and said in part:

> Chile's Communist Party, as in all other countries, is at the service of the political, economic, and military interests which inspire the Soviet Government's action, and to that effect it uses all possible resources in both the political and labor fields.

* It should be stated here that one of the most intriguing problems in the history of the Chilean Communist Party is its relationship with González Videla. Eudosio Ravines, who had much to do with establishing the Popular Front policy of the Chilean party, and others have maintained that González Videla had been a fellow traveller of the Communists since the late 1930's.

However, an important United States diplomat, who spent many years in Chile and knew González Videla intimately, told the author that González was never fooled by the Communists. This point of view was also reflected in an article by the Scripps-Howard writer, Parker La Moore, which appeared in the New York *World Telegram* on October 1, 1947. He said that there was consternation among Chilean politicians when González admitted three Communist ministers in his cabinet, and added:

"It is known now, however, that the wily President at that time privately told two conservative leaders that there was nothing to be excited about. . . . He said he intended to give the Communists a fair trial, but that he was convinced they would not last longer than three months."

In other words, the Communist Party has abandoned the ideals of the democratic left which it feigned to defend during the last war, and now it actually helps the nationalist interests of a foreign power. It also has divorced itself definitely from the ideals of freedom and justice cherished by Republican parties.

To attain its aims, it makes increasing economic demands, it foments and seeks to introduce disorder in the life of the people, paralyzing their essential activities, as well as those that are important in case of war or necessary for the continuation of Chile's industrial program and those of other democratic countries.

It uses as its instrument the masses of workers it controls through labor organizations, oblivious that in satisfying the foreign aims it serves, it inflicts disastrous damage to the national economy and to the very workers it pretends to defend.

Thus it uses the workman's desire for social justice to further the international aims it serves. . . .

Communist attacks on González Videla grew in violence. He countered these with increasingly stern measures against them. About the middle of 1948 he sent to Congress the controversial "Law for the Permanent Defense of Democracy." This law, which was finally signed on September 3, 1948, outlawed the Communist Party, removed registered Communist voters from the electoral lists, and gave the government the power to deport Communist leaders to outlying parts of the republic and keep them there.

The controversy over this law played directly into the Communists' hands, by splitting once again their chief rival among the workers, the Socialist Party. For several years the Socialists had been moving toward greater internal unity; the Partido Socialista Auténtico had been liquidated, and most of its members had rejoined the Socialist Party. However, González Videla's policy divided the Socialists once more.

The Law for the Defense of Democracy was not the only issue which split the Socialists. Another important controversy was, as always, whether or not the Socialists should participate in the government. Late in 1947 the Socialist Party had joined the González Videla government, but as the administration adopted increasingly repressive measures and showed itself incapable of dealing effectively with the country's serious economic problems, many of the Socialists opposed continued participation.

The Socialist legislators divided over the Law for the Defense of Democracy, some voting for and some against it. Soon afterwards, the party itself split. The anti-González Videla faction broke away to form the Partido Socialista Popular, under the leadership of Raúl Ampuero and Senator Salvador Allende.[64]

Meanwhile the Communists had suffered severely in the labor movement. The Railroad Workers Federation and other important union groups withdrew from the Communist-controlled C.T.Ch., which finally was reduced to the status of a general staff of the Communist Party in the labor movement.

However, the Party was not destroyed. Its organization remained strong in spite of persecution, and the Communists even continued to have members in parliament. With the exception of Pablo Neruda, the poet and Communist member of the Senate, who was finally expelled on the grounds of his personal insults to González Videla, none of the Communist members of Congress was removed. In January, 1949, most of the Communist leaders were freed from the deportation orders which had kept them in isolated parts of the country.[65]

As the 1952 presidential election campaign approached, the other parties began to seek the support of the Communists. At this time the rising star in the Chilean political scene was the ex-dictator, Carlos Ibáñez. Much time had passed since his dictatorship, and many people tended to forget its severity, remembering only that it had been a period of "peace" and "stability."

For a considerable period the Communists worked with Ibáñez. However, they apparently were unable to arrange a sufficiently attractive "deal" with him. Furthermore, the Partido Socialista Popular decided to join the forces of "Ibañismo," and its open support of the ambitions of the ex-dictator tended to cut the ground out from under the Communists. So the Communists looked around for other allies.

Meanwhile there was considerable opposition within the Partido Socialista Popular to the party's alliance with Ibáñez. This led to a split in the P.S.P. early in 1952. Senator Salvador Allende quit the party and rejoined the other Socialist faction, the Partido Socialista de Chile, at almost the same time announcing his candidacy for the presidency of the republic.

There then took place one of those sudden shifts in Chilean politics which make it so confusing and hard to follow for outside observers—and many people in Chile as well. Allende convinced his new colleagues of the Partido Socialista de Chile to back his candidacy and to accept Communist support for it as well. As a result, the Partido Socialista de Chile, which until then had been the most violently anti-Communist group in the Chilean political spectrum, joined with the Communists and small dissident factions of the Radical and Democratic Parties to form the so-called Frente del Pueblo (People's Front), backing Salvador Allende for President.

From the Communist point of view this was undoubtedly an able maneuver. It made it possible for the Party once again to function openly in the political sphere, through the medium of the Frente del Pueblo, of which it was by all odds the most important member.

The Socialists, too, thought that they would gain a good deal from the alliance. For the time being it would reduce the tension between the Socialists of the Partido Socialista de Chile and the Communists in the trade union movement and would assure the Partido Socialista de Chile more representation in Congress—if the alliance continued until the March, 1953, congressional election—than they could possibly obtain by themselves.

This sudden change of the Partido Socialista de Chile from the most violent opponent to the closest ally of the Communists was symptomatic of what had occurred to the Communists' chief rivals on the Chilean Left. The Socialists had acquired a profound feeling of inferiority in the face of the Communists, and were relieved to put an end to hostilities for the time being. Although not trusting the Communists, and knowing full well that the latter would abandon the alliance if it suited their purposes, they were glad to have a release of tension.

Again there were four candidates in the presidential election. Way out in front was Carlos Ibáñez. He was backed by the P.S.P. and by the Agrarian Labor Party, a group which had appeared after World War II and which was a peculiar amalgam of ex-Nazis, extreme nationalists, and socially minded intellectuals. Splinter groups from most of the other political parties also backed Ibáñez, but his strength did not come from any political party. It came from the general disillusionment of the masses of the people in the traditional parties, including the Communists, and a feeling verging on desperation, arising from the ever-mounting inflation.

The attitude of the Communists toward Ibáñez during this campaign remains something of a mystery. Officially they were opposed to him and were supporting the candidates of the Frente del Pueblo. However, the smallness of Allende's vote and the relatively mild behavior of the Communists towards Ibáñez during the campaign brought this into question.

Certainly, Ibáñez' program seemed to offer the Communists new opportunities. He promised to repeal the Law for the Permanent Defense of Democracy. His movement was an amorphous one, with no ideology or real program of its own, and if the Communists could operate inside it, it might be a fertile breeding ground for their Party.

The Partido Socialista Popular had operated on this principle.* Its leaders felt that Ibáñez was going to win anyway, and that the P.S.P. could influence the movement by joining it, but would be crushed if it attempted to buck the Ibañista forces.[66]

The second candidate in the 1952 election was Arturo Matte Larraín, son-in-law of the late Arturo Alessandri and nominee of the Liberal Party. Around him rallied all the elements of the Right in Chilean politics. He came in second in the voting.

The nominee favored by González Videla was Pedro Enrique Alfonso,

---

* By the end of 1955 the P.S.P. had become the most violent opponent of the Ibáñez government. Early in the following year, it entered yet another coalition with the Communists, the Frente de Acción Popular, together with the elements of the old Frente del Pueblo.

a member of the Radical Party, who had been González' Minister of Interior. He was backed by fractions of the parties which had made up the traditional Left. One element was a part of the Partido Socialista de Chile which had refused to go along with Salvador Allende and his alliance with the Communists, and which attempted to maintain a third Socialist Party under the leadership of Bernardo Ibáñez, Manuel Hidalgo, and other uncompromising anti-Communists. The bulk of the Radical Party also backed Alfonso, though minority Radical groups backed Allende and Ibáñez. Some of the Democráticos likewise backed Alfonso, as did the Social Catholic Falange Party. He received the third largest number of votes.

Allende was the fourth candidate, backed by the Frente del Pueblo, consisting largely of the Communist Party, the Partido Socialista de Chile, and minority elements of the Partido Democrático and the Radical Party. He came in last.

Whatever hopes the Communists may have had concerning the election of Ibáñez were not fulfilled. In spite of his promise to have the Law for the Permanent Defense of Democracy repealed, Ibáñez took no step toward accomplishing this. Some time after the election he announced that he had no intention of having the law repealed, that it was still necessary, since the Communists remained a menace to the nation.

However, the Communists did have virtually complete freedom to operate for a while after the inauguration of President Ibáñez. In the beginning the Law for the Preservation of Democracy was enforced hardly at all by the Ibáñez government. Although 40,000 Communist voters were still off the voting lists, there were few other handicaps to the free functioning of the Party.

The Communists took most advantage of their new freedom in the trade union field. The events of 1946-52 had reduced both C.T.Ch.'s to small groups. Many of the unions which the Communists had controlled in the earlier years had escaped from their grasp. This was particularly true of the miners—the copper workers had withdrawn from the Communist-dominated Miners Federation to form their own Confederación de Trabajadores de Cobre, under the political influence of the Partido Socialista Popular. It was also true among the maritime workers, where Communist influence had been reduced to a fraction of its former strength, and among the textile workers.

As a result of all of this, the Communists took up the slogan of "unity" in the labor movement. In doing so they hoped to short-circuit a move by Socialist trade unionists of both the P.S.P. and the Partido Socialista de Chile to unite all non-Communist unions in a new confederation.[67]

The original plans of the Socialists (which had the backing of the American Regional Organization of Workers, the O.R.I.T.) were to unite the Chilean organizations which were affiliated with or were willing to affiliate with the I.C.F.T.U. and the O.R.I.T., and to leave out the Communist-controlled unions. However, the Communists loudly played the tune of "labor unity," and persuaded the Socialist leaders to include them in the new unification of the Chilean labor movement. This led to the formation of the Central Unica de Trabajadores de Chile (known generally by its initials as the C.U.T.Ch.), in January, 1953. Virtually all the country's industrial union federations participated in the founding congress and joined the C.U.T.Ch.

There were six political groups in the C.U.T.Ch. founding congress: the Communists, the Partido Socialista de Chile, the Partido Socialista Popular, the Anarchists, the Social Catholics, and the Radical Party. There was much political horse-trading before the Executive Committee of the new organization was established. The upshot was a Committee with four Communists, four representatives of the P.S.P., four of the P.S.Ch., three Anarchists, one Radical, four Social Catholics, and one independent. One of the Catholics, Clotario Blest, and one member of the P.S.Ch., Baudillo Casanova, were out-and-out fellow-travellers of the Communists.[68]

Although the Communists were only a small minority of the C.U.T.Ch. Executive Committee, and although the Congress of the C.U.T.Ch. refused to join the Communists' World Federation of Trade Unions, the new group also refused to take an anti-Communist position and thus did not join the anti-Communist I.C.F.T.U. In the years that followed Communist and pro-Communist members of the C.U.T.Ch. executive attended Communist conferences in both hemispheres, "representing" the C.U.T.Ch., without being called to account publicly by the other members of the executive.

By the end of 1954 the Chilean labor movement presented a surprising case of the tail wagging the dog. The unions under the Communists' control were few—the much reduced Miners Federation, the now small Metal Workers Federation, the Construction Workers Federation. The Socialists, when their two parties were taken together, controlled by far the largest group—dominating the Railroad Workers, the Maritime Workers, the Hospital Workers, the Chemical and Pharmaceutical Workers, and numerous small unions. Most of the rest of the country's unions were controlled by one or another of the non-Marxist left-wing parties. In spite of this fact, on all crucial issues the non-Communist unions followed the Communists' lead. The Communists controlled many of the regional organizations of the C.U.T.Ch., including the all-important Santiago group. The Communists, by playing on the rivalries among their opponents and upon the personal vanity of many of the non-Communist union leaders, were able to keep the overwhelming majority of non-Communist unionists in a permanent position of inferiority.

The Communists had various weapons at their command, both inside and outside the labor movement. One of the most important of these was a subtle kind of bribery, represented by trips to the Soviet Union and other countries behind the Iron Curtain. In the late 1940's and early 1950's literally thousands of Chileans were the beneficiaries of such trips. Although some of those who visited the Communist countries returned disenchanted, many others were duly impressed and came back to sing the praises of the Soviet Union and its satellites.

Another powerful weapon was the myth of leftist unity. For 14 years after 1938 the country had been dominated by a coalition of left-wing forces. But the two right-wing parties, the Conservatives and Liberals, remained very strong. Much of the time they controlled Congress. They were a perpetual menace to the leftist hold on the country's politics.

The secret of the power of the right-wing parties was the fact that their control over the rural parts of Chile remained virtually untouched by the end of 1954. Chile was still suffering from a system of *latifundia,* or large landholding, which gave the landlords control not only of the earth, but also of the people who lived on it.

Until the election of 1952 it had been customary for the landlords to march their peons off to the polls to vote for the local Liberal or Conservative nominee. Thus, these two parties had always been assured of a sizable representation in Congress.

The most significant thing about the election of Carlos Ibáñez in 1952 had been the fact that for the first time, this control of the peasant vote had escaped from the Liberal and Conservative landholders. The majority of the rural workers and tenants voted for Carlos Ibáñez, much against their masters' wishes.

Had Ibáñez and his followers been fully aware of the significance of this fact, they might have undertaken the reform which is most needed in Chile—an agrarian reform. This would not only have broken the solid phalanx of the Right in Chilean politics, it would have made it possible for the first time to end the ever-climbing spiral of inflation. An agrarian reform would bring much more land into cultivation, resulting in larger crops and lower prices for agricultural products—largely foodstuffs—thus bringing a significant reduction in the cost of living, since most of the Chilean worker's budget is spent on food.

However, by the middle of 1956 no such agrarian reform had been undertaken, the inflation was as rampant as ever, and the solid right-wing bloc remained. Its existence made it possible for the Communists continually to invoke the legend of "left-wing unity." They could continue to insist that if the other left-wing parties did not accept an alliance with the Communists, they would be at the mercy of the Right, which historically has been true in Chile.

A third advantage which the Communists possessed was a source of abundant funds. The Communists have for years been the best-financed political group in Chile. In the 1930's much of their funds undoubtedly came from outside the country. In more recent years stories have circulated, which it is impossible to check, concerning the investments owned by the Communist Party in Chile. These are said to include bus lines, real estate projects, printing establishments, and numerous other money-making enterprises.

Whether their funds come from these sources or are "Moscow gold," it is certain that the Communists have long had ample financial resources. These constitute a bait, which can always be dangled before other parties, particularly the left-wing parties, which are poor. These funds also permit the Party to have a large corps of full-time functionaries, a luxury which other parties cannot afford. This is a particularly important weapon in the trade union field, and is one of the principal explanations for the Communists' predominant position in the labor movement.

Aside from its basic weakness among the populace, the greatest drawback to Communism's position in Chile is the volatility of the country's politics. The changeable nature of political alliances in the country has often given the Communists allies they might not have had in other nations. On the other hand, Chilean political alliances are disconcertingly short in their duration. The Communists, therefore, have never been able to consolidate their alliances and take full advantage of them. This, indeed, has been what has kept the Communists from gaining more influence than they now have, and from becoming a greater menace to the country's democratic tradition of government.

Thus, by the middle of 1956, although the Communists of Chile had power and influence out of all proportion to their membership or to the organizations which they controlled, they were still a long way from gaining control of the country's government. It remained clear, as it had been for over three decades, that Communism profited from the divisions among its opponents and from its rivals' failure to carry out a program which would deprive the Communists of the issues they have exploited by picturing themselves as the only true defenders of the nation's down-trodden. The only real answer to the Communists in Chile remained a social reform program which, beginning with an agrarian reform, would establish a firm economic basis for political and social democracy in the shoestring republic.

*Chapter XI*

# Communism in the High Andes

BOLIVIA, PERU, AND EQUADOR were all part of the Inca Empire when the Spaniards first landed on the West Coast of South America, early in the sixteenth century. A high degree of civilization had existed for at least a millennium among the Indians who peopled the high valleys of the Andes and the coastal areas between the mountains and sea. When the Spaniards arrived they succeeded in a short time in overthrowing the extensive Inca Empire. The conquerors divided the land and the people on it among themselves, and there began a four-century-long struggle between the Indians, and the Spaniards and their descendants. The Indians fought a rear-guard action to keep their land and to maintain their culture, religion, language. During most of the period since the Conquest the Indians have been the losers in this struggle. Having little standing in the white man's courts and no representation in his government, they have had to fight with the weapons of passive resistance, only occasionally resorting to sudden bursts of desperate violence.

The great majority of the Indians of the High Andes were converted into semi-serfs. In return for small bits of land which they were granted by the usurpers of their ancient communities, the Indians were expected to cultivate the holdings of the white landlords and to render personal service to their masters.

The landowning descendants of the Conquistadores became the rulers of the Andean countries. They dominated their society, their economic life, their politics. And they ruthlessly suppressed any attempts to dislodge them from positions of dominance.

However, even the Andean countries could not remain immune to the effects of the Industrial Revolution and modern capitalist society. Their rich deposits of minerals have been sought by the great industrial nations. So has their petroleum. Large-scale capitalist agriculture has produced goods for sale in the world market. Along the coast and in the larger cities, manufacturing industries have appeared.

These economic changes have brought social and political transformations. New social classes have appeared which have not been willing to submit indefinitely to the rule of the large landholders. In these new social classes, the Indians have found allies for the first time in many centuries.

Thus, the Andean countries are ripe for the Latin American social revolution, for agrarian reform, economic development, labor and peasant organization, and political democracy. In one of these nations, Bolivia, the revolution has already begun. In Peru it has been prevented during the last quarter of a century or more only by a series of military dictatorships. In the third nation, Ecuador, there are so far only faint glimmerings of this coming social, political, and economic change.

Such a situation should logically give the Communists a considerable opportunity. Indeed, the surprising thing about the situation in these three nations is that the Communists have made such little headway. The reason for this is that in the two countries where the social revolution has become an active threat or a reality, the Communists have been faced with indigenous national revolutionary groups which have taken the lead in the struggle to modernize the economies and politics of their respective nations. The Communists, as a result, have remained on the fringe of these countries' affairs, unable to sink deep roots or to arouse wide popular support.

A clearer picture of the situation can be gained from a more detailed analysis of each country.

## BOLIVIA

Bolivia's two-and-a-half-mile-high plateaus have probably been peopled by civilized human beings for a longer time than any other part of the American continents. Perhaps two millenniums ago, a prehistoric civilization, the remnants of whose stone cities may still be seen along Lake Titicaca, 13,000 feet above sea level, was built by the ancestors of present-day Bolivia's Aymara Indians. At the coming of the white man, more than four hundred years ago, the country was part of the Empire of the Incas, whose descendants form the other great Indian group in today's Bolivia, the Quechuas.

Both Indian races were subjugated by the conquering Spaniards, and only in recent decades have conditions changed so as to give the Indians new weapons with which to carry on their age-old struggle for the land and for full-fledged participation in the affairs of the nation. The coming of modern tin-mining created a compact group of Indians, who could be organized to demand their citizenship rights and a voice in how the community should be run. This group found allies among the growing Indian and mestizo (of mixed Indian and white ancestry) working class of La Paz and other cities.

These two groups—the tin miners and the urban proletariat—in 1952 brought about a revolution which put Bolivia on the path to social change and seemed destined to overthrow the white landowning aristocracy which had controlled the country for four hundred years.

Although a revolution of this kind would seem likely to give the Communists a special opportunity for agitation and organization, by the middle of 1956 they had been able to make but little progress. As was not the case with a somewhat similar situation in Guatemala, the Communists in Bolivia were faced with a strong rival in an ideological party which knew which way it wanted the revolution to go and how it wanted to take it there.

The present Communist Party of Bolivia was not established until December, 1949, though Communist groups had been active in the country for more than two decades. As early as 1923, Roberto Hinojosa, a young student leader from Cochabamba, described himself as being of the "extreme Left," and soon afterwards, when he was exiled, he made contact in Argentina with the Communist International.[1]

The country's best-known pro-Communist during the 1920's was Gustavo Navarro. In 1920 he was Bolivian consul in Paris, where he came to have much sympathy for the postwar revolutionary movements in Europe. He published a good deal about them, but did not wish to use his own name for these books and articles. He chose, instead, the name Tristán Maroff, one which he subsequently made famous.

In 1925 he returned to Bolivia, where he organized a Partido Socialista. This was not a Communist Party, and never affiliated with the Communist International, but it had great sympathy for the Soviet Union. The party was severely persecuted, its leaders were often arrested, its publications were banned. Its members were forced into hiding from time to time. Maroff himself was finally deported, and the party collapsed.[2]

By 1926 there were small groups of Communists active in La Paz, Cochabamba, and a few other places. However, they never formed an official Communist Party of Bolivia.[3] Some of these Communists worked inside Anarchist organizations. Thus Rigoberto Rivera reported in *La Correspondencia Sudamericana* of June 30, 1926, that in the Anarchist Centro Obrero Libertario "there are at the present time twenty members, almost all of them propagandists for Communism."

These early Communists were active in the labor movement, which was largely made up of mutual benefit societies and was under Anarchist influence. In 1929 the Communists were credited by *El Trabajador Latino Americano* (August-September, 1930) with leading a miners' strike in the city of Potosí.

At this time there was in existence a loose Confederación Boliviana del Trabajo, which had affiliates in various cities and its headquarters in Potosí. Although the C.B.T. was under Anarchist influence, it decided to send delegates to the continental trade union congress which the Red International of Labor Unions had organized in Montevideo for the spring of 1929. In stating its determination to attend the Montevideo Congress, the Confederación, was reported in *El Trabajador Latino Americano* of January 31-February 15, 1929, to have declared:

> The Confederación Boliviana del Trabajo, realizing the importance of this Congress, in which will be discussed questions of vital importance, both in the field of doctrine and in that of organization, as well as the creation of the Confederación Sindical Latino Americana, the principles which it should adopt as the Central Labor Organization of the continental labor movement, make it absolutely necessary that the Bolivian proletariat pledge its support of and accept the invitation to the conference. . . .

However, although the C.B.T. was represented in Montevideo, it did not join the C.S.L.A. The only Bolivian group actually to affiliate with the C.S.L.A. was the Federación Obrera de La Paz, under Communist influence. Its relations with the Anarchist-controlled Confederación Boliviana del Trabajo were not good, but the Communist group decided to accept an invitation issued by the C.B.T. for a national labor congress in Oruro on August 10, 1930. The Communists were in a minority in this congress, which decided not to join the Latin American Confederation. The Communists claimed to control not only the delegations of its own Federación Obrera of La Paz, but also similar groups from Sucre and Potosí, as well as the railroad workers' delegates from Uyuni and Oruro.[4]

The fighting between the Communists and their enemies in the trade unions was soon brought to an end by the outbreak of the Chaco War with Paraguay. As a result of this struggle, the whole labor movement was suppressed.

All the ideological groups in the labor movement opposed the war, but they did so in different ways. The Anarchists, the followers of Tristán Maroff, and a group of so-called "Communist nationalists" urged the workers to "desert and throw away your guns." The Communists opposed this point of view and argued that "individual desertion never can stop the war." Instead, they urged the workers to go to the front and there propagandize against the war and end it by revolution.[5] All working-class organizations were persecuted, strikes were broken, union leaders were jailed or sent to the front lines, where they were killed.[6]

During the war various groups of exiles were active in neighboring countries. One of these, the Grupo Obrero Tupac Amaru, in Argentina, was in contact with both the Socialist and the Communist parties there. Out of this group came people who were to be founders of the Trotskyite party, Partido Obrero Revolucionario, and of the predecessor of the Bolivian Communist Party, the Partido de la Izquierda Revolucionaria.[7]

The post-Chaco War period was marked by two revolutionary governments which for the first time showed some interest in the plight of the urban working class, those of Colonel Toro in 1936-37 and Colonel Germán Busch in 1937-39. Under Toro, the labor movement revived. In 1936 the Communist-controlled Federación Obrera de La Paz and the Anarchist Federación Obrera Local of La Paz signed a pact of unity as the basis for the establishment of a new national central labor organization. As a result of these negotiations, a congress was held which founded the Confederación Sindical de Trabajadores de Bolivia, first controlled by Tristán Maroff and his followers, who were closely associated with the Toro government. The pro-Communists were a minority in the new labor group, and at the last minute the Anarchists did not join it at all.[8]

The Communists were active in politics through the Comité Revolucionaria de la Izquierda, which later changed its name to Frente de Izquierda Boliviana. They were in close contact with the Chilean Communist Party. However, it was not until after the death of Colonel Busch and the installation of the moderate government of General Quintanilla that a Communist-oriented political party was established, the Partido de la Izquierda Revolucionaria (Party of the Revolutionary Left).[9] The P.I.R. was organized in 1940 by the Frente de Izquierda Revolucionaria and various regional political groups. It described itself as a "Marxist Socialist Party with full national autonomy," and denied being Communist.[10]

The P.I.R. sought influence in the labor movement. It organized party "brigades" in most of the unions, through which it tried to influence their policies.[11] It was the only party to so organize its trade union supporters, and within a short time they were the principal element in the C.S.T.B., displacing the followers of Tristán Maroff, who had controlled it during the regimes of Colonels Toro and Busch.

The new party received its baptism of fire in the 1940 presidential election. The government of General Quintanilla backed General Peñaranda, a hero of the Chaco War, as its candidate, and the P.I.R. put up José Antonio Arze, as the only candidate in opposition to the government nominee. He carried the towns of Cochabamba, Oruro, and Potosí. This election campaign made the P.I.R. a major factor in Bolivian politics.[12]

Two other important parties were organized at about this same time. In 1938 the Partido Obrero Revolucionario was established, its founders being most of the group who in exile had formed the Grupo Obrero Tupac Amaru. It was a Trotskyite organization and affiliated with the Fourth International. At first it made very little impression on the Bolivian workers, and it was not until the organization of the Federación Sindical de Trabajadores Mineros in the early 1940's that the P.O.R. began to get a foothold in the labor movement.

The other party which was organized at this time was the Movimiento Nacionalista Revolucionario, headed by a brilliant young economist, Víctor Paz Estenssorro. Its chief spokesman in the theoretical field was

Luis Peñaloza, who had been a member of the Grupo Obrero Tupac Amaru, but broke with it when the majority formed the P.O.R. The M.N.R. was a left-wing nationalist party. In its early years it was charged with having Nazi sympathies, an accusation which it subsequently declared to have been a calumny. Leaders of the party professed that it was similar to the Peruvian Aprista Party, and like the Apristas, they took particular interest in the Indians. They led the protests inside and outside of parliament when government troops fired on striking tin miners at Catavi, in December, 1942, a clash which ultimately brought down the Peñaranda government and made the M.N.R. a partner in the succeeding regime of President Gualberto Villarroel.

The Revolution of 1943 which overthrew President Peñaranda was a military *coup d'état* by a group of young officers, many of whom were widely suspected of being pro-Nazi, in conjunction with the M.N.R. Víctor Paz, the M.N.R. leader, became Minister of Finance.

Right after the Revolution, José Antonio Arze, the leader of the P.I.R., who was in the United States teaching at the Communist Party's Jefferson School, announced his and his party's support of the new regime. He then entered into negotiations with the new President, Major Gualberto Villarroel, proposing the formation of a coalition government to include the Army, the M.N.R., the P.I.R., the C.S.T.B. (which was under P.I.R. control), and "independent elements of a democratic point of view." Villarroel rejected this suggestion, and so Arze and the P.I.R. passed over to the opposition.

In March, 1944, Arze began touring the country to rally support for the P.I.R., as the chief opposition party. Arze was under arrest for a short time before he set out on his tour, and a few weeks later an attempt, widely attributed to the government, was made to assassinate the P.I.R. leader. It failed, but Arze again had to leave the country, going to the United States for hospitalization.[13]

Throughout most of the rest of the Villarroel regime, the P.I.R. remained one of the principal opposition groups. The government attempted to weaken the P.I.R. by breaking its control of the labor movement. A group of government supporters called a "third congress of the C.S.T.B.," which brought denunciation from the C.S.T.B. Secretary General, Donato Flores Gironda.[14] This congress founded a new C.S.T.B., headed by Víctor Chávez A., which claimed departmental federations in Sucre, Cochabamba, Santa Cruz, Tarija, and Oruro.[15]

During the latter part of the Villarroel regime, Roberto Hinojosa, who was by now a supporter of the Villarroel government, attempted to organize a Partido Comunista. It seems to have had no support from or connection with the international Communist movement and seems to have been principally an attempt to undermine the P.I.R. This Partido Comunista won little support and died with the death of its organizer, who was hung by a mob on the day the Villarroel government was overthrown.

However, the Villarroel government did not confine its labor activities to trying to seize control of the C.S.T.B. Under the lead of the M.N.R. ministers, the government took a sympathetic attitude toward attempts to organize the workers in the tin mines belonging to the Big Three mining companies, Patiño, Hochschild, and Aramayo. These workers were mainly Indians, many of whom worked only part time in the mines and returned to their small plots of land during harvest time.

The M.N.R. not only influenced the government to permit the organization of the miners, it took the lead in actually propagating unionism among them. By the end of the Villarroel regime in July, 1946, the great majority of the miners were organized in the Federación Sindical de Trabajadores Mineros, which was firmly under the control of the Movimiento Nacionalista Revolucionario.

In 1945 a new and important leader appeared among these workers when Juan Lechin, son of a Syrian merchant and a Bolivian woman, became Secretary General of the F.S.T.B. He belonged to the M.N.R., though he had certain sympathies for the Trotskyite P.O.R., whom he allowed to write the Federación's program and to whom he gave important posts in the organization.

In the last months of the Villarroel regime, the government attempted to make overtures to the continental Communist movement. In Mexico, the Bolivian ambassador, Carlos Montenegro, appeared on the same platform with Vicente Lombardo Toledano at a meeting to celebrate the anniversary of Bolivian independence. He paid tribute to "maestro Lombardo Toledano." For his part, Lombardo said that the C.T.A.L. had opposed the Villarroel government

> because we thought that it was a government which, regardless of its origin, had to prove that it had risen against the dictatorship of Peñaranda in order to change the situation of the people, and we said that insofar as the government demonstrated democratic leanings the Latin American workers' movement would lend it a hand and extend its aid.[16]

In spite of these exchanges, the P.I.R. played a leading role in the overthrow of the government. In the violent uprising which put an end to it, Gualberto Villarroel was hung in the Plaza Murillo in front of the presidential palace,* as was Roberto Hinojosa, head of the pro-government "Partido Comunista." Donato Flores Gironda, head of the Confederación Sindical de Trabajadores, and other P.I.R. leaders formed a part of the provisional government which ruled between the overthrow of Villar-

---

* When the M.N.R. again assumed the reins of government, in 1952, it converted the lamppost into a shrine to Villarroel's memory, placing a suitable plaque in front of it and stationing a soldier there as an honor guard, day and night.

roel and the establishment of a new constitutional government, that of President Enrique Hertzog, in the middle of 1947.

The P.I.R. supported Supreme Court Justice Guachalla, the opponent of President Hertzog, in the 1947 election, but in the first months of the administration, the P.I.R. had members in the Hertzog cabinet. Thereafter, the P.I.R. remained the "loyal opposition" to the Hertzog regime. Its relations with Hertzog's successor, Mamerto Urriolagoitia, were not so close. The P.I.R. finally passed into the opposition, and in the 1951 election it supported the M.N.R.'s presidential candidate, Víctor Paz Estenssorro. Although Paz was elected, he was not allowed to take office. Instead of recognizing the results of the election, President Urriolagoitia resigned and turned power over to a Military Junta, presided over by General Ballivián.

However, the P.I.R.'s early association with the Hertzog and Urriolagoitia governments did much to discredit it among the workers, who were its principal constituents. These two governments acted harshly toward the labor movement, which was largely controlled by the M.N.R. Whether or not this harsh policy had the approval of the Partido de la Izquierda Revolucionaria, the P.I.R. got much of the blame for it among the workers.

The association of the P.I.R. with the Hertzog and Urriolagoitia regimes caused much dissension within the P.I.R. itself. In December, 1949, a body made up largely of members of the party's youth group withdrew from the P.I.R. to form the Partido Comunista de Bolivia.

On April 9, 1952, the M.N.R. seized power, with the help of the workers of La Paz and the miners from the nearby tin towns. Víctor Paz Estenssorro, who had been elected President in 1951 but had not been allowed by the Military Junta to take office, was proclaimed Constitutional President by the revolutionaries. Three M.N.R. trade union leaders, including Juan Lechin as Minister of Mines, entered the Paz government.

After the Revolution of 1952 it became obvious that the P.I.R. had little or no popular support. As a result, a party congress was held in July, 1952, and the P.I.R. was formally liquidated.* Some of those who participated in this congress stayed on to form a second Partido Comunista, which came to be popularly called the Partido Comunista #2. In March, 1953, the two Communist groups united.[17]

The first three years of the Bolivian revolution which began in April, 1952, were marked by a great expansion of the labor movement. Not only were the Miners Federation and the Railroad Workers Confederation revived, but a National Confederation of Factory Workers was established, as was a Confederation of White Collar Workers. In preparation for the

* In 1955 some of the P.I.R. leaders who had refused to join the Partido Comunista revived the P.I.R. The P.I.R. and Partido Comunista ran a joint ticket in the election of 1956.

agrarian reform, a countryside network of peasant unions sprang into existence, under the patronage of the government.

The Communist Party was the third largest political group in this new labor and peasant movement. It continued to command a certain amount of sympathy among the railroad workers and made some slight headway among the miners. It gained considerable strength among the factory workers of La Paz, though it was not so strong in the National Confederation. It also had some influence among the La Paz Federation of White Collar Workers. It made little progress among the peasants.

The M.N.R. was overwhelmingly the dominant force in the labor movement. The miners and factory workers were firmly in its hands. The White Collar Workers Confederation was controlled for a while by the Trotskyite P.O.R. Among the peasants, the M.N.R. was dominant, though during the first year after the Revolution, the Trotskyites controlled the Cochabamba regional federation.

The Communists had representation in the Central Obrera Boliviana, the national confederation established a few weeks after the 1952 Revolution. During the first eight or nine months, the C.O.B. was under the control of the Trotskyites, but when they attempted to use it to criticize the government's policy on the nationalization of the tin mines, the M.N.R. ousted some of the P.O.R. delegates from the C.O.B. and assumed control. Both Trotskyites and Communists continued to be represented in the C.O.B., but they had more nuisance value than anything else.

The first Congress of the C.O.B., which met at the end of October, 1954, was completely dominated by the forces of the M.N.R. They rallied the Central Obrera to full support of the government, and though the Communists had a voice, they had few votes in the Congress. The Trotskyites were also weak.*

The principal reason for the continued weakness of both Stalinist and Trotskyite Communists in Bolivia was the fact that the moderate, nationalist-Socialist Movimiento Nacionalista Revolucionario had gained and held the support of the great majority of the country's workers, peasants, and intellectuals. In the first three years of the M.N.R. regime the Paz Estenssorro government had carried through a basic social revolution. It had ended the age-old, semifeudal landholding pattern by expropriating the *latifundia* and beginning the process of distributing it among the land-hungry Indian peasants. It had also expropriated the tin-mining industry, making it a government monopoly.

The government had also decreed a reorganization and expansion of the country's educational system and had begun to put into effect a plan

* Late in 1954 the Partido Obrero Revolucionario split into three quarrelling groups, while a fourth element, including the party's most important trade union leaders, joined the M.N.R. This virtually killed the Trotskyite party, which received only 2500 votes in the 1956 election.

which had as its objective the bringing of an appreciation of the modern world to the 75 per cent of the population who had hitherto been illiterate. Finally, the Paz government had launched a program of developing Bolivia's agriculture, mining, and industry, a program which by the end of 1954 had already registered spectacular success in the petroleum fields.

Although the Paz government was still faced with serious problems, particularly that of inflation, its accomplishments had been enough to prove that the administration was willing to carry out its promises. If it continued to put into effect its plan of ending the semifeudal economic and social system inherited from the time of the Spanish Conquistadores, and of laying the foundations for a prosperous and democratic nation in which both races and all classes could fully participate, it would continue to cut the ground out from under the Communists.

## PERU

The Peruvian Communists have been the handmaidens of virtually every dictatorship under which their country has suffered in the last quarter of a century. The reason for this has been the existence of the Peruvian Aprista Party, which has caught and held the imagination of the majority of the politically literate people of Peru, thus blocking the path of the Communists.

In the face of the Apristas' continuing strength, the alliance of the Communists and the dictators has been convenient for both groups. The Apristas, urging land reform, advanced labor legislation, industrialization, and the incorporation of the Indian masses into the civic life of the nation, have been a constant threat to the traditional regime in Peru, which has rested on the twin pillars of Army support and the wealth of the agrarian and commercial aristocracy.

At the same time, because of their advanced program and their hold on the urban masses and a considerable proportion of the Indians, the Apristas have been the chief stumbling block to the advancement of Communism. Therefore, it has been convenient for the Communists to seek allies among the Apristas' worst enemies—the dictators.

Both sides have sought advantages from this oft-renewed alliance. The dictators and the groups which back them have hoped to be able to build up through the Communists certain support among the people which they could not achieve by themselves, and thus counteract the influence of the Apristas. For their part, the Communists have sought to use government aid in building up their own influence in the trade unions and among the people in general. Thus, the Communists have played an important role in preventing the development of the social and economic revolution which is so long overdue in Peru. A land two thirds of whose population is descended from the ancient Incas, Peru has been the scene of a four-centuries-long struggle between these Indians and the heirs of their Spanish conquerors. The Indians have fought a rear-guard action to preserve the remnants of their ancient landholdings and to maintain their age-old culture and language.

For more than 25 years the Apristas have been advocating a revolution which would make the Indians truly a part of modern Peru. They have urged the return of the land to the ancient Indian communities from which it was stolen by the white landowners. They have sought universal education for the Indian masses. They have supported an economic program to develop the economy and end the dependence of the Indian peasant on a subsistence agriculture which has doomed him for centuries to a miserably low standard of living. It is for this reason that they have been so violently opposed by the white and near-white aristocracy. And it has been because of the constant struggle of the Apristas that the Peruvian Communists have never become a really decisive element in the political life of Peru.

The Communist Party of Peru had its origin in the Aprista movement. The latter arose from unrest among the students and workers at the end of the first World War. The students of the University of San Marcos in Lima organized a "popular university," to give classes in a wide variety of subjects to the members of the trade union movement of Lima and the port city of Callao. At the same time, a number of the student leaders, outstanding among them being Víctor Raúl Haya de la Torre, supported the workers' campaign for the eight-hour day and helped the workers to consolidate their trade union organizations. The Textile Workers Federation in particular owed its foundation to Haya de la Torre.

In 1923 President Augusto Leguía, dictator at that time, decided that the student-worker movement, of which Haya de la Torre was now the undisputed leader, was a menace to his regime. He arrested Haya and deported him to Panama. From there Haya moved to Mexico, then on to the United States and Europe. In all these places, Haya and the group of students which he gathered around him studied the various social and economic currents of the time and sought to work out a philosophy of and lay the foundations for a movement which would be particularly adapted to Latin America and to Peru.

In 1924 the Alianza Popular Revolucionaria Americana (A.P.R.A.) was established by Haya in Mexico. Around this organization gathered a group of Peruvian students studying abroad. Local branches of A.P.R.A. were established in Mexico, Buenos Aires, Paris, and other centers. The leader of the Paris branch was Eudosio Ravines, later the founder of the Communist Party of Peru.

During his years in Europe Haya visited Britain—where for a short while he was a student at Cambridge—France, Germany, and finally

Russia. He went there in company with Bertram Wolfe, then a leader of the United States Communist Party, on his way to Moscow for the Fifth Congress of the Communist International. There Haya talked with many of the Soviet leaders and became convinced that Communism as it had evolved in the Soviet Union was a Russian phenomenon which was not applicable to Latin America.

Back in Western Europe, Haya and Ravines attended the Anti-Imperialist Congress which the Communists organized in Brussels in 1928. The Aprista delegates were the minority in the Congress and objected to many of the resolutions passed there. Frequently the resolutions were passed with the note that they were accepted by the Aprista delegates only "with reservations."[18]

Meanwhile, in Peru, two trends had been evident. In the first place, the group of labor leaders with which Haya had been most closely connected, the textile workers, had been keeping his memory fresh. Haya frequently had articles in their paper, they celebrated the day on which he was expelled as a day to be commemorated by the labor movement, and they continuously pictured him as a martyr for the Peruvian workers.[19]

On the other hand, another group of students and intellectuals had formed around José Carlos Mariátegui. He had been a brilliant student while at the University and had been chosen by Dictator Leguía to receive a government scholarship for travel and study in Europe in the early 1920's. He returned home a Marxist and founded a magazine, *Amauta*, which was one of the most brilliant intellectual journals in Latin America. Contributions to it came from all over the Continent and from leading left-wing intellectuals of Europe as well.

Mariátegui was more clearly a Marxist than was Haya de la Torre. Although Haya maintained in later years that Mariátegui was basically in agreement with his own position, the activities of the Mariátegui group were oriented toward the foundation in Peru of a Communist Party.[20]

Their first step was to send Julio Portocarrero, a pro-Communist trade union leader and a member of the group, to Moscow to attend the Fifth Congress of the Red International of Labor Unions and while there to make contact with the Communist International itself. He returned with a series of suggestions or orders from the Comintern. The last of these said: "There exist in Peru isolated Communists who are in accord with the program and tactics of the C.I. These elements should take the initiative to form a Peruvian C.P. The Secretariat of the C.I. will do all possible to aid this work."[21]

As a direct result of this communication, the founding meeting of the Partido Socialista del Perú was held on September 16, 1928, at a spot halfway between Lima and the beach of Herradura, with six people present: Julio Portocarrero, Avelino Navarro, Hinojosa, Borja, Ricardo Martínez de la Torre, and Bernardo Regman. Mariátegui was sick and unable to attend, but his ideas were presented by Martínez de la Torre, and he was considered as the seventh member of the founding group.

Several weeks later, on October 7, the group met once again, with Luciano Castillo and Chávez León added to their number. At this meeting they formally declared the Partido Socialista to exist and named Mariátegui as Secretary General. Portocarrero was elected trade union secretary, Martínez de la Torre secretary of propaganda, Bernardo Regman treasurer. Navarro and Hinojosa were made assistant trade union secretaries.[22]

Soon afterwards Mariátegui drew up the Program of the Party, which consisted of an analysis of the situation of Peru at that particular time and a detailed program of both immediate demands and long-range objectives of the party. It proclaimed that "the basis of Marxist socialism in the present period is Marxism-Leninism," though it did not announce the party's intention of affiliating with the Comintern.[23]

Delegates of the Socialist Party attended the continental Communist Congress in Buenos Aires in May, 1929. However, their thesis that Communism in Peru should first be organized under the cover of a Socialist Party was sharply criticized by representatives of the Comintern and by the Argentine Communist leader, Victorio Codovilla, among others.[24] Soon after this conference, and only a few days before the death of Mariátegui, the Peruvian party received a letter from the Comintern, directing them to proceed immediately to change the name of their group to Partido Comunista.[25]

The events in Buenos Aires and the letter from the International produced a crisis in the Partido Socialista. However, before it was resolved, Mariátegui, who had long suffered from tuberculosis, was dead.

The Communists' relations with Mariátegui have remained one of the more intriguing chapters in the history of the Peruvian Communist Party. Although his position on Peruvian affairs was decisively rejected by the Comintern, Mariátegui died before he could make up his mind which position he should finally adopt, and the Communists therefore took his name for their banner.*

George Paz, a writer in the New York *Daily Worker*, in commenting on Mariátegui's death on May 12, 1930, said, "His value as a Marxist-Leninist theoretician is unquestioned." He might have added, "by anyone except the Communist International." Paz noted, too, that Mariátegui's funeral ceremonies were conducted by the "Communist Party of Peru."

The crisis among the Peruvian Communists caused by the action of the Buenos Aires Conference was finally resolved by a split in the group and the formation of two different parties. The Executive Committee of the

---

* Mariátegui apparently never made any public statement concerning his attitude. Theories on what he really felt differ widely. Eudosio Ravines told the author that Mariátegui favored submission to the Comintern's order; Ricardo Martínez de la Torre told him that Mariátegui expressed his opposition to this action.

Partido Socialista* resolved to change the name of the organization to Partido Comunista and apply for full affiliation to the Comintern. Only Ricardo Martínez de la Torre voted against the move. He withdrew from the Communist Party, but did not form any group of his own.

However, one of those who had at first favored obeying the Comintern's dictum, Luciano Castillo, later changed his mind, and soon after the re-christening of the Partido Socialista, he withdrew from the Communist Party and formed a new Socialist Party.[26] This was the first democratic Socialist Party to be successfully established in Peru. It gained considerable influence in the northern coastal areas, where it soon won control of the oil workers' organizations. It has continued through a quarter of a century to be the principal political element among this group of workers, and when permitted by the government, the petroleum workers usually elected members of the Socialist Party to the Chamber of Deputies and the Senate.

The first Secretary General of the newly christened Partido Comunista was Eudosio Ravines. He had been a close associate of Haya de la Torre for several years, and the chairman of the Aprista group in Paris. However, he had broken with Haya in 1928, and had decided to help form a Peruvian Communist Party. In 1930 he returned to America, stopping a while in Chile and then going on to Peru.

The Communists had meanwhile turned their attention to trade union affairs. The program of Mariátegui's Partido Socialista had pledged them to seek the establishment of a national trade union confederation, but the task of building one was difficult. In June, 1927, the government, on the excuse of a "Communist uprising," had closed virtually all the unions, and they were able to renew their activities only slowly.

The April, 1929, number of *El Trabajador Latino Americano* announced the formation of the Comité Pro Confederación General de Trabajadores del Perú. This group issued a May Day Manifesto which was signed by the most important trade unions then existing in Peru, including the Chauffeurs, Textile Workers, Railroaders, and Trolley-car Workers Federations, the brewery workers, and the Agricultural Workers Federation.[27]

On May 1, 1929, a meeting was held in the headquarters of the Chauffeurs' Federation, attended by delegates from the groups which had signed the May Day Manifesto, at which it was decided to establish a Provisional

---

* The Executive Committee of the Partido Socialista included an interesting group of men. Mariátegui was a member, as was Eudosio Ravines, first Secretary General of the Communist Party, who turned bitterly anti-Communist in the 1940's and remained anti-Aprista. A. Franco, Hugo Pesco, who remained with the Party for many years, also belonged to the Executive, as did Luciano Castillo, founder and still head of the second Socialist Party. Another important member was Julio Porto-carrero, who was for several years the Party's representative in Moscow. Several other members dropped out of politics altogether soon after the formation of the Communist Party.

Committee of the Confederación General de Trabajadores del Perú. On May 17 a further meeting was held which elected this Committee, and this date is generally accepted as the founding day of the C.G.T.P.[28]

A delegation from the C.G.T.P., headed by Julio Portocarrero, took part in the founding congress of the Communists' Confederación Sindical Latino Americana in Montevideo in May, 1929. Portocarrero was elected to the General Council of the C.S.L.A.[29]

The C.G.T.P. greeted with approval the overthrow of the Leguía dictatorship by a military *coup d'état* on August 22, 1930, and presented a list of demands to the new Military Junta which took over the government. Among other things, it demanded release of trade unionists then in jail, recognition of basic trade union rights, abolition of various existing forms of forced labor, and improvement of a workmen's compensation law.[30]

Both the C.G.T.P. and the Communist Party itself were able to work more or less openly for some time after the overthrow of Leguía. Their activities were multitudinous. Many new unions were organized. Together the C.G.T.P. and the Communist Party established "popular universities" in the unions, copied after those which had given rise to the Aprista movement after the first World War. They called them Universidades Populares José Carlos Mariátegui. They also formed local groups and a national committee of the Anti-Imperialist League, one of the international Communist front organizations of that period.

The new military government was worried by the increased Communist activity. In response, it issued a decree on "sedition" which made it possible for civilians to be tried in military courts for actions against the regime.

However, a more serious block to the growth of the Communists than any the government created was the Partido Aprista Peruano. After the fall of Leguía, the Aprista students who had been scattered throughout America and Europe returned home. Their first moves were to join with non-Communist trade union leaders in forming a political party, the Partido Aprista Peruano, and to name Haya de la Torre as candidate for the presidency.

Haya himself returned and immediately started on an electoral tour around the country. The trip was a veritable triumph. The party made converts not only among the urban workers—whose old Anarchosyndicalist leaders generally joined the new Aprista Party—but also among the middle class, and among the Indian masses of the highlands. The Aprista movement caught the imagination of the great majority of the republic's humble citizens.

The Communists' attitude toward the Apristas was that of the Communists throughout the world toward other left-wing parties in the Third Period. They attacked the Apristas as "social fascists" and compared their ideas with those of Mussolini. *El Trabajador Latino America-no*, the Communists' continental trade union paper, in an article in its May, 1932, edition, referred to Haya as the "Apra-Fascist leader," and accused him of "using all the counterrevolutionary arsenal of Trotskyism to combat the C.P." The paper alleged that Haya "uses the names of Marx and Lenin to disfigure the ideas of those chiefs of the world proletarian revolution and to give an honorable appearance to the national fascist demagoguery of his party." The article went on:

> Haya de la Torre does not want the expropriation of the imperialists nor the liquidation of the *latifundias*. He does not want to liberate the Indians, the majority of the population, he does not wish that they be given back land stolen from the communities so that they can do as they please with them, even so far as to separate and form Quechuan and Aymaran republics.*
>
> Haya de la Torre is, then, a conscious enemy of the agrarian and anti-imperialist revolution in Peru.

The Communists met serious Aprista competition in the trade unions. Although non-Communist trade union leaders in such organizations as the Textile Federation had helped to organize the C.G.T.P., they chafed under Communist control, particularly after the Aprista Party had been formally organized.

The Communist leaders of the C.G.T.P. launched an offensive against the Apristas. In the second number of the C.G.T.P. periodical, *El Trabajador*, which appeared in November, 1930, the editors wrote, "We assert that Aprismo is an instrument of the bourgeoisie," and proceeded to attack the Aprista program for the unification of the middle and working classes to fight against the foreign imperialists and the native landlords.[31]

The Apristas and other left-wing groups attacked the C.G.T.P. for its submission to the Communist Party "line." The C.G.T.P. responded to this by attempting to disclaim any Communist orientation. *El Trabajador* of March 19, 1931, claimed, "The C.G.T.P. does not have a Communist orientation, but a revolutionary one, a class-conscious one, which in many cases coincides with that of the Communists."[32]

The Communist Party went to the defense of the C.G.T.P. The party's periodical, *Hoz y Martillo* (Hammer and Sickle), in its issue of November 4, 1931, accused "the chiefs of Aprofascism" of "attacking the revolutionary class-conscious unions." It accused the "Aprista unions" of trying "to domesticate the workers, to sow confusion, to practice class collaboration, that is, betrayal of the proletariat in the interests of the bourgeoisie and imperialism."[33]

---

* It is interesting to note in this denunciation an echo of the "self-determination of the Black Belt" propaganda in which the United States Communists were indulging at the same time. In Peru, in conformity with the Comintern's Third Period "line," they advocated "self-determination" for the country's Indians.

The trade union rivalry of the two parties became more intense in 1934 when the Aprista-controlled unions withdrew from the C.G.T.P. and formed the Central Sindical de los Trabajadores Peruanos. The *Boletín Sindical* of the Communists' continental trade union group, the C.S.L.A., accused the Apristas of "unifying the less prepared elements of the proletariat . . . along with the most unscrupulous provocative elements," in the Central Sindical. It also accused the Aprista trade union group of "impeding by every means conceivable the fight for the workers' immediate needs, of destroying the proletarian movement . . . of betraying, hamstringing, and selling out any action of the workers which is undertaken without them. . . ."[34]

Both the Communist and Aprista union groups were outlawed by the dictatorship of General Oscar Benavides, after the failure of a strike called by the Central Sindical at the end of 1934. This was part of a general crackdown on the opposition by General Benavides.[35]

Benavides had succeeded to the presidency when his predecessor, Colonel Sánchez Cerro, had been assassinated the year before. Sánchez Cerro himself had been elected President in the August, 1931, poll, in which Haya de la Torre had been the Aprista nominee. The Communists apparently had nominated no candidate in this election, and are alleged by the Apristas to have supported Sánchez Cerro.[36]

During the months before the 1931 election, the Communists had had wide freedom to organize and recruit members. From July 15 to September 15, 1931, the Peruvian Communist Party had had a "revolutionary competition agreement" with the Chilean Party to enlist new members. The Peruvian Party had sought to increase its membership of 500 by some 980, but claimed to have actually recruited 1739 new members. Its drive had been particularly successful among the students, artisans, and peasants.

Unemployed Indian Communist miners had been sent back to their villages and haciendas to recruit new members for the Party, and were reported to have been very successful. Industrial workers, according to the June 7, 1932, issue of the Comintern's *International Press Correspondence*, which reported on this campaign, had not received enough attention in the drive. Only 45 per cent of the Party's membership had consisted of workers at the end of the drive. The article also criticized the Peruvian Communist Party for not organizing mass demonstrations of industrial workers and for not participating sufficiently in strikes in progress during this period.

Although President Sánchez Cerro had allowed civic freedom for a few months after his election, he had soon clamped down and re-established a dictatorship. By the end of 1931 the Aprista Party had been outlawed, its deputies expelled from the Chamber, and Haya himself arrested. In May, 1932, in a notable trial, at which Haya had used the opportunity to present the Aprista Party program, he had been sentenced to jail.[37]

In July, 1932, the Apristas had staged a revolt in the northern city of Trujillo. The rebellion had lasted for seven days, and had been followed by one of the bloodiest massacres which has occurred in Latin America in this century. Hundreds of rebel prisoners had been taken to the outskirts of the city, where they had been shot. Many had been submitted to long-drawn-out torture before being killed. These incidents had won Sánchez Cerro the undying hatred of the Apristas.[38]

The Communists had had little to do with this revolt. They had never had much influence in the Trujillo section of Peru, and they had made no move to support the revolt in other parts of the country. The Apristas allege that after the Trujillo Revolt Sánchez Cerro became very tolerant of the Communists in the hope of using them against his Aprista foes.

However, the Communists had aroused the government's ire again early in 1933, when they participated in a demonstration in Lima against the threatened war with Colombia over the Leticia border region. As a result, Eudosio Ravines, the Party's Secretary General, had been jailed. While in jail, he had gone on a hunger strike against prison conditions.[39]

On April 30, 1933, Colonel Sánchez Cerro had been assassinated. Then and since it has been widely suspected that the Apristas were behind his murder. In any case, the government of General Benavides, which took over when Sánchez Cerro was killed, had given the country a brief period of political respite. Haya de la Torre had been released, and the political parties had been allowed to function once again. This lenience continued until the general strike of late 1934.

Meanwhile the Communist International had passed from the Third Period to the Popular Front era. As a result, the Communist Party of Peru in the spring of 1935 issued an *Open Letter to Haya de la Torre*. After enumerating the woes of the world, it pointed to developing Popular Front movements in other Latin American countries, and urged the need for such a front in Peru. It asked, "In the present condition of our country, is it possible for one political party to lead the national emancipation struggle of the peoples of Peru?" and then answered its own question, "No it cannot."

The *Letter* then went on to explain, with rather surprising candor, "The Communist Party has emerged from the propagandist period of recent years, when it was building up the basic proletarian cadres in irreconcilable struggle against bourgeois and petty bourgeois views on Peruvian affairs and therefore carrying on a determined fight against the views of the A.P.R.A."

The Communists then announced:

> We reject in advance with the greatest determination any arguments, no matter from whom they come, that the sharpness of the struggle which has hitherto taken place between our parties can be

any serious hindrance to the joint defense of the people's interests and declare such statements to be anti-popular and utterly unconvincing.

Finally, the *Open Letter* proposed a Peoples' Front in Peru, to be made up of the Communist Party and the A.P.R.A., based on a ten-point program, which included labor demands, a general amnesty, repudiation of foreign debts, nationalization of imperialist enterprises, and "participation in an anti-war congress, the people's arbitration commission in the Chaco,* close alliance with the national liberation alliances of the Latin American countries and all the oppressed classes and peoples." It suggested that differences in policy of the two parties on the Indian question be disregarded, because "these questions will be decided by the Indians themselves."[40]

The Apristas refused these overtures on the part of the Communists. The Communist International's publication, *International Press Correspondence,* reported on October 19, 1935:

> The answer of the A.P.R.A. leaders shows that they have not yet found the energy to put the real interests of the Peruvian nation above petty personal feeling . . . the answer of the A.P.R.A. was that as the suggested platform was that of the A.P.R.A., all the Communists had to do was to expel Ravines from their ranks and join the A.P.R.A.

The Communist periodical went on to claim that the followers of A.P.R.A. were not in agreement with their leaders, and favored a united front with the Communists. It stated that "This fact is so general that the leader of the A.P.R.A. refugees in Buenos Aires, Seoane, placed a ban on reading the Ravines letter." It added that the letter "has greatly contributed to dispelling the doubts of the A.P.R.A. adherents as to the sincerity of our proposals of united action."

Failing to persuade the Apristas to be their allies, the Communists soon found a new ally in Manuel Prado, General Benavides' choice as his successor in the presidency. Even before the election of Prado, General Benavides took a relatively lenient attitude toward the Communists. In 1938 he permitted the legal recognition of the Chauffeurs' Union, led by Communist Juan P. Luna.[41]

During the election campaign of 1939, a Democratic Front was formed around Prado's candidacy.** The Front was composed of a number of small parties and personal friends and followers of Prado, and was backed by the still illegal Communist Party.[42] Manuel Prado wanted a few genuine workers on his congressional ticket. Luna, as head of the Chauffeurs'

---

* A Communist "attempt to solve" the Chaco War between Bolivia and Paraguay, which was then raging.

** An election had been held in 1936. Although the government had not permitted the Apristas to name a candidate at this time, a nominee backed by the Apristas was winning when General Benavides suddenly suspended further counting of the ballots, and had Congress elect him for an additional period of three years.

Union, qualified under this definition, so the Communist trade unionist was given a position as candidate for deputy on the Prado ticket.[43]

During the Prado administration, which lasted from 1939 to 1945, the Communist Party gave full backing to the administration. It did so, according to Juan P. Luna, in conformity with the C.T.A.L.'s orders to support those regimes in Latin America which had a correct position on the war.[44]

Although the Prado regime kept in force the laws of its predecessors which provided for police surveillance of trade union and political meetings, the government did allow a considerable development of the trade union movement. The Communist Party suffered little or no persecution during the Prado administration. According to the regime's Director General of Labor, Jorge Fernández Stoll, the Communists offered to back the regime, and their offer was accepted, with the result that the government took little action against them. During the latter part of the Prado regime, they were allowed to publish a paper, *Democracia y Trabajo*.[45]

The principal figure in the Party during these days was Juan P. Luna, the Communists' member of the Chamber of Deputies. He did yeoman work for the Party, giving it most of his salary as deputy, getting out of jail trade unionists who were incarcerated, and allowing Party and union meetings to be held in his house, which, as the residence of a deputy, was presumably immune from search by the police.

The older leadership of the party was expelled during this period. In a Party Congress held in 1942 Ravines, Portocarrero, and others were accused of being "Trotsky sympathizers." The Congress sent a mission to Chile to try to win over Aprista leaders Manuel Seoane and Luis Alberto Sánchez, whom it considered "pro-Ally," but with no results.

An important event in the wartime history of the Communist Party was a visit in 1942 by Vicente Lombardo Toledano, President of the Communist-controlled Latin American Confederation of Workers (C.T.A.L.). He was received by President Prado,[46] and spoke at a mass meeting in the Municipal Theater.[47] In this speech he urged the workers not to go out on strike, since this would hurt the Allied war effort, and emphasized the necessity for the workers to intensify their efforts and work harder. It is reported that before speaking to the country's labor leaders, Lombardo Toledano conferred at length with the local leaders of the Communist Party.[48]

One result of Lombardo's visit was that the government gave the green light to the formation of a national labor confederation under Communist leadership. Another step toward this was the formation of the Unión Sindical de Trabajadores as the central organization of the unions in Lima early in 1943.

A few months after Lombardo's visit to Peru, a Peruvian delegation consisting of Communists, Apristas, and independents, attended the Congress of the Confederation of Workers of Chile. There they signed a pact promising to push the unification of the Peruvian workers. As a result, the Comité de Unificación Nacional de los Trabajadores Peruanos was formed. It existed until May 1, 1944, when the Confederación de Trabajadores del Perú was founded.[49]

The first Secretary General of the C.T.P. was Juan P. Luna, who remained chief of the group until after the 1945 election. At that time the Apristas took control of the Confederation, though the Communists had begun to lose their grip on the labor movement some months before.[50]

As the time approached for the 1945 presidential election, all political groups began to prepare for it. In 1944 a Democratic Front was launched in Arequipa, which included the Apristas, the Communists, and certain independent elements. The Prado government was anxious to break up this coalition, and Director General of Labor Jorge Fernández Stoll was commissioned to do the job.

Fernández Stoll had to go to Arequipa to settle a strike in which the Communists were deeply involved. The Communists proposed to Fernández Stoll that if he would settle the strike—which was of key importance to them in relation to prestige in the area—on terms favorable to them, they would withdraw from the Democratic Front. He agreed, and they withdrew. However, the walkout was not settled on the terms for which the Communists had hoped, and several local leaders of the Party were expelled as a result. This was the end, however, of Communist participation in the building of a National Democratic Front in preparation for the 1945 election.[51]

As the election campaign progressed, two candidates appeared. The government's nominee was General Ureta; the opposition candidate was José Luis Bustamante. The latter was backed by a National Democratic Front which included the Aprista Party and various independent groups and which the Communists were allowed to join just a few weeks before the election.[52]

In preparation for the election both the Aprista and Communist Parties were given legal recognition (though not allowed to register under their customary names), and were allowed to participate openly in the campaign. The Apristas took the name "Partido del Pueblo" for the purpose of the election; the Communists selected the name "Vanguardia Socialista del Perú."

The Vanguardia Socialista held a meeting in the Teatro Bolívar in Lima to celebrate its legal recognition. The National Democratic Front's presidential candidate, Bustamante, was the star speaker. He said that the meeting had great significance for him because it indicated the Communist Party's "respect for the laws of the nation and its renouncing of the extreme aspects of its doctrinaire program." According to the Lima newspaper, *Jornada*, on June 16, 1945, the meeting cheered all references to national unity in the Allied countries during the war. There was "applause" for every reference to the U.S.S.R. and Great Britain, and "great applause" for every reference to the United States.

The Communists won a number of seats in the Chamber of Deputies in the 1945 election. However, in spite of these victories, they fared badly as a result of Bustamante's election as President. The biggest winners in the election were the Apristas, who gained control of one house of parliament and came within a few seats of a majority in the other and for a while were the most important element in the government of President Bustamante.

The Apristas routed the Communists in the labor movement. Even the Chauffeurs Federation, which had long been a Communist bastion, was captured by the Apristas. Arturo Saboroso, veteran Aprista leader of the Textile Workers Federation, succeeded Juan P. Luna as Secretary General of the Confederación de Trabajadores del Perú.

During the three years of the Bustamante regime, the Communists enjoyed the same freedom as other political parties. They gained a good deal in terms of membership from this new-found freedom. Their membership increased from an estimated 1500 in 1945 to 35,000, which they claimed in 1947.[53]

A few months after Bustamante came to power, the Communists began to seek to form an alliance against the Apristas. They hoped to include in it if possible the personal followers of ex-President Manuel Prado, with whom they had worked so well in the past, and the former associates of ex-President Benavides, who had died soon after the 1945 election.

Relations between Bustamante, who owed his election to the votes of the Apristas, and Haya's followers got worse as time went on. Finally, on October 3, 1948, a dissident element of the Aprista Party led a mutiny of the naval garrison at Callao. Although the Aprista Party leadership did not support this revolt, President Bustamante took advantage of the uprising to outlaw the Aprista Party once again.

Three weeks later Bustamante himself was overthrown by an armed uprising led by General Manuel Odria. Soon after seizing power, Odria officially outlawed the Communist Party. He claimed to have done so in conformity with the agreement of the Ninth Inter American Conference in Bogotá in April, 1948, which provided that American states would do everything possible to avoid being victimized by "international Communism and any other totalitarian regime."[54]

However, the Communist Party had split by this time. During the Bustamante regime two factions had developed in the Party, one led by the trade unionist, Juan P. Luna, the other by the Party's Secretary General, Jorge del Prado. Even before the fall of Bustamante, Luna officially quit the Party, with many of his followers.

The official Party remained under the control of Jorge del Prado, and this was the group outlawed by the Odria government. The Luna group aligned itself with General Odria's regime. Because he had been more than two years out of the official Communist Party, Luna was legally eligible to be a candidate for Congress in the elections held late in 1950. He headed a ticket put up by the Workers Independent Electoral Committee, organized with the backing of the Odria government, and consisting of members of the Luna faction of the Communists. He was elected to the Senate, and several others on the ticket became members of the Chamber of Deputies.[55]

The Peruvian Communists thus followed the policy of "dual Communism" which became popular with the Latin American Parties in the late 1940's. One faction, the "official" Party, was in open opposition to the Odria regime, and its leader, Jorge del Prado, fled to Argentina. His successor as Secretary General, Manuel Ugarte, was arrested early in 1954. The other faction, headed by Juan P. Luna, was in the inner councils of the Odria dictatorship.

However, neither Communist faction was a major force in Peruvian politics by the end of 1956. Although the official Party had gained some influence among Aprista Party members who were disillusioned by the apparent support given to Odria by the United States Government,* it still had not made significant inroads among the great mass of the Aprista Party's followers. The Luna Communists gained what minor influence they had largely from their close connection with the dictator. Thus, Peru was a prime example of the fact that the chief stumbling block to Communism in Latin America is a democratic leftist party, and likewise gave ample evidence of the Communists' willingness to work with Latin American dictators and vice versa.

During the election of 1956 the official Communist Party supported the candidacy of Fernando Belaunde Terry, while the Luna faction supported General Odria's candidate, Hernan Lavalle. The election was won by a third nominee, ex-President Manuel Prado, to whom the Apristas gave their support at the last moment.

With the inauguration of Prado, the Aprista Party was made legal once again. There began a period of cooperation between the Apristas, still the country's majority party (though not directly represented in the new Congress, which was elected before the legalization of the Aprista Party), and the Prado administration. The Apristas were anxious to have a period of peace during which they could reorganize their forces, with a view to winning the 1962 presidential and congressional elections. On his side, Prado seemed to represent a group among the country's big land-

* In the middle of 1953 President Eisenhower conferred on Odria the Order of Merit, accompanying the award by a citation praising him for having suppressed "Communists and subversive elements," the latter phrase seeming to refer to the Apristas.

holding and commercial interests who had reached the conclusion that continued military domination of the country's affairs was more danger- ous to their interests than the Aprista Party functioning in a democratic atmosphere would be.

In the meanwhile, the official Communists cooperated with Belaunde Terry in his efforts to establish a political party, the Partido Acción Popular. They played a major role in this organization, particularly in Southern Peru, where it had its greatest importance. By the end of 1956 it was too early to say whether the Belaunde group would develop into a new popular force which would be able to challenge the hold which the Apristas had had on public opinion for over a quarter of a century, or would merely become a "front" for the Communists.

## ECUADOR

Ecuador, the smallest of the Andean countries, has so far felt com- paratively little of the impact of the Latin American social revolution. Indeed, it has perhaps been less affected by the modern white man's civi- lization than any other country in South America. The greater part of its population is composed of Indians, tilling the soil in the valleys and plateaus of the Andes. They are still living under the yoke of the white landowner which was riveted on their necks by the Spanish Conquista- dores and has been little lightened by succeeding movements for national independence or by the countless revolutions and counterrevolutions which are a constant feature of the nation's political life.

Relatively small groups of industrial workers have in recent years come into existence in the capital city of Quito, the port of Guayaquil, and one or two provincial towns. They, together with the more numerous artisans, the new class of white-collar workers, the railroaders, the oil workers, and the few thousand employees of the modern plantations along the Pacific Coast, make up the urban working class of Ecuador. A recent study of the country has estimated that there are only some 50,000 privately employed wage earners and 40,000 public employees in the whole nation.[56]

Political activity in Ecuador is confined almost completely to the urban centers. Only the Communists have made any serious attempt to work among the stolid Indian masses of the highlands, and their success has been limited in the extreme. Indeed, that they have been active in this field at all is perhaps due more to the personal interest of the Party's founder, Dr. Ricardo Paredes, than to any conscious policy of the Party.

Unlike its neighbors, Peru and Bolivia, Ecuador had not by the middle of 1956 been seriously shaken by the continent-wide movement of social revolution. No party of social change had caught the imagination of the country's masses, although the movement which put José María Velasco Ibarra in the presidency for the third time in 1952 perhaps presaged a fundamental change in the country's political pattern.

Among the small but influential group of city workers, the Communist Party of Ecuador has played a key role for over a quarter of a century. The history of this Party demonstrates what a well-organized though small Communist group can do, even when it is faced with a rival radical party which is more powerful numerically, if that rival party does not have a well-defined program and dynamic political leadership. The history of the Ecuadorean Communist Party shows it to have been one of the two best manipulators of fellow-travellers in the whole continent, the other being the Communist Party of Chile. But unlike the Chileans, the Ecuadorean Communists have not had a rival who fell to pieces organizationally. On the contrary, the Ecuadorean Socialists, who are the Communists' chief competitors, have maintained a united party for more than twenty years, but in spite of this have been "managed" by the smaller, but better-organized and more determined Communist group during much of this period.

The Communist Party of Ecuador was founded in the mid-1920's as the Partido Socialista Ecuatoriano. The Party emerged out of a small group which before the Revolution of 1925 began editing in Quito a biweekly newspaper *La Antorcha* (The Torch). This periodical was launched in the last months of 1924 by a group of young intellectuals who later were to play leading roles in the country's political and cultural life. Ricardo Paredes, a medical doctor who in time became the dean of Ecuadorean Communists, was the director of the periodical. Among its chief contributors were: Jorge Carrera Andrade, who became one of the nation's leading novelists and in later years was a Socialist, not a Communist; Juan Pablo Múñoz, who later was head of the National Musical Conservatory; and Luis Maldonado Estrada, who was to be a leading figure in the Socialist Party.

The paper attacked the government of the day very severely, and because of an article entitled "The Disciples of Mephistopheles," which assailed ex-President Leonidas Plaza Gutiérrez (successor of the great Liberal *caudillo*, Eloy Alfaro, and in 1924 the power behind the government), the periodical was closed down for a month.[57]

The content of various numbers of *La Antorcha* showed the political orientation of those who were editing it. One of the first articles it published was entitled "Toward a Socialist Party." There were articles by the Spanish Socialists, Fernando de los Ríos and Marcellino Domingo, as well as one by Maxim Gorki. It had an underlying tone of sympathy for the Soviet Union, though it was in no sense a Communist periodical as yet.

The paper continued to appear for a period of about six months, its last number coming out a few weeks before the July 9, 1925, Revolution. Around *La Antorcha* there formed a group which in January, 1925, took the name "Grupo Socialista *La Antorcha*."[58] Its membership was drawn largely from the younger elements in the dominant Liberal Party. The

group immediately sought to gain influence in the mutual benefit associa-
tions which were Quito's only labor movement at that time. Soon after
its organization the Grupo Socialista put up candidates for office in the
Sociedad Artística e Industrial de Pichincha, the largest and most important of the workers' organizations, but its nominees were defeated.[59]

Meanwhile the *La Antorcha* group was seeking a more definite political orientation. In the February 7, 1925, issue of its paper, the Grupo
Socialista *La Antorcha* put forth its first political program. This bore evidence of the Liberal origins of the authors. It could perhaps best be described as a Liberal program with socialistic overtones.

The Quito Socialist group soon served as a model for the establishment of similar societies in other cities. Soon after the announcement of
the founding of the Grupo Socialista *La Antorcha*, a Grupo Socialista
*La Reforma* was established in the northern city of Tulcán. The Liberal
background of the members of this group was evident from its adoption
of the Liberal Party motto of "Dios y Libertad."[60]

The Revolution of July 9, 1925, was an important event in the life of
the fledgling *La Antorcha* group. This movement was led by a group of
radical army officers. It was particularly supported by people of the mountain region (the Sierra), who resented the political domination of the
country by the bankers and businessmen of the coastal region. The President of the first Revolutionary Junta formed by the rebels was Luis
Napoleón Dillon, one of those who had helped found and edit *La
Antorcha*. Other members of the *La Antorcha* group were also active in
the 1925 Revolution.

As a result of the Revolution of 1925 the leaders of the Grupo Socialista
*La Antorcha* decided to launch a political party. The Partido Socialista
Ecuatoriano was therefore established on May 16, 1926. Luis Napoleón
Dillon was a charter member.

The first periodical to be published by the new Partido Socialista was
*La Vanguardia* (a name copied from that of the Argentine Socialist
Party's paper), which appeared in the last months of 1927. This paper had
considerably more of a Communist orientation than had *La Antorcha*. It
published various official proclamations of the Comintern, such as the Report of A. Lozovsky on the meeting of the Communists' Pan Pacific Labor
Congress.[61]

In the early days of the Partido Socialista there also existed an avowedly
Communist group within the party known as "Amigos de Lenin," of
which Ricardo Paredes was the leader. This group published its own
periodical, *La Fragua*, which printed frequent Comintern proclamations
and those of the Red International of Labor Unions, the Young Communist International, and the Red Peasants International. It urged the
workers to form trade unions and opposed the older mutual benefit
societies.

The Socialist Party ran its first candidates in the 1928 Constituent Assembly election. There were five candidates from Quito, none of whom was elected. However, Dr. Rigoberto Ortiz was elected a deputy from Guayaquil. He was later expelled from the party for voting in the Assembly in favor of Dr. Isidro Ayora—the dictator at that time—for President of the Republic. The first successful Socialist Party candidate from Quito was elected in 1929.

Ricardo Paredes, one of the founders of the Grupo *La Antorcha* and Secretary General of the Partido Socialista, went to Moscow late in 1927 and stayed through most of the year 1928. While there he attended the ceremonies in celebration of the tenth anniversary of the Bolshevik Revolution, and the Sixth Congress of the Communist International. At this Congress[62] Paredes represented both the Partido Socialista and the Amigos de Lenin. The Congress accepted the request of the Partido Socialista Ecuatoriano for admission as a fraternal member of the Comintern.[63]

With its affiliation to the Communist International, the Partido Socialista adapted its activities more closely to the policies of the International. It established an Anti-Imperialist League, as other Communist Parties were doing throughout the continent.[64] It also established a party training school, the Escuela Lenin, in Quito, for leadership cadres.[65]

The Communist orientation of the Partido Socialista after Paredes' return from Moscow was shown in the names and policies of the party's periodicals. Although the Quito provincial organization of the Partido Socialista revived *La Antorcha* in 1929, in the next year *La Hoz* (The Sickle) appeared as the official organ of the Partido Socialista. It was an avowedly Communist sheet, and it advocated changing the party's name to Partido Comunista and full adhesion of the party to the Comintern. The official publication of the Juventud Comunista Ecuatoriano was *Frente Rojo*, which first appeared in October, 1929. (The youth group was already known as "Communist," though the party was still "Socialist.") The transformation of the Partido Socialista Ecuatoriano into a Communist Party was completed in 1931, when it changed its name to Partido Comunista.

In the early 1930's there was formed in Guayaquil an extremist Communist group, known as Grupo Comunista and issuing an organ it called *El Comunista*, which was outside of and opposed to the Partido Socialista. Its leaders included Dr. Rafael Coello Serrano, who in the 1950's was leader of the Unión Popular Republicano of José María Velasco Ibarra; and Carlos Guevara Moreno, who in the 1940's was a minister in the cabinet of the same Velasco Ibarra, and during the next decade was Mayor of Guayaquil and *caudillo* of the whole coastal area.

The Grupo Comunista joined the Partido Socialista after the latter had changed its name to Partido Comunista, in 1932. However, Guevara Moreno was expelled from the Party the same year and left the country for France. There also he joined the Communist Party, and in due time was once again expelled.[66]

Meanwhile an important element in the Partido Socialista had opposed the increasingly Communist orientation of the party. Many of the dissidents withdrew to form other groups. One was established in Quito in 1930 and at first took the name "Transformación Social," later changing it to "Partido Socialista." Although it had some members in Guayaquil, the larger number of dissidents in the port city formed "Renovación Social," which soon took the name "Partido Social Cooperativista."[67]

The Communist Party was bitter in its attacks on the dissidents, who in 1933 united to form a new Partido Socialista Ecuatoriano. Following the Comintern's Third Period policy of hostility toward Socialist parties, the Ecuadorean Communists called the Socialists "betrayers" and "social fascists."[68]

With the change in the Comintern line, the Communists changed their attitude towards the country's other left-wing parties. As early as March, 1934, they called for the formation of a United Front with the Socialist Party, following the lead of the French Communists. Some months passed, however, before such a front was formed. When it was established, the Socialists, Communists, and Liberals united in opposition to the regime of the President, José María Velasco Ibarra, and this coalition was instrumental in bringing about his overthrow.[69]

Relations between the Communist and Socialist Parties remained more or less cordial during the rest of the 1930's. During this period the Socialists became one of the country's major parties. At one of the numerous constitutional conventions, that of 1938, the Socialists had one third of the members. They were closely allied with the President at this time, General Henríquez.[70]

After this period of the middle and late 1930's, the Socialists maintained their "friendly" relations with the Communists for the next twenty years, with some interruptions. The reasons for this are undoubtedly various.

For one thing, all the left-wing elements in Ecuador have lived in constant fear of the Conservative Party and right-wing elements generally. There has been a general feeling that a division of the Left would mean a victory of the Right, and a return of Church control over the country's political life. The Conservatives have remained the country's largest party, and until the middle 1950's only left-wing unity was able to prevent their control of the nation.*

Those Socialists who favored continuing "unity" with the Communists —generally the majority of the party—have used this fear of a Conservative victory as an excuse. This argument has been particularly effective in the labor movement where during the late 1940's and early 1950's the

* A three-way split in the Left in the 1956 election resulted in the election of a Conservative President, Dr. Camilo Ponce Enriquez, for the first time in 61 years.

Socialists, though in the majority, generally followed policies dictated by the Communists.

Another reason for the Socialists' continued subservience to the Communists was the fact that the Communists were a much better organized, more determined, and better indoctrinated group than their Socialist rivals. The Communists never have lacked for money. They were reported in the late 1940's to have 15 to 20 full-time party workers in Guayaquil alone. In 1942 when there was a discussion as to whether the government would help pay for a projected labor congress, Pedro Saad, the principal Communist trade union leader said that if the government would not help, he had 30,000 sucres from the Communist-controlled Confederación de Trabajadores de América Latina which could be used. It was estimated that the Communists spent 150,000 sucres in the 1945 election campaign.[71]

The Communists took an active part in election activities. In the presidential election of 1932 they nominated Antonio Ruiz Flores, leader of the Consejo Central of the Agricultural Workers Union of the coastal region of Milagro.[72] In the following year Ricardo Paredes was the Party's candidate in yet another presidential poll.[73]

Although they remained a relatively small group, the Communists had influence in the trade union movement and in the Indian organizations from the very beginning. The work among the Indians was largely the personal endeavor of Ricardo Paredes. An avid student of the Indian problem in Ecuador, he won a certain degree of confidence from the aborigines. In 1944 he organized the Federación de Indios Ecuatorianos, which was completely under Communist control. At its founding congress, the Federación elected Paredes as a delegate to the latest of the country's Constituent Assemblies.[74]

During the latter half of the 1930's Communists and Socialists cooperated in the trade unions, and in 1937 united labor organizations were founded in both Guayaquil and Quito. Several attempts to form a national trade union federation failed, however. The first of these took place at a meeting in Guayaquil in 1937. Another attempt was made in 1938, at a congress in the city of Ambato. Due to factional fighting among the delegates, this was not successful. As a result of a visit to Ecuador by the pro-Communist continental labor leader, Vicente Lombardo Toledano, it was agreed to make another attempt in March, 1943, to establish a national labor confederation. The Congress met on schedule in Quito, but was closed down by the government, and most of its leaders were jailed for five months. However, before the Congress was dissolved, it succeeded in electing a National Committee of Unification, with both Socialist and Communist trade unionists as members. When they got out of jail, a second meeting of the National Committee of Unification was held in August, 1943. Its business was discussion of a revolutionary plot to overthrow President Carlos Aroyo del Río.[75]

The labor group worked closely with the Alianza Democrática, which had been formed among the Conservatives, Liberals, Socialists, and Communists to bring about the overthrow of the President. There was considerable opposition to this alliance by one faction of the Socialist Party. Led by Luis Maldonado Tamayo, member of that party's national Executive Committee, this group opposed the Socialists' cooperating with the Conservatives on the one hand and with the Communists on the other.[76]

In spite of this opposition, the Socialists remained in the revolutionary group, and the plot against President Aroyo del Río was successful in May, 1944. The rebels installed a Junta, composed of representatives of all the parties which participated in the revolt. The Communist representative on the Junta was Gustavo Becerra.[77]

The revolutionaries called ex-President José María Velasco Ibarra back from exile, and for almost a year Velasco Ibarra governed with the left-wing parties, the Liberals, the Socialists, the Communists, and the small Revolutionary Socialist Vanguard. They controlled the Constituent Assembly, which met on President Velasco's summons.[78]

Soon after the Revolution of 1944 a successful National Workers Congress was finally held. Out of it emerged the Confederación de Trabajadores del Ecuador, with Communist leader Pedro Saad as its first Secretary General.[79] The C.T.E. joined the Communist-controlled C.T.A.L. and sent delegates to the founding congress of the World Federation of Trade Unions in Paris in October, 1945. Pedro Saad and the Socialist union leader, Juan Isaac Iobato, were the C.T.E.'s representatives. Saad served on the Credentials Committee of the W.F.T.U. Congress[80] and made a speech urging "strong action" against Franco and Perón by the new world labor federation.[81]

In spite of the fact that both Socialists and Communists were represented in the C.T.E., from the beginning it followed the Communist line on international affairs. Thus, *Trabajadores*, official organ of the C.T.E.'s Quito Regional Federation, in its October 9, 1945, issue, backed the Russian position at the London Foreign Ministers' Conference then taking place. This article claimed the United States, in advocating that all countries participating in the second World War should have something to say about the peace, only took this position because it controlled a group of "virtually colonial nations." A victory of the United States point of view under these circumstances would mean "the defeat of the true interests of world democracy."

A month later the C.T.E. itself issued a message which was published in the New York *Daily Worker* on November 21, 1945, urging Latin American labor to fight "United States monopolies." It accused the United States of trying "to make Ecuador an exclusively agricultural country, merely a source of raw materials for U.S. industry and a market for the North American imported products."

"The North American attitude," said the proclamation, "undoubtedly results from pressure of North American imperialist circles."

The Communists continued to control the Confederación de Trabajadores del Ecuador until the organization's second Congress in November, 1946. The Socialists captured control in that meeting, gaining seven members of the C.T.E.'s Executive Committee, compared to four Communists.[82]

In spite of the fact that the Socialists gained control of the Confederación de Trabajadores del Ecuador, they made no attempt to participate in the movement to organize a rival organization to the Communist-controlled Confederacíon de Trabajadores de América Latina. The Socialists argued that to withdraw from the C.T.A.L. and join the non-Communist continental group, the O.R.I.T., would split the C.T.E. This would weaken both the Socialists and Communists in the face of the continuing right-wing threat from the Conservatives and, in the early 1950's, from the followers of José María Velasco Ibarra.[83]

Meanwhile the Communists had gone through various vicissitudes with the turns and twists of Ecuadorean politics. Velasco Ibarra, put in power largely by the left-wing parties in 1944, turned against these parties in March, 1946, and ousted the left-wingers from his cabinet. The principal leaders of the leftist parties, as well as the trade unions, were jailed from March to September, 1946.[84]

For the rest of Velasco Ibarra's tenure of office, the President governed with the Conservative Party. He was finally overthrown by an Army coup in September, 1947. After some confusion, Galo Plaza, son of the late President Leonidas Plaza, was elected President in 1948. President Plaza presided over one of the most democratic regimes in the country's history.

The elections at the end of the Galo Plaza administration resulted in ex-President José María Velasco Ibarra being elected chief executive for the third time. The Communists succeeded in getting a member of the Senate in this same poll, when Pedro Saad was named to that body as a "functional" Senator, to represent the organized workers of the coastal region of the republic. Saad was the only Communist elected, although the Party had had three members in Congress during the Plaza regime. The Socialist representation in Congress fell from fifteen to eight with this same 1952 election.[85]

By the end of 1956 the Communists of Ecuador still constituted a small party. They still were able to get the Confederación de Trabajadores del Ecuador to follow their policies, in spite of the fact that the Socialists formally controlled the Confederation. Although late in 1954 a concerted effort was launched in the C.T.E. by the anti-Communist wing of the Socialist Party to withdraw the Confederation from the C.T.A.L. and affiliate it with the continental free trade union movement, this move was defeated.

Although President Velasco Ibarra had threatened to outlaw the Communist Party, he did not do so, and Pedro Saad was re-elected to the Senate in the 1956 election. The victory of a Conservative, Dr. Camilo Ponce Enriquez, in this poll opened a new chapter in Ecuador's history. Although President Ponce promised fundamental reforms in the country, including even an agrarian reform, the Left was highly suspicious of his regime, and the effect of Ponce's election was to tighten the unity among the Liberal, Socialist, and Communist parties. Hence, the Communist Party of Ecuador remained one of the most successful Communist groups anywhere in the continent as a manipulator of "fellow travellers," though it had failed to gain much of a mass base for itself.

*Chapter XII*

# Communism in the Bolivarian Republics

## COLOMBIA

COLOMBIA'S COMMUNIST PARTY presents yet another instance of the fact that the most certain way to defeat the Communists is through a rival political movement which can catch the imagination of the workers and peasants who otherwise become the backbone of the Communist movement. Twice the Communist Party of Colombia promised to become one of the most powerful organizations of its kind in all Latin America. Twice its career was cut short. First, it was destroyed in 1930 with the coming of the Liberal Party to power, and second, in the middle 1940's, it fell victim to the rise of the demagogic, popular Liberal leader, Jorge Eliécer Gaitán.

The origins of the Columbian Communist Party go back to the middle 1920's. In 1924 there arrived in the country a Russian immigrant, Silvestre Savisky, who took great pride in the Russian Revolution and had the enthusiasm of a missionary. He soon gathered around himself a group of students and workers in Bogotá who formed what they called the Grupo Comunista.

These early Communists included many people who later were to play a leading role in Colombian politics, though not as Communists. For instance, there was Guillermo Hernández Rodríguez, who became President of the Council of State under the Liberal government in the 1930's, and Diego Mejía, who had a distinguished diplomatic career in the 1930's and 1940's. Gabriel Turbay, who later became a leading Liberal Party politician and diplomat and a Liberal Party candidate for the presidency of the republic, also belonged to the Grupo Comunista.

The members of the Grupo Comunista were avid readers of Russian literature, most of it translated into Spanish. Particularly popular was a series of works called the "Red Library," published by a Spanish firm.

The group established organizations similar to its own in various provincial towns. In the banana zone the leader of the group was José Russo; in the West it was Ignacio Torres Giraldo, working out of the city of Cali; and in Medellín, the country's main industrial center, the principal leader of the Grupo Comunista was a woman, María Cano. The purpose of this proselytizing was the ultimate formation of a Communist Party.

The Savisky group was much persecuted by the police. Savisky himself was deported, and the Grupo Comunista in Bogotá was dissolved. However, the Communists received support from the Liberal Party press, particularly from Luis Cano, director of the important Liberal newspaper, *El Espectador,* who went Savisky's bail when he was arrested. The persecution only served to stimulate the enthusiasm of the Communists and to arouse support for them, particularly among the workers.

In 1925, a labor conference, which was labelled the Second Workers Congress, met in Bogotá. Its president was Ignacio Torres Giraldo, of the Grupo Comunista of Cali, but the majority of the delegates were Anarchosyndicalists. After considerable struggle between the Anarchosyndicalist and pro-Communist tendencies in the Congress a compromise was reached, whereby an Anarchist program was adopted but it was agreed that the Confederación Obrera Nacional, which emerged from the Congress, would join the Communists' Red International of Labor Unions. Torres Giraldo was elected President of the C.O.N.

The Third Workers Congress, which met in 1926, was torn by a discussion of the idea of launching a labor party. There were three factions in the Congress. One group, headed by Torres Giraldo, did not think the time was ripe for organizing such a party. An extreme Left group proposed the immediate formation of a Communist Party. The majority favored neither of these courses. Led by Francisco de Heredia, one of the earliest propagandists of Socialist ideas in Colombia, it proposed the formation of a party to be called the Partido Socialista Revolucionario, which would be Communist in orientation but not in name, and which would not affiliate immediately with the Comintern. This group carried the day, with the result that the extreme left wing—led by Naftalí Arze, who had spent some time in Russia—withdrew from the Congress. Some months later, however, Arze joined the new party.

The Central Committee of the new P.S.R. included three people: Torres Giraldo, Tomás Uribe Márquez (later a leading Liberal politician), and Guillermo Hernández Rodríguez. The P.S.R. was for the most part a propaganda organization, to spread the ideas of Communism. María Cano and Torres Giraldo toured the country, visiting all the *Departmentos* (equivalent to states in the U.S.A.), and established local organizations in many places. In some cases they encountered trouble with the police and were even jailed for short periods.

The Second Congress of the P.S.R. met in 1927. Torres Giraldo suggested at this meeting that the party affiliate to the Third International. One of the purposes of this proposal was to take the wind out of the sails of the small left-wing group which had been active outside the P.S.R. since the 1926 Congress. Affiliation was adopted.

The application of the P.S.R. for admission to the Communist International as a "fraternal" member was accepted, and thenceforward the party played an active role in the affairs of the Comintern. Two delegates, Guillermo Hernández Rodríguez and Naftalí Arze, were sent to the celebration of the tenth anniversary of the Russian Revolution in Moscow in November, 1927. Ignacio Torres Giraldo became a member of the Presidium of the Red International of Labor Unions. Tomás Uribe Márquez became a member of the Central Committee of the Communist International itself. Diego Mejía was sent to the Lenin school in Moscow for training. Finally, Alberto Castillón was the Colombian delegate to the Sixth Congress of the Comintern in 1928.

There were several factions in the P.S.R. One, clearly Marxist, was led by Torres Giraldo. The other group was composed of people who were essentially Liberals, who wanted to use the P.S.R. as a means to the violent overthrow of the Conservative Party regime then in power. They organized militia, gathered arms, manufactured bombs. At the same time, they opposed normal work among the trade unions and were against aiding any partial strikes, such as the 1928 banana strike, wanting to conserve all the party's energies for a final general strike and *coup d'état*.

During the heyday of the Partido Socialista Revolucionario the party had a daily newspaper in Cali called *La Humanidad*, which began originally as a weekly. It also had a weekly, *La Justicia*, in Medellín and another weekly, *Vox Populi*, in Bucaramanga. Other party papers appeared less frequently in other towns.

The high point of the P.S.R.'s history was the banana workers' strike in 1928. The labor movement among the banana workers had been started by an Anarchosyndicalist, Raúl Mahecha, who had previously led two unsuccessful walkouts among the oil workers along the Atlantic Coast.

Being aware of Mahecha's activities and knowing that a strike among the banana workers was inevitable, the Marxist element in the P.S.R. sought to gain influence with these workers. Torres Giraldo and María Cano were sent to Baranquilla, to organize a Solidarity Committee among the local unions and local members of the Partido Socialista Revolucionario to support the forthcoming walkout. A leading member of this Committee was Augusto Durán, destined in later years to be Secretary General of the Communist Party.

After the strike began, the P.S.R. sent Alberto Castillón into the area, to try to bring the walkout to a successful conclusion. Two other Communists, a Frenchman who went by the name of Rabate, and an American, Joseph Zack Kornfedder, were also on the spot as agents of the Comintern.

Meanwhile the government, after some days of hesitation, had ordered the workers back to their jobs, and the strikers held a meeting to protest this order. The meeting was under the chairmanship of Alberto Castillón, who made the principal speech. During the demonstration the troops shot at the workers, resulting in an estimated 86 deaths. With this massacre, the strike was broken.

Soon after, the P.S.R. began to decline in membership and influence. The reason for this was that all those members of the party who were essentially Liberals withdrew to support the 1930 election campaign of the Liberal Party, in which, for the first time in many years, the Liberals appeared to have a chance to win.[1] The P.S.R. received only a few hundred votes for its presidential nominee, Alberto Castillón.[2]

The Liberals won the 1930 election, and Enrique Olaya Herrera became President. Several of the ex-members of the P.S.R. played leading parts in the Olaya Herrera administration and succeeding Liberal governments. As a result of their deserting the P.S.R., it was reduced to a very minor role in the country's political life.

The ultimate fate of the P.S.R. was decided in Moscow in a discussion in the Latin American Secretariat of the Communist International. Those who participated in this discussion were Stefani, an Austrian who dealt with Latin American affairs for the Comintern; Manuilsky, then President of the International; Trilla, a Spaniard; Guillermo Hernández Rodríguez; Joseph Zack Kornfedder; and the wife of Hernández Rodríguez. It was decided that the P.S.R. should change its name to Partido Comunista and direct its energies toward the labor movement.

A commission composed of Hernández Rodríguez, his wife, and Joseph Z. Kornfedder was appointed to go to Colombia to carry out the Moscow decision. They arrived in Colombia in July, 1930, and soon afterwards a party conference was called, which changed the organization's name to Partido Comunista. Hernández Rodríguez was elected Secretary General, a post which he kept until 1932, when he was expelled from the Party for "indiscretions."[3] He was succeeded by Luis Vidal, who has been described as "an intellectual, and a generous, fervent, and honorable man."[4]

The Communists carried on an active campaign against the Leticia border war between Colombia and Peru in 1933. They held antiwar demonstrations in Bogotá, Baranquilla, and other towns, and the Communist press reported, "Many revolutionary unions issued antiwar manifestoes." In reprisal for these activities the offices of the Communist periodical, *Tierra*, were smashed, and the paper was banned. The headquarters of the Communist Party were raided, and it was reported that five hundred Communists were arrested.[5]

In conformity with the Comintern's Third Period line, the Colombian Communists concentrated much of their propaganda activity on the Indians, many of whom were agricultural workers. They also cooperated with Indian groups in the Department of Tolima, where agricultural workers struck against their employers. According to *International Press Correspondence* of October 17, 1935, "All these movements . . . are mostly spontaneous, owing to the immaturity of the Communist Party, and because the trade unions and peasant organizations are weak." In accordance with this Third Period policy of wooing racial minorities, the Colombian Communists chose an Indian peasant, Estiquio Timote, as their nominee in the presidential election of 1934.[6]

The 1934 election brought to the presidency the second Liberal Party President, Alfonso López. López represented the Liberals' left wing, and he carried out an extensive reform program during his four years in office. He revised the tax system, to increase the payments of those in the higher income brackets, gave encouragement to organized labor, and carried out other reforms.

However, the left-wing policies of the López administration were not enough to win him the immediate support of the Communists. As late as September 28, 1935, a year and a half after the election of López, the Comintern's *International Press Correspondence* reported, "The position of the masses . . . has not improved one hair's breadth," and called the Liberal Party "the political form in which the young industrial bourgeoisie and the old landowning class exercise their role jointly in spite of certain differences in their economic interests." Finally, the article claimed that Lopez "no longer enjoys the slightest sympathy among the masses."

The changes of the Comintern's Popular Front Period were soon reflected in Colombia, however. On May Day, 1936, President López and Communist leader Gilberto Vieira both spoke from the presidential palace in a demonstration to celebrate the occasion. Vieira, according to Stephen Naft, "came out in support of the reformist and democratic policies of President López."[7]

The new policy of Communist-Liberal cooperation first became evident in the trade union field. During the Third Period the Communists had organized a central labor organization of their own, which they called the Central Obrera y Campesina de Colombia. Established in 1929, the new organization was supposedly set up on the basis of industrial unionism, but it never gained much support.[8]

In the summer of 1935 those trade unions controlled by the Liberals joined to form the Confederación Sindical de Colombia. Some sixty unions were reported by *International Press Correspondence* of September 28, 1935, to have participated in the founding of the C.N.S. By the end of 1937 the C.N.S. has been said to have contained "practically all unions in Colombia, radical and moderate." At that time its Central Committee consisted of eight moderates, of whom four were labelled "socialists," four were Communists, and one was an Anarchosyndicalist.[9] The C.N.S., the name of which was changed to Confederación de Trabajadores de Colombia (C.T.C.), was one of the four principal organizations participating in the formation of the Confederación de Trabajadores de América Latina in Mexico in September, 1938.[10]

A struggle developed within the Party during this Popular Front period. Augusto Durán, Baranquilla leader of the Party, and Gilberto Vieira, one of the founders of the Partido Comunista, led the fight against Ignacio Torres Giraldo, who had become Secretary General of the Party after his return from Moscow in 1934. At the Party's Fourth Congress in 1939 Giraldo was removed, and Augusto Durán became Secretary General, while the post of President of the Party was created for Vieira.[11]

Another change in the Communist International line destroyed trade union unity once again during the first year and a half of the second World War. The C.T.C. split into two groups, one Liberal and one Communist. It was not until Russia was brought into World War II that the two forces were again brought together in one labor organization. A convention in December, 1941, re-formed the united C.T.C.[12]

The reunification of the labor movement was brought about by a renewal of the Communists' former policy of cooperation with the Liberals. They went much further during this period than they had during the pre-war Popular Front Period. Following the example of the United States and Cuban Communist Parties, the Colombians even changed the name of their Party, adopting the name "Partido Social Democrático."[13]

During the second World War period the Communists made considerable gains, among both the workers and the intellectuals. Important lawyers and literary figures, such as Diego Montaña Cuellar and Alvaro Pío Valencia, joined the Party. Its voting strength increased rapidly, reaching a peak in 1944, when the Partido Social Democrático received 30,000 votes and won a senatorship, four posts as deputies, seventeen seats in Departmental Councils, and fifty posts as municipal councillors.[14]

However, soon after this election the decline of the Communists began. It was very rapid. Its cause was the rise of Jorge Eliécer Gaitán as the new apostle of Liberalism. The principal leadership of the Liberal Party had been in the hands of a small group of coffee planters and publicists since it had come to power in 1930. By the middle 1940's considerable dissatisfaction with these old-line leaders began to appear among the rank and file members of the Liberal Party. One evidence of this was the rapid gain in strength of the Communists.

During much of the Liberal period Gaitán had been a member of Congress and had participated, in a small way, in the Liberal administrations. However, as a chaotic situation developed during the second administration of President Alfonso López (1942-46) and López seemed to have ceased to be the leader of the party's left wing, the Liberal masses looked around for other leadership. They found it in the person of Gaitán.

Jorge Eliécer Gaitán launched a vigorous campaign against the "Liberal oligarchs," as he called the old-line leaders of the party. He did not present a concrete program, but his rhetorical speeches gained him wide support among the workers and peasants who made up most of the Liberal Party membership.

One result of the rising popularity of Gaitán was the rapid decline of the Communists. The rout of the Communist Party became complete in the election of 1946. There were three presidential candidates: The opposition Conservative Party nominated Mariano Ospina Pérez, a moderate businessman from the industrial city of Medellín. The Liberal Party split, the moderate element naming Gabriel Turbay, who returned from his post as Ambassador to Washington to accept the nomination, the dissident faction in the party supporting Gaitán and gaining more votes than Turbay.

Under the leadership of Durán, the Communists vacillated during this campaign. First, they backed the candidacy of Darío Echendía, who was being put forward by Alfonso López as the Liberal Party nominee, at the same time denouncing Turbay as an oligarch and plutocrat. However, when Echandía's candidacy failed, the Communists, instead of backing Gaitán as might have been expected, backed the more conservative of the two Liberal candidates, Turbay. During the campaign they denounced Gaitán as a "fascist." However, when both Liberal nominees were defeated by Ospina Pérez and in the debacle Gaitán took over leadership of the Liberal Party, the Communists made still another switch and pledged all-out support to Gaitán, in spite of the things they had said about him in the campaign.[15]

The result of this equivocal position of the Communists on key national problems was that the Communist Party lost virtually all the support which it had gained during the early 1940's. The 1946 election, on which the Party had little influence, showed this clearly, and the congressional and local elections in the following year confirmed it. The Communists lost their senatorship, and all seats in the Chamber of Deputies and elected only one member of a Departmental Council, that of Cundinamarca, the department in which the capital city, Bogotá, is located.[16]

The decline of Communist strength brought conflicts within the Partido Social Democrático to a head. The Party began to split. Early in 1947 Montaña Cuellar, attorney and principal leader of the Petroleum Workers Federation, who had joined the Communist Party in 1944, was forced to quit the Party's ranks. He was attacked by Augusto Durán as an "intellectual" and "bourgeois," and knowing that he was going to be expelled, he quit, taking the Petroleum Workers with him, outside the Communist Party's control. Another blow to the P.S.D. came from its Youth Section. The young people of the Party abandoned the Communists in a body and joined the followers of Gaitán.

The chief opposition to Durán's control of the Partido Social Democrático came from the Party's President, Gilberto Vieira. The Vieira faction accused Durán of being responsible for the Party's dubious behavior in the 1946 campaign, a line of conduct opposed by Vieira, who had urged that the Party back Gaitán from the beginning.[17] Vieira claimed that even after Earl Browder had fallen from grace in the United States Party, Durán had championed the position of the American Communist leader against that of Jacques Duclos and the International.[18]

The final scission in the Partido Social Democrático came at the Party's Fifth Congress in July, 1947. The Durán and Vieira factions split, the Vieira group rechristening their part of the Party "Partido Comunista," Durán's followers taking the name "Partido Comunista Obrero." The Montaña Cuellar group stayed independent for the time being. The Vieira Partido Comunista became the "official" Communist Party, recognized by the Cominform.

A few months after the split, an incident occurred in Bogotá which won the Colombian Communists much undeserved publicity. This was the insurrection which took place in the Colombian capital while the Ninth Inter American Conference was meeting there in April, 1948. This revolt, which held the city in its grip for more than two days, left the center of the town in ruins reminiscent of London after the blitz. Many of those present in Bogotá at that time, including United States Secretary of State George Marshall, immediately accused the Communists of responsibility for the uprising.

However, the present writer believes that the "Bogotazo" as most Latin Americans call these events, was in no way the work of the Communists. They did not have the prestige or influence to cause the kind of thing that happened on April 9, 1948.

The facts are that the Liberal leader Jorge Eliécer Gaitán, was murdered by an assassin whose exact identity has never become known. The strongly Liberal masses of Bogotá, who idolized Gaitán, were swept with sudden anger and descended upon all those buildings and individuals which were most closely associated with the Conservatives whom they felt were responsible for Gaitán's death.

Had the Communists been behind the Bogotazo the result of these events would have been much different. The mob was in control of the city for 48 hours, and with determined leadership could have overthrown President Ospina Pérez. One of the notable things about the Bogotá insurrection was the fact that the government did not fall. Instead, the President maintained his position, and the formation of a new coalition government of Conservatives and Liberals was the only immediate political consequence of the revolt.

The Communist leaders were nowhere to be seen during most of the

Bogotazo. It is widely believed that Gilberto Vieira spent most of the time hiding in the offices of *El Tiempo*, the Liberal newspaper, which naturally was immune from attack.

The Communists continued to lose ground after the Bogotazo. They finally lost control of the national organization of the Confederación de Trabajadores de Colombia. A split in the organization between the Liberals and Communists in 1947 was patched up, but in 1951 the C.T.C. finally broke into two groups. The majority of the C.T.C. continued under Liberal Party control with its old name.* The Communists established a C.T.C. Independiente. The Liberal C.T.C. joined the I.C.F.T.U., while the Communist group maintained the old C.T.C's affiliation with the W.F.T.U.

In spite of the split in the C.T.C., the Communists continued to control many of the regional federations of the Liberal C.T.C. In the departments of Valle and North Santander the Communist control was particularly notable. The Liberals were prevented by the government from holding departmental C.T.C. conventions, and thus were unable to purge the Communists from these organizations.[19]

Meanwhile the position of both factions of the Confederación de Trabajadores de Colombia had been greatly weakened by the growth of two new labor groups, neither of which was under Communist influence. The first of these was the Unión de Trabajadores de Colombia (U.T.C.), set up in 1946 under the patronage of the Jesuits, which had the tolerance, if not the support, of various Conservative Party governments and by the early 1950's was the strongest labor group in Colombia. It was affiliated with the O.R.I.T. and the I.C.F.T.U.

The second group was the Confederación Nacional del Trabajo, set up in 1953 with the support of the Peronistas. Although well financed, it ran into considerable difficulties because of the increasingly anticlerical position of Perón, which was not palatable to the workers of strongly Catholic Colombia. The C.N.T. was affiliated to the Peronista continental labor group, A.T.L.A.S., and had few if any Communists in its ranks. It dissolved soon after Perón's overthrow, and its unions rejoined the C.T.C.

By the end of 1956 the Communist Party of Colombia had been reduced to a minor factor in the country's politics. On the suggestion of President Rojas Pinilla, the Party was outlawed by the National Constitutional Assembly in August, 1954. Its position in the labor movement had been virtually destroyed. It had profited little from the chaotic situation in which the country had been living since the assassination of Jorge Gaitán in April, 1948, although some Communist groups took part in the four-year-

---

* The Liberals suffered severe persecution under President Laureano Gómez (1950-53). When Gómez was overthrown by General Rojas Pinilla, the C.T.C. offered Rojas its support. It continued to back him even after the Liberals had broken with Rojas.

long guerrilla warfare of desperate Liberal elements which preceded the *coup d'état* of General Rojas Pinilla, in June, 1953.*

The future of the Communist Party of Colombia appeared at the end of 1956 to depend on the general trend of political events. President Mariano Ospina Pérez had been succeeded in July, 1950, by President Laureano Gómez, the leader of the extreme right wing of the Conservative Party, who had been elected late in 1949 in a contest in which the Liberals had refused to participate.

President Gómez attempted to pave the way for a fascist corporate state, patterned more or less after that of his personal friend, Spanish Generalísimo Francisco Franco. In order to do this, he attempted to purge from all government positions those elements of his own party who were in disagreement with him, including the friends of his predecessor, Ospina Pérez. When in June, 1953, he attempted to oust Army General Staff Chief General Rojas Pinilla, the military leader ousted the President in a bloodless coup.

It was widely hoped that the *coup d'état* of Rojas Pinilla would bring peace to the country. In fact, all political elements except the Gómez Conservatives and the Communists pledged their support to the new regime. Liberal guerrilla bands which had been operating in much of the rural area of the country since soon after the Bogotazo laid down their arms. General Rojas promised a government "above parties."

However, two years later the country still had not settled down completely. The Rojas Pinilla regime had been converted into a purely military dictatorship, and had alienated virtually all political groups. This was indicated by an agreement signed in the middle of 1956 by Liberal leader, Alberto Lleras Camargo, and Conservative chief Laureano Gómez, to which most leaders of both major parties adhered. This pledged the two traditional parties to cooperate in fighting the Rojas regime and in establishing a successor government.

It seemed unlikely that the country would find peace until new political forces developed which would provide a means for participation in the country's political life of the masses, who had never had much say in the management of either the Liberal or Conservative Party. Whether the Communist Party would be able to become one of the vehicles for this popular expression remained a question by the end of 1956, though it

---

* There is one small region in the department of Cundinamarca—consisting of a number of haciendas some distance from any town of importance—which the Communists dominated for two decades after the middle 1930's. Their power based on unrecognized agricultural workers' unions which terrorized the local Conservative landowners, the Communists had virtually their own government. They had their own armed forces, they administered justice and even carried out executions. During the anti-guerrilla campaigns of the late 1940's and early 1950's, the Colombian Army never went near this area, which was virtually isolated from the rest of the country. In the middle of 1955 the Communist-oriented periodical *Latin America Today* reported Government troops moving into this region.

seemed unlikely, since the Party had been seriously discredited during the previous decade.

A new wave of guerrilla warfare might well strengthen the position of the Communists. They might be able to succeed the second time where they had failed the first to organize a sizable guerrilla force of their own, which would be a danger equally to the Conservatives and the Liberals. Civil peace and social progress remained the only cures for Communism in Colombia.

## VENEZUELA

The oil bonanza has made Colombia's sister republic of Venezuela one of the most important, strategically, of the nations in the western hemisphere. Since the beginning of large-scale exploitation of petroleum during World War I, Venezuelan oil production has expanded steadily. By the late 1940's Venezuela was the second largest producer and the largest exporter of the black gold.

Venezuela's politics have not been as happy as its recent economic history. The country has suffered under an almost unbroken series of dictatorships since the resignation of its first President, Simón Bolívar, in 1830. The first third of the present century was marked by the tyranny of Juan Vicente Gómez, widely known as "the tyrant of the Andes." After a dozen short years of relatively democratic development, the country was plunged in 1948 into another period of dictatorial rule, equal in ferocity to that of Gómez, which by the end of 1956 was still in existence.

During the short period of democratic development from the death of Gómez late in 1935 to the installation of the Pérez Jiménez dictatorship in November, 1948, there developed four principal political parties. The largest of these was the Democratic Action Party (Acción Democrática), headed by Rómulo Betancourt, who served as President of the Republic for two years, 1945-47, during which his party aroused the imagination and gained the loyalty of a large part of the laboring people, middle class, and peasantry of Venezuela.

Acción Democrática has been the chief stumbling block to the progress of the Communists in Venezuela. An "Aprista" party, it has preached a program of moderate socialism and moderate nationalism and has made its appeal principally to the same groups to which the Communists looked for support. Its history has demonstrated the fact that the best antidote to Communism in Latin America is a vigorous party of the democratic Left.

Communist agitation and organization in Venezuela began before the end of the Gómez dictatorship. The first Venezuelan to figure in the councils of the Communist International was Ricardo Martínez, a young man who had fled from Gómez' dictatorship in the 1920's and had gone to live in the United States. There he joined the Communist Party of the United States and came to be regarded as an "expert" on Latin American problems, particularly those of the Caribbean area.

Martínez went to Moscow for the Comintern's Sixth Congress at the end of 1928 and stayed for the meeting of the Red International of Labor Unions some time later. At a meeting of the Latin Americans then present in Moscow, presided over by Alexander Lozovsky (then head of the R.I.L.U.), Martínez was selected as the Latin American resident representative in the Moscow headquarters of the R.I.L.U. According to Eudosio Ravines, his selection was due to the machinations of Victorio Codovilla, the Argentine Communist leader, who feared the influence of Martínez' principal rival for the position, Julio Antonio Mella of Cuba.[20]

However, as yet there did not exist a Communist Party in Venezuela itself. It was not officially organized until 1931. The Party had its origins among a group of university students who had declared a general strike against the Gómez regime in 1928. Most of these young men were deported from Venezuela and were scattered in various countries of the hemisphere.[21]

One of the principal figures in this movement was Rómulo Betancourt, who sought refuge in Costa Rica where he took an active part, with Manuel Mora, in forming the Communist Party of Costa Rica. However, he quit this group in 1935.[22]

Another element among the students in exile formed the Partido Revolucionario Venezelano, headed by Gustavo Machado, which became a part of the Communists' continental "Anti Imperialist" front organization. Machado went to Nicaragua, where he made contact with the rebel, Augusto Sandino. Subsequently, he became Sandino's representative in Mexico for a short while.

Machado joined a military opponent of Dictator Gómez, General Rafael Urbina, in an attempted revolt late in 1929. The insurrection was launched from the Dutch island of Curaçao, and before taking off for their homeland the Venezuelans seized control of the island, taking prisoner the Governor and Chief of Police and seizing the ship *Maracaibo*, which belonged to a steamship line owned by the Venezuelan dictator. Upon landing on Venezuelan soil, the rebels returned the Governor of Curaçao to his dominion.[23] In spite of initial success in forcing the surrender of the garrison at Coro, the uprising was defeated by the Gómez forces. This was the last serious revolt attempt before the death of the dictator.

Some of the students of the "generation of 1928" who remained in Venezuela joined in March, 1931, to found the Communist Party of Venezuela. A few months after its establishment, most of the Party's principal leaders were arrested.[24] They were very roughly handled by the police, and after being released a number of them were expelled from the Party on charges of having disclosed information about the Party while being tortured by police officers.[25]

The possibility of Communist agitation, or any other kind of opposition political activity, was extremely limited so long as Gómez lived. However, in 1934, when tension was high between Venezuela and Colombia over a border dispute in the San Faustino Valley, the Venezuelan Communists cooperated with their Colombian comrades in antiwar agitation.[26]

The Venezuelan Communists were represented in various international Communist gatherings. Besides Martínez, who remained in Moscow during most of the 1930's, one Ribas attended the Seventh Congress of the Comintern in 1935.[27] The Venezuelan Communist Party, which heretofore had been a "sympathetic" party, was admitted to full membership in the Communist International at this 1935 Congress.[28]

Juan Vicente Gómez died in his sleep late in December, 1935. His successor, President Eliazar López Contreras, Gómez' son-in-law and Minister of War, began immediately to modify the dictatorship. He allowed the exiles to return and for a short while permitted a considerable degree of political activity by the opponents of the Gómez regime.

Most of these opposition elements joined to form a group called the Organización Revolucionaria Venezolana (more commonly known by its initials as O.R.V.E.). This organization rallied most of the "generation of 1928" as well as many leaders of the trade unions which became active right after the death of Gómez. The O.R.V.E. soon changed its name to Partido Democrático Nacional.[29]

López Contreras soon clamped down on the leaders of the opposition, many of whom were expelled from the country once more. Only Rómulo Betancourt and one other important non-Communist leader remained in the country. The Communists were more fortunate, since many of the more important figures in their movement were unknown, having returned from training in Moscow soon after Gómez' death, but having remained in the background during these early months of López Contreras' administration.[30]

Dissension soon arose within the Partido Democrático Nacional between the Communists and non-Communists. The latter insisted that the party should be a strictly Venezuelan organization and that the Communists should break all connection with the international Communist movement. This the Communists, naturally, refused to do. The result was that late in 1937 the two groups split. The non-Communists continued to use the name Partido Democrático Nacional, and the Communists came out openly as the Partido Comunista de Venezuela.[31]

Both the non-Communist forces, led by Betancourt, and the Communists, led by Juan Bautista Fuenmayor and the Machado brothers (Eduardo and Gustavo), concentrated much of their attention on the labor movement. For the first half-dozen years or so after Gómez' death the Communists were the dominant element in the trade unions, and particularly among the petroleum workers, who were the largest single group of organized workers.[32]

However, Betancourt was particularly successful in enlisting the intellectuals behind the banner of the Partido Nacional Democrático. José Peña, writing in the New York *Daily Worker*, on October 28, 1945, commented on this situation: "During this period he gathered about him some of Venezuela's principal intellectuals—writers, economists, professionals—as for instance, Rómulo Gallegos, Andrés Eloy Blanco and Carlos D'Ascoli. With these figures in the direction, he later organized the Acción Democrática."

The Venezuelan Communists followed the various twists and turns of the international Communist "line." During the first part of World War II they denounced the conflict as "imperialist," and the Communist members of the Venezuelan Students Federation withdrew from the organization because they refused to sign an anti-fascist manifesto which the Federation issued.[33] With the attack on the Soviet Union, the Venezuelan Communists suddenly became the most violent opponents of the Axis.

Both the Communists and the Betancourt forces were severely persecuted during most of the López Contreras regime, though this dictatorship was by no means as tyrannical as that of Gómez. Both parties opposed the election in 1941 of General Isaias Medina Angarita, whom López Contreras had chosen to succeed to the presidency.

Although they knew that he had no chance of winning, since the election of the President was in the hands of the López-controlled Congress, the Betancourt forces, who by now had rechristened their group Acción Democrática, nominated Rómulo Gallegos for the presidency. Gallegos was the country's leading novelist, a figure highly respected throughout the Spanish-speaking part of the hemisphere, who had associated himself in a general way with Acción Democrática, though he had not as yet joined the party. Around his name Acción Democrática conducted a widespread propaganda campaign, which was the party's first nation-wide effort and established the organization on a firm basis.

The Communists, too, opposed Medina's candidacy. The day Congress elected Medina, a Communist-led demonstration outside of the legislative palace was broken up by the police. The Communists then circulated throughout America an article which they entitled "With Clubs and Gunfire General Medina Commences His Regime." They explained their action by saying that they thought that Medina was going to be a fascist-minded President, since he had announced himself an admirer of Mussolini and they suspected him of sympathies with the Axis.

However, Medina turned out to be a rather different kind of chief executive. Although he remained essentially a dictator, he moved in a democratic direction. He allowed Acción Democrática to organize as a legal party. He never persecuted or jailed the Communists, and had the Constitution revised so as to eliminate Paragraph Six, which had outlawed the Communist Party. Even before this, he permitted the Communists to organize a legal political group, known as Unión Popular.

Medina carried through various reforms. He had the Constitution amended so as to have Congress chosen by direct instead of indirect election. He launched a number of social laws and carried out a housing program in Caracas.

The Communists, in the meanwhile, changed their attitude toward Medina. This change cannot be judged solely from the point of view of internal Venezuelan politics. It must be borne in mind that the policy of the Communists throughout the hemisphere during the second part of World War II was to support any Latin American government which declared itself pro-Ally, which Medina's did.

Following this general line, the Venezuelan Communists became ardent friends of the Medina administration. They developed close relations with President Medina himself and with some members of his government. Subsequently, Juan Bautista Fuenmayor admitted to the author that the Communists had probably gone too far in their all-out support of the Medina administration.

The Communists' most serious setback during the Medina regime was loss of control of the trade union movement, as a result of the failure of the Second Workers Congress, which met in Caracas early in 1944. Vicente Lombardo Toledano of the C.T.A.L. was present at this meeting, which had the purpose of launching a national central labor organization. During the election of the Executive Committee for the new group, one of the delegates who belonged to Acción Democrática suggested that representation on the Committee should be half Communist and half Acción Democrática, since those were the two political groups represented among the delegates. A Communist objected to this, saying that since the Communists had a majority among the delegates, they should have the majority on the new Executive Committee.

The Acción Democrática members then withdrew from the Congress. President Medina called a special Cabinet meeting to discuss this question, and the government resolved to withdraw legal recognition from all unions whose delegates had remained in the Congress after the departure of the Acción Democrática group, and had thus labelled themselves Communists.

The exact reasons for this action by the government remain a mystery. Certainly it was a political error, so far as Medina was concerned. Acción Democrática was the chief opposition group, and the Communists were at that time cooperating closely with the government. The upshot of the move was that the Acción Democrática people were able to reorganize a number of the unions whose legal recognition had been withdrawn, and were able to capture many others. From 1944 on they controlled a considerable majority of the organized labor movement.[34]

This defeat and the general policy of Communist support of the Medina regime brought about a split in the ranks of the Communist Party. The origins of this division went back to 1942. At that time Medina had allowed the Communists to establish a legal Party, Unión Popular, and in return the Communists supported Medina's candidates in the congressional elections of that year. This aroused a good deal of opposition within the Party.

Unión Popular came to be controlled by the anti-Medina faction, headed by Gustavo and Eduardo Machado and the Communist trade unionists, Luis Miquilena and Rodolfo Quintero (which came to be known as the Machamiques, from the names of Machado and Miquilena). Miquilena and his two principal aides, Cruz Villegas and Horacio Scott, had been expelled from the Communist Party in 1940, but had been permitted to become members of Unión Popular when it was established.

The other faction was led by Juan Bautista Fuenmayor. Tension between his group and the Machamiques mounted after 1942. This culminated in a public meeting in 1944 during which supporters of the Machamiques booed Fuenmayor. When Fuenmayor protested this treatment to the National Executive Committee of the Unión Popular, Quintero and Miquilena backed the action of their supporters. As a result, Fuenmayor and his followers withdrew and re-established the open Partido Comunista.[35] At the same time the Machamiques "expelled" Fuenmayor from the Unión Popular.[36] They rechristened their group Partido Comunista Unitario early in 1945.[37]

On October 18, 1945, President Medina was overthrown by a *coup d'état*. The partners in this movement were Acción Democrática and a group of young military leaders, whose principal figures included Captain Mario Vargas, Major Carlos Delgado Chalbaud, and Captain Marcos Pérez Jiménez.

The action of Acción Democrática in cooperating in this insurrection has been a subject of hot controversy ever since. It seemed to conflict with Acción Democrática's democratic philosophy and the general trend toward democratic civilian government which had marked the Medina administration. The explanation of the A.D. leaders was twofold. First, they argued that Medina had indicated his intention of naming his own successor, to be elected by Congress, which he controlled; that he had refused all suggestions to change the Constitution so as to provide for popular election of the new chief executive; and that he had also refused all offers by Acción Democrática to select jointly a compromise candidate whom both Medina and Acción Democrática could support.

Second, the Acción Democrática leaders have maintained that the military men were determined to carry out the *coup d'état* whether or not

Acción Democrática cooperated with them. The Acciondemocratistas feared that if the revolt occurred without any civilian participation, it would result in the re-establishment of something comparable to the Gómez regime. Furthermore, Betancourt and his friends refused to co-operate in the uprising until the military men agreed that the resulting government would be civilian in character and that the party would have a majority in the new ministry.[38]

The Communists opposed the *coup d'état*. Both factions took up arms to defend the Medina regime. However, when they found out that Acción Democrática, and not ex-President López Contreras, was behind the up-rising, the Fuenmayor faction withdrew from the fight and declared its neutrality.[39] The Machamiques, on the other hand, continued to fight until the uprising was successful.[40]

For a short while after the uprising, which made Rómulo Betancourt the country's Provisional President and established a government domi-nated by Acción Democrática, the government kept some of the principal Machamique Communist leaders in jail. However, by the first of Decem-ber, 1945, most of them had been released:[41]

Betancourt made clear his position with regard to the Communists. He said he "would refuse to cooperate with the Communists as his predeces-sor had done," but would not interfere with their legitimate political ac-tivities. The only warning which Betancourt gave to the Communists was that they had better not attempt to "pervert" the Army.[42]

The conflict between the two factions of the Venezuelan Communist movement continued. Each group sought to get the new government to recognize it as the Communist Party of Venezuela. Both groups sent dele-gations to neighboring countries, particularly to Cuba, which was the center of Caribbean Communist activities at that time, to get the support of the international Communist movement. Both groups also besieged the new Russian Ambassador, who had arrived as a result of the resumption for the first time since the Russian Revolution of diplomatic relations be-tween Venezuela and the Soviet Union.[43]

In February, 1946, the Fuenmayor Communist Party held its Fifth Con-gress. It agreed to put up a list of candidates, headed by Fuenmayor, for the Constituent Assembly elections which had been called by the Betan-court government. It also agreed to support conditionally "progressive acts of the present provisional government."[44]

This attitude of appeasement toward the Betancourt government as-sumed by the Fuenmayor Communists was in strong contrast to the posi-tion of the Machamiques. They continued to follow an extremist policy, using their power in the labor movement to call strikes whenever possible and refusing all contacts with the Betancourt regime. They became a frankly oppositionist group, as they had been under Medina.[45]

The two Communist factions put up a joint list of candidates for the

Constituent Assembly elections held on October 27, 1946. They elected two deputies, Juan Bautista Fuenmayor and Gustavo Machado. However, they received only 51,179 votes out of a total of 1,390,263 and came in fourth among the four parties which elected delegates to the Assembly. Acción Democrática received 1,053,761 votes, the Catholic Social Party, Copei, got 150,273, and the moderate left-wing party, Unión Republicana Democrática, polled 54,893 votes. Acción Democrática elected 137 of the 160 deputies in the Assembly.[46]

Meanwhile an attempt was made to unite all the Venezuelan Communists in one Party. A Preparatory Committee for a Unity Congress was established on which were represented the Fuenmayor group, the Machamiques, and a third group of independent Communists which was outside both these major factions. Although the Machamiques withdrew from the Preparatory Committee, their delegates were present at the Unity Congress, which met in November, 1946.

The Unity Congress did not end the conflict among the Communists of Venezuela, although it did considerably alter the balance of forces between the two main groups. The Congress resulted in the unification of the Fuenmayor Party, the independent Communists, and a part of the Machamiques, to form what came to be recognized by the government and the Communist International as the Partido Comunista de Venezuela. The most important change in allegiance as a result of this meeting was that of the Machado brothers, one of whom, Gustavo, became a member of the Political Bureau of the new Party.[47]

Some idea of the importance which the international Communist apparatus assigned to this Congress can be gathered from the presence of fraternal delegates from other Communist Parties. Representatives were present from the Communist Parties of the United States and Mexico, the Popular Socialist Parties of Cuba and the Dominican Republic, the Partido Socialista Democrático of Colombia, and the Communist Party of Spain and the United Socialist Party of Catalonia.[48]

The fact that the new Fuenmayor-Machado Party was recognized by the international Communist movement as the official organization is demonstrated by a letter written to Fuenmayor, Machado, and Luis Emiro Arrieta by William Z. Foster, head of the Communist Party of the United States. The letter, written on June 23, 1947, congratulated these three leaders of the Partido Comunista de Venezuela "for the historical conquest you have achieved by establishing a united Communist movement in Venezuela."[49]

The report of the Credentials Committee concerning the 248 delegates who attended this Congress gave some interesting information about the nature of the Party which was formed there. About 42 per cent of the delegates were industrial workers, almost 25 per cent were agricultural and unskilled workers, 26 per cent were white-collar workers, and 6½ per cent were professional people. Half the delegates were under thirty years of age; and the delegates had been in the Party on an average of nearly six years. Almost 55 per cent of the delegates were active members of their trade unions, and 32½ per cent of them were elected officials of their respective unions.[50]

However, the Communists still had relatively little weight in the nation's politics. Acción Democrática had without any doubt won the support of the great majority of the workers, peasants, and intellectuals of Venezuela. It had taken long strides in the direction of building in Venezuela a democratic, civilian society.

Under the rule of Acción Democrática civilian organizations of all kinds flourished. Four important political parties were firmly established, so firmly that they resisted many years of buffeting under the dictatorship which supplanted Acción Democrática late in 1948. Among these was Acción Democrática itself, which had been strongly established even before the party came to power, but succeeded in extending its influence considerably after the October, 1945, revolution.

The second party in terms of importance was the Comité Popular Electoral Independiente, known generally by its initials as the Copei. It was established by Rafael Caldera, a young lawyer who had been Attorney General in the first months of the Betancourt regime, but had resigned because of disagreements with the Acción Democrática members of the government. Its general orientation was Social Catholic, though it had its greatest influence in the traditionally conservative Andean mountain states along the Colombian frontier.

The third party was the Unión Republicana Democrática. It was a left-wing party which did not differ essentially in its ideology from Acción Democrática. Its leader was Jovito Villalba, who had been one of the leaders of the 1928 student movement against Gómez and had been one of the original leaders of O.R.V.E. after the death of Gómez. He had had personal differences with both Betancourt and the Communists and had not joined either of their groups, though he did not organize a party of his own until after the October, 1945, revolution. During most of the Acción Democrática regime he and his party were bitterly opposed to A.D., and were accused by A.D. of giving refuge to many elements of the old Medina and López Contreras administrations.

Finally, there were the Communists. In spite of all efforts to unite the various factions of the Venezuelan Communist movement, it remained split throughout the Acción Democrática regime. The Fuenmayor group came to be known as the "Red Communists," since they adopted the color red as their insignia for the 1947 presidential and congressional election; while the rival group, led after the defection of Gustavo Machado by Rodolfo Quintero and Luis Miquilena, came to be known as the "Black Communists," from their use of black as their electoral color.

The growth of political parties was not the only achievement of the Acción Democrática regime. The government launched a policy of "sowing petroleum," as Rómulo Betancourt summed up the economic policy of the regime. The Acción Democrática leaders felt that Venezuela should gain as much as possible from the oil bonanza which was then already under way. First of all, the Betancourt government renegotiated the agreements with the oil companies operating in the country, adopting the "50-50" principle, whereby the companies agreed to give Venezuela half the profits from the exploitation of the country's oil resources. It was agreed that if, at the end of the fiscal year, the oil companies had not returned 50 per cent of their profits, negotiations would be conducted to determine what extra payments the companies should make.

Then the government set about to make the best possible use of its share of the return. Betancourt established the Venezuelan Development Corporation to channel government investments into agriculture and industry. The government undertook extensive road building and irrigation projects. It started a program combining the encouragement of immigration with the settlement of immigrants and Venezuelans in new agricultural colonies. This had as its objective the ending of the anomalous situation in which Venezuela was importing a large part of its foodstuffs, in spite of the fact that most of the country's population was still engaged in agriculture.

The government also undertook to carry out an extensive social program. It established the Venezuelan Institute of Social Security, which aimed to provide health insurance and other benefits to the urban and rural workers of the nation. Betancourt also undertook to augment greatly the housing program begun by the Medina regime, by extending it to the provincial regions and putting the emphasis on the provision of individual houses instead of apartments for as many workers as possible.

The Acción Democrática regime also undertook an extensive program of agrarian reform. This was combined with the immigration and colonization program and was designed to create an extensive small-landholding class, as well as to experiment with various types of collective agriculture. Unfortunately, the program was just getting under way when the Acción Democrática regime was overthrown.

The political changes under the Acción Democrática regime were also of profound significance. The government called elections in October, 1946, for a Constituent Assembly. These were the first elections ever held under a system of universal adult suffrage. Illiterates were enabled to vote through a system under which each political party was assigned a different colored ballot, and voting was by party list.

The Constituent Assembly wrote a new basic document for the nation, which confirmed the principle of universal adult suffrage and provided for the first time for direct popular election of the President of the Republic. It also followed the current fashion in Latin American constitutions by writing into the document a considerable amount of social legislation.

The first election under this new Constitution was held in 1947. Acción Democrática supported Rómulo Gallegos, world-famed novelist, for the post of chief executive. The Copei nominated Rafael Caldera, while the Communists nominated Gustavo Machado. Gallegos won overwhelmingly, and was inaugurated as the first popularly elected President in impressive ceremonies early in 1947.

Both Communist groups participated in these 1947 elections. The Reds elected oil workers' leader Jesús Faria to the Senate and Juan Bautista Fuenmayor and Gustavo Machado to the Chamber of Deputies.[51] They polled 48,000 votes. The Blacks, now calling themselves Partido Revolucionario Proletario (Comunista), had no presidential nominee and had less success at the polls, failing to elect any members of Congress.[52] However, in subsequent municipal elections, they did succeed in winning a few seats in town and city councils, particularly in the eastern oil fields.[53] They received 20,000 votes in the 1947 congressional poll.[54]

One of the most important aspects of the Acción Democrática regime was the growth of the trade union movement. In less than two years after the seizure of power by Acción Democrática the number of legally recognized trade unions increased from about two hundred to almost nine hundred. Half of these new organizations were established among agricultural workers, whom previous governments had not allowed to organize.[55] The number of organized workers increased from 40,000-50,000 in October, 1945, to about 300,000 by June, 1948.[56]

Not only did the trade unions greatly increase in numbers, they were for the first time able to establish a national central labor organization. The great majority of the unions were under Acción Democrática leadership, and the Acciondemocratistas moved cautiously in the direction of a national labor group. First, they established a large number of industrial and regional labor federations.

Finally, in November, 1947, the various federations were brought together in the Confederación de Trabajadores de Venezuela, of which Acciondemocratista Pedro Pérez Salinas became the Secretary General. It included the great majority of the country's labor organizations in its ranks.[57]

The two Communist groups adopted different tactics towards the Acción Democrática-controlled labor movement. The Red Communists of Fuenmayor, having a policy of friendship, more or less, toward the Acción Democrática government, generally worked within the federations and the Confederación de Trabajadores de Venezuela, which were controlled by Acción Democrática. In Caracas, where the labor movement was split by the Black Communists, the Red Communist unions, which at first were divided between the Acción Democrática-controlled group and the Black Communist-controlled group, finally all entered the Acción Democrática-controlled Federación de Trabajadores del Distrito Federal y Estado Miranda, which was affiliated with the C.T.V.[58]

However, relations between the Red Communists and the Acción Democrática people in the unions amounted at best to an armed truce. Occasionally, they flared into open conflict. This occurred early in 1948, when Acciondemocratistas and Red Communists in the Petroleum Workers Federation clashed over the details of a new contract which the Federation was negotiating with the oil companies. As a result of this conflict, the Acciondemocratista majority expelled the Communist members of the Executive Committee of the Federation, who were forced to set up their own organization, which they called the Comité de Unidad y Democracia Sindical.[59] This split continued after the overthrow of the Acción Democrática regime, which resulted in the suppression of all oil workers' organizations.

The Black Communists were more openly in conflict with the Acciondemocratistas in the labor movement. The Black Communists' principal trade union strength was in the Federal District (Caracas) and in the eastern oil fields. Before the 1945 revolution the unions under their control formed part of a united Federation of Workers of the Federal District, of which Black Communist Rodolfo Quintero was the Secretary General and Acciondemocratista Augusto Malave Villalba was President.

After the 1945 revolution the two political groups in the Federation clashed, and the Federation did not function in fact for some months. When time came for the regular election of officers of the Federation, early in 1946, Malave Villalba did not summon the requisite meeting on the basis which Quintero desired. So Quintero called his own meeting to elect new officers for the Federation. Only Communist-controlled unions sent delegates to this meeting, and a solid slate of Communist officers was elected.

The Acción Democrática unions soon afterward held their meeting, elected another new slate of officers to their own liking, and continued to call their organization the Federation of Workers of the Federal District. However, the Quintero group claimed that theirs was the organization which was legally recognized by the government.[60] This problem of government recognition was never resolved during the Acción Democrática administration.

On November 24, 1948, President Rómulo Gallegos was overthrown by a military coup led by three of the officers who had originally cooperated with Acción Democrática in the 1945 revolution—Colonels Carlos Delgado Chalbaud, Marcos Pérez Jiménez, and Felipe Llovera Paes—who formed a Military Junta to run the government. This closed what was virtually Venezuela's only period of democratic development.

As had been the case in the two preceding regimes, the two Communist factions took different positions with regard to the new government. Here, as in other dictatorial countries of Latin America, the Stalinists followed the policy of "dual Communism," having one faction opposed to the dictatorship and another siding with it.

After a slight hesitation, the Red Communists aligned themselves with Acción Democrática in the opposition. Their newspaper, *Tribuna Popular*, was suppressed for three days by the Junta Militar on the last day of November, 1945.[61] Subsequently it was suppressed entirely, and the Red Communist Party was outlawed by the regime.

This alignment was particularly evident in the trade unions. The Red Communists sided with Acción Democrática. The unions under Red control participated in the oil workers' strike, led by Acción Democrática, which occurred in February, 1950, and resulted in the government's cancelling the legal recognition of the Federation of Petroleum Workers and all its affiliated unions.

This attitude of the Red Communists met opposition from Juan Bautista Fuenmayor, who had long been one of the principal figures in the Party. He objected to using the oil workers for political strikes. At the Party's Sixth Congress he criticized this policy of the Party for making it little more than a tail of the Acción Democrática kite. He was defeated in the Congress, which expelled him from the Party, and he was subsequently exiled by the military government.[62]

In spite of their attempts to work with Acción Democrática in the trade union field, the Red Communists' overtures were not welcomed by A.D. With the suppression by the government of the C.T.V. and the Federation of Workers of the Federal District, to which both Acciondemocratista and Red Communist unions belonged, the formal unity of these two elements in the trade union movement disappeared. The unions remaining under the control of the two parties set up separate headquarters in Caracas. Both groups were severely persecuted by the government, their headquarters were frequently raided by the police, their chief leaders were jailed, and the government made it exceedingly difficult for them to function.

In the political field, the Red Communists tried several times to create a united front with Acción Democrática against the military government. In December, 1951, they issued a public letter, urging such joint action, to the National Executive Committee of Acción Democrática—which was still functioning in Venezuela—to which the Acciondemocratistas did not reply.

A year later the Red Communists issued another call for a united front with Acción Democrática. They proposed that it be based on the following program:

1. Re-establishment of constitutional guarantees.
2. Freeing of political prisoners.
3. Free elections presided over by a provisional government.
4. Defense of the demands of the workers.
5. Nomination of a joint ticket to defeat the electoral farce.

The Communists also proposed that Acción Democrática and the Red Communists join in forming the provisional government which they demanded. This appeal, like its predecessor, went unanswered.[63]

In December, 1952, the government permitted relatively free elections for a new Constituent Assembly. Although neither Acción Democrática nor the Communists were allowed to put up candidates, the other parties had considerable freedom to campaign. However, when the returns began to indicate an overwhelming victory for the Unión Republicana Democrática, which had been backed by Acción Democrática, the government suspended the counting of the ballots. Then, a few days later, they announced that the government party, F.E.I., had "won" after all. At the same time the leaders of the U.R.D. were rounded up and sent into exile.

Right after these events the Red Communists issued another manifesto. They attacked both Acción Democrática and the U.R.D., blaming the former's "vacillations" for the Fall of Gallegos in 1948, and the "vacillations" of U.R.D. for its defeat in 1952. The manifesto then went on to argue that "today the most necessary revolutionary task is unity—unity of all labor, peasant, democratic, and popular elements."

The Red Communists denounced those who opposed such a united front, and announced that "The Communist Party of Venezuela calls for the establishment of this unity by the masses, over the heads of those leaders who oppose it, to struggle for the granting of ALL POWER TO A LEGITIMATE CONSTITUENT ASSEMBLY."[64]

Early in 1955 the Red Communists were still dangling the bait of "unity" before the members of Acción Democrática. The latter were as firmly rejecting it. *Venezuela Democrática*, an A.D. publication in Mexico, in its issue of April, 1955, carried a long article opposing this Communist maneuver. The heart of it was contained in the following:

> Communist participation [in unified action against the regime] would mean an attempt to convert what should be an instrument of struggle against the Venezuelan dictatorship into an apparatus for struggle and propaganda against the United States in its controversy with the Soviet bloc. Starting from a just assertion—the share of Yanqui imperialism in the responsibility for the maintenance of the Latin American dictatorships—this propaganda would seek principally to undermine the United States to the benefit of its adversary. This, in the last analysis, is a nationalistic aim, but has nothing to do with us, the interests of the Soviets being different from ours. As a consequence, we would have to renounce—without any compensa-

tion—all possibility of aid from the liberal and democratic sectors in the United States, from whom we can expect useful aid, as is evidenced by the recent pronouncements of the A.F.L. and C.I.O. against the coming meeting in Caracas of the World Petroleum Commission.

The Black Communists took an entirely different tack. Although they did not come out and frankly support the military regime, they did give it their tacit approval. For its part, the military government left the Black Communists relatively free to operate, particularly in the labor movement. For several years the government was unable to build a labor movement of its own, and it was anxious to have trade unions in existence, which could help the regime politically if necessary and in the meanwhile could act as a rebuttal to the charges of the opposition and of the International Labor Organization that it was suppressing the freedom of organized labor.

The Black Communists' trade union movement thus served the government's purpose. A few days after the overthrow of Gallegos the officials of the Black Communist Federation of Workers of the Federal District applied to the government for legal recognition of their own group. They were granted such recognition, which by the end of 1954 they still possessed.[65]

The Federation of Workers of the Federal District, headed by Rodolfo Quintero, was permitted by the government to continue to function. It made no secret of its Communist nature. It continued to be an affiliate of both the C.T.A.L. and the World Federation of Trade Unions. Rodolfo Quintero attended the Congress of the W.F.T.U. in 1951 and later was the guest of the Hungarian trade unions for a tour around that Iron Curtain country.[66] In spite of the official denunciation of his group by the Cominform, Quintero thus continued to have considerable recognition from the international Communist movement.

The extent to which the government permitted the activities of the Black Communist labor movement was shown by a report which appeared on January 30, 1952, in *El Nacional* (a newspaper owned and operated by Miguel Otero Silva, for long one of the leading lights of the Venezuelan Communist movement, though not affiliated with either the Black or Red faction). This report concerned a convention of the Black Communist labor groups in Barquisimeto a few days before.

The Barquisimeto Congress was preceded by a large public meeting, attended by some 9000 workers. The Congress itself went on record in support of the Communists' "peace" campaign, and pledged its support to the C.T.A.L. and the World Federation of Trade Unions. Such a meeting would have been absolutely impossible without the approval of the military regime.

The Black Communists were not only able to continue with their Caracas federation. but were also able to organize in other states. In the eastern oil state of Anzoátegui they were able to establish a second state federation, which was also legally recognized by the government.[67]

However, this pro-government attitude of the Black Communists was not unanimous. Luis Miquilena and Cruz Villegas, two of the leaders of the Federation of Workers of the Federal District, objected to the position which Rodolfo Quintero had taken in more or less supporting the government's resolution of an oil workers dispute early in 1951. The government had refused to allow the remaining oil workers' unions to sign a contract with the companies, and had itself signed the contract "on behalf of the workers."

During the preparations for the 1952 May Day demonstration, the dispute between the Miquilena-Villegas group and the Quintero faction broke into the open. The result was a split in the Federation, with Quintero taking the great majority of the group with him to a new headquarters. He soon gained the legal status which the united federation had previously possessed.[68] By the end of 1954 the Miquilena-Villegas group had disappeared.[69]

The danger to the continued cooperation between the Black Communists and the military government—which after December, 1952, was presided over solely by Colonel Pérez Jiménez—was the action of the government in creating its own trade union group, the so-called M.O.S.I.T. (Movimiento Obrero Sindical Independiente de Trabajadores). This was established early in 1952 and received ample support from the government, including the gift of a magnificent "Trade Union House" built by the government in the capital city. Significantly enough, most of its principal leaders were ex-Communists.

However, by the end of 1954 the Black Communists' Federation of Workers of the Federal District and the State of Miranda was still functioning. Rodolfo Quintero had left the country early in 1954, prior to the Tenth Inter American Conference held in Caracas in March. According to Rafael García, head of the M.O.S.I.T., when interviewed by the author on June 25, 1954, Quintero had left the country "at the request of the government," so as not to embarrass it during the Conference.

The Black Communists' Federation still claimed to have 22 unions affiliated by the end of 1954. Early that year it held a conference to plan for the formation of a national confederation. However, this confederation had not been established by the middle of 1956. The Federation held a May Day, 1954, demonstration in its headquarters which its leaders claimed was attended by some 2000 delegates from various labor organizations.[70]

The Black Communists confined their activities to the trade unions during the military dictatorship. They did not name any candidates for the 1952 Constituent Assembly elections. In the middle of that year they declared the Partido Revolucionario Proletario (Comunista) dissolved, on the grounds that they wished to facilitate the unification of the country's Communist movement.[71] However, their bid was not accepted by the Red Communists, and by the end of 1956 the Venezuelan Communist movement was still split between the Red and Black factions.

The Communists remain a comparatively minor element in the political life of Venezuela. The great majority of the people undoubtedly are still loyal to the country's two major parties, Acción Democrática and Copei. The Unión Republicana Democrática gained considerable prestige and perhaps increased popular support because of its electoral struggle against the dictatorship in the Constituent Assembly poll of December, 1952, which it won, but out of which it was counted by the government. The U.R.D.'s victory was due to various factors, including the fact that it was the most radical opponent of the government allowed to function at that time, and the fact that Acción Democrática underground forces supported the U.R.D. ticket.

Still divided, and playing the game of "dual Communism," the Venezuelan Communists found that their best ally was the United States Government. The United States had shown a willingness not only to maintain formally friendly relations with the highly unpopular military dictatorship, but to go out of its way to pay homage to this regime.

Two events late in 1954 would almost seem especially designed to play into the Communists' hands. President Eisenhower bestowed the Order of Merit upon Dictator Pérez Jiménez, accompanying it with a citation which praised the dictator for his activities "before and after becoming president." Since his activities before becoming President included the overthrow of a democratically elected government, the maintenance of concentration camps, the outlawing of the country's majority party, the suppression of the trade union movement, and the stealing of an election, this was passing strange. A few weeks later after Pérez Jiménez was honored, the head of the government's secret police, Pedro Estrada, was received with high honor during an official visit to Washington.

This United States support for the Pérez Jiménez regime was the greatest asset which the Communists possessed in the middle 1950's. It made increasingly difficult the position of those parties, such as Acción Democrática and U.R.D., which spoke for the democratic Left, and tried to maintain an attitude of friendship for the United States. It seemed to confirm all the bad things which the Communists—under the limited protection of the same military dictatorship—were saying about the United States being a "fascist" country internally and "imperialist" in its foreign policy.

The United States Government attitude of friendliness towards the dictator was creating an increasingly explosive situation inside Venezuela. Its continuation might well result in the Communists of Venezuela becoming for the first time a major force in the political life of that nation.

# Chapter XIII

# Stalinism in the Pearl of the Antilles

CUBA, THE "PEARL OF THE ANTILLES," has been the scene of operations of one of the most important and powerful of the Latin American Communist Parties. The Cuban Party has been of key importance for a number of reasons. It was the first such Party to place one of its members in the national Cabinet; it demonstrated most graphically the way in which the Communists have often used cooperation with a dictator to achieve power in the labor movement and politics; and more recently the Cuban Communists have given a rather new twist to the continental policy of "dual Communism" as a tactic in dealing with the typical military *caudillo* of Latin America.

The labor and radical movement of Cuba, like those of most Latin American countries, was much influenced by the Russian Revolution. During the early 1920's various small groups of people calling themselves Communists appeared in different parts of the republic. In 1925 these scattered nuclei were brought together to form the Partido Comunista de Cuba.

The Cuban Communist Party was founded during the period when the administration of President Gerardo Machado, elected by popular suffrage in 1924, was hardening into a dictatorship. A few weeks after the Communist Party was formed its leaders were arrested, and the Party was forced to go underground.

During the 1920's the Communists worked to organize their usual "front" organizations, of which the Anti-Imperialist League was the most important. The League's activities were typified by its organization of a group of 150 workers to distribute leaflets denouncing the Pan American Congress being held in Havana in 1928. The Party published an illegal weekly newspaper, *El Comunista*, with a circulation of 1000 to 1500 copies during the late 1920's.[1]

The first General Secretary of the Cuban Communist Party was Julio A. Mella, a young man who as a student in the University of Havana had been active in organizing workers' education classes among the unions of the city. He also led a strike movement among the students, which resulted in Machado's closing down the University for a time in 1925.

A few months later Mella and some of his close associates were arrested for a supposed "bomb plot" and, after engaging in a 19-day hunger strike, were finally deported to Mexico. There Mella became active in the Mexican Communist Party, serving for a few months in 1928 as secretary general of that party.

On January 10, 1929, he was assassinated on the streets of Mexico City. His murder is still shrouded with mystery. Although the Cuban Communists have since his death used his name as a banner, claiming that he was killed by agents of Gerardo Machado's police force, the fact seems to be that Mella had been expelled from the Mexican Communist Party two weeks before his assassination.[2]

There is considerable suspicion that Mella was done away with by the Communists themselves. Carlos Contreras, an Italian Communist, who has served as a Communist agent in half a dozen countries in Europe and America,* has been implicated in his death. A recent writer, Víctor Alba, in his *Historia de los Partidos Comunistas de América Latina*, suggests that Mella may have been killed by a "double agent," someone working for both the Communists and Machado.

The Communists were particularly active in the trade union movement. They organized "revolutionary fractions" in several of the unions, notably the railroad workers', the weavers', and the tobacco workers' unions.[3] They took a leading part in the Confederación Nacional Obrera Cubana, a central labor body which had been formed in 1924 under Anarchosyndicalist leadership. After the assassination of its first Secretary, Alfredo López, in the late 1920's the C.N.O.C. passed under the control of the Communists, and one of their number, César Vilar, became its second Secretary General.

The Communists participated amply in the growing resistance to the dictatorial Machado regime. Under their leadership, the C.N.O.C. called a one-day, anti-Machado general strike on March 20, 1930, and organized an important May Day demonstration that same year.

Although the C.N.O.C. was outlawed by the Machado government, its constituent unions continued to engage in strikes. Important walkouts took place among textile workers, shoemakers, and cigar workers, and in transportation. These culminated in a sugar workers' walkout early in 1933.

This sugar strike was organized at a national sugar workers' conference under C.N.O.C. sponsorship in Santa Clara in December, 1932, to which the Communists claimed workers from 32 sugar mills sent representatives. The walkout occurred several months later, and the Communists maintained that about 20,000 workers participated in it. The concrete result of the walkout was the formation of the Sindicato Nacional

* Most recently "Carlos Contreras" has gained notoriety in Europe as Vittorio Vidale, head of the Communist Party of the Free State of Trieste.

Obrero de la Industria Azucarera, the country's first national sugar workers' union.

During this final part of the Machado regime the Communists were also active in other fields. They made some inroads among the farm workers, forming "regional peasant leagues" among them. They also attempted, less successfully, to penetrate the Army.[4]

The Communists played a very equivocal role in the general strike which brought the overthrow of the Machado dictatorship. Although J. Gómez, in *International Press Correspondence*, September 15, 1933, writes that Machado's overthrow was "the result of the real revolutionary struggle of the broad masses of the toilers, whose chief leader was the heroic Communist Party of Cuba," and that Machado was ousted "by the revolutionary pressure of the masses of the toilers," which "had been prepared by the whole of the previous work of the Communist Party in Cuba and was led chiefly by this Party," these boasts were something less than the truth.

Another *International Press Correspondence* writer, R. Bychovsky, in the May 4, 1934, issue, came nearer the truth when he said that the Communist Party's Central Committee "considered that the armed struggle against Machado would lead directly to imperialist intervention, and the Central Committee called on the workers to stop the general strike at a time when it had already grown into a spontaneous armed insurrection."

That the Communists futilely urged the calling off of the general strike which overthrew the Machado dictatorship is certain. The only subject for conjecture is their reasons for doing so. Bychovsky and other Communists before and since have argued that they acted thus in fear of United States invasion. Those opposed to the Communists have argued that they did so for quite different reasons.

One anti-Communist labor leader told the author that, in the face of a general strike which was reaching alarming proportions, Machado called in the leaders of the Communist-controlled C.N.O.C., attempting to make a deal with them if they would call off the strike. According to this source, the President offered to legalize the Communist Party and the C.N.O.C., and to give the C.N.O.C. money with which to carry on its operations, if it would order the cessation of the general walkout. An agreement to this effect was said to have been signed by César Vilar for the C.N.O.C. with Machado's Minister of the Interior.[5]

Whatever their motives for wanting to call off the general strike, the Communist leaders failed in their attempt. As a result, Machado was forced to leave, giving up his office to Manuel de Céspedes. De Céspedes himself was overthrown three weeks later in a coup organized by a group of noncommissioned officers of the Army, and the Directorio Estudiantil, a group of university students led by Dr. Ramón Grau San Martín, Professor of Medicine at the University of Havana.

Grau San Martín became President of Cuba, and the leader of the non-commissioned officers, Sergeant Fulgencio Batista, took over the post of Chief of the General Staff, with the rank of Colonel. The new government was socialistically inclined and vigorously nationalistic, opposed particularly to the influence of the United States business firms which held a large part of the island's economy in their hands.

The Grau San Martín government decided to default payment on outstanding government debts to United States citizens. It ordered a reduction of 45 per cent in the gas and electric rates, and when the United States-owned electric company refused, the government nationalized the firm. Grau began a program for distribution of government land to landless peasants, with $33\frac{1}{3}$ acres going to each family. Finally, he issued a decree which specified that at least 50 per cent of all workers in any firm had to be of Cuban nationality.[6]

In spite of the fact that this was a very radical program for Cuba and was aimed principally at United States enterprises operating in the country, the Grau San Martín government met the blind opposition of the Communist Party. As a writer in *International Press Correspondence* of October 10, 1935, pointed out, the Communist Party "failed to draw a demarcation between the national revolutionary camp on the one hand, and the feudal-imperialist counter-revolutionary camp on the other. This explains the hostile attitude taken by the Party towards the government of Grau."

The Communists bitterly attacked Grau San Martín. For instance, a pamphlet published by the United States Communist Party while Grau San Martín was still in power wrote of him: "Like a last hope of the ruling class, Ramón Grau San Martín stands before the masses, as a 'revolutionary' president—in the shadow of the American dreadnaught, the U.S.S. Mississippi and thirty-seven other fighting vessels."[7]

The Cuban Communists adopted a typical Third Period attitude towards the Grau San Martín government. They raised the slogan of "A workers' and peasants' government." Typical of their attitude was an article written in September by G. Sinani, one of the Comintern's bosses of Latin American affairs, and published in the December, 1933, issue of *The Communist*. In it he wrote:

> The situation of the San Martín government is becoming more and more unstable. The presidential palace is guarded day and night by machine gun posts. According to the latest information, San Martín himself has already informed the political groups which support him of his resignation.
>
> Nevertheless, the present situation in Cuba is noteworthy precisely as a *transition* situation. . . .
>
> . . . The question of the further development of the Cuban anti-feudal and anti-imperialist revolution, bourgeois-democratic at its

first stage, can only be solved in mass fights. The internal conditions, as we have seen, are undoubtedly favorable at the present moment for rallying the majority of the proletariat around the Communist Party and for the winning of the leadership in the peasant revolution, *i.e.*, for forming the conditions which are most favorable for the victory of the revolution. The situation in the army, which is becoming more and more difficult for the exploiting class to utilize against the revolution, increases these chances many times.

The Communists openly called for the overthrow of Grau San Martín. On the anniversary of the Russian Bolshevik Revolution, November 7, their newspaper, *Bandera Roja*, urged that it should be "a day of struggle against the bourgeois-landlord government of Grau San Martín, for the establishment of the workers and peasants government on the basis of soviets."

Following this policy, the Communists actively engaged in setting up "soviets" in various parts of the island. In this connection their newspaper, *El Trabajador* (predecessor of *Bandera Roja*), declared:

> Workers! Peasants! In those places where our mass struggle has reached the level of civil war, *i.e.*, the armed struggle against the ruling classes under the leadership of the proletariat and the Communist Party, fraternize with the soldiers, and in those places where there are no local governments, organize soviets of workers', peasants', and soldiers' deputies.

The Comintern later criticized this proclamation, noting that it "does not correspond to the correct tactics actually conducted by the Party," which carried through "the organization of soviets, as organs of preparation for the seizure of power, as organs of the revolutionary mobilization of the masses for the struggle for power" even where there still was an effective local government in existence.[8]

The Communists issued instructions to their "soviets." They ordered them to form two basic committees, the first "to improve immediately the living conditions of the population," the second "to defend the workers' and peasants' government."

Under Communist leadership, peasants seized the land upon which they had been working and formed armed "Red Guards" to defend it. The most important of these soviets was at Realengo 18 in the mountains at the eastern end of the island, near the United States naval base of Guantánamo. The leader of the soviet was a Negro Communist, León Alvarez. The Communist regime there was reported to have taken steps to diversify the agricultural production of the area and to raise the educational level of the people, during its domination of the region. The Realengo 18 soviet survived the overthrow of the Grau San Martín government for a few months.

The Communists also put forward the slogan "formation of a workers' and peasants' government" on a national scale. However, according to Bijowsky, writing in the April 5, 1934, issue of *The Communist International*, the Party "having published the program . . . did not propagate and did not popularize it further, did not make it the starting point for a systematic and clear explanation to the masses as to what the soviets could give them in the near future, what concretely is meant by the revolutionary way out of the crisis, proposed by the Communist Party."

The Communists were very active in the labor movement during the three and a half months of the Grau San Martín government. The C.N.O.C. brought within its ranks most of the country's trade unions. The fourth Congress of the C.N.O.C. was held early in January, 1934, with 10,000 delegates representing a claimed 300,000 workers. A report of this Congress in the *New Masses* of January 23, 1934, noted that "One of the delegates was from the 'Macay sugar mill. He told the Congress how the first soviet in Cuba was set up in his mill."

The Communist opposition to the Grau San Martín government, expressing itself as it did largely in insurrectionary activities, was one of the principal factors bringing about the downfall of the Grau San Martín regime and the substitution for it of a conservative military dictatorship. The continuous Communist activities in the cities and countryside gave the United States, which did not like the Grau San Martín government, ample opportunity to maintain that that government "did not have effective control of the country," and that therefore the United States could not recognize it.

As a result of continued United States refusal to recognize the Grau San Martín government, Colonel Batista, unquestioned chief of the armed forces, decided that something must be done about the situation. He therefore ousted Grau about the middle of January, 1934, thus beginning one of the classical political enmities of Cuban history. In Grau's place, Batista installed Colonel Mendieta, a man much more to the liking of the United States State Department. Within a short time United States recognition was achieved.

For more than a year after the fall of Grau, and in the face of a growing campaign of restrictions upon the labor unions and free political activity, the Communists continued to level most of their attack at Grau San Martín and other left-wing nationalist elements. This, of course, was quite in conformity with the general policy of the Third International during that period. The Comintern was insisting that the "real enemies of the working class" were not the reactionaries and the fascists, but rather the socialists, whom they labelled "social-fascists," and Grau's lower-middle-class nationalists, whom they insisted on calling "petty bourgeois servants of the landlords and imperialists."

Characteristic of this Third Period attitude during 1934 was an article of Joaquín Ordoqui, one of the principal leaders of the Cuban Communist Party, in the December, 1934, issue of *The Communist* in which he said:

> The Party . . . has exposed the policy of Grau San Martín and Guiteras (his "Left"), a policy of "retreat," that is to say, of support for the policy of the ruling classes. Guiteras calls upon the masses to trust that he, with his "revolution," will solve the situation. As the C.P. of Cuba has correctly stated, what Guiteras, with his "Left" demagogy, is preparing is a *coup d'état* in which a faction of certain elements of the army that are antagonistic to Batista will take part.

The Communist Party of Cuba held its Second Congress April 20–22, 1934, and this was reported in the June 14, 1934, issue of *International Press Correspondence*. There were 67 delegates present, of whom 43 were reported to be workers. Among these were 13 sugar workers, 9 tobacco workers, 6 transport workers. There were 14 Negroes among the delegates.

The Congress decided to concentrate the Party's efforts behind the slogan "worker control, confiscation and distribution of the land of the Yankee and native landlords." It also endorsed the idea that the Negro problem in Cuba should be handled "as a national rather than a 'racial' question," and advocted "self-determination of the Negroes in the Black Belt of Oriente Province," wording almost identical with that used by the United States Communist Party at the same time.

The Congress was addressed by Robert Minor, representing the Communist Party of the United States, which sent its greetings. Greetings were also received from and sent to the Communist Parties of the Soviet Union, Germany, China, and various Latin American countries.

One of the Communists' principal "front" organizations, the Defensa Obrera Internacional (the Cuban version of what in the United States was the International Labor Defense), also held a Congress during this period, on May 16–17, 1934. There were 92 delegates present at their secret conclave, of whom 65 were members of the Communist Party or the Young Communist League. It devoted most of its deliberations to the conduct of a campaign to gain legal status for the Communist Party.[9]

The first year of the Mendieta regime was marked by constant labor unrest, with frequent strikes, and continuing minor insurrections in the countryside. These culminated in the general strike of March, 1935. The Communists were active in most of these movements, although the masses of the workers and peasants followed the lead of Grau San Martín's Cuban Revolutionary Party* and Guiteras' Young Cuba party, rather than the Communist Party.

* The followers of Grau called their party the Partido Revolucionario Cubano (Auténtico) and came generally to be known as the "Auténticos." They merged with Guiteras' "Young Cuba" after the latter's untimely death, and rallied to their ranks most of the non-Communist Left.

The general strike of March, 1935, began among the students in the last weeks of February. Several hundred thousand students and teachers walked out, throughout the island, demanding school breakfasts, better equipment, increase of teachers' salaries. The non-Communist unions were the first to come out in sympathy with them. The movement took on a political character and became frankly directed toward the overthrow of the Mendieta government. The slogan of "a civil government without Batista" was raised by the strikers.

However, as is admitted by V. Cortés, writing in the June 5, 1935, issue of *Communist International*, the Communists did not take the lead in this movement which might have been expected of them. The C.N.O.C., completely under Communist control, did not call for a general strike until March 10, several weeks after the movement had got under way. When it did call the workers out, it was too late, and although "during the strike armed conflicts between the strikers and armed forces of the government took place, as well as spontaneous attacks upon police stations," the movement was finally suppressed by the Mendieta-Batista government.

Just before the events of March the Communist Party of Cuba began to adopt the worldwide Communist policy of the Popular Front, which had already been launched by the European and United States Communist Parties. This change in line took place in the Fourth Plenum of the Central Committee of the Party on February 28, 1935. As a result of the decisions of this meeting, V. Cortés reported that "The language and tone adopted in the Communist press have begun to change, the superfluous and not always well-founded attacks hitherto to be found in the polemics have been disregarded (for instance, as regards the national revolutionary group of Guiteras . . . and the National Agrarian Party)."

Cortés went on:

> This is a splendid beginning. The Party is ridding itself of the mistaken idea which restricted its initiative, the idea that the proletariat is opposed by one reactionary front composed of all parties from the A.B.C. to the Guiteras group. It is beginning to differentiate in its approach to these organizations. It is beginning to seek its allies—albeit even inconsistent and temporary allies—in the organization of a genuine national revolution. . . .

However, this change came too late to be of any particular use in the struggle against the Mendieta-Batista dictatorship. For the next two and a half years, the country groaned under a regime which almost matched that of Machado in its terror and its suppression of civil liberties.

Near the end of it Batista, who was the real boss of the country, having ousted Mendieta and two of his successors when these proved not to be sufficiently subservient to his bidding, began to change his policy. There has been much speculation on this change of heart in Batista. It seems most likely that it was due to the fact that Batista came to realize that if he continued to run the country as he had done since January, 1934, he would go down in his country's history with the reputation of being as hated a tyrant as Gerardo Machado himself. This he did not want.

For whatever reason, Batista began to modify his government's position. One of the first evidences of this was his permitting the organization by the Communists of a "front" party, the Partido Unión Revolucionaria, late in 1937. The head of this new group was Juan Marinello, one of the country's principal poets and intellectuals.

The P.U.R. was notable for the group of intellectuals which it rallied to its banner. These included not only Marinello, but Salvador García Agüero, the party's first Vice President, and a leading Negro teacher and literateur; Nicolás Guillén, the nation's outstanding poet; Augusto Rodríguez Miranda, head of the Grand Lodge of Cuban Masonry; and Dr. Antonio Macías, leading intellectual light of the province of Matanzas.[10]

The country's small Socialist group also entered the P.U.R. At various times the Socialists, whose principal figure was maritime union official Juan Arévalo, had unsuccessfully attempted to launch an effective Cuban Socialist Party. They were now welcomed into Marinello's group.

In December, 1937, Batista backed a general political amnesty.[11] Soon afterward he took up the suggestion, put forward first by the Partido Unión Revolucionaria, for the calling of a Constituent Assembly to write a new basic document for the republic.

Although the Communist Party was still illegal, Batista allowed it to commence publication of a daily newspaper, *Hoy* on May 1, 1938, under the editorship of Aníbal Escalante, a member of the Communists' National Executive Committee. Two months later the Party held its Tenth Plenum, which resolved that the Communists must adopt "a more positive attitude toward Colonel Batista, compelling him, by means of it, to take yet more democratic positions, in order that real guarantees for the exercise of democratic rights shall be established."[12] The Plenum also referred to Batista as "no longer the focal point of reaction, but the defender of democracy."

Blas Roca (the pseudonym for Francisco Calderio), the Secretary General of the Party, addressed this Communist meeting. He commented that "When Batista found the path to democracy, the Party helped him."[13]

A week after this Plenum Blas Roca and Joaquín Ordoqui were invited to confer with Batista at his headquarters in Camp Columbia, on the outskirts of Havana. Exactly what agreements were reached during this fateful meeting, probably only the two Communist leaders and Batista knew. However, enemies of the Party have maintained that the Communists agreed to back Batista's plans for calling a new constitutional assembly, in return for legal recognition of the Party and permission to reorganize the trade union movement under Communist control.[14]

That there is a good deal of truth to these charges is indicated by what followed the Batista-Communist interview. Similarly, it seems very possible from subsequent events that the Communists also promised to use their influence to get the Auténticos of Grau San Martín, and other opposition groups, to support the Batista program. The Communist Party, in any case, officially backed a proposal, first put forward by Juan Marinello and the P.U.R., for the formation of a "unity party," to include the P.U.R., Auténticos, National Agrarian Party, and other groups. The Auténticos rejected this invitation.[15]

Shortly after the Batista-Communist interview, Batista called together the newsmen of Havana for an announcement. To them he said: "The Communist Party, according to its constitution, is a democratic party which pursues its ends within the framework of a capitalist regime and renounces violence as a political means, and consequently it is entitled to the same status as that of any other party in Cuba." Following this statement, the Communist Party was legalized for the first time in its 13-year history, on September 25, 1938.[16]

The Party's first public bow came on November 12, when more than 80,000 people paid to attend a Communist Party rally in the Polar Stadium. The speakers at this meeting included Blas Roca, Joaquín Ordoqui of the Cuban Communist Party, and James W. Ford of the Communist Party of the United States.

The Party held its Third National Congress January 10–15, 1939, in the provincial city of Santa Clara. Three hundred and forty-seven delegates were in attendance, of whom 259 were said to be workers, and 25 were listed as peasants. They represented a claimed Party membership of 23,300. There were also 72 fraternal delegates, including representatives of the Mexican, Canadian, Venezuelan, and United States Communist Parties. William Z. Foster represented the C.P.U.S.A.

The Third Party Congress adopted a typical Popular Front period Communist program. It was summed up by Blas Roca in these words:

> We fight for the unity of the people of Cuba, for the unity of the revolutionaries, and for a great united national front, to realize immediately an urgent practical program; to achieve a free and sovereign Constituent Assembly; to establish democracy with equal rights for Negroes and women; to aid the unemployed; to protect the peasants against evictions; to apply the social laws; to extend culture; to save the thousands of Cuban debtors by means of a law for the revaluation of mortgages; for defense of the national economy; for defense of our country from Nazi-fascist invasion; help for Spain and China; collaboration with the democratic countries, etc.

With the Communist Party now legal, the need for the Partido Unión Revolucionaria had disappeared, and its virtual liquidation was provided for at this Communist Congress. It was agreed that the P.U.R. and the

Communists would run a joint slate of delegates to the Constituent Assembly, in elections which were being scheduled for later in 1939.[17]

The close relations between the Cuban Communists and those of the United States was not only indicated by the presence of leading North American Communists at important Cuban Party meetings, but by a visit of Blas Roca to the United States in October, 1938. In an interview with the New York press he praised the Roosevelt Good Neighbor Policy and then went on to say that he was in the United States seeking moral support for the Cuban workers, and, according to *The New York Times* report of October 21, "to assure continued financial aid from the Communist Party here."

The Communists took a leading part in the reorganization of the trade union movement, which came once again under their domination. Cuban delegates of various political shades attended the founding conference of the Confederación de Trabajadores de América Latina in Mexico City in September, 1938. Among those present were Sandalio Junco* and Eusebio Mujal of the National Labor Committee of the Auténtico Party. Also there were Lázaro Peña and Carlos Fernández R., of the Communist Party, and independents, such as Angel Cofiño and Juan Arévalo.

At that meeting the Committee for a Workers National Convention was established, under the chairmanship of Lázaro Peña, Communist tobacco workers' leader. It summoned a convention of workers' organizations from all over the island, which met on January 23, 1939, in Havana. There were eight hundred delegates present, who proceeded to organize the Confederación de Trabajadores de Cuba. Lázaro Peña became the first Secretary General, and the control of the organization was solidly in the hands of the Communist Party.[18]

From that time until the end of Batista's administration in 1944, and even for a few years after that, the Communists were favored by officials of the Ministry of Labor. Under their control of the C.T.C., the Cuban unions developed the habit of avoiding direct collective bargaining and taking virtually all grievances and collective disputes to the Ministry for resolution.

The opponents of the Communists in the labor movement maintain that Labor Ministry officials lent a much more sympathetic ear to workers' complaints when they were taken to the Ministry by a Communist union leader than when they were presented by an Auténtico or Independent trade unionist. These opponents also maintain that the Ministry itself was thoroughly padded with Communist Party members and sympathizers until well after the end of President Batista's administration.[19]

* Junco had been one of the leading Communists in the 1920's, but led the Trotskyite split in the Party. The Trotskyites did not maintain a separate party for very long. With the formation of the Partido Auténtico, Junco took his group into its ranks. They formed the backbone of the labor group in the Auténtico Party.

The Communists threw themselves into the campaign for the election of a Constituent Assembly. In the party registration period in July, 1938, the Communists claimed to have registered 75,000 voters, and the P.U.R. some 73,000. However, election officials cut down this total to 90,000 for the two parties combined.

The Communist and P.U.R. parties ran a joint slate in all six provinces of the republic. Their candidates included the leading figures of the two groups, such as Juan Marinello, Salvador García Agüero, Blas Roca, and important labor leaders such as César Vilar, Lázaro Peña, and José María Pérez.

The attitude of the Communists toward the parties which were not on friendly terms with Batista had undergone a considerable change. This is shown by an article written by Robert Clark from Havana, for the *Sunday Worker* of New York City, published early in 1939. Clark refers to "Dr. Ramón Grau San Martín's Cuban Revolutionaries (Auténticos), once a revolutionary force but now tainted by Trotskyism and its leader's blind ambition to be president."

The Communists, with their two parties now united under the name Unión Revolucionaria Comunista, won six seats in the Constitutional Convention, elected late in 1939, which sat during the first months of 1940. The Communist delegation was led by Juan Marinello and included Blas Roca as one of its principal members.

Marinello told the author on August 12, 1947, that the Communists were principally responsible for the fact that the 1940 Constitution was one of the most advanced, in terms of labor and social provisions, of any in the hemisphere. There is no doubt that they were a powerful·influence in this direction, although the Auténticos and some other groups shared the Communists' enthusiasm for these sections of the new basic document.

Blas Roca presented a list of provisions which the Communists suggested should be included in the new Constitution. These included the statement that "Work is a fundamental right of the Cuban in his country. The state will employ all means within its power to assure work to every Cuban who desires it." Other suggestions, which were adopted, included recognition of the right of the workers to organize into unions, federations, and confederations of labor, and the right of unions to strike and boycott.

Other legislation suggested by Blas Roca and written into the Constitution included provisions for written collective contracts, enforceable by law, for minimum wages, for the eight-hour day and 48-hour week, prohibition of the work of children under 14, and provision of social security. He also suggested that the law whereby 50 per cent of all workers in a firm must be Cubans, which had first been passed during the Grau San Martín revolutionary regime in 1933 and had at that time met stiff Communist opposition, should be written into the Constitution.[20]

The Unión Revolucionaria Comunista delegates had to meet several attacks upon their Party by its opponents in the Constitutional Assembly. Attempts were made to introduce resolutions which would have dissolved the U.R.C. and the Confederación de Trabajadores de Cuba on the ground that they were "international" in nature, and Blas Roca bore the brunt of the fight against these measures.[21]

In the elections which were held in July, 1940, following the completion of the work of the Constitutional Convention, the Communists supported the candidacy of Fulgencio Batista for the presidency of the republic, forming part of his Socialist Democratic Coalition. This collaboration of the Communists with Batista paid off very handsomely for the Unión Revolucionaria Comunista.

The Communists elected not only ten members of the Chamber of Deputies, but more than one hundred members of city councils throughout the island. A Communist, Justo Salas, was elected mayor of the city of Santiago de Cuba, second largest town in the republic, and another Communist was elected mayor of Manzanillo. In the city of Havana, where Juan Marinello was the Party nominee for mayor, the Party added 10,000 votes to the number which it had received in the election for members of the Constituent Assembly in November, 1939.[22]

The Communists followed the international Communist line of opposition to the Allies during the first year and a half of World War II. Typical of the attitude of the Communists during this period was an article in *Acción Socialista*, then published by members of the Unión Revolucionaria Comunista, in July, 1940, which talked about "the promoters of the Anglo-French war-makers and their social-democratic lackeys." This article ended "Down with Imperialist War! Down with capitalist reaction! Peace in all countries! Long live the U.S.S.R., bulwark of peace, of liberty, and of socialism! Long live the fraternal alliance of the workers of all countries!"

The Communists even went so far as to criticize their new-found allies in the Batista government on the war issue. Thus Juan Marinello attacked "elements in our government who adopt a warlike attitude on the pretext of defending democracies which don't exist."[23]

This attitude on the war issue brought about a minor split in the Partido Unión Revolucionaria Comunista in 1941, when the Socialist group which had formed part of the Unión Revolucionaria, and then of the P.U.R.C., broke away to re-form a Partido Socialista de Cuba. The spokesman for this group was the periodical *Acción Socialista*. As early as August, 1940, it began to be critical of the position of the Communists on the war. In an article in its September, 1940, issue, Juan Arévalo stated the objections of the Socialist group to the Communists' position:

> . . . For us, it is not a matter of indifference whether Germany or Britain triumphs. Victory of the former will signify the death of free

thought and of the free action of peoples. No one can deny that the English are a more tolerant, more liberal people than the Germans. . . . The English bourgeoisie exploits, like any other; but it does not prevent the workers from fighting for their emancipation. The triumph of Germany and of Italy, on the contrary, will signify the extinction of popular, liberal, and emancipating movements.

Between the evil of English imperialism and the evil of Nazi-Fascist imperialism, we prefer the former, because we consider it the lesser evil. And it is in this that we differ from the Communist comrades.

In January, 1941, the Socialist group definitely withdrew from the Partido Unión Revolucionaria Comunista. A number of important trade union leaders withdrew from the Communist ranks during this split, particularly leaders of the Maritime Workers, and the Electric Light and Power Workers Unions, including such people as Ramón León Renterría, Juan Arévalo, and Ignacio González Tellechea of the former, and Angel Cofiño of the latter.[24]

However, this split did not break the momentum of Communist growth during the Batista administration. The Communists continued to dominate the labor movement. They used their control of the unions to line up the C.T.C. in support of their opposition to the Allies. When the delegates of the Maritime Federation attempted to introduce a pro-Ally resolution at the Second Congress of the C.T.C. in December, 1940, the resolution was strongly defeated.[25]

With the entry of Russia into the war, the Communists hastened to agree with the other supporters of Batista on this important issue. Thus, when the Ministry of National Defense solicited voluntary enlistments for the armies of the Allied powers after Pearl Harbor, Blas Roca, Communist leader and member of the Chamber of Deputies, was one of the first to volunteer.[26]

In conformity with the hemisphere's Communist pattern, set by the Communist Party of the United States and followed by those of Colombia, Costa Rica, and Panama, the Cuban Communists changed their name. Abandoning Unión Revolucionaria Comunista, they adopted the title Partido Socialista Popular.

Juan Marinello, in an interview with the author on August 13, 1947, explained this change in name as a maneuver to limit the effectiveness of the campaign being waged by "reactionaries" against the Communists on the basis of the "Comunista" part of their title. He went on to say that the change in name was a very successful move and gained the Party just what it wanted, a big increase in strength.

The Communists maintained their strength in Congress, and became an official part of the coalition supporting President Batista, along with the Liberal, the Democratic, and (after March, 1943) the A.B.C. parties. In March, 1943, Marinello entered the Batista Cabinet as Minister Without

Portfolio, thus making the Communists' rapprochement with Batista complete. Marinello was the first Communist in any Latin American country to become a member of the government.

The Communists grew violent in their attacks on the opposition Auténtico Party. André Simón,* in the New York *New Masses* on September 28, 1943, wrote:

> The interests backing the Auténticos are very concrete: American corporations, Spanish Falangistas, and Cuban Trotskyites are behind the Partido Revolucionario Cubano, which is neither revolutionary nor genuinely Cuban. Its unbridled demagogy follows the Nazi pattern, and although the party's program is not fascist officially, there are sufficient grounds for fearing that if ever it comes to power it will follow the road to a totalitarian state.

The Communists enjoyed wide influence not only in parliament and the government, but among the masses as well. The number of registered Communist voters rose from 90,000 in 1940 to 150,000 six years later. They had a daily newspaper, *Hoy*, with one of the biggest circulations in the city of Havana, and published various other periodicals as well. A "theoretical" organ, *Fundamentos*, appeared every month.

One of the most powerful propaganda instruments which the Communists possessed was Radio Station 1010. Opponents of the Communists claimed that they got control of this illegally, since the money to finance it was originally raised in the name of the Confederación de Trabajadores de Cuba, but the Communists made sure that the radio station was under the control of members of their Party, and even when they lost control of the C.T.C., Station 1010 continued to be an organ of the Communist Party.[27]

During the election of 1944, to choose a successor to President Batista, the Communists supported Batista's nominee as a member of the Democratic-Socialist Coalition. Batista's men were defeated by the Auténicos' chieftain, Dr. Ramón Grau San Martín, but the Communists scored a considerable triumph on their own account. For the first time three of their number, Juan Marinello, César Vilar, and Salvador García Agüero, were elected to the Cuban Senate, and the Party placed nine members in the Chamber of Deputies, including C.T.C. leader Lázaro Peña.[28]

The election of Grau San Martín was undoubtedly a blow to the Communists. It threatened their position in the labor movement, since there were large elements in the Confederación de Trabajadores de Cuba and its affiliated unions who were under Auténtico Party leadership, and who were anxious to take over control of the Confederación and its constituent groups.

* André Simón, whose real name was Otto Katz, returned to his native Czechoslovakia after World War II. He was shot when the followers of Rudolf Slansky were purged in the early 1950's.

However, the rather precarious situation of the Grau government upon taking office made it inadvisable for the Auténtico people in the labor movement to carry out an all-out offensive at once. The Army was still largely loyal to outgoing President Fulgencio Batista. Grau lacked a majority in Congress. A general strike, called by Communist-led labor unions, might well have resulted in the overthrow of newly installed President Grau.

However, it was some time before a modus vivendi was worked out between Grau and the Communists. Before taking office, Grau gave an interview in which he said that the C.T.C. needed reorganization, "so that it would not be used as the political peon of a little group," and added that the C.T.C. was "a legitimate child of the Auténtico Party." Eusebio Mujal, head of the National Labor Committee of the Auténtico Party, also made an attack on the Communist leadership of the C.T.C.[29]

Lázaro Peña answered these Auténtico attacks vigorously for the Communists, though speaking in the name of the C.T.C. His retort, reported by the pro-Communist *Allied Labor News* on June 9, 1944 was:

> In the face of such threats, and reflecting the feelings of the workers of the nation, in the name of the C.T.C. executive committee, I am certain that the new government will not be successful in interfering with the C.T.C.'s development . . . the C.T.C. does not need reorganization by this government because this is the concern of the workers only.

The position of the Communists was strengthened because of the fact that the third element in the C.T.C., the so-called Independents, composed mainly of the old-time Socialists, who had withdrawn from the P.U.R.C. in 1941—did not side with the Auténticos in the beginning of their controversy with the Communists. This brought down on the head of Juan Arévalo, the most vulnerable of these Independents, a violent attack by Senator Eddy Chibas, one of the more fiery Auténtico politicians, who lashed out against Arévalo on his popular weekly radio program.[30]

This crisis was overcome by a series of conferences. First of all, Lázaro Peña led a C.T.C. delegation to speak with the President. Grau San Martín told the labor leaders:

> I am pleased with this visit of the Cuban workers, since our triumph in the elections was of all the Cuban people. We fight for the improvement of workers' living standards. This interview is a commentary on the possibility of guaranteeing unity, so that the nation can continue on its progressive path and make its maximum contribution to the war effort.

Lázaro Peña replied in kind, saying:

> The Cuban workers are satisfied with your words with respect to the maintenance of wages. We agree with you that the workers must

cooperate with capital to increase production. We are interested in a harmonious solution to our problems and pledge all our strength to aid victory for the Allies.[31]

The next move was a conference between the C.T.C. leaders and the National Labor Committee of the Auténtico Party, a meeting arranged at the suggestion of the Independents in the C.T.C. The Auténtico group was represented by Eusebio Mujal, Emilio Suri Castillo, Auténtico leader among the sugar workers, Alfredo Fleitas, Secretary of Finances of the Auténtico Committee and leader of the Salesmen's Union of Havana, and several others. The C.T.C. was represented by Lázaro Peña, Angel Cofiño, Jesús Menéndez, Communist sugar union leader, Carlos Fernández R., "brain trust" of the Communist trade unionists, and various others.[32]

The agreement finally reached between the Auténticos and the Communists was that the two groups were to have equal representation in the leadership of the C.T.C., that Lázaro Peña was to continue as Secretary General, and that there would be no substantial changes made in the Ministry of Labor. This was a victory for the Communists, since it maintained intact their dominant position in the labor movement.[33]

Agreement was also reached between the Communists and Grau on political matters. During the first months of his administration Grau was able to govern largely through emergency powers granted the President during World War II. However, when Congress opened late in 1945 these powers expired. Grau therefore needed a parliamentary majority. The Communists agreed to support the Auténtico candidate for President of the Senate, thus giving him the margin of victory.[34] For their part, the Auténticos supported the candidacy of Juan Marinello for Vice President of the Senate, the first Communist to win that post.[35]

Subsequently, during the 1946 congressional elections, the Communists joined with the Auténtico Party and the small A.B.C. party in a coalition. This coalition was successful, and as a result of it Grau's party won a majority in both houses of Congress. The Communist position stayed much the same as it had been in the previous election.[36]

By this time the Communist-Auténtico alliance had become highly insecure. The Auténticos were eager to gain control of the labor movement, and after having won a majority in Congress and gaining a better grasp on the Army, Grau no longer needed the Communists' support or at least toleration, as he had done during his first months in office.

The break in the Communist-Auténtico alliance came in May, 1947, on the occasion of the Fifth Congress of the Confederación de Trabajadores de Cuba. The Auténticos first tried to get an agreement with the Communists which would have permitted the replacement of Lázaro Peña by an Auténtico. This the Communists rejected. The Auténticos then proposed that an Independent, Angel Cofiño, be elected Secretary General in place of Peña. This, too, the Communists refused.

The delegates gathered in Havana for the Congress in an atmosphere of high tension. The night before the Congress was to meet, one of the Auténtico delegates was assassinated, while leaving the building in which the Credentials Committee of the Congress was receiving delegates' mandates. The Auténticos immediately blamed this murder on the Communists.

The Minister of Labor, Carlos Prío Socorrás thereupon moved swiftly to suspend the meeting of the Congress, and suggested that both sides name members of a committee, to which the Ministry of Labor would also name several individuals. This committee would then plan for the calling of the Fifth Congress of the C.T.C. some time later in the year. The Auténticos accepted this proposition, but the Communists did not.

The Communists postponed "their" convention a short while, and then held it in Havana. Lázaro Peña was re-elected Secretary General, and maritime workers' leader Ramón León Renterria and some other Independents were named to its Executive Committee. The Communists claimed that there were 24 Communists, 12 Auténticos, two members of the new Ortodoxo Party, two Independents, six Liberals, and one member of the Democratic Party on the 47-man Executive Committee of the C.T.C.[37]

The Auténticos, for their part, waited a couple of months, then held "their" C.T.C. convention. Angel Cofiño was elected Secretary General of the Auténtico C.T.C., and power in the group was divided between the Auténticos and the Independents who followed Cofiño.

For a while the government stayed "neutral" in this fight. The only move of the Minister of Labor was to oust the Communists from the as yet uncompleted "Palacio de los Trabajadores," which the Grau administration had been building as the headquarters of the C.T.C., when Lázaro Peña and his friends attempted to seize it by force as a demonstration that they were the "real" Confederación de Trabajadores de Cuba.

It was uncertain for several months which way some of the most important unions of the C.T.C. would go. The Maritime Workers Federation, led largely by Independents, at first sided with the Communist group, but after the government extended official recognition to the Auténticos' C.T.C., late in 1947, the Maritime Federation switched sides. The Sugar Workers Federation was headed by Communist leader Jesús Menéndez, and for a while several Auténticos on its Executive Committee served on the Executive Committee of the Communist C.T.C. However, in November, 1947, a sizable group, headed by Emilio Suri Castillo, broke away to organize another Sugar Workers Federation in the Auténtico C.T.C. It soon had the great majority of the sugar workers in its ranks.

The Tobacco Workers Federation, of which Lázaro Peña had originally been a leader, also hesitated for some time. However, finally it, too, went over to the Auténtico Confederación.

Communist strength in the labor movement declined steadily after the split in the C.T.C. After the government gave official recognition to the Auténtico C.T.C. the Communists attempted to reorganize their forces with the name Confederación de Trabajadores de Cuba Independiente, with Lázaro Peña still as Secretary General. However, though Peña continued to go abroad to meetings of the World Federation of Trade Unions "in representation of the workers of Cuba," by the early 1950's the Communists had only a skeleton organization left in their hands. It was not until after the *coup d'état* by Batista in March, 1952, that the Communists began to recover some of their lost ground.

The struggle between the two labor factions often burst into violence. Several leading Communist trade unionists were killed in gun-fights. The most important of these was Jesús Menéndez, leader of the Communist sugar workers and member of the Chamber of Deputies, who was murdered by a police captain, in a clash near a sugar plantation.[38] Another important Communist slain was Aracelio Iglesias Díaz, Secretary of what remained of the Communists' Maritime Federation, killed in October, 1948. The Communists accused an anti-Communist maritime leader, Alberto Gómez Quesada, of this killing.[39]

The splitting of the C.T.C. led also to a violent political break between the Communists and the Auténticos, particularly those Auténticos following the leadership of Carlos Prío Socarrás, the Minister of Labor who had recognized the Auténtico C.T.C. The Communists violently denounced Prío in the months following the C.T.C. split, referring to him in their speeches as "Carlos Prío Machado Socarrás."

The Communists were equally uncomplimentary toward the Auténtico C.T.C. They never failed to refer to it as the "C.T.K.," substituting the word *krumiro*, or strikebreaker, for the last word of the Confederación's name.

They launched a campaign against an alleged attempt by the Auténticos to re-elect President Ramón Grau San Martín in the 1948 presidential poll, using this as an excuse to criticize the regime. When the Auténticos finally named Prío Socarrás as their candidate for the presidency, the Communists attacked him and his party without quarter.

Throughout the administration of President Prío, the Partido Socialista Popular violently attacked the principal measures of the government. Thus, though the Communists had long advocated the establishment of a National Bank, when the Prío government introduced into Congress a measure to establish such a bank the Communists assailed it. Communist leader Aníbal Escalante, writing in *Fundamentos*, February, 1949, commented thus on the government's National Bank proposal:

The government forces have pictured the project as the best possible, but we have assumed the only correct position: The project was not good. The National Bank Law was drawn up as a species of conservative compromise, which weakens the effectiveness of this proposed institution in the national economy. The government made concessions to foreign bankers and to the private capitalist interests which eliminate from the National Bank a long series of effective weapons, and the Bank will therefore be born weak and restricted. In other words, another government a little less alien to the interests of the nation would have been able to produce a law which would have been a little less bad.

The Communists also violently opposed the Prío government's proposal to raise a loan of several hundred million dollars in the United States for public works projects. Another article by Escalante, in the September, 1949, issue of *Fundamentos,* pictured this as a "sell-out to Yankee imperialism," and said that "It forms part of the plan to please and satisfy the Yankee magnates, by raising an official scandal over the supposed necessity of giving guarantees to foreign capital, that is to say, reducing wages, eliminating paid vacations and collective contracts, etc."

The Communists repeatedly attacked one of the weakest links in the armor of the Grau and Prío administrations—their corruption. Early in 1948, even before the Communist-Auténtico feud had really got well under way, the P.S.P. issued an Open Letter to President Grau, demanding the dismissal of two members of his Cabinet who were reputed to be most corrupt, Minister of Commerce Casas and Minister of Education Alemán.[40]

With the approach of the 1952 election for the successor to Prío, and the naming by the Auténtico national convention of Carlos Hevia, a distinguished engineer who had been Prío's Minister of Public Works, the Communists became furious in their denunciation of Hevia and the party which had named him. Blas Roca, writing in the February, 1952, issue of *Fundamentos* said:

> The program drawn up by the Auténtico convention rejects the nationalist and progressive Auténtico program of 1934; it is a program of betrayal of anti-imperialism, of betrayal of Cuba.
> The candidacy of Hevia is the concretization in the form of a single individual of this betrayal. . . . The candidacy of Hevia is not only the candidacy imposed by the Presidential Palace, it is a denial of the very basis of the Auténtico Party, it is a symbol of surrender to imperialism, since Hevia is the nominee of Annapolis and the Bacardí Rum Co., which has long ago ceased to be Cuban, being converted into a Cuban-American company, more American than Cuban.

The official election program of the Partido Socialista Popular in 1952, as published in the same issue of the Party periodical, *Fundamentos,* started off with the statement that "The core of the electoral struggle of 1952 is the aspiration of the overwhelming majority of the people to throw out the government." The P.S.P. then went on to urge the formation of a united front of all anti-government parties, in which the Communists offered to participate. Being unsuccessful in this plea, in view of the certainty of the major opposition party, the Ortodoxos, that it was going to win the election and the unwillingness of the other opposition nominee, ex-President Fulgencio Batista, to withdraw, the Partido Socialista Popular had not as yet definitely announced whom it was supporting, when the whole campaign was brought to a sudden halt by General Batista's *coup d'état* of March 10, 1952.

The Prío government, for its part, wasted no love on the Communists. It moved to deprive them of some of their most effective instruments, particularly their daily paper, *Hoy*, and their Radio Station 1010. The grounds for this move were that the Communists had diverted money originally raised for the C.T.C. to finance the building of its Workers Palace Headquarters to buying these two outlets for Communist propaganda.

The move to seize the radio station was successful, and it was finally sold to a non-political, commercial broadcasting company. However, the courts checked the Prío government's move to deprive the party of *Hoy* and ordered it returned to the Partido Socialista Popular, in whose hands it remained until some time after the fall of the Prío government.[41]

One of the principal reasons why the Communists turned so strongly against the Grau and Prío regimes was the ability of those administrations to get along with the United States. The P.S.P. of Cuba, after pursuing a strongly "Browderite" program of "national unity" in national affairs and in favor of "Big Four unity" in the international sphere, followed the violent international Communist shift against these concepts in the post World War II period.

The extent to which the "national unity" theme was adopted in the last years of the war is demonstrated by a statement of the Communist-controlled Confederación de Trabajadores de Cuba in the June 28, 1944, issue of the Havana daily newspaper, *El Mundo*. This statement of the C.T.C. was in response to an announcement of the National Association of Cuban Industrialists to the effect that it intended to maintain present wage scales and thus avoid any serious labor controversies.

The C.T.C. announcement, published by *El Mundo* at the labor group's request, said: "The Resolutions adopted by the National Association of Industrialists coincide fundamentally with the policies maintained by the C.T.C. These policies are the keeping of the present wage scales . . . protecting the buying power of the laborer and, at the same time, maintaining the present scale of living."

The statement went on:

The C.T.C. repeats its decision announced at the Ninth National Council . . . calling upon all workers and employers and the government to continue the cooperation existing at present in order to avoid breaks in production; to respect established wage scales; and calling upon all classes to maintain national unity in the face of current problems.

This pronunciamento coincides curiously with similar statements being made at about the same time by the Confederación de Trabajadores de México and other national trade union groups, which, like the C.T.C., were affiliated to the Communist-controlled Confederación de Trabajadores de América Latina.

With the end of World War II and the beginning of the struggle between the Western Powers and the Soviet Union, the Cuban Communists drastically altered their policy. In February, 1946, Blas Roca published a pamphlet, *Al Combate*, which embodied the new program adopted by the Party Congress in Havana a few weeks before.

The Blas Roca pamphlet pointed to the Party's "error" in the recent past, which it blamed on the nefarious influence of the now deposed Earl Browder, of urging national cooperation with the country's capitalist elements. It stressed the necessity of renewing the struggle against "United States imperialism," in which fight the pamphlet pledged the Party to try to achieve Latin American unity. It violently attacked the United States press, the A.F. of L., and the F.B.I. as "imperialistic agents."[42]

The Cuban Communists reacted strenuously against every move by the United States in the international field. Typical of one of their milder outbursts was their reaction to the Truman plan for aiding Greece and Turkey in the spring of 1947. An unsigned article in the June, 1947, issue of *Fundamentos* said of this:

The true meaning of Truman's message is that it proclaims openly the North American pretensions toward the supremacy and domination of the whole world. It cannot help but affect the vital interests of all peoples and all States, large and small. But in the present epoch, after the defeat of the Fascist aggressors and in the presence of the powerful impulse of the democratic forces throughout the world, the plans for world hegemony of any power or bloc of powers are more illusory and unrealizable than ever.

The Cuban Communists established the full range of postwar "front" organizations. A national group of the World Federation of Women was established, under the control of the long-time Communist leader Esperanza Sánchez. In the middle of 1949 a call was issued for a National Congress of Peace and Democracy, which, according to *Fundamentos* of September, 1949, "was signed by intellectuals, artists, university professors, youth leaders, feminist leaders, Negro representatives, Masons and Catholics, Protestants and atheists."

The Russian Embassy seems to have played an important role in this Cuban Communist agitation against the United States. By the end of World War II it had a staff of over fifty people, though there were few Russians in the country and there was little trade between Cuba and the U.S.S.R. Its main work seemed to consist of propaganda in Cuba and neighboring countries.[43] However, during the last two years of the Prío regime, the Soviet Embassy began to reduce its activities. The New York *Times* reported on April 6, 1952, that "During the last two years the legation gradually withdrew from the prominent position that it had occupied in the capital's social and diplomatic life. The lavish fiestas, which used to be so popular with the upper class, became more and more infrequent."

During the Prío Socarrás administration the Communists lost considerable ground among the masses of the people. In the 1950 elections the Communists were forced to run on a ticket of their own, no other party agreeing to coalesce with them. As a result, they lost the three seats which they had previously held in the Senate, although they maintained their nine seats in the Chamber of Deputies. In the province of Havana they ran only 10,000 votes behind the coalition list, which received the minority representation in the Senate from that province.[44] The Party's registration fell from 150,000 in 1948 to only 55,000 two years later.[45]

The Communists had lost out almost completely in the labor field. In the last Congress of the C.T.C. before the Batista coup there were only 11 Communists out of a total of 4500 delegates. It was reported that only twenty of the country's three thousand unions were clearly in Communist hands.[46]

The Batista *coup d'état* of March 10, 1952, opened a new chapter in the history of the Cuban Communist Party. This coup was carried out almost singlehanded by Batista, who seized Camp Columbia with the aid of a few of his friends among the officer corps there, in the middle of the night, and then, in the face of the vacillation of President Prío and his followers, proceeded to gain control of Havana, then of all Cuba.

For a short time the Communists hesitated in deciding on an attitude toward the new regime, and Batista likewise vacillated concerning what position he would take toward his old allies of the P.S.P. A few days after the coup Juan Marinello told the author that he did not think it likely that the old alliance with Batista would be resumed so long as the latter remained "anti-Communist, pro-United States, and anti-democratic." Rather, he foresaw an alliance between the Communists and other opposition parties for a civil struggle against Batista. However, he seemed to leave the door open for patching things up with the P.S.P.'s old friend, saying that the Communists had influence inside and outside the unions which might be useful to the dictator.

Batista at first announced that he did not intend to outlaw the Communist Party or any other party in Cuba. A kind of armed truce seemed to prevail between him and his former allies.

However, in April, 1952, the Soviet Union broke off diplomatic relations with the Batista government when the Cuban regime refused to allow two diplomatic couriers coming to the island from Mexico to bring in their diplomatic pouches without going through regular customs inspection. This seemed to indicate the position which the P.S.P. was supposed to take. The Party became increasingly hostile to the regime.

Batista himself soon moved against the P.S.P. His first move was to change the electoral law, making it necessary for a party to register 8 per cent of the electorate in order to gain legal recognition, something which the Communists were unable to do.[47] Then, late in 1953, the Party's principal leaders were arrested, or went into exile, and finally the Batista government outlawed the Partido Socialista Popular.

However, the Cuban Communists showed the adaptability demonstrated by their comrades in other Latin American countries under the yoke of dictators who felt it necessary, in order to gain the approval of Washington, officially to suppress the Communist Party. They adopted the policy of "dual Communism." The Communists had long maintained two organizations, one legal—the P.S.P.—and the other illegal—in preparation for emergencies such as that of 1952. Blas Roca was official head of both groups, though most of the other members of the secret group were unknown—except perhaps to the intelligence officials of the Cuban government. Fabio Grobart, a Pole, had long been the leading light in the underground organization, but he was forced to leave the country by the Prío Socarrás government.[48]

This existence of an underground organization made it comparatively easy for the Cuban Communists to give a new twist to the "dual Communism" technique. Instead of having a formal split, resulting in a second Communist Party which under another name could take its place among the dictator's supporters, the Cuban Communists actually entered Batista's own party.

Batista and his associates were happy to have these new recruits. The fact was that Batista came to power with very little support among the masses of the people, and most particularly among the organized workers. Although there had existed for some time a "Workers' Bloc" in Batista's Partido de Acción Unitaria (soon after his coup renamed by Batista the Partido Acción Progresista), it had few supporters among the rank and file, and none among the leadership of the C.T.C. and its affiliated unions. Therefore, Batista's followers welcomed elements who promised to provide the working-class backing Batista so sorely needed.

Among the Communists who turned up in the Bloque Obrero of the P.A.U., or elsewhere in the new Batista administration, was Julián Sotolongo, who until 1952 was Provincial Secretary of the P.S.P. in Camaguey and was that Party's candidate for deputy in 1946, 1948, 1950, and 1952. Others were Gilberto Galán, a local labor leader, Mercedes Chirino, Manuel Alonso, and Guillermo Pérez Lamy. The last was a Communist labor lawyer who was named legal advisor of the Ministry of Labor soon after the Batista regime seized power.[49]

The C.T.C. leaders claimed that various old Communist figures bobbed up in the Ministry of Labor after Batista's coup.[50] One of those to whom they most objected was Arsenio González, who had been the lawyer of the Communists in their attempt to wrest legal control of the C.T.C. and its property from the Auténtico leaders before March, 1952, and who became Sub-Secretary of Labor under Batista.[51]

Thus by the end of 1954 the Communist Party of Cuba was illegal, though important Communist and pro-Communist elements had obtained positions within the Batista party, and even within his administration. The Party was in a position to keep on its feet, no matter what happened.

By the end of 1956 the Batista administration seemed to be firmly in the saddle, its chief having been elected "Constitutional President" in October of the previous year, in an election in which he had no opposition as a result of the last-minute withdrawal of Grau San Martín from the race. However, Batista still seemed anxious to govern as mildly as possible, and so was not likely to create too many serious hindrances to the functioning of the Communists' illegal Party machine, which had never been dismantled even in the P.S.P.'s palmiest days. At the same time, the branch of Cuban "dual Communism" which was working within the Batista party ranks was free to make the most of the opportunities presented by the ex-sergeant's hold on the reins of power.

*Chapter XIV*

# Communism in the Caribbean

THE ISLANDS OF THE CARIBBEAN SEA were once referred to, injudiciously but truthfully, by President Herbert Hoover as "America's poorhouse." For more than a century they seemed to have been by-passed by the stream of history. They had been one of the finest prizes of empire during the seventeenth and eighteenth centuries, when all Europe was anxious to acquire the product of the famous "sugar islands." (In 1763 Britain hesitated some time before deciding to keep Canada instead of Guadeloupe and Martinique as spoils of the Seven Years War.) During the nineteenth and early twentieth centuries, however, they languished in squalor, dire poverty, and virtual oblivion.

Only in recent years have the West Indies begun again to come into their own. At the turn of the century the biggest of the islands, Cuba, achieved its independence, and Puerto Rico began its experience of life under the United States flag. With the opening of the Panama Canal the region took on a new strategic importance, and with the growing imperial interests of the United States, this country began to become aware of what was going on in its own back yard.

In the late 1930's the whole of the British West Indies seemed to burst into flame, with a series of violent strikes and political demonstrations on practically every island. At the same time mounting nationalistic feeling was demonstrated in Puerto Rico. The region began to be caught up in the Latin American social revolution.

The West Indies which have emerged in the last quarter of a century are quite different from those fabulous "sugar islands" of the seventeenth and eighteenth centuries. The earlier history of the area saw them all ruled as colonial dependencies by small groups of white European landowners. The great majority of the people were slaves. Now the descendants of the slaves and the remaining descendants of the landholders have tended to merge into a new nationality in each island. The dominant political groups are no longer white, but brown and black. The landholding system itself has begun to crumble, or at least to be transformed.

It is in this atmosphere that the Communist movements of the Caribbean have appeared. It would seem likely that they would find ample ground in which to sow their seed. However, so far the Communists have made comparatively little headway, aside from a short period of importance and power in Cuba. In the British islands they have generally been checked by socialist and native left-wing nationalist movements which have "stolen their thunder." The same was true in Cuba and Puerto Rico. Peculiar circumstances in Haiti and the Dominican Republic have limited their expansion in those two countries.

The present chapter will deal with the situations of the Communists in the three island nations of Haiti, the Dominican Republic, and Puerto Rico, and in the British West Indies. Because of the longer history and peculiar importance of the Communist movement in Cuba that has been dealt with in another chapter.

## HAITI

The Haitians are a proud and independent but primitive people. The great majority of the three million souls packed into the over-populated western third of the romantic tropical island of Hispaniola are small farmers, each having an acre or two of land, where he grows small quantities of coffee, bananas, and corn, and a reed and mud house with a thatched roof, overrun with children and domestic animals.

The fact that most Haitians have a small bit of land has not prevented poverty, but it has prevented the development of bitter social conflicts. The tenant-landowner relations which plague most of the Latin American countries were eliminated in 1804 when the new Haitian Republic confiscated all the country's colonial estates and turned the land over to the ex-slave peasantry. Labor problems have been of limited dimensions, since the country has been until recent years virtually without industries and has had but few plantations.

Economic and social conditions in Haiti, therefore, have not been very conducive to the development of a Communist movement. Furthermore, during virtually its entire history the country has suffered under a series of dictators, who have prevented not only the development of the Communist Party, but the organization of any parties whatsoever.

The Haitian Communist Party was organized illegally in 1930 by two intellectuals, Max Hudicourt and Jacques Romains. It spent its first sixteen years as an underground party. Romains, one of the country's leading poets and novelists, was deported to Mexico, where he died. Hudicourt was also exiled, spending much of his time in the United States.

With the overthrow of the dictatorship of Élie Lescot in January, 1946, the country entered on a short period of democratic government. Presided over by Dumarsais Estimé, the administration allowed a degree of political freedom which had previously been unknown in Haiti, and launched an ambitious program in the fields of education and economic development. It also allowed the development of a trade union movement for the first time.

Right after the overthrow of the dictatorship, political parties were formed. These included a Christian Democratic Party (the Parti Social Chrétien) and an Aprista-like group, the Mouvement Ouvrier Paysan, led by Deputy Daniel Fignolé.

One of the first parties to appear was the Parti Comuniste, organized by Félix Dorlean Just Constant, a young Episcopalian minister. Raymond Pace Alexander, writing in *The Nation* magazine of May 4, 1946, said of this group:

> The Communist Party in Haiti is not actually a Marxist party. It is a strong socialist movement to end the oppression of the working classes and the corruption in the government. It wants to institute an educational program for the masses, still 75 per cent illiterate; to legalize labor unions; to end the granting of monopolies to foreign-owned corporations, chiefly American; and to begin an era of intelligent planning for Haiti's economic, social and cultural recovery. Its leaders hope to see the Haitian-American Cooperative Commission on Education, of which our State Department is sponsor, broadened to become a vital part of Haitian cultural and economic life.

The party also urged an end to United States control of Haitian finances—a legacy of the United States occupation of the 1920's—and better-balanced commercial relations with the United States. It issued a fiery journal, *Combat,* which sounded more like a Third Period Communist periodical than a Communist publication of 1946.[1]

Another Communist Party soon appeared, in the shape of the Parti Socialiste Populaire. This group, whose name was copied from that of the Cuban Communist Party, was the Party founded by Hudicourt and Romains, with a different title. Hudicourt arrived from New York City, soon after the overthrow of Lescot, to assume its leadership. The real nature of the P.S.P. was obvious from the position which it took on various international issues. It carried on intensive propaganda against the Marshall Plan—though what that had to do with Haiti was hard to see. It dwelt incessantly on the dangers of "American imperialism," and attacked the Estimé government for being "subservient" to the Americans.

The Parti Comuniste and the P.S.P. bid for official recognition by international Communist authorities. The decision taken by these authorities was indicated by the Cuban Communist paper, *Hoy,* on February 22, 1946, when it declared:

> The Popular Socialist Party of Haiti is based on the principles of Marxism and an immediate program which is conscious of the pressing needs of the Haitian people. The Communist Party of Haiti is filled with infantile concepts, which tend to make it sectarian, and which separate it from the masses.

The Parti Comuniste of the Rev. Mr. Constant soon afterwards declared itself "dissolved."

In the 1946 election the P.S.P. succeeded in electing Max Hudicourt Senator and another Party member to the Chamber of Deputies. However, a few months after his election Hudicourt was assassinated, while the deputy was soon expelled by the Party.[2]

The Communists of the P.S.P. were particularly active in the trade union movement. They controlled the first central labor group established after the 1946 Revolution, the Fédération des Travailleurs Haïtiens. However, the F.T.H. soon split, with a group of pronounced anti-Communists establishing the Fédération Haïtien du Travail, which took over most of the unions formerly belonging to the Communist-dominated Federation.[3] The Communist trade union soon lapsed into inactivity.

The P.S.P. issued a daily newspaper, *La Nation*, which was credited by its political enemies with a circulation of only 400 copies, compared with the 2600 enjoyed by the paper with the largest circulation in Port-au-Prince at that time.[4]

Relations between the Communists and the Estimé government were the subject of some dispute. Although the P.S.P. criticized what it called the "subservience" of the Estimé government to the Yankees, the opponents of the P.S.P. claimed that the Party was a close supporter of the Estimé government.

As President Estimé's term of office began to draw to an end, a move was launched to amend the Constitution to permit his re-election. This provoked loud protests from all the political parties, and early in December, 1949, President Estimé ordered the dissolution of the country's political parties and the suspension of their newspapers. A few weeks later President Estimé himself was overthrown by the Army, thus paving the way for the assumption of the presidency by General Paul Magloire. Under the Magloire dictatorship all partisan political activity was banned, and the Parti Socialiste Populaire, like all the others, was able to function only underground. There was no evidence by the end of 1956 that the Party had any significant following.

## DOMINICAN REPUBLIC

Potentially one of the most powerful and dangerous Communist Parties of Latin America is that of the Dominican Republic. Although by the end of 1956 the Dominican Partido Socialista Popular (as the local Communists are called) had only a handful of supporters, and was forced to operate very much underground, Generalissimo Trujillo had prepared the soil for a sudden development of the Communist seed.

Trujillo presides over the most complete dictatorship in the American hemisphere. His control over the government is absolute, whether he is officially President or has another member of his family in this post. No opposition group can work openly in the country, and a man has to be exceedingly brave to work even clandestinely against the dictator. Trujillo's police hover over the whole republic and his espionage system is reported to spread throughout the hemisphere.

This kind of atmosphere is certainly preparing the way for Communism in the Dominican Republic. It is preventing the growth of healthy democratic parties which might challenge the appeal of the Communists to the masses of the peasants, workers, and intellectuals. It is equating all opposition to Trujillo with "Communism," thus clouding people's minds concerning the real nature of the Communist international movement, its aims, objectives, and methods of operation.

With the cynicism characteristic of dictators, Trujillo has not been dogmatic about his opposition to the Communists, and upon one famous occasion allied himself with them and gave them an opportunity to organize and agitate, though this chance was denied to all other non-Trujillo groups. The Dominican Republic perhaps presents the most blatant example of the Communist's willingness to work with the Latin American dictators and the dictators' willingness to work with them, if it is convenient for both sides.

The Trujillo regime came to power soon after the United States Marines left the Republic in 1930, ending an occupation begun during World War I. The Marines left Trujillo as commander of the Army which had been set up "to preserve order." He soon seized control of the government.

Ruling for a quarter of a century, Trujillo was unstinting in heaping praise upon himself. He rechristened the Republic's capital, which Columbus named Santo Domingo when he founded it in 1493, Ciudad Trujillo (Trujillo City). He built monuments to himself in the capital and in the provincial towns. He named provinces after members of his family.

Yet, in the economic field the dictator followed intelligent policies. He diversified the nation's agriculture, while at the same time extending the sugar industry, the nation's principal foreign exchange earner. He also pushed a moderate industrial development program.

Trujillo has followed a social policy similar at least on paper to that of most Latin American countries of this period. He set up a social security system and established a government-controlled labor movement. Although the trade union movement was completely under the dictator's thumb, it seemed likely by the middle of 1956 that the disappearance of Trujillo or any relaxation of his rule would probably result in great gains by the Communists inside this labor movement, such as had occurred in 1946, when Trujillo worked with Communist labor organizations for a time. Even before that time, the Communists had been much better able to work in the kind of atmosphere maintained by the dictator than were any of his democratic opponents.

The Communist Party of the Dominican Republic originated with a group of Spanish Communist exiles, who migrated to the Republic after the end of the Spanish Civil War. It has been estimated that of the nine hundred Spanish refugees who entered the country after 1939, between one hundred and one hundred and seventy were Communists. Once there, they established branches of both the Communist Party of Spain and the so-called United Socialist Party of Catalonia, which had been the Comintern affiliate in the northeastern section of the Spanish Republic.

The Spanish Communist exiles established a network of organizations and publications, although they were careful not to call any of them, openly, Communist. These organizations included a Catalan Club, a League of Wounded of the Spanish War, and a Commission for Solidarity with Spanish Refugees. Their publications included *Por la República, Juventud Española, Boletín de Información Sindical,* and a considerable number of pamphlets and booklets.

The Spanish Communists did their utmost to proselytize the local people. Dominicans were invited to attend and address the meetings of Spanish Communist "front organizations." Some young people, particularly among the university students, were interested in the Party, and ultimately joined to form the Dominican Communist Party.

Trujillo himself began to make overtures to the international Communist apparatus during World War II. In 1943 his pet "labor confederation," the Confederación Dominicana del Trabajo, was ordered to join the Communist-controlled Confederación de Trabajadores de América Latina (C.T.A.L.), and a delegate from the C.D.T. attended the Third Congress of the C.T.A.L. in Cali, Colombia, in December, 1944.[5] The C.D.T. remained affiliated with the C.T.A.L. until 1948.[6]

At the same time Trujillo courted the Soviet Union itself. In June, 1945, he named a Minister Plenipotentiary to Moscow, Ricardo Pérez Alfonso. In sending to the Senate a request for the confirmation of Pérez Alfonso's nomination, Trujillo wrote:

> . . . In fact, for many years before the present war, ships flying the Soviet flag have visited our ports, receiving friendly treatment of the authorities and of the people; Russian artists have been among us as ambassadors of the rich musical sensibility of that people; works of Russian writers, ancient and modern, from Turgenev to Stalin occupy important places in our book stores and public libraries, where they have always been at the free disposition of everyone.
> . . . As a result of their noble and powerful contribution to the victory of the United Nations, and of the imminent constitution, in the historic Conference of San Francisco, of the world organization for the perpetuation of peace, security, justice, and cooperation, the

Soviet Union, whose material power has been made evident in defense of a high cause, will always be recognizd as one of the great forces for good and progress upon which the democratic world can count.[7]

Meanwhile a Communist Party was being formed. The leader of this group was Pericles Franco, Jr., known generally by the diminutive of his name, Periclito. The son of a high official of the Trujillo regime, he had gone to Chile as a student in 1938 and had become a Communist there. Returning to his own country in 1942, he entered the University of Santo Domingo, where he encountered other students who had come under the influence of the Spanish Communists. Together they established the Dominican Communist Party.

The second most important figure in the Party was Francisco Henríquez, usually known as "Chito." He had come to know various Spanish Communists in the Dominican Republic, and had had contact, as well, with the Communist Party in Cuba, where he had spent some time. The Ducourdray brothers were also important figures in the Party.

The Communists functioned underground from 1942 until 1945. In the summer of the latter year the police arrested several students who were distributing propaganda at the University, and the leaders of the Communist Party sought diplomatic asylum. Franco took refuge in the Colombian Embassy, and Henríquez in the Venezuelan one. Periclito spent the next few months travelling widely around South America and finally arrived in Cuba, where Henríquez and other young Communist leaders had also sought refuge.

About the middle of 1946 Generalissimo Trujillo, who was preparing an "election" which would permit him once again to become chief executive, sent an emissary to make contact with the Dominican Communists in Cuba. This person was Ramón Marraro, an intellectual who had been a fellow traveller.

The reasons for Trujillo's attitude were probably several. On the one hand, the area was experiencing a wave of democratization. Dictators had fallen in Peru, Brazil, El Salvador, and Guatemala, and the tenure of office of others was uncertain in various countries. Even Trujillo felt that it was necessary to appear "democratic." How could he be more so than to permit the Communists to organize openly in his bastion?

But there was undoubtedly another motive behind Trujillo's move. He was anxious to make it appear that he was truly "popular" and that the only real opponents of his regime were the Communists. Thus, if they ran against him, the results of such an election could be duly treated as "constitutional" and "democratic."

Marraro was successful in his mission. The Communist leaders agreed to return. All except Franco himself, who remained behind for some time

as a precautionary measure, returned to their native soil. There they
openly established the Partido Socialista Popular, a name borrowed from
their Cuban comrades.

The P.S.P. received official recognition from the Trujillo government.
Trujillo, answering the Communists' request for official registration as a
legal political party, wrote J. M. Bonetti Burgos, then the Secretary of the
Interior, recommending that the Party's registration be accepted. In this
letter, which was published in *La Nación* of Ciudad Trujillo on October
16, 1946, Trujillo wrote:

> . . . Communism, whose existence in the Republic is now an im-
> portant fact, has its undoubted origin in the organizations of the
> Union of Soviet Socialist Republics, and in order to understand its
> role in guiding political and social activities, it would be well not to
> forget the self-sacrificing cooperation which the U.S.S.R. gave to the
> democracies in the recent World War. Its existence among us is, fur-
> thermore, a round and eloquent rebuttal to those calumniators who
> without foundation accuse the Dominican Republic of not being a
> democratic country. . . .

The Communists were very active during the months in which they
operated legally in the Dominican Republic. They succeeded in building
up a membership of two thousand in this short time.[8] The P.S.P. recruited
several important trade union leaders, including Mauricio Báez, leader of
the sugar workers. The Party held a series of public campaign meetings in
all the important provincial cities and towns.

However, the Party suffered from internal dissension even in the short
period of its legal operation. Francisco Henríquez was expelled from the
Party on charges of "deviationism," and Trujillo tried to entice him into
the President's camp. Henríquez resisted this and went into exile in Cuba.
Mauricio Báez also withdrew from the Party before it was again suppressed by Trujillo.

The excuse for suppressing the Partido Socialista Popular, shortly before
the 1947 election, was a mass meeting which the Party held in the capital
city as the culmination of its recruiting campaign. A group of Trujillistas
invaded the meeting, and it broke up in a melee. The P.S.P. was immediately accused of having caused a riot, and promptly suppressed. Its
principal leaders were put in jail, where they remained for two years or
more.[9] They were finally released from prison and were allowed to go to
Cuba. However, they were not permitted by the Prío government to stay
there, so they proceeded to Guatemala, where they established their
headquarters. There they published a weekly periodical, *Orientación*,
which was smuggled back into the Dominican Republic. With the fall of
the Arbenz government in Guatemala, the Dominican Communist leaders
were reported as going to Mexico.

During this period of exile, the Communists were even more bitter in their attacks on the other opposition parties than they were in chastising Trujillo. A particular butt of their attacks was the Partido Revolucionario Dominicano, a democratic left-wing group which worked closely with the United States trade union movement and the Inter American Regional Organization of Workers (O.R.I.T.). The P.R.D. seemed the most likely group to challenge the Communists in a post-Trujillo Dominican Republic. A party of a general "Aprista" orientation, it sought support particularly among the organized workers and peasants.

The Communists denounced the members of this group as "agents of Yankee imperialism," and accused them of being "really allies of Trujillo." The P.R.D. leaders, for their part, attacked the Communists on the same grounds, alleging that the latter had never really broken with Trujillo.*[10]

The Communists sought to turn all anti-Trujillo sentiment into opposition to the United States. This campaign was aided by the continued policy of United States Ambassadors to the Dominican Republic of treating the Dominican dictatorship as a respectable member of the brotherhood of democratic nations. Comments such as that reportedly made by the United States Ambassador early in 1954 to the effect that if Trujillo had been born in the United States, he certainly would have become President of that country, played directly into the hands of the Communist propagandists.

By the end of 1956 there was no doubt that the Communists were still active in the Dominican Republic. The complete lack of democratic liberties in that country meant that the Communists, more fitted for and more skilled at underground operations than were democratic elements, were undoubtedly laying the groundwork for a rapid development whenever the Trujillo regime relaxed or was in one way or another done away with.

## PUERTO RICO

The Commonwealth of Puerto Rico, though constitutionally part of the United States, is culturally, economically, and socially part of Latin America. This little island, with its two and a half million people, is becoming increasingly important as a bridge between the two Americas.

Viewed superficially, Puerto Rico would seem the perfect background for the rise of one of the strongest Communist movements in all Latin America. Not only is there bleak poverty on the island, but it is subject more than any other Latin American area to "Yankee imperialism," since it was militarily conquered by the United States and remains legally a

* That there may be some truth in this charge is indicated by a curious incident which occurred shortly after the disappearance in New York of one of Trujillo's most vocal opponents, the Basque leader, Jesus de Galindez. Norman Thomas, who had several times accused Trujillo of having Galindez kidnapped and killed, received an invitation to come to the Dominican Republic to see what progress the Trujillo regime had brought the country. The invitation came from the Partido Socialista Popular.

part of the U.S.A., though it is Spanish-Negro in race, culture, and outlook.

Yet Puerto Rico's Communists have never represented more than an infinitely small proportion of the island's electorate, they were only of fleeting importance in the country's labor movement, and they have never achieved any importance whatsoever in Puerto Rico's public administration. The reason for this peculiar lack of success is that a robust popular movement grew up during the 1940's which caught and held the imagination of the great masses of the people and was able not only to promise, but to go a long way toward carrying out, the reforms which the Communists usually claim they are the only people capable of achieving.

The nemesis of the Puerto Rican Communists has been the Popular Democratic Party, led by Luis Muñoz Marín, since 1948 the elected Governor of the island. Launching his movement in the late 1930's, Muñoz promised to right the social wrongs of the country's humble, diversify and develop the economic life of the island, and work out a new relationship between Puerto Rico and the mainland giant to which it "belonged."

That the Communists have been fully aware of the damage which Muñoz has done to their chances of success in the island is shown by the evolution of their attitude toward Muñoz and the Popular Democrats. Though at first supporting the Partido Popular Democrático in the hope of taking it over, or at least of influencing it in the direction of opposition to the United States, the Communists have in the last decade adopted an attitude of intransigent hostility to Muñoz and his regime and have allied themselves instead with the minuscule, terroristic Nationalist Party, led by Pedro Albizu Campos.

Small Communist groups first appeared in the island in the early 1930's. At this time there was great discontent among the people, particularly among the sugar workers. Unemployment was tremendous, intensified by the rapid growth of the population. The Puerto Ricans chafed under the rule of "continentals" as they called the United States citizens from the mainland.

The Communist International, in *International Press Correspondence*, June 18, 1931, outlined the activities which it felt the Puerto Rican comrades should pursue during this Third Period era. These included the organization of "left-wing" groups in the trade unions, organization of the unemployed, unionization of the sugar plantation workers, and leadership of "the movement for national freedom for Puerto Rico."

The Communists were unwilling to work with any of the other parties which at the time were seeking one or more of these objectives. They characterized the veteran labor and Socialist Party leader, Santiago Iglesias, as "the arch betrayer" and accused the Nationalist Party, which was then gaining some influence among workers and students, of being "more demagogic than the Socialist Party"; the International urged that "the Communists must expose this demagoguery with the utmost energy."

The International urged the Puerto Rican Communists to get together and get to work. It ordered: "The members of the existing Communist groups must be immediately organized into shop and street nuclei. They are regularly to pay their monthly dues at their unit meetings." The *International Press Correspondence* writer added "We feel certain that the above-given suggestions as to the immediate tasks of our comrades, if carried out, will ensure the way to the formation of a strong, militant, and mass Communist Party."

The Communist Party of Puerto Rico was formally organized in September, 1934, as a direct affiliate of the Communist International, rather than being affiliated through the Communist Party of the United States. In the December 5, 1939, issue of the *New Masses*, it was described by Jane Speed de Andreu, American-born wife of one of its principal leaders, as having a budget of less than $300 a month, with which it maintained 15 full-time organizers. It issued both a weekly party newspaper, *La Verdad*, and a trade union journal. It had offices in 11 cities in the island, with its chief headquarters in the capital, San Juan.

The first Secretary General of the Party was Alberto Sánchez, described by Mike Gold, in the June 2, 1940, issue of the New York *Daily Worker*, as "one of the most modest and self-sacrificing pioneers who glorify the name of Communist." He had spent some years in the States, where he had become active in the labor movement and had joined the Communist Party. Returning to the island, he helped to organize the Puerto Rican Communist Party.

Sánchez was of key importance in this early period of the Communist Party's history, because he was Secretary General of the Chauffeurs' Union, one of the most important in the island, with a total membership reported by Gold to be 15,000. The President of the union at this time was Francisco Colón Gordiany, then described by Gold as a "left-wing Socialist."

The island was not unaffected by the C.I.O. organizational drive on the mainland in the late 1930's. Communist trade unions joined with others to form the Comité Progresista de Organización Sindical, which Jane Speed de Andreu, in the *New Masses* of December 5, 1939, described as "a young and struggling trade union center." It was a rival to the A.F. of L.'s insular affiliate, the Free Federation of Workers. The Comité was succeeded in 1940 by the Confederación General de Trabajadores (C.G.T.). Although the C.G.T. was not immediately affiliated with the C.I.O., it was generally aligned with it, and for five years it was the island's largest labor organization.

The Communists played a leading role in the organization of the C.G.T. For a short time they were able to use their position in the Confederación to wield considerable influence in the general political affairs of the country.

Meanwhile, however, the Popular Democratic Party (P.P.D.) had appeared. Organized by Luis Muñoz Marín, the son of Louis Muñoz Rivera, the man who had been the island's principal political leader during the first 17 years of United States occupation, the P.P.D. was something new under the Puerto Rican sun. Luis Muñoz Marín broke with the tradition of making the question of the status of the island the chief issue in the country's politics.

The Popular Democratic Party concentrated its attention on social and economic issues. It urged a program of economic diversification and growth for the island, including the nationalization of the country's electric power resources and their expansion so as to meet the needs of the people and to create the possibility of industrial development of Puerto Rico.

Muñoz and his followers also urged the establishment of a social security system, the passing of minimum-wage and maximum-hour laws suited to the island's needs, the launching of a sizable housing program, and other social legislation. Finally, they urged an agrarian reform program, which would assure each peasant at least a small plot of land upon which to build his hut and have his garden.

This program won the approval of the great majority of the country's electorate. In the first election in which the party participated, that of 1940, it won a majority in the Insular Senate and nearly a majority in the House of Representatives. In succeeding elections it won full control of the elective part of the island's government, a control which by 1948 gave it all but one seat in the Senate and two in the House.

The Communists at first tried to penetrate the new party. Rexford Guy Tugwell, who was the wartime Governor of the island, in his book *The Stricken Land* (Doubleday, 1947)* describes the attempts in 1943 and 1944 by Communists and other independence advocates to capture the P.P.D. He says:

> Some part was taken in this movement to capture the party by a small group of "Comunistas," who were by now active in the Confederación General de Trabajadores. . . . These "Comunistas" were, for the moment, because it was a party policy, in favor of the war, and so somewhat cautious about the use of the strike. But in typical Communist fashion they worked night and day, admitted no scruples in making decisions and conducted themselves in ways which indicated their contempt for such bourgeois concepts as promises and contracts. . . . About this time we became aware of the affiliations being encouraged by the "Comunistas" between Puerto Ricans and

* Acknowledgment is made herewith to Doubleday & Company for permission to quote the following passages from Rexford Tugwell, *The Stricken Land*.

Communist organizations elsewhere. The leaders in Puerto Rico were quietly visiting abroad, especially in Cuba and Mexico, and emissaries were being received in San Juan.

Dr. Tugwell asserts that "because they were allied with the 'independentistas' Muñoz granted them too much. So he came to extend a dangerous tolerance to the 'Comunistas', forgetting that they had no direct interest in Puerto Rico but were only using independence as a means of causing trouble for another 'capitalist' nation."

He notes, also, that the Communists were active in engendering strikes in the enterprises which the Muñoz government had taken over or established—the public utility system and the factories built by the Industrial Development Corporation. He adds, "It was obvious that the 'Comunistas' were getting ready for the day when the party line of international communism would diverge from policies of the United States."

In retrospect it appears that Dr. Tugwell's fears were only partly justified. The fact was that the momentum of the Muñoz Marín movement was so strong that Muñoz could afford the relative tolerance with which he at first viewed their activities. Furthermore, during the war period it was unlikely that they would turn against Muñoz or the United States either, in view of the Communist support of the war. In any case, they did not gain sufficient ground to make them a really vital force in the country's economic or political life.

The Communists continued their friendly relations with Muñoz Marín for a short while after World War II. Although by April 5, 1946, the Communist periodical, *El Popular*, of Mexico City was attacking Muñoz as a "tyrant" and accusing him of having "betrayed the fight for national independence" and of being "a very clever tool of the Yankee imperialists," the United States and Puerto Rican Communists were somewhat more cautious. Helen Simon, writing in the New York *Daily Worker*, on May 9, 1946, said:

> The Communists criticize the many instances of mismanagement of the program and realize its limitations, but they back every effort to industrialize, despite the imperialist grip. They feel that in this way the free Puerto Rico they demand will start out on firmer footing.
>
> The Communists differ from the Populares in perspective. The P.D.P. thinks in terms of private ownership; even when the government develops an industry, it is for eventual sale to private enterprise. The Communists want government factories to remain in the people's hands. They demand: Nationalize the basic industries and the land, with or without compensation to the present owners.
>
> With all its hesitations, mistakes, short-sightedness and impatience with criticism, however, the P.D.P. has done a remarkable job. I think it would be tragic were all its works to be destroyed by the whim or policy of an unfriendly governor. . . .

The Puerto Rican Communists followed the vagaries of the United States Communist Party. Thus, near the end of World War II, the Party "dissolved" and reorganized as the Puerto Rican Congress of Independence. In March, 1946, again following the United States example, the Puerto Rican Communists reorganized anew as the Partido Comunista de Puerto Rico, at the same time denouncing their former policy as "Browderism."[11]

Whatever influence the Communists had during the second World War was dissipated in the years that followed. The C.G.T., in which they were active, broke into two groups at its 1945 Convention, held at the University of Puerto Rico. One faction, which incorporated and henceforth was known as the Confederación General de Trabajadores Inc., was headed by the Populares' Senator Barreto Pérez and Speaker of the House Ramos Antonini. It remained more or less closely associated with the Populares.

The other faction, which took the name Confederación General de Trabajadores Auténtica, was headed by Francisco Colón Gordiany as President and Juan Sáez Corales as Secretary General. Sáez Corales was a Communist, so the Party still had considerable importance in this faction of the C.G.T. However, soon after becoming Secretary General of the C.G.T.A. he was drafted into the United States Army. Although his post was kept vacant for him while he was in the armed forces, difficulties arose when he returned and attempted to resume the Secretary Generalship.

The upshot was that Juan Sáez Corales and other Communist unionists left the C.G.T.A. and formed the Unidad General de Trabajadores, of which Sáez Corales became Secretary General. However, the U.G.T. was the smallest of the island's various central labor groups, having its main strength among the workers of the Coca-Cola Bottling Company and among the construction workers, one of whose several unions was affiliated with the Unidad General.

The Communists ran into added difficulties with the passing of the Taft-Hartley Act, which became valid in the island as well as in the continental United States. The officials of the U.G.T. and its affiliated unions were the only group of labor leaders to refuse to fill out non-Communist affidavits as required by the law. Their unions, therefore, could not make use of the facilities of the Federal National Labor Relations Board.[12]

However, the continuing progress of the Muñoz Marín government after World War II did a great deal more damage to the Puerto Rican Communists than any particular piece of legislation. The administration launched a large industrialization program, not only trying to entice continental companies to establish plants on the island, but encouraging local business people to go into manufacturing as well. The results of this program were demonstrated during the fiscal year 1953-54, when although there was a sharp decline in the price of sugar, the country's principal agricultural export, the total value of exports of the island increased, due to the large number of manufactured goods its factories were by then shipping to the continental United States.

The Muñoz regime's economic development program was very effective in agriculture as well. Not only did the coffee and tobacco business revive with government aid, to the point where in 1954 the country was again exporting the former, but the regime was successful in encouraging the growth of fruit and vegetable cultivation, on the basis of which a sizable canning industry developed. Benefits of the economic development program were widely shared. Governor Muñoz maintained that real wages had increased by 170 per cent in the first thirteen years of the Populares' domination of the country's administration.[13]

In the political field the Muñoz regime led the island towards a new kind of status. After persuading President Truman in 1947 to appoint the island's first Puerto Rican Governor, Muñoz then sought and got the election of the Governor and other officials heretofore appointed by the President of the United States. Still further progress was made when, in 1952, a specially elected Constituent assembly wrote the first Constitution for what now came to be known as the Commonwealth of Puerto Rico.

In spite of the Muñoz regime's rather remarkable achievements, the Communist attitude toward the administration became one of extreme bitterness. This change in position regarding the regime came as the Cold War grew more intense and as it became increasingly clear that Muñoz had given up his old ideas on independence and was seeking to work out some arrangement concerning the island's status which would keep it as part of the United States, while giving Puerto Rico complete internal self-government.

The Communists, both in Puerto Rico and among the large number of Puerto Ricans who had migrated to New York City, came to work more and more closely with the Puerto Rican Nationalists. The latter were extreme advocates of independence, who did not believe in making use of the normal democratic processes to attain their objective, but resorted instead to violence.*

The general campaign of the United States government against the Communists in the U.S.A. finally was felt by the Communist Party of Puerto Rico in October, 1954. At that time ten of the leaders of the Puerto Rican party were arrested as violators of the Smith Act, the same law under which most of the top leaders of the United States Communist Party had been jailed.

Those rounded up included Juan Sáez Corales and his wife and César

---

* The Nacionalistas are not to be confused with the Independentistas, a party which appeared as the main opposition group in the late 1940's, which uses constitutional methods and declares that when it gets a legislative majority it will proclaim independence.

Alberto Andreu, the party's General Secretary and his wife, Jane Speed de Andreu, born in the United States, who was the Secretary of Education of the Party in San Juan. Others were Juan Santos Rivera, described by the F.B.I. as "Moscow-trained," and Juan Emanuelli, who was the Puerto Rican Party's liaison man in New York with the Communist Party of the United States.[14]

Although the arrest of these leading Communist figures might serve to make them martyrs in their home island, it seemed likely that it would also do their Party further damage. However, it was likewise eminently clear that the most important factor in preventing the rise of a really important Communist movement in Puerto Rico was the success of the reform program of the Popular Democrats—an integral part of the Latin American social revolution. By the end of 1956 the remaining Puerto Rican Communists constituted a very small group.

## THE COLONIAL WEST INDIES

Although the British and Dutch West Indies are outside the scope of a strictly Latin American study, the similarity of their problems to those of the Spanish-, Portuguese-, and French-speaking parts of the southern half of the hemisphere and their geographical propinquity to these countries make it essential to say at least a word or two about the Communist movements in the colonial West Indies.

In most of the islands of the colonial West Indies the Communists carry little or no weight. Although there may be individuals and very small groups of Communists operating in these areas, there is no organized Communist movement of any importance. The only parts of the region where Communism has been a real problem are Jamaica, Trinidad, and the South American colony of British Guiana. (No Communist movements have appeared in the Dutch colonies of Curaçao and Aruba. In Surinam, otherwise known as Dutch Guiana, on the northern coast of South America, it was reported early in 1954 that Communist elements were active in the Surinam Miners Union, the country's most important trade union group. Nevertheless, politically the Communists remained a group of negligible importance in Surinam, a country which has developed indigenous non-Communist leaders who have shown their ability to carry out a constructive program.)

All the Communist movements of the area are a product of the Revolt of the Caribbean, which took place just before the outbreak of the second World War. In 1937 and 1938 a series of strikes, which were more often violent than pacific, broke out in the British colonies in the West Indies. Sweeping from British Guiana and Trinidad through the chain of islets in the Windward and Leeward Islands and on up to Jamaica, these walk-outs and demonstrations spread like an uncontrolled blaze.

In most cases the leadership of these movements was completely without ideology. A series of picturesque and sometimes demagogic leaders, including Ayube Edun of British Guiana, Uriah Butler of Trinidad, and William Alexander Bustamante of Jamaica, appeared suddenly on the scene. They and their followers struck out more or less blindly against the evils under which their countries had been suffering for so long.

However, there grew up alongside the movements of these original demagogic leaders, elements which were more serious and more influenced by doctrine and less by emotion. Outstanding examples were the Socialist-inclined People's National Party of Jamaica and Labor Party of Barbados and the Communist-controlled People's Progressive Party of British Guiana. After the first effervescence, these more serious parties took over the leadership of the Revolt of the Caribbean.

This movement has had two principal aspects. First of all, it has been a revolt against the social and economic conditions under which the people of the West Indies have lived for a century or more. Thus there suddenly appeared in 1937-38 trade unions and peasant organizations which sought to raise wages and improve the conditions of their members. The movement also soon developed plans and programs for putting an end to these countries' excessive dependence on one crop—usually sugar—and for the diversification of the economies of the islands.

The second aspect of the movement has been a revolt against political colonialism. Demands immediately were voiced for a revision of the constitutions of the British and Dutch colonies in the West Indies, so as to give the masses of the people participation in the government and to give the colonial areas greater freedom from the control of the respective "mother countries."

Thus the Revolt of the Caribbean has been essentially a part of what we have called in this volume the Latin American social revolution. The English- and Dutch-speaking Americans of the West Indies were as influenced as their Spanish-, Portuguese-, and French-speaking brothers by the currents of the times. Spontaneously they developed more or less the same kind of programs as those which appeared elsewhere in the region—programs for economic development, social and labor legislation, national self-expression, and political democracy.

The Communists have played a comparatively minor role in all this. In most of the areas they have been stopped by the development of Socialist or indigenous native reform groups which seized the leadership and, insofar as they were able, began to put their programs into effect.

In Jamaica the Communists for many years worked inside the People's National Party and its associated trade union group, the Trade Union Council. The leadership of the T.U.C., composed mainly of Frank and Ken Hill, Richard Hart, and Arthur Henry, were from the beginning the left wing of the People's National Party. Their labor group joined the World Federation of Trade Unions at the W.F.T.U.'s founding Congress in Paris and continued to belong to the W.F.T.U. after the British T.U.C. and other democratic union groups had withdrawn in 1949.

There is no doubt that this left-wing group carried on a certain amount of "educational" activity among the rank and file of the P.N.P. and the T.U.C. However, it was not until the early 1950's that a showdown took place between the left-wing leadership and the more moderate leaders, such as Norman Manley, N. V. Nethersole, and others.

By 1952 Manley and the other leaders of the party became greatly concerned with the possible influence of the pro-Communist element on the P.N.P.'s prospects for winning control of the island and of conducting an effective government after having won election. Manley and others had not objected to the left-wing attitudes of the T.U.C. leadership so long as the latter group did not try to organize a party within a party. By the early 1950's Manley was convinced that this was what was happening.

As a result, in March, 1952, the Hill brothers, Hart, and several other left-wingers were charged with disloyalty to the party and its democratic Socialist principles and of trying to organize a Communist group within the P.N.P. After a public trial by the executive of the P.N.P., the left-wing group were expelled.

The expulsion of virtually the whole Trade Union Council leadership presented a serious problem for the People's National Party. Its electoral support was based largely on the trade union membership, and so it became essential for the P.N.P. to start another trade union group. The result was the establishment late in 1952 of the National Workers Union, headed by F. A. Glasspole, who had been National Secretary of the T.U.C. but was not in sympathy with the pro-Communist leanings of the majority of the T.U.C. leadership. The full influence of the P.N.P. was thrown behind the National Workers Union, and within two years it was the second largest and the most solidly organized trade union group in the island.

Those expelled from the P.N.P. had meanwhile split among themselves. Richard Hart, who had always been the firebrand among the left-wingers, accused the Hills and other T.U.C. leaders of being afraid to make a clean break with the P.N.P. and of wanting to return to its fold. As a result the Congress of the T.U.C. in August, 1953, was marked by a further division. Hart and a small nucleus broke away from the T.U.C., to form the Jamaica Federation of Trade Unions, which consisted only of a few small sugar workers' unions and one or two other scattered groups.

There is no doubt that the Hart group was and is the genuine Communist element in the Jamaican political picture. Hart teamed up with Ferdinand Smith, ex-Secretary of the National Maritime Union of the United States. Smith had been deported from the United States late in the 1940's and had gone to Europe, where he had worked in the headquarters of the W.F.T.U. About the time of Hart's break with the Hills,

Smith returned to Jamaica as the Caribbean representative of the W.F.T.U., of which he was an Assistant General Secretary.

The Communist Party of Jamaica is known as the People's Freedom Movement. It was founded as the People's Educational Organization and was reorganized as a formal party early in 1954. The Party maintains a bookstore in the center of Kingston, which is like any Communist bookstore anywhere in the world, selling a wide line of Cominform, W.F.T.U., and other Communist periodicals and pamphlets. The Hart group failed to elect any of its candidates to the House of Representatives in the January, 1955, general election.

The Hill brothers and the T.U.C. remained in a somewhat anomalous position. They organized a political group, the National Labor Party, but it did not seem to have any real place in the country's political spectrum.

In 1954 the N.L.P. tried to make an alliance with the Jamaica Labor Party of Prime Minister Bustamante, but failing in this, the N.L.P. went it alone in the January, 1955, elections. Neither of its two candidates for the island's House of Representatives was elected.

Meanwhile the T.U.C. was being sniped at from three directions. The Communists' Jamaica Federation of Trade Unions took off a small part of the T.U.C. when it split away. The P.N.P.'s National Workers Union and Bustamante's own Bustamante Industrial Trade Union continually raided the T.U.C. However, in 1956 a virtual truce was declared by the T.U.C., B.I.T.U., and N.W.U. The T.U.C. had joined the International Confederation of Christian Trade Unions late in 1955.

By the middle of 1954, therefore, the Communists were out in the open in Jamaica for the first time. They constituted a very small element in the country's political and trade union life, but they were tightly organized and, like Communists everywhere, were willing to wait for the future, taking the long-term view of affairs.

With the victory of the People's National Party in the January, 1955, elections, it did not seem likely that in the near future they would be able to gain much influence. The new government organized by Norman Manley had a constructive and dynamic program, which seemed likely to hold the loyalty of the island's electorate for some time to come. It also promised to provide leadership in the fight for democratic social change throughout the rest of the British West Indies, which had hitherto been lacking. This kind of leadership is particularly necessary in Trinidad and British Guiana.

The Communist movement in Trinidad is small, but the political and economic conditions there have until recently been propitious to its future growth. After the first impetus of the 1937-38 upheaval had spent itself, the prestige of Uriah Butler, who had led the strikes of that period, declined rapidly. Butler had no program and came to be regarded by the people of Trinidad as too much of a demagogue.

However, his passing from the scene left a vacuum in Trinidad's politics. It coincided with the death of Captain Cipriani, who in the 1920's and early 1930's had been the first important organizer of trade unions and a popular political party (the Trinidad Labor Party). The result was that by the late 1940's the island's political life was in the hands of a large number of small parties, most of which were some politician's personal vehicle to power, and few of which had any well-defined ideology or program.

Under these circumstances, the island until 1956 seemed ripe for the appearance of some new leader or party able to present a concrete program and bring together the scattered groups in the colony who would support an attempt to further development of the island's economy, extend its social legislation, and make more meaningful the extensive self-government which it already possessed. If this leadership had come from the Communists, they might have been able to repeat in Trinidad what they accomplished in British Guiana in the early 1950's.

During 1956 a party appeared which seemed destined to end the long-existing political vacuum. Dr. Eric Williams, the island's leading intellectual, resigned his post as Economic Adviser to the Caribbean Commission, and returned home to found the People's National Movement. This party was patterned after the Jamaican People's National Party, and immediately aroused enthusiastic support, particularly in the cities and towns. In elections held early in October, 1956, the new party swept the polls and Dr. Williams was inaugurated as the island's first Chief Minister. It seemed highly likely that the rise of the People's National Movement would close the doors to Communist political advance for some time to come.

The Trinidad Communists continued to be of some importance in the trade union movement. Among those who had been leaders in the rise of Trinidad trade unionism in the early 1940's were Quintín O'Connor and P. Rojas. They had succeeded in building up strong unions among government employees and oil workers, respectively, and on the basis of these two groups had established the Trinidad Trade Union Council, which for some years was the island's only central labor organization.

The Trindad T.U.C. affiliated with the World Federation of Trade Unions in 1945 and stayed with it after the withdrawal of the British T.U.C. and other democratic groups. However, an important element in the T.U.C., led by the Seamen and Waterfront Workers Trade Union, which was headed by a dynamic ex-longshoreman, C. P. Alexander, broke away from the T.U.C. and formed a rival group, the Federation of Trade Unions of Trinidad, which joined the I.C.F.T.U. The trade union movement is thus divided between these two groups.

The principal element in the island which had not been organized successfully by the end of 1954 was the sugar workers. Although both the pro-Communist element and the anti-Communists had unions in the field, neither group had been able to make any appreciable headway. At the end of 1954, however, the I.C.F.T.U. and the British Trade Union Congress gave considerable amounts of money to the democratic union group to undertake a serious organizing campaign among these workers, who make up the largest single working force in the island. In 1955 most of the sugar workers' organizations were brought into a united effort to organize these workers, with the help of the Federation of Trade Unions of Trinidad.

The Communists of Trinidad are organized in the West Indian Independence Party, established in the late 1940's. It has only a small electoral force and did not have any members in the island's legislature by the end of 1956. However, it carries on intensive activities aimed against "British imperialism" and "Yankee imperialism" and espousing the cause of the workers of the island.

The Communists had rough going in the early 1950's. The government was very hostile to them in spite of the fact that its principal Minister, Alfred Gomes, had once been a fellow traveller himself. At the "suggestion" of the government, the Trinidad T.U.C. officially withdrew from the W.F.T.U. in 1953, and O'Connor and Rojas officially "resigned" from the West Indian Independence Party. However, these measures were purely formal, to avoid trouble with the government, as the leaders of the trade union group were free in admitting. The Trinidad Communists were certainly not, in 1956, an element which could be completely discounted for the future.

The most successful Communist group in the British West Indies was that of British Guiana, on the northern coast of South America. This colony, vast in area and small in population, has one of the lowest standards of living of the whole region. Its population is heterogeneous, consisting of East Indians and Negroes in about equal proportion, with smaller groups of Portuguese, American Indians, Chinese, and British.

Until 1950 politics had been largely a matter of personal and racial rivalries. Parties formed around individuals and tended to be either Negro or Indian, but seldom both. However, in 1950 there appeared a group which ended this situation.

The People's Progressive Party was formed in that year. Its principal leader was Cheddi Jagan, a young Indian dentist, who had studied in the United States and while there had married an American girl who was reported to have been an active member of the Young Communist League. Unlike other Guianese parties, it cut across racial lines. Its principal figures included a young Negro attorney, L. F. S. Burnham, and a young Negro trade union leader, Ashton Chase, who had studied at Ruskin College, Oxford, and had returned to assume leadership of the country's oldest trade union group, the British Guiana Labor Union. Another important figure was Dr. Lachmansingh, an Indian physician, who for years had been attempting to establish a sugar workers' union in opposition to the older Man Power Citizens Association.

The new party set to work with great energy, and its ideas caught hold quickly. It urged full self-government for the colony; it urged that something be done to overcome the colony's dire poverty; it urged that Indians and Negroes and other groups sink their racial differences in larger issues.

That the P.P.P. was Communist in its orientation is certain. Its periodical, *Thunder*, participated fully in all the Communists' international campaigns, for "Stockholm Peace Petitions," about "germ warfare," and the like. It had frequent contributions from Communists outside the colony, notably Paul Robeson. It was unyielding in its picturing of everything British and North American as bad and "imperialistic" and everything Russian as "peaceful" and "constructive." Cheddi Jagan was officially listed in the World Federation of Trade Unions' monthly periodical as the W.F.T.U. representative in British Guiana. However, there was also a fairly strong non-Communist, and even anti-Communist, element in the P.P.P.

Late in 1952 British Guiana was given a new Constitution, providing for a large degree of internal self-government. Elections under this Constitution were held in April, 1953, with the result that the P.P.P. won 18 out of the 24 seats filled by election in the colony's legislature. During the first week in June, 1953, a P.P.P. Cabinet was formed, with Cheddi Jagan as virtual Prime Minister.

This P.P.P. administration remained in power only five months. During that period tension mounted in the colony. The P.P.P. was intent upon getting full control of the colony's labor movement and pushed through the legislature a law which would have made that possible. However, the government seems to have done little toward developing a program for the economic reconstruction of the country. The fact is that the election of the P.P.P. ministry took the P.P.P. leaders themselves by surprise, and they needed a good deal of time to develop a program. Furthermore, they were undoubtedly awaiting the issuance of the report of an economic survey mission of the International Bank for Reconstruction and Development which had visited British Guiana early in 1953, a report which they did not receive until about three weeks before they were ousted from office.

In October, 1953, the British Governor of the colony announced that he had dismissed the P.P.P. ministry and had suspended the Constitution. At the same time troops were landed in the colony to "keep order." The Governor charged that the P.P.P. was preparing a coup against constituted authority in the colony, that it had been undermining the police forces and otherwise had been preparing to seize full and dictatorial power. No very concrete evidence was ever made public to back up these charges.

The fact is that the P.P.P. government was in an almost impossible position. It did not control the police, the armed forces, or the finances of the administration, and thus was not in a position to establish a Communist dictatorship. On the other hand, it was dogmatically unable to carry out a program which would have assured that it would maintain wide popularity for a long period of time. To develop the resources of British Guiana, a great deal of capital is needed, an amount which British Guiana itself does not possess. However, for ideological reasons, the P.P.P. was not willing or able to seek such capital where it might have been found— the Colonial Welfare and Development Fund, the United States Export-Import Bank, the International Bank, or private foreign investors.

Thus hemmed in by the Constitution and their own dogma, the only alternative for the P.P.P. leaders was a campaign against the British. With this nationalistic tactic, the P.P.P. could expect to whip up and maintain popularity. It seems to the author, therefore, that it was inevitable that the P.P.P. government sooner or later would have clashed with the British. The surprising thing was that it happened so soon, and that the British authorities handled the situation as they did.

Many observers inside and outside British Guiana felt at the time that there was no reason to suspend the Constitution. They pointed out that the Governor had ample powers to veto any measure of which he did not approve, and that suspension of the Constitution should have been at last resort, when it was found that the Constitution would not work.

Its fall from power did not hurt the P.P.P. politically for some time. It held the support of those who had voted for it in April, 1953, and picked up backing among many who had not. That this was true was shown by the report of a special Constitutional Mission sent by the British government in 1954 to study the situation caused by the suspension of the basic document. This Commission recommended that no new Constitution be granted at that time, since the P.P.P. would undoubtedly win again, perhaps by a bigger majority, if elections were held in the near future.

The government and elements in the colony opposed to the P.P.P. took various measures in 1953 and 1954 to counteract the P.P.P.'s influence. These included police restrictions on the movements and activities of the principal P.P.P. leaders, the formation of a unified opposition party, and the enactment with British help of a large-scale development program to provide land for the landless, increase the output of foodstuffs, and develop certain manufacturing industries.

Meanwhile dissension was growing in the ranks of the P.P.P. The non-Communist faction chafed under the control of the Jagans and their allies. When a party conference was held early in 1955, Cheddi Jagan was deposed as party leader in favor of L.F.S. Burnham. The result was a wide-open split in the party.

Both sides proceeded to elect new Executive Committees, with the Communist faction supporting Jagan, and the non-Communists—including four of the six Ministers in the P.P.P.'s short-lived government, Burnham, Lachmansingh, J. Narain Singh, and Ashton Chase—taking the Burnham side. The Jagans retained widespread support among the workers on the sugar plantations, while the strength of the Burnham faction was more notable in the towns.

The causes for this split seem to have been personal rivalries among the leadership and the Communist issue. Burnham maintained that the Jagans had always been the left wing in the party and were responsible for its debacle in 1953. The Jagan faction, of course, attacked Burnham and his friends as "betrayers," and "tools of British imperialism."

The fact seems to be that Burnham had been opposed to the Jagans' pro-Communism, but that so long as it did not imperil the program for autonomy and social progress in the colony, he did not fight it. However, by January, 1955, he seems to have reached the conclusion that the party would never again be allowed to get on its feet until the Communist taint was removed from it.

In September, 1956, it was announced that a new constitution would be granted and elections would be held under this constitution sometime during 1957. There was no doubt that the Jagan party would be weaker than it had been four years before, as a result of the split in the P.P.P. However, whether a new popular force would arise, capable of taking the leadership in the fight for social reform and colonial autonomy away from the Communists, depended on whether the Burnhamite P.P.P. and other groups could unite to form such a party. In any case, the Communists were likely to remain a considerable political force in British Guiana for some time to come.

## Chapter XV

# Communism vs. the Mexican Revolution

MEXICO'S REVOLUTION antedates that of Russia. This fact has been the country's best guarantor against Communism. Busy concentrating on their own great social transformation, the Mexicans have resisted every attempt to convert it from an indigenous Mexican movement into an appendage of the Russian Revolution.

The Mexican Revolution was the first of the twentieth-century Latin American social upheavals. Centered as it has been on agrarian reform, industrialization, the rights of organized labor, the raising of standards of living, the achievement of political democracy, the Mexican Revolution has represented an attempt to deal pragmatically with the problems which faced the nation. It is notable for the fact that it has not produced any theory or any great ideological leader.

Although individual leaders of the Mexican Revolution have from time to time worked with the Communists, and a few have even belonged to the Communist Party for longer or shorter periods of time, the Communists have generally found the ranks of the Mexican revolutionaries impervious to their propaganda. This fact is all the more remarkable because of the great wave of nationalism—and consequent anti-Yanquismo—which has been an integral part of the Revolution itself.

The Communist Party of Mexico was founded in an atmosphere of *opéra bouffe* and international intrigue. For several years before 1919 there had existed a small Mexican Socialist Party. Late in 1917 it was joined by an American, Linn A. E. Gale, who was supposed to have left the United States in order to avoid the draft. Gale, who established a small periodical which became the official organ of the party, soon came to dominate the organization.

However, early in 1919 he ran into serious opposition. The leader of the dissident element within the party was M. N. Roy, an Indian Nationalist turned Communist. Roy was working closely with Borodin, a Russian who (according to the memoirs of Carleton Beals, who himself took a hand in these events) had been sent to Mexico by the Soviet leaders, to create a diversion in the rear of the United States and prevent it from joining a general war against the Soviet Union.

According to Beals, Roy had been promised by Borodin that if he could convert the Mexican Socialist Party into a Communist Party and get himself elected as a delegate to the 1920 Congress of the Comintern in Moscow, he, Borodin, would see to it that Roy got help for his fight against British imperialism in India.

So Roy set about attempting to win converts in the Mexican Socialist Party for the idea of transforming it into the Communist Party of Mexico. He was bitterly opposed by Gale, but Roy had a good deal of money at his disposal and succeeded in packing Gale's party to such a degree that he was finally able to expel Gale from the organization. Then, in a sudden switch, Gale held a rump meeting of his faction the very night of his expulsion from the party and formed a new organization, which he promptly labelled the Partido Comunista of México.

Roy, in the meantime, was still having difficulties in convincing the Socialists that they should join the Comintern and change the name of the party. In the end he lost the battle and was himself expelled from the party. However, his followers, upon withdrawing, formed a second Partido Comunista de México.[1]

For some time the two parties each claimed to be the "authentic" Communist Party and sought the blessing of the Comintern. Gale's group had a certain advantage because of his friendly relations with President Venustiano Carranza. Its principal leaders were: Refugio Rodríguez as Secretary General; Timoteo García as Agricultural Secretary; C. F. Tabler, an American, as Mining Secretary; Vicente Ortega as Railway Secretary; Francisco Cervantes López as Industrial Secretary; Maclovio Pacheco as Construction Workers' Secretary; and Gale himself as Publicity Secretary.

However, early in 1920 President Carranza was overthrown by a military revolt, led by Alvaro Obregón and Adolfo de la Huerta—the last successful military insurrection of the Mexican Revolution. Soon after the inauguration of de la Huerta as Provisional President, the government deported Gale.[*2]

---

* Upon his return to the United States Gale was arrested as a draft-dodger. While in jail he recanted his radical ideas. His attorney, Samuel Castleton, was reported in the New York *Call* of September 17, 1921, as writing to Roger Baldwin of the American Civil Liberties Union:

". . . my client has authorized me to make public the information that he has renounced his former political beliefs and convictions, that he has completely severed his connections with the radical movement, and consequently would not be justified in receiving any further aid or support from them.

"My client, Linn Gale, desires to state that he is absolutely sincere in the repudiation of his former radical opinions, as expressed through *Gale's Magazine,* and that at no time in the future will he engage in radical activities."

The rival Communist group finally received the blessings of the Comintern because of the endorsement of Borodin, who had the confidence of the Soviet leaders. M. N. Roy and an American, Charles Phillips, were the Party's delegates to the 1920 Congress of the Communist International. Roy did not return to Mexico, and in its first years the Mexican Party remained under the leadership of Phillips.

Phillips had also gone to Mexico to avoid the United States draft, having been a pacifist in the United States and active in the Student Anti-War Society at Columbia University. As Mexican delegate to the Comintern, he was honored by Lenin with a long interview, during which they discussed the Mexican Revolution and the role which Mexico could play in the World Revolution.[3]

Phillips and the other leaders of the Mexican Communist Party sent to Moscow very optimistic reports about the activities and prospects of the Mexican Communist Party. There seemed to be some basis for this optimism. Several of the important leaders of the Mexican Revolution joined the Communist Party in this early period, including General Mújica, Governor of the State of Michoacán, and Governor Felipe Carrillo Puerta of Yucatán, the head of the powerful Partido Socialista de Yucatán, who, however, refused to rechristen his party and affiliate it with the Comintern.[4] None of these military and political leaders stayed in the Party long.

Apparently the Comintern did not take too seriously the reports of Phillips and his associates. They sent Sen Katayama, the famous Japanese Communist and member of the Executive Committee of the Comintern, to investigate the real situation of the Mexican party and to survey the general possibilities of Communist organization in Latin America.[5]

Accompanying Katayama to Mexico, also as a Comintern representative, was Luis Fraina, one of the principal figures in the Communist Party of the United States. Among the instructions which they took to the Mexican Communists was that they must engage in election campaigns. This idea did not sit well with the Mexican comrades, among whom Anarchist ideas were particularly well entrenched.

However, although they did not agree with the point of view of the Comintern representatives, they were eager to get the money which the Communist International was offering them. So, like the old Spanish Viceroys in America, they decided to "obey but not execute" the orders of the International's representatives.

They received money from the Comintern delegates for a "political campaign" during the 1922 election. They had posters printed and brought these and other evidences of the campaign to Fraina, but never really conducted such a campaign. The money supposed to be spent on electoral activities was spent by the Party on other things.

This incident is reported to have been the cause of Fraina's downfall in Comintern circles and in the United States Communist Party. The hoax which had been perpetrated upon him by the Mexican Communists soon became known to Fraina, and when he returned to the United States he was so ashamed of having been hoodwinked that he would not account for the money which he had paid out to them. He thus came under a cloud and was soon expelled from the United States Communist Party.[6]

Meanwhile the Communist Party of Mexico had acquired a number of distinguished recruits among the increasingly important group of artists who were gaining world-wide renown by painting the story of Mexican history and the Mexican Revolution on walls and canvases throughout the country. Early in 1922 they had formed a "trade union," the Sindicato Revolucionario de Obreros Técnicos y Plásticos. Most of the members of the Sindicato soon joined the Communist Party. They included Diego Rivera, José Clemente Orozco, David Alfaro Siqueiros, and others.

The artists' union published a magazine, *El Machete,* which soon became the official organ of the Communist Party. Bertram Wolfe, writing in *The New Leader* of October 11, 1954, has vividly described this periodical:

> It was vast, bright and gory, an oversized bedsheet of a newspaper, its masthead a huge woodcut of a machete, 16½ inches long by 5 deep, printed in black and overprinted in blood red. Each issue carried a number of wonderful propaganda cartoons, cut directly on wood or linoleum or etched on metal by the artists themselves. Today, the copies of "El Machete" are an art collector's item. Its editors were Xavier Guerrero, Alfaro Siqueiros and Diego Rivera.

After the entry of these artists into the Party, they tended to dominate it completely. The working-class members of the Party's Executive Committee were no match for *El Machete's* editors, all three of whom were elected to the Committee in 1923. As Wolfe has said in the article we have already noted, "From a party of vaguely revolutionary politicians, the Mexican Communist party was now converted into a party of vaguely revolutionary painters."

This new leadership gave the Comintern repeated headaches. A leading member of the American Communist Party, Bertram Wolfe went to Mexico in 1923 to work as a teacher. Upon his arrival he found that the Communists were deeply involved in the struggle for the presidential succession, and he felt that they were backing the wrong candidate.

The choice of a successor to General Alvaro Obregón, who had become President late in 1920, lay between General Adolfo de la Huerta, who had been Provisional President in 1920, and General Plutarco Elías Calles, who had the support of Obregón. The Communists were backing de la Huerta, from whom they were receiving a subsidy, and had agreed to back him in a revolutionary attempt if that became necessary.

When Wolfe became aware of this situation, he raised a commotion in the Party's Executive Committee. He was convinced that de la Huerta's candidacy had become the rallying point for the country's more conservative elements and that those who wished to continue the Revolution were generally backing Calles.

Wolfe finally succeeded in convincing the Party leaders of the error of their ways. When the de la Huerta revolt finally came, late in 1923, the Communists supported the Obregón-Calles group and in the State of Vera Cruz, where the Party had considerable influence, actually put troops in the field to support the government.

Although he was successful in getting the Communists to abandon de la Huerta's cause, Wolfe was not successful in getting them to give up the habit of receiving outside subsidies. With the victory of Calles, the Communists became subsidized by him, and throughout most of the next thirty years the Communist Party of Mexico got a larger or smaller subsidy from the Mexican government.[7]

The leadership of the Party was reorganized in April, 1924. Every member of the old Executive Committee except one either resigned or was thrown out. Rafael Carrillo, leader of the Communist Youth, was made Executive Secretary of the Party, and a new Executive, of which Bertram Wolfe was a member, was elected.[8]

The Secretary General of the United States Communist Party, Jay Lovestone, attended the enlarged Executive Committee meeting of the Mexican Communists at which these changes took place as delegate of the Comintern. He was particularly insistent that the Party's Anarchosyndicalist tendencies be curbed and that the organization and discipline of the Party be strengthened. These aims were achieved. Wolfe was elected as the Party's delegate to the Fifth Congress of the Comintern, to be held later in the year.[9]

The Third Congress of the Mexican Communist Party was held in April, 1925. In *International Press Correspondence*, on June 18, 1925, Wolfe wrote that this Congress

> was both the summing up of their work and the small beginning of a real Communist Party in Mexico. The delegates from revived locals, once more accustomed to meet, pay dues, obey discipline and carry on Communist tasks, surveyed the work of the emergency executive and expressed their approval of it.

The Congress drew up an extensive program for future activities. It stressed the importance of Communist Party members' work in the newly established Anti-Imperialist League. It also pledged the Party members to organize a national peasants' league out of various state leagues then in existence.

The Congress was very critical of the Calles government. According to Wolfe, it pledged the Party to "expose the Calles government as the Left arm of American imperialism, the Right arm of which is fascism and intervention," and called the Calles government "the gendarme of the Yankee bankers and petroleum companies."

The meeting also attacked the Confederación Regional Obrera Mexicana, the labor organization closely associated with the Calles government, which was headed by the Minister of Industry and Labor, Luis Morones. According to Wolfe, the meeting pledged the Communists "to expose the leaders of the Confederación Regional Obrera Mexicana as paid agents of the government and instruments of American imperialism in Mexico," and to "campaign against their sowing of divisions in labor's ranks, their attacks against the independent unions not affiliated with them, their betrayal of all strikes against American capital, their class collaboration and anti-strike theories and their servility to the government."

The Communists, though attacking the leadership of the C.R.O.M. and the Anarchosyndicalist trade union group, the C.G.T., warned their members against ever making an attack "on the organizations or their masses." They decided to establish Communist cells in both of the labor groups and to establish a Communist trade union "educational" group, patterned on the Trade Union Educational League of the United States.

A new Executive Committee was elected. It consisted of Rafael Carrillo as Executive Secretary, and Xavier Guerrero, Bertram Wolfe, Alfaro Siqueiros, Carlos Rendón, and Manuel Ramírez as members.

In spite of their verbal attacks on the government of Calles at this Congress, the Communists continued to receive subsidies from it. They were also given one seat in the Senate by the Calles government.[10]

The Communists' principal popular support in the 1920's lay among the peasants. A Communist, Guadeloupe Rodríguez, was founder and leader of the Peasants League and of the Labor Party of the State of Durango and was elected to the Executive Committee of the National Peasants League in 1926. In 1927 he went to Moscow to participate in the celebration of the tenth anniversary of the Bolshevik Revolution.[11]

In the State of Vera Cruz the local League of Agricultural Communities decided as early as 1924 to join the Communists' Peasant International. Its resolution of affiliation said that "The Peasant International in Moscow is the only organization which satisfies the hopes and demands of the workers; our Congress will take action to join the Peasant International as soon as possible." Two leaders of the Vera Cruz group, Manuel Díaz Ramírez and Ursulo Galván, were elected to the Presidium of the Peasant International soon afterward.[12]

A national peasants' group was established under Communist leadership in 1926. It affiliated with the Peasant International. Ursulo Galván became the principal figure in this national organization. However, in September, 1929, Galván was accused of having gone over to the government, and so "on account of this treachery" he was expelled from the Peasant International, which announced that "Any attempt on the part of Galván to speak in the name of the Peasant International is a deception of the masses." The International appealed to all members of the National Peasant League to fight against Galván and to continue "their merciless struggle . . . for the establishment of a real workers and peasants government in Mexico."

The Communists made comparatively little progress in trying to capture the labor movement during the 1920's. Their activity in the labor movement began as soon as the Party was organized. In 1920 a Confederación Comunista Obrera was organized. It was reported at the time that "It repudiates political action, insists upon industrial organization, denounces government job-holding on the part of union leaders, attacks the A.F. of L. and the affiliation of the C.R.O.M. with the A.F.L. Its purpose is summed up in direct action and recognition of the Third International."[13]

When the Confederación General de Trabajadores was established in 1921, the Communists participated in it along with the Anarchosyndicalists. A delegate from the C.G.T., one Ramírez, took part in the 1921 Congress of the Red International of Labor Unions. However, the Communists were not able to oust the Anarchosyndicalists from control of the C.G.T., and Ramírez, writing in *International Press Correspondence* of April 5, 1923, reported that "The leading circles of the Federation . . . continue to attack the R.I.L.U., the Russian Revolution and Soviet Russia."

However, the Communists did not confine their activities to the C.G.T., which was in any case the minority group in the Mexican labor movement. They tried eagerly to get the C.R.O.M., the majority labor group, to join the Red International of Labor Unions. The Mexican Labor Attaché in Moscow, a leader of the C.R.O.M., attended a meeting of the Executive Bureau of the R.I.L.U. The Bureau welcomed the establishment of direct relations between the C.R.O.M. and the R.I.L.U., and the Mexican representative extended an invitation to send a representative of the Red International of Labor Unions to the next convention of the C.R.O.M., which was accepted.[14]

However, the behavior of the first Soviet Minister to Mexico, who arrived about this time, did as much as anything to make impossible any kind of cordial relationship between the C.R.O.M. and the R.I.L.U. The first Minister from the Soviet Union was Petskovsky, described by Carleton Beals as "a big booming man with gnarled tobacco teeth showing through a dark beard." Before the Minister's arrival in Mexico, Soviet Foreign Minister Tchitcherin announced that Mexico would become the center of Communist activities in the New World, to which President Calles immediately replied that Soviet diplomats in Mexico would have to obey international law and respect Mexican sovereignty.[15]

This incident was only a prelude to what was to come. Soon after his arrival Petskovsky was invited to address the C.R.O.M. leaders at a formal dinner. Although he could not come, the First Secretary of the Legation substituted for him. A dour-looking man, with a shaved, egg-shaped head, the First Secretary was notable more for candor than for diplomacy. He delivered a speech at the banquet in which he denounced his hosts, the C.R.O.M., as "reformists" and "traitorous," and added that the Russians considered anyone who maintained friendly relations with the A.F. of L.—which the C.R.O.M. did at that time—as being traitors to the best interests of the workers.[16]

From then on relations between the C.R.O.M. and the Communists, both nationally and internationally, were bad indeed. The C.R.O.M. repudiated the invitation which the Mexican Labor Attaché had extended to the R.I.L.U. to send a delegate to the next C.R.O.M. Congress, whereupon, according to *International Press Correspondence*, February 18, 1926, "The R.I.L.U. asked the C.R.O.M. Executive to pass a unanimous resolution at their next Congress . . . in favor of the only International which unites all workers of all Continents." However, the C.R.O.M. refused to affiliate with any international group, least of all the R.I.L.U. at that time.

Nevertheless, the Communists continued to work among the rank and file of C.R.O.M. members. David Alfaro Siqueiros, writing in *El Trabajador Latino Americano* of October 15, 1928, noted that

> As to the revolutionary influence in the organizations of the C.R.-O.M., one can say that it is quite important and is constantly expanding. For instance, six months ago there was no such influence in the textile centers; now there exists great influence in Puebla, which is the most important textile region of the country.

He added, "In general, we can say that there are many *sindicatos* under revolutionary influence."

The Communists also had influence in various autonomous labor groups. David Alfaro Siqueiros himself was the leader of the Federación de Mineros del Estado de Jalisco, with four thousand members. The Federación de la Alimentación de Méjico, with 72,000 members, cooperated with the Communists, and joined a committee which the Communists organized to establish a Mexican affiliate of their continental trade union confederation, the Confederación Sindical Latino Americano.[17]

With the beginning of the Communist Third Period the Mexican Communists were faced with a crisis. The switch in the Comintern's policy coincided with a change in the Mexican political situation. As the presidential term of Plutarco Elías Calles drew to a close, a hot contest developed for the succession. The leading candidate was ex-President Alvaro Obregón. Although the Constitution forbade the re-election of any President, the way for Obregón's candidacy was cleared by amending the Constitution.

During this campaign the Communists had their own candidate, Pedro V. Rodríguez, an old-time revolutionary. He was officially the nominee of the Workers and Peasants Bloc, organized by the Communists, with the participation of the National Agrarian League, some Communist labor groups, and some small political parties. The Executive Committee of the Bloc consisted of Diego Rivera as President, Galván of the National Agrarian League, Hernán Laborde of the Railway Workers Party, and various others.[18]

Obregón was elected, but before he could take office he was assassinated by an extreme right-wing student. A well-known lawyer, Emilio Portes Gil, became Provisional President, and at the end of 1929 General Ortiz Rubio was elected to fill out Obregón's unexpired term.

Meanwhile, however, in March, 1929, a group of military men, led by Generals Escobar and Aguirre, initiated a revolt against the government of President Portes Gil. With the help of ex-President Calles, who took charge of the troops in the field, the government won out. It had in this the backing of the Communist Party, which pictured the government's role as defense of the "revolution" against "reaction."

This attitude of the Mexican Communists was roundly condemned by the Communist International. It claimed that Mexican Communists had "misinterpreted" the situation in their country. The 1929 revolt, according to the Comintern, was in fact a struggle between American and British capital, with the Americans supporting the government and the British backing the rebels. The Communists should not have had any part in such a struggle, declared the Comintern.[19]

The result of this disagreement between the International and the Mexican Party leadership was a purge of the Mexican Party. The chief victim of the purge which occurred in 1929 was Diego Rivera, the famous artist, who had twice been in the Party's Executive Committee. Eliminated from the Communists' ranks for reasons which remain obscure, he soon afterward joined the international Trotskyite movement and became Mexico's principal supporter of the exiled Russian revolutionary.

Among those also expelled from the Communist Party at this time were many of the Communists' agrarian leaders, including Ursulo Galván. This was a serious loss for the Party, because the expelled peasant leaders were particularly strong in some of the Mexican states, especially Puebla. There they allied themselves with "left-wing" politicians who were not on particularly good terms with the Federal Government.

This alliance was demonstrated at the Puebla State Agrarian Congress in February, 1931, which was addressed by Governor Leónidas Andreu Almazán, as well as by the Governors of the States of Vera Cruz and Guanajuato, and was presided over by Julio Cuadros, a follower of the peasant leader, Galván. It was also addressed by other ex-Communists, including Germán List Arizubide, who had once been a leading Latin American figure in the Comintern.[20]

Even before the new leadership had assumed control of the Party, the

Communists had taken the first step in the direction of the Third Period policy of the Comintern in trade union matters by establishing a central labor organization under purely Communist control.

They first set up the Comité Nacional Pro Defensa Proletaria y Pro Confederación Sindical Latino Americana. To this were affiliated the Confederación de Sindicatos Obreros y Campesinos of Nayarit State, the Liga Obrera y Campesina of the State of Coahuila, the Federación Obrera of Tamaulipas, the Confederación Obrera of the State of Jalisco, and the National Peasants League.[21]

At the end of January, 1929, the Comité Nacional sponsored a Congress which established the Confederación Sindical Unitaria de México. It was attended by 397 delegates from union groups, and 102 other unions were reported as sending letters or telegrams of support for the meeting. In addition there were delegates from "revolutionary minority groups" in unions not controlled by the Communists. Fraternal delegates were present from the Trade Union Educational League of the United States, and the Communist trade union confederations of France and Czechoslovakia sent greetings.

The declaration of principles of the C.S.U.M. stated that the Confederación was intended to unite all labor unions opposed to capitalism. It rejected "that narrow unionism which preaches the abstention by trade union organizations from all activities which are not exclusively trade union, exclusively concerned with wages, collective contracts, etc." It maintained that the fight against "reaction" was much broader than that. However, the C.S.U.M. pledged that "under no circumstances" would it take part in electoral political campaigns.

The C.S.U.M. declared itself against trade union bureaucracy, for strict discipline among its affiliates, and against "leaderism and *caudillismo.*" Its declaration stated, "The Confederación Sindical Unitaria de México will be completely opposed to any compromise with the governing petty bourgeois forces which are fighting desperately to maintain the control which they have hitherto exercised over the labor organizations of Mexico."[22]

A "pact of solidarity" was signed between the C.S.U.M. and the Trade Union Educational League of the United States. It pledged "mutual solidarity . . . against all exploiters, native as well as foreign, of the proletarian and agrarian masses." The two groups promised to "fight together against the menacing danger of a new imperialist war and for the most energetic defense of the Union of Soviet Socialist Republics," and to "carry on a war to the death against the Pan American Federation of Labor and the 'Labor Monroe Doctrine.' "[23]

The Second Congress of the C.S.U.M. was held in June, 1930. It took up problems of organization, relations with the peasants, and relations with other Communist-controlled organizations, such as International Red Aid and the Anti-Imperialist League. It also discussed disciplinary measures against members of the Executive and Confederal Councils of the C.S.U.M. against whom charges were pending, and the election of new executive bodies.[24]

At the end of 1929 a new President, General Ortiz Rubio, was chosen to serve out the unexpired term of the late General Obregón. He was distinctly more conservative than his predecessors. Not only did he suspend the agrarian reform program, he launched a violent "anti-Communist" campaign.

When the anti-Communist campaign began, three hundred leading members of the Party, including its Executive Committee, officials of the Anti-Imperialist League, Communist trade union leaders, and officials of the Young Communist League, were arrested in raids conducted by the Chief of Police of Mexico City. The Communist paper, *El Machete*, and publications of the Communist unions were suppressed, and their presses were destroyed. Communist peasant leader Guadelupe Rodríguez was murdered.[25]

As part of the anti-Communist campaign, the Ortiz Rubio government broke off relations with the Soviet Union. The Communists, for their part, demonstrated violently in several foreign countries, including the United States, against the Mexican government's persecution of their Party.[26]

In 1932 President Ortiz Rubio resigned as President, and his place was taken by General Abelardo Rodríguez. However, Rodríguez' government continued its predecessor's anti-Communist drive. Strikes by Communist-led unions were broken by troops, and numerous additional Communist leaders were jailed.[27]

The Communists continued to have rather rough going until the inauguration of General Lázaro Cárdenas as President in December, 1934. The advent of the Cárdenas administration changed drastically the whole picture of Mexican politics.

Lázaro Cárdenas surprised virtually everyone. He had been chosen by ex-President Calles, and it was more or less expected that he would reign, but Calles would rule. However, such was not the case. Even in his election campaign Cárdenas showed originality. He campaigned very vigorously, making tours throughout the country during which he talked over the points of his "Six Year Plan" of government with workers, peasants, businessmen, intellectuals, in all parts of the country.

Once he was President, Cárdenas was his own boss. It was his ambition once again to quicken the tempo of the Mexican Revolution, which had slackened considerably since the mid-1920's. He sought to carry to conclusion the agrarian reform, and to follow a policy of economic nationalism by returning to Mexican control industries which were foreign-owned.

This program of increased revolutionary activity by the Cárdenas government ran into severe opposition from Calles and many of the other revolutionary *caudillos*. Cárdenas deported Calles and Luis Morones, head of the C.R.O.M., to the United States, from which exile Calles never returned.

In spite of the comparative ease with which Cárdenas got rid of Calles, he felt that his government had a certain instability, and that it was necessary to enlist the humbler elements of the population to support the government politically and, if necessary, militarily. With this in mind, Cárdenas distributed arms widely among his supporters in the rural areas and sought to build up powerful organizations of peasants, workers, and middle-class government supporters.

For Cárdenas one of the first necessities was to reunite the labor movement. The relative unity of organized labor which had existed during the heyday of the C.R.O.M. in the 1920's had disappeared. As a result of the 1928 election campaign, in which the C.R.O.M. chief, Luis Morones, had been an active candidate for the presidency but had been passed over when the government nomination went to Alvaro Obregón, relations between the C.R.O.M. and the government had grown cooler and cooler. Furthermore, many of the State Governors, who had considerable latitude in political action, were antagonistic to the C.R.O.M.

As a result of this, various splits had occurred in the organization. The C.R.O.M. in the Federal District broke away, for a while continued to use the name, and then took the title Cámara Nacional del Trabajo. Various State organizations separated from the C.R.O.M. In 1929 the Communists succeeded in rallying some C.R.O.M. organizations to their Confederación Sindical Unitaria de México. Finally, in 1932, Vicente Lombardo Toledano, who had been one of Morones' right-hand men, quarreled with his chief and led another split in the C.R.O.M., establishing his own Confederación General de Obreros y Campesinos de México. Cárdenas was anxious to unite all these groups, as well as the old C.R.O.M. and C.G.T. if possible, to form a labor organization which could be a firm support for his government.

The aims of Cárdenas were forwarded by the change in the international Communist line. The Comintern had entered the Popular Front period, and this made it possible for the Mexican Communists to join the Cárdenas camp—in the labor movement and elsewhere. However, it took them some time to do so.

Although early in 1935 Cárdenas legalized the Mexican Communist Party for the first time in half a dozen years, it was slow to rally to his support, because the shift from a Third Period to a Popular Front policy had not been completed. The Communists' attitude during the first months of Cárdenas' administration was explained by Serrano, one of the Mexican delegates to the Seventh Congress of the Comintern, as reported in *International Press Correspondence* of August 17, 1935:

The Party has been unclear in its attitude towards the national government and the anti-imperialist struggle. . . . The Party thought that the antagonisms between Cárdenas and Calles are only a quarrel between fascist groups. But the Cárdenas government stands for reform measures, whilst Calles' aims are reactionary. Our attitude toward the Cárdenas government must be dictated by the demand for the independence and freedom, of the Mexican people. The Communist Party must win over for the united front those adherents of Cárdenas who are prepared to carry on the anti-imperialist and anti-reactionary struggle, in order that a broad movement for the People's Front may be launched.

The Party's slowness in backing Cárdenas was emphasized in an article by Serrano in the December 2, 1935, issue of *International Press Correspondence*. He again urged that "In this situation our party must concentrate its fire against Calles . . . at the same time the Party must develop a mass movement on the basis of a struggle for economic, political and anti-imperialist demands." He pressed the Communists to "find an approach to the left wing of the national revolutionary party. . . . I propose a united front with the movement of the Cárdenists." However, Serrano added:

We shall criticize the vacillating attitude of Cárdenas and expose his concessions to the imperialists and at the same time reject the tendency, which appears in trade unions and even in the ranks of our party, to consider Cárdenas as a national revolutionary leader. We must make it clear to the masses that this is not a maneuver to expose Cárdenas, but a sincere desire on our part to extend and develop the people's front of struggle against imperialism.

Following the general Popular Front Communist line toward patriotism, which brought the United States Communists to proclaim that "Communism is twentieth-century Americanism," Serrano in this same article advocated a new attitude toward the "patriotic traditions and the revolution of 1910." He said, "We must win back the heritage and revolutionary traditions of the people and transform September 16, the anniversary of independence, and November 20, the anniversary of the 1910 revolution, into two dates of the national liberation movement."

The first field in which the change in the Communist line toward Cárdenas was felt was the trade union movement. Following the Comintern directive to dissolve purely Communist trade union groups and merge them with the stronger "reformist" union movements, the Mexican Communists cooperated in Cárdenas' attempts to establish a new united trade union center as a firm political base for his administration.

The first step in this direction was taken on June 15, 1935, when a Pact of Solidarity was signed among many of the principal union organizations, including the C.S.U.M. This Pact pledged the different groups not to raid one another, and to work toward the formation of a single national trade union center. The associated unions agreed on a policy of "non-collaboration with the capitalist class" and support of "an eminently revolutionary tactic."

The groups which entered into this Pact of Solidarity were the independent trolley-car workers, printing-trades workers, railroad workers, miners, and electricians, and three central labor groups: the Confederación Sindical Unitaria, the Cámara Nacional del Trabajo, and the Confederación General de Obreros y Campesinos. As a result of the Pact, the Comité Nacional de Defensa Proletaria was established.[28]

The work of the Comité Nacional de Defensa Proletaria culminated in a National Congress at the end of February, 1936; this set up the Confederación de Trabajadores de México, of which Vicente Lombardo Toledano became Secretary General. At the Congress an incident occurred between the Communists and Lombardo Toledano's C.G.O.C.M. during the election of the new Confederation's National Committee. The Communists nominated Miguel A. Velasco of their labor group as Secretary of Organization of the new union, while Lombardo Toledano's followers supported Fidel Velázquez. The controversy became acrid, but finally a compromise was achieved by giving Velázquez the organization post and making Velasco Secretary of Education of the C.T.M.[29]

The Communists thus had representation on the Executive Committee of the new C.T.M. They gained considerable importance in the leadership of the constituent unions of the Confederation, including key miners' and railroad workers' organizations. But their relations with Lombardo Toledano and the majority of the executive of the C.T.M. remained strained for some time.

About a year after the formation of the C.T.M., in April, 1937, it suddenly split. The unions under Communist influence broke away and formed a rival group with the same name. Although the dissidents denied that the Communist Party had anything to do with this trade union split, the fact was that the seceding unions were primarily Communist-controlled groups.

Lombardo Toledano denounced the split as a maneuver of the Communists. He said:

> The problem basically is this: that the comrades of the Communist Party have not wished to understand that the C.T.M. is a United Front of the Proletariat, a general front of the proletariat and not a homogeneous organization, not an organization which is coherent in ideology, not an organization which must obey one single opinion and one single tactic. . . .[30]

Lombardo Toledano accused the Communists of trying to use their positions of authority in the C.T.M. to recruit members by force. He said:

On being in contact with the working class for the first time in their history, the Mexican Communists have worked to obtain a mechanical control of the directive organizations of the unions, and a mechanical control also of new members. The membership of the Communist Party is increasing in a way which seems to me irregular and false, because it is coming about not because people are joining out of conviction, but is an artificial increase, brought about by social and political pressure, which is inflating the membership of the small Communist Party. As a result many of those who are now in the Communist Party are not really Communists, but are recruited only because it is convenient for the Communists to have them in their ranks.

Lombardo then proceeded to read the Mexican Communists a lesson, telling them that their comrades in other countries acted in a much more reasonable manner. He cited particularly the Communist Party of the United States which, he said, "conducts its affairs in an intelligent, sane, sincere, and revolutionary manner." In passing, he said, "Comrade Browder is my friend, as are other members of the Political Bureau. . . ."

Finally, Lombardo Toledano argued that the Mexican Communists, in splitting the C.T.M., were acting against the Comintern's Popular Front policy.[31] That this was true and that the Communists were actually responsible for the division of the C.T.M. is indicated by the way in which the matter was resolved.

Both the Communist faction and Lombardo Toledano sent reports on the split to the New York *Daily Worker*, official publication of the Communist Party of the United States. Earl Browder, then Secretary General of the United States Party, made the unusual move of permitting the *Daily Worker* to publish Lombardo's version of the dispute.* In this account, which appeared on July 4, 1937, Lombardo stated "that the C.T.M. is not opposed to Communism, but objects to certain tactics of the leaders of the Communist Party in union affairs."

The publication of Lombardo's side of the C.T.M. controversy in the *Daily Worker* aroused the ire of the Mexican Communist leaders. After numerous telephone conversations between Communist headquarters in Mexico and the United States, the Mexican Party sent a delegation post haste to New York City. There, after long conferences, the Mexican Communist leaders agreed to end the split in the C.T.M. However, the Mexicans asked that Browder come to Mexico to "explain" the decision to an emergency meeting of the Mexican Party which would be called for the purpose. This Browder agreed to do.

The change in the Communists' position was officially adopted at an

* Browder's relations with the Mexican Communist leaders had not been friendly for some time. Theirs was the one Communist Party in the Caribbean region which was not receiving "advice" from him at that point. In addition, Browder may well have thought that the Mexicans were violating the Comintern line by splitting the C.T.M. at that stage.

amplified meeting of the Central Committee of the Mexican Communist Party which was held from June 26 to June 30, 1937. It was agreed, according to the official C.T.M. report, "that the resolutions of the Fourth National Council of the C.T.M. must be respected, and the National Committee of the C.T.M. must receive loyal cooperation in its endeavor to strengthen proletarian unity, and to have the decisions of the representative institutions respected."[32]

Browder attended this meeting. He took advantage of his presence in Mexico to have long conversations with Lombardo Toledano and with President Cárdenas. Browder feels that these discussions with Lombardo were the real beginning of the latter's orientation in a Communist direction.[33]

There is little doubt that Lombardo increasingly made common cause with the Communists in the Confederación de Trabajadores de México after the healing of the 1937 breach in the organization. For a decade after the incident the control of the C.T.M. rested in the hands of Lombardo, those who had been associated with him in the C.G.O.C.M. (such as Fernando Amilpa and Fidel Velázquez), and the Communist or pro-Communist elements of various hues.

For some time there existed a small opposition group, which had at first been closely associated with Lombardo and sought to win him over to a democratic Socialist point of view, but which became increasingly alienated from him as he more and more played the Comintern's game. Although this Socialist group toyed for a while with the idea of splitting the C.T.M., they did not do so, and as a result were forced out or resigned from the leadership of the Confederación one by one.[34]

Lombardo Toledano evolved more and more in the Communist direction and acquired increasing importance in the international Communist apparatus. After the reunification of the C.T.M. he seldom veered from the Communist line on international affairs. He followed the twists of Communist policy during the second World War, violently denouncing the conflict while the Soviet Union was allied with Germany and becoming an equally violent champion of the Allied cause after the Soviet Union was attacked by the Nazis.

There is no doubt that the Party found Lombardo very useful in Mexico in spreading the international Communist line, whatever it happened to be at any particular time. The government contributed considerable amounts of money for the maintenance of the so-called "Workers University" run by Lombardo, which published a considerable amount of material on international labor and political matters, faithfully adhering to the international Communist position. Government funds were also enlisted by Lombardo for the publication of *El Popular*, a daily newspaper which hewed closely to the Communist line. It continues down to the time of writing (December, 1956) to be the principal spokesman for international Communism in Mexico, and perhaps in all Latin America.

After September, 1938, Lombardo was the head of the Confederación de Trabajadores de América Latina. Although this was at first a true "Popular Front" group, having national union affiliates which were Communist, Socialist, Aprista, and of other political tendencies, during the second World War it became completely Communist-dominated.

Lombardo, as the spokesman for the C.T.A.L., became the most important Communist-oriented trade union leader in the hemisphere. He loyally carried out the Comintern's program for subordinating the interests of the workers of Latin America to the overriding aim of victory for the Soviet Union and its allies. He maintained friendly relations with all the governments—dictatorial or democratic—which pronounced themselves against the Axis. He urged the workers not to "cause trouble," but to concentrate on production for the war effort.

In spite of this growing importance in the Comintern hierarchy, Lombardo never joined the Communist Party of Mexico. He had no particular respect for its leaders, regarding the Party as a noisy group of people without much real political importance in Mexico, and as a group which might endanger his close association with Lázaro Cárdenas, upon which rested Lombardo's political importance in Mexico itself. The international Communist leaders, who found him ever ready to work with them in the broader Latin American field, apparently never insisted upon his joining the official Stalinist Party in Mexico. He was more useful to them in any case as an "independent Marxist" than he would be as an official Communist.

Relations between Lombardo and the Mexican Communist Party showed no outward signs of friction after the patching up of the C.T.M. split in July, 1937. They undoubtedly gained a good deal from their association with him in running the country's largest trade union center.

The Communists made gains during the Cárdenas period not only in the labor movement, but among the peasantry as well. The Cárdenas epoch saw the virtual completion of the splitting up of the land among the peasants. Basking in the Popular Front atmosphere, the Communists strongly backed this program of Cárdenas for land reform, and won back much of the ground they had lost among the peasants during the sectarian Third Period.

The Communists were particularly strong in the La Laguna cotton-growing area in the northern state of Coahuila. They dominated the local peasants' union, of which a young Communist, Dionisio Encina, was the chief, and led it in a bitter strike in 1936. President Cárdenas settled this walkout by expropriating all the land involved under the agrarian reform legislation and turning it over to the peasants to be run collectively.

The Communists would probably have gained much more among the peasants if President Cárdenas had not intervened. Realizing the political potential of the peasantry, Cárdenas was anxious to control it himself. He therefore decided that the tradition of having the peasants belong to the trade union central labor organizations should be broken. He patronized the establishment of a separate peasants' organization, the Confederación Nacional Campesina, and made sure that it was under his own personal influence, not that of the Communists or any other potentially inimical political group.

Cárdenas' handling of the problem of peasant organizations was characteristic of his method of government. He never put all his eggs in one basket. While strengthening the unions through the establishment of the C.T.M., he kept the peasants' and government employees' unions out of the Confederación de Trabajadores de México. While following a radical social and economic policy, he sought a certain reconciliation with the Church. While assuring his own control over the Army, he countered the military by arming large numbers of peasants and workers.

He did much the same in his relations with the Communists. Although there is no doubt that he gave them full freedom of action and propaganda, and even subsidized some of their activities, he checked them among the peasants and even more violently in regard to Leon Trotsky.

The Russian exile had had a hectic life since his expulsion from the Soviet Union in 1929. He had sought refuge first in Turkey, then in France, and finally in Norway, and had been expelled by all these countries under pressure from the Stalin government. His last expulsion, from Norway, occurred as a result of the Moscow Trials of 1936-37, during which the victims "confessed" that they had cooperated with Trotsky in making plans to turn the country over to the Nazis and Japanese.

Trotsky's situation seemed desperate. The Norwegian government acceded to Moscow's pressure, and it seemed as if Trotsky would have nowhere to go. At that moment, Diego Rivera, who was then Mexico's leading Trotskyite, approached President Cárdenas with the idea that the Russian leader be given refuge in Mexico. Cárdenas agreed.

Leon Trotsky arrived in Mexico early in 1937. He was the guest of Rivera for some months, when the temperamental natures of the Mexican painter and his guest clashed, and Trotsky took up residence in a large house a few blocks from Rivera's home in Coyoacán, on the outskirts of Mexico City.

The presence of Trotsky on Mexican soil was a standing grievance of the Mexican Communist Party. The Party mobilized all its forces for a propaganda campaign against the Russian exile. They pushed their campaign against Trotsky in the C.T.M., and although it was politically impossible for the labor group to go on record condemning Cárdenas' action, the C.T.M. in January, 1937, did adopt a resolution "placing on the government of Mexico the full responsibility for the presence of Trotsky on Mexican soil," and strongly attacked Trotsky's political position.[35]

The Mexican Communists cooperated fully with the G.P.U.'s moves to murder Trotsky. The first attack which was made on Trotsky's fortified house in May, 1940, was led by David Alfaro Siqueiros, one of the principal leaders of the Mexican Communist Party. That the Mexican Communists also cooperated in the second, and successful, attack on Trotsky several months later is fully indicated in the story of Trotsky's murder as told in *Así Se Mataron a Trotsky*, by General Leandro Sánchez Salazar, who was in charge of the police investigations of his murder.

Communists did not allow disagreements over Trotsky's presence in Mexico to disturb their increasingly friendly relationship with the Cárdenas administration. It had taken the Communists a long time to decide to give all-out support to Cárdenas. As late as the beginning of 1937, Ricardo Martínez, writing in the February 13 issue of *International Press Correspondence,* had denounced "sectarian tendencies" in the Mexican party which

> are expressed by confusing the independent line of the Party with a too ready and superficial criticism of the inconsistencies of the Government and the leadership of the C.T.M. instead of carefully giving serious thought to the causes responsible for the mistakes, presenting the responsibility on each occasion, explaining it patiently and clearly to the masses, and in that way helping the Government in correcting its mistakes.

By the end of 1937—partly as a result of the *faux pas* of their split with the C.T.M. leadership, no doubt—the Mexican Communists had finally learned their lesson and were giving loud and virtually uncritical support to the Mexican President. This was indicated by an article by the Party's General Secretary, Hernán Laborde in *The Communist* of February, 1938. Laborde commented:

> It has been seen that there exists in fact in Mexico a People's Front, in that all the people's organizations, particularly the C.T.M., and including the peasant, youth, and women's organizations, and naturally, the Communist Party, support the government and the National Revolutionary Party (P.N.R.). It is equally clear that the policy of Cárdenas is a highly advanced People's Front policy.

Laborde added that in Mexico the conditions for the Popular Front were different from those in France and Spain.

> In Mexico the National Revolutionary Party is the party of the revolution in power and has the support of all the people's organizations. Having leadership in national politics, this party does not consider it necessary to share its power with other organizations in a united front which would place upon it determinate obligations and restrictions.

. . . Under these conditions, the People's Front is possible only within the *National Revolutionary Party* (P.N.R.); that is to say, by transforming the P.N.R. into a bloc-party, in a broad united front, formed by the C.T.M., the Peasant's Federation, the Communist Party, and all the organizations accepting the common program.

Laborde's article praised the program of the Cárdenas government—its aid to the unions, its agrarian reform efforts, its economic nationalist program, and its aid to Loyalist Spain. He commented, "The only inconsistency exhibited by Cárdenas . . . is his inexplicable backwardness in failing to renew diplomatic relations with the U.S.S.R. and his lamentable hospitality to Trotsky."

Laborde gave in this article some interesting information on the gains which the Communists had reaped from their cooperation with Cárdenas. He commented that "the party is growing in political authority and numerical strength," and noted that its membership had risen to 20,000 and it was hoped that by the end of 1937 it would increase to 25,000. The circulation of its paper had risen to 20,000 copies and was pushing toward 30,000.

The Communists strongly supported Cárdenas' move to transform the National Revolutionary Party from an individual membership organization, consisting mainly of government employees, into a coalition party, to which the C.T.M., the Peasants Confederation, and other groups would be organizationally affiliated. Alfred Miller, writing in *International Press Correspondence* of January 8, 1938, hailed it by saying "The old P.N.R. is gone, and the way is open for the Party to become the *People's Front of Mexico*, to unite in itself all the elements, all the different strata and groups of the population that are today supporting Cárdenas and his reforms."

The outbreak of World War II brought the Communists and fellow travellers of Mexico considerable difficulty. The Mexican government apparently became concerned with the concentration of Communist International bigwigs in Mexico in 1940 and the anti-Allied and anti-United States propaganda not only of the official Communists, but of Lombardo Toledano and the C.T.M., which at this time was under his control.

The first casualty of this situation was Lombardo Toledano himself. In September, 1940, he was removed as Secretary General of the C.T.M., his place being taken by Fidel Velázquez.[36] Although Lombardo remained head of the Confederación de Trabajadores de América Latina, there is no doubt that his star was dimmed for some time, and the C.T.A.L. was deprived of the extensive funds which it had hitherto had at its command, funds which probably owed their origin to the Mexican government.

The official Communists also had their troubles. A bill was introduced in Congress providing for the outlawing of the Communist Party. Although this was never enacted into law, it gave some indication of the shift of opinion in official circles concerning the Party.

The Mexican Communist Party was also faced with internal dissension. There were many who could not stomach the Stalin-Nazi Pact and the events which followed it, and *The New York Times* reported on January 27, 1940, that the Party was busy expelling those who opposed this new turn in the international Communist line.

A few months later there occurred a wholesale purge in the leadership of the Party. It appears that this was carried out on orders from the Comintern itself. Present in Mexico at that time were: Dmitri Manuilsky, former head of the Comintern; Leon Haikiss, former Soviet Ambassador to Spain and in 1940 Secretary of Organization of the Comintern; and James Ford, leading figure of the Communist Party of the United States.[37] It was also reported that Victorio Codovilla, leader of the Argentine Communist Party and one of the Comintern's principal Latin American "gauleiters," was in Mexico, on the way home from service as one of the International's chief "advisors" to the Spanish Loyalist Government.[38]

Early in March, 1940, Hernán Laborde, Secretary General of the Party, and Valentín Campa, its outstanding trade unionist, were ousted from their positions as "leading secretaries" of the Party. No public explanations for their removal were given at that time.[39]

An Extraordinary Congress of the Party was called two weeks later. Its principal feature was a speech by Andreas García Salgado, described by the New York *Daily Worker* of March 24, 1940, as "president of the Special Control Commission which led the fight against the class enemy in the party." He violently denounced Ramírez, National Education Secretary of the Party, and two minor figures in the leadership and called for their expulsion.

García Salgado extended his attack to Hernán Laborde and Valentín Campa, who, he said, were "fully aware of the past of these men." He attacked the Laborde-Campa leadership further because "The party surrendered its independence in Yucatan, accepting the subsidy of the Governor there," and he asserted that "Laborde fostered corruption, censuring the Communist leader of the Teachers' Union for exposing graft in the organization, and insisted that the grafter remain in the union."

Finally, García Salgado warned:

> The work of cleaning the party is not finished. It must continue on the basis of the knowledge and application of the political line approved here. The party must clean out enemies and traitors, and lead the struggles for the people's demands as the best guarantee of the smashing of reaction and uprising.

James W. Ford of the United States Communist Party was one of the principal speakers at this Extraordinary Congress. The *Daily Worker* noted that his speech was "vigorously applauded" when he "declared that President Roosevelt's 'good neighbor' policy is dead and called for the unity of Latin and North American peoples in the face of the increasing aggressiveness of Yankee imperialism."

The real reasons for this split still remain something of a mystery. Although it was not mentioned at the time, Campa later claimed that he had "quit" the Party because of the Stalin-Hitler pact.

Whatever the reason for the removal of Laborde and Campa from the leadership of the Mexican Communist Party, they and their followers were soon expelled from the official Communist Party and established one of their own, the Partido de Obreros y Campesinos de México. It continued to use the hammer-and-sickle insignia, and to follow the international Communist line. It was still in existence in mid-1956 and was still complaining that this split in the Mexican Communist movement was all a mistake.[40]

The Mexican Communists—of the official brand, the Laborde-Campa variety, and the Lombardo Toledano stripe—followed the varying twists of the Communist line during World War II. An example of the kind of propaganda to which they resorted was a cartoon in the April, 1940, issue of Lombardo's magazine, *Futuro*, picturing a spider web in which flies representing Austria, Ethiopia, Spain, China, Albania, Poland, and Czechoslovakia had been caught and were being devoured by a spider with the Union Jack painted on its back.

As soon as the Soviet Union entered the war, however, everything changed for the Mexican Communists. All three branches of Mexican Communism strongly supported the Allied war effort from then on. The Mexican Communists of all factions followed the world-wide pattern of calling for all-out support of the Allies, and particularly of the Soviet Union. For the time being, Lombardo and the official Communists alike were full of praise for the Good Neighbor Policy of Roosevelt. Lombardo was a frequent visitor to Washington, where he conferred with State Department and trade union officials. Upon one occasion the Communist front group, the Council for Pan American Democracy, held a testimonial dinner for Lombardo at which Philip Murray was the principal speaker.[41]

Foreign Communists continued to play an important role in Mexican Stalinist activities. Mexico was one of the principal refuges of exiled Europeans during World War II. Both Communist and anti-Communist refugees from Germany, France, Spain, Austria, Czechoslovakia, and various other countries resided there. The Communist refugees had a particularly tight-knit series of organizations, "Free Austria," "Free Czechoslovakia," etc. Active in them were individuals who were to become leading figures in the postwar European Communist Parties. These included André Simon (*né* Otto Katz), who became a leading figure in the Czech government, but was eliminated in the purge of Rudolf Slansky, with whom Simon-Katz was closely associated; and Egon-Erwin Kisch and Paul Merker, who became leading figures in the East German regime after the second World War.

All these exiled Communist groups cooperated closely with the local Stalinists. A Federation of Organizations for the Aid of Foreign Refugees was established under the leadership of Professor José Mancisidor of the Mexican Communist Party. Many of the Communist exiles were given posts at Lombardo's "Workers University," while all of them had free access to his newspaper, *El Popular*.[42]

The position of the Communists, local and foreign alike, was strengthened early in 1943 by the arrival of Constantine Oumansky as Soviet Ambassador, when the Mexican Government recognized the Soviet Union for the first time in a dozen years. Camille Cianfarra, writing in *The New York Times* of November 28, 1943, noted that Oumansky's embassy was very popular both socially and politically.

Cianfarra explained this as follows:

> The predominant view among the members of Mexico's ruling class seems to favor closer relations with Moscow in order to counteract what is thought to be Washington's influence here. There is no question in the mind of observers here that, despite the consistency and loyalty with which the United States is pursuing a good-neighbor policy, a great deal remains to be done before the diffidence, dislike and uneasiness which Mexicans feel toward the "Colossus of the North" can be erased. Washington's repeated gestures of good-will . . . have undoubtedly improved the atmosphere, but they have not been decisive.

While supporting the European Communists in their midst, the Mexican Communists carried on a violent campaign for the expulsion of strong anti-Communists who had also sought refuge in Mexico. The leading figures against whom this campaign was directed were: Victor Serge, an exiled Russian ex-Communist opponent of the Stalin regime; Marceau Pivert, left-wing French Socialist; and Julián Gorkin, one of the leaders of the Spanish left-wing Socialist P.O.U.M. party.

The English-language *Mexican Labor News*, published by Lombardo's Workers University, launched attacks on these three which were typical of the Communists' campaigns. In replying to an article by Richard Rovere in *The Nation* about the situation of the anti-Communist refugees in Mexico, the February 17, 1942, *Mexican Labor News* declared:

> Pivert, the French Trotskyite, is described as head of a small "Socialist" party. This is similar to calling Hitler the head of a large "Socialist" party, as Pivert's party advocated French national socialism and worked in close cooperation with the Bonnet gang of fascist

terrorists, known to have been supplied with funds by the Nazi Intelligence Service.

Gorkin is described as a "leader of Spain's P.O.U.M.," which is
true, but Rovere did not add that Gorkin was condemned for treason
by the Republican government; that is, condemned for being in
league with the enemy, the fascist Franco, after the May revolt in
Barcelona.

Needless to say, these charges against Pivert and Gorkin were entirely
untrue. Pivert was readmitted to the French Socialist Party after World
War II and became a member of its National Executive. Gorkin became
one of the moving spirits in the World Congress for Cultural Freedom.

As the end of the war approached, the Mexican Communists followed
the Stalinist line in urging "national unity." Like Communists in other
countries, they supported the move to have the principal labor and employer organizations sign a pact. The C.T.M. did sign such an agreement
with the National Manufacturers Association of Mexico. The significance
of this pact was indicated by the New York *Daily Worker*'s Latin American specialist, Juan Antonio Corretjer, in the issue of September 16, 1945:

> The pact is a coalition of the main anti-imperialist elements in the
> national body; that industrial bourgeoisie which assumes an anti-
> imperialist role in the dependent countries, and the proletariat. The
> coalition is based on the anti-imperialist coincidence of interest be-
> tween that section of the bourgeoisie and the proletariat; complete
> political independence for the nation; complete economic develop-
> ment of the national resources; raising the living standard of the
> population.

The official Mexican Communist Party, unlike most of the Latin American Communist groups, lost rather than gained in membership during the
second part of World War II. Late in 1946 the Mexican Communist Party
was claiming only 13,000 members, compared with the 30,000 which it
had claimed just before the outbreak of World War II.[43] This fall in
membership came with the backwash of the Party's success during the
Cárdenas period, and reflected as well the existence of rival Communist
organizations in the country.

The Communists continued to have influence in the labor movement,
but it declined rather than increased during the war. The official Party,
as it emerged from the war, still commanded considerable influence among
the oil workers, the miners, and several other federations. The Laborde-
Campa group completely controlled the Railroad Workers Federation,
while having some power in other union groups. Lombardo, of course, remained a leading figure in the C.T.M., which continued to be affiliated
with the Confederación de Trabajadores de América Latina, of which he
remained President.

Lombardo took a leading part in the development of the World Federation of Trade Unions. He went to the conference in London early in 1945 which laid the basis for the establishment of the W.F.T.U., and was lionized there, particularly by the Communist delegates to that meeting. He also was a delegate to the W.F.T.U.'s founding Congress in Paris in October, 1945, and served on its Constitution Committee.[44]

The Communists of all brands supported the government's presidential nominee in the 1946 election, Miguel Alemán. The C.T.M. was the first important organization to nominate him, and it did so on the motion of Vicente Lombardo Toledano.[45]

In the postwar. years the Communists, of all factions, lost virtually their entire strength in the labor movement, though they continued to wield considerable influence among the country's intellectuals. The first major defeat for the Communists was the expulsion of Lombardo Toledano from the Confederación de Trabajadores de México, as the result of his attempt to organize his followers formally into a political party.

Soon after the war Lombardo proposed the idea of launching a new political party, the Partido Popular. He insists that when he first proposed this, the leaders of the C.T.M. were all in favor of it.[46] A resolution supporting the idea of establishing such a party as the political spokesman for the labor movement was passed in the C.T.M. Congress of March, 1947.[47]

However, the majority of the leaders of the C.T.M. did not want to go along with Lombardo's new party. They felt that it would be suicidal for the C.T.M. to divorce itself from the government party, the Partido Revolucionario Institucional.* The C.T.M. was one of the three principal bases of the P.R.I., the other two being the National Peasants Confederation and an organization of middle-class groups brought together as the Confederation of Popular Organizations.

Through this association with the P.R.I., the leaders of the C.T.M. had considerable influence on the policies of the government. In some parts of the country the C.T.M. was the real base of the P.R.I., since the other elements either did not exist or functioned only at election time. Hence, the C.T.M. leaders felt that their organization had a good deal more to lose than to gain from attempting to set up a "labor party."

No doubt the growing tenseness of the Cold War had its effect on the thinking of the C.T.M. leaders. The government of Miguel Alemán had taken its place on the side of the West in this conflict, and it would not be good internal politics for the C.T.M. to continue in the international Communist orbit.

Whatever its reasons, the C.T.M. leadership refused to go along with Lombardo in the establishment of the Partido Popular. When Lombardo

---

* The government party of Mexico has changed names three times. When it elected Cárdenas it was the National Revolutionary Party. When he reorganized it in 1938 it took the name of Partido de la Revolución Mexicana. In the middle 1940's it was changed once again to Partido Revolucionario Institucional.

actually announced his decision to launch this party late in 1947, the Thirty-Second National Council of the C.T.M. reversed the decision of the March, 1947, C.T.M. Congress, which had specified that officials of the labor group must join the new party. The Council even went further, and three members of the Secretariat of the C.T.M. who had joined the Partido Popular were relieved of their jobs.[48]

Although the C.T.M. leaders tried to dissuade Lombardo from going through with the formal establishment of the Popular Party, Lombardo refused to be persuaded. Victor Serge, writing in the *New Leader* of November 1, 1947, maintained that Lombardo had announced his decision to launch the Partido Popular after returning from a meeting of the Executive Committee of the World Federation of Trade Unions, where presumably he had received orders to establish the new party.

Lombardo finally went through with his program for establishing the Partido Popular at a Congress held in Mexico City, June 20-21, 1948. The new party's general program was not formulated particularly in Communist terms. It promised full support for the economic development of Mexico, the continuation of the agrarian reform, and the development of political democracy. Perhaps the only part of its program which gave some indication of its real orientation was Article 81, which began, "The expanionist policy of North American imperialism constitutes the principal menace for the sovereignty of the Latin American countries, as well as the major obstacle to the rapid and adequate industrialization and the full economic development of these countries."[49]

The real significance of the Partido Popular was better shown by its membership than by its program. The founding members of the party included most of the well-known fellow travellers among the Mexican intelligentsia—Lombardo himself, Narcisso Bassols, Diego Rivera (who after his break with Trotsky had evolved more and more toward the Communist Party, and was finally to be readmitted to it in 1954), David Alfaro Siqueiros (who had been formally expelled from the Party after the fiasco of his attempt to murder Trotsky in 1940), and many others.

With the establishment of the Partido Popular, with Lombardo Toledano as its President, the erstwhile Secretary General of the C.T.M. virtually read himself out of the labor organization which he had founded. The Thirty-Third Council of the C.T.M., meeting in January, 1948, formally expelled Lombardo Toledano.[50]

The Lombardista Communists established a new central labor organization. At first called the Alianza de Obreros y Campesinos de México, the group finally took the name of Unión General de Obreros y Campesinos de México. Although boasting the longest name of any of the Mexican labor groups, it had the smallest membership. None of the country's large industrial unions belong to the U.G.O.C.M., and its membership was concentrated in a few regions, such as the Laguna cotton-growing area, where the official Communist Party continued to have some influence. In 1954 it merged with another small labor group, the Confederación de Obreros y Campesinos de México, headed by Mario Suárez.

The Communists experienced other defeats in the labor movement. Their attempts at the 1947 Congress of the C.T.M. to increase their influence in the executive bodies of the Confederation were roundly defeated by the more conservative group, headed by Fidel Velázquez and Francisco Amilpa.

All three Communist factions were allied in this attempt to keep control of the C.T.M. Their nominee for Secretary General of the Confederation was Luis Gómez Z., of the Partido Obrero y Campesino de México, while the non-Communist officials of the C.T.M. supported Fidel Velásquez.

When the Communists failed in their attempt to have Gómez Z. elected Secretary General, they took steps to launch another confederation. The lead in this was taken by the petroleum, railway, and miners' unions, which called a congress to launch the new group. The result was the Confederación Unica de Trabajadores, of which Luis Gómez Z. became Secretary General.

Most of the money for the new Confederation—some $50,000—was supplied by the railroad workers' union, whose principal leaders were Gómoz Z. and Valentín Campa. However, in 1949 the P.O.C.M. leaders were ousted from control of the railroad union, and the new officials of the union brought about the indictment of Gómez Z. and Campa on the grounds that they had stolen this money and used it without the approval of the other leaders of the railroad workers union.[51]

The C.U.T., in spite of the 350,000 members which it claimed when it was founded, soon became a minor factor in the Mexican labor movement. Apparently the government hesitated for a while as to whether it should support the C.T.M. or the C.U.T., since the Secretary of Labor, Andreas Serra Rojas, attended both the founding Congress of the C.U.T. and the Congress of the C.T.M. which was held at approximately the same time.[52]

The Communists soon lost their influence in the important national industrial unions which had first joined the C.U.T., including the petroleum and railroad workers. These national unions therefore withdrew. Both the petroleum and railroad unions were lost to the Communists in 1949.[53]

Aside from their activities in the labor movement, the Communists of all three factions were very busy with the customary Communist international campaigns. These reached a high point in a Continental Congress for Peace, held in Mexico City, September 5-9, 1949.[54] As sponsors of this Congress and of various "World Peace Congresses" held in Warsaw and elsewhere, the Communists were able to line up numerous important intellectuals and politicians. Among those who allowed their names to be used in these campaigns were ex-President Lázaro Cárdenas, General Heriberto Jara, who became head of the Mexican Peace Committee, and numerous figures in the art, music, and literary circles of Mexico.

In spite of their success in getting important Mexicans to allow their names to be used for international Communist programs and campaigns, the Communists remained a relatively small element in the Mexican political picture in mid-1956. Some idea of the size of the official Party may be gained from the fact that the Federal District organization of the Party prided itself on having increased the sales of the Party paper, *Voz de México*, from 200 to 600 a week between 1948 and 1949.[55]

The election campaign of 1952 presented serious problems for the three Communist factions. All three were on bad terms with the Alemán government. The official Party stated its attitude in an article in the Cuban Communist magazine, *Fundamentos*, of January, 1950. According to this article:

> In the government of Alemán there has been taking place a realignment of forces which has given preponderance to the reactionary elements and the capitulators to imperialism, which support the granting of concessions to the Yankees, the liquidation of the agrarian reform and of the progressive principles of the Federal Labor Law, and seek an alliance with the Sinarquistas [a Fascist party outlawed by the Alemán regime].

In the 1952 campaign there were four candidates. The government nominee was Adolfo Ruiz Cortines, who had been for a long time a Minister in Alemán's Cabinet. The right-wing opposition candidate was J. Luna, nominee of the Partido Acción Nacional. The principal opposition nominee was General Miguel Henríquez Guzmán, onetime Minister in Cárdenas' Cabinet, who had organized his own Federation of People's Parties to support his candidacy. The fourth candidate was Vicente Lombardo Toledano, named by the Partido Popular. Lombardo's party formed an alliance with the official Communist Party for this campaign, and also had the support of the Partido Obrero y Campesino de México. However, the alliance of Lombardo's party with the other Communists was an unstable one. The official Party sought to get Lombardo to withdraw in favor of Guzmán.

The Communist Party issued a statement of its position in *La Voz de México* of March 23, 1952. This statement said:

> The Mexican Communist Party, hearing the clamor of the masses of the citizens of the country, who are asking for the unity of the democratic forces to defeat the anti-popular, reactionary, and traitorous policy of the Government and its imposed candidate, has several times approached the independent parties, urging upon them the necessity for unity to secure triumph over the imposed candidate, the

candidate of national betrayal, the candidate of the P.R.I., Adolfo Ruiz Cortines.

The statement went on to condemn the attitude of the Partido Popular, which was refusing to withdraw Lombardo Toledano's nomination. Meanwhile the Communists, in spite of an agreement with the Partido Popular to put up a joint ticket of nominees for the Senate and Chamber of Deputies, accepted positions on the list of Henríquez Guzmán's followers. In the State of Coahuila the Federation of Popular Parties named Dionisio Encina (the Communist Secretary General) for Senator and the head of the State Committee of the Communist Party for Deputy.[56]

Throughout the campaign the Communist Party continued to urge Lombardo to withdraw. When he failed to do so, the official Party switched its support in the last days of the campaign and officially endorsed General Henríquez.

In mid-1956 the Mexican Communists remained divided and relatively weak. The P.O.C.M. was still urging the unification of the Partido Obrero y Campesino de México and the Partido Comunista. However, the official Party was completely unreceptive to the idea. *La Voz de México* in its February, 1954, issue attacked the P.O.C.M. as a "bank of agents—provocateurs of imperialism" in the "service of Yankee imperialism," and as "Trotskyists without quotation marks." It claimed that "these shameless people have descended to the lowest depths of moral depravity and have converted themselves into a band of vulgar provocateurs whose favorite weapon is slander."

Unity between the Partido Comunista and the Partido Popular did not seem any nearer than unity between the former and the P.O.C.M. Lombardo Toledano continued to be the Communist's foot in the government camp. He remained a close friend of ex-President Lázaro Cárdenas, who was still the "strong man" behind the Mexican government. Many observers were convinced that the reason why Lombardo had not withdrawn in the 1952 elections was that he was playing the government's game in splitting the opposition to Ruiz Cortines. Although officially outside the government's fold, he remained the Mexican Communist who was most friendly to the regime.

For a while in 1954 the Lombardo Communists had a more than platonic relationship with the government. For some months Narcisso Massols, one of the founders of the Partido Popular, was an advisor to President Ruiz Cortines on foreign policy, and his influence was generally credited with having swung the Mexican government to a position of opposition to the United States on the famous "anti-Communist resolution" which the latter sponsored at the Tenth Inter American Conference at Caracas, in March, 1954. However, a few months later Bassols was dismissed, and direct relations between the Ruiz government and the Lombardo group were thus broken.

Lombardo remained a key figure in the international Communist hierarchy. He continued as Secretary General of the Confederación de Trabajadores de América Latina, which was reduced to a purely Communist labor confederation. The C.T.A.L. was given increased prestige and importance in December, 1949, when the Peking Congress of the World Federation of Trade Unions, which Lombardo attended, granted the C.T.A.L. headquarters the task of issuing and distributing all Spanish-language publications for the world Communist labor group. Lombardo continued to be a member of the Executive Committee of the W.F.T.U.

The official Communists were frankly in the opposition. They had several years before lost their electoral registration as an official party, and had been reduced to tiny proportions in the general political picture. The third group, the P.O.C.M., differed little from the official Party, either in its position on international affairs, its relationship to the government, or the extent of its influence.

The only field in which the Mexican Communists have been able to make some headway—and this has brought them few actual members in any of their parties—has been among the intellectuals. Impelled by a strong nationalist feeling, and being violently anti-United States, many of the Mexican intellectuals have been willing and anxious to express whenever possible their defiance of "Tío Sam." Thus they have frequently joined in Communist campaigns against one or another aspect of United States foreign policy.

This attitude of the Mexican intelligentsia was strikingly demonstrated during the troubles in Guatemala in the middle of 1954, when the Communists were particularly successful in organizing groups of "Friends of Guatemala" and in getting signatures for violent proclamations against alleged "Yanqui intervention" in that country. However, this does not mean that the vast majority of even anti-Yanqui intellectuals in Mexico have been willing to join the Communist Party, or forswear allegiance to the Mexican Revolution in favor of the Russian Revolution.

The fundamental reason for the failure of the Communists to make significant headway in Mexico has undoubtedly been the fact that they have been busy trying to sell a foreign revolution to a country which was going through a fundamental revolutionary change of its own. In constantly advertising the virtues of a Communist revolution à la Soviet Union, the Mexican Communists were not only running counter to the trend of events in Mexico itself, but were also defying the patriotism of the Mexican people, for whom their own revolution has become virtually synonomous with present-day Mexico.

The Communists have consistently maintained that the Mexican Revolution was "incomplete," that it could not be "successful" until it became a "proletarian" revolution, led by the Communist Party. This was made clear in discussions within the Communist International as far back as

1928, when a Mexican delegate to the Sixth Congress of the Comintern, Travín, maintained that in the Mexican Revolution "the Socialist traits relegate to a back seat bourgeois democratic traits"; he was taken to task by the Comintern's Latin American "expert," Humbert-Droz, who said that the Mexican Revolution could not reach its fruition until the proletarian revolution under the leadership of the Communist Party had been carried out.[57]

The theme recurred in an article by Ladislao Carvajal in the Cuban Communist magazine, *Fundamentos,* of February, 1952. Carvajal maintained that:

> The great struggles of the masses and of the peasant movement were directed by the Mexican bourgeoisie which has shown itself incapable of conducting them victoriously. . . . The working class, small, weakly organized, and under the ideological influence of anarchosyndicalism, showed itself incapable of leading the movement. . . . The lack of direction of the peasant movement by its natural leader, the working class, impedes the achievement of a complete victory.

Carvajal went on:

> In the course of the revolution there was lacking a basic condition for its triumph: the alliance between the workers and the peasants. The workers, weak ideologically, politically, and organizationally, were prisoners of the national bourgeois interests. . . . Only the existence of a proletariat which acts as an independent class, as an independent political force, oriented by an independent political organization, with a program differentiated from the rest of the parties and truly a Marxist-Leninist-Stalinist party, a Communist Party, will conduct the Mexican Revolution to its full triumph.

Such an analysis, calling upon the Mexican people to follow in the footsteps of another country instead of continuing on the path which the leaders of the Mexican Revolution have set for it over nearly half a century, has not gained the support of any appreciable portion of the Mexican populace. There are few Mexican revolutionaries who would maintain that there is nothing wrong with what has been accomplished since 1910, or that the work of the Mexican Revolution has been completed. But there are few who wish to be told that everything which the Mexicans have accomplished in the last four and a half decades has been for naught, that it is really unimportant, and that the Mexicans should throw it all overboard and set out to imitate another country, which started its revolution later than Mexico and, most Mexicans feel, has little to teach them.

*Chapter XVI*

# Communism's Bid for Power in Guatemala

IN GUATAMALA THE COMMUNISTS gambled and lost—at least temporarily. With the overthrow of President Jacobo Arbenz in July, 1954, the Communists of Guatemala lost the power which had brought them nearer than any of their comrades to gaining control of a Latin American government.

For ten years the Communists, though small in numbers, had been able to capitalize on a broad movement of unrest and social change. They had met no serious opposition from any other advanced left-wing party and for a decade had been able to play on the political ignorance and the preoccupations of their associates. They had found in Jacobo Arbenz the perfect tool for entrenching themselves in the centers of political power.

Thus, although they had contributed little or nothing to the social revolution through which Guatemala was passing, they had been able to identify this revolution almost completely with themselves. They had managed to divert a healthy movement for bringing democracy and social progress to Guatemala down the blind alley of international Communist propaganda aimed at serving the ends of Soviet foreign policy. As events moved to a climax, Communists bore a major part of the blame for the overthrow of the revolutionary government.

The Guatemalan Communist Party was first organized soon after World War I, in the wake of the overthrow of the twenty-year dictatorship of President Estrada Cabrera. A group of workers in the government arsenals established an organization which they called Unificación Obrera, in which students and some Liberal Party politicians participated. This organization led a successful strike among the arsenal workers.

The students in the organization took the lead in urging that all "bourgeois" politicians be ousted from Unificación Obrera, and on May Day, 1921, the group was reorganized and rechristened Unificación Obrera Socialista. A system of red membership cards was established, and a directing council of twenty members was set up.

The government took action against the group soon after this change, intimidating the print shops of the capital city so that the Unificación Obrera Socialista was unable to publish its manifestoes and periodical. However, the U.O.S. soon set up its own printing establishment.[1] In an exchange of open letters with the Communist Party of Mexico, which was published in *International Press Correspondence* of June 9, 1922, the U.O.S. noted that until recently, "Our organizations were persecuted; our wives and children were killed in the streets of the Capital, and many workers were shot down." The letter added that under the new regime of President Orellana, which had just come to power, the principal U.O.S. leaders were being jailed, and "Nothing has changed."

At the 1922 Congress of the Communist International, Alfred Stirner, a Swiss who was in charge of affairs in Latin America for the International, noted that the only group "which stands near us and in connection with us" in Guatemala was the Unificación Obrera Socialista. Stirner reported that the group had ninety members in Guatemala City and a few in the mining areas, and that in spite of the fact that the U.O.S. was illegal, its "propaganda in the country is well organized." As a result of Stirner's report, the Communist International advised the Unificación Obrera Socialista to form a legal organization "even if it be under the guise of social democratic slogans."[2]

In April, 1923, the Unificación Obrera Socialista sent a delegation to Mexico to ask the Communist Party of that country to instruct them in Communism and the means of transforming their organization into a Communist Party. This mission was successful, and the U.O.S. was renamed Partido Comunista and began to publish a periodical called *El Socialista*. The Party joined the Communist International at the Comintern's Fifth Congress in 1924.

Soon after, a new wave of persecution by the government destroyed the Party's press and library. In spite of these attacks, the Communists were able to establish the first trade union under their control, the Sindicato General de Panificadores (Bakers) of Guatemala City.

In 1925 the Party held a meeting in memory of Lenin. The government took the occasion to close down the Communist press again. Del Pinar, one of the leaders of the Party, was arrested and kept in jail for thirteen months. The International Red Aid affiliates in Mexico and Argentina were called upon to assist the campaign to free Del Pinar, and a delegation from the Mexican Communist Party went to Guatemala and succeeded in obtaining the release of the Guatemalan leader.

The Communists were constantly persecuted by the government. In 1924 their publication, *Nuestra Palabra*, was suppressed. In the following year the Party issued a new periodical, *Vanguardia Proletaria*, one thousand copies of which were distributed among the workers more or less regularly for a short while. This newspaper was also suppressed, and its

editors were jailed. During the next five years the Party did not attempt
to publish any other periodical, "for financial reasons, since the labor organizations have scarcely enough funds to keep going," as it reported in
the Communists' continental trade union periodical, *El Trabajador Latino
Americano*, of January-February, 1930.

The Communists concentrated much of their energy on work among
the trade unions. In 1925 the headquarters of Communist Central American trade union activities was established in Guatemala City, with the organization there of the Consejo Obrera Centro-Americano. The office of
this Consejo was staffed by members of the Guatemalan Communist
party.[3]

The Communists soon became the dominant force in the Federación
Regional de Trabajadores de Guatemala, which was established in May,
1926. The Federación Regional, which joined the Communist continental
labor confederation, the C.S.L.A., when it was established in 1929, included bakers unions in various cities, tobacco workers, chauffeurs, and
other groups.[4]

The Communists tried to extend union organization to the workers on
the United Fruit Company's banana plantations and on the International
Railways of Central America. A strike which they succeeded in organizing among the banana workers was broken by the Army.[5]

The Chilean labor historian, Moisés Poblete Troncoso, writing in the
September, 1929, issue of the *Monthly Labor Review*, said of the Communist trade unions in Guatemala at that time: "Guatemala also has a
separate Communist organization, which is composed of a small group of
workers and which has not been successful. The government has taken
energetic measures against this organization, and the greater number of
industrial workers do not wish to have any connection with it."

In the middle of 1929 the government cracked down on the Communist
unions. Their headquarters were closed, and many of their leaders were
jailed. A number of the principal figures in this union movement were
unable to stand up against this persecution, turned against the Federación,
and were promptly denounced in the international Communist press.[6]

The Guatemalan Communists participated amply in the international
activities of the Comintern. Two of their leaders, Luis Sánchez Obando
and José Luis Chiguichón, attended the Sixth Congress of the Communist
International in 1928.[7]

Following the Comintern's policy of opposition to "Yanqui imperialism," the Guatemalan Communists organized a demonstration on Sixth
Avenue in Guatemala City in the summer of 1930 against a loan which
Guatemala was about to contract with United States interests. The meeting was broken up by the police, and 150 of the demonstrators were
jailed. Several of the principal Communist leaders were severely tortured.[8]

As a result of the failure of the Communist-led revolt in El Salvador in January, 1932, a number of the Salvadorean Communist leaders fled to Guatemala. Perhaps the most important of them was Miguel Mármol, who, having been left for dead by a Salvadorean government firing squad, was actually only wounded and succeeded in making his escape across the border. He and other fleeing Communist leaders were jailed by the Guatemalan government of General Ubico, and they stayed in prison for several years.[9]

At the same time Ubico put an end to Communist activities in his own country. Seventy-six Guatemalan Communist leaders were arrested. Ten of them, including Luis Chiguichón, Juan Pablo Wainwright, and Luis Sánchez Obando, were executed.[10]

During the Ubico regime there was little Communist activity in Guatemala. On October 6, 1933, the Guatemalan Party was reported by *International Press Correspondence* to be one of ten communist Parties to sign a manifesto in support of the Cuban Revolution and in favor of the establishment of a Cuban Soviet Government. On May 20, 1935, the *Communist International* reported that the Guatemalan Party had "collapsed" and that attempts were being made to revive it. However, no successful effort to rebuild the Communist Party of Guatemala was made until after the fall of the Ubico dictatorship in the middle of 1944.

The Communist Party of the late 1940's and early 1950's grew up as part of the profound social revolutionary movement which began after the ousting of Dictator Ubico. This revolution was not in itself Communist. In general outline it followed the pattern of the Mexican Revolution of 35 years before, and its principal aims were to integrate the Indian—who makes up two thirds to three fourths of the country's population and who had been held in bondage by the white man for four centuries—into the general life of the community, modernize the country's government, encourage the growth of the labor and peasant movements, enact advanced social legislation, and give impetus to the economic development of the country.

The governments which came after the 1944 Revolution took many steps to carry out this program. A new Constitution was adopted in 1945. In 1947 a Labor Code was adopted, and a couple of years later it was amended to permit the organization of agricultural as well as urban workers. A Social Security Institute was established. A Development Institute was inaugurated to give impetus to the diversification of agriculture and the building up of industry.

The revolutionary governments had a strong nationalistic tinge, which the Communists were able to use to their own advantage. The administrations of Juan José Arévalo and Jacobo Arbenz sought to reduce the hold which the United Fruit Company and allied firms had on the Guatemalan economy. For this purpose they began the construction of a port on the Atlantic Coast to rival the United Fruit-owned port of Puerto Barrios, and of a highway from Guatemala City to the new port, to divert traffic from the United States-owned and United Fruit-affiliated International Railways of Central America.

The government after 1944 was in the hands of the young military men and ex-students who had been largely responsible for the Revolution of 1944. Although these men had a fairly clear idea of what kind of reforms they wanted to carry out in Guatemala, most of them were naïve and unsophisticated concerning the wider issues of the Latin American social revolution. They were unaware of the basic differences between the indigenous national revolutionary movements and the international Communist Movement and its objectives.

The reasons for the naïvete of the leaders of the 1944 Revolution were several. First of all, under the Ubico dictatorship they had not had much opportunity to learn distinctions between Socialism, Communism, Aprismo, and other such movements, since the Ubico government had regarded all these trends as "subversive" and labelled them as "Communist."

In the second place, the opposition to the Revolution likewise made little distinction between such things as labor legislation, social security, and agrarian reform on the one hand, and Stalinism on the other. They lumped together all these things as "Communist," thus adding greatly to the real Communists' prestige. The Communists, therefore, were able to equate an attack on "Communism" with an attack on the Guatemalan Revolution.

Further, the 1944 revolutionaries came to power at a time when everything seemed to be sweetness and light between the democrats of the great Western Powers and the Communists inside and outside the Soviet Union. The Guatemalan revolutionary leaders never got over this wartime honeymoon.

The 1944 revolutionaries were too busy to have time to make the kind of distinctions which were necessary for guiding their movement along democratic channels. Moreover, no grave issue arose during the ten years between 1944 and 1954 on which the policies of the Communist Party and those of the non-Communist revolutionaries seemed seriously to clash. The latter could therefore go on thinking of the Communists as "just another revolutionary party," without ever awaking to the danger which Communist influence represented to the whole movement for social change in Guatemala. Only after the downfall of the government of President Arbenz, did some of the non-Communists begin to understand the ulterior motives with which the Communist International was operating in Guatemala.

The Communists cultivated the natural nationalistic feelings of the leaders of the other revolutionary parties. Due to the geographical location of Guatemala and the influence which United States-owned companies had on the economic and social life of the country, these nationalistic feelings more often than not ran against the United States, and the Communists capitalized upon this fact to carry on their extreme anti-Yanqui propaganda which, if it did not always have the approval of the leaders of the other parties, at least did not particularly offend them.

Contributing to this situation was the attitude of some of the American enterprises operating in the country, particularly the International Railways of Central America and the United Fruit Company. These firms, in their labor relations and general dealings with the Guatemalans, found it impossible to shake off the proprietary attitude and authoritarianism which they had developed over four decades of operations in Guatemala.

In the last months of the Arbenz administration the stand taken by the United States government also played into the Communists' hands. The protests which the State Department made against the expropriation of lands of the United Fruit Company under the agrarian reform convinced most politically conscious people in Guatemala that the concern of the United States in Guatemala was with the fate of the United Fruit Company rather than with the menace of Communism, a point of view which the Communists naturally cultivated. And the position taken by the Secretary of State, Mr. Dulles, at the Tenth Inter American Conference in Caracas in March, 1954, and the way in which it was countered by the Guatemalan delegation, led by Foreign Minister Guillermo Torriello, unified the forces around the Arbenz regime on an issue concerning which the Communists seemed to them to be right and the United States appeared wrong.

Finally, the Guatemalan revolutionaries of 1944 were unfortunate in their leadership. There did not appear on the scene any penetrating thinker who saw clearly the necessity for the Guatemalan Revolution's seeking its own path, unencumbered by the international commitments and dictatorial ambitions of the Stalinists. President Arévalo was a rather fuzzy thinker who, though aware of the nature of the Communists, was more interested in avoiding trouble than in having a showdown with them.

His successor, President Arbenz, was unequivocally in the Communists' corner. Under his administration all attempts to establish a clearly anti-Communist or even non-Communist party supporting the government met with the opposition of the President of the Republic. Rightly or wrongly, Arbenz considered the Communists his closest allies, and he strongly opposed any attempt to isolate them. The power of the President of Guatemala being as great as it is, this was a conclusive argument for many of those members of the revolutionary camp who might otherwise have wavered on the Communist issue.

Thus, although several revolutionary parties were formed between 1944 and 1954, none of them had a well-defined program or drew a sharp distinction between its own doctrines and those of the Communists. The latter were able to infiltrate the ranks of the other revolutionary parties, and to split them with impunity when that seemed convenient. The Communists were also able, particularly during the Arbenz administration, to seize the leadership and to exert influence out of all proportion to their numbers or popular support. The other parties, themselves confused ideologically, developed a decided inferiority complex in the face of the Communists, who always seemed to know what they wanted and why they wanted it, and who seemed able to explain in theoretical terms the most minute maneuver on the political chessboard.

The Communists did not establish an open party of their own immediately after the 1944 Revolution. It was not until 1949 that the Communist Party of Guatemala was officially reorganized, and not until 1952 that it was registered as a legal political organization.

However, as early as December, 1945, elements in the Confederación de Trabajadores de Guatemala discussed seriously the possibility of establishing an open Communist Party. The project was dropped when the plan was exposed prematurely by a prominent labor leader, who was approached by the group with the offer of a candidacy for deputy if he would join the new Party.

In 1947 a secret organization known as the Vanguardia Democrática was established as the nucleus for the future Communist Party. Among its founders was José Manuel Fortuny, who was at that time Secretary General of the Partido Acción Revolucionaria. This organization came out into the open on May 25, 1950, when José Manuel Fortuny led a group out of the P.A.R. to form what they first called "Octubre Comunistas." A year later they adopted the name Partido Comunista.

Daniel James notes that Fortuny took with him a large part of the leadership of the P.A.R. Among those joining Fortuny were: Bernardo Alvarado Monzón, the P.A.R.'s Youth Secretary; Humberto Ortiz, its Secretary for Rural Affairs; Antonio Ardón, Secretary for Social Affairs; and Pedro Fernández and Alfredo Guerra Borges, members of the P.A.R.'s Political Committee.[11]

In June, 1950, Victor Manuel Gutiérrez, the head of the Confederación de Trabajadores de Guatemala, who had quit the P.A.R. some months previously, announced the formation of a second Communist Party, under the name of Partido Revolucionario de Obreros Guatemaltecos, having a program almost identical with that of the Octubre Comunistas. The two parties continued their parallel existence until Gutiérrez' return from an extended trip to the Soviet Union in November, 1951. A few weeks after this he suddenly announced the dissolution of the P.R.O.G. and urged its members to join the Partido Comunista.[12]

By the time the Communists came out into the open, they were the dominant factor in the labor movement. Trade union activity got under way soon after the overthrow of Ubico, and it was from the beginning oriented and aided by Mexicans and Central American refugees, working in the interests and under the direction of the Communist-controlled Confederación de Trabajadores de América Latina. One of the chief advisors to the new trade unions was Miguel Mármol, the Salvadorean Communist.

The first central labor group established was the Confederación de Trabajadores de Guatemala, founded early in 1945, which affiliated with the C.T.A.L. However, within a few months of its organization, there was a split led by those opposed to growing Communist influence in the C.T.G. The railroad workers' and most factory workers' unions of Guatemala City withdrew to form the Federación Sindical de Guatemala. This dissident group for some time resisted Communist influence, and was even on friendly terms with the American Federation of Labor and the anti-Communist Inter American Confederation of Workers (C.I.T.). However, early in 1951 the F.S.G. also joined the C.T.A.L., thus paving the way for the reunification of the labor movement under Communist leadership.

Meanwhile the C.T.G. devoted much of its energies to attempting to organize the agricultural workers and Indian peasant communities. The Labor Code was modified in 1949 over the protest of landowners' groups, to make it possible legally to establish trade unions among rural workers. The penetration of the countryside by the C.T.G. was undoubtedly intended by the Communists to set the stage for Communist leadership in the forthcoming agrarian reform. Another organization, the Confederación Nacional Campesina, composed in large part of tenant farmers, was not subject to Communist influence until the summer of 1952.

One of the most effective methods of Communist penetration of the labor movement was through a "training program" for union leaders. A "leadership training school," Escuela Claridad, was established in 1945, and the Communists succeeded in getting the Confederación de Trabajadores de Guatemala to send all current and potential union leaders to this school, where they received not only training in trade union activities, but indoctrination in Communist ideas and methods of organization.[13]

The unification of the Guatemalan trade union movement came in January, 1952, when a Unity Congress established the Confederación General de Trabajadores de Guatemala. Chosen as Secretary General of the new group was Victor Manuel Gutiérrez, a young school teacher, who was also a Communist Party member of the Chamber of Deputies. Other important Communist leaders of the C.G.T.G. included its Grievance Secretary, Carlos Manuel Pellecer, a successful Communist candidate for the Chamber of Deputies in the 1952 election; its Agrarian Secretary, César

Montenegro Paniagua, another Communist deputy; and Max Salazar, the Secretary of Organization.

The Communists' influence in the labor movement was one of the keys to their expanding power in Guatemalan political life. In August, 1949, the trade unions showed the importance of their loyalty to the government of President Juan José Arévalo, when they helped to thwart an attempted military *coup d'état* by calling a general strike of protest against an Army uprising.

The Arévalo administration, though giving the Communists wide freedom to operate, held them somewhat in check. Leading Communists such as Enrique Muñoz Meany and Carlos Manuel Pellecer were "exiled" for several years to diplomatic posts in Europe and elsewhere. Arévalo refused to allow the registration of the Communist Party as an official political organization. He also put some curbs on its "educational" activities.

Meanwhile the Communists had succeeded in infiltrating other political groups supporting the administration of Arévalo. Communist influence in the Partido Acción Revolucionaria (P.A.R.), one of the first parties to appear after the 1944 Revolution, was one of the reasons for the split in that party which occurred in 1948, resulting in the formation of the Partido Frente Popular Libertador.[14]

Communist influence in the Partido Frente Popular Libertador was cited several years later as a reason for the formation of the Partido Socialista by dissident members of the former group, led by Augusto Charnaud McDonald, who was frequently thereafter referred to by the Communists as "our Tito with the exotic names."

In the middle of 1952 there was a move to unite all the pro-government parties except the Communists in a new organization, to be known as the Partido de la Revolución Guatemalteca (P.R.G.). The first step was a declaration by the P.A.R. and the Partido Socialista of their intention to unite, and their invitation to the Partido de Renovación Nacional and other small pro-government groups to join the new party.

The Partido de la Revolución Guatemalteca was established on July 2, 1952. As a united party, it lasted less than a month. Its dissolution was largely the result of Communist pressure. The Communist leaders made little attempt to hide their opposition to the P.R.G. José Manuel Fortuny wrote two articles in the Communist weekly paper, *Octubre*, analysing it. He accused it of "uniting all the bourgeois and petty burgeois groups supporting the Arbenz administration." He charged that its main objective was "to isolate the Communists both from the masses and from the government." Hence, he and his associates took a dim view of the P.R.G.

In his second article Fortuny hinted that there were "certain elements" of the P.A.R. who were not in agreement with the amalgamation with the other groups to form the P.R.G. These "certain elements" burst into the open late in July, when a group of ex-P.A.R. leaders withdrew from the P.R.G. to re-form the P.A.R. Several weeks later Renovación Nacional was also re-established.

This attempt to form a strong non-Communist if not anti-Communist party supporting the Revolution thus came to naught. Even the remnants of the P.R.G. were still infiltrated by the Communists. The Secretary General of the party was Abel Cuenca, a Salvadorean who had been one of the younger leaders of the 1932 Communist revolution in his native country, and who in private conversations made no secret of his continued loyalty to Moscow.

As a result of this demonstration of Communist influence, virtually no supporter of the Revolution dared to say that he was against the Communists after 1952. The Communists had succeeded in making it appear that opposition to Stalinism was opposition to agrarian reform, democratic government, a labor code, trade unionism, and all the other things which had been gained since 1944.

The Communist Party was legalized just before the 1952 congressional election. In their Second National Congress, held December 11-14, 1952, the Communists changed the Party's name to Partido Guatemalteco del Trabajo, thus clearing the way for its inscription as a legal party. Before this there had been some doubt as to whether they could be recognized under the electoral law, since the 1945 Constitution forbade registration of parties with international affiliations. Ostensibly, this change of name cut international ties.

The Second Congress of the Communist Party, which changed the organization's name, had three basic subjects for discussion: A report on the work of the Party since the last Congress, made by José Manuel Fortuny; a report on the Program of the Party, submitted by Alfredo Guerra Borges, the organization's Propaganda Secretary; and a report on the proposed reforms of the Party's statutes, submitted by Bernardo Alvarado, Secretary of Organization.

In his report Fortuny took credit for the agrarian reform, the unification of the labor movement; "the fight in defence of bourgeois-democratic freedoms now under continual threat by feudal-imperialist reaction which conceals its subversive activities under the Hitler mask of anti-Communism," and various other matters. He laid particular stress on the "electoral democratic front" in the 1952 elections, in which the government parties supported certain Communist candidates. However, Fortuny criticized "the poor contact of the Party with the masses."

Fortuny also noted "lack of clarity in the attitude of the Communists in the matter of eliminating the feudal backwardness of the country and in the matter of its bourgeois development." He said they tended to look on the Guatemalan Revolution "from the standpoint of the classical revolutions of this type (in France, etc.)," and thus thought that a long capitalist period was necessary, and that the leadership of the Revolution must therefore remain with the bourgeoisie. This Fortuny denied.*

A bit later in his report Fortuny made a bid for Communist participation in the government when he announced that one of the Party's principal objectives must be "the formation of a more democratic and more popular, genuinely anti-imperialist government in which all the forces of the national patriotic front would be represented, a government which would fight for the economic development of Guatemala, for national independence and for peace."[15]

This Party Congress was attended by 184 delegates, who represented 14 times more members than had been represented at the Party's first Congress. It was noted that the Party in 1949 had had no newspaper, while in 1952 it had an eight-page weekly, *Octubre*, the circulation of which had risen from about 800 copies in June, 1950, to 3000 copies in December, 1952. At times, some 7000 copies were sold. This compared with the average circulation of 20-22,000 copies sold by the biggest Guatemalan daily paper.[16] (A few months before the fall of the Arbenz government, the Communists launched a daily paper, *Tribuna Popular*.)

The Communists participated in the congressional elections of December, 1952. They had two candidates, José Manuel Fortuny in the city of Guatemala and Carlos Manuel Pellecer in the province of Escuintla. In both cases, they won the endorsement of the other pro-government parties for their candidates, though there was much grumbling in those other parties against this move. Pellecer was victorious, but Fortuny lost out in Guatemala City, where the pro-government forces generally did poorly.

During the administration of President Jacobo Arbenz the Communists made rapid gains in influence. They had been early supporters of Arbenz, long before he had become the government candidate for the presidency in the 1951 election. His attitude toward the Party was summed up in his speech opening Congress on March 1, 1954, when he commented that some people "are asking that the Communists be put in quarantine, as well as those who are alleged to be Communists." He then went on:[17]

> The democratic and progressive forces of Guatemala are not something isolated from the democratic and patriotic program of these same forces, which were grouped around my candidacy and which now firmly support my government. To attempt to combat certain democratic and progressive forces without attacking at the same time

---

* In this connection it is interesting to note a speech by Augusto Charnaud McDonald, Minister of Interior and generally considered to be a convinced anti-Communist, though an opportunist. Speaking to a convention of the P.R.G., of which he was the leader, he said early in 1954 that the P.R.G. as a "bourgeois" party was historically destined to disappear, that the future leadership of the Guatemalan Revolution lay with the party representing "the working class." Although he did not say so specifically, he implied the necessity at some future date for the P.R.G. and other non-Communists to abdicate all leadership to the Communists.

our program is not only paradoxical but presumes an ingenuousness on our part in agreeing to lose the support of what has been the basis of the conquests achieved through that program and regime. This would be equivalent to suicide for the democratic and revolutionary movement of Guatemala.

Arbenz not only permitted the Communists to operate freely, he gave them key posts in the public administration. The National Agrarian Department, charged with carrying out the agrarian reform, was largely under the control of the Communists. Its second-in-command was closely allied with them, if not a secret member of the Party, and a majority of the Agrarian Inspectors, who carried out the actual work of transferring land from the landlord to the peasants, came from the Communists' ranks.

The agrarian reform carried out by the Arbenz government was the most important single aspect of its program. Although they had not been happy about the terms in which it was drawn up, the Communists took full advantage of their key position in its administration to drive home to the peasants receiving land that they owed this gift to the Arbenz government, and more particularly to the Communist Party, which, they said, was the strongest supporter of the agrarian reform program. They were not particularly punctilious about taking over only land which was eligible for expropriation under the terms of the Agrarian Reform Law. Communist Deputy Carlos Manuel Pellecer was particularly active in leading peasants to seize land which was clearly not supposed to be taken over under the law. Through these and other measures, he built up in the Department of Escuintla the most solid stronghold of the Communist Party anywhere in Guatemala.

The Communists also controlled the National Radio Station. An instance of how their control operated occurred during the sessions of the Congress of the National Peasants Confederation (C.N.C.) in March, 1952. The C.N.C. was not under Communist Party control, and the officials of the Radio Station were at first unwilling to broadcast its sessions. At last, however, they agreed to put the opening meeting on the air. The Congress came on the air for the singing of the national anthem, which opened the meeting, and then as soon as the non-Communist C.N.C. Secretary General, Leonardo Castillo Flores, began his opening speech, the session was taken off the air, to return only when Victor Manuel Gutiérrez, Communist Deputy and Secretary General of the General Confederation of Workers, began to give his speech as a fraternal delegate.[18]

The Communists also made headway among the police. Colonels Cruz Wehr and Jaime Rosenberg, in charge of the police under Arbenz, were closely associated with, if not members of, the Communist Party. In the latter months of the Arbenz administration they were particularly active in persecuting enemies of the Communists.

The newspapers of the pro-government parties were all under Communist control. They cooperated fully with the Communists on issues such as "germ warfare in Korea," the "Stockholm Peace Petition," and other international Communist campaigns. So did *Diario de Centro América*, the official daily of the Guatemalan government, until it suspended publication early in 1954.

Leading figures in the Arbenz administration were officials of various Communist "front" groups. The President's wife was head of the National Women's Alliance, affiliated with the Communists' International Federation of Women; Julio de la Hoz, President of Congress, was head of the Communists' Guatemalan Peace Committee, and other leaders of all the government parties were active in this group. In other Communist "transmission belts" there were dignitaries of the Arbenz administration of equal importance.

The Communists thus were able to divert the Guatemalan Revolution from its course and convert it into one more weapon of Soviet foreign policy. In doing so they not only brought disaster to the Revolution, but, for the time being at least, oblivion to themselves. The insurrectionary movement led by Colonel Carlos Castillo Armas, which overthrew the Arbenz government in July, 1954, certainly would not have had the toleration of the United States government and the active cooperation of the Honduran regime, had it not been for the extensive Communist influence in the Arbenz government.

In the months which preceded the downfall of the Arbenz regime widespread terrorism was employed against anti-government elements. One case of this terrorism involved the leaders of the Unión Nacional de Trabajadores Libres, guilty of attempting—without too much success—to organize a rival to the Communist-controlled C.G.T.G., who were suddenly arrested, tortured, and then dumped across the Honduran and Mexican frontiers. A second instance was that of Oscar Luna, head of the so-called Workers' Anti-Communist Committee, who disappeared and the next day was found floating head down in Lake Amatitlán.

During these last months the tension mounted in Guatemala City. The Communists increased their pressure on the government and on the non-Communist groups allied with the Communists. There is little doubt that Communist pressure had much to do with the growing violence of the Guatemalan government's attacks on the government of the United States. Communist influence was undoubtedly decisive, too, in getting the government to acquire the boatload of munitions from behind the Iron Curtain which arrived in March, 1954.

At the same time the Communists were moving to gain absolute control over their partners in the government coalition. They sponsored the formation late in 1953 of a Front of Democratic Parties, apparently patterned on the "popular fronts" established in the "people's democracies" soon after World War II. The four government political parties

—P.A.R., P.R.G., Renovación Nacional, and the Communists—were represented in this Front, as were the Confederation of Workers and the National Peasants Confederation.

In this coalition the Communists automatically controlled two votes—their own and that of the C.G.T.G. In most cases, they could probably have counted on fellow travellers in official positions in a couple of the other parties, and would thus have had a majority. Their confidence that this would be the case was shown by their pressure during the last few months of the Arbenz regime to impose "the discipline of the Front of Democratic Parties" on its constituent organizations.

However, the Castillo Armas revolt occurred before this process had reached its logical conclusion—the formation of a real "people's democracy" in Guatemala. The revolt, beginning early in June, 1954, was launched from Honduran soil by a handful of civilians and ex-Army officers. The rebels captured the city of Chiquimula, but fought few battles.

There is small doubt in the mind of the author that the movement was largely an internal affair. The United States and several neighboring governments had made no secret of the fact that they did not like the Arbenz regime. However, the author has found little evidence that the United States State Department or the United States Embassy in Guatemala City took any active part in producing the "invasion" of the country by Castillo Armas or in securing its triumph,* though there is also small question that the governments of Honduras and Nicaragua did give some help to the invading forces.

The essential reason for the downfall of the Arbenz government was the fact that the Army refused to fight against Castillo Armas. Although the Arbenz regime had done all it could to assure the loyalty of the Army, there were still elements among the high officers who had doubts about the President's cooperation with the Communists. They felt that he had brought the Castillo Armas invasion on himself, and they did not want to fight the rebel group. After much shadowboxing, several of the top-ranking officers finally demanded the resignation of Arbenz. Twenty-four hours later they likewise demanded the resignation of Colonel Díaz, to whom Arbenz had turned over power.

Even before the full triumph of the Castillo Armas movement, the Communist Party was outlawed by the short-lived government of Colonel Enrique Díaz. Although a round-up of Communist leaders was ordered by Díaz, most of them escaped and took refuge immediately in various foreign embassies in Guatemala City. Only Victor Manuel Gutiérrez, among the leading figures of Guatemalan Communism, stayed in hiding for a few weeks, attempting to organize the underground fight against the Castillo

* The author, of course, cannot pass judgment on any activities which secret agencies of the United States Government—such as Military Intelligence or the C.I.A.—may have contributed to this movement.

Armas regime. Late in August, 1954, he also went into the Argentine Embassy and thence into exile.

The result of the success of the Castillo Armas revolt was the destruction, for the time being at least, of all the Communist-controlled organizations in Guatemala. All the front groups were suppressed, as was the Confederación General de Trabajadores. Small-fry Communists were rounded up, given steep jail sentences, or in some instances killed.

Among those Guatemalans who had taken refuge in Mexico after the fall of Arbenz, a split occurred between the Communists and pro-Communists on the one hand and the non-Communists on the other. The latter group saw that the Communists had been to a large extent responsible for driving their government into a position of obstinate and blind opposition to the United States, and within the country had unnecessarily aroused resistance to the regime.

Although President Carlos Castillo Armas was himself a liberal-minded man, the elements around him were principally those who were not only opposed to the Communists, but to the Guatemalan Revolution as well. As a result, the Castillo regime tended to reverse the 1944 Revolution. The agrarian reform was halted, and most of the land expropriated under the Arbenz regime was returned to the landowners. Only a great deal of pressure from abroad kept the government from cracking down once and for all on the labor movement—which was reorganized with an anti-Communist, but radical, leadership.

All the parties which had grown up during the revolutionary period were suppressed. The organizations which took their place were composed principally of "friends of the President." None of the groups which appeared was a defender of the 1944 Revolution.

Whether the Guatemalan Communists would be able to make a comeback with the next turn of political fortune in the country seemed to depend by the end of 1956 on what occurred in the ranks of the opponents of the Castillo Armas government. If they continued their 1944-54 policy of cooperation with the Communists, the latter's future would be a bright one. However, if they learned from the experience of this revolutionary decade that the Communists would betray a national revolution if it suited the convenience of their foreign mentors, a new nationalist democratic Left group might well appear to take the leadership of the Guatemalan social revolution. There was some indication that the non-Communist Left in Guatemala had indeed learned its lesson.

## Chapter XVII

# Coffee, Bananas, and Communism in Central America

THE SIX NATIONS of Central America are among the smallest of the Latin American countries. Theirs are classic examples of "semi-colonial" economies. They are all overwhelmingly agricultural. Four of them gain most of their foreign exchange from the sale of coffee; one depends largely on the export of bananas. The sixth country, Panama, depends principally on the proceeds from the Canal Zone for the purchase of the imports which are fundamental to its economic life.

All but two of the Central American countries have almost unbroken traditions of dictatorial government. Alliances of landowners and military *caudillos* have dominated these four countries virtually since they achieved independence. Only Costa Rica has any deep-rooted tradition of democratic government, while Panama's fifty years of independence have been marked by chronic instability and intermittent dictatorship.

The Central American countries have been involved in the Latin American social revolution. To a greater or less degree, they have begun the attempt to diversify their economies, have enacted labor and social legislation, and have at least incipient labor movements.

The most spectacular Central American incident in the Latin American social revolution occurred in Guatemala, where after 1944 an ambitious program of widespread social change was undertaken. As we have seen, it was sidetracked by the Communists, who by 1954 came virtually to control the course of the Guatemalan Revolution, and were largely responsible for the setback which it suffered with the Castillo Armas "invasion" of July, 1954.

Guatemala is not the only country in Central America where the Communists came near to government power. For a few short years in the middle 1940's they had great influence in Costa Rica, ended only by the civil war of 1948, which brought José Figueres to office for the first time.

In the rest of the Central American isthmus the Communists had by the middle of 1956 made relatively little headway. However, there as elsewhere in Latin America, the future depends on the progress of the Latin American social revolution and the development of non-Communist parties capable of leading it.

## EL SALVADOR

El Salvador is one of the two countries in Latin America where the Communists ever seriously undertook an armed revolution. It was the first Central American country in which they gained appreciable influence. Although the Salvadorean Communist Party has been illegal for all but a few months of its thirty-year history, the Party was for some years in the late 1920's and early 1930's a real force in the political life of the country, and in the last decade it has been a constant preoccupation and cause for uneasiness of the governments of this little coffee republic.

The country is a fertile field for Communist propaganda. The extremes of wealth and poverty are greater in El Salvador than in any other Central American country. The economy is dominated by a tightly knit group of coffee planters who not only control the cultivation of this principal Salvadorean crop, but dominate sugar growing, grazing, and most of the banking system, and whose power is feared by the most independent of cabinet ministers.

There is a large rural proletariat among whom the Communists can carry on their propaganda and organizational activities. Most of the peasants of El Salvador have no land of their own and work as wage laborers on the coffee or sugar or *henequén* plantations belonging to the small group who dominate the nation's economic life. In the cities there is a growing industrial working class, a natural target for the efforts of the Stalinists.

The Communist Party of El Salvador was founded in 1925 as a result of a visit by delegates from the Communist Party of Guatemala, which had been instructed by Communist leaders in Mexico to extend its activities into neighboring republics. Its first adherents were groups of students and workers from San Salvador, the capital.

One of the first steps taken by the small Communist group was to organize an Anti-Imperialist League, which was active throughout the rest of the 1920's and was particularly effective in rallying support among the intellectuals. However, most of the Communists' energies were concentrated in the labor movement. The labor activities of all the Central American Communist Parties were directed by a Consejo Obrero Centro Americano, with headquarters in Guatemala. To this were affiliated a scattering of unions in the various countries of the isthmus.

However, in 1926 a wider field of activity opened up for the Communists in the labor movement of Central America. In that year there was organized the Confederación Obrera Centroamericana (C.O.C.A.), with affiliates in virtually all the Central American republics. It began as a relatively conservative organization and was wooed both by the Pan American Federation of Labor, which paid for the transportation of delegates from various countries, including El Salvador, to the 1927 P.A.F.L. Convention in Washington, and by the International Federation of Trade Unions, the predominantly Socialist trade union group with headquarters in Amsterdam.

The Communists were also active in trying to win over the C.O.C.A. and its affiliated groups. Several of the regional affiliates of the C.O.C.A., including the Federación Regional de Trabajadores de El Salvador, sent delegates to the founding Congress of the Confederación Sindical Latino Americana in Montevideo in May, 1929. The C.O.C.A. virtually ceased to exist after this Congress. With the affiliation of the Federación Regional de Trabajadores de El Salvador to the C.S.L.A., the Communist influence in the organization grew by leaps and bounds.

Communist activities in the unions were coordinated with their activities in other fields. Thus the Federación Regional undertook to patronize the organization of a section of the International Red Aid, the worldwide Communist "Red Cross," established for the legal defense and financial aid of those in their ranks who got into difficulties, an organization of which the International Labor Defense in the United States was an important affiliate. In El Salvador, the I.R.A. took the name of Liga Pro-Luchadores Perseguidos (League for the Defense of Persecuted Fighters). The Federación Regional de Trabajadores gave instructions to its local affiliates to undertake organization of local groups of the Liga Pro-Luchadores Perseguidos throughout the Republic.

The contact between the Salvadorean Communists and the Comintern was close, being maintained particularly through the International Red Aid. Augustín P. Martí, one of the chief Salvadorean Communist leaders, was the Representative of the Caribbean Bureau of the I.R.A. in El Salvador.

The Communists participated in the presidential election of 1930, backing Dr. Arturo Araujo, who was a candidate on the ticket of the Partido Laborista. However, Araujo did not allow himself to fall under Communist influence, and early in 1931 he ordered the arrest of Martí and one or two other Communist leaders.

As a result of Martí's arrest, the Communists issued a violent denunciation of Araujo, labelling his regime "a government of assassins and criminals," and calling all "the workers and poor peasants of the world to demonstrate their solidarity with their brothers of El Salvador." This same manifesto said: "The Communist Party calls all the workers and poor peasants of El Salvador to relentless struggle against the national bourgeoisie, UNCONDITIONAL ALLY OF YANKEE IMPERIALISM, and against its servile instrument: the government which assassinates workers and poor peasants, that of Arturo Araujo."

Partly as a result of this agitation, partly as a result of growing discontent in the Army, the Araujo government was overthrown in December, 1931. He was succeeded by the First Vice President, General Maximiliano Hernández Martínez.

At first Martínez sought to woo the support of the Communists, and permitted them to present candidates under their own name in the municipal and congressional elections held in January, 1932. The Communists claimed to have won these elections, but the government did not so count the ballots. All attempts of the Communist leaders to see General Martínez about the problem were to no avail, and an interview which they had with his Minister of War, Colonel Joaquín Valdés, brought them little satisfaction.

The Communists then determined on a revolutionary attempt to seize power. They had succeeded to a considerable degree in infiltrating the Army, particularly among the enlisted men and noncommissioned officers. (On December 18, 1931, for instance, they had organized a Barracks Committee in the First Cavalry Regiment.) Upon these military supporters they began to base their insurrectionary plans.

On January 9, 1932, the Central Committee of the Communist Party established a Revolutionary Military Committee and set January 22, 1932, as the date for the insurrection. The Revolutionary Military Committee was to function as the General Staff of the Salvadorean Red Army, and "commanders" were named from among the Communist-inclined soldiers in the various regiments and barracks throughout the country. Detailed instructions were sent to these "commanders," notifying them of the date of the intended revolt and informing them that they would get further detailed instructions on that day as to how to proceed.

However, Martínez got wind of what was happening through the Ubico government in Guatemala, which had inadvertently received information and documents concerning the revolutionaries' activities. As a result, Martínez began to move against the would-be rebels. On January 18 a state of siege was proclaimed in San Salvador and the principal departments implicated in the revolt plot. The Communist paper, *Estrella Roja*, was suppressed, and its editors, Mario Zapata and Alfonso Luna, were jailed. The principal Communist military leader, Agustín P. Martí, was captured.

The other Communist leaders, thus caught unawares, attempted to cancel the orders for the uprising, but only succeeded in causing greater confusion. Not all the local groups received these countermanding instructions, and as a result isolated revolts occurred in various parts of the country. There was no such coordination from the center as had been planned, and so, though the revolt was serious, it failed miserably.

Martínez was ruthless in suppressing it. Thousands of peasants were machine-gunned in cold blood. Virtually all the leaders of the Communist Party were captured, court-martialed, and shot. The terrorism of the Martínez government on this occasion is still a vivid memory in El Salvador.

A few Communist chiefs succeeded in escaping, among them the Cuenca brothers, Abel and Max, and the trade union leader, Miguel Mármol, Treasurer of the Federación Regional de Trabajadores. They reached Guatemala, where they were promptly jailed by Dictator-General Ubico.[1]

The suppression of the revolt of 1932 destroyed the Communist Party, all its front organizations, and the labor movement as well, and installed Martínez as dictator of a regime which lasted for a dozen years. It was 1936 before the Communist Party was reorganized. Even then its members operated at great danger to themselves, and there was little field for activity, since the Martínez government did not permit the reorganization of any species of labor movement.[2] It was not until 1942 that the regime allowed the reactivation of the mutual benefit societies and the Communists were again able to conduct their underground activities with some degree of success.[3]

Martínez was finally overthrown by a general strike of students and workers in May, 1944. His downfall was followed by a feverish period of political activity, supposedly leading up to a presidential election. Most of the more advanced political groups supported the candidacy of a mildly leftist teacher, Arturo Romero, and his Partido Unión Democrática; and the Communists, then in the full bloom of wartime "collaboration" with other left-wing forces, also backed Romero.

In the few months during which this campaign flourished, the Communists were particularly active and successful in the labor movement. Trade unions were rebuilt virtually overnight. By October, 1944, the Unión Nacional de Trabajadores, founded after Martínez' downfall, claimed to have 50,000 members in its ranks, including railroaders and truck drivers, textile workers, miners, and factory workers in San Salvador and provincial cities. The U.N.T. was largely under Communist influence and inspiration. Old pre-1932 Communist leaders, including Miguel Mármol, Dagoberto Marroquín, and others, were active in the U.N.T.[4]

However, another setback was experienced in October, 1944, when Colonel Osmín Aguirre, who had been Martínez' Chief of Police, seized power and re-established a dictatorship along the Martínez lines. Under his regime, the trade union movement and virtually all political activity were suppressed. A "government-in-exile" was established in Guatemala, headed by Dr. Miguel Tomás Molina, who had been elected provisional chief executive by the National Assembly, but had not been allowed by Osmín Aguirre to take office.

After some months Osmín Aguirre held elections in which General Castañeda Castro was elected President. During the latter's administration the dictatorship was modified, but the labor movement was not allowed to revive and the Communist Party remained illegal, many of its leaders, including Mármol, going to Guatemala, where Communist activities were getting under way in earnest.

In December, 1948, Castañeda Castro was overthrown by a group of more or less socially minded young officers. One of them, Major Oscar Osorio, was elected President early in 1949. The Osorio regime followed a cautious program of social legislation, establishing a social security system, passing and enforcing factory legislation, and giving discreet encouragement to the trade union movement.

The government after 1949, though carrying out a moderate social program and being sympathetic with organized labor, was very much afraid that the Communist Party would grow to influential proportions once again. This fear was intensified by the rapidly increasing influence of the Communists in neighboring Guatemala under the Arbenz regime.

As a result the Osorio government, although it allowed the reorganization of individual unions, for some time did not permit the formation of national trade unions, and throughout his administration President Osorio refused to give permission for the formation of a central labor organization.

The Osorio administration kept close watch on the Communists. Mármol and other exiled Communist leaders returned to El Salvador during the early years of the regime and were active among the shoemakers and other craft unions. Several times the Communists formed informal central labor groups of their own.

Soon after the 1948 Revolution the Comité de Reorganización Obrera Salvadoreña was established under Communist influence. However, it was officially dissolved by the government a few months after Osorio took the reins of office. In 1951 its place was taken by the Comité Pro-Defensa Derechos Laborales, which was also under Communist influence.

The Communists' strength was greatest in the organizations of small craftsmen, such as the shoemakers, barbers, and others, though they also had considerable influence in the Electrical Workers Union. The two central labor groups established by the Communists, the C.R.O.S. and the C.P.D.D.L., had headquarters in which were located most of the craft union groups of the capital city.

Late in 1952 the government closed the headquarters of the Comité Pro-Defensa Derechos Laborales, declared the Comité itself dissolved, and ordered the arrest of a number of the important Communist trade union leaders. Some of them were subsequently deported to Guatemala. Others returned there on their own initiative, including Miguel Mármol, who by now was the dean of Salvadorean Communist trade unionists. Many Communist labor leaders were jailed, and a number were barbarously treated by the police.[5]

After 1952 the Osorio government did not allow the Communists to establish any other union group. They lost control of many of the unions which had been under their influence, including the electrical workers, and by 1956 their general influence in El Salvador had reached a low ebb.

The Osorio regime realized that mere suppression was no answer to the Communist problem, and its policies were designed to steal the Communists' thunder. Its social program included the construction of a considerable number of workers' homes, the establishment of a social security system, and a sympathetic attitude towards organized labor. The Osorio government also undertook the economic development of the country, through building hydroelectric dams, encouraging further industrialization, and attempting in a small way to diversify agriculture.

However, by the middle of 1955 the Osorio government had not tried to touch the country's major social problem, that of the landless peasants. The power of the landholders was still too great for even a progressively minded regime to dare to come to grips with it. It seemed unlikely, however, that the latent potentialities of Communist growth would be permanently destroyed until something serious was done about this problem. Suppression was but a stopgap, and although the government's social program for the cities was useful in counteracting Communist propaganda there, little had been done to reduce its appeal to the simple, hard-working but landless country folk.

The presidential election of 1956 did not bring any fundamental change in the Salvadorean regime. Lieutenant Colonel José Maria Lemus, a close associate of Colonel Osorio, was the successful nominee. Soon after his inauguration he gave some indication that he would permit the organization of a central labor body, and that his government might undertake a mild program of land distribution to landless peasants, principally with areas still owned by the government. However, there was no indication that the new administration's attitude towards the Communists would be different from that of its predecessor, or that the Lemus government would undertake any fundamental reform program which might end once and for all the potential threat of the Communists.

## HONDURAS

Honduras is the real Banana Barony of Central America. For nearly two generations its economy has been ruled by the growing and exportation of the golden fruit. The country's whole North Coast is dominated by two banana firms, the United and Standard Fruit Companies, which command what are virtually states within a state, not only owning the land, but providing practically all the public and social services and controlling the whole economic and social and, until the 1950's, the political life of the region.

Most of the rest of the country is still primitive. A mountainous nation, Honduras is divided into a series of valleys, separated by low mountain chains. Most of the people live in these valleys, but transportation facilities between them have been scanty, and only in the late 1940's did the government undertake a program of road-building to bind the country together.

The population is centered largely on the North Coast and in the West, near the Salvadorean frontier. Much of the eastern part of the nation, which is flatter and is thought to be potentially good agricultural land, has only a scanty population.

Like most of the Central American countries, Honduras has suffered from an almost interminable series of dictatorships. There has been little opportunity for free development of political parties, Communist or any other kind. After a period of relative freedom in the late 1920's and early 1930's, the 16-year-long dictatorship of Tiburcio Carías Andino blotted out virtually all political activity. Only with the installation of Juan Manuel Gálvez as President, in 1948, did the political atmosphere begin to clear and political activity of all kinds become possible once again.

Functioning in such an atmosphere, the Communist Party of Honduras never achieved the size or influence of its fellow Parties in neighboring Guatemala and El Salvador, though for a few years in the 1920's and 1930's it made some progress, and under Gálvez the Communists again became active.

Communism in Honduras began in the late 1920's, and the first labor organization in which the Communists were reported to have gained some influence was the Railroad Workers Union, established and recognized by the government in 1926. In this period the Communists were also active among the banana workers of the North Coast.

The most picturesque leader of these early Honduran Communists was Juan Pablo Wainwright, the footloose son of an English father and Honduran mother. As a stripling he had gone to the United States, where various misadventures landed him in jail. Some time later he enlisted in the Canadian Army during World War I and fought in France. After his discharge he wandered widely in Europe, Africa, and the Far East, returning home only in 1924.

However, the misfortunes of Honduran politics soon had him on the move again, this time visiting neighboring Guatemala and El Salvador. In the latter country he became a Communist, and in 1928 he returned home once again, this time to throw himself into the work of organizing the banana workers. After leading a violent strike among them in 1930 he was jailed, but succeeded in escaping to Guatemala.

Throughout this period he was a principal figure in Communist activities in Guatemala, El Salvador, and his native country. He was implicated in the Communists' revolutionary attempt in El Salvador in January, 1932, but succeeded in making good his escape to Guatemala. However, there he was captured once again, and was finally executed by the orders of General Ubico.[6]

During the 1920's the most important labor organization in Honduras was the Federación Obrera Hondureña, the local affiliate of the Confederación Obrera Centro Americana. The Communists at first worked inside this group, but unlike their comrades in Guatemala and El Salvador were unable to gain control of the organization. The Federación Obrera refused to join the Communist-dominated continental labor group, the C.S.L.A., and as a result, in 1929, the Communists in conformity with the Comintern's Third Period policy organized their own national labor group, the Federación Sindical Hondureña.

The Federación Sindical was established by a Congress held on May Day, 1929, in Tela on the north coast. It claimed to have within its ranks all the important unions in the country "among them the embattled Unión Ferrocarrilera de Honduras" (the railroad workers' organization). Its headquarters were established in Tegucigalpa, the capital, in the center of the country, although most of its affiliates were on the north coast. The Federación resolved to establish its own paper, *El Trabajador Hondureño*.[7] The chief officials of the Communist union group were Abraham Ramírez, Secretary General, and F. Armando Amaya, its Secretary of Internal Affairs.[8]

The C.S.L.A. headquarters in Montevideo severely criticized the work of the Honduran Communist trade unionists. In correspondence with the C.S.L.A., the Honduran Communists themselves summed up their deficiencies thus:

> . . . the ideological orientation has been diverted in a petty bourgeois and opportunist direction; the base of the F.S.H. is in small industry and the artisan class, etc.; we still have no influence among the agricultural workers of the banana centers of the North Coast; in spite of the fact that it has been in existence for a year, our Federation does not have a really class-conscious attitude; we have not carried out even one of the resolutions of the C.S.L.A.; the way in which we have been asking for labor laws of the State merits the most severe criticism from you.[9]

The second Congress of the Federación Sindical Hondureña, which met on May Day, 1930, tried to remedy these "defects." It resolved to concentrate activities in the banana fields, where "action committees" would be established, since full-scale trade unions were impossible because of "persecution." The Congress also resolved to send a delegate to "the world congress of Moscow."

Soon afterward the Communists made a serious attempt to carry out the decisions of their trade union group. They called a general strike in the banana fields for July 4. But on June 18 the government cracked down on them, and most of the leaders of the F.S.H. were jailed or exiled to desolate and isolated parts of the country.

In spite of this temporary setback, the Communists continued their work. They coordinated their activities closely with those of their comrades in neighboring Guatemala and El Salvador. Six weeks before the attempted Communist revolution in the latter country, the Salvadorean Communist leader Augustín P. Martí wrote Honduran Communist Antonio Gil in Puerto Cortés, Honduras, urging upon him the necessity "to fulfill your promises to our . . . association."[10]

Whether in conjunction with the Salvadorean movement or not, the Communists launched a second general strike among the banana workers of the north coast of Honduras early in January, 1932. President Colindres declared martial law and rushed troops to the area. They and the United Fruit Company's police rounded up the strike leaders and deported them to El Salvador, whence they never returned.

The year 1932 marked the ascension to power in Honduras of President Tiburcio Carías Andino. His regime ruthlessly crushed not only the Communist Party, but all dissident political activities, and completely destroyed the trade union movement. For more than sixteen years the Communist Party of Honduras was driven so far underground as virtually to cease to exist.

It was not until after the inauguration of President Juan Manuel Gálvez, late in 1948, that the political situation in Honduras began to change once more. Moving slowly, Gálvez took steps to allow the reorganization of the political parties. The opposition Liberal Party returned to lusty life, and a new party appeared upon the political horizon, the Partido Revolucionario Democrático Hondureño, usually known by the initials P.R.H.

In the beginning many left-wing Liberals joined this new group, but it soon came under the control of the Communists.[11] Although it was not an avowedly Communist Party, the P.R.H. became the front behind which the Communists worked to rebuild their forces.

As usual, they were active in the labor movement. Although President Gálvez did not allow the reorganization of trade unions until the summer of 1954, numerous mutual benefit societies did appear.

One of these mutualist groups, the Sociedad de Artes Gráficas, was organized in Tegucigalpa in 1949 and began publishing a periodical, *Voz Obrera*. Early in 1950 *Voz Obrera* undertook to establish a labor-organizing committee under the name of Comité de Coordinación Obrera. It included in its ranks the printing-trades workers, the shoemakers, the tailors, and other groups.

*Voz Obrera* meanwhile became increasingly pro-Communist in its orientation. Articles by Vicente Lombardo Toledano appeared, and in various issues the paper announced its adherence to the Communist continental trade union group, the C.T.A.L., and the World Federation of Trade Unions. It also gave great publicity to events in neighboring Guatemala.

In September, 1953, President Gálvez moved against *Voz Obrera* and the P.R.H. The newspaper was suppressed, its principal editors took refuge in the Guatemalan Embassy and left for that country, while the party was outlawed.[12]

Meanwhile the Communists had once again been exceedingly active among the banana workers. There is no doubt that many Hondurans crossed the loosely guarded frontier between Honduras and Guatemala, and received training in the Communist schools in Guatemala City. There they were taught the basic principles of trade union organization, were coached in public speaking, and were indoctrinated with Communist ideas and ideology.

The Honduran Communists got what seemed like their great opportunity in the strike which broke out in the banana fields along the north coast in May, 1954. It is a subject of much controversy whether or not the Communists were responsible for organizing this walkout. President Gálvez asserted to the author that he had proof that the banana strike was originally intended as an attempt to overthrow his government. He claimed that Guatemalan Communist leaders José Manuel Fortuny, Victor Manuel Gutiérrez, and Carlos Manuel Pellecer were in Livingston, near the Honduran frontier, whence they directed the movement. They hoped that Gálvez would move troops in to break the strike, after which the defeated strikers would retreat to the nearby Guatemalan frontier, where arms were to be ready for them, and they would return as a conquering army. Gálvez' refusal to break the strike and the interception of a ship loaded with arms with the destination of Puerto Barrios, Guatemala, impeded the fulfillment of these plans, according to Gálvez. While President Gálvez and the officials of the United Fruit Company maintained that the spark was lit by the Communists, the strike leaders, Communist and non-Communist alike, maintained that the movement was spontaneous.

Whether or not they began it, there is little doubt that pro-Communist elements became the first leaders of the walkout. However, after the strike had been in progress for about a month, these leaders were deposed from the Central Strike Committee, and thereafter the leaders of the strike, and the negotiators of the final settlement, early in July, were strongly opposed to the influence of the Communists and the P.R.H.

After the strike was over, the struggle for control of the newly organized banana workers continued. The Central Trade Union Committee (the old Central Strike Committee), firmly in the hands of the non-Communists, summoned a conference in order formally to organize a union among the United Fruit Company's employees. Its efforts were opposed by the P.R.H. faction.

The P.R.H. leaders controlled the workers' groups in the principal *terminales*, that is, the company towns scattered throughout the U.F.C. holdings. The representation at the union convention was so arranged that the plantation workers, who make up the great majority of the company's employees, were adequately represented.

The founding Conference of the new banana workers' union met on August 28, 1954. Most of the P.R.H. elements boycotted the meeting, and it was completely in the hands of the non-Communists. The P.R.H. elements meanwhile had set about the organization of what would amount to a rival union among the United Fruit workers. The control of the banana workers of the Standard Fruit Company remained firmly in the hands of the non-Communists.

In October, 1954, another threat to the nation's political stability arose as a result of the presidential elections to choose a successor to President Juan Manuel Gálvez. There were three candidates: ex-dictator General Tiburcio Carías Andino of the Nacionalista Party; Abraham Williams of the Reformista Party; and Ramón Villeda Morales of the Liberal Party.

The election campaign took place in a tense atmosphere. Threats of civil war if they lost "unfairly" emanated from all three parties. It seemed almost certain that the election would deteriorate into armed conflict.

Although the Liberal Party received more votes than either of its opponents, and many observers felt that it had really elected its candidate, no nominee was recognized as having received the majority of 51 per cent of the popular vote which was required by the nation's Constitution. The election was thus thrown into Congress, but no party had the two-thirds majority of the house which was necessary for election.

A deadlock thus occurred. President Gálvez took "sick leave" and went to Panama, leaving the presidency in the hands of his Vice President, Juan Lozano. When the constitutional time limit for the election of a President was reached, Acting President Lozano declared a "constitutional dictatorship." Announcing that no new chief executive had been elected, he declared that the newly elected Congress was dissolved and that he would continue in office for two years, after which he would call new elections for both the presidency and Congress.

This solution of the crisis was accepted by all parties. The Acting President was able to form a three-party Cabinet in which the key posts were held by members of the Liberal Party. A National Consultative Assembly, also composed of members of all three parties, was set up as a substitute for Congress.

A resort to arms was thus avoided. Honduran politicians of all three major parties showed a maturity of political judgment which was new to Honduran politics.

However, a new crisis occurred in October, 1956. President Lozano had decided to stay in power, in spite of his promises not to do so when he originally took over two years before. He presided over elections for a constitutional assembly, which were unanimously won by Lozano's supporters, who had announced in advance that they intended to name the Provisional President as constitutional chief executive.

After a few days of protest by the forces opposed to Lozano—the Liberals and the Nationalist followers of ex-dictator Carias—the President was overthrown by a military coup. The members of the new junta announced that they had seized power because of the fraudulent nature of the elections presided over by Lozano and the fact that the majority of the people were opposed to his regime.

The Communists played no part in this political crisis. The peaceful resolution of the situation prevented them from capitalizing on a civil war, which might well have given them a chance to offer "support" to one faction or another, thus enabling them for the first time to become a significant factor in the nation's public life.

Whether or not the Communists would continue to be a minor element in Honduran politics seemed to depend upon the general development of the country's civic life. A peaceful evolution toward free elections and regularized constitutional government would probably prevent their gaining any real significance.

Although for the first time in many years the Communists had an important base among the banana workers of the north coast, they were faced with a serious opponent in the Liberal Party. Although one of the nation's traditional parties, the Liberals developed a new, younger, more socially minded leadership during the Gálvez administration. These leaders supported the banana workers' strike in the summer of 1954, and aroused the imagination and support of most of the banana workers and of many workers and peasants in the rest of the country. By the middle of 1955 they seemed likely to be able to forestall any considerable growth by the Communists, working through the Partido Revolucionario Hondureño.

## NICARAGUA

Two names have dominated the history of Nicaragua for the last generation: Agusto Sandino and Anastasio Somoza. The first was a military man and politician who achieved world-wide fame when he resisted for half a dozen years the incursions of United States Marines, in the last of the century-long series of United States military interventions in the small Central American republic. The second was the man who seized control of his nation's government after the Marines left and was able to maintain that control for more than two decades.

Sandino became a hero for all those elements, both inside and outside of Latin America, who in the 1920's were opposed to the United States pre-Good-Neighbor policy of open, armed intervention in the internal affairs of its Latin American neighbors. Whether Sandino was indeed a hero or merely a grandiose bandit is still a subject of fervent discussion in Nicaragua itself.

The Communist International attempted to capitalize upon the exploits of Sandino during the late 1920's and early 1930's. There were very few Communists in Nicaragua itself, but abroad the Communists for a while looked upon Sandino as virtually the incarnation of "anti-imperialism." They tried to "capture" him, and when they finally failed to do so, they turned violently against him.

The Sixth Congress of the Communist International, meeting in Moscow in 1928, adopted a resolution proposed by the Communist Parties of the United States and Mexico, which started off: "The Sixth World Congress of the Communist International sends fraternal greetings to the workers and peasants of Nicaragua, and the heroic army of national emancipation of General Sandino, which is carrying on a brave, determined struggle with the imperialism of the United States." It called upon "all working-class organizations, and the entire proletariat of all countries" to support Sandino.[13]

The Communists organized a Hands Off Nicaragua Committee (generally known by its Spanish initials as "Mafuenic"), in the name of which they carried on a continent-wide fund-raising campaign. They attempted to picture this Committee as the only organization authorized by Sandino to raise funds on his behalf, whereas, in fact, he had an official agent in Mexico, Pedro José Zepeda, who was his authorized representative for fund-raising and all other activities.

The Communists did all they could to discredit Dr. Zepeda. They circulated false rumors to the effect that he had misappropriated funds which he had raised on behalf of Sandino. When Dr. Zepeda sent a considerable amount of money from Mexico to Sandino, *El Machete*, the Mexican Communist Party paper, reported that the money had been raised and sent by Mafuenic, not by Zepeda.

Mafuenic actually raised a paltry $1000 for Sandino. It was sent to Nicaragua via Gustavo Machado, the Venezuelan exile who was later to become a leading figure in the Communist Party of his native country. However, Machado is reported to have spent $400 of this sum for his trip from Mexico to Nicaragua, and to have asked Sandino for $350 more for the costs of his return. Sandino authorized the Communists to spend the remaining $250 for the publication of a pamphlet on his behalf, a pamphlet which Víctor Alba maintains never appeared.

When Sandino made a trip to Mérida, Mexico, in 1929 to confer with ex-President Plutarco Elías Calles, the Communists tried to dissuade the Nicaraguan, arguing that Calles was urging him to come to Mérida in order to poison him. As a result of this "misunderstanding," Sandino fired his private secretary, the Salvadorean Communist leader, Augustín Martí.

The Communists succeeded for a while in "capturing" Sandino's brother, Sócrates. They paraded him around their meetings in Mexico and neighboring countries and used him to give the impression that they and only they were defending Sandino. However, Sócrates broke with them over a rumor, first circulated by the Communists, that the guerrilla chief had accepted a bribe of $60,000 from the United States Government to lay down his arms. The Communists themselves were forced to have the Anti Imperialist League "investigate" this rumor and "clear" Sandino of the charge.

Relations between Sandino and the Communists continued to grow worse. Sandino denounced their activities "on his behalf" in a letter to Hernán Laborde, then Secretary General of the Mexican Communist Party, dated January 2, 1930. From April, 1930, on, Sandino had no further correspondence with them.[14]

Soon after United States troops were withdrawn from Nicaragua, Sandino agreed to cease his operations and make peace with the government. Then the Communist International turned savagely on its erstwhile hero. The Comintern organ, *International Press Correspondence,* on March 24, 1933, accused him of "betrayal of the Nicaraguan independence movement," and commented that Sandino's insistence on confining his struggle merely to a fight against invading United States troops "was bound to lead to his finally betraying the movement."

There were few Communists in Nicaragua at this time, and as late as May 20, 1935, the periodical, *Communist International,* reported that there was no Communist Party in that country. However, a number of the country's handful of Communists were arrested by President Sacasa at the time of Sandino's surrender.[15]

Throughout most of the 1930's the Nicaraguan Communists operated within the Partido de Trabajadores Nicaraguenses, which maintained friendly relations with the Communist International.[16] In 1937 this party split over the issue of supporting the presidential candidacy of General Anastasio Somoza.[17]

Somoza had been one of the principal figures in the National Guard, the army which the United States Marines organized to fight Sandino. He was widely regarded as having been responsible for the assassination of Sandino when the rebel came into the capital city to discuss the terms of his surrender. By the end of 1936 Somoza had maneuvered himself into control of the government and now sought to assume the presidency formally.

The Communist faction in the Partido de Trabajadores Nicaraguenses, led by Juan Lorio, Manuel Pérez Estrada, Carlos Pérez Bermúdez, Augusto Lorio, and Armando Amador, withdrew from the party and established their own organization, the Partido Socialista.* [18] The first Secretary General of the party seems to have been Francisco Hernández Segura, who was editor of a paper, *Senderos*.[19]

In 1939 the Partido Socialista was closed down by the Somoza government, and many of its leaders fled into exile. One of them, Armando Amador, went to Costa Rica, where he played an important role in the Costa Rican Communist Party.[20]

After Russia's entry into the second World War the Nicaraguan Communists followed the general international policy of making friends with any Latin American ruler who would proclaim himself on the side of the United Nations, something which Somoza had hastened to do soon after the entry of the United States into the conflict. The first step towards a rapprochement between Somoza and the Communists was a visit which Lombardo Toledano, head of the Communist-controlled Confederación de Trabajadores de América Latina, made to Nicaragua in the course of a tour around Latin America in May, 1943. During this visit he not only conferred at length with both the Central Committee and the Executive Committee of the Partido Socialista, but he also conferred with President Somoza, spoke over the government radio, and reviewed a parade of the members of Somoza's Liberal Party.[21]

Apparently on this visit Lombardo convinced the Nicaraguan chief executive that it would be to his advantage to allow the organization of a labor movement under Partido Socialista control, and to give the Partido Socialista itself more freedom of operation. In any case, in May, 1944, a national labor congress met in Nicaragua. The pro-Communist *Allied Labor News* of May 3, 1944, reported this congress as being "sponsored" by Somoza, who addressed the gathering and announced that he was going to promulgate the country's first Labor Code. The three hundred delegates present founded the Confederación de Trabajadores de Nicaragua.

The C.T.N. was very successful. It succeeded in organizing regional labor federations not only in Managua, but in the departments of Matagalpa, Granada, León, Corinto, and Chinandega. It organized virtually all the country's urban wage workers.

The Partido Socialista, with Juan Lorio now Secretary General, became strong. It completely controlled the trade unions, as was shown by the fact that Blas Roca, member of the Politburo of the Cuban Communist Party, was the official guest of the C.T.N. at a reception in the Casa

---

* The Communist International now being in its Popular Front stage, it was no longer required that all Communist Parties adopt the Communist label.

Obrera, a building constructed by the Somoza government for the C.T.N. to use as its headquarters.

Communist fractions operated in most of the unions, and were able to control most of the unions' activities. Within the unions the members of the Partido Socialista held key posts controlling membership records and finances of the organizations.[22]

By the end of World War II the Somoza regime was in serious difficulties. As was true of most of the other dictators of Latin America, Somoza's position had been greatly weakened by the victory of the United Nations in a war fought under slogans of democracy and freedom, in spite of the fact that Somoza's regime had itself been a member of the United Nations. The Nicaraguans, like the Brazilians, Peruvians, and others, felt that if democracy was worth fighting about in Europe or Asia, it was something worth practicing in their own country.

In seeking popular support, Somoza tried to make a deal with the Communists. He permitted for the first time the open organization and propaganda of the Partido Socialista, which held its first public meeting in the Gimnasio Nacional on July 6, 1946.

There is considerable evidence available that during this period the Communists were very well financed, and that their funds came from abroad. There are indications that these funds came from the Soviet Embassy in Mexico City, though they were sent through El Salvador, with checks to leaders of the Partido Socialista of Nicaragua being drawn on a Salvadorean bank.[23]

The Communists made the most of the opportunity to function without government interference. By December, 1946, they claimed 1500 members and the support of 25 per cent of the electorate.[24]

Since Somoza relied considerably on the Partido Socialista for support, the Communists began to press him for influence within the government. They wanted government jobs, and even put in a bid for seats in Congress. However, Somoza resisted this pressure.

At the same time the opposition, which was preparing for the elections of 1947, also sought the Communists' support. It offered to name six Communists on its ticket for members of the Chamber of Deputies, including Juan Lorio and Armando Amador. In the end the Communists threw their support to the opposition candidate, Enoch Arguedo.

Since Somoza counted the votes, his candidate, Dr. Leonardo Arguello, won the election. Arguello was an old man, who had been a perennial candidate for the presidency. He was no friend of Somoza, but apparently the dictator felt the need for naming someone who would appear to be a genuine democrat. Somoza apparently felt that he could control Arguello, though he soon found out that such was not the case. Arguello, immediately upon being inaugurated, turned against his sponsor and attempted to launch the government on an independent, anti-Somoza policy.

The Communists supported him in these efforts. A commission of the Party, consisting of Federico Hernández Segura and Salvador Cuadro, leader of the Commercial Employees Union, waited upon Arguello and offered him their support. The Army at this time was divided, and the Communists—along with many other political observers—felt that Arguello stood a better than fair chance of triumphing over Somoza.

However, Arguello lasted less than a month. He was overthrown by Somoza, who had remained Commander-in-Chief of the National Guard. All factions of the Liberal Party came to Somoza's support, and an attempted demonstration in favor of Arguello, supported by the Partido Socialista, was a failure.

Relations between the Communists and Somoza worsened rapidly. Finally, in January, 1948, at a meeting of the Executive Committee of the Party, at which Armando Amador, who had recently been in Guatemala, was giving a report on instructions he had received there, the police broke in and arrested all the top leaders. At the same time the Confederación de Trabajadores de Nicaragua was dissolved by the government, and all its leaders were arrested.[25]

For almost a year the labor movement and the Communist Party remained dormant. The principal leaders were in jail, and neither the Party nor the unions could function. However, near the end of 1948, through the intervention of two Argentine Labor Attachés who were then in Managua, a group of leading trade union figures was brought together, and a new central labor group was founded, the Confederación General de Trabajadores.[26]

The Communists soon came to dominate the new C.G.T. They succeeded in getting the organization to go on record against the United Nations action in Korea and to take other decidedly Communist positions. However, at the end of 1950 a revolt against Communist influence in the C.G.T. ranks succeeded in ending their control of the organization. The C.G.T. from that time on became a Peronista-inclined group.

The Communists, having lost control of the C.G.T., formed their own trade union central organization, the Unión General de Trabajadores, which, however, was unable to get legal recognition, and was the smallest of the Nicaraguan central labor groups.* It contained shoemakers, printing-trades workers, mosaic workers in Managua, and several agricultural laborers' groups.

Some of the Communist-controlled unions were legally recognized by the government. However, when a group of them endorsed a Communist

---

* As a result of splits in the C.G.T., there were also formed in the early 1950's the Confederación Nacionalista de Trabajadores Democráticos, the Comité Democrático de Sindicatos Libres, and the independent Federación de Transportadores Unidos de Nicaragua. All of these had friendly relations with the O.R.I.T., while the C.G.T. joined the Peronista continental labor group, the A.T.L.A.S.

"peace" petition, and this endorsement was published in the Partido Socialista's illegal newspaper, *Orientación,* the government withdrew this
recognition.[27]

In mid-1956 the Partido Socialista de Nicaragua was still illegal and
persecuted by the government. The trade union central organization under its control was also illegal. The Communists thus had been reduced,
for the time being, to a relatively unimportant factor in the country's
political life. Their attempt to work with the local dictator had failed,
largely due to their own mistaken analysis of the strength of the dictatorial regime.

The assassination of President Anastasio Somoza late in 1956 presaged
fundamental changes in the Nicaraguan regime. However, at the time this
is being written it is too early to say whether these alterations will make
the task of the Communists in Nicaragua easier or more difficult.

## COSTA RICA

Although the Communist Party of Costa Rica has had its ups and
downs, and at the time this book is being written is of relatively minor
importance in the country's politics, its history is of peculiar interest for
several reasons. It provides an early demonstration of the ability of the
Communists to use friendly relations with a government to entrench
themselves in the public administration. It was particularly notable because of the Communists' attempt—largely successful for a short time—
to cultivate friendship with the Church. Finally, it presents a good illustra-
tion of the fact that the best and only sure way to defeat the Communists
is through a movement of social reform which actually does some of the
good things the Communists, as a means of getting to power, promise to
do.

Costa Rica is a small country of less than a million people. Unlike
most of the Central American countries, it has a population made up
largely of small farmers, living on the country's central plateau, which,
because it is several thousand feet above sea level, has a temperate climate.
On both coasts there are tropical areas, where the banana industry has
developed.

The people of Costa Rica are largely of Spanish extraction, though
there are sizable groups of Negroes and Nicaraguan mestizos on the two
coasts. The nation is comparatively little industrialized, and only in recent
years have urban social problems become a pressing matter. Labor relations problems in the banana industry date back farther.

Costa Rica has democratic traditions of long standing, and has prided
itself for a considerable time on the fact that it possessed more public
school teachers than members of its armed forces. The temper of the
people has long been conservative, and only in the last two decades have

social problems begun to grow acute. The Communists were the first to profit from this change.

The Communist Party of Costa Rica was founded in 1929 by Manuel Mora, a young university student, barely nineteen years of age. For a decade after it was established the Communist Party was virtually the only outspoken supporter of the rights of the workers, the small peasants, and the downtrodden in general. Mora and his Party captured the support of intellectually curious and socially conscious university students throughout most of the 1930's. They also succeeded in building up a certain base among the artisans of San José and provincial towns and the banana workers of the ubiquitous United Fruit Company.

Soon after the founding of the Party, the Communists began to organize trade unions in San José. The first group they succeeded in establishing was the Carpenters Union, and in 1930 Mora founded the Unión General de Trabajadores, as the country's first central labor organization. However, it did not last long.

In 1930 Mora began his work in the banana fields on the Atlantic Coast. Here, in the great holdings of the United Fruit Company, were the only true "proletarians" of Costa Rica at that time, large numbers of wage workers, laboring for a common employer and with common grievances. The organization of these workers presented many problems, not only because of Company opposition and government suspicion, but because of rivalries among various groups of workers. Most of the United Fruit employees were foreigners—either English-speaking Jamaicans, brought in in the early days of the Company's operations, or Nicaraguans, who came to the plantations to work a bit later. These groups were suspicious of one another, and both were unfriendly toward the native Costa Ricans.

In spite of these difficulties, Mora and the other Communists were able to achieve a certain degree of organization among the workers. The first test of this union came in 1934, when the country's first major strike hit the United Fruit Company. Nearly all the workers—some 15,000 in number—participated in the walkout.

The strike was led by Mora, who had the year before been elected the first Communist member of the Costa Rican Congress. The list of demands which he and other union leaders presented to the Company and the small planters working for the Company sought the abolition of payment of the workers by tokens cashable only at company stores, the improvement of housing conditions, provision of anti-snake-bite serum and quinine at readily available spots on all plantations, and other general improvements.

Mora, as leader of the strike, had several interviews with President Ricardo Jiménez, whom Mora in later years characterized as "one of the real liberals in the history of Costa Rica." In their first talk, Jiménez admitted to Mora that Mora could undoubtedly overthrow Jiménez if he wanted to, but that a Communist government would not last more than a week. Mora denied any such intentions and said he was merely leading the banana workers in a justified economic strike.

The walkout went on for a month, and after a second interview between the President and the Communist leader, Jiménez ordered the Company to negotiate with the workers. It agreed to do so, but balked when the workers named Manuel Mora as their chief representative. However, the Company finally agreed to accept whatever terms the small banana planters were willing to agree to, and the walkout was brought to a successful conclusion.[28]

At this time the Costa Rican Communist Party was recognized as a "fraternal member" of the Communist International. In this capacity it was one of ten Communist Parties to sign a manifesto supporting the Cuban Revolution, which had overthrown Gerardo Machado, and urging the establishment of a Soviet Government in Cuba.[29]

One of the early leaders of the Costa Rican Communist Party was a young exile from Venezuela, Rómulo Betancourt. A student leader in his own country, Betancourt had been exiled by the tyranny of Juan Vicente Gómez and had sought refuge in the little Central American republic. A few years older than Mora, he quickly took a leading position among the Costa Rican Communists.

Betancourt urged the withdrawal of the Costa Rican Communist Party from the Comintern and its reorganization as a purely national group. In later years Betancourt maintained that even Mora favored this action at the time.[30] However, with the resignation of Betancourt from the party in 1935 the move was dropped, and in the Seventh Congress of the Communist International in August, 1935, the Costa Rican Party was accepted as a member of the International.[31]

In spite of their success in organizing the banana workers, the Communists did not make any spectacular political gains during the rest of the 1930's. Although Mora was regularly reelected to Congress, the Communists did not add to their representation there. The withdrawal of the United Fruit Company from operations along the Atlantic Coast of Costa Rica made it impossible for the Communists to consolidate the gains they had made in that part of the country as a result of the 1934 strike.

However, in the early 1940's the Communist Party began to make strides both as to numbers and influence. This was due to a variety of circumstances. Among the most important factors was the alliance which was formed between the Communists and President Rafael Calderón Guardia.

Calderón Guardia was elected President in 1940. He was a doctor of medicine who had gained great popularity through his work among the poorer elements of the population of San José. As President, he quickly lost his popularity. Rumors of graft in his administration were widespread, and in any case Calderón suffered from the swing of the political pendulum—almost any Costa Rican government becomes unpopular after a longer or shorter period in office.

As a result of his loss of popular backing, Calderón Guardia looked around for new allies. The most useful prospects were the Communists. They were already strong supporters of his regime, in accordance with the wartime policy of the Communist International, after the entry of Russia into the second World War, of supporting any government in Latin America which backed the Allied war effort. Calderón Guardia and Mora spoke from the same platform at a war rally right after Costa Rica's entry into the conflict in December, 1941. Costa Rica was the first American country officially to enter World War II, declaring war, on December 7, 1941, even before the United States Congress did.

There is no doubt that the Communists had great influence in the administrations of Calderón Guardia and his successor, Teodoro Picado. They became close advisors of the President on political affairs as well as on social and economic matters. They deserve much of the credit for the passage of the Labor Code, for the establishment of a social security system, for the enactment of workmen's compensation, for the inauguration of an income tax. They had a key role not only in proposing these measures, but in setting up and administering the organizations to carry them out.

Communist political influence grew with association with the government. By 1945 there were four Communist members of Congress, and by 1948 their number had increased to seven.[32]

The Costa Rican Communists followed the wartime policy of many American Communist Parties in changing their name so as to make themselves more acceptable to other left-wing and to moderate elements. On June 13, 1943, a National Conference of the Party was called by the Politburo, and it resolved to "dissolve" the Communist Party and to found a new organization, to be labelled Vanguardia Popular. Manuel Mora remained the Secretary General in the new party, and virtually all the old leaders retained their posts.

The program of the "new" party was moderate and mentioned nothing about the class struggle, the socialization of the means of production, or other parts of the orthodox Communist program. Instead, it called for a limited agrarian reform, the guarantee of agricultural prices, the launching of an economic development plan.

The party announced its support of "the social policy of President Calderón Guardia, based on the Papal Encyclicals, and the promulgation of a Labor Code which will guarantee to the workers of city and country their rights without hindering the development of industry or of agriculture."

In the international field it urged "profound and constant collaboration with the United States and the other powers which are confronting in the field of battle Nazi Fascist savagery, formulating with the United States treaties guaranteeing the political and economic independence of the country after the war. . . ."[33]

This change in the party's name and modification of its program won the approval of wide segments of the community. President Calderón Guardia, in an interview with the United Press on December 26, 1943, commented that "Costa Rica never will be a Communist menace in Central America" and stressed that Vanguardia Popular was not a Communist group.

Most striking was the attitude of the Catholic Church toward the rechristened party. Archbishop Víctor Sanabria, the head of the Church in Costa Rica, commented that "The substitution of the Vanguardia Popular for the Communist Party constitutes an event of great importance and merits the applause and gratitude of their fellow citizens."[34]

Subsequently Sanabria went a good deal further than this statement. He was a man of social conscience, who realized that Costa Rica was destined to go through social changes, and apparently at this time he hoped that if the Communists could be separated from the International and made a genuinely Costa Rican party, they might be the means of bringing about these changes.

Vanguardia Popular sought the tolerance, if not the active support, of the Church hierarchy. It addressed a letter to Sanabria, the key sentence of which was a question: "Do you believe, Señor Archbishop, that there exists any obstacle to a Catholic citizen's collaborating or allying himself with the Partido Vanguardia Popular?"

To this question, Archbishop Sanabria sent a long reply, which read in part:

> There was in Costa Rica a party called the Communist Party which had a leader and a program. In this, according to the claims of its leader several times in his speeches and his writings, and as he demonstrated with documents which merit our good faith, nothing was contained which imperiled religion or which opposed the Catholic conscience . . . but the dissolved party had a name, that of the Communist Party, a name which in Costa Rica and everywhere else the Church has to interpret as a program, and as a program the synthesis of whose ideas are condemned by the Church many times, in official documents of great solemnity. . . . The Party decided to dissolve as a party and then form a new group which neither in its name nor in its program contains anything which signifies the word COMMUNIST. . . . The chief of the new party is neither in a worse nor a better condition in abstract and theoretical terms, than the chiefs of the other parties. His proposals, or rather, those of his party are those

which would conform to the Constitution and the laws with the same will . . . as the other parties.

After citing the Vanguardia Popular statement in favor of the Papal Encyclicals, Sanabria went on: [35]

> Can I condemn the new Party? No, I cannot condemn it. And if I condemned it I should have to give reasons for condemning it and I do not have any. . . . I am not saying to Catholics that they should enter this or any other party, or that they should not enter this or any other political group. All of the parties start at the same place as does the Partido Vanguardia Popular.

This position of the Church was no doubt of considerable help to the Communists during World War II in gaining adherents among the workers. For the first time they were able to establish a successful national central labor organization. On October 4, 1943, the Confederación de Trabajadores de Costa Rica was organized, at a convention of delegates who claimed to represent 96 unions and 10,000 workers. [36]

The close connection between the new C.T.C.R. and the Vanguardia Popular was clear from the leadership of the two groups. The Secretary General of the C.T.C.R., Rodolfo Guzmán, was also Trade Union Secretary of Vanguardia Popular; the Secretary of Propaganda of the Party was C.T.C.R. Secretary of Organization for the Pacific Zone; and the Agrarian Secretary of the Party was also Secretary of Agrarian Affairs of the C.T.C.R.

In the election of 1944, in which Calderón Guardia's candidate, Teodoro Picado, was victorious over ex-President León Cortés, the Communists were members of the triumphant government coalition, along with Calderón's National Republican Party. [37]

Relations between the Calderón regime and the opposition had been growing worse for some time. In 1942 José Figueres, an engineer and one of the country's leading agriculturalists, was exiled, after he had given a series of radio speeches in which he denounced the alleged corruption of the Calderón regime. He returned to manage León Cortés' campaign in 1944.

The situation did not improve after the 1944 election. In February, 1944, the country's principal newspaper, *Diario de Costa Rica*, owned by Otilio Ulate, announced that it and the daily, *La Hora*, were closing down indefinitely because "Costa Rica has entered a dictatorial regime, in which the Communist Party shares authority." [38] Two years later the opposition claimed that the government won the congressional election by foul means.

As the time of the 1948 presidential election approached, tension between the government and the opposition mounted. In the summer of 1947 there occurred a general strike in San José, supported by most of the merchants and by the "Rerum Novarum" trade union confederation, the chief rival of the Communists' C.T.C.R. in the labor field.

This movement was brought to an end by an accord for the conduct of the 1948 elections. It was agreed that the administration of the poll would be placed in the hands of an independent, three-man Election Tribunal, one member of which would be named by the President of the Republic, one by the Congress, one by the Supreme Court.[39] The presidency and the Congress were both controlled by the Calderón Guardia forces.

Calderón was a candidate for re-election in 1948. His opponent was Otilio Ulate, publisher of *Diario de Costa Rica.* When the votes were counted by the Election Tribunal, the majority were certified to favor Ulate.

The Calderonistas, who controlled Congress, decided to nullify the verdict of the Electoral Tribunal. Although Calderón has been reported as willing at first to accept the results of the election, Manuel Mora is credited with having persuaded him to change his mind.[40] Mora denies this, saying that he advised Calderón to accept the Electoral Tribunal decision, since the Calderonistas, with their majority in Congress, could make the new administration follow its wishes.[41]

With the nullification of the election of Ulate by the Calderonista Congress, civil war broke out in Costa Rica. The leader of the movement was José Figueres, who had returned home in 1944 and from then on had been a leading figure in the opposition. The war lasted for about one month, during which time the government forces in San José were divided among the Calderonistas, the personal followers of President Picado, and the Communists.

The forces of Figueres won the war. In the negotiations which put an end to the conflict an agreement was signed between the representative of the Figueres forces and Manuel Mora, promising that the new regime would carry on the social policies begun by Calderón Guardia and continued by the Picado administration. Subsequently, it was claimed that the Figuerista representative had agreed that no harm would come to Vanguardia Popular. The truth seems to be that no such assurance was given, but that the Communist leaders were forced to tell their followers such an agreement had been made, in order to get them to lay down their arms.[42]

The revolutionaries established what they called the Junta de Gobierno de la Segunda República, which stayed in power for 18 months and then handed the presidency over to Otilio Ulate, elected in the 1948 poll. This Junta decreed several measures which did great damage to the Communist Party.

The Figueres government officially dissolved the Communist Party (Vanguardia Popular), and the Costa Rican Supreme Court decreed the end of the Confederación de Trabajadores. A Constituent Assembly elected under the Junta's auspices wrote into the new Constitution an article making it unconstitutional for any future regime to recognize the Communist Party as a registered political organization.

Many of the Communist leaders went into exile during the Junta period, and the Communist-controlled labor movement was demoralized. Some of the unions formerly belonging to the C.T.C.R. joined the Confederación Costarricense del Trabajo "Rerum Novarum," the anti-Communist trade union group, whose Secretary General, Father Benjamín Núñez, became Minister of Labor in the Junta administration.

With the inauguration of President Otilio Ulate in November, 1949, restrictions on the Communists were relaxed. The exiled Communist leaders, including Manuel Mora, returned from exile. The Communists renewed activity in the trade union field and soon re-established regional federations in the principal provinces of the Republic.[43] They regained considerable strength in the southern part of the Pacific Coast banana fields. In 1953 they finally succeeded in re-forming a central labor body, the Confederación General de Trabajadores.

The Communists played no independent role in the 1953 presidential elections. They first attempted to establish a "front" party, under the name of Partido Progresista Independiente. Although no leading figures in the Communist movement appeared as founders of this organization, it was finally denied recognition by the Electoral Tribunal, on the grounds of its being a Communist-controlled group and thus unconstitutional.[44]

When it became impossible to have a candidate of their own, the Communists backed Fernando Castro Cervantes, who also had the support of Calderón Guardia and of some close associates of retiring President Otilio Ulate.

The victor in the 1953 election was the old enemy of the Communists, José Figueres. After retiring from the presidency of the Junta de Gobierno late in 1949, Figueres set about the organization of a political movement which would bring him and his associates back into control of the government. The Figueristas attempted to organize an ideological party, a party which was not merely the personal vehicle of a political leader, but a principled party, with a platform and program of government—the second such attempt in Costa Rican history, the first having been made by the Communist Party.

During the year and a half of the Junta, the Figueristas had given evidence of their progressive orientation. They had nationalized the country's banks, imposed a capital levy, and renegotiated the government's contract with the United Fruit Company. They had established a system of guaranteed prices for the country's farmers.

While out of the government, Figueres and his associates developed a wider and more extensive program, including plans for economic development, public housing, electric power development, amplification of the country's labor and social security legislation, and renegotiation once again of the contract under which the United Fruit Company operates in the country. They organized the Partido Liberación Nacional as their ideological party.

This program and the character of José Figueres ("Don Pepe," as most Costa Ricans called him) won the overwhelming support of the people of Costa Rica. The Communists whose influence had been growing rapidly throughout most of the 1940's, were stopped in their tracks. This was due much more to the fact that Figueres and his group captured the imagination of many of those workers and small peasants who had turned toward the Communists during the early 1940's than to the relatively mild persecution which the Communists suffered during the Junta government and the prohibition on presentation of Communist candidates under the 1949 Constitution.

The future of the Costa Rican Communist Party thus depended by the middle of 1956 on the success of the Figuerista movement. Like similar "Aprista" parties in other countries, the Partido Liberación Nacional had proved its ability to undermine the Communists by presenting the workers and peasants with a program couched in national terms for the solution of the nation's principal economic and social problems through democratic procedures. The degree of success of the Aprista party in carrying out its promises was likely to determine whether or not the Communists would once again become an important factor in the political life of Costa Rica.

## PANAMA

No country could have more strategic value for the Communists than Panama. Sitting as it does astride the "Big Ditch," Panama is of key importance to the defense of the United States and the whole Western Hemisphere, and a strong Communist Party there would be an important potential ally of the Soviet Union in case of hostilities with the United States.

However, the Communist Party of Panama is surprisingly small. It has never been a major force in the political life of the Republic, has never even elected a member of the National Assembly. In spite of widespread anti-Yanqui feeling and resentment against racist and domineering attitudes adopted by authorities of the Canal Zone, Communism has never found fertile soil in Panama.

The small size of the working class in Panama and the importance of the workers of the Zone, who might be reluctant to be mixed up in Communist activities because of the peril to their jobs, perhaps help to explain this paradox. Important, too, is the fact that most Panamanians have either supported the country's traditional political parties or, when they broke away from their allegiance to them, supported non-Communist movements which promised most of the things the Communists offer, but had no connection with Moscow.

The first Communist group in the country was the Partido Laborista, formed in 1925 after a strike in which Communist prapaganda first appeared. It was established on the initiative of the Sindicato General de Trabajadores. The party was a fraternal affiliate of the Communist International, but was described by its delegate to the 1929 Continental Communist Congress in Buenos Aires as "not completely Communist."[45]

The Partido Laborista entered candidates in the 1928 election and received one thousand votes in the city of Colón. However, although the Communists claimed that they received enough votes to elect two members of the National Assembly, no Partido Laborista candidate was certified as having been victorious.

Fear was expressed during the Buenos Aires Comintern Congress that "This party will escape from Communist control." As a result of this fear, and in conformity with Communist International policy during the Third Period, the Communist Party of Panama was officially organized in 1930. One of its leaders, Eliseo Echévez, was sent to Moscow to confer with the leaders of the Comintern.

Early in 1929 the Communists took the lead in organizing a new central labor group for the Republic. Most of the country's handful of unions were in the new organization, the Confederación Sindical de Obreros y Campesinos de Panamá, which joined the Confederación Sindical Latino Americana. The groups affiliated included carpenters, journalists, painters, shoemakers, maritime workers, and a few agricultural workers' groups, 14 unions in all.[46]

The Communists used the trade unions under their control to give more of an appearance of solidity to their political activities. Thus in June, 1930, the Confederación Sindical joined with the Communist Party and a few independent unions and agricultural workers' organizations to form a Workers and Peasants Bloc, for political purposes.[47]

In 1933 a new force entered the labor movement to challenge the Communists' domination. The Socialist Party of Panama was established under the leadership of Demetrio Porras, the son of a onetime President of the Republic. Throughout the 1930's it fought with the Communists for control of the country's small trade union movement. Sometimes both sides resorted to violence.[48]

In the late 1930's still another political group entered the scene to steal much of the Communists' thunder. This was the party of Arnulfo Arias, brother of ex-President Harmodio Arias, who gained popularity with a stridently nationalist program. This program brought him to the presidency in 1940. For a short while the Communists were more or less allied with him because of his hostile attitude towards the United States and sympathy for the Axis powers, which fitted in with the Communists' policy during the Stalin-Nazi Pact days.

However, the Communist Party remained very small. Early in 1941 it was reported to have only fifty members. Eliseo Echévez, who had spent some time in the Soviet Union during the 1930's, was one of its leaders, as was Cristóbal Segundo, a lawyer.

During the latter part of World War II the Communists gained considerable ground in Panama, as they did in most of the Latin American countries. They made progress especially in the trade union movement. Their influence was given a fillip in September, 1943, when Vicente Lombardo Toledano visited the country.[49] A couple of months later a Comité Organizador de los Trabajadores was established with the avowed aim of organizing "thousands and thousands" of Panamanian workers without regard to political or religious creed or racial background.[50]

While the war was still in progress, in October, 1944, a national labor congress was held in Panama City under the auspices of the Comité Organizador de los Trabajadores, at which was founded the Federación Sindical de Trabajadores de Panamá.[51] The Secretary of the new F.S.P. was Efraim Morel, a Communist.[52]

For the first time the Communists made substantial headway among the workers of the Canal Zone. This penetration was not achieved by the Panamanian Communist Party itself, but rather via the United Federal Workers, a Communist-controlled United States union, at that time belonging to the C.I.O. The founding meeting of the U.F.W.'s Union of Workers of the Panama Canal Zone was held in May, 1946; it claimed to represent 10,000 workers.

For three years this union remained in the C.I.O. During this period it contained perhaps one half of the 14,000 Panamanian workers employed by the Canal Zone administration. In 1949, after the United Federal Workers was expelled from the Congress of Industrial Organizations as being under Communist control, the Communists lost their hold on the Canal Zone workers. Virtually all those workers who remained in the union went over to a new Civic Workers Organizing Committee, which was established by the C.I.O. This was under strictly non-Communist control.

During the second World War the Communist Party of Panama had followed the lead of brother Parties of the hemisphere in changing its name, adopting the title Partido del Pueblo. It participated in a number of elections, though it never succeeded in electing any candidate to the National Assembly. By 1947 the total vote it could muster for its candidate for President, Cristóbal Segundo,* had fallen to about one thousand.

The Panamanian Communists turned violently against the United States

---

* Cristóbal Segundo was sworn in temporarily as a Supreme Court Justice in February, 1948, to replace Gregorio Miró, a member of the Court then on vacation.

as the international Communist line changed after World War II. They played an important part in the demonstrations in December, 1947, against a proposed treaty with the United States which would have permitted the latter to keep a number of the air bases it had built in the Republic for protection of the Canal during World War II.

With the return of Arnulfo Arias to power in 1948, the Communists found rougher sledding. In April, 1950, Arias and his Cabinet signed a resolution outlawing the Partido del Pueblo. However, the decision was later declared unconstitutional by Attorney General Carlos A. López, and it was suspended.[53] The Party was finally outlawed by President José Remón late in 1953.[54]

By the mid-1950's the Communists had lost most of their support in the trade unions. The Federación Sindical de Trabajadores de Panamá was split several times after World War II, and by 1954 it was reduced to three officially recognized trade unions: the tailors, led by Domingo Barria; the Power and Light Workers Union of Colón; and the bus drivers of Panama City. The F.S.T.P. also claimed two other unions which did not have legal recognition: the Port Workers Union of Colón and the Mechanics and Metallurgical Workers Union.

In the summer of 1954 the Communist-controlled Bus Drivers Union called a strike which lasted four days and was partially won by the workers. However, as a result of this walkout the Bus Drivers Union decided that it was the better part of wisdom for them to withdraw from the Federación Sindical de Trabajadores.

The Communists made some attempts to penetrate non-Communist labor organizations. They attempted to get into the O.R.I.T. affiliate, the Confederación Agraria Nacional, headed by Tomás Dionisio Arauz. However, these endeavors were defeated by Arauz' vigilance and the opposition of the workers.[55]

The decline of the Communists' support in the unions was matched by the general decline of their popularity. First Arnulfo Arias and then José Remón, who became President at the end of 1952, captured the support of many of those who might otherwise have been subject to Communist influence. Remón's administration appealed to local nationalism by seeking a revision of the treaty by which the United States has control of the Canal Zone. It sought to clean up the corruption which had become a serious problem in Panama's public administration, and to institute a program of economic development.

Writing in the January 4, 1954, issue of *The New York Times*, Sydney Gruson reported thus on the effect on the Panamanian Communists of certain other aspects of the Remón administration:

> President José R. Remón successfully maneuvered a bill through Congress recently outlawing Communists in Panama. The party has

been seriously weakened during the past year by internal feuds. Observers who only a year ago considered it a serious threat to the Panama Canal now believe that the combination of harassment by Remón's police and intra-party feuding have destroyed its immediate effectiveness.

However, it is recognized that the party's unity could be decreed from outside if necessary. The necessity would arise, it is believed, in the event of war between Russia and the West when sabotage of the Panama Canal might be a major Communist military operation.

Remón was assassinated early in 1955. Although it was first reported that the Communists had had something to do with the President's murder, there seemed to be no evidence that they had had any part in it. His death resulted from rivalries among some of his own followers.

By the middle of 1956 the Communists, who never had had much political strength in Panama, were weaker among the general public than they had been in two decades. Although they remained a danger, insofar as possible sabotage of the Canal was concerned, they were only a very minor menace to the political stability of the Republic of Panama.

# Part Three

*The Communist Movement in Latin America and United States Policy*

*Chapter XVIII*

# The Right and the Wrong
# Fight Communism in Latin

A FEW CONCLUSIONS can be drawn from such a survey of Communism in Latin America as is presented in the foregoing pages. First, the Latin American Communists are real Communists. They are not "agrarian reformers," or "another kind of radical," but part of the world-wide Communist movement.

Second, Communism in Latin America is not now principally a military problem, but rather a political one.

Third, the Latin American Communist Parties are operating in a region which is going through those political, social, and economic changes which accompany the Industrial Revolution in an "underdeveloped" area.

Fourth and finally, the most effective opponents of Communism in Latin America are those elements of the Democratic Left which are trying in a democratic way to bring about the social revolution which is so necessary to the future of Latin America.

From these conclusions follow certain truisms about the struggle against Communism in the region. First, anyone anxious to see the triumph of democracy over totalitarianism should be concerned with the problem of the Communists in our neighboring republics.

Second, Communism in Latin America should be dealt with primarily in terms of healthy social growth rather than suppressive police action.

Third, Communism is less likely to prosper if the Industrial Revolution is ushered in in such a way as to occasion the least possible violence and dislocation in the lives of the common people of Latin America.

Finally those interested in seeing democracy triumph over Communism in our hemisphere should give their utmost support to the Democratic Left, no matter how much its economic and social ideas may differ from those which are popular in the United States.

One of the handicaps in all attempts to deal with Communism in Latin America is the lack of interest displayed by the government and people of the United States and of the other free countries in the problems of

merican peoples. United States Presidents and Secretaries of State
ent years have been absorbed by the problems of Europe, Asia, and
ca, so that they have had little time for Latin America. They have
egated this field of international affairs to their subordinates, who have
ften been capable, well-intentioned men, but men who in attempting to
manage United States relations with Latin America have lacked the prestige and authority of President or a Secretary of State.

Even less fortunately, the turnover in the post of Assistant Secretary of
State for Latin American Affairs (the chief United States diplomatic official charged with relations with the other republics of the hemisphere),
has been startling. This situation has been aggravated by the circumstance
that almost every new Assistant Secretary has started out with a new set
of policies toward the countries within his responsibility. In many cases—
notably in dealings with Perón—each Assistant Secretary has had to learn
over again the lessons of his predecessor. Frequently, each succeeding Assistant Secretary has apparently had to commit over again the errors
which his predecessors first made and then repented. This has all led to
confusion in United States dealings with Latin American countries.

The only times when the top officials of the United States Government have paid much attention to events in the Latin American countries
have been such moments of crisis as the Guatemalan affair in 1954. At such
times, badly informed and unaware of the deeper currents which direct
the thinking of the Latin Americans, they have often made errors which
anyone cognizant of the trend of affairs in Latin America would have
avoided.

To cite but one instance, the behavior of Secretary Dulles during the
Tenth Inter American Conference at Caracas, Venezuela, in March, 1954,
shocked many seasoned observers of Latin American developments. Not
only did Dulles use the full weight of the United States Government to
induce the Conference to take a position uncongenial to the majority of
the Latin American countries, he did it in a manner likely to lose friends
and alienate the peoples of the southern part of the hemisphere.

Concerned with almost nothing but the "Anti-Communist Resolutions"
aimed at Guatemala, Dulles seemed to the Latin Americans indifferent to
their feelings, their fears of "Yankee Intervention," and the concentration
of their interest on entirely different problems. He stayed at the Conference only long enough to see adoption of the Resolution. Then he took
a plane home the very day the Resolution was passed, leaving his subordinates to deal with the economic and social questions which were the
primary concern of the Latin American delegations.

Not only did Mr. Dulles thus slight the feeling of dignity of the Latin
American diplomats, but he also disappointed the democratic aspirations
of the great majority of the Latin American common people. The Conference was held in the capital of one of the most notorious dictatorships

in the hemisphere, but Mr. Dulles had not a word to say about the problems of militarism and dictatorship which are of overwhelming importance to the peoples of Latin America. Interested only in the threat of Communist dictatorship, he seemed oblivious to that of the military *caudillos* which are the actual obstacle in the struggle toward democracy in most Latin American countries.*

The people of the United States are even less concerned with the real problems of Latin America than is their government. Here the fault lies largely with the newspapers and other organs of information and opinion. With a few honorable exceptions, such as *The New York Times* and the *Christian Science Monitor*, the United States press pays little or no attention to events in Latin America, unless it be to give passing note to some new revolution or *coup d'état*.

The result is that the people of the United States, when they have any idea at all about what is going on in Latin America, receive a distorted view of events there. There is little attempt by the American press to give the kind of background and careful analysis which it devotes to the problems of France, India, or even faraway Nepal.

Thus the average United States newspaper reader gets the impression that Latin Americans are picturesque but childlike, that they are prone to cheer a dictator one day and hang him the next, that there is little to be taken seriously in the affairs of the Latin American countries. The average North American is utterly shocked when something like the Guatemalan affair suddenly bursts into the headlines of his daily newspaper. He has no background, he tends to get panicky, and he certainly does not understand what is really going on.

The result of this lack of interest on the part of the United States Government and the United States public in the affairs of Latin America is that pressure groups with interests in the area have an inordinate amount of influence. The policy of the United States towards Perón, for example, tended to be determined not on the basis of what was best for the United States in the general situation of the Cold War, or what was best for inter-American relations, but rather in terms of how it could be made possible for United States businessmen to invest capital and make money in the Argentine Republic.

Only the self-sacrificing activity of small groups of United States citi-

* It should be noted, however, that the prompt action of the United States at the time of the invasion of democratic Costa Rica by forces supported by dictator Anastasio Somoza of Nicaragua in January, 1955, gave evidence for the first time in many years that the United States Government was becoming aware of the dangers to future democratic development in the hemisphere and to the fight against Communism represented by the military dictatorships. The United States, by urging the Organization of American States to move to prevent the invasion and to aid Costa Rica to resist it, not only raised the prestige of the O.A.S., but heartened tremendously the democratic elements in Latin America who are fighting a two-front war against both military dictatorships and the Communists.

zens interested in Latin American affairs keeps the situation from being worse than it is. Among the groups which should be mentioned particularly in this connection is the United States labor movement. Both the A.F. of L. and C.I.O. (especially the former), took a lively interest in Latin American problems after the end of World War II and used their influence consistently on the side of Latin American democrats and in favor of United States economic aid for Latin America. This policy has been continued by the united labor movement.

Of importance, too, has been the Inter American Association for Democracy and Freedom, headed by Miss Frances Grant of New York City. Through its publications, such as its monthly magazine, *Hemispherica*, its sponsoring of the causes of exiled Latin Americans, and its support for democratic Latin American governments such as that of President José Figueres of Costa Rica, it has helped to influence the United States Government and to inform at least a small part of the United States reading public of the state of affairs in the other American republics.

Thus, the first necessity in the struggle against Communism in Latin America is for the people and government of the United States to take more interest in the affairs of the Latin American countries, to become better informed, and to act in an enlightened and intelligent manner toward our Latin American neighbors. How important this is, most North Americans hardly understand. People who have not travelled widely in the area have trouble comprehending the importance of the pronouncements and actions of the United States Government, and even of private American individuals, in determining policy in the Latin American nations.

One element in the United States Government which has shown some interest in the situation in Latin America has been the military. Unfortunately, its influence, by and large, has been detrimental. Guided, as they must necessarily be, largely by military considerations, the United States armed forces have tended to make the situation in Latin America worse rather than better, have helped the Communist leaders in that area rather than hindered them.

As these pages have argued already, the Communist problem in Latin America is not primarily a military one. It is a problem of winning or keeping the loyalty of the peoples of Latin America for the democratic way of life and of fortifying them in their determination not to succumb to the blandishments of the Communists.

This struggle is made more difficult by the existence of dictatorships in many, and on occasions most, of the Latin American countries. This prevalence of dictatorship gives the Communists two advantages. First, they are able to join with other groups in a "democratic" fight against a particular dictator while often another faction of the Party is collaborating with the tyrant. Second, charges that the Communists themselves want to establish a dictatorship are of less importance to democratic elements in those countries where the immediate fight is not against a Communist dictatorship, but rather against a home-grown military one.

Since World War II the United States Government, and particularly the Defense Department, has followed a policy of arming the Latin American governments, and the Latin American dictators in particular. This is making the struggle for democracy in these countries increasingly difficult.

In the old days, when the Latin American dictatorships were armed only with rifles and small arms, and perhaps a few venerable cannon, it was no great task for the civilian population to rise in arms against a tyrant and overthrow him. This becomes increasingly difficult—indeed, with a few exceptions, virtually impossible—when the Latin American armies are provided with tanks, high-powered artillery and rifles, and, most important of all, with airplanes.

Such an arming of the Latin American military is all the more dangerous in view of the uselessness of these armed forces insofar as actually protecting their countries against a major enemy is concerned. It is doubtful if the armies and navies of more than two or three of the Latin American countries could put up enough opposition to hold off such an enemy even long enough for the United States to fly in reinforcements.

The Latin American armies, therefore, serve little purpose except to "maintain order" in their respective nations, which more often than not means maintaining dictatorial power over the people of those countries. Hence United States action in arming these military forces has the result of riveting existing tyrannies on the helpless civilian populations of Latin America.

The United States armed forces have used not only their military influence, but their political influence, on behalf of the Latin American dictators. Especially since the inauguration of the Eisenhower administration, this has had disastrous results on the struggle for democracy in other American countries. It has led the United States to confer high honors on at least two of the military dictators of the hemisphere—President Manuel Odría of Peru and President Marcos Pérez Jiménez of Venezuela.

These actions have been all the more disastrous in terms of United States prestige and democracy's cause in Latin America, because they have been widely publicized, while actions which the United States Government has taken to support democratic regimes in Latin America have received no publicity. Thus, the dispatch of six jet airplanes in the fall of 1954 to defend the administration of President José Figueres of Costa Rica against invasion by Nicaragua received virtually no publicity whatsoever. (This incident occurred several months before the actual invasion attempt in January, 1955, when, also, the United States Government came to Costa Rica's aid.)

The United States Government has tended to look at the situation in

Latin America entirely too much in military terms. The North American public, almost completely uninformed about events to the south, has offered little or no opposition to this over-narrow orientation. Even those newspapers which carry a reasonable amount of Latin American news have protested little against the continuing policy of arming the Latin American dictators.

The real problems of Latin America are economic and social, not military. Latin America is trying to put her vast natural resources to work, to build an industrial civilization, to raise the standards of living of her long-oppressed masses. At the same time, she is throwing off the social and cultural patterns which have endured since the Spanish and Portuguese first conquered the southern part of this hemisphere.

These are the problems with which the United States Government and people should be concerned in Latin America. The United States is in a position to be of great help in this process of development, and to aid in guiding the Latin American social revolution down democratic channels. The degree to which this course is pursued will go far toward determining whether the Communists will be the ultimate victors in the struggle for power in Latin America.

Of course, the United States has given some aid to Latin American industrial development. Private investors first developed the mines and some of the agricultural resources, built some of the railroads and power plants, and constructed many of the factories. United States public investment, through the Export-Import Bank and the International Bank for Reconstruction and Development, has to some degree forwarded economic growth in recent years.

However, United States aid to Latin America has been piddling, at least when compared with the investments which this country has made in Europe, and even in Asia, since World War II. Such aid as has been given has been dealt out in driblets, without any central plan or coordination of the United States's efforts with those of the Latin American countries.

Something more extensive is needed if the battle against Communism in Latin America is to be won. Farseeing Latin American politicians, and some people in the United States, have for nearly a decade been urging the need for some kind of Marshall Plan for Latin America.

What is required is a long-range program for pooling the hemisphere's resources in order to develop the Latin American countries. What is further required is for the United States to present the Latin Americans with the same kind of a proposition as that presented the Europeans in 1947. What the United States should do is to propose to the Latin American nations that they get together and draw up a five to ten year plan for economic development, coordinating their own efforts insofar as possible and taking into full account the capital which could be raised in Latin America. Then the United States should join Latin America in working out a program for the provision of United States capital for those parts of the general plan which would call for otherwise unavailable foreign currency.

Such an undertaking would mean a considerable amount of United States public investment in Latin America. It is foolish to think that the job can be done adequately by United States private investors. Secretary of the Treasury George Humphrey seemed to many observers extremely doctrinaire and ignorant of Latin American conditions when he urged Latin American delegates to the Rio Economic Conference, late in 1954, to depend almost exclusively on private sources of funds for any foreign investment they needed.

In the first place, the kind of United States private investment which characterized the first third of this century is a thing of the past. Investment must henceforth be concentrated in fields which the Latin Americans consider most vital and under conditions in which United States investors do not receive special privileges, unavailable to Latin American nationals. Contracts such as that negotiated between the Standard Oil Company of California and the Perón government in April, 1955, giving the Company exemption from many of the nation's laws, are exceptional.

In the second place, the Latin Americans, rightly or wrongly, feel strongly that considerable portions of their economy should be in the hands of their own nationals. Public utilities, land transportation, some heavy industry, to a certain degree mining and petroleum, are closed to private foreign investors from now on.

Hence, public investment by the United States will be required in these areas. While opposed to the development of their resources by United States private firms, the Latin American countries are anxious to obtain intergovernmental loans and grants which will enable them to develop these resources themselves. Furthermore, there is a vast range of "social investment" which it would not be profitable for private investors to undertake. Such things as roads, technical training, health services, educational facilities—requiring more or less foreign exchange—will almost never be financed by private investors.

There will still be ample opportunity for private foreign investment, in manufacturing industries particularly, to a lesser degree in commerce and in other service industries. In order to stimulate such investment, measures might be taken in the United States to insure United States firms against possible losses in Latin America, a system which was used to a limited degree in Europe during the Marshall Plan days.

The adoption of a Marshall Plan for Latin America could have the same disastrous results for the Communists in that part of the world which it had for the Communists in Europe. No longer could they claim that the United States is unconcerned with Latin American problems. Latin Americans would have tangible proof that the United States was conscious of their desire to modernize and raise the productivity of their economies and to increase the standard of living of the people.

A Marshall Plan for Latin America would provide a tangible substitute for the promises of the Communists, which sometimes seem so alluring. One great asset of the Communists, in Latin America and in the other "underdeveloped" parts of the world, is the apparent success with which Communist Russia, and now Communist China, have been able to develop economically. A Marshall Plan for Latin America would counteract this favorable impression, demonstrating that the free world, too, knows how to raise the productivity and enhance the well-being of the underdeveloped countries, and can achieve this without the terrible cost in human lives and human misery which Communist methods exact.

The United States might reduce the need for a Latin American Marshall Plan by working out with the Latin Americans some means of assuring stable prices for the area's principal raw material and food exports. Most of the Latin American countries are dependent upon one or two or at best a narrow range of mineral or agricultural exports for all their foreign exchange. Periodically their economies are endangered by wild fluctuations in the prices of these products, which tend to vary much more rapidly and much more extremely than do those of the industrial products making up the bulk of United States exports to Latin America.

Ever since World War II the Latin American countries have been urging the United States to consider plans to establish "buffer stocks" or other mechanisms for assuring stable prices for their exports over a reasonably long period of time. Most Latin Americans would be willing to settle for a good deal less than maximum prices for their exports if they could be assured of price stability. The United States has steadily refused such arrangements.

Of course, such international price-fixing mechanisms are complicated and create new problems of their own. However, until some means can be found for levelling off the extreme variations in the prices of Latin America's principal exports, the countries to the south of us are going to remain at the mercy of international markets over which they have little or no control. In consequence, it is infinitely more difficult to plan and carry out an orderly program of expanding production and raising the standard of living for the 150,000,000 Americans in the other twenty republics of the hemisphere.

Economic measures are not enough. The United States must rekindle the democratic idealism which President Franklin D. Roosevelt seemed to many Latin Americans to have ignited. The United States must show that it is deeply concerned not only with the fight against Communist dictatorship, but also with the fight against the native variety of dictatorship which flourishes so widely in Latin America.

This does not mean overt intervention in the internal affairs of the Latin

American countries. Former Assistant Secretary of State John Moors Cabot is correct when he says that democracy cannot be imposed by force on the Latin American countries.[1] However, the United States can bring considerable pressure to bear on behalf of democracy, and there can be much greater activity on the part of the United States Government and the people of this country in defense of Latin American democratic elements.

These democratic elements are numerous. They include the parties which throughout this book we have called the "Aprista" parties—the Peruvian Apristas, the Venezuelan Acción Democrática, Pepe Figueres' Liberación Nacional Party in Costa Rica, the Puerto Rican Popular Democrats, to name but a few. They include the democratic Socialists of Uruguay, Argentina, and Peru, and sections of the Socialist parties of Chile and Ecuador. They include the Liberals of Colombia, Ecuador, and Honduras. They include Social Catholics in various countries. They include certain indigenous groups such as the Batllistas of Uruguay, the government's P.R.I. party in Mexico, and others.

These are the groups in Latin America who are able to meet the Communists on their own ground, to promise and in a democratic way to deliver to the humble and ambitious people of the continent the fruits of the Latin American social revolution. The United States must not allow them to turn away from this country in bitterness and frustration, or to be undermined by the Communists as a result of apparent United States support of dictatorship.

So far as the United States Government is concerned, the relighting of the torch of political democracy means that, while maintaining formally "friendly" relations with the dictator countries of Latin America, this Government should never make it appear that it actually supports and approves of dictatorial regimes. Certainly this means that a halt should be called to the policy of handing out medals to the dictators.

But United States policy must be more than merely negative. The President and Secretary of State and other high officials of this government should make it clear that they support democracy in the Americas as well as in Europe and Asia. Certainly it would not be too much to expect of the leading officials of this country, which claims to be the champion of liberty, that from time to time they take occasion to deplore the prevalence in this hemisphere of imprisonment for political reasons. In receiving Latin American ambassadors, in commemorating Latin American historical occasions, and when other appropriate opportunities present themselves, the President and Secretary of State should make it plain that the United States actively approves of the democratic regimes in Latin America and disapproves of the dictatorships.

Of course, such a policy of encouraging democracy in Latin America involves delicate diplomatic problems. However, so does the policy which has been followed in recent years of showing open support for the dictatorships. An expressed democratic policy would take the hollowness out of the United States' exhorting the nations of the world to freedom, a hollowness particularly audible to Latin Americans subject to native tyrannies. Only in this way can our country scotch the Communist propaganda line, which puts the chief onus for the existence of the Latin American dictatorships on the United States. Only thus can the United States Government demonstrate that "democracy" in America does not mean dictatorship, as the Communists claim.

Responsible groups of United States citizens can also encourage democracy in Latin America, and so cut the ground out from under the Communists. Forward-looking North Americans can express more frequently their support for the Democratic Left in Latin America. The newspapers of the country can open their columns more fully to the democratic leaders of Latin America—both those who can function in their own countries and those who are forced to live in exile.

Only if the United States Government and people throw their support to those elements in Latin America which are working for political democracy and social change can the fight against the Communists be won. Dictatorships in Latin America are at best transitory. They are poor dikes against the Communist flood, and in the long run serve only to insure that once the flood starts to roll it will be stronger than ever before. The only real victors against Communism will be those groups which can arouse the imagination of the Latin American peoples.

# Bibliographical Note

In the course of travels throughout the American hemisphere extending over a decade, during which he has been concerned principally with collecting material on labor and political conditions in Latin America, the author has had occasion to interview leading figures in virtually all of the area's Communist Parties. He has also frequently encountered ex-Communists, many of them figures of importance in the earlier years of their respective Parties, who have been willing to talk at considerable length concerning the activities of these organizations. Therefore, much of this book is based on interviews with Communist leaders, ex-Communists, and others in a position to know something about the Communist movement in Latin America. Among the ex-Communists, special mention should go to Bertram Wolfe and Earl Browder once of the Communist Party of the U.S.A.

Documentary material is ample, though scattered. Only one Latin American Communist Party, to the author's knowledge at least, has had an official history of its organization written. This is the Argentine Party, whose history, published in 1947, is very useful, if properly discounted, for a rounded view of the activities of that country's Stalinists.

In the other countries, it is necessary to piece together the history of the Party from other sources. Most of the more important Communist Parties of the hemisphere have turned out voluminous amounts of pamphlet material, giving interesting and important information on particular aspects and periods of their history. Several of the more important groups—including those of Cuba, Brazil, Argentina, and Chile—put out "theoretical" journals, which contain much information not only on their own activities and ideas, but on those of other Latin American Communist Parties as well. The present volume has borrowed more or less heavily from the Cuban Communists' periodical *Fundamentos*, the Brazilians' *Problemas*, and the Argentine's *Nueva Era*.

Reports of congresses and conventions of the different Communist Parties and of continental Communist organizations are of great value. The reports of the 1929 congresses of Communist trade unionists and Communist Parties, the reports of the different congresses of the C.T.A.L., and published accounts of conventions of individual Parties and trade union groups have been fruitful sources of information for the present book.

The international Communist publications have been particularly informative concerning Latin America's Communist Parties. During the period of the Comintern these publications were numerous. They included: *International Press Correspondence,* issued by the International itself; *La Correspondencia Sudamericana,* published by the South American Bureau of the Comintern; *El Trabajador Latino Americano,* put out by the International's Latin American trade union apparatus. Other important periodicals of this epoch were the English-language *Communist International* and *The Communist.* Since World War II, the Cominform's *For a Lasting Peace, For a People's Democracy* frequently has published material on our subject.

Several official and unofficial publications of the United States Communist Party have also been very useful. These include the New York *Daily Worker, New Masses,* and the wartime *Allied Labor News.*

Of course, numerous non-Communist sources were also used: interviews with various non-Communists; several metropolitan newspapers in the United States, such as *The New York Times* and the *Christian Science Monitor;* news magazines in this country, Mexico, and Colombia; journals of opinion such as *The New Leader* and *The Nation.*

In writing the present volume, the author has found the following books helpful. Martin Ebon's comprehensive *World Communism Today* devotes relatively few pages to Latin America, but contains many informative details. Víctor. Alba's *Historia del Comunismo en América Latina,* published in Mexico in 1954, is small and makes no pretense of giving a detailed history of the movement. However, it contains some worthwhile insights and some interesting information on such things as the relations of the Communists with Augusto Sandino, for instance.

Daniel James's *Red Design for the Americas: Guatemalan Prelude* is very good in its discussion of the Guatemalan Communist bid for power, though it is somewhat less valuable when it attempts to generalize for the area as a whole.

A number of volumes deal extensively with the Communist Parties of individual countries. Jorge Schlesinger's *Revolución Comunista* has useful information and documentary material on the early Communist movements of Guatemala and El Salvador. Ricardo Treviño's *Espionaje Comunista* contains some interesting details about the situation in Mexico, though the reader must beware of his confusion of passion with fact. Ricardo Martínez de la Torre's monumental collection of documents concerning the labor and radical movement of Peru, *Apuntes para una Interpretación Marxista de la Historia Social del Perú,* in four thick volumes, is particularly valuable for that country.

Carleton Beals's book of reminiscences, *Glass Houses,* is interesting on the early years of the Communist Party of Mexico. Two lives of Luiz Carlos Prestes, by Abguar Bastos and Jorge Amado, have been useful for the history of the Brazilian Party and of Prestes' association with it.

Full details concerning the specific sources consulted will be found in the List of Footnotes which follows this Bibliographical Note.

# FOOTNOTES

### Chapter III

[1] Eudosio Ravines, *The Yenan Way* (New York, Charles Scribner's Sons, 1951), pp. 54-69.
[2] Víctor Alba, *Historia del Comunismo en América Latina* (Mexico, Ediciones Occidentales, 1954), p. 40.
[3] *Ibid.*, pp. 35-37.
[4] *Ibid.*, pp. 94-95.
[5] Ravines, *op. cit.*, p. 146.
[6] *Ibid.*, p. 260.
[7] *Ibid.*, p. 263.

### Chapter IV

[1] Diego Abad de Santillán, *La F.O.R.A.—Ideologia y Trayectoria del Movimiento Obrero Revolucionario en la Argentina* (Buenos Aires, Ediciones Nervo, 1933), pp. 269-275.
[2] Alexander Lozovsky (head of the Red International of Labor Unions), in *International Press Correspondence* (the Communist International publication), December 27, 1922.
[3] Alexander Lozovsky, *El Movimiento Sindical Latino Americano—Sus Virtudes y Sus Defectos* (Montevideo, Ediciones C.S.L.A., 1928).
[4] *International Press Correspondence*, October 17, 1925.
[5] *La Correspondencia Sudamericana* (organ of the South American Bureau of the Communist International), April 15, 1926.
[6] *International Press Correspondence*, December 22, 1927.
[7] *Resoluciones de la Conferencia Sindical Latino Americana* (Montevideo, Ediciones C.S.L.A., 1928).
[8] *Bajo la Bandera de la C.S.L.A. Resoluciones y Documentos Varios del Congreso Constituyente de la C.S.L.A. . . . en Montevideo, en Mayo de 1929* (Montevideo, Ediciones C.S.L.A., 1929).
[9] Interview with Ignacio Torres Giraldo, former Secretary General of Communist Party of Colombia, in Bogotá, Colombia, July 15, 1947.
[10] Francisco Pérez Leirós, *El Movimiento Sindical en América Latina* (Buenos Aires, Imprenta La Vanguardia, 1941).
[11] Confederación de Trabajadores de México, *C.T.M. 1936-1941* (Mexico, 1941).
[12] Pérez Leirós, *op. cit.*
[13] Vicente Lombardo Toledano, *El Proletarido de América Latina Ante los Problemas del Continente y del Mundo* (Mexico, C.T.A.L. Publications, 1942).
[14] *Hoy*, July 27, 1943 (daily paper of Cuban Partido Socialista Popular).
[15] Confederación de Trabajadores de América Latina, *Reunión de Montevideo* (Mexico, C.T.A.L. Publications, 1944).
[16] Confederación de Trabajadores de América Latina, *Segundo Congreso General de la Confederación de Trabajadores de la América Latina* (Mexico, 1945).

### Chapter VII

[1] *Voz do Povo* (Anarchist periodical), May 1, 1921.
[2] *A Plebe* (Anarchist periodical), May 7, 1924.
[3] Interview with Roberto Morena, ex-Anarchist, Communist trade union leader, in Rio de Janeiro, August 28, 1946.
[4] *A Plebe*, December 19, 1922.
[5] Stephen Naft, Labor Movements of Latin America (unpublished manuscript), p. 3.
[6] *International Press Correspondence*, December 14, 1922.

7 Arnold Roller (Stephen Naft) undated memorandum, prepared for Tass News Agency.
8 Octávio Brandão in *International Press Correspondence*, September 9, 1926.
9 Octávio Brandão, leader of Partido Comunista do Brazil, longhand manuscript, dated March 14, 1926.
10 Arnold Roller memorandum, *op. cit.*
11 *A Plebe*, May 10, 1924.
12 Interview with Roberto Morena, August 28, 1946.
13 *International Press Correspondence*, January 22, 1928.
14 *El Trabajador Latino Americano* (Latin American Communist trade union periodical), October 15, 1928.
15 Interview with Roberto Morena, August 28, 1946.
16 *Ibid.*
17 *La Correspondencia Sudamericana*, September 15, 1926.
18 *International Press Correspondence*, February 2, 1928.
19 Interview with João da Costa Pimenta, in São Paulo, June 17, 1953.
20 *International Press Correspondence*, October 17, 1928.
21 *Ibid.*, July 25, 1928.
22 *Ibid.*, August 1, 1928.
23 *Ibid.*, November 21, 1928.
24 Interview with ex-Communist leader Hilcar Leite, in Rio de Janeiro, June 11, 1953.
25 *Ibid.*
26 Interview with ex-Communist, ex-Trotskyite, Socialist leader Plinio Mello, in São Paulo, June 16, 1953.
27 Augusto Machado, *Caminho da Revolução Operária e Camponêza* (Rio de Janeiro, Calvino Filho, 1934), pp. 100-101.
28 *Ibid.*, p. 102.
29 Interview with Plinio Mello, June 16, 1953.
30 Abguar Bastos, *Prestes e a Revolução Social* (Rio de Janeiro, Editorial Calvino, 1946), p. 248.
31 Interview with Plinio Mello, June 16, 1953.
32 Jorge Amado, *Vida de Luis Carlos Prestes* (São Paulo, Libraria Martins, 1946), p. 126. This volume contains one of the best accounts of the wanderings of the Prestes Column, in a somewhat romanticized form.
33 Interview with Hilcar Leite, June 11, 1953.
34 Interview with Aristides Lobo, ex-Trotskyite, Socialist leader, in São Paulo, June 17, 1953.
35 Cited by Bastos, *op. cit.*, p. 264.
36 Bastos, *op. cit.*, p. 229.
37 *Ibid.*, p. 252.
38 *Ibid.*, p. 271.
39 *Ibid.*, p. 272.
40 *Ibid.*, pp. 272-274.
41 *Vanguarda Socialista*, September 21, 1945.
42 Interview with Luiz Carlos Prestes, in Rio de Janeiro, August 27, 1946.
43 Interview with Ignacio Torres Giraldo, ex-leader of Colombian Communist Party, ex-member of Executive Committee of Red International of Labor Unions, in Bogotá, July 15, 1947.
44 Bastos, *op. cit.*, p. 317.
45 Interview with Luiz Carlos Prestes, August 27, 1946.
46 Bastos, *op. cit.*, p. 317.
47 "Struggles of the Communist Party of South and Caribbean America," *Communist International*, May 20, 1935.
48 *El Trabajador Latino Americano*, October-November, 1935.
49 "Luis Carlos Prestes," *Communist International*, March-April, 1936.
50 *International Press Correspondence*, August 20, 1935.
51 "Luis Carlos Prestes," *Communist International*, March-April, 1936.
52 Amado, *op. cit.*, p. 117.

53 *Ibid.*, p. 107.
54 Stephen Naft, "Fascism and Communism in Latin America," *Foreign Policy Bulletin* (1937), p. 229.
55 *International Press Correspondence*, December 2, 1935.
56 "Luis Carlos Prestes," *Communist International*, March-April, 1936.
57 *International Press Correspondence*, December 21, 1935.
58 "Luis Carlos Prestes," *Communist International*, March-April, 1936.
59 *International Press Correspondence*, June 20, 1936.
60 Naft, "Fascism and Communism in Latin America," p. 230.
61 *International Press Correspondence*, February 20, 1937.
62 *Ibid.*, May 15, 1937.
63 *Ibid.*, June 20, 1936.
64 Octávio Brandão, in *ibid.*, July 24, 1937.
65 Naft, Labor Movements of Latin America, p. 4.
66 Octávio Brandão, in *International Press Correspondence*, January 2, 1937.
67 Interview with Herminio Saccheta, ex-Secretary General of Partido Socialista Revolucionario, in São Paulo, June 16, 1953.
68 Interview with Hilcar Leite, June 11, 1953.
69 Interview with Pedro Viadero, President of Graphic Arts Workers Union of São Paulo, in São Paulo, August 22, 1946.
70 Associated Press, March 14, 1944.
71 Mexico City *El Popular* (daily newspaper of Vicente Lombardo Toledano) June 5, 1944.
72 *Tiempo* (weekly news magazine, Mexico City), July 20, 1945.
73 *Christian Science Monitor*, July 28, 1945.
74 Astrogildo Pereira (Brazilian Communist leader), in *Allied Labor News*, September 28, 1945.
75 *Allied Labor News*, October 5, 1945.
76 New York *Daily Worker*, June 9, 1945.
77 Ernie Hill, in *Chicago Daily News*, November 24, 1945.
78 Interview with Luiz Carlos Prestes, August 27, 1946.
79 Associated Press, August 17, 1945.
80 *Vanguarda Socialista*, February 8, 1946.
81 New York *Daily Worker*, November 1, 1945.
82 *Washington Post*, November 25, 1945.
83 Mexico City *El Popular*, January 27, 1946.
84 Interview with Manuel Lopez Coelho Filho, leader of Rio de Janeiro Metal Workers Union, leading Communist trade unionist, in Rio de Janeiro, August 29, 1946.
85 Interview with Manuel Lopez Coelho Filho, in Santiago, Chile, December 18, 1946.
86 *The New York Times*, January 22, 1947.
87 *Ibid.*, May 8, 1947.
88 *Ibid.*, October 30, 1947.
89 Andres Silva Paraguassu, "A Luta dos Trabalhadores do Brasil Contra O Jugo Imperialista dos Estados Unidos," *Problemas* (Brazilian Communist periodical), November-December, 1952.
90 Interview with Maria da Graça, member of the Editorial Committee of the Communist daily, *Imprensa Popular*, and Vice President of the National Journalists Federation in Rio de Janeiro, June 10, 1953.
91 João Amazonas, "Pela Paz, Pela Libertação Nacional," *Problemas*, July-August, 1951.
92 Interview with Maria da Graça, June 10, 1953.
93 Silva Paraguassu, *op. cit.*
94 Interview with Maria da Graça, June 10, 1953.
95 Interview with Roberto Morena in Rio de Janeiro, June 10, 1953.
96 Interview with José Gomes Talarico, President of the National Journalists Federation, in Rio de Janeiro, June 9, 1953.
97 Interview with João Bautista Almeida, President of the National Maritime Federation, in Rio de Janeiro, June 14, 1953.

98 Interview with Remo Forli, President of Metal Workers Union of São Paulo, in São Paulo, June 16, 1953.
99 Interview with João Bautista Almeida, June 14, 1953.
100 Interview with Maria da Graça, June 10, 1953.
101 Interview with Plinio Mello, June 16, 1953.
102 Interview with Darle Lara, Socialist Party leader, in São Paulo, June 16, 1953.


CHAPTER VIII

1 Montevideo *Justicia*, April 25, 1921.
2 Interview with Emilio Frugoni, leader of the Socialist Party, in Montevideo, November 25, 1946.
3 *El Sindicato Rojo*, April, 1923.
4 Manuscript report to Rosta News Agency from Gilberto Schiappapietra, dated January, 1926.
5 *El Trabajador Latino Americano*, October 30, 1928.
6 *Ibid.*, February 28-March 15-30, 1929.
7 *Ibid.*, February 28-March 15-30, 1929, and June-July, 1929.
8 *Ibid.*, November-December, 1931.
9 Schiappapietra report, *op. cit.*
10 *La Correspondencia Sudamericana*, November 15, 1926.
11 Schiappapietra report, *op. cit.*
12 *El Movimiento Revolucionario Latino Americano, Versiones de la Primera Conferencia Comunista Latino Americana, Junio de 1929* (Buenos Aires, Editorial La Correspondencia Sudamericana, 1929), p. 137.
13 *El Trabajador Latino Americano*, September-October, 1931.
14 *Ibid.*, January-February, 1932.
15 Francisco Pintos, *Historia del Uruguay (1851-1938). Ensayo de Interpretación Materialista* (Montevideo, Ediciones Pueblos Unidos, 1946), p. 173.
16 *Ibid.*, p. 197.
17 *Ibid.*, p. 198.
18 *Ibid.*, p. 171.
19 *Ibid.*, p. 196.
20 Interview with Esteban Kikich, Trotskyite leader, in Montevideo, October 10, 1946.
21 Speech by José Cardoso, Socialist leader, reported in *El Sol* (Socialist Party periodical), Second Week, May, 1945.
22 Interview with Nicasio Zeballos Calzada, trade union leader of Independent Nationalist Party, in Montevideo, October 14, 1946.
23 *Ibid.*
24 Interviews with Juan Acuña, Socialist union leader, and Humberto Gómez, packing-house workers leader, in Montevideo, on October 7, 1946, and October 16, 1946, respectively.
25 Interview with Nicasio Zeballos Calzada, October 14, 1946.
26 Eugenio Gómez, *Uruguay Unido en el Frente de la Libertad* (Montevideo, Editorial Amoa, 1941).
27 Eugenio Gómez, *El Pueblo Votará Por la Unión Nacional* (Montevideo, Ediciones Justicia, 1942).
28 *The New York Times*, November 25, 1950.
29 *Ibid.*, November 28, 1950.
30 *El Trabajador Latino Americano*, November 15-30, 1929.
31 Teodoro Vázquez, in *El Trabajador Latino Americano*, November 15-30, 1928.
32 *El Trabajador Latino Americano*, May, 1932.
33 *International Press Correspondence*, March 9, 1934.
34 Report of Bernardo de Jesús Leiva to Congress of Confederación de Trabajadores de América Latina, published in *Congreso de Cali—C.T.A.L., Diciembre 1944* (Mexico, C.T.A.L. Publications, 1945).
35 Virginia Prewett, in *PM*, December 16, 1945.

[36] Martin Ebon, *World Communism Today* (New York, Whittlesey House, 1948), p. 335.

CHAPTER IX

[1] Interview with Victorio Codovilla, Argentine Communist leader, in Buenos Aires, November 19, 1946.
[2] "Report Transmitted to the International Socialist Party and to all Socialist Parties, 1919," *Weekly People* (organ of the Socialist Labor Party of the United States), July 24, 1920.
[3] Interview with Victorio Codovilla, November 19, 1946.
[4] *Ezbozo de Historia del Partido Comunista de la Argentina* (Buenos Aires, Editorial Anteo, 1947). The official Communist Party version of its own history, this is hereafter referred to as "Official Communist *History*."
[5] "Report Transmitted to the International Socialist Party and to all Socialist Parties, 1919," *Weekly People*, August 21, 1920.
[6] *Ibid.*
[7] Official Communist *History*, p. 23.
[8] *Ibid.*, p. 25.
[9] "Report Transmitted to the International Socialist Party and to all Socialist Parties, 1919," *Weekly People*, August 14, 1920.
[10] Official Communist *History*, p. 25.
[11] *Ibid.*, p. 41.
[12] *Ibid.*, p. 43.
[13] *Ibid.*, p. 40.
[14] Diego Abad de Santillán, *La F.O.R.A.—Ideologia y Trayectoria del Movimiento Obrero Revolucionario en la Argentina* (Buenos Aires, Ediciones Nervo, 1933), p. 301.
[15] *Ibid.*, p. 300.
[16] Interview with Sebastián Marotta, ex-Secretary General of F.O.R.A. IX, in Buenos Aires, November 27, 1946.
[17] Unión Sindical Argentina, *Memoria y Balance del Comité Central Presentados al Primer Congreso, 1924* (Buenos Aires, 1924), p. 30.
[18] Rodolfo Ghioldi, La Correspondencia Argentina, typewritten manuscript, signed, undated but 1926.
[19] Interview with Italo Gerassi, Central Committee member, and Marcos Panteléon, Administrative Secretary, of the Communist Party of Argentina, in Buenos Aires, November 19, 1946.
[20] Official Communist *History*, p. 38.
[21] *Ibid.*, p. 43.
[22] *Ibid.*, p. 55.
[23] *Ibid.*, p. 43.
[24] *Ibid.*, p. 44.
[25] *Ibid.*, p. 45.
[26] All the foregoing material on splits in the Communist Party of Argentina is drawn from Official Communist *History*, Chapters IV and V.
[27] Interview with Attilio Biondi, onetime Treasurer of Unión Sindical, in Buenos Aires, November 30, 1946.
[28] *El Trabajador Latino Americano*, September 15, 1928.
[29] *Ibid.*, October 30, 1928.
[30] Interview with Attilio Biondi, November 30, 1946.
[31] *El Trabajador Latino Americano*, June-July, 1929.
[32] *Ibid.*, November, 1932.
[33] *Ibid.*, November-December, 1931.
[34] Official Communist *History*, p. 74.
[35] Rodolfo Puiggros (former member of the Politburo of the Communist Party of Argentina, head of Movimiento Obrero Comunista), in *La Crítica*, May 19, 1953.
[36] Official Communist *History*, p. 76.

37 Interview with Benito Marianetti, member of the Central Committee of the Communist Party, in Mendoza, Argentina, December 3, 1946.

38 Interview with Dr. Emilio Levy Ferrer, Secretary General of the Mendoza Socialist Federation, former leader of the Partido Socialista Obrero, in Mendoza, December 2, 1946.

39 Official Communist *History*, p. 84.

40 *Ibid.*

41 *Ibid.*, p. 85.

42 Rodolfo Puiggros, in *La Crítica*, May 22, 1953.

43 Interview with Italo Gerassi and Marcos Panteleón, November 19, 1946.

44 Interview with Cándido Gregorio, Secretary General of the Socialists' Unión Obrero Textil, in Buenos Aires, October 31, 1946.

45 Official Communist *History*, p. 86.

46 *Ibid.*, pp. 74 and 89.

47 *Ibid.*, p. 89.

48 *Ibid.*, p. 88.

49 See Jesús Hernández, *Yo Fúi un Ministro de Stalin* (Mexico, 1953). Hernández was Communist Minister of Education in the Republican Government during the Spanish Civil War.

50 Rodolfo Puiggros, in *La Crítica*, May 20, 1953.

51 Rodolfo Puiggros, in *La Crítica*, May 21, 1953.

52 Interview with Cándido Gregorio, October 31, 1946.

53 Official Communist *History*, p. 94.

54 *Ibid.*

55 *Ibid.*, p. 107.

56 This information is drawn from interviews with various principals in this split, including Francisco Pérez Leirós, in Buenos Aires, on October 30, 1946, and José Domenech, in Rosario, November 11, 1946.

57 Official Communist *History*, p. 116.

58 Interview with Earl Browder, in Yonkers, New York, March 23, 1953.

59 Rodolfo Puiggros, in *La Crítica*, May 26, 1953.

60 Data on the Communist-Tessaire negotiations came from an interview with Rodolfo Puiggros, who carried on the negotiations for the Communists, in Buenos Aires, August 4, 1952.

61 Official Communist *History*, p. 119.

62 *Ibid.*, p. 126.

63 Interview with Arturo Frondizi, President of the Unión Cívica Radical, in Buenos Aires, July 15, 1954.

64 Interview with Rodolfo Puiggros, in Buenos Aires, June 27, 1953.

65 *Ibid.*

66 Interview with Rodolfo Puiggros, August 4, 1952.

67 Interview with Eliseo Barrios, member of the Trade Union Committee of the Socialist Party, in New Brunswick, N.J., April 8, 1954.

68 Official Communist *History*, p. 131.

69 *Resoluciones del Comité Central Ampliado del Partido Comunista, Reunido en la ciudad de Rosario durante los dias 28 y 29 de julio de 1951* (Buenos Aires, Editorial Anteo, 1951).

70 Interview with Rodolfo Puiggros, June 27, 1953.

71 Victorio Codovilla, *Defender la Linea Independiente del Partido, para Construir el Frente de la Democracia, de la Independencia Nacional y la Paz* (Buenos Aires, Editorial Anteo, 1953).

Chapter X

1 Fernando Alegría, *Recabarren* (Santiago, Editorial Antares, 1938), p. 155.

2 Interview with Manuel Hidalgo, onetime chief of the Chilean Communist Party, in Santiago, Chile, December 17, 1946.

3 Interview with ex-General Juan Bennett, one of three members of the Junta de Gobierno, September, 1924-January, 1925, in Santiago, Chile, March 11, 1947.

4 Interview with ex-President Arturo Alessandri, in Santiago, April 3, 1947.

5 Interview with Elías Laferte, President of the Chilean Communist Party, Senator, in Santiago, January 13, 1947.

6 Interview with Manuel Hidalgo, December 17, 1946.

7 Interview with Elías Laferte, January 13, 1947.

8 "Chile, the Economic Situation," *Communist International*, June, 1928.

9 Interview with Manuel Hidalgo, December 17, 1946.

10 Interview with Elías Laferte, January 13, 1947.

11 "Chile, the Economic Situation," *op. cit.*

12 *En defensa de la Revolución—Informes, Tesis y Documentos Presentados al Congreso Nacional del Partido Comunista a Verificarse el 19 de Marzo de 1933* (Santiago, Editorial Luis E. Recabarren, 1933), p. 29. This is a report of the first post-Ibáñez Congress of the Hidalgo Communist Party.

13 *Hacia la Formación de un Verdadero Partido de Clase—Resoluciones de la Conferencia Nacional del Partido Comunista realizada en Julio de 1933* (Santiago, Gutenberg Press, 1933), p. 26. This is the report of the first post-Ibáñez Congress of the Laferte Communist Party.

14 Interview with Oscar Weiss, onetime leader of the Hidalgo Communist Party youth group, in Santiago, March 17, 1947.

15 *En defensa de la Revolución, op. cit.*, p. 22.

16 Partido Socialista, *Política Sindical del Partido Socialista—Tesis Sindical Aprobada por el V Congreso del Partido Celebrado en Santiago en Diciembre de 1938* (Santiago, 1939).

17 Elías Laferte, in *El Trabajador Latino Americano*, September-October, 1931.

18 *En Defensa de la Revolución, op. cit.*, p. 112.

19 *El Trabajador Latino Americano*, September-October, 1931.

20 Interview with Oscar Weiss, March 17, 1947.

21 *Ibid.*

22 Interview with Elías Laferte, January 13, 1947.

23 Interview with Salvador Ocampo, Communist Senator and ex-Secretary General of Federación Obrera de Chile, in Santiago, January 14, 1947.

24 *En defensa de la Revolución, op. cit.*, p. 26.

25 Interview with Salvador Ocampo, January 14, 1947.

26 *The New York Times*, December 26, 1931.

27 Interview with Marmaduque Grove, leader of 1924, 1925, and 1932 revolutions, onetime head of the "Socialist Republic," in Santiago, December 26, 1946.

28 From a throwaway issued by the Socialist Republic on the day the Junta de Gobierno took office, June 4, 1932.

29 *El Trabajador Latino Americano*, May, 1932.

30 Interview with Oscar Weiss, March 17, 1947.

31 Interview with Julio Corvalán Jáunez, who was in 1932 Treasurer of the Communist Party of Chile, in Santiago, December 22, 1946.

32 *En defensa de la Revolución, op. cit.*, pp. 57-62.

33 *Hacia la Formación de un Verdadero Partido de Clase, op. cit.*, pp. 20-25.

34 *Ibid.*, p. 30.

35 *En Defensa de la Revolución, op. cit.*, p. 30.

36 *Hacia la Formación de un Verdadero Partido de Clase, op. cit.*, p. 32.

37 *En Defensa de la Revolución, op. cit.*, p. 110.

38 Interview with Oscar Weiss, March 17, 1947.

39 Interview with Salvador Ocampo, January 14, 1947.

40 Interview with Bernardo Ibáñez, Secretary General of the Confederación de Trabajadores de Chile, in Santiago, January 7, 1947.

41 René León Echaiz, *Evolución Histórica de los Partidos Políticos Chilenos* (Santiago, 1939), p. 188.

42 *International Press Correspondence*, May 1, 1937.

43 Carlos Contreras Labarca, *Adelante en la Lucha por el Programa del Frente Popular* (Santiago, Ediciones del Comité Central del Partido Comunista, 1940), p. 32.

44 Humberto Abarca and Salvador Ocampo, *La Unidad del Pueblo Defenderá las Conquistas Democráticas—Discursos Pronunciados en la Cámara por los Diputados Comunistas* (Santiago, Ediciones del Comité Central del Partido Comunista de Chile, 1941), p. 4.

45 Elías Laferte, *Como Triunfaremos en las Elecciones de 1941* (Santiago, Ediciones del Comité Central del Partido Comunista de Chile, 1940), p. 4.

46 Partido Socialista, *Chile y América en su Orbita Espiritual del Socialismo* (Santiago, Departamento de Publicaciones, 1941).

47 *The New York Times*, December 22, 1940.

48 New York *Herald Tribune*, December 5, 1940.

49 *The New York Times*, March 15, 1941.

50 New York *Herald Tribune*, March 9, 1941.

51 Partido Socialista de Trabajadores, *El Camino del Pueblo—Resoluciones del Tercer Congreso del Partido Socialista de Trabajadores, Santiago, 1 al 3 de Mayo de 1942* (Santiago, Chile, 1942), p. 15.

52 Interview with César Godoy Urrutia, onetime leader of the Partido Socialista de Trabajadores, Communist deputy at the time of the interview, in Concepción, Chile, February 22, 1947.

53 Daniel Palma R., *La Unidad Juvenil Aplastará el Fascismo* (Santiago, Chile Editorial Juventud, 1941), p. 4.

54 Interview with Bernardo Ibáñez, January 7, 1947.

55 *Allied Labor News*, February, 1943.

56 Radio Agriculture, Santiago, February 25, 1943.

57 Interview with Bernardo Ibáñez, January 7, 1947.

58 *Pacto de Acción Política—Partido Socialista Auténtico y Partido Comunista de Chile—Documentos* (Santiago, Chile, 1946).

59 Interview with Bernardo Ibáñez, January 7, 1947.

60 Partido Socialista, *Una Etapa de Clarificación Socialista* (Santiago, Chile, 1944), pp. 27-28.

61 *The New York Times*, November 1, 1946.

62 *Ibid.*, October 23, 1947.

63 Interview with Bernardo Ibáñez, in New York City, December 27, 1947.

64 Interview with Bernardo Ibáñez, in New York City, October 22, 1948.

65 *The New York Times*, January 28, 1949.

66 Interview with Raúl Ampuero, Secretary General of Partido Socialista Popular, in Santiago, August 8, 1952.

67 Interview with Manuel Ovalle, President of the Copper Workers Confederation, in Santiago, August 9, 1952.

68 Interview with Luis Quiroga, Christian Social member of the Executive Committee of the C.U.T.Ch., in Santiago, July 21, 1954.

CHAPTER XI

1 Roberto Hinojosa, longhand manuscript autobiography, undated but 1925.

2 Interview with Gustavo Navarro (Tristán Maroff), in La Paz, Bolivia, May 26, 1947.

3 Interview with Sergio Almarás, Secretary General of Communist Party of Bolivia, in La Paz, July 9, 1953.

4 *El Trabajador Latino Americano*, August-September, 1930.

5 *Ibid.*, January-February, 1933.

6 Interview with Aurelio Alcoba, José Antonio Orellana, and Luis Gallardo Velasco, leaders of the pro-Communist Confederación Sindical de Trabajadores de Bolivia, in La Paz, May 29, 1947.

7 Interview with Nicolás Sánchez, leader of the Partido Obrero Revolucionario, in La Paz, June 3, 1947.

[8] Interview with Anarchist leader José Mendoza Vera, head of the Federación Obrera Local, in La Paz, May 30, 1947.

[9] Interview with Hernán Sánchez Fernández, member of the Executive Committee of Tristán Maroff's Partido Socialista Obrero Boliviano, in La Paz, May 28, 1947.

[10] Partido de la Izquierda Revolucionaria, *Programa de Principios, Estatutos y Otros Documentos* (La Paz, Editorial Trabajo, 1941).

[11] Interview with José Antonio Arze, chief of the Partido de la Izquierda Revolucionaria and President of the Chamber of Deputies, in La Paz, May 27, 1947.

[12] Interview with Hernán Sánchez Fernández, May 28, 1947.

[13] Interview with José Antonio Arze, May 27, 1947.

[14] La Paz *El Diario*, November 23, 1945.

[15] La Paz *La Noche*, November 13, 1945.

[16] Mexico City *El Popular*, August 7, 1945.

[17] Interview with Sergio Almarás, July 9, 1953.

[18] Interview with Víctor Raúl Haya de la Torre, leader of the Apristas, in New York City, January 26, 1948.

[19] Interview with Arturo Sabroso, Aprista trade union leader, in Lima, June 28, 1947.

[20] Interview with Víctor Raúl Haya de la Torre, in Lima, June 18, 1947.

[21] Ricardo Martínez de la Torre, *Apuntes Para Una Interpretación Marxista de la Historia Social del Peru* (Lima, 1948) Vol. II, p. 396.

[22] *Ibid.*, p. 397.

[23] *Ibid.*, pp. 398-402.

[24] *Ibid.*, pp. 409-433.

[25] *Ibid.*, pp. 497-506.

[26] Interviews with Ricardo Martínez de la Torre, in Lima, June 27, 1947, and Luciano Castillo, in Lima, June 26, 1947.

[27] Martínez de la Torre, *op. cit.*, Vol. III, pp. 10-13.

[28] *Ibid.*, pp. 13-14.

[29] *Ibid.*, p. 55.

[30] *Ibid.*, Vol. IV, p. 85.

[31] *Ibid.*, Vol. III, pp. 551-553.

[32] *Ibid.*, p. 557.

[33] *Ibid.*, p. 563.

[34] *Ibid.*, p. 578.

[35] Interview with Juan La Torre, Aprista labor leader and head of the Chauffeurs Federation, in Lima, June 18, 1947.

[36] *Ibid.*

[37] Fernando Cossío del Pomar, *El Indo Americano* (Lima, Editorial Nuevo Día, 1948).

[38] *Ibid.*, pp. 295-296.

[39] *International Press Correspondence*, February 9, 1933.

[40] *Ibid.*, November 25, 1935.

[41] Interview with Jorge Fernández Stoll, Director General of Labor under Benavides and Prado, in Lima, June 20, 1947.

[42] Interview with Juan P. Luna, Communist leader, in Lima, June 28, 1947.

[43] Interview with Jorge Fernández Stoll, June 20, 1947.

[44] Interview with Juan P. Luna, June 28, 1947.

[45] Charles E. Hutchinson, in *Revue of Labor and Social Developments in Latin America*, July 31, 1945.

[46] Interview with Eliseo García, Trade Union Secretary of the Communist Party, in Lima, June 20, 1947.

[47] *Ibid.*

[48] Interview with Alberto Lizarzaburu, textile workers union leader, in New Brunswick, New Jersey, March 3, 1954.

[49] Interview with Eliseo García, June 20, 1947.

[50] Interview with Alberto Lizarzaburu, March 3, 1954.

[51] Interview with Eliseo García, June 20, 1947.

[52] Hutchinson, *op. cit.*

53 Martin Ebon, *World Communism Today* (New York, Whittlesey House, 1948), p. 327.

54 *The New York Times*, November 3, 1948.

55 Interview with Juan P. Luna, in Lima, Peru, June 28, 1947.

56 Lilo Linke, *Ecuador* (London, Royal Institute of International Affairs, 1953), pp. 66 and 71.

57 This information, unless otherwise noted, was drawn from an interview with Ricardo Paredes, Secretary General of the Communist Party of Ecuador, in Quito, July 5, 1947.

58 Quito, Ecuador, *La Antorcha*, January 17, 1925.

59 Interview with Ricardo Paredes, July 5, 1947.

60 Quito *La Antorcha*, June 8, 1925.

61 Quito *La Vanguardia*, December 15, 1927.

62 Interview with Ricardo Paredes, July 5, 1947.

63 Quito *La Vanguardia*, November 15, 1928.

64 *Ibid.*, August 6, 1929.

65 *Ibid.*, July 22, 1929.

66 Interview with Ricardo Paredes, July 5, 1947.

67 Interview with Dr. Carlos Palacio Sáenz, leader of the Partido Socialista, in Guayaquil, May 2, 1947.

68 *Bandera Roja*, second half, October, 1933.

69 Interview with Ricardo Paredes, July 5, 1947.

70 Interview with Luis Maldonaldo Tamayo, Secretary General of the Socialist Party of Ecuador, in Quito, July 6, 1947.

71 Interview with Dr. Carlos Palacio Sáenz, May 2, 1947.

72 *Bandera Roja*, October 20, 1932.

73 Interview with Ricardo Paredes, July 5, 1947.

74 *Ibid.*

75 Interview with Pedro Saad, ex-Secretary General of the Confederación de Trabajadores del Ecuador, in Guayaquil, July 2, 1947.

76 Interview with Luis Maldonaldo Tamayo, July 6, 1947.

77 Associated Press, May 29, 1944.

78 *Allied Labor News*, July 25, 1944.

79 Interview with Pedro Saad, July 2, 1947.

80 Mexico City *El Popular*, September 26, 1945.

81 *Allied Labor News*, October 5, 1945.

82 Interview with Miguel Angel Guzmán, Vice President of the Confederación de Trabajadores del Ecuador, in Quito, July 4, 1947.

83 Interview with Pablo Duque, member of the Executive Committee of the Confederación de Trabajadores del Ecuador, member of the anti-Communist Party faction of the Socialist Party, in Quito, August 21, 1952.

84 Interview with Miguel Angel Guzmán, July 4, 1947.

85 Interview with Hugo Larrea Benalcazar, editor of the Socialist daily, *La Tierra*, in Quito, August 20, 1952.


CHAPTER XII

1 All this information came from an interview with Ignacio Torres Giraldo, July 15, 1947.

2 *American Labor Year Book 1930* (New York, Rand School Press, 1930), p. 228.

3 Interview with Ignacio Torres Giraldo, July 15, 1947.

4 *La Semana* (weekly news magazine, published in Bogotá), July 5, 1947.

5 William Simons, "The Expanding Inter-Imperialist Wars in South America," *The Communist*, December, 1932.

6 *The New York Times*, February 11, 1934.

7 Stephen Naft, "Fascism and Communism in Latin America," *Foreign Policy Bulletin* (1937), p. 233.

[8] *El Trabajador Latino Americano,* February 28-March 14-31, 1929.

[9] Naft, *op. cit.,* p. 234.

[10] Ricardo Martínez, "The Significance of the Latin American Trade Union Unity Congress," *The Communist,* November, 1938.

[11] Interview with Renato Arango, former leader of the Communist Party of Colombia, in Bogotá, July 14, 1947; and *La Semana,* July 5, 1947.

[12] Bogotá *El Tiempo* (Liberal Party daily newspaper), December 23, 1941.

[13] Interview with Gilberto Vieira, President of the Partido Social Democrático, in Bogotá, July 12, 1947.

[14] Interview with Renato Arango, July 14, 1947.

[15] *La Semana,* July 5, 1947.

[16] *Ibid.*

[17] Interview with Renato Arango, July 14, 1947.

[18] Interview with Gilberto Vieria, July 12, 1947.

[19] Interview with Víctor Julio Silva, former Secretary General of the Confederación de Trabajadores de Colombia, in Bogotá, August 5, 1954.

[20] Eudosio Ravines, *The Yenan Way* (New York, Charles Scribner's Sons, 1951), p. 58.

[21] Interview with Mercedes Fermin, leading figure in the Partido Acción Democrática, in Caracas, July 25, 1947.

[22] Interview with Rómulo Betancourt, head of the Partido Acción Democrática, in San José, Costa Rica, September 1, 1952.

[23] Interview with Juan Bautista Fuenmayor, head of the Communist Party of Venezuela, in Caracas, July 29, 1947.

[24] *El Trabajador Latino Americano,* August 31-September 15, 1929.

[25] *Communist International,* October, 1936.

[26] *International Press Correspondence,* February 23, 1935.

[27] *Ibid.,* August 17, 1935.

[28] *Ibid.,* August 31, 1935.

[29] Interview with Juan Bautista Fuenmayor, July 29, 1947.

[30] Interview with Rómulo Betancourt, September 1, 1952.

[31] Interview with Juan Bautista Fuenmayor, July 29, 1947.

[32] Interview with Rodolfo Quintero, head of the "Black" Communists, Secretary General of the Federation of Workers of the Federal District, in Caracas, July 30, 1947.

[33] *El País* (Acción Democrática daily newspaper), July 25, 1947.

[34] Interview with Juan Bautista Fuenmayor, July 29, 1947.

[35] *Ibid.*

[36] Interview with Luis Miquilena, a leader of the "Black" Communists, in Caracas, July 25, 1947.

[37] Interview with Juan Bautista Fuenmayor, July 29, 1947.

[38] Interview with Rómulo Betancourt, September 1, 1952.

[39] Interview with Juan Bautista Fuenmayor, July 29, 1947.

[40] Interview with Luis Miquilena, July 25, 1947.

[41] *The New York Times,* December 1, 1945.

[42] *Ibid.,* December 12, 1945.

[43] *Ibid.,* February 27, 1946.

[44] Havana, Cuba, *Hoy* (Communist daily paper), February 13, 1946.

[45] Interview with Cruz Villegas, a leader of the "Black" Communists, in Caracas, July 23, 1947.

[46] *Fundamentos* (theoretical organ of the Cuban Communists), January, 1947.

[47] Interviews with Juan Bautista Fuenmayor, July 29, 1947, and Cruz Villegas, July 23, 1947.

[48] *Fundamentos,* January, 1947.

[49] *Ibid.,* August, 1947.

[50] *Ibid.,* January, 1947.

[51] Interviewed with José Vargas, an official of Acción Democrática trade unions in Caracas, June 26, 1948.

[52] New York *Daily Worker,* January 11, 1948.

53 Interview with Rodolfo Quintero, in Caracas, June 28, 1948.
54 New York *Daily Worker,* January 11, 1948.
55 Interview with Raúl Leoni, Minister of Labor, in Caracas, July 28, 1947.
56 Interview with P. B. Pérez Salinas, Secretary General of the Confederación de Trabajadores de Venezuela, in Caracas, June 30, 1948.
57 *Ibid.*
58 Interview with Juan Bautista Fuenmayor, in Caracas, June 28, 1948.
59 *Ibid.*
60 Interview with Cruz Villegas, July 23, 1947.
61 *The New York Times,* December 2, 1948.
62 Interview with Rodolfo Quintero, in Caracas, July 23, 1952.
63 *Boletín Sindical* (periodical of the Communists in Caracas), August 23, 1952.
64 *Fundamentos,* February, 1953.
65 Interview with Cruz Villegas, in Caracas, July 21, 1952.
66 Interview with Gonzalo Travieso, "Black" Communist leader, in Caracas, July 23, 1952.
67 Interview with Rodolfo Quintero, July 23, 1952.
68 Interviews with Rodolfo Quintero, July 23, 1952, and Cruz Villegas, July 21, 1952.
69 Interview with Luis González, Assistant Secretary of the "Black" Communist labor federation, in Caracas, June 25, 1954.
70 *Ibid.*
71 Interview with Rodolfo Quintero, July 23, 1952.

CHAPTER XIII

1 Interview with Carlos Fernández R., leading Communist trade unionist, historian of the trade union and radical movement of the island, in Havana, August 11, 1947.
2 *The Militant* (weekly newspaper of the United States Trotskyites, New York), January 15, 1931.
3 Interview with Carlos Fernández R., August 11, 1947.
4 R. Martínez Villena, "The Rise of the Revolutionary Movement in Cuba," *The Communist,* June, 1933.
5 Interview with Fausto Waterman, Auténtico trade union leader, in Havana, August 9, 1947.
6 *International Press Correspondence,* January 15, 1934.
7 Martin Kaye and Louise Perry, *Who Fights for a Free Cuba?* (New York, Workers Library Publishers, 1933), p. 9.
8 Mijowsky, "Weaknesses and Mistakes of the Communist Press in Cuba," *Communist International,* April 5, 1934.
9 *International Press Correspondence,* July 13, 1934.
10 New York *Sunday Worker,* March 15, 1939.
11 New York *Herald Tribune,* September 25, 1938.
12 New York *Daily Worker,* October 1, 1939.
13 Arthur Pincus, "Cuba's Puppet Democracy," *The Nation,* December 17, 1938.
14 Interview with Fausto Waterman, August 9, 1947.
15 Abed Brooks, in *World News and Views* (formerly *International Press Correspondence*), December 24, 1938.
16 Pincus, *op. cit.*
17 William Z. Foster, in *World News and Views,* February 18, 1939.
18 Interview with Fausto Waterman, August 9, 1947; and José María Pérez, "How Cuban Labor United," New York *Sunday Worker,* June 6, 1943.
19 Eusebio Mujal, quoted in *CTC* (organ of the Confederación de Trabajadores de Cuba), June, 1944.
20 Blas Roca, *Siempre Firmes* (Havana, Ediciones Sociales, 1940), p. 44.
21 *Acción Socialista,* May, 1940.
22 New York *Sunday Worker,* July 21, 1940.
23 Juan Marinello, *Unión Revolucionaria y la Constitución de 1940* (Havana, Ediciones Sociales, 1940), p. 12.

[24] *Acción Socialista*, January, 1941.

[25] *Ibid.*

[26] *The New York Times*, November 17, 1942.

[27] Interview with Samuel Powell, violently anti-Communist labor leader of the Auténtico Party, in Havana, March 17, 1952.

[28] Interview with Juan Marinello, President of the Partido Socialista Popular, in Havana, August 13, 1947.

[29] *CTC*, June, 1944.

[30] *Acción Socialista*, July, 1944.

[31] *Allied Labor News*, July 28, 1944.

[32] *Acción Socialista*, November, 1944.

[33] *World Report* (weekly news magazine), August 20, 1946.

[34] Radio Havana, November 23, 1945.

[35] Interview with Juan Marinello, August 13, 1947.

[36] *World Report*, August 20, 1946.

[37] Interview with Carlos Fernández R., leading figure in the Communist CTC, August 11, 1947.

[38] Benjamin Davis, in New York *Daily Worker*, March 7, 1948.

[39] New York *Daily Worker*, October 19, 1948.

[40] *Ibid.*, March 9, 1947.

[41] Interview with Samuel Powell, March 17, 1952.

[42] *The New York Times*, February 24, 1946.

[43] *Ibid.*, March 27, 1945.

[44] Interview with Juan Marinello, in Havana, March 18, 1952.

[45] *The New York Times*, April 6, 1952.

[46] Interview with Víctor Federico Alegría, Secretary General, Federación Nacional de Trabajadores de Seguros, in Havana, Cuba, July 24, 1953.

[47] Interview with Carlos Fernández R., in Havana, July 25, 1953.

[48] Interview with Luis Serrano Tamayo, Secretary General of Federación de Trabajadores del Tabaco, ex-Communist, in Havana, March 19, 1952.

[49] Interview with Jesús Artigas, Treasurer of Confederación de Trabajadores de Cuba, in Havana, July 24, 1953.

[50] Interview with Samuel Powell, member of Executive Committee of Confederación de Trabajadores de Cuba, in Havana, March 17, 1952.

[51] Interview with Jesús Artigas, July 24, 1953.

CHAPTER XIV

[1] Martin Ebon, *World Communism Today* (New York, Whittlesey House, 1948), p. 304.

[2] Interview with Roger Leonard, editor of Parti Socialiste Populaire daily paper *La Nation*, in Port-au-Prince, Haiti, August 30, 1949.

[3] Interview with Milien Josué and Molière Compas of Federation Haitien du Travail, in Port-au-Prince, Haiti, June 23, 1948.

[4] Interview with Paul Cassagnol, President of Parti Populaire Social Chretien, in Port-au-Prince, Haiti, August 29, 1949.

[5] *Congreso de Cali, C.T.A.L., 1944* (Mexico, C.T.A.L. Publications, 1945), pp. 110-111.

[6] Interview with Julio César Ballester, Secretary General of Confederación Dominicana del Trabajo, in Ciudad Trujillo, Dominican Republic, August 18, 1949.

[7] Ciudad Trujillo *La Nación*, June 13, 1945.

[8] Ebon, *op. cit.*, p. 305.

[9] All of the above information is from an interview with Jesús de Galindez, United States Representative of Basque Government-in-Exile, and former official of Dominican Republic Ministry of Labor, in New York City, November 30, 1954.

[10] Interview with Angel Miolán, Labor Secretary of Partido Revolucionario Dominicano, in Havana, Cuba, March 20, 1952.

11 Ebon, *op. cit.*, p. 307.
12 Interview with Hipolito Marcano, President of Federación Libre de Trabajadores de Puerto Rico (A.F. of L. state organization), in San Juan, Puerto Rico, August 15, 1949.
13 Interview with Governor Luis Muñoz Marín, in San José, Costa Rica, November 9, 1953.
14 New York *Post*, October 20, 1954.

CHAPTER XV

1 Carleton Beals, *Glass Houses, Ten Years of Free-Lancing* (Philadelphia, J. B. Lippincott Company, 1938), pp. 50-51.
2 *The New York Times*, September 3, 1920.
3 Interview with Roberto Haberman, long-time adviser of leaders of Confederación Obrero Regional Mexicana, in New York City, March 4, 1953.
4 Bertram Wolfe, "The Strange Case of Diego Rivera," in *The New Leader*, October 11, 1954.
5 Víctor Alba, *Historia del Comunismo en America Latina* (Mexico City, Ediciones Occidentales, 1954), p. 15.
6 Interview with Bertram Wolfe, former leader of the United States Communist Party, in New Bruswick, New Jersey, March 22, 1954.
7 Interview with Bertram Wolfe, in New York City, November 4, 1947.
8 Bertram Wolfe, "Bolshevisation and Immediate Tasks of the Mexican Communist Party," *International Press Correspondence*, June 18, 1925.
9 Interview with Jay Lovestone, in New York City, April 6, 1954.
10 Interview with Bertram Wolfe, November 4, 1947.
11 *International Press Correspondence*, June 7, 1929.
12 *Ibid.*, February 11, 1925.
13 Carleton Beals and Roberto Haberman, "Mexican Labor and the Mexican Government," *The Liberator*, October, 1920.
14 *International Press Correspondence*, October 29, 1925.
15 Beals and Haberman, *op. cit.*, p. 339.
16 Interview with Roberto Haberman, March 4, 1953.
17 *El Trabajador Latino Americano*, September 30, 1928.
18 *International Press Correspondence*, March 29, 1929.
19 "Problems of the Mexican Communist Party," *The Communist*, May, 1930.
20 New York *The Militant*, April 1, 1931.
21 *El Trabajador Latino Americano*, January 15, 1929.
22 *Ibid.*, February 28-March 15-30, 1929.
23 *Ibid.*, April 15-30, 1929.
24 *Ibid.*, August-September, 1930.
25 *International Press Correspondence*, January 23, 1930.
26 *Ibid.*, March 6, 1930.
27 *Ibid.*, February 9, 1933.
28 *El Trabajador Latino Americano*, October-November, 1935.
29 Confederación de Trabajadores de México, *C.T.M. 1936-1941* (Mexico, 1941), pp. 57-59.
30 *Ibid.*, p. 260.
31 *Ibid.*, pp. 260-265.
32 *Ibid.*, p. 256.
33 Interview with Earl Browder, in Yonkers, New York, March 23, 1953.
34 Interview with Rodrigo García Treviño, former leading official of the Confederación de Trabajadores de México, head of the Grupo de Socialistas Mexicanos, in Mexico, August 22, 1951.
35 *C.T.M. 1936-1941, op. cit.*, p. 268.
36 *The New Leader*, November 30, 1940.

[37] *The New York Times*, April 14, 1940.
[38] Rodolfo Puiggros, in *La Crítica*, May 20, 1953.
[39] New York *Daily Worker*, March 16, 1940.
[40] New York *The Militant*, April 5, 1954.
[41] New York *Daily Worker*, February 23, 1943.
[42] Victor Serge (exiled Russian ex-Communist), in *The New Leader*, May 13, 1944.
[43] *The New York Times*, September 23, 1946.
[44] Mexico City *El Popular*, September 26, 1945.
[45] United Press, June 7, 1945.
[46] Interview with Vicente Lombardo Toledano, in Mexico City, August 25, 1948.
[47] Ricardo Treviño, *El Espionaje Comunista* (Mexico, 1952), p. 47.
[48] *Ibid.*
[49] *Razón Histórica, Principios, Programa y Estatutos del Partido Popular* (Mexico, 1948).
[50] Treviño, *op. cit.*, p. 48.
[51] *The New Leader*, February 11, 1950.
[52] *The New York Times*, March 24, 1947.
[53] *Ibid.*, January 4, 1950.
[54] Treviño, *op. cit.*, p. 49.
[55] "El Partido en el Distrito Federal de México," *Fundamentos*, September, 1949.
[56] *La Voz de México*, March 23, 1952.
[57] *International Press Correspondence*, October 17, 1928.

## Chapter XVI

[1] *El Movimiento Revolucionario Latino Americano, Versiones de la Primera Conferencia Comunista Latino Americana, Junio de 1929* (Buenos Aires, Editorial La Correspondencia, 1929), p. 224.
[2] *International Press Correspondence*, November 13, 1922.
[3] *El Movimiento Revolucionario Latino Americano, op. cit.*, pp. 225-226.
[4] *El Trabajador Latino Americano*, January-February, 1930.
[5] Charles Kepner, *Social Aspects of the Banana Industry* (New York, Columbia University Press, 1936), p. 188.
[6] *El Trabajador Latino Americano*, November 15-30, 1929.
[7] Jorge Schlesinger, *Revolución Comunista—¿Guatemala en Peligro?* (Guatemala City, Unión Tipográfica Castañeda, Avila y Cía, 1946), p. 48.
[8] *El Trabajador Latino Americano*, August-September, 1930.
[9] Interview with Alfredo Schlesinger, collector of materials on the Communists of Central America, in Guatemala City, August 23, 1954.
[10] *El Trabajador Latino Americano*, January-February, 1932.
[11] Daniel James, *Red Design for the Americas: Guatemalan Prelude* (New York, The John Day Company, 1954), p. 70.
[12] *Ibid.*, pp. 71-73.
[13] Interview with Luis Felipe Balcarcel, Secretary General of the Federación Autónoma Sindical, former Secretary of Organization of the Confederación de Trabajadores de Guatemala, in Guatemala City, August 23, 1954.
[14] Interview with Paulino Ovalle, Sub-Secretary of Organization and Propaganda of the Partido Frente Popular Libertador, in Guatemala City, August 11, 1948.
[15] José Manuel Fortuny, *Informe Sobre la Actividad del Comité Central del Partido Comunista de Guatemala* (Guatemala City, Ediciones del Partido Guatemalteco del Trabajo, 1953).
[16] Alfredo Guerra Borges, "Results of II Congress, Guatemala Party of Labour," *For a Lasting Peace, For a People's Democracy*, February 6, 1953.
[17] Guatemala City *El Imparcial*, March 2, 1954.
[18] Interview with Leonardo Castillo Flores, Secretary General of the Confederación Nacional Campesina, in Guatemala City, March 30, 1954.

Chapter XVII

1 Jorge Schlesinger, *Revolución Comunista—¿Guatemala en Peligro?* (Guatemala City, Unión Tipográfica Castañeda, Avila y Cía, 1946); interview with Alfredo Schlesinger, August 23, 1954.
2 *Congreso de Cali, C.T.A.L., 1944* (Mexico, C.T.A.L. Publications, 1945), p. 98.
3 Interview with Miguel Mármol, in Guatemala City, July 22, 1953.
4 *Congreso de Cali, C.T.A.L., 1944, op. cit.,* p. 98; interview with Eduardo Alfonso Figeac, in San Salvador, August 7, 1948.
5 This information was gathered in interviews with various labor and political leaders during several visits to El Salvador in the late 1940's and early 1950's.
6 This is taken from Schlesinger, *op. cit.*
7 *El Trabajador Latino Americano,* June-July, 1929.
8 *Ibid.,* September-October, 1929.
9 *Ibid.,* August-September, 1930.
10 Schlesinger, *op. cit.,* p. 222.
11 Interview with Juan Angel Muñoz Aguilar, former Liberal Party leader and an early member of the Partido Revolucionario Hondureño, who withdrew when he discovered Communist influence in it, in Guatemala City, January 25, 1954.
12 This information about *Voz Obrera* comes from a diplomatic source which the author is not free to name.
13 *International Press Correspondence,* September 1, 1928.
14 Víctor Alba, *Historia del Comunismo en América Latina* (Mexico City, Ediciones Occidentales, 1954), pp. 86-88.
15 *International Press Correspondence,* April 13, 1933.
16 *Ibid.*
17 Interview with a former leader of the Partido Socialista de Nicaragua, who has requested the author not to divulge his name. Hereafter, he will be referred to as "P.S.N. source."
18 P.S.N. source.
19 *Tiempo* (Mexico City news magazine), June 1, 1945.
20 P.S.N. source.
21 *Ibid.*
22 *Ibid.*
23 *Ibid.*
24 *The New York Times,* December 30, 1946.
25 P.S.N. source.
26 *Ibid.*
27 *Ibid.*
28 Most of the facts concerning these early years are drawn from an interview with Manuel Mora, in San José, Costa Rica, September 1, 1952.
29 *International Press Correspondence,* October 6, 1933.
30 Interview with Rómulo Betancourt, in San José, Costa Rica, September 1, 1952.
31 *International Press Correspondence,* August 31, 1935.
32 Interview with Manuel Mora, September 1, 1952.
33 *Noticias Católicas* (published by the National Catholic Welfare Council, Washington, D.C.), July 2, 1943.
34 *Ibid.,* July 9, 1943.
35 *Ibid.*
36 *Trabajo* (newspaper of Vanguardia Popular), October 8, 1943.
37 San José *La Tribuna,* February, 1944.
38 *Diario de Costa Rica,* February 8, 1944.
39 Interview with Manuel Mora, September 1, 1952.
40 Interview with Arturo Volio Guardia, ex-Secretary of Congress, ex-member of the National Republican Party, July 31, 1948.
41 Interview with Manuel Mora, September 1, 1952.
42 The author is not at liberty to disclose his source of information concerning the negotiations. However, it is an individual closely connected with these events.

[43] Interview with Manuel Mora, September 1, 1952.

[44] *The New York Times,* July 15, 1953.

[45] *El Movimiento Revolucionario, op. cit.,* p. 99.

[46] *El Trabajador Latino Americano,* April 15-30, 1929.

[47] *Ibid.,* June-July, 1930.

[48] Interview with José Brouwer, leader of the Partido Socialista de Panamá, in Caracas, Venezuela, July 24, 1947.

[49] Panama City *El Trabajo,* September 15, 1943.

[50] *Ibid.,* November 15, 1943.

[51] *Allied Labor News,* August 9, 1945.

[52] Interview with José Brouwer, July 24, 1947.

[53] *The New York Times,* June 1, 1950.

[54] *Ibid.,* January 4, 1954.

[55] Interview with Tomás Dionisio Aráuz, head of the Confederación Agraria Nacional, in Panama City, August 6, 1954.

## CHAPTER XVIII

[1] See John Moors Cabot, *Towards Our Common American Destiny* (Boston, Fletcher School of Law and Diplomacy, 1955).

# Index

## DATE DUE